SIXTH EDITION

Criminology

A Canadian Perspective

Rick Linden

University of Manitoba

NELSON EDUCATION

NELSON EDUCATION

Criminology: A Canadian Perspective, Sixth Edition

by Rick Linden

Associate Vice President, Editorial Director:
Evelyn Veitch

Editor-in-Chief:
Anne Williams

Executive Editor:
Cara Yarzab

Marketing Manager:
Heather Leach

Senior Developmental Editor:
Rebecca Ryoji

Developmental Editor:
Mark Grzeskowiak

Permissions Coordinator:
Sheila Hall

Content Production Manager:
Christine Gilbert

Production Service:
Newgen

Copy Editor:
Wendy Thomas

Proofreader:
Eileen Kramer

Indexer:
Ann Blum

Senior Manufacturing Coordinator:
Joanne McNeil

Manufacturing Coordinator:
Loretta Lee

Design Director:
Ken Phipps

Managing Designer:
Katherine Strain

Interior Design:
Newgen

Cover Design:
Dianna Little

Cover Image:
James Lauritz/Getty Images

Compositor:
Newgen

Printer:
Edwards Brothers

Printed and bound in The United States of America
1 2 3 4 10 09 08

For more information contact Nelson Education Ltd., 1120 Birchmount Road, Toronto, Ontario, M1K 5G4. Or you can visit our Internet site at http://www.nelson.com

Library and Archives Canada Cataloguing in Publication Data

Criminology : a Canadian perspective / [edited by] Rick Linden. — 6th ed.

Includes bibliographical references and index.
ISBN 978-0-17-644190-6

1. Criminology—Canada—Textbooks. I. Linden, Rick

HV6807.C76 2008 364.971
C2007-907342-5

To Christopher, who gave so much and asked so little

and

Dan Koenig, a wonderful colleague and friend

Brief Contents

PART I: CRIME AND SOCIETY

CHAPTER 1 **Crime, Criminals, and Criminology / 3**

CHAPTER 2 **The Origins and Role of Law in Society / 29**

CHAPTER 3 **Criminal Law / 68**

CHAPTER 4 **Counting Crime / 103**

CHAPTER 5 **Correlates of Criminal Behaviour / 137**

CHAPTER 6 **Feminism and Criminology / 183**

PART II: EXPLANATIONS OF CRIME

CHAPTER 7 **Early Theories of Criminology / 219**

CHAPTER 8 **Psychological Perspectives on Criminality / 247**

CHAPTER 9 **Strain Theories / 282**

CHAPTER 10 **Conflict Theories / 310**

CHAPTER 11 **Contemporary Critical Criminology / 339**

CHAPTER 12 **Interactionist Theories / 371**

CHAPTER 13 **Social Control Theory / 397**

PART III: PATTERNS OF CRIMINAL BEHAVIOUR

CHAPTER 14 **Conventional or "Street" Crime / 429**

CHAPTER 15 **Organized Crime / 463**

CHAPTER 16 **Corporate and White-Collar Crime / 498**

GLOSSARY / G1

CREDITS / C1

INDEX / I1

Contents

Preface xi

PART 1: CRIME AND SOCIETY 1

CHAPTER 1 Crime, Criminals, and Criminology / 3
Rick Linden, University of Manitoba

■ A Violent Crime: The Sand Brothers 3 ■ A White-Collar Crime: The Downfall of Conrad Black 6 ■ What Is Criminology? 9 • Why Should We Study Crime? 9 • The Discipline of Criminology 12 • Overview of the Book 13 ■ Rules and Laws 14 • The Regulation of Behaviour 14 • What Is a Crime? 15 • Crime Is Socially Defined 18 • The Relativity of Crime 19 ■ Who Makes the Rules? Conflict Versus Consensus Theories of Law 19 • The Consensus Approach 20 • The Conflict Approach 20 ■ Criminology Is an Evolving Discipline: The New Field of Green Criminology 21 • Green Criminology 22 • Issues in Green Criminology—Crimes Involving Food 24 • **Summary 25 • Questions for Critical Thinking 26 • Net Work 26 • Key Terms 27 • Bibliography 27**

CHAPTER 2 The Origins and Role of Law in Society / 29
Rodney Kueneman, University of Manitoba

■ Patterns of Human Social Organization 30 • Small-Scale Society 31 • Dispute Settlement in Small-Scale Society 34 ■ The Transformation from Small-Scale Society to the State 37 • The Slow Emergence of Social Power 37 • The Evolution of Inequality 39 • Transformation in the Forms of Dispute Settlement 40 ■ Modern State Systems 42 • From Tribalism to Feudalism 42 • The Emergence of the Centralized State 43 • The Coalition of Merchants and Monarchs 44 • Commerce, Contracts, and the Primary Role of Law 45 • The Consolidation of Bourgeois Ascendance 46 • State, Law, and Interest Groups 47 • Regulation by Law 47 • The Failure to Regulate: The Eclipse of the State? 51 ■ A Coming Crisis in State Legitimacy? 55 • The Dilemma and Challenge for the Modern State 56 ■ Full Circle: Restorative Justice and a Return to Original Forms of Dispute Settlement? 57 • **Summary 62 • Questions for Critical Thinking 62 • Net Work 63 • Key Terms 63 • Suggested Reading 64 • Bibliography 65**

CHAPTER 3 Criminal Law / 68
Simon N. Verdun-Jones, Simon Fraser University

■ What Is a Crime? 68 ■ What Is Criminal Law? 70 ■ The Sources of Criminal Law 70 • Federal Legislation and Criminal Law 70 • Federal and Provincial or Territorial Regulatory Legislation: Quasi-Criminal Law 72 • Judge-Made Criminal Law 72 ■ Impact of the Canadian Charter of Rights and Freedoms on Criminal Law 73 ■ The Basic Elements of a Crime: *Actus Reus* and *Mens Rea* 76 • The *Actus Reus* Elements of a Crime 76 • The *Mens Rea* Elements of a Crime 78 • Subjective and Objective *Mens Rea* 79 • *Mens Rea* and Regulatory Offences 82 ■ Becoming a Party to a Criminal Offence 83 ■ The Use of Criminal Law as a Preventative Tool: Inchoate Offences 85 • Counselling an Offence That Is Not Committed 85 • Criminal Attempt 86 • Conspiracy 88 ■ Defences to a Criminal Charge 88 • Mental Disorder as a Defence to a Criminal Charge 89 • General Defences to a Criminal Charge 90 • **Summary 97 • Questions for Critical Thinking 98 • Net Work 99 • Key Terms 100 • Suggested Reading 100 • Cases Cited 101**

CHAPTER 4 Counting Crime / 103
John Evans, President, Management and Policy International, Inc.
Alexander Himelfarb, Foreign Affairs and International Trade, Canada

■ Controversies over Counting Crime 104 ■ Statistics on the Criminal Justice System 107 • From Records to Statistics 107 • Canadian Criminal Justice Statistics 109 ■ How Much Crime? 110 ■ Official Statistics: Canadian Uniform Crime Reports 111 ■ Victimization Surveys 120 • Highlights 121 ■ Self-Report Studies 126 ■ The Future of Crime and Criminal Justice Statistics 131 • **Summary 132 • Questions for Critical Thinking 133 • Net Work 133 • Key Terms 134 • Suggested Reading 134 • Bibliography 135**

CHAPTER 5 Correlates of Criminal Behaviour / 137
Timothy F. Hartnagel, University of Alberta

■ Correlates Defined 137 ■ Age 139 • Peak Ages for Crime 139 • Maturational Reform 142 ■ Sex 144 • Sex Differences and Crime Trends 144 • Role Convergence? 148 ■ Race 149 • Race and Crime 149 • Over-Representation of Canadian Aboriginal People in the Criminal Justice System 152 • Explanations of Aboriginal Over-Representation 155 ■ Drug Misuse and Criminal Behaviour 159 ■ Social Class 163 • Conflicting Evidence? 163 • Reconciling the Apparent Conflicts 166 ■ Region 169 • **Summary 173 • Questions for Critical Thinking 173 • Net Work 174 • Key Terms 174 • Suggested Reading 174 • Bibliography 175**

CHAPTER 6 Feminism and Criminology / 183
Elizabeth Comack, University of Manitoba

■ The Invisibility of Women 184 • Theories of Women's Crime 184 • The Mainstream Theories of Crime 188 • The Generalizability Problem 190 • The Gender-Ratio Problem 190 • The Women's Liberation Thesis 191 • Criminalized Women 192 ■ Violence Against Women 195 • The Cultural Construction of Rape 195 • The Law's Role in Condoning Male Violence Against Women 197 • Criminology's Complicity 198 • Breaking the Silence 199 • The Montreal Massacre 200 • Recent Developments in Law's Response to Violence Against Women 201 ■ Blurred Boundaries: Women as Victims and Offenders 204 ■ Gendered Violence 205 • **Summary 209 • Questions for Critical Thinking 209 • Net Work 209 • Key Terms 210 • Suggested Reading 210 • Bibliography 210**

PART 2: EXPLANATIONS OF CRIME 217

CHAPTER 7 Early Theories of Criminology / 219
Tullio Caputo, Carleton University
Rick Linden, University of Manitoba

■ The Classical School 224 • The Classical Theory of Crime 225 • Assessing the Contributions of the Classical School 227 ■ The Statistical School: Social Structure and Crime 229 ■ Lombroso and the Positive School 232 • The Contribution of the Positive School 235 ■ Biological Theories in the Early 20th Century 236 • Crime and Physical Characteristics 236 • Crime and Intelligence 239 • **Summary 243 • Questions for Critical Thinking 243 • Net Work 244 • Key Terms 244 • Suggested Reading 244 • Bibliography 245**

CHAPTER 8 Psychological Perspectives on Criminality / 247
Patricia A. Zapf, John Jay College of Criminal Justice
Nathalie C. Gagnon, Kwantlen University College
David N. Cox, Simon Fraser University
Ronald Roesch, Simon Fraser University

■ Psychological Theories of Crime 248 • Psychoanalytic Theory 249 • Theories of Moral Development 252 • Eysenck's Theory of Crime and Personality 255 • Social Learning Theory 256 • Operant Conditioning 259 ■ Antisocial Personality 260 ■ Crime and Mental Illness 267 • **Summary 273 • Questions for Critical Thinking 274 • Net Work 274 • Key Terms 275 • Suggested Reading 275 • Bibliography 276**

CHAPTER 9 Strain Theories / 282

James C. Hackler, University of Victoria

■ **Durkheim: The Functions of Crime and Anomie 283** • Anomie and Normlessness 283 ■ **Merton: The Gap Between Aspirations and Means 284** • Strain as a Feature of Society (Rather Than of Individuals) 286 • Responding to Opportunistic Crimes of the Powerful 288 • Strain as a Feature of Individuals 289 • Coercion and Strain 289 ■ **The Shift from Control to Opportunity Structures 290** • Kobrin: Opportunities in the Community 291 • Richard Cloward: Illegitimate Opportunity Structures 292 • Marginal Opportunity Structures 294 ■ **From Albert K. Cohen: The Middle-Class Measuring Rod to Elijah Anderson: The Code of the Street 296** ■ **Assessing Strain Theories 299** • The Static State of Strain Theories 299 • The Convergence of Strain Theory and Other Perspectives 300 ■ **Uses of Strain Theory 301** • John Braithwaite: Greater Class Mix and the Reduction of Crime 302 • Reducing Upper-Class Crime 302 ■ **Policy Implications 303** • **Summary 305** • **Questions for Critical Thinking 306** • **Net Work 306** • **Key Terms 306** • **Suggested Reading 307** • **Bibliography 307**

CHAPTER 10 Conflict Theories / 310

Danica Dupont

■ **Cultural Conflict Theory 310** ■ **Group Conflict Theory 311** ■ **Marxist Conflict Perspectives in Criminology 315** • Instrumental Marxism 317 • Structural Marxism 319 • Crimes of the Powerless 323 • Crimes of the Powerful 324 ■ **Socialist Feminism 326** ■ **Left Realism 329** • **Summary 331** • **Questions for Critical Thinking 332** • **Net Work 333** • **Key Terms 333** • **Suggested Reading 333** • **Bibliography 334**

CHAPTER 11 Contemporary Critical Criminology / 339

Bryan Hogeveen and Andrew Woolford, University of Alberta and University of Manitoba

■ **What Is *Critical* about Critical Criminology? 340** ■ **Critical Criminology in English Canada 343** ■ **Governmentality and Power: Foucault and Criminology 346** ■ **Actuarialism, Risk, and the Risk Society 349** ■ **Cultural Criminology 352** ■ **A "Field Theory" of Criminology 354** ■ **Agamben—Sovereignty and the State of Exception 356** ■ **Jacques Derrida: Deconstruction *Is* Justice 360** • **Summary 365** • **Questions for Critical Thinking 366** • **Net Work 366** • **Key Terms 367** • **Suggested Reading 367** • **Bibliography 367**

CHAPTER 12 Interactionist Theories / 371

Robert A. Stebbins, University of Calgary

■ **The Deviant Career 372** • Primary Deviation 373 • Agents of Social Control 375 • Secondary Deviation 378 • Reactions to Commitment 383 ■ **Socialization into Crime 385** • Differential Association 385 • Criminal Identities 388 ■ **Limitations 389** • The Neo-Marxist Critique 389 • The Empiricist Critique 390 • The Ethnomethodological Critique 390 ■ **Implications 391** • **Summary 392** • **Questions for Critical Thinking 393** • **Net Work 393** • **Key Terms 394** • **Suggested Reading 394** • **Bibliography 394**

CHAPTER 13 Social Control Theory / 397

Rick Linden, University of Manitoba

■ **Theories of Social Disorganization—Durkheim, Thrasher, and Shaw and McKay 398** • Durkheim and Social Integration 398 • Thrasher and *The Gang* 398 • Shaw and McKay—Ecological Analysis 399 ■ **Early Social Control Theories—Reiss and Nye 400** ■ **Hirschi and the Social Bond 401** • Attachment 401 • Commitment 402 • Involvement 402 • Belief 402 • Self-Control—The General Theory of Crime 402 ■ **Family Relationships 404** • Strength of Family Ties 404 • Parental Supervision and Discipline 404 • Parental Role Model 405 ■ **Schooling 406** ■ **Religion 407** ■ **Female Criminality 409** ■ **Issues with Social Control Theory 410** • How Does Control Theory Explain Upper-World Crime? 410 • Does Everyone Have the Same Motivation to Deviate? The Role of Delinquent Peers 411 • Is Control Theory a Conservative Theory of Crime? 413 ■ Policy Implications of Control Theory 416 • Policy Implications—The Family 416 ■ The Schools and Social Policy 419 • **Summary 420 • Questions for Critical Thinking 421 • Net Work 421 • Key Terms 422 • Suggested Reading 422 • Bibliography 422**

PART 3: PATTERNS OF CRIMINAL BEHAVIOUR 427

CHAPTER 14 Conventional or "Street" Crime / 429

Daniel J. Koenig, Formerly of University of Victoria
Rick Linden, University of Manitoba

■ The Routine Activities Approach 430 • Who 432 • Where 433 • When 433 ■ Critique of Routine Activities Theory 433 ■ Patterns of Specific Crimes 434 ■ Murder and Other Criminal Homicides 435 • Legal Meanings of Types of Homicide 435 • The Dynamics of Homicide 438 ■ Assaultive Behaviours 441 • The Increased Incidence of Assault in the 1980s and 1990s 442 • Family Violence—Child Abuse and Elder Abuse 442 ■ Robbery 444 • Incidence 444 • Victims 444 • Offenders 445 • Pattern 446 ■ Break and Enter 446 • Incidence and Patterns 447 • A Crime of Opportunity 448 ■ Motor Vehicle Theft 449 ■ Preventing Crime 451 • Situational Crime Prevention 451 • Reducing Motivated Offenders 452 • Selective Incapacitation 454 • **Summary 456 • Questions for Critical Thinking 457 • Net Work 458 • Key Terms 458 • Suggested Reading 458 • Bibliography 459**

CHAPTER 15 Organized Crime / 463

Rodney T. Stamler, Assistant Commissioner RCMP (Rtd)

■ What Is Organized Crime? 464 • What Distinguishes an Organized Crime Group from a Terrorist Group? 467 ■ How Organized Is Organized Crime? 468 • The Roots of Organized Crime 468 ■ Who Is Involved in Organized Crime? 471 ■ Major Organized Crime Groups in Canada 472 • The Italian-Based Mafia 473 • Outlaw Motorcycle Gangs 475 • Triads and Other Asian Organized Crime Groups 479 • The Russian Mafia and Eastern European Crime Groups 482 • South American, Colombian, and Mexican Cartels 483 • Other Canadian Ethnic-Based Crime Groups 484 ■ The Nature of Consensual Crime Activity 485 ■ Money-Laundering Schemes 486 ■ Controlling Organized Crime 489 • Legalization of Illicit Goods and Services 489 • Enforcement 490 • National Criminal Laws and Procedures 491 • International Cooperation 492 • **Summary 493 • Questions for Critical Thinking 493 • Net Work 494 • Key Terms 494 • Suggested Reading 494 • Bibliography 495**

CHAPTER 16 Corporate and White-Collar Crime / 498

John Hagan, Northwestern University
Rick Linden, University of Manitoba

■ The Extent and Nature of Corporate and White-Collar Crime 499 • The Extent of Corporate and White-Collar Crime 499 • The Nature of Corporate and White-Collar Crime 501 ■ Class, Crime, and the Corporations 502 • Occupation, Organization, and Crime 502 • Social Class and Crime 504 ■ White-Collar Crime and the Social Organization of Work 508 • Crime and the Corporation 508 • The Criminogenic Market Structure 510 • Corporate Accounting Scandals 512 • Consumer Safety Issues 516 ■ White-Collar Crime and Legal Sanctions 517 ■ Occupational Crime 521 • Unprofessional Conduct and Malpractice 521 • Investment and Securities Fraud 524 • Internet Fraud 525 • Tax Fraud 525 • Political Corruption 528 • Blue-Collar Crime 529 • Employee Fraud 530 • **Summary 531 • Questions for Critical Thinking 531 • Net Work 532 • Key Terms 532 • Suggested Reading 532 • Bibliography 533**

Glossary G1
Credits C1
Index I1

Preface

Since it was first published in 1987, *Criminology: A Canadian Perspective* has been used to introduce this field to more than 50 000 students across the country. At that time, most criminology courses in Canada were taught using American texts. It was our intention to provide a text that was written *by* Canadians, *for* Canadians. Over the past three decades, the discipline of criminology has grown from a few widely scattered faculty members to a large community of academics, researchers, practitioners, and students. The sixth edition of *Criminology: A Canadian Perspective* continues to reflect their work. That said, criminology remains a small and underfunded discipline in Canada. As a result, much of the new theoretical and empirical work in the field continues to come from the United States and Europe. This sixth edition represents our continued effort to provide you with the best Canadian scholarship in combination with the most relevant research from other countries.

Advantages of a Multiauthored Text

The many different theories proposed to explain criminality are continually being revived and revised. Often the popularity of a particular theory owes as much to ideological commitment and academic fashion as it does to the explanatory power of the theory. As a result of this unresolved diversity, the pages of many texts are littered with the bodies of straw men, set up only to be sacrificed to the author's favourite approach. The authors of this text are among Canada's leading criminologists. The advantage of having such a multiauthored text is that the diverse perspectives of criminology can be fairly represented. In this book, each chapter is written by someone who has used the perspective in his or her own research and who understands its strengths and weaknesses.

Organization of the Text

This book is intended as a text for a one-term course in introductory criminology. While the book deals extensively with theories about the causes of crime (which have largely been developed elsewhere), its purpose is to provide students with information about crime in Canada.

The chapters of this text have been organized into three parts. Part 1, "Crime and Society," provides some of the basic information about crime: the sources of criminal law; the legal elements of crime; the sources of information about crime; the social correlates of criminal behaviour; and a discussion of women and crime. This part provides the student with the background necessary to assess the theories of crime causation presented in Part 2. In this part, entitled "Explanations of Crime," all the major theories are covered, including biological, psychological, and sociological explanations. In Part 3, "Patterns of Criminal Behaviour," many of the most serious and frequent types of crime are discussed. The way we have arranged the chapters is our suggestion for presenting the material, but instructors are encouraged to assign these chapters in whatever order best suits their course needs.

Features of the Text

Each chapter begins with a brief *Introduction* and a list of *Learning Objectives* and concludes with a *Summary, Questions for Critical Thinking, Net Work* (an Internet activity), a list of *Key Terms, Suggested Readings*, and a *Bibliography*. This text also features *Web Links* to interesting related websites, a *Running Glossary*, which defines the key terms in the margin next to the paragraph in which they first appear, and a full *Glossary* at the end of the text.

The following ancillary products are also available to augment teaching and learning inside and outside the classroom and to facilitate testing: a computerized test bank, a printed study guide, PowerPoint slides, and a website (www.lindencriminology6e.nelson.com). The PowerPoint slides are available for instructors to download at the website.

New to the Sixth Edition

This edition of *Criminology: A Canadian Perspective* provides us with the opportunity to update crime statistics, to add new research material, and to make some major revisions that have been suggested by reviewers. These major revisions include two new chapters and significant changes to several others.

The two new chapters are Chapter 10, "Conflict Theories," written by Danica Dupont, and Chapter 11, "Contemporary Critical Criminology," written by Bryan Hogeveen and Andrew Woolford. These authors represent a new generation of Canadian criminologists and bring a fresh perspective to these topics. Chapter 10 replaces an earlier chapter covering conflict theories. The theories covered in this chapter include cultural conflict theory, group conflict theory, instrumental and structuralist Marxism, socialist feminism, and left realism. Chapter 11 covers material about critical criminology that is not covered in many criminology texts, including the work of theorists such as Foucault, Bourdieu, Wacquant, Agamben, and Derrida.

Major revisions have been made to Chapter 1 ("Crime, Criminals, and Criminology"), which now includes a lengthy discussion of Conrad Black and his conviction for fraud and obstruction of justice and a section on green criminology, one of the newest sub-fields in the discipline. Chapter 5 ("Correlates of Criminal Behaviour") has extensive new material on race and crime, including a discussion of racial profiling of Blacks in Toronto and new data on Aboriginals and crime. It also has a lengthy new section on drug misuse and criminal behaviour. Chapter 7 ("Early Theories of Criminology") has three new boxes dealing with the Enlightenment, Eugenics, and Criminology in Nazi Germany. A new section on Elijah Anderson's "Code of the Streets" has been added to Chapter 9 ("Strain Theories"). There is a new box on the problems of the Davis Bay Innu in Chapter 13 ("Social Control Theory"). Chapter 14 ("Conventional or Street Crime") now includes a critique of routine activities theory and a new box on the social problems in Vancouver's downtown eastside. The statistical material in Chapter 14 has been updated and several redundant sections have been cut. Chapter 16 ("Corporate and White-Collar Crime") now includes a discussion of criminal and unethical behaviour in sports, a section on consumer safety issues including the recalls of pet food and toys manufactured in China, and new material on political corruption, including a discussion of the Gomery Inquiry.

ACKNOWLEDGEMENTS

It has become traditional for authors to thank families for not making demands, and spouses, or close friends, both for moral support and for those unspecified but essential services that writing seems to require. Since my wife and children had already reached their tolerance limit with my work schedule, I decided that I couldn't just disappear into my office and reappear two years later with a book. Thus it is to them that I owed my wise decision to get help from the friends and colleagues who co-authored the text. For the time I did spend writing, I thank for their support Olive, Brad, Chris, Robin, Shawn, T.J., and Amanda. By the time of the fourth edition, all my children were old enough that they no longer cared about my working hours. However, their place at my work table was taken by pets, and I thank Nicholas, Morris, Annie, and Edward for ensuring that each page in this manuscript has been stepped on or slept on by an orange cat. Callie has recently added some black cat hair to my computer keyboard.

As usual, working with the people at Nelson Education Ltd. has been a delightful experience. For significant improvements in this sixth edition, I thank Cara Yarzab and Rebecca Ryoji and their colleagues who have worked on the book. As usual, Diane Symbaluk has done a wonderful job with the ancillary material.

Special thanks to the reviewers who have given us good advice over the various editions: Bill Avison, Marilyn Belle-McQuillan, Thomas Bernard, Augustine Brannigan, David Brownfield, Tullio Caputo, Elaine DeCunha-Bath, Sange de Silva, Robert Drislaine, Karlene Faith, Thomas Gabor, Colin Goff, Jim Hackler, Sheilagh Hodgins, Carl Keane, Gail Kellough, Heather A. Kitchin, John Martin, Norman Okihiro, Robynne Neugebauer, Gary Parkinson, Michael Petrunik, Karen Richter, Vincent F. Sacco, Les Samuelson, Bernard Schissel, Alfredo Schulte-Bockholt, Phillip C. Stenning, Lee Stuesser, Diane Symbaluk, David Ryan, Heather A. Kitchin, Norman Okihiro, and Austin T. Turk.

I would also like to thank each of the authors who contributed to the book. I appreciate your enthusiastic responses to revision suggestions and your efforts to meet deadlines. I continue to enjoy and to learn from your work.

Individual authors wished to make the following acknowledgements: J. Evans and A. Himelfarb (Chapter 4)—"The authors wish to thank the Canadian Centre for Justice Statistics for providing much of the data presented in this chapter." T.F. Hartnagel (Chapter 5)—"I wish to thank Kerri Calvert of the Sociology Information Centre, University of Alberta, for her help in locating references and generally keeping me informed of recent material. I also wish to acknowledge the research assistance of Marianne Nielson, Hannah Scott, Cora Voyageur, and Xavier Cattarinich, who helped me with the various editions of this text."

Rick Linden
University of Manitoba

PART 1

Crime and Society

Part 1 of this book provides some basic information about crime: the origins of our criminal law, the legal elements of crime, the sources of information about crime, and the social correlates of criminal behaviour.

Chapter 1 introduces you to the discipline of criminology, which is the scientific study of crime and criminals. This chapter explores the role played by rules and shows how these rules are sometimes formalized in laws. The chapter also looks at several different ways of defining crime and points out that because crime is socially defined, the definition of crime can change over time. "Green" criminology is one of the newest sub-fields of criminology and is used to illustrate the changing nature of criminology.

In Chapter 2, we learn how our system of law has developed as we have evolved from simple hunting and gathering societies to modern industrial ones. With the increased complexity and growth of modern societies comes the need for a formal legal system to maintain order. We also learn why some social harms are defined as illegal, while others are not.

The legal elements of a crime are *actus reus* (the physical element) and *mens rea* (the mental element). These are discussed in Chapter 3, along with defences available to an accused, a history of criminal procedure, and an outline of the social factors affecting the definition of specific types of crime.

We cannot study crime systematically unless we can measure it. Chapter 4 details some of the ways we count crime, such as official government statistics, victimization surveys, and self-report surveys. None of these methods is completely adequate; you will learn the strengths and weaknesses of each.

Before we can explain a phenomenon such as crime, we must know something about the way it is distributed demographically. In Chapter 5, a number of correlates of crime are discussed, including age, sex, race, and social class. In recent years, there has been an increased recognition of the importance of looking at the issue of women and crime. Because of this, Chapter 6 considers this correlate in more depth. The explanations of crime discussed in Part 2 should be judged according to how well they account for these regularities.

Crime, Criminals, and Criminology

1

Rick Linden

UNIVERSITY OF MANITOBA

Canadians seem to have an endless fascination with crime. Our daily newspapers and television news programs are saturated with stories about crime and criminals. Movies, television shows, and video games are often filled with depictions of violence and other criminal behaviour. While crime is a matter of public concern and a favourite form of entertainment, it is also the subject of serious academic study. This chapter will introduce you to the discipline of criminology, which is the scientific study of crime and criminals.

Learning Objectives

After reading this chapter, you should be able to

- Define the term *criminology*.
- Understand the different subject areas studied by criminologists.
- Explain the role played by rules in our daily lives and understand how these rules can become formalized in law.
- Understand the different ways of defining crime. These are a strict legal definition, an expanded legal definition that goes beyond just considering the criminal law, a definition based on the protection of people's human rights, and a definition that places acts of deviance and crime on a continuum ranging from minor acts of deviance to serious offences that almost everyone agrees are wrong.
- Explain how crime is socially defined and how people's ideas about crime can change over time.
- Understand the two main theoretical perspectives on how some acts get defined as criminal and others do not. These are the conflict and consensus perspectives.
- Understand the new sub-field of green criminology.

A Violent Crime: The Sand Brothers

Robert and Danny Sand grew up in an Alberta family with their father, Dennis, and their mother, Elaine. Robert was born in 1978 and Danny was born in 1980. Dennis Sand, who had served time in jail in his youth for a variety of crimes including armed robbery, gave up crime when he was 20 and later supported his family by doing a variety of jobs. He lives in a small Alberta community where Elaine runs a business, and both are respected community members (Staples, 2002). As youngsters, Robert and Danny were constantly in trouble, along with several of their closest friends who made up a group composed of the only mixed-race boys in their town. The boys had difficulty in school and often refused to do any work. Their behaviour couldn't be controlled by their parents and the boys were frequently suspended from school. In junior high they got into more serious trouble, including intimidating other students. At age 15 Danny was sent to a youth centre for beating up another student. The boys began to steal cars and to use a variety of drugs, including crack cocaine. Newspaper reporter David Staples described the situation of the brothers and their friends:

> Their contact with adults was minimal. No teachers, because the teens had all dropped out. No parents, because most didn't live at home. They relied on each other to figure out the world, believing their friends were closer and wiser than any adult. They're all there to protect each other, and they can't see past that, says [one of the mothers]. The teens suffered from the moral blindness of those who have achieved nothing in life and have nothing to lose. But they weren't entirely lacking in vision. They had an inkling of the difference between right and wrong. They certainly understood when someone did wrong to them, or to one of their closest friends. They just didn't see it as a problem to rob or injure someone outside of their group. It was us vs. them, with them being teachers, the RCMP, car owners, property owners, anyone with something they wanted to grab. (Staples, 2002, D2)

In 1998, after several armed robberies, Robert received a seven-year jail sentence. He became a model inmate, though counsellors said he could never explain why he had behaved the way he did. Danny also ended up in jail for a number of crimes, including attacking a police officer. After his release, Danny got involved in another incident that foretold the crime that would result in his death. An Edmonton police officer used his cruiser car to block an alley where Danny Sand was suspiciously parked in a stolen truck. Instead of giving up, Danny sped toward the cruiser and seemed to swerve toward the police officer. After this incident, he joined Robert in Drumheller Penitentiary, where he continued to get into trouble and where he got a stomach tattoo saying "Fearless, Painless, Senseless." After his release Danny told people that he would never go back to jail.

In October of 2001, Robert was released to a halfway house. He could find only menial work and began to fear that he had cancer. He reunited with Laurie Bell, a former girlfriend who was a heavy drug user. He left the halfway house, violating his parole. On December 18, Robert and Laurie, along with Danny, who was also violating his parole, headed for the Maritimes, where they had vague plans for making a new life. They never made it past Manitoba.

In the midst of a crime spree that included robbing a bank, breaking into homes, and stealing several vehicles, the three made it to the town of Russell, Manitoba. Shortly after midnight on December 21, Danny drove onto the main highway without first stopping at a stop sign. When RCMP constables Brian Auger and Dennis Strongquill tried to stop the vehicle because of this violation,

Robert fired several shotgun blasts at the police. When the police drove away, Danny chased the police SUV into town. He rammed the SUV after it stopped at the Russell RCMP Detachment. Robert jumped out of their truck and fired several shotgun blasts at Constable Strongquill, who was trapped in the damaged police vehicle. Four of the shots hit Constable Strongquill, who died almost immediately.

After a manhunt, the RCMP found the trio at a motel near Wolseley, Saskatchewan. A police sniper fatally wounded Danny Sand, and Robert Sand and Laurie Bell were captured and charged with first-degree murder. While in prison awaiting trial, Robert kept a diary in which he reflected on the shooting:

> I was in one of my moods so I asked to see the pictures again of my case. There are pics of trucks burnt, crashed shot up etc. Homes broken into, property of ours and others and of course pics of the dead cop, shot up cop cars and Dan. Now I've seen them before and without emotion, I've no more tears to shed. But I was looking at this man, on a table. And I started to think, he's just a man, and shouldn't be dead. He had a family and friends, and now he's a body on a table. I realized it's not the man I hated, but the uniform he wore. His flag, colours of war. But seeing him without his uniform I felt bad for the loss of his life. But then I flipped to the pics of Dan, and my thoughts changed. Cause now I felt that the other man is right where he should be. And losses on both sides are to be expected, only Dan took my place. And when I looked upon the cop car I felt pride, and remembered the battle, I remembered how these enemy soldiers fled in fear and cowardess. I saw how much damage I'd caused to their unit and smiled, from the knowledge that the enemy isn't as strong as they want us to believe. But they should beware that the moment they fly their flag, wear their uniform. That they're at war and people die in war, everyone has their enemies. (McIntyre, 2003, 195)

Robert Sand, who physically attacked his own lawyer in court at the end of his trial, is now serving a life sentence after being convicted of first-degree murder; Laurie Bell was convicted of manslaughter.

One of the challenges of the discipline of criminology is to make sense of cases such as this one. Why did the Sand brothers live such wild and undisciplined lives? Why did they aggressively pursue Constable Strongquill and his partner? Why did Robert see the world as a war zone? Is there anything we can do to prevent tragedies like this in the future?

Criminologists have considered a wide range of theories to explain crime, and you will learn about many of these theories in this text. Some focus on biology—could Robert and Danny have inherited traits from their parents that made their criminality more likely? Others look at an individual's psychological make-up—were the Sand brothers psychopaths or could other mental conditions have caused their behaviour? Other theories are sociological—what role did their family and friends play in their violence? Could the schools have done a better job motivating the brothers to study and to become involved in legitimate outlets for their energy? What role did racism and the brothers' poor economic prospects play in their lives?

These questions are very complex and we may never be able to adequately explain individual cases such as this one. However, even if we could explain the factors that led Robert Sands to kill Constable Strongquill, would the same explanation apply to another homicide case that was being dealt with at the same time as Robert Sands was facing the court on murder charges? Diego Zepeda-Cordera, a Toronto barber, was a member of the Missionary Church of Christ (Galloway, 2003). His 19-year-old son, Walter, began to behave in a way that troubled Zepeda-Cordera, who was very devoted to his religious beliefs. Walter began to go out to bars, he smoked, and he wouldn't help out around the house. His parents found a satanic magazine in his room. His father became extremely concerned when Walter began to speak in gibberish at a religious meeting. Believing his son was possessed by the devil, Mr. Zepeda-Cordero and a friend tied Walter to two metal chairs in their apartment building. Their minister and many church members came to the home to pray over Walter in order to exorcise the devil they believed was inside him. Walter remained tied to the chairs, often with duct tape over his mouth, for seven days before he died of dehydration. Although the judge in the case believed that the men genuinely thought Walter was possessed and sought to help him, he sentenced them to four years in jail after they pleaded guilty to manslaughter.

As these two examples suggest, there are many different patterns of homicide that have little in common other than the death of a victim. Some involve intoxicated people who stab friends during drinking parties; others involve a settling of accounts among organized criminals; some abusive men kill their wives and children; some corporate executives kill their customers by selling defective products in order to enhance their profits; some corporate executives kill their employees by providing unsafe working conditions; and some predators kill children after having sex with them. In your criminology course, you will learn about these and many other patterns of criminal behaviour. The case of Conrad Black, accused of several white-collar crimes, further illustrates the diversity of the behaviour studied by criminologists.

A White-Collar Crime: The Downfall of Conrad Black

For much of the spring of 2007, the Canadian media covered the trial of Conrad Black and several co-accused who were charged in the United States with a variety of offences relating to the fraudulent acquisition of funds that should have gone to shareholders of Hollinger International, but which instead were taken by the accused, who were managers of the company.

Black's background was very different from that of the Sand brothers. His father was a wealthy businessman and Conrad had a very comfortable childhood. As a boy he attended Upper Canada College, an elite private school, but was unhappy with its regimentation and discipline. While at the college, he broke into school offices and stole and altered school records. On one occasion, he and several accomplices broke into the central office and stole several final exam papers. Perhaps anticipating his later business career, Black had previously taken copies of the academic records of all the students in the school, so he knew which students would be prepared to pay the most for the exam papers. His motivation was not entirely commercial:

> I was going to reduce the school's whole academic system . . . to utter chaos while achieving a spectacular mark for myself having done virtually no work. . . . By the last week of the school year, I had almost completely undermined the system. . . . I had more power than our jailers. I penetrated the Masters' Common Room and reassigned the faculty to supervisory tasks by typing up and substituting my own assignment sheet, assuring among other things that our examinations were presided over by the least vigilant people available, the music and printing teachers, as I recall. (Black, 1993, 15)

The scheme unravelled when one of Black's customers confessed to cheating and Black was expelled from the school.

After graduating from Laval University's law school, Black began a career in the newspaper business when he and two partners bought a small Quebec paper, the *Sherbrooke Record*. The paper was losing money and Black and his partners quickly discovered a formula that would eventually make them very rich. They fired 40 percent of the employees (a step that Black was reported to have described as "drowning the kittens" [Plotz, 2001, n.p.]), modernized the production process, and almost immediately began to make a profit. They cut costs relentlessly. When one employee brought Black's partner David Radler a petition signed by newspaper staff complaining about some of the cost-cutting measures taken by the new management, Radler deducted 2 cents from the man's pay for wasting the piece of paper (Black, 1993). At the same time Black reports beginning a pattern of behaviour that later led to serious legal problems:

> [At the same time as they were cutting even the most minor expenses at the newspaper] we operated . . . what amounted to a modest slush fund for our preferred causes and tenuously business-connected expenses. (Black, 1993, 72)

Throughout his business career Black attempted on several occasions to transfer money from the corporations he ran—but which were owned by public shareholders—to his personal accounts.

Black began buying other small papers and eventually acquired a very important British paper, the *Telegram*, as well as the *Jerusalem Post*, Canada's *National Post*, and the *Chicago Sun-Times*. At one point through his corporation Hollinger International, he ran hundreds of daily papers including 60 percent of the papers published in Canada and controlled the world's third-largest newspaper chain (McNish and Stewart, 2004). Black was extremely wealthy and had a very high public profile. He moved to London, and in 2001 he gave up his Canadian citizenship so that he could accept admission to the British House of Lords and the title of Lord Black of Crossharbour. Shortly after taking his seat in the House of Lords in 2001, Black's financial empire began to unravel when he was challenged by investors at Hollinger's annual shareholders meeting. Some investors began to demand to know why their investment in

Hollinger was not profitable while Black and other senior executives were getting very wealthy. He was ultimately forced to step down from his position as chief executive officer of Hollinger and an investigation committee established by the board of directors accused Black and other executives of running a "corporate kleptocracy" that conspired to steal $400 million from Hollinger that should have been paid out to shareholders. The report concluded that "Black and Radler were motivated by a 'ravenous appetite for cash' . . . and Hollinger International, under their reign, 'lost any sense of corporate purpose, competitive drive or internal ethical concerns' as the two executives looked for ways to 'suck cash' out of the company" (McNish and Stewart, 2004, 288). In 2005 this action was followed by criminal fraud charges filed in the United States against Black and three other executives.

During much of the period when his actions were under investigation, Black demonstrated the imperious attitude that had characterized his career. In response to criticisms of his extravagance in things like his use of company jets, he responded:

> There has not been an occasion for many months when I got on our plane without wondering whether it was really affordable. But I'm not prepared to reenact the French Revolutionary renunciation of the rights of nobility. We have to find a balance between an unfair taxation on the company and a reasonable treatment of the founder-builder-managers. We are proprietors, after all, beleaguered though we may be. (McNish and Stewart, 2004, 92)

Black and several colleagues were charged with conspiring to take funds from Hollinger International for their own personal gain. This is illegal because the corporation was owned by shareholders, not by the men who ran the company. How did they take the money? Over a period of years, Black sold off Hollinger's newspapers. When he sold the papers, the buyers also paid for agreements that Hollinger would not start competing papers in those markets. However, rather than these non-compete fees going to Hollinger and its shareholders, they went directly to Black and his colleagues. They were alleged to have diverted over $83 million in these transactions. In some of the cases, the non-compete agreements were not even requested by the purchasers but were put in the agreement at the request of Black and his colleagues. The money to pay these fees was simply diverted from the purchase price, so the funds that went to Black were essentially taken from Hollinger's shareholders. In one transaction in which Black himself purchased a newspaper from Hollinger, Black was even paid a fee to agree to not compete with himself. In other transactions, Black and his colleagues received personal non-compete fees and additional fees were also paid to a company that they owned (McNish and Stewart, 2004). In effect, they were being paid twice for the same thing at the expense of Hollinger shareholders who actually owned the papers being sold.

Black was also charged with misusing corporate money for personal expenses. One of the key examples of this presented by the prosecution at his trial was using over $40 000 of Hollinger money to pay for a lavish birthday party for his wife. Another charge was obstruction of justice because of an incident when he and his chauffeur were videotaped violating a court order by removing a number of boxes of documents from his Toronto office. Key to the case against Black was testimony from his partner, David Radler, who had pled guilty and received a relatively lenient 29-month sentence in exchange for his testimony against Black.

Black's defence was relatively straightforward. His lawyers claimed that the non-compete payments were approved by Hollinger's board of directors and were therefore legal. They also claimed that his use of Hollinger funds for parties, trips, and other expenses was legal because the expenses were business-related. For example, his wife's birthday party was held after a board meeting and involved making contacts with other business people. Also, Black paid a portion of the expenses from his own funds to cover the personal component of the event. Finally, they claimed that David Radler was lying in order to get lenient treatment. In fact, Radler had consistently lied about his involvement prior to his guilty plea and he did receive lenient treatment, so his testimony was vulnerable to those charges by the defence.

In July 2007 Black was convicted on four charges and acquitted on nine others. He was convicted of obstruction of justice because of the documents he removed from his office. The other convictions related to non-competition agreements that were not requested by the buyers of several Hollinger newspapers and to the sale in which Black was paid handsomely for agreeing not to compete with himself. Black's sentence was not known at the time this chapter was written, but it will almost certainly be for a much lengthier prison term than he would receive in Canada, where white-collar criminals are treated very leniently in comparison to the United States (see Chapter 16).

What Is Criminology?

The term **criminology** is used in a number of different ways. Detectives in mystery novels and forensic scientists and crime analysts on television shows are sometimes referred to as criminologists. The term is also sometimes applied to physicists and chemists who specialize in studying the trajectories of bullets or the ink used in counterfeit money. Most commonly, the term is applied to academics who study crime and the criminal justice system. In this text, we will follow the definition of the discipline given by two famous American criminologists, Edwin Sutherland and Donald Cressey: "Criminology is the body of knowledge regarding crime as a social phenomenon. It includes within its scope the processes of making laws, of breaking laws, and of reacting to the breaking of laws. . . . The objective of criminology is the development of a body of general and verified principles and of other types of knowledge regarding this process of law, crime, and treatment" (1960, 3). This definition implies that criminologists take a scientific approach to the study of crime.

criminology
The body of knowledge regarding crime as a social phenomenon. It includes the processes of making laws, breaking laws, and reacting to the breaking of laws. Its objective is the development of a body of general and verified principles and of other types of knowledge regarding this process of law, crime, and treatment.

Why Should We Study Crime?

There are three reasons why it is important for us to know more about crime. First, social scientists feel that it is intrinsically worthwhile to understand more about all aspects of our social lives, including criminal behaviour and society's response to this behaviour. Learning about crime can tell us a great deal about

FOCUS

BOX 1.1 Crime and the Media

Most Canadians learn about serious crime through the media rather than from first-hand experience. Stories on television and radio and in newspapers, magazines, and books shape our views about crime and criminals. Writers of television series and movies use violence to attract viewers and to sell tickets. Newspaper editors and television reporters also select the crime news we hear about and construct the way in which this news is presented to us in order to attract an audience.

Unfortunately, the picture of crime we receive from the media is often not accurate. For example, while most crime is property crime, most stories in the media deal with violent crime. Typical of research in this area was a review of all the crime-related stories reported over two months in an Ottawa newspaper (Gabor, 1994). Over half the stories focused on violent crimes, particularly murders. However, violent crimes made up only 7 percent of reported crimes in Ottawa, and the city averaged just six murders per year. While violent crimes were over-reported, property crimes rarely received much attention, and white-collar and political crimes were almost never discussed. Between 1990 and 1996, the homicide rate in Canada declined by almost 20 percent while the murder coverage on CBC and CTV national television news programs increased by 300 percent. Calgary had 12 murders in 1996, a year in which the *Calgary Herald* published 1667 murder-related stories (National Media Archive, 1997).

The portrayal of crime in the fictional media is even more distorted. Consider the partial list of the 221 violent acts depicted in *South Park: Bigger, Longer & Uncut*, the R-rated movie based on the animated series *South Park*, and ask whether the list reflects the reality of the lives of today's young people:

> 130 weapons fire (with multiple killings), 18 electric shocks, 10 blows to the body, 8 blood spatterings, 3 burnings, 3 hanging-body scenes, 1 breaking of body in half, 1 assault with chain saw, 1 attempted electrocution, and 1 dog attack. (Media Index, 1999)

The popularity of programs such as *CSI* has affected people's perceptions of the justice system. Some prosecutors have spoken about the *CSI* effect, which they feel has caused crime victims and juror members to expect more definitive forensic evidence than is available outside the fictional laboratories of a television show (Dowler et al., 2006).

Why do the media misrepresent crime? The primary goal of the media is to make profits by selling advertising. Stories that attract viewers or readers will boost ratings and circulation even if these stories do not represent the reality of crime. The informal news media rule "If it bleeds, it leads" reflects the fact that the public is fascinated by sensationalized, bloody stories such as mass murders or attacks against helpless senior citizens. Commenting on his experience with the media, the executive director of the Nova Scotia Bar Society said, "If there's no blood and gore, or there's no sex, it's not newsworthy. And if it falls into the category of being newsworthy, then

our society. For example, the United States has a much higher rate of violent crime, particularly firearms crime, than Canada. The United States also has a much harsher justice system than Canada (see Box 12.1). These differences highlight important value differences between the two countries. Similarly, changes in the patterns of crime over time can help us to identify and to understand changes in our society. Second, if we wish to reduce crime we need to understand it. Just as an understanding of a disease helps medical scientists to develop cures, we must understand crime in order to prevent it. For example, Richard Tremblay conducted several studies tracking the behaviour of children

FOCUS

BOX 1.1 Crime and the Media *(Continued)*

they have to show the dead body. They've got to show the corpse" (McCormick, 1995, 182).

The media's misrepresentation of crime has several consequences. First, Canadians greatly over-estimate the amount of violent crime and have a fear of crime that is higher than the actual risk of victimization. Crime stories lead us to see Canada as a violent and dangerous place although it is in reality a safe country. Second, the media provide a distorted stereotype of offenders. Violent crimes are most often committed by relatives, friends, and acquaintances, not by the anonymous stranger so many of us fear. Consider even our image of the mass murderer. Everybody in Canada knows about Clifford Olson and Paul Bernardo. However, few recognize the names of mining executives Clifford Frame, Gerald Phillips, and Roger Parry, who may have been responsible for the deaths of 26 miners in the 1992 Westray Mine disaster in Stellarton, Nova Scotia. Our fear of crime and our image of the criminal have an impact on government policy toward crime. Actual crime trends are irrelevant—if the public feels crime is out of control, it demands that government do something about it. Although crime rates are declining, a combination of increasing media coverage of crime and pressure from a variety of interest groups has led the federal government to tighten several laws, including those dealing with immigration, young offenders, and firearms.

The media may also contribute to crime. There is some evidence that children who are exposed to a great deal of television violence are more likely to be violent themselves, but this linkage is complex and people disagree about the degree to which television influences behaviour rather than simply reflecting an interest in violence. However, there is some anecdotal evidence that the media do play a role in individual cases. For example, Virginia teenager Josh Cooke was a fan of the movie *The Matrix*. He had a large poster from the film in his room and had a trench coat like the one worn by Neo, the character Keanu Reeves played in the movie. He also bought a shotgun similar to one used by Reeves in his movie fight against the "agents." In 2003, Cooke used the shotgun to kill his father and mother and then turned himself in to the police. His defence was that he was attempting to escape the matrix. Several other killers across the United States have also claimed to be affected by *The Matrix*, and two of these accused have been found not guilty by reason of insanity (Jackman, 2003). Lee Boyd Malvo, the young man accused of being one of the Washington snipers who killed 10 people in 2002, has written,

> Wake up! Free your mind, you are a slave to matrix "control." . . . The outside force has arrived. Free yourself of the matrix "control". Free first your mind. Trust me!! The body will follow. Remove fear, doubt, distrust, watch the change then. (Jackman, 2003, 3)

While it is obvious that most people who see movies such as *The Matrix* do not commit murders, many researchers believe that media exposure can influence people who are already vulnerable or predisposed to commit violence.

in Montreal as they grew up. One of his more interesting findings was that boys whose violent behaviour had not followed the normal pattern of declining by age 16 were more likely than other boys to be the sons of young mothers with low levels of education. Based on this research, he has worked with the Quebec government to develop support programs for mothers who fit these risk profiles to see if this support will help to reduce the criminality of their children (Blumstein, 2003). Finally, crime directly or indirectly affects all of us. Many of us have been victims of crime and all of us pay for the costs of crime and the crime control system. Also, many Canadians are employed in the justice system or in security-related businesses.

Criminal Code of Canada
laws.justice.gc.ca/en/C-46/index.html

The Discipline of Criminology

The discipline of criminology includes six major areas: the definition of crime and criminals; the origins and role of law; the social distribution of crime; the causation of crime; patterns of criminal behaviour; and societal reactions to crime.

The Definition of Crime and Criminals

Not all social harms are criminal nor are all criminal acts harmful. Thus it is necessary to specify what kinds of acts are defined as crimes. Also, while it might at first seem obvious, there is also some question concerning who should be defined as a criminal for purposes of criminological research. For example, should we include someone who has been charged with a criminal offence but has not been convicted? What about the person who has committed a criminal offence but not been charged? And how about the person who has been convicted of violations of laws governing a safe workplace after an employee was killed on the job, when these laws are not part of the Criminal Code?

The Origins and Role of the Law

It is important to understand the social origins of our laws as well as the role that law plays in society. Why do some acts get defined as criminal, while others are dealt with under other types of legislation or are not sanctioned at all?

The Social Distribution of Crime

In order to understand crime we must know such things as the characteristics of people who commit crimes; trends in the occurrence of crime over time; and differences between cities, provinces, and countries in the rates and types of crime. These and other dimensions of the social distribution of crime help criminologists to understand the causes of crime.

The Causation of Crime

One of the most important questions for criminologists is why some people commit crimes, while others live more law-abiding lives. In this text you will learn about a wide variety of explanations of criminal behaviour ranging from the biological to the individual to the social.

Patterns of Criminal Behaviour

Criminal acts are defined by law in particular categories such as homicide, theft, and sexual assault. Criminologists have conducted a great deal of research analyzing the patterns of these offences. Among the questions asked by criminologists are these: Who are the offenders? Who are the victims? Under what social circumstances are offences most likely to take place? What are the consequences for the victims of crime? How can particular types of crime be prevented?

Societal Reactions to Crime

Historically, societies have responded to crime in many different ways, and the issue of how best to deal with offenders is an important one. In our society we normally process law violators through a criminal justice system that includes the police, the courts, and the corrections system. Criminologists have studied each of these institutions very extensively.

While this text does not cover the criminal justice system, a brief overview of the system will help you to understand how people charged with criminal offences are dealt with in Canada. As you will learn in Chapter 3 ("Criminal Law") under the Constitution Act of 1867, the federal Parliament has exclusive jurisdiction over criminal law and procedure. This means that the provinces and territories cannot pass or amend the criminal law. However, the provinces are responsible for the administration of justice. Because of this division of power, the Canadian criminal justice system is quite complex. For example, there are many different levels of responsibility for policing. We have a federal police force, the Royal Canadian Mounted Police, which enforces some federal laws, such as the Controlled Drugs and Substances Act, for which it is responsible in all provinces and territories. However, it also acts as a provincial police force in all jurisdictions except Ontario, Quebec, and Newfoundland, which have their own provincial police forces. The provinces pay the RCMP for these services under a provincial policing contract. The RCMP also acts as a municipal police force in some communities. While most of these are small communities, they also do urban policing under contract in larger communities, most notably in the Lower Mainland of British Columbia. Thus while the city of Vancouver has its own municipal force like most of Canada's larger municipalities, the adjoining cities of Burnaby and Richmond are policed by the RCMP. In 2006, there were almost 62 500 police officers in Canada (Statistics Canada, 2006).

The courts also come under both federal and provincial jurisdiction. The provinces are responsible for appointing some judges and for administering the "lower" courts that deal with most criminal cases, including those involving young offenders. Higher-level courts that try serious criminal cases are the responsibility of the federal government as are the provincial appeal courts. Appeal courts do not try cases, but hear appeals of cases decided by other courts. At the top of the hierarchy of courts is the Supreme Court of Canada, which hears appeals of decisions made by provincial courts of appeal.

Sentenced offenders who receive sentences of less than two years are dealt with by the provincial government. This includes offenders who receive community dispositions such as probation or restitution. Those who are imprisoned go to institutions that are run by the provinces. A sentence of two years or more must be served in a federal institution that is run by the Correctional Service of Canada. This service also supervises offenders who are released into the community prior to the expiration of their sentences. The release decision is made by a separate body, the National Parole Board.

Overview of the Book

In the first three chapters of this text you will learn about the definition of crime and criminals and about the origins of law and the legal system. Chapter 4 describes how we obtain data about crime and criminals and Chapter 5 outlines the social distribution of crime in Canada. Chapter 6 deals with issues involving women and crime and introduces you to some of the theories that criminologists have developed to explain crime. Chapters 7 to 13 deal with early theories of crime and its causation, and with psychological and sociological explanations of criminality. The last section of the book deals with patterns of crime, including conventional or "street" crime (Chapter 14), organized crime (Chapter 15), and corporate and white-collar crime (Chapter 16). This text will not discuss the police, courts, and corrections because at most colleges and universities the operation of the criminal justice system is usually covered in a separate course.

Rules and Laws

The Regulation of Behaviour

norms
Established rules of behaviour or standards of conduct.

All groups have rules that guide their members' behaviour. Society cannot function without them—if we are to live and to work with others, rules are necessary. We must also have a reasonable expectation that other people will obey the rules. Think of the chaos that would result if each driver decided which side of the road she would drive on each day, or which stop sign he would decide to obey. Most of the time most of us conform to the **norms** our group prescribes. Of course, not all members of the group obey all the time. All of you have broken many rules, perhaps some of them important ones. In this text, we shall consider the topic of crime—behaviour that breaks the rules. How do rules get established? Why do people break them? How do groups respond to this violation?

We learn most rules so well that we follow them without thinking about them. Following accepted ways of walking and talking is almost automatic as these norms have been internalized. Often we cannot even specify all the rules that govern a particular behaviour, we just follow them. For example, when you try to learn a foreign language you suddenly become aware of all sorts of rules, such as those governing verb tenses, that you aren't consciously aware of when you are using English. Other rules are not followed in this routine fashion. Many of us may wish to drive above the speed limit, park illegally, or use marijuana but refrain from doing so because of our fear of penalties. Others may break these rules whenever they get a chance.

Think of some of the informal rules (or folkways) that govern your conduct. When you were younger, your parents probably tried to persuade you to eliminate some of your favourite habits such as eating with your fingers, dipping food in your milk, and banging your toys on the furniture. These are very basic rules—others can be more complex. For example, how do you address the Queen or the lieutenant-governor if you meet them? Whose name do you mention first when you introduce your 22-year-old spouse to your 60-year-old employer? What are we to make of these rules that seem, on their face, to be trivial or silly? Rules help us to select from the vast numbers of potential behaviours of which we are capable. Do we bow, kiss, or shake hands as a greeting? Which of two persons holds a door for the other? Who gets served first and last at dinner? How do we handle the important milestones in life such as marriage and death? While the way each society solves these little problems may vary widely, each society has provided solutions. Not only do these solutions avert potential chaos, but following the rules enhances our sense of belonging. The penalties for not following these rules are normally informal ones—the disapproval of family, friends, or colleagues or perhaps a reprimand from an organization to which the violator belongs. However, we normally don't think of the penalties, but continue to obey these rules because we have been taught to obey them and because they are part of belonging to the group.

In our society, not all actions are governed only by these informal means of social control. Why do some informal rules become more formal regulations or laws? Consider the early days of the automobile. Driving was not regulated and the only rules of the road were those that applied to horse-drawn carriages. When automobiles were open and speeds slow, drivers gave right of way to other drivers who had higher social status, just as was done when walking down the street. However, as speeds became higher and as drivers ranged farther from their homes, this became impractical, and the state had to establish more formal regulations. In this and in many other cases, we might say that the law exists when order can no longer be maintained through informal rules. The law also deals with behaviour that is too serious to be left to informal mechanisms.

What Is a Crime?

As you will read in Chapter 2 (The Origins and Role of Law in Society), the concept of crime has been developed relatively recently. That does not mean that people didn't do harmful things to one another in earlier times, but this harmful behaviour was handled quite differently than it is now. Prior to the 18th century, in most societies offences were handled privately by the wronged individual and his or her family. The early courts in Europe and North America dealt with religious and civil law rather than with criminal law.

The Legal Definition of Crime

The most common **definition of crime** is a *legalistic* one that defines a crime as an act that violates the criminal law and is punishable with jail terms, fines, and other sanctions. This legal definition is satisfactory for most purposes and will fit most of the crimes discussed in this text. However, some criminologists have argued for a sociological definition of crime that encompasses a broader range of harmful behaviour than this strict legal definition provides. Among the strongest advocates of this broader approach have been Edwin Sutherland, Herman and Julia Schwendinger, and John Hagan.

legal definition of crime
Crime is an act that violates the criminal law and is punishable with jail terms, fines, and other sanctions.

Is White-Collar Crime Really Crime?

Edwin Sutherland was one of the most important figures in the development of criminology and you will read about his work on crime causation later in this text. In his famous presidential address to the American Sociological Association in 1939, Sutherland (1940) argued that focusing only on violations of the criminal law had led criminologists to present a misleading picture of crime. Limiting criminological research to offences that were dealt with in the criminal courts, such as burglary, assault, and theft, led to the conclusion that crime was primarily a lower-class phenomenon. However, Sutherland pointed out that many **white-collar crimes** were committed by middle- and upper-class people in the course of their business activities. Criminologists neglected these crimes because they were not dealt with by the criminal courts:

white-collar crime
Crime that is committed by middle- and upper-class people in the course of their legitimate business activities.

> The crimes of the lower class are handled by policemen, prosecutors, and judges, with penal sanctions in the form of fines, imprisonment, and death. The crimes of the upper class either result in no official action at all, or result in suits for damages in civil courts, or are handled by inspectors, and by administrative boards or commissions, with penal sanctions in the form of warnings, orders to cease and desist, occasionally the loss of a license, and only in extreme cases by fines or prison sentences. (Sutherland, 1940, 8)

Sutherland argued that even though they may not be dealt with in criminal court, the great harm caused by white-collar criminals made it imperative that criminologists study them. Thus he was suggesting that the legal definition of crime be expanded to encompass the violation of other types of laws.

Human Rights Violations as Crime

human rights
The minimum conditions required for a person to live a dignified life. Among the rights set out by the Universal Declaration of Human Rights are the right to life, liberty, and security of the person; the right to be free of torture and other forms of cruel and degrading punishment; the right to equality before the law; and the right to the basic necessities of life.

Another attempt to expand the definition of crime was made by Herman and Julia Schwendinger (1970), who advocated a definition of crime based on **human rights** rather than on legal statutes. If an action violated the basic rights of humans to obtain the necessities of life and to be treated with respect and dignity, criminologists should consider it a crime. Thus government policies that create poverty and homelessness should be studied as crimes along with other practices that cause social harm, including imperialism, sexism, and racism. Advocates of this critical or humanistic approach feel that the criminal law has been established by those who control the power in society so that acts committed by powerful people are not criminalized and the law is biased against the poor. The Schwendingers' proposal explicitly places criminology on the side of the poor and powerless. While this approach has not received a great deal of support from other criminologists, it does play a useful role in drawing attention to the way in which we view social harms.

WWW

Universal Declaration of Human Rights
www.un.org/Overview/rights.html

A Continuum of Crime and Deviance

While few criminologists today would limit their work to the strict legal definition of crime, most would also not make the definition as broad as the human rights approach would suggest. John Hagan (1985) has proposed another approach to defining crime that reflects the way most criminologists view their discipline. Hagan says that a definition of crime must encompass not only violations of the criminal law, but also "a range of behaviors that for all practical purposes are treated as crimes (e.g., Sutherland's white-collar crimes), as well as those behaviors that across time and place vary in their location in and outside the boundaries of criminal law. In other words, we need a definition that considers behaviors that are both actually and potentially liable to criminal law" (1985, 49). Hagan proposed that deviance and crime be considered as a continuum ranging from the least serious to most serious acts. Seriousness can be assessed on three dimensions:

- *The degree of consensus that an act is wrong.* Most people feel that mass murder is wrong, but there is much less agreement over the issue of using marijuana.

FIGURE 1.1 Hagan's Varieties of Deviance

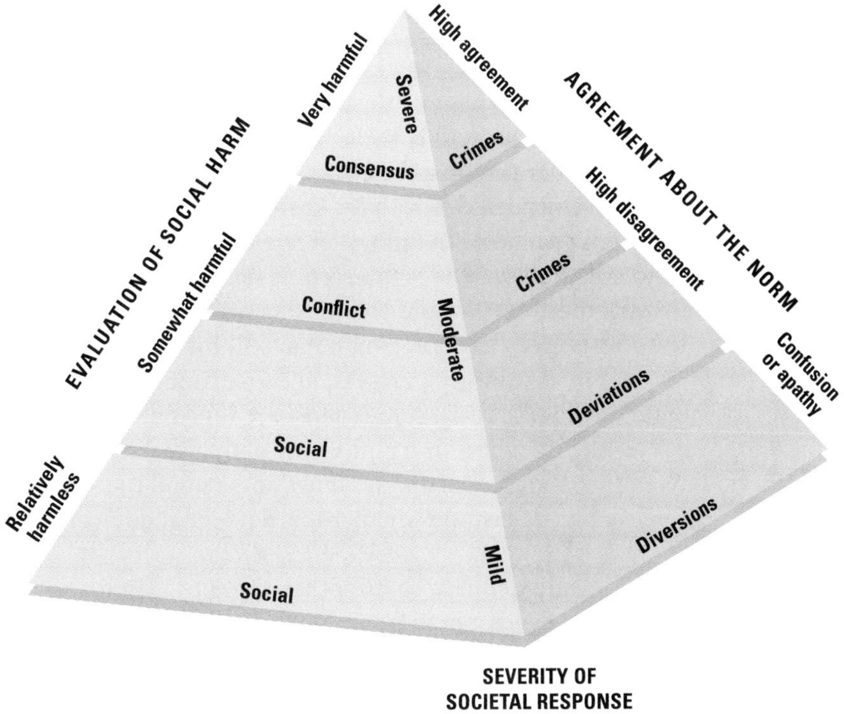

Source: John Hagan. (1991). *The Disreputable Pleasures: Crime and Deviance in Canada*, 3rd ed. Toronto: McGraw-Hill Ryerson, p. 13. Reprinted by permission.

- *The severity of the society's response to the act.* Murder is punishable by death in some societies and life imprisonment in others. On the other hand, possession of small amounts of marijuana may be ignored by the police, and in 2003 the government proposed to decriminalize this behaviour (though the subsequent Conservative government dropped this proposal).
- *The assessment of the degree of harm of the act.* Drug use, illegal gambling, and prostitution are often considered to be "victimless" crimes that harm only the offender, while serious crimes of violence are considered to be very harmful.

Although these three dimensions are normally closely related, this is not always the case. For example, the operators of the Westray mine, whose unsafe practices resulted in the death of 26 miners in Nova Scotia, caused a great deal of harm (see Box 16.1). However, even though most Canadians would probably agree that this negligence was wrong, none of the people responsible for the mine were penalized for their actions. This approach recognizes that "the separation of crime from other kinds of deviance is a social and political phenomenon" (Hagan, 1985, 49) and allows criminologists to consider a broad range of behaviours, including some types of deviance that may not be against the law. Hagan's approach is illustrated in Figure 1.1, which shows four major categories of crime and deviance: consensus crimes; conflict crimes; social deviations; and social diversions. Although this text will not specifically consider social deviations and social diversions, the distinction between consensus and conflict crimes is an important one that will be discussed in several chapters of this text.

Crime Is Socially Defined

Can you think of any type of behaviour that everybody condemns? Most people might consider killing another person to be an act that is always evil, but this is not the case. Soldiers are considered heroes for killing the enemy during time of war. Society allows police officers to kill under some circumstances, and all of us have the right to kill a person who is threatening us with lethal force. Even those who commit what most of us would call murder are not always classified as murderers by the courts. For example, a man may kill his neighbour and be found not guilty by reason of insanity (now called "not criminally responsible on account of mental disorder"). If the same man were sane but intoxicated at the time of the offence, he might be found guilty only of manslaughter. Even for an act as serious as killing another person, we must understand the social context of the act before we can determine whether it is deviant and how it should be classified.

Just as murder is socially defined, so are other types of crime and other forms of deviance. An act is deviant only from the point of view of a set of rules and regulations, and these vary widely from society to society and from group to group. There are some broad similarities in acts that are defined as deviant. For example, most societies, most of the time, frown upon members killing one another or plotting the violent overthrow of the government. However, there are also great differences between societies and within societies over time. Some societies consider as unlawful many acts that are tolerated or even encouraged in Canada while others permit practices that we restrict. For example, in Saudi Arabia women are not permitted to drive cars or wear short skirts, in Singapore it is unlawful to possess chewing gum (it creates messy streets and transit vehicles), and on some French beaches it is unlawful to wear clothes. All these practices are quite acceptable here. On the other hand, Canada and most western countries have laws against helping a terminally ill person to commit suicide (see Box 3.1), while in Holland doctor-assisted suicide is common.

Thus there is nothing inherent in any act that makes it unlawful. We can define deviance as behaviour that violates the rules, whatever those rules may be. However, this definition leaves us with problems. Whose rules are to be followed? Consider the case of the Muslim father living in Winnipeg who went to court because he wanted his 14-year-old daughter to marry her 27-year-old fiancé. However, such a marriage is not permitted by Manitoba law, which sets the minimum age for marriage at 16 (*Winnipeg Free Press*, 1993). Thus behaviour that is normative from the father's perspective is considered deviant from the province's perspective. What about a person who belongs to an outlaw motorcycle gang? Behaviour that conforms to the standards of the group will often violate the rules of the broader society. The same is true of those who use terrorism to fight what they feel is an unjust political system. If the revolution is successful, they will be heroes. Many political leaders, including Menachem Begin of Israel, Fidel Castro of Cuba, and China's Mao Zedong, began their political careers by using violence to achieve power. However, if the revolution fails, the leaders will be killed or imprisoned. This important question of "Who sets the rules?" will be discussed more fully later in this chapter.

The Relativity of Crime

Another implication of the fact that crime is socially defined is that the rules can change. A situation in the United States a few years ago highlighted just how relative the law can be. Because of pressure from the federal government, many states raised their legal drinking age from 18 to 21. At least one state did this in stages, with the drinking age rising one year each January 1. In a television interview, one university student whose 18th birthday was in late November described what he was facing for the next three years. Each year, he would be able to legally drink alcohol from his November birthday until midnight on December 31. Since the drinking age changed with the new year, he had to return to soft drinks until the following November when he turned 19. This would go on every year until he was 21, which meant that he could legally drink for less than 6 months out of the 36 months between his 18th and 21st birthdays.

A more important example is the fact that only a few decades ago, the sexual acts of gays and lesbians were prohibited by the Criminal Code and subject to maximum penalties ranging from five to fourteen years, depending on the specific act (Rodgers, 1962). When former prime minister Pierre Trudeau was the Minister of Justice, he declared that the "state has no place in the bedrooms of the nation" and removed these sections from the Criminal Code. Since that time there have been dramatic changes. Gays and lesbians now have the right to get married and as this chapter is being written, Scott Brison, a former cabinet minister, has just become the first Member of Parliament to marry another man.

These examples point out the fact that criminal and non-criminal are not two distinct categories. There is an overlap between the two, and the line between them can be very ambiguous. We often speak as if the world were divided between criminals and non-criminals. However, we have all broken the law at times—does this mean we are "criminals"? In fact, phrases like "everybody does it" are used to justify crimes that are committed by "respectable" people, including stealing from employers, not reporting tips and other income on tax forms, and copying computer software (Gabor, 1994). How do people draw the line between respectable citizens who occasionally do bad things and those they consider "criminals"? What are the implications of thinking of crime as being a matter of degree?

Who Makes the Rules? Conflict Versus Consensus Theories of Law

Of course the law is not completely subjective or arbitrary. Many criminal laws reflect serious social harms that are illegal in most societies and that most people condemn. However, as you have learned, the exact form of the laws and the specific behaviour prohibited vary greatly in different places and at differ-

WWW

Department of the Solicitor General of Canada
www.ps-sp.gc.ca

ent times. Why do some acts become subject to criminal sanctions while others do not?

One of the most important questions in the study of criminology is "Who sets the rules?" Who decided that selling marijuana is illegal, while selling cigarettes is a respectable business? Who determined that an impaired driver who causes the death of a pedestrian can be severely sanctioned, while an employer whose violation of workplace safety rules causes death may receive only a small fine? We have seen that rules can take many different forms, so the issue of how rules come to have a specific content is an important one. There have been two distinct approaches to this question, the consensus and conflict perspectives.

WWW
Department of Justice Canada
canada.justice.gc.ca

The Consensus Approach

consensus theory
Laws represent the agreement of most of the people in society that certain acts should be prohibited by the criminal law.

value
A collective idea about what is right or wrong, good or bad, and desirable or undesirable in a particular culture.

Consensus theorists believe that law represents the consensus of the people. That is, the law is simply a codification of the **values** shared by most members of a society. For example, several Muslim countries have institutionalized sharia law, which is explicitly based on the Koran, so the law reflects those societies' religious values. Similarly, many of the early European settlers in the United States were Puritans who left England for the colony of Massachusetts so that they would be free to practise their religious beliefs. Not surprisingly, the legal code of the new colony reflected these beliefs. Much of their legal code of 1648 was taken directly from the Bible, and many crimes were punishable by death. These capital crimes included "idolatry, witchcraft, blasphemy, bestiality, sodomy, adultery, rape, man stealing, treason, . . . cursing or smiting of a parent, stubbornness or rebelliousness on the part of a son against his parents, and homicide committed with malice prepense, by guile or poisoning" (Haskins, 1969, 37). Of course, religious values are not the only ones enshrined in law, but they do illustrate how values become codified in law.

Support for the consensus view is also found in the fact that there is a broad agreement regarding many laws, particularly those that deal with street crimes such as robbery, burglary, and murder. Several studies have asked people to rate the seriousness of a broad range of criminal offences. These studies have demonstrated that there is considerable agreement among people from Canada and the United States concerning the rankings of these offences (Normandeau, 1966, Akman et al., 1967).

The Conflict Approach

class conflict theory
Laws are passed by members of the ruling class in order to maintain their privileged position by keeping the common people under control.

Conflict theorists do not share the view that our laws reflect a consensus of members of society. This is particularly apparent in the work of **class conflict theorists,** who take the view that laws are passed by members of the ruling class in order to maintain their privileged position by keeping the common people under control. Activities that threaten those with power are defined as illegal, and the legal mechanism of the state is used to enforce the laws. One example from Canada's early history shows how the law can be used to further the aims of the politically powerful at the expense of the common people. After the Riel Rebellion in 1885, Hayter Reed, the assistant commissioner of Indian Affairs, used his powers under the Indian Act to control the Aboriginal population. He deposed many of the chiefs he felt were disloyal and undermined the authority of other chiefs and headmen by instructing his staff to deal directly with individuals and families rather than with the bands. He also confined Indians to their reserves by ordering the implementation of a pass system that had no justification in law:

> Officials of the [North West Mounted Police] were never comfortable with the absence of any legal foundation for the pass system. The lack of a legal basis in this case undermined the validity of all NWMP operations: they were trying to demonstrate to the Indians that the police enforced a rational system of laws that operated to the benefit of all. . . . In 1893 a circular letter was issued directing all police officers to refrain from ordering Indians without passes back to their reserves.
>
> Hayter Reed would have none of these weak-kneed, legalistic concerns. He urged the police to continue enforcing the pass system on the grounds that the "moral responsibilities of the Indian Department transcended treaty obligations." Reed's views triumphed. By at least 1896 the police had reversed their position. In that year Commissioner Herchmer issued a circular letter instructing police who encountered any Indian without a pass to "use all possible pressure to persuade him to return to his reserve." (Carter, 1990, 153–54)

The pass system was eventually ended, but it did restrict the movement of Aboriginal people for 20 years. In this case, the legal system was used to restrict the movement of people who represented a threat to those holding power—the government and the white settlers who were moving onto the Prairies.

Consensus and conflict theories each provide explanations of the formation and persistence of some laws. However, as Hagan's definition of crime suggests, neither provides a complete explanation. While the majority of the populace does support many laws, some do benefit the powerful at the expense of the rest of us. Others fit in neither category. For example, there is no consensus in our society about the propriety of abortion, gambling, prostitution, or marijuana use, but laws regulating these behaviours do not reflect any particular class interest. Thus some feel that the most accurate way of describing the process of law formation is group conflict theory. This perspective recognizes that all laws are the result of a political process, and that this process typically involves a conflict or a debate between different interest groups. You will learn more about these theories later in this text.

Criminology Is an Evolving Discipline: The New Field of Green Criminology

Like other academic disciplines, criminology is constantly changing. One of the newest areas of study is green criminology. Over the past decade, environmental concerns have grown steadily throughout the world. In keeping with these concerns, some criminologists have begun to develop a "green criminology" because they feel the discipline should contribute to the debate about the causes and consequences of environmental destruction and should use their expertise to help deal with this problem.

Green Criminology

Green criminology begins with the view that criminology should not just study actions that violate the criminal law but also actions that are socially harmful. Some environmental harms are illegal. One of Canada's most serious environmental disasters was a case of water pollution on Walkerton, Ontario that caused over 2000 people to fall seriously ill and led to seven deaths. The operators of the water treatment plant who failed to test the water and who falsified test results were successfully prosecuted, but politicians such as former Ontario premier Mike Harris, whose government's policies contributed in a major way to the tragedy (O'Connor, 2002) were not prosecuted. However, many actions that are much more serious in the long term such as the emission of huge quantities of greenhouse gases in the production of oil from Alberta's tar sands and clearcutting tropical rainforests are not against the law. Green criminologists argue that the damage to the Earth caused by destructive environmental practices can be far more serious than the illegal acts that have traditionally been the subject matter of criminological study (Lynch and Stretesky, 2007) and are the proper concern of criminology.

Green criminology encompasses a broad range of behaviours ranging from acts that are clearly harmful, such as dumping toxic waste in the ocean, to acts that many people consider to be acceptable, such as eating meat or wearing leather shoes. Green criminology has its roots in the environmental and animal rights movements, though more green criminologists have focused on environmental issues than on animal rights. The environmental focus of green criminology covers the study of environmental damage, including air and water pollution and harm to natural ecosystems such as oceans and forests. Those interested in animal rights study "individual acts of cruelty to animals and the institutional, socially-acceptable human domination of animals in agribusiness, in slaughterhouses and abattoirs, in so-called scientific experimentation and, in less obviously direct ways, in sports, colleges and schools, zoos, aquaria and circuses" (Beirne and South, 2007, xiv) (see Box 1.2). These theorists have introduced the concept of "speciesism," which refers to discrimination against non-human animals.

The range of work done by green criminologists has been outlined this way:

- It has documented the existence of law-breaking with respect to pollution, disposal of toxic waste and misuse of environmental resources.
- It has raised questions relating to the destruction of specific environments and resources, in ways that are "legal" but ecologically very harmful to plants, animals, and humans.
- It has challenged corporate definitions of good environmental practice and emphasized the claims of non-human nature to ecological justice.
- It has emphasized the dynamic links between distribution of environmental "risk" and distinct communities, and particularly how poor and minority populations experience disproportionate exposure to environmental harm.

FOCUS

BOX 1.2 Animal Cruelty Laws in Canada

In several chapters of this book you will learn that laws do not just happen, but are the result of a complex social process. Whether or not particular laws are passed depends on the influence of individuals and groups whose interests would be affected by the law. Green criminologists are very critical of the fact that the voices of environmentalists are often not heard by politicians who are also being lobbied by corporate interests who can profit from environmental damage. Current attempts to improve Canada's animal cruelty legislation shows how different groups try to ensure that legislation does not interfere with their interests.

Canada has not updated its animal cruelty legislation since 1892, and there is widespread agreement that stronger laws are needed to prevent animal abuse. Many critics of the current legislation cite an Edmonton case in which two men tied a dog to a tree and beat it to death with a baseball bat. The men were not convicted of animal cruelty because the evidence showed that the dog had died when it was first hit with the bat so it did not suffer cruelty. It is also very difficult to get convictions for people who neglect their animals because the Crown must prove that the neglect is "wilful." Thus a farmer whose animals have starved to death will be acquitted unless it can be proved that he acted wilfully. As a result, very few people in Canada have been convicted of animal abuse.

New animal cruelty laws have been before Parliament since 1999. However, the proposed legislation has been opposed by hunters, trappers, farmers, and medical researchers who experiment on animals, who fear that the laws would affect their livelihoods. In 2007 there were two bills before Parliament. The first (Bill C-213) would make minimal changes other than making the penalties tougher for existing offences. The second (Bill C-373) would add significant protection for animals. The second bill is supported by many groups, including the Canadian Veterinary Medical Association and virtually all of Canada's humane societies and animal support organizations. On the other side are groups such as the Canadian Sportfishing Industry Association which has claimed that the proposed legislation will jeopardize the $10 billion-a-year sportsfishing industry by making it "possible for a Grandfather to face a federal criminal prosecution for taking his grandchildren fishing" (Canadian Sportfishing Industry Association, 2007). Other opponents have claimed that the bill would give animals the same legal standing as humans and would encourage animal rights "terrorists" to keep attacking medical researchers (Senate Committee on Legal and Constitutional Affairs, 2006). Proponents of Bill C-373 argue that the bill excludes harming animals for lawful reasons such as hunting and medical experimentation, but this interpretation has been challenged by opponents. This debate has effectively paralyzed Parliament and it is unlikely that legislation will be passed soon.

- It has investigated the specific place of animals in relation to issues of "rights" and human–non-human relationships on a shared planet.
- It has criticized the inadequacies of environmental regulation in both philosophical and practical terms.
- It has exposed corporate attempts to stifle environmental critique and dissent through the use of public relations propaganda and strategic lawsuits against public participation.
- It has reconsidered the nature of victimization in relation to environmental changes and events, including social and governmental responses to this victimization.

- It has explored the ways in which law enforcement officials—particularly the police but also environmental protection authorities—have intervened with regard to regulation of fisheries, prosecution of polluters, and conservation of specific environs and species. (White, 2007, 33–34).

The work of green criminologists is grounded in the philosophy of ecological citizenship. This means that notions of morality and rights should be extended to "non-human nature" (White, 2007, 35) and that societies should adopt a notion of ecological citizenship that obliges them to recognize that the environment must be protected for future generations.

Issues in Green Criminology—Crimes Involving Food

In 2007 hundreds of thousands of Canadian pet owners learned that the food they had been serving their pets was contaminated with melamine and that the animals were at risk of kidney failure. An unknown number of animals died as a result of the contamination, which came from a protein supplement purchased from China by Menu Foods, a major Canadian pet food supplier. While this particular incident did not involve food used by humans, it is an example of crimes involving the food chain. Hazel Croall (2007) has conducted research that has shed light on a type of crime that many of us know little about. The consequences of food crime can be very serious. Croall cites incidents in which over 250 people in Spain died after consuming tainted cooking oil and 21 people in Scotland died of *E. coli* poisoning spread by contaminated meat.

Using a definition of "crime" that is somewhat broader than many criminologists would feel comfortable with, Croall has examined how crimes can take place at each stage in the food chain from production to consumption. At the level of *food production*, Croall discusses the use of genetically modified crops (which are legal in many jurisdictions, but regulated in the European Union), cruelty to farmed animals, and the use of illegal immigrant labourers who are often exploited because their immigration status means they cannot complain about mistreatment without being deported. The fish industry has been involved in illegal activities ranging from environmental pollution in fish farms to catching more fish than is allowed under national and international agreements.

Crimes can also take place during the *manufacturing of food*. Perhaps the most common of these involve additions to food products such as adding water to poultry and meat so that sellers can charge for a heavier weight and adding potentially harmful chemicals to change the flavour and consistency of food. In the Canadian pet food case mentioned earlier, a chemical was added to make protein levels appear higher because it was cheaper than raising protein levels by using natural ingredients. Rule violations during *food preparation* are very common. Every municipality has inspectors who visit restaurants in order to ensure that they meet hygiene standards. They frequently close restaurants because of violations such as the presence of pests, including rats, mice, and insects or the failure of staff to wash their hands properly. Finally, illegal practices are common in the *marketing of food*. These practices include labels that conceal ingredients or make false health claims and using needlessly large packages to try to persuade the consumer that they are getting more product than is actually the case.

Croall suggests that the study of food crime is consistent with several evolving trends in criminology. Perhaps the most important of these is the fact that food issues are global and cannot be understood without knowledge of global trends in production and trade. Illegal agricultural labour practices often involve immigrant workers, and giant multinational food corporations routinely play one government against another in their quest for larger food production subsidies. Global corporations are also able to influence the effectiveness of attempts to regulate their socially and environmentally harmful behaviour by threatening governments that they will simply move their businesses to another country with more business-friendly regulations. One result has been that environmental damage has been the greatest in poor countries that are the most desperate for any development (Chunn et al., 2002).

Summary

- The *term criminology* is used in a number of ways. In this text it will refer to the body of knowledge regarding crime as a social phenomenon. It includes within its scope the processes of making laws, breaking laws, and reacting to the breaking of laws. The objective of criminology is the development of a body of general and verified principles and of other types of knowledge regarding this process of law, crime, and treatment.
- The discipline of criminology includes six major areas. These are the definition of crime and criminals; the origins and role of law; the social distribution of crime; the causation of crime; patterns of criminal behaviour; and societal reactions to crime.
- Our behaviour is strongly influenced by norms, many of which we have internalized. Much of the time we don't even consciously think about the rules that govern our behaviour. Most of the time, rules are enforced through informal means such as the disapproval of our family and friends. However, in some cases the rules are formalized into laws.
- The strict legal definition of crime is an act that violates the criminal law and is punishable with jail terms, fines, and other sanctions. Sociologists have expanded this definition in a number of different ways. In his discussion of white-collar crime, Sutherland said that criminologists should also include violations of other types of laws in addition to criminal law. The Schwendingers proposed that crime be defined as a violation of human rights. Hagan felt that criminologists should consider deviance and crime as a continuum ranging from the minor acts of deviance to serious crimes.
- Crime is socially defined. No behaviour is inherently good or evil, and we must understand the social context of an act before we can determine whether it is deviant and how it should be classified. Also, the form of laws and the specific behaviour that is prohibited vary greatly in different places and at different times.

- Consensus theorists believe that laws represent the will of most of the people in a particular society. On the other hand, conflict theorists feel that law reflects power relationships in society, as those with power use the law to help maintain their position. Some laws fit each of these perspectives.
- Like other disciplines, criminology continually moves into new research areas. One of the newest sub-fields in criminology is green criminology, which studies environmental and animal rights issues.

QUESTIONS FOR CRITICAL THINKING

1. Look at Figure 1.1 (see page 17), which shows different types of crime and deviance. Can you think of examples of behaviours that fit into each of the four categories (consensus crimes, conflict crimes, social deviations, and social diversions)? How can particular behaviours move from one category to another? Can you think of examples of behaviours that have moved from one category to another?
2. Look at the way your local newspaper handles crime stories. What picture of crime in your community is provided by the newspaper? If you have a tabloid paper (such as the *Toronto Sun*, the *Winnipeg Sun*, or the *Vancouver Province*) in your community, does it handle crime stories in a different manner from other newspapers?
3. Think of a law people are currently lobbying to change. What kind of changes to the law are being advocated? Why do some people want to change the law? If anyone is resisting the legal change, why are they offering this resistance? What do you think will be the outcome of this attempt at legal change?
4. Discuss some of the advantages and disadvantages of the Schwendingers' suggestion that crime be broadly defined as a violation of human rights.
5. Many college and university students have used drugs, and some who work as restaurant servers do not declare all of their income on their tax forms. Should these students be called criminals? Why do you feel they should or should not be called criminals?

NET WORK

A group led by criminologist Delbert Elliott has established a website dedicated to the prevention of violence. The group has assessed over 600 violence prevention programs and has selected a small number that have a demonstrated ability to reduce violence. Go to the website for Blueprints for Violence Prevention at **www.colorado.edu/cspv/blueprints/model/overview.html**. Look at three of the model programs that have been selected by the project. For each of these programs, can you determine what aspect of the child's social environment the program planners are trying to change? What does the success of the three programs you have selected tell you about the causes of crime?

KEY TERMS

class conflict theory; pg. 20
consensus theory; pg. 20
criminology; pg. 9
human rights; pg. 16
legal definition of crime; pg. 15
norms; pg. 14
value; pg. 20
white-collar crime; pg. 15

BIBLIOGRAPHY

Akman, D.D., A. Normandeau, and S. Turner. (1967). "The Measurement of Delinquency in Canada." *Journal of Criminal Law, Criminology and Police Science* 58:330–37.

Beirne, Piers, and Nigel South. (2007). *Issues in Green Criminology: Confronting Harms Against Environments, Humanity and Other Animals*. Portland: Willan Publishing.

Black, Conrad. (1993). *A Life in Progress*. Toronto: Key Porter Books.

Blumstein, Alfred. (2003). "The Kid Whiz: Richard Tremblay." *Time* May 26:54.

Canadian Sportfishing Industry Association. (2007). "Federal Animal Cruelty Legisltion." http://www.csia.ca/media/FEDERAL_ANIMAL_CRUELTY_LEGISLATION.pdf. Accessed 18 August 2007.

Carter, Sarah. (1990). *Lost Harvests*. Montreal: McGill-Queen's University Press.

Chunn, Dorothy, Susan Boyd, and Robert Menzies. (2002). "'We All Live in Bhopal': Criminology Discovers Environmental Crime." In Susan Boyd, Dorothy Chunn, and Robert Menzies (eds.), *Toxic Criminology: Environment, Law and the State in Canada* (pp. 7–24). Halifax: Fernwood.

Croall, Hazel. (2007). "Food Crime." In Piers Beirne and Nigel South (eds.), *Issues in Green Criminology: Confronting Harms Against Environments, Humanity and Other Animals* (pp. 206–29). Portland: Willan Publishing.

Dowler, Ken, Thomas Fleming, and Stephen Muzzatti. (2006). "Constructing Crime: Media, Crime and Popular Culture." *Canadian Journal of Criminology and Criminal Justice* 48: 837–50.

Gabor, Thomas. (1994). *Everybody Does It: Crime by the Public*. Toronto: University of Toronto Press.

Galloway, Gloria. (2003). "Parents Sentenced for Exorcism Gone Wrong." globeandmail.com. www.theglobeandmail.com/servlet/story/RTGAM.20030522.ue. Accessed May 28, 2007.

Hagan, John. (1985). *Modern Criminology: Crime, Criminal Behaviour, and Its Control*. New York: McGraw-Hill.

Haskins, George Lee. (1969). "A Rule to Walk By." In Richard Quinney (ed.), *Crime and Justice in Society* (pp. 33–54). Boston: Little, Brown and Company.

Jackman, Tom. (2003). "Murder Defendants Claim Connection with Hit Movie." HoustonChronicle.Com. www.chron.com/cs/CDA/printstory.hts/nation/1923147. Accessed May 28, 2007.

Lynch, Michael J., and Paul Stretesky. "Green Criminology in the United States." In Piers Beirne and Nigel South (eds.), *Issues in Green Criminology: Confronting Harms Against Environments, Humanity and Other Animals* (pp. 248–69). Portland: Willan Publishing.

McCormick, Chris. (1995). *Constructing Danger: The Misrepresentation of Crime in the News*. Halifax: Fernwood Publishing.

McIntyre, Mike. (2003.) *Nowhere to Run: The Killing of Constable Dennis Strongquill.* Winnipeg: Great Plains Publications.

McNish, Jacquie, and Sinclair Stewart. (2004). *Wrong Way: The Fall of Conrad Black.* Toronto: Viking Canada.

Media Index. (1999). "South Park Gets Nasty at Record-Setting Pace." *Austin American-Statesman*, July 16:E1.

National Media Archive. (1997). "T.V. Coverage Down: Murder Rate Up Slightly." *On Balance* 10(7). Vancouver: The Fraser Institute.

Normandeau, Andre. (1966). "The Measurement of Delinquency in Montreal." *Journal of Criminal Law, Criminology, and Police Science* 57:172–77.

O'Connor, The Honourable Dennis R. (2002.) *Report of the Walkerton Inquiry: Part One: Summary.* Toronto: Queen's Printer for Ontario.

Plotz, David. (2001). "Conrad Black." *Slate*, 31 August. http://www.slate.com/id/114605.

Rodgers, R. S. (1962). *Sex and Law in Canada: Text, Cases and Comment.* Ottawa: Policy Press.

Schwendinger, Herman, and Julia Schwendinger. (1970). "Defenders of Order or Guardians of Human Rights." *Issues in Criminology* 5:123–57.

Senate Committee on Legal and Constitutional Affairs. 2006. "Evidence." 4 December, 2006.

Staples, David. (2002). "Fearless, Painless, Senseless: The Sand Brothers." *Edmonton Journal*, March 31: D1.

Statistics Canada. (2006). "Police Personnel and Expenditures." *The Daily.* 15 November. Ottawa: Statistics Canada.

Sutherland, Edwin. (1940). "White-Collar Criminality." *American Sociological Review* 5:1–12.

Sutherland, Edwin, and Donald Cressey. (1960). *Principles of Criminology*, 6th ed. Philadelphia: J. B. Lippincott.

White, Rob. (2007). "Green Criminology and the Pursuit of Social and Ecological Justice." In Piers Beirne and Nigel South (eds.), *Issues in Green Criminology: Confronting Harms Against Environments, Humanity and Other Animals* (pp. 32–54). Portland: Willan Publishing.

Winnipeg Free Press. (1993). "Law, Religion Clash over Child Marriage." September 24.

The Origins and Role of Law in Society

2

Rodney Kueneman

UNIVERSITY OF MANITOBA

People in all forms of human society have disputes, and every human group has developed mechanisms for restoring social order. Today the law plays a prominent role in the restoration process, but not all communities have relied on formally enacted laws that are enforced by the power of a state. In small-scale societies, victims or their relatives were responsible for settling disputes, and the major goal of dispute settlement processes was to restore harmonious relationships between the conflicting parties. In this chapter, you will learn how our system of formal laws has developed.

Learning Objectives

After reading this chapter, you should be able to

- Trace the changes from community-based dispute resolution processes in small-scale societies to state-controlled processes in more complex societies.
- Explain why knowledge of social context is important in understanding the existence and operation of different dispute settlement systems.
- Understand the emergence and consolidation of social and economic power in human societies and how the consolidation has made it difficult to control the actions of those who have power.
- Explain why the rule of law has become a primary force in modern societies and understand the limitations of law as a means of controlling behaviour.
- Understand the importance of restorative dispute settlement processes in small-scale societies and explain why they are once again becoming popular.

Throughout most of human existence, we lived in small hunting and gathering communities. Cooperation, mutual aid, and kinship within these communities were the essential means of preserving harmony and restoring order. The absence of a centralized power structure meant that these communities had to rely on these different mechanisms to keep the peace. One of the tasks of this chapter is to show how different dispute settlement mechanisms can be understood only within their social context. As patterns of societal organization changed, different forms of dispute settlement emerged. The general role of dispute settlement processes in all societies is the restoration of order; however, the nature of these different social orders and the groups who have received the most benefit from order within them have changed significantly. As we shall see, dispute settlement processes are intimately involved in the structuring of social relationships.

This textbook is about crime. It is important to realize that crime does not exist in all societies. In a technical sense, a crime is a violation of a law, and not all societies have had formulated laws. While each society has had to develop a moral order complete with stated expectations for acceptable behaviour, not all societies have developed laws to restrain their members. The formulation of law requires the existence of a central body such as a **state** that develops law and enforces compliance with it. This is not only a matter of semantics. For much of human history, social order was maintained by other means. It is equally important to note that criminal law, as we know it, has not been part of the social fabric for most of human history. Harms between individuals were resolved by various forms of redress in societies without a state. Even in societies with a state apparatus, many disputes are regulated by civil law. Under civil law, the state adjudicates between the parties to the dispute in an effort to repair the damage. Criminal law comes into existence at the point when the state declares itself to be the injured party for certain types of infractions. In its narrowest sense, criminology is concerned with this limited subset of laws and social infractions. But in order to understand the broad question of social order, it is important to see criminal law within an historical and social context that considers the full spectrum of dispute settlement practices.

state
As defined by Max Weber (1864–1920), the state is an institution that claims the exclusive right to the legitimate exercise of force in a given territory through the use of police to enforce laws or the army to maintain civil stability. While there have been stateless societies, most complex societies have state systems of formal government and administrative bureaucracies.

Finally, it is important to reflect on the human condition. The human animal does not rely on the use of instincts. In place of the instincts that order so much of the lives of other animals, human beings must fashion their collective stability by way of culture. While humans share common emotional, intellectual, and motivational attributes, they have produced an amazing variety of solutions to the problems they have faced. Equipped with a powerful imagination, members of our species have introduced both inspiring and terrifying innovations to their communities. This human imagination has contributed to the development of human culture. But it is also a principal source of instability that has threatened to erode, weaken, and destroy the social fabric it has created. Humans have the ability to create disputes and to upset social arrangements. Law and other forms of dispute settlement are at the heart of our efforts to limit and to recover from the harm that is inflicted. Although there are many differences between societies, each social order must be recognized as a response to the need to construct a moral, or at least a legal, order.

It will not be possible here to provide a detailed description and analysis of the vast array of human cultures. Instead, our inquiry will examine two patterns of social organization: hunting and gathering societies and industrial societies.

Patterns of Human Social Organization

Cultures have been classified in many different ways. Lenski (1966) emphasized the **mode of production** used by societies. He developed the following classification: hunting and gathering, pastoral, horticultural, agricultural, and industrial societies. This chapter will focus primarily on the hunting and gathering and the industrial forms because they provide the greatest contrast with respect to dispute settlement practices.

mode of production
The dominant form of social and technical organization of economic production in a society. Historically, a variety of modes of production can be distinguished based on both technology and the structure of social relationships.

The **hunting and gathering society** has been a dominant form of social order in the history of the human species. For example, Michalowski (1985) argues that humans have lived in small-scale societies for the vast majority of the time that we have been in existence:

> Acephalous [headless, leaderless] societies were the only type of human community for 30 000 of the 40 000 years since the evolution of modern humans. It is also highly probable that archaic humans had been living in acephalous social arrangements for the preceding 200 000 years. Acephalous societies are small, economically cooperative and relatively egalitarian societies with simple technology and division of labor based mainly upon age and sex. Stratification in terms of differential access to material goods and political power does not exist. While these societies lack rulers or governments with the power to command, direct and correct the behavior of others, acephalous societies are generally characterized more by order and cooperation than by chaos and competition.

Some of these **acephalous societies** did change their mode of production and were transformed into pastoral and horticultural forms. Under certain conditions, some of them were further transformed into agricultural and industrial societies. The hunting and gathering form, however, persisted in many parts of the world into this century. It has been virtually eliminated by contact with the Western world.

The change in the mode of production to the pastoral or horticultural form created new possibilities for patterns of social organization. These new patterns slowly and inexorably transformed some human cultures and are now visible in modern industrial society. The emergence of surplus, **stratification**, technological innovations, social power, and large populations has made possible the growth of the industrially based social system (Newman, 1983).

The rest of this chapter will outline the basic characteristics of the dominant social forms and will show how the dispute settlement processes used in these different settings were a part of the social fabric. It will become clear that the discussion of custom, law, and dispute settlements must be placed within a social context in order to understand how each settles the troubles that spring up in all human societies.

Small-Scale Society

In this section, the general characteristics of small-scale societies will be described as a prelude to a discussion of their typical practices for settling disputes. Although such attributes are not present in all small-scale societies, they do appear in virtually all hunting and gathering societies and hence are useful as "**ideal types**" for the purposes of analysis.

Without underestimating the often harsh realities of the small-scale society or succumbing to the propensity to romanticize it, there is no question that such communities were characterized by a strong **collective solidarity**. Whether living in the High Arctic, on the plains, or in the tropical rainforests, hunters and gatherers were well aware that they were part of a natural

hunting and gathering society
Probably the earliest form of human society that still persists in remote regions of the world, to some extent. These societies have an economic base that rests on the use of the naturally occurring animal and plant resources of the environment. They do not practise agriculture or raise animals.

acephalous society
Literally "headless," meaning that the society is without any formalized or institutionalized system of power and authority. Collective decisions are made in a variety of ways, including informal community gatherings, which will change according to circumstances.

stratification
A social division of individuals into various hierarchies of wealth, status, and power. There is disagreement about how to describe stratification systems; some sociologists favour the concept of class and others discuss status differentiations.

ideal type
An abstract model of a classic, pure form of social phenomenon. It is a model concept and does not necessarily exist in exact form in reality. An example is Ferdinand Tönnies's (1855–1936) dichotomy *Gemeinschaft* and *Gesellschaft*.

collective solidarity
Similar in meaning to Émile Durkheim's term *mechanical solidarity*, this refers to a state of social bonding or interdependency that rests on similarity of beliefs and values, shared activities, and ties of kinship and cooperation among members of a community.

ecosystem that had forces they could not control. They were aware of their individual vulnerability and realized that their collective life was an exercise in mutual survival. The cooperative, mutual-aid character of these societies was not accidental. The near certainty of death for those who lacked the assistance of the group strengthened the group's solidarity.

The Need for Self-Restraint

Hunting and gathering groups were small communities of approximately 50 members who had closely related kin ties. In these small, face-to-face communities, social networks were dense and were characterized by a high degree of social visibility. The mutual-aid character of such social relationships meant that there was an expectation of continuity of relationships over time. The absence of a complex division of labour made it necessary for each individual in the group to fulfill a number of roles with other members. This **diffuseness of roles** placed a premium on cooperation since each member was intimately involved with other members. Continuous interaction with other members of the group provided each member with feedback from others concerning the acceptability of certain types of behaviour and created a climate for the development of common norms and the cultivation of a consensus.

diffuseness of roles
A characteristic of relatively simple societies in which people encounter one another in a variety of overlapping roles—there is little occupational specialization and no clear separation of private and public spheres of life. People are continuously reminded of their extensive bonds with others.

In such close and intimate quarters, members were reluctant to offend one another because of their mutual interdependence. Each member learned to cultivate personal restraint and the control of impulse in order to prevent the breakdown of a working order. Colson (1974) shows how these social circumstances fostered the development of forbearance, the avoidance of disputes, the sharing of resources, and the tolerance of human foibles. She relates how the Tonga of Zambia attempted to sidestep controversial issues and were reluctant to allow others to drag them into disputes. The Tongas' social structure worked against the outbreak of violence, the fear of attack by sorcerers, or other forms of retaliation. This contributed to the development of self-restraint.

Colson also reminds us that it is not that these people lacked "occasion for quarrels and hostility but they learn that they must control their hostility, their greed, and their envy if they are to survive" (61). Such communities could easily punish any individual who consistently went his or her own way. The self-restraint that members exercised stemmed not only from the close, intimate, and friendly ties that are a product of common life, but also out of the fear of reprisal and the desire to keep hostilities from surfacing and disturbing the business of living. Rupert Ross (1989), a Crown attorney in northern Ontario, relates how the principle of emotional restraint still operates in some remote Ojibway communities (see Box 2.1). The practice of "burying" old disputes and declining to revisit the emotions that they evoke was an exercise in individual restraint that kept these disruptions of the past from damaging current social relations.

Mutual Dependence

Living in a subsistence economy, where little or no surplus could be generated, created the necessity for the group to share the fruits of a day's hunting or foraging. Typically, the spoils were distributed in such a way as to ensure that

FOCUS

BOX 2.1 The Principle of Emotional Restraint in the Ojibway Community

Grief, anger and sorrow [should] be quickly buried. They should not be expressed, for that only serves to burden the person who hears. They should not be explored or indulged privately, for doing so results in a lessened capacity to contribute the fullest energy, attention and skills which the hunter-gatherer society needed to maintain survival. Expressions of anger or criticism would serve only to create friction, a dangerous luxury to a people who required the maximum cooperation of all. Even the *thinking* of critical thoughts about others was to be avoided. Quite simply, the past was the past, and its negative parts were to be buried and forgotten as quickly as possible. . . .

While such overt observances of these rules are declining, it remains a central tenet of life in many communities that it is wrong to speak of your hurts and angers and criticisms, wrong to indulge your private emotions. Instead, you bury and you carry on, resisting the backwards glance. I recall one teenage rape victim who refused to testify when her assailant finally came to trial more than a year after the event; her reason was simply that he should have paid his penalty by now and be getting on with his life. For her, it was simply too late to put him through it. The past was the past.

Asking a Native accused to explain what it was that aggravated him to such a degree that he attacked his victim is the subject of a special constraint, already referred to, which forbids the criticism of others.

Source: Rupert Ross. "Leaving Our White Eyes Behind: The Sentencing of Native Accused." [1989] 3 *Canadian Native Law Reporter* 1 at 4.

everyone received an equal and adequate share, regardless of the extent and nature of each one's contribution. In such a distribution system, there may have been collective scarcity if food was not found, but there was never poverty in the sense that some ate while others went hungry. Though a member was not expected to love everyone else, each one was expected to care for all members of the community. This ensured that all members would be cared for in the nonproductive times of their life such as childhood and old age, and during times of sickness. This bond of mutual dependence helped to keep greed and the desire for advantage in check.

A Community of Belief

The structure of small-scale society fostered both moderation and compassion, which acted as powerful curbs to selfishness. A shared system of customs and patterns of behaviour in domestic, economic, and political life grew out of the personal and interpersonal accommodations that were required of such intimate social actors. There is no question that this type of society was coercive; there was virtually no freedom of belief. One's location in the kinship system established basic duties, obligations, rights, and privileges. Failure to meet obligations jeopardized one's relationship with many members of this primary group and, especially, the face-to-face interaction with one's immediate kin. The notion of collective responsibility, which was prevalent in such communities, made kin groups accountable for the behaviour of their members. The positive dimension of community membership was that throughout the life cycle, the customary ways provided meaning for members. This sense of purpose helped foster commitment to community beliefs and practices.

The Absence of Surplus, Stratification, and the State

The life of the hunters and gatherers was an exercise in cooperative living. The inability to produce or to keep large amounts of food on hand meant that food gathering was a regular activity that included all able-bodied members. The division and distribution of foodstuffs to all community members underscored the understanding that everyone had a right to the fruits of this collective activity; they were a group possession to be shared by all. The need to move regularly acted to limit the amount of personal belongings a person could accumulate, and since each member had access to the same raw materials, there was little difference in the individuals' limited possessions. The possibility of generating any significant **surplus** under these conditions was limited. Small-scale society, then, acted as a brake on the human tendency to secure an advantageous individual position. By identifying one's "self" with the interests of the entire group, the individual self so familiar to our society was superseded by a social or collective self-concept.

surplus
The excess of production over the human and material resources used up in the process of production. In simple societies, there was often little if any surplus since the production from hunting and gathering was entirely used up in subsistence. With the development of animal herding and settled agriculture, production exceeds immediate subsistence needs, and social inequality and class division become possible when particular individuals or groups are able to take control of this surplus.

The absence of surplus was a strong force that suppressed the emergence of economic stratification and any form of state-like structure or political institution. Small-scale societies have been characterized as acephalous (without a head) because there was no distinct source of social power or authority independent of the collective will. The only form of power available to special individuals in such societies was influence. Influence was based on status derived from hunting skill, sex, wisdom, or generosity, and not on differential access to, and accumulation of, material resources. Social status was a group property, not a personal attribute. The members of the group could give it and take it away. Hoebel (1973) comments on the position of the Inuit headman:

> The headman possesses no fixed authority; neither does he enter into formal office. He is not elected, nor is he chosen by any formal process. When other men accept his judgement and opinions, he is headman. When they ignore him, he is not.

Thus, if an esteemed individual became arrogant or tried to force others to comply in ways that were deemed inappropriate, the special status was removable. All aspects of group life worked in a systematic fashion to control and limit the will of the individual in the best interests of the group. This is the type of society to which Tönnies (1887) applied the term ***Gemeinschaft***, where human beings "remain essentially united in spite of all separating factors."

Gemeinschaft
A German word, translated as "community," used by sociologist Ferdinand Tönnies (1855–1936) to define an ideal type or model of a society in which social bonds are personal and direct and there are strong shared values and beliefs. Characteristic of small-scale, localized societies, it is in contrast to *Gesellschaft*, which refers to complex, impersonal societies.

Dispute Settlement in Small-Scale Society

The major goal of dispute settlement in small-scale societies was to restore harmonious relations between parties that could not interact because of some conflict. It was essential that problems be settled as quickly as possible in mutually agreeable ways for all involved parties so as not to impede group life.

The absence of an independent political institution meant that disputants typically had to resolve their differences without the assistance of an adjudicator (Gulliver, 1979). Community pressure was applied to the parties in a dispute to meet and to bring an end to the discord. Each party had to give and to receive information from the other in order to learn of the other party's needs and expectations. In a series of such educational exchanges, an attempt was made to move toward a mutually agreeable outcome and the restoration of harmonious interaction.

This type of approach to discord led to a general airing of all the issues that created friction between the parties. This ensured that an effort was made to keep the conflict from escalating and to lead the discordant parties to a mutually satisfying conclusion to their problem. Potential troublemakers had to recognize that at some point they would have to confront those whom they had directly harmed, rather than being part of some abstract system of justice with a victim who was a stranger. Inside this general framework, there was some variation in the types of disputes and the form of the settlement practices.

Types of Disputes and Their Settlement

Newman (1983) provides rich detail concerning the types of disputes that arose in hunting and gathering societies. Many disputes among hunting and gathering peoples concerned women. Because women were valuable producers, adultery, failure to honour marriage agreements, and the taking of a woman by an enemy caused serious disruptions. While women were not necessarily considered the property of their fathers or husbands, there was an interest in controlling them as valuable resources to the kin system. Other causes of conflict involved such acts as improper food distribution, asymmetrical gift exchange, laziness, stinginess, theft, and murder. Theft was an infrequent offence among nomadic foragers because of the relative absence of property. Murders were relatively infrequent and almost always resulted from disputes concerning women. Because of the emergence of the notion of property among sedentary food collectors, however, there was a greater incidence of theft and disputes over the use of land in those societies.

The primary method of redress in small-scale society itself was self- or kin-based redress. Other methods, used less frequently, were advisor or mediator systems.

Self- or Kin-Based Redress The range of responses available in self- or kin-based redress included public criticism, shaming rituals, temporary ostracism, or expulsion from the group, blood feuds, and reprisal killings. Some sedentary food gatherers also developed a scale of fines for certain types of infractions. This list in no way exhausts the full range of responses that were employed, but it does encompass those used most frequently. Less harsh methods were often employed initially, and only when they failed were more punitive responses called forth. In some instances, a disputant may simply have chosen to leave the group and join another on a temporary or permanent basis.

The injured party had to initiate the dispute process because there was no centralized authority. This does not mean that the victim was free to do to an offender whatever the victim chose. The society had customary expectations about the appropriateness of different reprisals. Too harsh a response could evoke group disapproval and sanctions. For example, among the Aranda of Australia, the socially defined punishment for adultery included cuts around the shoulder blades of the offending man inflicted by the cuckolded husband during hot pursuit of the offender. If the cuts were too deep and exceeded the standard of acceptable punishment, however, the husband stood to forfeit his wife. Among the Mataco of South America, if the reprisal was considered to be more serious than the original offence, the initial offence was expunged and the offender became the injured party. An individual could lose the support of his or her family by retaliating too vigorously. It is important to emphasize here that self-redress is a regulated social process. The image of small-scale societies as violent and constantly feuding is inaccurate. The ordered independence, which was the hallmark of such social formations, did not allow for anarchy when wrongs were redressed. While it is true that disputes did escalate into blood feuds and cycles of revenge killings, even these proceeded in an orderly fashion. Furthermore, small-scale society had a body of custom that was coupled with the fear of reprisal and that acted as a brake on such escalation by defining an appropriate level of redress for various offences.

Clearly defined notions of right and wrong behaviour existed in spite of the absence of third-party authority figures. It should be noted that formalized civil or criminal law was not present or necessary for these small, kin-based communities to restore order. If an individual violated a custom, he or she suffered the consequences. His or her kin did not provide protection from legitimate retaliation. If the punishment was too harsh or unfairly exacted, a retaliation was initiated, and conflict continued until both sides were satisfied with the resolution of the situation. An exchange of gifts often signalled the end to hostilities.

Advisor Systems The advisor system was really only an extension of the self-redress method of dispute settlement because it was once again ultimately the victim or kin who would enforce any retaliation. Disputants approached advisors, who tended to be men who were distinguished warriors, hunters, or speakers. They were mature, although not always the oldest men of the community, and were regarded as public repositories of wisdom about customs and rituals. In general, they were not selected because of birth right.

The process of dispute settlement was activated when one or both parties sought out one of these high-status figures. They were not required to turn to this third party, but it was expected that they would do so. Each party presented its case, and after considering the facts, the advisor recommended what should be done. He interpreted the case with respect to custom, and it was his role to ensure that the social group's conception of appropriate behaviour was protected. He was a moral authority, but he could not enforce compliance. He could, however, attempt to influence disputants with shaming rituals and his ability to make compelling arguments. Among some groups, the advisor could take a more active role by indicating which side his own kin group would back in the event of a reprisal. Here, too, the advisor could not direct his kin group, but only report its position with reference to the dispute. The advisor was, essentially, a communication link between parties and attempted to coordinate a settlement without violence. An advisor gained status by being able to settle disputes without the outbreak of revenge activity. A demonstrated ability to resolve disputes peacefully strengthened his moral authority. If the advisor overstepped his bounds and tried to make his authority too exacting, the community would stop using him in his capacity of advisor. Thus the advisor system was still firmly controlled by the community.

Most hunting and gathering societies relied on self-redress; a smaller proportion developed an advisor system.

In general, the dispute settlement processes used by small-scale societies were designed to restore social integration and harmony. These societies tried to surround and contain problems involving members of the community and sought to resolve them through compromise and reconciliation. Each member was tied to other members for a variety of social purposes. The discord created by disputants interfered with these other positive and necessary ties. These people simply could not afford to have long-standing anger and discord. As Ross (1989) points out, traditional Inuit and Ojibway dispute settlement mechanisms provide a poignant contrast to the assumptions of the Canadian criminal justice system (see Box 2.2).

On the whole, small-scale society had considerable success in avoiding the outbreak of serious trouble. Each member of the community was able to exercise some measure of control over others, so power remained diffuse. As a community, members were able to deal with discord in such a way that victim and offender could once again enter into harmonious interaction after a mutually agreeable settlement of a dispute had been made.

The Transformation from Small-Scale Society to the State

Within the last 6000 to 8000 years, most hunting and gathering societies have been transformed into pastoral, horticultural, agricultural, and industrial societies, as a result either of their own development or the invasion of an outside culture. The transformation of some small-scale societies to state societies will be outlined in this section, along with a discussion of the way in which this transformation affects the dispute settlement process.

The Slow Emergence of Social Power

Hunting and gathering communities were long able to resist any aspirations to autonomy and power by their members. While positions of influence did exist for those who made special contributions to the group, this status was not consolidated by greater access to material resources. Influential members still had to be responsive to the opinions, expectations, and judgments of the rest of their community in order to retain their special status.

At some point, the mutuality of **tribalism** was ruptured. The emergence of the concept of property slowly and progressively created social power for

tribalism
Where social bonds are based primarily on people's real or assumed common descent from an ancestor or group of ancestors, and this shared identification distinguishes the group from outsiders. In such societies, all social relationships tend to be direct and quasi-familial.

FOCUS

BOX 2.2 Traditional Inuit and Ojibway Dispute Settlement

The practice in one Inuit village was to call the entire village together and to put the actual event forward as a *hypothetical* event which might happen some time in the future. All people, including the miscreant and his victim, were required to put forward their views as to how things might be handled peacefully and properly were the situation ever to arise. There was no blaming, no pointing of fingers, and no requirement of explanation; nor was there ever any discussion, much less imposition, of either punitive or restitutionary response. At an Ojibway Reserve in my district similar dynamics governed. While the miscreant and his victim were summoned before an Elders Panel, there was never any discussion of what had happened and why, of how each party felt about the other or of what might be done by way of compensation. Nor was there any imposition of punishment. Each party was instead provided with a counselling Elder who worked privately to "cleanse his spirit." When both counselling Elders so signified by touching the peace pipe, it would be lit and passed to all. It was a signal that both had been "restored to themselves and to the community." If they privately arranged recompense of some sort, that was their affair. As far as the community was concerned, the matter was over. While I have not learned what the private counselling did consist of, I have been told that it did not involve retrieval and re-examination of the past in either its factual or emotional facets. It concentrated upon the future, and its spiritual component was central.

As a footnote, such ethics also cast the behavior of native victims in a very different light. Refusal or reluctance to testify or, when testifying, to give anything but the barest and most emotionless recital of events, may of course have been prompted by fear of the accused, by fear of the court, by love for and forgiveness of the accused or by any other such "sensible" reason (including the possibility, of extreme rarity in my experience, that they are uncomfortable because they are lying). Another reason, culturally foreign to us, could be that giving testimony face to face with the accused is simply considered wrong. It was not part of the traditional processes described above, where in fact every effort seems to have been made to *avoid* such direct confrontation. I recall one Indian woman who repeated her entire story of abuse to me in vivid detail before going into court and then asked me to do whatever I could to have the court send her very dangerous assailant to jail for as long as possible. Ten minutes later she took the witness stand and absolutely refused to say anything of an accusatory nature. When such witnesses regularly ask why they have to repeat their stories in court when they have already told "us" (meaning the police and the Crown), I have come to suspect that it is more than fear or embarrassment at work. I suspect instead that it is perceived as ethically wrong to say hostile, critical, implicitly angry things about someone *in their presence*, precisely what our adversarial trial rules have required. . . . In fact, we have taken this legal challenge into our daily lives, exhorting each person to open up with the other, to be honest and up front, to get things off our chests, etc., all of which are, to traditional native eyes, offensive in the extreme. When they refuse to follow the exhortations of our rules, we judge them as deficient in rule-obedience or, worse still, rule-less. In our ignorance we have failed to admit the possibility that there might be rules other than ours to which they regularly display allegiance, an allegiance all the more striking because it is exercised in defiance of our insistent pressures to the contrary.

Source: Rupert Ross. "Leaving Our White Eyes Behind: The Sentencing of Native Accused." [1989] 3 *Canadian Native Law Reporter* 1 at 5–6.

families and individuals. Privately owned land and livestock meant that the more fortunate members of the community were in a position to generate a surplus (Newman, 1983). This surplus increasingly gave them and their progeny the ability to rely less on the community for their survival. Under such circumstances, some of the ancient patriarchs began to define women as property, to secure not only control of their labour, but also their reproductive capacities "in order to ensure that there would be determinate heirs to function as the designatable future owners of individually held accumulations of private property" (Clark and Lewis, 1977).

The Evolution of Inequality

The power constellation of small-scale society was "horizontal" or "flat" and under the control of the community as a whole. It was the community that moved against the interests of individuals or factions when their undertakings were viewed as a serious threat to the good of the group. New forms of power inaugurated important changes. The emergence of surplus, stratification, and the basis for factional power gave rise to the "pyramidal" power constellation of modern societies and the development of the state in rudimentary form. The changing role of mediators, elders' councils, restricted councils, and then chieftainships shows the slow, yet progressive, development and consolidation of a social form of power independent of the community as a whole.

In small-scale society, each individual was expected to discharge his or her obligations directly to other community members. Slowly, the social elites were able to redirect this exchange to consolidate and to enhance their position in the changing social order. The goods that had been readily available to all members in a simple economy of sharing became distributed in patterns that reflected the stratified nature of pastoral, horticultural, agricultural, and industrial orders. These new modes of production made it increasingly possible for powerful groups and individuals to extract surplus value from those who turned to them in order to make a living. The ability to have other people help generate their personal wealth greatly accelerated the formation of stratified inequality. Less powerful segments in society found it increasingly difficult to resist those social forces that were compromising their interests.

Ultimately, the state emerged in agricultural society, and it championed and represented the interests of the powerful. The growing size, technological sophistication, and complexity of social systems gave rise to the need for large bureaucracies and a class of officials whose personal interests would become fused with those of the state. Human history was firmly established on a course that would generate hitherto unseen levels of surplus, poverty, and social inequality. The interests of whole groups of individuals were devalued and subordinated to the interests of powerful factions and the state. The equality of condition in small-scale society had been replaced by a class system rife with disparities.

The dispute settlement practices that emerged with these different social forms and the types of offences committed in such societies reflected the basic changes in social structure that have been outlined in this section. Attention will now be focused on the dispute process and the changes that took place that created law as it exists today.

Transformation in the Forms of Dispute Settlement

As societies changed their form, social relationships became complex and the types of disputes that arose in these societies changed. For example, with the emergence of private property, theft became possible. The concepts of rent and the violation of contracts became grounds for disagreement. When individuals began writing wills, problems emerged concerning appropriate or disputed inheritance. The emergence of contracts and wills contributed to the need for more codified conventions and a body of civil law. Finally, the emergence of surplus meant that disputes could be settled by the payment of various types of fines to compensate the party who had been wronged. For example, under Anglo-Saxon law, if a woman was raped, a compensatory fee was paid to either her husband or her father, depending on who exercised the rights of ownership over her at the time of the offence. The fee was not paid directly to the woman herself as she was not considered to be the person who had been wronged by the act (Clark and Lewis, 1977).

Increased productive capacity resulted in disputes concerning property, accompanied by increasingly complex legal codifications to deal with them. The creation of chiefdoms, and eventually states, was accompanied by the emergence of offences such as treason, slander, and libel, and, in general, the possibility for criminal law as defined as offences against the Crown. Failure to pay taxes or to work on public projects became offences and sources of litigation. In this section, some of the basic features of elders' councils, chieftainships, and paramount chieftainships will be examined. These are the dominant structural elements in dispute settlement that distinguish societies lying between small-scale societies and state systems.

Elders' Councils

Elders' councils performed legal, political, economic, and administrative functions. Disputants were required to submit their dispute to these councils, whose verdicts were binding. There were often several levels of councils, including local and regional councils with different powers; for example, one level would hear appeals. The membership in these councils was representative of the influential segments of the society. The members of the council may have included all married males or the oldest male in each family. In all instances, each family was represented, and hence membership was basically democratic. Participation was not contingent upon wealth, although there was a clear sex bias. Eventually, most men in the community would have occasion to sit on the elders' councils.

Council procedures were marked by a high degree of formality. This is uncharacteristic of the forms of dispute settlement discussed so far. Formal language, recourse to precedents, and rules of conduct all marked the seriousness of the occasion. The conclusions of these councils carried considerable weight because they were made by a representative group of elders who were charged with the duty of determining a dispute in the best interests of the community. Community pressure dictated the obligation to accept the judgment of the council. If an individual was recalcitrant, the council could enlist local men to threaten the offender and deprive him or her of property, or direct the kinsmen of the victim to retaliate. This was the only type of self-redress that was available in these systems.

Chieftainships

A chief was the highest political authority in the community and was recognized as having the ultimate power in settling disputes. The chief's decisions were binding, although others may have been required to enforce them. Chieftainships tended to be based on heredity or supernatural knowledge. Chiefs were primarily rich men from influential families. They also were expected to display oratorical skills, wisdom, and knowledge of customary ways. Chiefs usually served on a permanent basis and held office through their productive years, either voluntarily relinquishing it when they judged themselves incapable of continuing or being overthrown by rebellions when they fell from popularity. Chiefs often had the right to select their successor, although this was contingent upon community approval.

Chieftainships made possible a formalization and institutionalization of the legal system. The chief was able to intervene in a dispute without being requested to do so and heard appeals if more informal attempts to settle a dispute failed. Chiefs had the power to order executions, beatings, public reprimands, and economic sanctions such as fines and destruction or confiscation of property. No form of self-redress was allowed unless the approval of the chief had been secured. Considerable power was placed in the hands of the chief, although he often consulted community members prior to making a decision.

Paramount Chieftainships

The **paramount chieftainship** was a form of social order that took a significant step away from the participatory and democratic features of other models. Paramount chieftainships were much like kingdoms. They were based on hereditary aristocracies and drew together a large number of communities or villages that retained some level of local autonomy. Paramount chieftainships were complex, hierarchical structures. The chief was surrounded with retainers and nobles who performed judicial and administrative tasks. Many such chieftainships had a "civil service" recruited from the ranks of royalty to handle daily affairs. This apparatus allowed a more formal and structured legal system to develop. In this way, the paramount chief was able to extend control over a large geographical region and a sizeable population.

paramount chieftainship
A political system similar to a kingdom that brings together a number of partly autonomous villages or communities under the hierarchical rule of a grand chief.

The paramount chief held court in a capital city, and the paramount chief's court served as the highest court of justice. District or circuit courts were used as a first resort to settle disputes, but more serious cases came under the jurisdiction of the paramount chief, who had the final authority to make binding decisions. In many societies, the chief had an advisory council made up of royalty. However, the final decision in settling cases rested with the chief, who had a full range of options available. From the structure of paramount chieftainship, it was a small step to the creation of the state.

The transformation of the hunting and gathering social form and the attendant dispute-settling processes are dramatic when considered in this comparative framework. But the changes occurred so gradually that the historical actors barely noticed them. Once the checks on the accumulation of wealth and power that bound small-scale society together were undercut, there seemed to be an inevitable chain of events that led to the emergence of a state system. Some of the reasons for this steady and cumulative development have been discussed in general terms. In the next section of this chapter, the modern state system will be examined in greater detail. Implicit in this analysis will be a comparison of modern social and legal structures with those of small-scale society.

Modern State Systems

The full emergence of the state in the past 3000 or 4000 years has created a rich and complex social tapestry. We will outline the essential changes in social-power constellations that transformed land-based **feudalism** into the modern capitalist state. This historical outline will be somewhat detailed in order to provide an adequate basis for a sophisticated analysis of the key structural changes that would ultimately result in the emergence of modern commercial, industrial society. The case of England provides the basis for the analysis of the emergence of law in Western democratic states. This focus is clearly appropriate when seeking to understand the legal system in Canada and the United States of America. The analysis of law in state systems in other historical circumstances is beyond the scope of this chapter.

feudalism
A system of economic and social organization found historically in several areas of the world.. In western Europe, feudalism was at its height between about 1000 and 1500. The economic foundation of the system was the feudal manor that included a central farm owned by the landlord and small land holdings for a class of bonded farm labourers (serfs). The serfs were required to work the central manorial farm and to provide the lord with produce and money payments in return for their right to use the land. The system gradually declined as cities and towns grew and power became centralized in nation-states under monarchies.

From Tribalism to Feudalism

The primary basis for social order prior to feudalism was tribal kinship. In this social order, military leaders had already begun to emerge in a class system where conquered individuals became followers tied to their leaders with reciprocal obligations (Jeffery, 1969; Kennedy, 1976). A patchwork of local fiefdoms under the control of local lords began to develop. The invasions of England, especially the Norman Invasion, accelerated the full development of a feudal order. In essence, feudalism was a social system based on the tenure of land, which was the dominant form of capital in an agrarian mode of production. The use of land was granted to the vassal in return for military service or, in later years, for rent. Those who held land had obligations to protect and to provide food for their serfs in hard times. These serfs were typically tied to the land and were required to deliver labour service, tribute, and the like. This relationship, while based on subjection, had a quasi-familial tone. Land was not a commodity that was for sale. The right to use the land was controlled by the lord. A serf could lose the right to land use only for neglect of the land or failure to meet obligations.

No central power existed in the early period of feudalism. Social order was maintained through the kinship system as well as the developing land tenure system in which the vast majority of individuals were eventually required to have a lord. In tribal times, blood feuds were the primary dispute settlement mechanism. In medieval England, the secure emergence of local fiefdoms resulted in intervention by the local lord, who had the authority to administer a variety of different sanctions. As feudalism developed and the notion of collective responsibility was replaced with that of individual responsibility, money settlements and fines were used to settle serious disputes, with the exception of those committed by outlaws, who were slain without fear of reprisal. By the year 871, feuds could be resorted to only if other forms of compensation had been requested and denied. Compliance with such standards was through local custom since no centralized source of power had emerged to enforce them. Local lords were not willing or able to become involved in all disputes. For example, only the rape of wealthy, propertied virgins would typically secure the involvement of the powerful lords who protected them (Brownmiller, 1975).

Once these Anglo-Saxon lords were able to consolidate some power in England, they began to develop a body of law to deal with disputes. Under this system, trial by ordeal (using such methods as walking on hot coals or reaching into boiling water to pick up a pebble) was the means to establish guilt or innocence for those disputants who could not find some other way to settle a dispute. The pattern is clear; kin-based dispute settlement practices were being continuously undermined and replaced by feudal lords and their laws.

The Emergence of the Centralized State

With the success of the Norman Invasion in 1066, William the Conqueror declared himself the "supreme landlord" of all England, so that all individuals who held land held his land. Over the succeeding centuries, the English kings slowly expanded and consolidated their power over the feudal landscape. Harms committed in disputes between individuals increasingly were seen to harm the *mund*, or the king's region. As a result, compensation was paid to kings, lords, and bishops, rather than to kinship groups. Originally, the *King's Peace* referred to his ability to protect his own person, but, as Jeffery argues, the development of the central state meant that "gradually it was extended to include the king's court, army, servants, hundred-court, and finally the four main highways of England." The Norman kings saw themselves as the injured party when a crime was committed since the harm was against their peace. Since some crimes were now against the Crown, criminal law became a reality. The Crown replaced the victim as the injured party, and compensation to the victim's family was replaced by punitive fines that were payable to the Crown.

This trend continued, as the king could enforce his increased claims to **sovereignty** with force. A central authority had emerged in England to replace the authority of feudal lords. By 1180, Henry II had introduced a system of royal courts and a system of royal writs. Thus **common law** came into existence as the law of the Crown available to all individuals. As Jeffery (1969) has stated, "The family was no longer involved in law and justice. The State was the offended unit, and the State was the proper prosecutor in every case of crime." The pivotal role that law and the courts played in this undertaking to consolidate centralized political and economic power is of primary significance. Another major factor was the growth of trade and the rise of the merchant class. These developments led to the decline of the feudal system and to the rise of towns and cities at the expense of the rural manors. Cities began to arise during the reign of King John (1199–1216) and, although they were situated on

WWW

"Historical Origins of Government's Monopoly on Criminal Justice" National Center for Policy Analysis (USA)
www.ncpa.org/studies/s181/s181c.html

sovereignty
The authority possessed by the governing individual or institution of a society. Sovereign authority is distinct in that it is unrestricted by legal regulation since the sovereign authority is itself the source of all law.

common law
The common law tradition found in English Canada derives from feudal England, where it had become the practice for the king to resolve disputes in accordance with local custom. Customs that were recognized throughout the country were called common custom, and decisions made by the king and by subsequent courts set up to settle disputes became known as common law. Common law is considered a source of law.

land controlled by feudal lords, they fell under the jurisdiction of the Crown. A new system of social relationships developed that was based on commerce instead of on feudal obligations.

The Coalition of Merchants and Monarchs

William the Conqueror had established a state apparatus when he made all nobles take an oath to establish him as their feudal overlord. With this came the power to create laws to govern the kingdom, royal officials to protect the king's interests, and royal courts to dispense the king's justice. This state apparatus was superimposed on feudalism. While feudalism was dominant, the king used the state apparatus to defend the common interests of feudal lords. However, the breakdown of feudal obligations and the feudal tax system also meant a loss of revenue for the Crown, which needed to find new ways to finance war and the state. This was accomplished by going outside the feudal system to negotiate loans with merchants, using land as collateral. The king wanted his power consolidated and needed political support and financial assistance, while the merchants wanted a unified and safe trading area (Chambliss, 1969; Hall, 1969a). The state was to become the vehicle that the Crown and its merchant allies would use to defeat the resistance impeding the development of the new social order. In return for their support, Henry VIII conceded that Parliament would have control over tax revenues and the legislative function. Thus the state, which was staffed with the **bourgeois class**, would become the mechanism for change by statute. Laws would be passed by Parliament.

bourgeois class

The term *bourgeois class*, or *bourgeoisie*, was used by Marx to refer to the capitalist or ruling class in modern societies.

The merchants benefited from this new arrangement because they were able to gain greater access to land. The feudal lords' losses in war brought the merchants the land that the lords had put up as collateral for loans. When Henry VIII expropriated church land, over one-sixth of the land in England was removed from its connection to feudalism. Henry sold this land to friends and allies, for whom he created peerages with seats in the House of Lords. This action more than doubled his revenue, placed a large block of land outside feudal control, and made this land available for the money market. As the feudal system declined, many lords were tied into feudal land arrangements of rent, which were driving them into financial ruin. Eventually, their lands also were freed of feudal ties and became part of the commodity market to be bought and sold as private property in the interest of profit. In 1540, Henry VIII also gave his support to the Statute of Wills, which made most land in England transmittable by will. The role of the Crown had changed from that of shared owner of land under feudalism to that of land regulator via the state, which was becoming a separate and sovereign entity.

The labour of serfs, which had been tied to the land under feudalism, was freed from the land, as were the lords. In addition, much of the land that had been controlled by the church was also made available as commons for serfs to graze their animals. However, the new owners enclosed a great deal of this land for wool production and thoroughly disrupted the lives of the commoners. The right of commoners to hunt, fish, and gather wood on their lord's manor was extinguished under the new property relations. The Black Act of 1723 increased the number of offences for which the courts could impose the death penalty.

These harsh measures were seen as necessary to encourage the common people to abandon these feudal practices (Thompson, 1976). The new land regulations displaced the rural workforce, which then became the new workforce of the factories made possible by technological innovation.

These fundamental changes contributed to the increased importance of commerce and money. The close and personal ties of fealty and its reciprocal duties and obligations were being eclipsed by the abstract and anonymous transactions of money in commercial enterprise. The growth of banking institutions, the use of paper currency, and other instruments of credit created new occasions for theft by trusted third parties. The famous Carrier's Case of 1473 made it clear that the law of theft would need to be refined in order to prevent intermediaries from keeping goods put in their possession for transport (Hall, 1952). International trade, which was spurred by Britain's colonial empire, also necessitated an expansion and refinement of the concept of theft. Hall (1969b) recounts how the law governing embezzlement was enacted to make theft of paper money and commercial bonds a crime. If a business was run by members of a household, behaviour was regulated by custom and by family ties. However, when businesses grew they needed to hire employees from the larger communities who had no other ties to the owners. Transactions between anonymous parties would henceforth be regulated by law because of the absence of customary ties between them.

The role of law and the place of lawyers would figure prominently in the regulation of the new social relationships. In order to chart the consolidation of state power within the context of law, it is essential to study the activities of various interest groups with respect to commerce and contract law. The consolidation of a new form of social life based on contract was achieved within the context of commerce and the rise of the bourgeois class.

Commerce, Contracts, and the Primary Role of Law

The growth of commerce, spurred by the Industrial Revolution and the expansion of trade, required greater uniformity and enforceability of trading arrangements. Towns, cities, and even nation-states realized that a system of law, and a court system to apply it, would be essential if trade was to stabilize and grow. The volume of trade, its growing impersonality, the practice of joint ventures, and the long distances involved in international trade created the need for a mechanism to secure the interests of traders. Legal contracts, which had existed since Roman times, became the dominant mechanism that would tie social relationships together in the new social order. Tönnies (1887) argued that the ***Gesellschaft*** (i.e., the modern society) came to exist as a superior power to enforce the terms set out in the contracts of the merchants and capitalists. Lawyers grew in number and importance as new contract forms were developed to meet the increasingly complex trade arrangements of the time. Contracts, which had been private agreements, now became widely used to bind together individuals in the new social order. This new reliance on contract required changes in the court structure. In the feudal era, common law had developed to settle disputes. This law was applied in church courts, as well as in the King's Court.

Gesellschaft
A German word, translated as "society-association," used by Ferdinand Tönnies (1855–1936) to refer to an ideal type or model of a society in which social bonds are primarily impersonal, instrumental, and narrow. Characteristic of large-scale, complex societies, with a strict division between private and public spheres of life, it contrasts to the community-oriented life of the *Gemeinschaft*.

During the mid-1500s, the king sought to consolidate power, and he found that great inroads could be made into common law by throwing his support behind merchant law in support of the merchant class. In return for taxes and loans, the Crown placed the power of the state behind the laws of commerce and enforced these laws. The merchant class supported the legislative and judicial power of the Crown in exchange for the development of legal mechanisms that would further strengthen their class position, increase their fortunes, and consolidate their power. The law and lawyers had been guaranteed a primary role in the new industrial, capitalist mode of production. The bourgeois had helped to strengthen the power of the monarch in order to be protected by his state apparatus. The king's support of merchant law as the law of the land helped to stabilize the necessary social and legal conditions for commerce.

The power of the nation-state was solidified around the interests of commerce, and the role of custom and kinship was eroded. The basis for the new social order was predicated on law, in the realm of both commercial and criminal activity. While the primary interest of this chapter is criminal law, it is important to track the rise of the institution of law in the modern state—and this was primarily within the context of merchant interests.

The merchant class had supported the aspirations of the Crown because its members needed a stable and modified system in order to conduct their affairs. However, once the land had been redistributed and feudal village life had been disrupted, the bourgeois became interested in forming a new alliance so as to curb the Crown's ability to restrict trade. Tigar and Levy (1977) document the new alliance with common-law lawyers.

The Consolidation of Bourgeois Ascendance

Contracts under merchant law were enforced in merchant courts, as well as in chancery and admiralty courts. Common-law lawyers realized that the portion of law that they administered was shrinking with the decline of the landed nobility. Some of them were eager to have merchant law enforced in their courts. The bourgeois were supportive of such a development, as it would make them less dependent on the king and his special courts. Common-law lawyers made a concerted effort to make their courts more receptive to bourgeois legal principles. By 1600, an alliance between the common-law lawyers and the bourgeois was finding success in introducing the bourgeois theory of contract into common-law courts. A conflict between the Crown and the merchant class ensued because the Crown wanted to control merchant activity through the monarch's court, and the bourgeois wanted to evade the Crown's attempts at controlling trade by having matters handled through the common-law courts.

The merchant class gained a strong hold on the Parliament as the landed aristocracy's power waned. Parliament used its control over tax revenues in its efforts to limit the king's control of trade. This conflict was resolved in the English Civil War of 1642–48 by a reduction in the power of the monarchy and the establishment of the bourgeois-controlled Parliament as the sole source of political control.

Peasants and workers were not represented in this early Parliament, and the modern state developed under the influence of the bourgeois. The rise of the labour movement would come later, but as Miliband (1969) has convincingly displayed in his book *The State in Capitalist Society*, the power of organized labour has never managed to match that of organized business. Whatever advances have been made in democratizing the state apparatus, it remains a political and legal structure to protect the interests of property. In the arena of modern political life, various interest groups bring pressure on the state to protect their interests under the rule of law.

State, Law, and Interest Groups

As the structures of feudalism declined, the state became the dominant institution regulating social order and settling disputes. State decisions were backed up by military and police organizations. The state stood as the superior force behind the contractual arrangements of business and property in order to ensure that the terms of these agreements were observed.

In this context, the law has become the dominant means to regulate human affairs: legislation and administrative directives are the legal apparatus that create the bases of modern nation-states; property, commerce, real estate, labour, and contractual agreements are all regulated by law; municipalities and corporations are governed by law; the protection of the environment is regulated by law; and disputes over person and property are handled through family, civil, and criminal law. In short, the law is the principal means whereby human activity is prohibited, permitted, or required, and the state and the law are intimately meshed in the creation of the modern social order.

As shown in earlier sections, the merchant class was quite successful in promoting and protecting its interests as it helped shape the nature of the state and the law. But business interest groups are not the only ones that approach the state to promote their interests. A variety of cultural, ethnic, minority, class, economic, and political interest groups lobby the state in order to promote their own interests. The modern state has become a vehicle sought after by a variety of groups, each seeking certain guarantees and protections. The heterogeneous nature of modern societies and the antagonistic relationships between various groups ensure that the state cannot promote the interests of all groups. Choices need to be made. Given the nature of electoral politics, the state is under some pressure to promote the values and interests of the majority and of powerful minorities in order to maintain legitimacy and popularity. In the remainder of this chapter, several examples will be reviewed to provide some insight into the range of interest groups seeking to influence the content and role of law in modern society. Given the sheer volume of law and the complexity of modern society, this review is meant to be only illustrative of the role of law in modern society.

Regulation by Law

Some authors argue that the law reflects the values of the majority of the population, while others analyze various laws to show that powerful minority interests have shaped the content of the law. There is no reason to conclude that only one of these positions is correct. It is clear that some legal enactments reflect the values of the majority, and it is also clear that other laws clearly do not reflect the values of the majority but instead reflect the values of powerful minorities. The significant impact of powerful interests on the content of law is a topic that is subject to much debate. In this section, examples that demonstrate both points of view will be discussed.

Consensus and the Law

Under some circumstances, there is broadly based consensus about limiting certain forms of behaviour. There is general consensus regarding laws that seek to protect individuals from common assault in public places, from breaking and entering, and from theft of property from their residence. There is also considerable agreement about what constitutes serious crime. Rossi and Waite (1974) replicated the earlier work of Sellin and Wolfgang (1964) on the ranking of seriousness of crimes and came to the following conclusion: "The norms defining how serious various criminal acts are considered to be, are quite widely distributed among blacks and whites, males and females, high and low socio-economic levels, and among levels of educational attainment" (237). This basic consensus about what constitutes crime against person and property should not be understated.

Interest Groups and the Law

Most of the research on law, however, shows the operation of interest groups. Chambliss demonstrates how various interest groups have been able to influence the content and the use of vagrancy laws (see Box 2.3).

Hagan and Leon (1977) and Platt (1969) show the operation of various "moral entrepreneurs" who were part of a child-saving movement, and the responsiveness of the state in creating legislation and a separate juvenile court. West and Snider (1985) have also documented the operation of interest groups in this movement, but they expand the argument by suggesting that their motives were not only to save children, but also to deal with an excess labour supply.

Research on drug legislation also shows the state responding to various forms of pressure. Becker (1963) attempts to demonstrate that drug legislation in the United States was the result of the efforts of a civil servant, Harry Anslinger, who was primarily a moral entrepreneur. Dickson (1968) further argues that this bureaucrat was able to use his access to government services not only to foster particular moral objectives, but possibly also to save his organization and help it expand. The research of Shirley Small (1978) into Canadian narcotics legislation suggests that strong racist sentiments against Asians were a motivating force in the push for drug laws. Comack (1985) suggests that these anti-Asian sentiments were grounded in labour disputes that were being handled in racial terms instead of in class terms.

Graham's (1976) analysis of amphetamine legislation clearly demonstrates the operation of special interests. In spite of strong support from the American public and the president, attempts to change the Federal Drug Administration's (FDA) control of amphetamine production failed because of pressure from the powerful drug companies. A legislative remedy would have gone a long way in promoting the common good with regard to this significant problem, but the power of a sizeable lobby stifled the attempted changes. This fact was hidden from public view.

FOCUS

BOX 2.3 The Origin and Evolution of Vagrancy Law

In sum, the vagrancy laws constituted a legislative innovation designed to provide an abundance of cheap labor to England's ruling class during a period when serfdom was breaking down and the pool of available labor was depleting. They hit at the "idle" and "those refusing to labour." With the breakup of feudalism, the utility of these laws disappeared. The increased dependence of the economy upon commerce and trade made the former use of the vagrancy statutes irrelevant. In the early 17th century, the emphasis turned to "rogues," "vagabonds," and others suspected of criminal activities. During this period, the statutes embraced "roadmen" who preyed upon citizens transporting goods from one place to another. The increased importance of commerce to England during this period brought forth protective laws. The vagrancy statutes originally aimed at providing serfs for feudal landlords became a weapon in this new enterprise.

In the United States during the late 19th and early 20th centuries, vagrancy statutes were used, much as they had been in England, to create a labor force. The end of the Civil War left Southern plantation owners and Northern industrialists wishing to industrialize the South without an adequate work force. The Emancipation Proclamation and the passage of the 13th and 14th Amendments freed the slaves, but a system of wage labor did not exist. Also, there was unwillingness on the part of the plantation owners or industrialists to pay wages where slavery had previously provided cheap labor. A solution to the dilemma posed by the abolition of slavery was to arrest "free Negroes" for vagrancy and then force them to labor by leasing them to landowners, mining companies, or industrialists.

The use of vagrancy statutes to create and control the labor force in the United States is not limited to the South or to the period immediately following the Civil War. Until very recently, during times of harvest people were arrested for vagrancy and given the option of either working as a farm laborer or being sent to jail. These statutes were also used to control "undesirables." California used them to limit the immigration of unemployed persons during the depression. Vagrancy statutes also came to serve the police as a catch-all to permit them to arrest, harass, or jail persons whom they found to be a nuisance or suspected of being potential criminals.

The very nature of vagrancy statutes as catch-all categories pinpointing a status rather than an act makes them swim in vagueness. . . . Because of the vagueness of the statutes and the unbridled discretion granted law enforcers, the enforcement of these statutes has culminated in a large body of appellate court decisions. In 1972, a group of people arrested under the Jacksonville, Florida, statute appealed to the U.S. Supreme Court arguing that their arrest [was] unconstitutional because the statute was too vague. . . . The Supreme Court [supported] the defendants' appeal. . . . As a practical matter, the long, disreputable history of vagrancy statutes in the United States ended with this decision.

Source: William Chambliss. (1988). *Exploring Criminology*. New York: Macmillan, pp. 109–11. Reprinted by permission of the author.

The analysis of the history of rape legislation (Brownmiller, 1975; Clark and Lewis, 1977; Kinnon, 1981) shows that such laws were enacted to protect the transmission of property in the male line of descent. Fathers used rape laws to avoid transferring property to men of whom they disapproved but who had taken their daughters by bride capture. They also sought compensation for the reduction of bride price that they suffered because their daughters had lost virginal status. Husbands wanted to secure control over their wives' reproductive capacity to ensure that they transferred their property to their own sons. Therefore, women and children became the property of the man of the household, and the act of rape became an offence against the husband. Over time, and as the result of concerted feminist activity, the act of sexual assault has been reconceptualized as a crime against the woman who has been victimized, and in some jurisdictions, including Canada, the husband can now be prosecuted for the rape of his wife (Chapter 5). This, of course, means that women have succeeded in having themselves redefined as persons and not merely as the property of their fathers or husbands.

Research conducted on anti-combines legislation in Canada also provides the kind of evidence that demonstrates the operation of class-based interest groups in the framing of the law. Smandych (1985) outlines the confrontation that was brewing in the 1880s between labour and capital. The Knights of Labour movement specifically focused on the monopolistic nature of industrial capitalism and demanded the elimination of combines. A royal commission was established, and it submitted its report in the same year that the first anti-combines legislation was enacted. But as Goff and Reasons (1978) point out, the wording of the statute was weakened in comparison with proposals in preliminary drafts. So the statute appeared to constrain capital interests when, in fact, it hardly did so. More changes to this statute in the 1970s further liberalized the circumstances under which mergers were permissible. Thus not only was the state unwilling to champion the interests of organized labour in the legislation, but as Goff and Reasons, and Snider (1980) have shown, the act has been applied only to small firms in Canada. In spite of the evidence of higher prices under conditions of oligopoly and in spite of protests by organized labour, the Canadian government has been unwilling to regulate the larger corporations in order to make Canada competitive in the international market. The government appears to fear the loss of investor confidence and the flight of capital.

The Canadian Centre for Occupational Health and Safety
www.ccohs.ca

The history of occupational health and safety legislation is also very instructive. Friedman and Ladinsky (1980) trace the changes in the law governing industrial accidents and relate that, initially, employers were held responsible for injuries to workers under tort law, even if such injury resulted from the negligence of another employee. But this doctrine of *respondeat superior* was slowly replaced by the fellow-servant rule, which did not allow an employee to sue the employer in the case of injury unless harm was caused by the employer's personal misconduct. This move effectively prevented thousands of lawsuits in the United States, but the large number of accidents generated a continuing series of cases. Pressure was exerted by workers and their unions, and, in some jurisdictions, legislation was introduced to exclude the application of the fellow-servant rule. Workers' compensation schemes were proposed, but employers showed little interest in them until judges began awarding damages to employees. The compensation legislation that was finally enacted was based on a compromise position. Employers and employees would both contribute to the cost of the program, which would guarantee the injured employee compensation based on statutory schedules. However, the employer would be protected from the bulk of civil liability litigation because employee claims would be handled by an administrative agency instead of by the courts.

While this compensation program has been more or less acceptable to workers and owners, Walters (1983) shows how the Ontario government has undertaken changes in occupational health and safety legislation in an effort to reduce the cost of running its health-care system. It has been estimated that $1.4 billion is added to the health-care system's bill every year because of industrial accidents. Here is an interesting case of the state enacting legislation not to promote or protect the interests of any specific interest group, but rather to reduce its own deficit. It is interesting to note that Snider (1994) found that the greatest gains in the regulation of dangerous corporate behaviour have been in the realm of occupational health and safety.

These examples demonstrate that the process of law creation is heavily influenced by various interest groups and the pressure that they bring to bear on the state. It seems quite clear that the state often does find itself in situations in which it can make decisions based on the wishes and interests of the majority. At other times, it finds itself hard pressed to regulate effectively some of the special interest groups.

The Failure to Regulate: The Eclipse of the State?

There is growing concern among some analysts that transnational corporations operating in countries all over the globe have amassed so much economic power that they are getting beyond the control of nation-states. These corporations are expanding at two to three times the rates of growth of national economies, and the scale of such organizations gives them considerable power to resist the efforts of nation-states to regulate them. These corporations can, and do, bring considerable pressure to bear on national governments. If a government is too restrictive in its regulatory policies, a **transnational corporation** can relocate operations to another country with laws more to its liking. It is clear that corporations are responsible for behaviour that is harmful to various other interest groups and that these harms are not being effectively controlled by the state and the rule of law. The following examples help make the point.

transnational corporation
A corporation that has sales and production in many different nations. As a result of their multinational reach, these corporations are often thought to be beyond the political control of any individual nation-states.

Victims of Avoidable Harms

Reasons et al. (1981) recount numerous instances in which Canadian workers were needlessly exposed in the workplace to risks that resulted in injury and death. Many of these dangers are known to employers and are avoidable, leading Reasons et al. to suggest that these casualties are "victims without crimes," and that such injuries should be conceptualized as "assaults" on the worker. Stone (1975) recounts cases of corporate actions involving injury that would have resulted in criminal trials and possibly death sentences had they been committed by individuals. Dowie (1977) reports that the design problems of the Ford Pinto that resulted in passenger injury and death were known by the auto manufacturer, that these problems could have been addressed by cost-effective measures, and that the corporation chose not to make the improvements. Internal Ford memos reveal that the costs of design changes were compared to the costs of potential litigation for death, dismemberment, and injury, and that the company decided to put Pinto passengers at risk. It is hard to conceive of the death and injury created by the Pinto as accidental when such injury and death were anticipated and could have been avoided. It could be argued that these deaths were homicides and that such harmful behaviour ought to come under the control of the Criminal Code. Ford was, in fact, charged with homicide for one of the Pinto accidents, but was acquitted by an Indiana jury. These cases are common and make it clear that the modern consumer-citizen is not being protected under the rule of law from dangerous corporate misbehaviour.

The courts could move in the direction of holding corporations and their managers accountable for harms such as the one that took place in Cook County, Illinois. On July 1, 1985, three former executives of a silver-recycling plant were convicted of murder, and each received a sentence of 25 years in prison and a fine of $10 000 for the death of an employee. The company had exposed workers to cyanide gas by intentionally concealing warnings of hazards from immigrant workers. These murder convictions are believed to be the first in the United States of corporate officials in a job-related death. But to date, governments have not pursued a vigorous policy of bringing such corporate harms under the appropriate sections of the Criminal Code. This case turned out to be a rarity and not a harbinger of greater corporate accountability.

The Asbestos Institute Online
www.asbestos-institute.ca

Finally, Brodeur (1985) has provided a detailed analysis of problems associated with the asbestos industry in the United States and Canada. It has come to light that the industry had been aware of the health hazards related to the inhalation of asbestos particles since the 1930s, but that it withheld this information from workers and did not take steps to improve the safety of the workplace. *Facts on File* has kept track of the significant developments related to the claims against asbestos companies. The key developments will be tracked here in some detail because they demonstrate the legal complexities involved as the various stakeholders attempt to use the law to protect their interests against those of other interested parties. It is estimated by a U.S. Federal Appeals Court "that the number of current and future claimants [is] expected to reach several million" (*Facts on File*, 1997). Further, "analysts estimated total asbestos liability to be as high as $50 billion" (*Facts on File*, 2000). Asbestos firms have been flooded with lawsuits in which courts have been finding them responsible for the resultant illnesses and deaths and have awarded victims sizable punitive damages. "$53.5 million dollar judgment [was awarded] in favor of the estate of Stephen Brown, a former mechanic who died of mesothelioma in December 2000. The verdict handed down in a State Court in New York City, was the largest ever awarded to a single asbestos plaintiff" (*Facts on File*, 2002). In 1982, the Johns-Manville Corporation, with assets of more than $2 billion, filed for bankruptcy in the United States in an effort to escape paying the damages assessed for its harmful business practices. By 2000, 25 companies had filed for bankruptcy protection due to asbestos litigation. The U.S. government was put under considerable corporate pressure to grant this request. However, it was also faced with pressure to hold corporate citizens accountable to the same laws that ordinary citizens are bound to obey. It is increasingly clear that the government's response to this situation is to make use of *civil* rather than *criminal* courts. Reasons et al. (1981) make a compelling case in arguing that many "accidents" in the workplace are not unforeseen and therefore are not accidents. They argue that they should properly be conceptualized as "assaults on the workers" and handled by way of the Criminal Code rather than by occupational health and safety legislation, offering the following example: "It has been revealed that asbestos companies continued to expose workers to that substance in spite of the fact that they had had evidence concerning its fatal effects for some thirty years. Such conscious, premeditated, and rational behaviour undoubtedly led to thousands of deaths and disabilities. Nonetheless, asbestos companies are only liable to civil lawsuits" (6).

The court system initially declined to allow victims to bring forward class action suits, but finally, in 1991, the judicial panel on multidistrict litigation allowed more than 26 000 personal injury cases involving asbestos to be consolidated "in order to reduce delays and rising costs in asbestos litigation, which many lawyers said had reached a crisis level, with plaintiffs dying or depleting their resources before a verdict was handed down" (*Facts on File*, 1991). Since then, other courts have also consolidated asbestos cases because they are the largest number of civil cases in U.S. federal courts. This decision has made it easier for victims to gain access to damage awards. (Similar class action, or "mass tort," cases are also being used or contemplated in actions against tobacco companies as well as the manufacturers of the Dalkon Shield, Agent Orange, and silicone breast implants.) In an effort to limit their liability in future claims, large asbestos companies proposed a settlement under which "220 companies and their insurers would resolve outside of court as many as 100,000 new asbestos-injury claims for $1 billion over the next decade" (*Facts on File*, 1993). This settlement was an attempt by the companies to set a limit on monetary damages that they would be liable to pay to claimants after the number of claims and the size of settlements being awarded threatened to bankrupt many of them. An appeals court struck down the settlement package in May 1996. The appeals court ruled "that the agreement, which would bar individuals from pursuing future claims against the manufacturers, could compromise the rights of people who were currently unaware that they had been exposed to asbestos" (*Facts on File*, 1997). This decision was upheld by the Supreme Court on June 25, 1997. So the outcome of this episode of corporate deviance is far from settled. The state finds itself in the middle between the rights of individuals to damages and the needs of the corporations to limit damages so that they can remain in business. The state clearly has an interest in keeping corporations in business because they are the major employers in an industrial economy. Many jurisdictions are considering legislation that could limit the amount of damages for which corporations could be sued. It remains to be seen whether the United States is prepared to hold major corporations responsible under the law for their reckless and harmful behaviour. The asbestos companies are encountering financial fallout in any event. For example, in December 7, 2001, Halliburton, a multinational corporation with operations in over 120 countries, "saw its stock tumble 42% after a Baltimore, Md. jury that day had ordered the company to pay $30 million in damages in an asbestos exposure lawsuit" (*Facts on File*, 2001). Halliburton also has Energy Services Group, which provides technical products and services for *oil* and *gas* exploration and production, and had a subsidiary, KBR, which undertook major construction of *refineries*, *oil fields*, *pipelines*, and *chemical plants*. It was KBR that was involved in the asbestos litigation. In 2004, the U.S. Bankruptcy Court approved a deal between Halliburton and Equitas, a reinsurance firm, that would pay Halliburton $575 million (25% of the $2.3 billion that Halliburton sought) to finance an asbestos trust fund (*Facts on File*, 2004). In 2005, Halliburton "finalized a $5.1 billion settlement that ended its past and future liability to asbestos lawsuits" with regard to claims by more than 400 000 people (*Facts on File*, 2005). On April 5, 2007, Halliburton announced that it had broken ties with KBR, which had been its contracting, engineering, and construction unit for 44 years.

Transnational corporations exist to make profits for investors, but the pursuit of profit has often been maximized by reckless and dangerous behaviour. The growing evidence of the serious harm to employees, customers, and the environment that has resulted suggests that a very powerful set of human actors is currently operating beyond the control of law. For example, Marchak (1991) describes some of the serious harms that stem from the creation of free trade zones within Third World countries. **Free trade zones** are created by countries within their borders to attract corporations to set up businesses. The corporations that work within these zones have often been able to negotiate very favourable terms, including freedom from taxation, exemptions from labour and environmental legislation, and very favourable labour regulations that allow them to hire workers very cheaply. One of the more harmful practices discussed by Marchak is the use of noncitizen, female workers from neighbouring states in microchip production and the garment industry. For example, "Singapore has imported Malaysian, Thai, Filipina, and Indonesian women as guest workers. These women have no citizen rights and no civil rights, and are deported if their eyesight or productivity fails to please, or if markets slow down" (Marchak, 1991, 147). When they are sent back home, they receive no compensation or benefits and typically face severe financial difficulties.

free trade zone
A specially designated geographical area within a nation that is exempt from the regulations and taxation normally imposed on business. These zones are intended to facilitate cross-border production and trade. Examples of these zones are found along the United States–Mexico border, where they are referred to as *maquilladora*.

At present, many such harms cannot be brought to the courts for remedy because the state has not defined them as disputes or crimes. It may be asked whether the modern state has truly established the rule of law when serious sources of harm escape regulation and control. In some important ways, the legal power of the state has been superseded by the economic power of the modern corporation. The law cannot function to restore order in areas of social life where the state does not establish its jurisdiction. The absence of protection from the raw economic power of corporations places individuals, and perhaps even humanity, in harm's way.

Snider (1999, 2000) carefully illustrates many of the acts of corporate impropriety in Canada and documents the steps taken by the Canadian government to "make corporate crime disappear." She recounts how, in 1986, the House of Commons passed legislation that abolished the Combines Investigation Act and replaced it with the Competition Act. Among other things, this change removed criminal sanctions from the merger and monopoly sections and removed the public interest criterion that had previously been used when evaluating proposed mergers. She documents how these changes have further eroded the weak record of Canadian government scrutiny and intervention in corporate mergers that have been harmful to other groups in Canadian society. She notes that "the significance of the disappearance of corporate crime speaks volumes about the potential of state law to harness capital. The corporate counter-revolution illustrates how profoundly dependent the promulgation and enforcement of nation-state law is on the balance of powers operating within a society" (Snider, 1999, 204). She notes that when unions or social movements are strong, such as in Europe or Scandinavia, corporate "downsizing and decriminalization will be resisted longer and more effectively" (204). When they are weak, as in Canada and the United States, corporate wrongdoing is increasingly decriminalized and subject to decreasing scrutiny. Further, she stresses that progressive social movements have a vital role to play in developing and applying pressure on the state to use law as a mechanism for controlling harmful corporate behaviour.

The unwillingness or inability of the state to regulate forms of behaviour that have serious deleterious consequences has resulted in growing cynicism about the legitimacy of an ineffective "social contract" and "rule of law." It is important to reflect on some of the serious concerns raised about the harm caused by the state's failure to protect us from corporate crime (see also Chapter 16).

A Coming Crisis in State Legitimacy?

An essential role or function of the law is to foster a willingness to comply with legal prescriptions of good conduct. The rule of law depends in large measure on the willingness of the majority of citizens to comply with legal prescriptions and prohibitions. In situations of widespread, sustained levels of disobedience, the social control apparatus may be unable to cope or even be overwhelmed. Thus it is essential that the state system be seen as providing peace, security, good government, and protection from harm. Any state that fails to live up to its end of the social contract sooner or later faces a crisis of nonconfidence. In numerous quarters, dissatisfaction is growing with the evident failure of the nation-state system to regulate serious forms of harmful behaviour that have not been criminalized or limited by legal sanctions. If this situation is allowed to persist, it is reasonable to expect an increase in cynicism, which may lead to a crisis in the legitimacy of the "rule of law." Four of the most glaring examples of uncontrolled harm are the following:

- The un(der)regulated business practices of major corporations result in the daily introduction of massive amounts of toxins into the air, water, soil, and food chain, which is having serious and evident consequences for human health. The rapidly growing incidents of cancers, birth defects, sterility, and other humanly created misery are clear signs that the state has not been fully effective in providing basic security from harm. Its limited effectiveness in regulating corporate behaviour is of growing concern. The responsibility to curb the harm caused by irresponsible corporations properly falls within the jurisdiction of the state since corporations are created by charters of incorporation that are approved by the state. The history of incorporation clearly documents how the American state has forfeited the tight control of corporations that had been imposed when they were first brought into being (Grossman and Adams, 1993). This ineffectiveness may make people critical not only of the corporations but also of the state itself.
- The systematic assaults on entire ecosystems, in the pursuit of profit maximization, have resulted in loss of diversity, loss of habitat, species extinctions, and deformities of plant and animal life forms. The cumulative consequences

are so serious that they threaten the very integrity of the world's ecosystem and have been referred to as an "ecocide" (Broswimmer, 2002). The fact that such destructive behaviour is not criminalized undermines the legitimacy of the nation-state system. Citizens expect the state to protect them and future generations from human-created sources of harm.

- Extreme levels of economic inequality continue to grow. When "the world's 587 billionaires are now worth more than the combined income of the bottom half of humanity [3.2 billion]" (Cavanagh and Mander, 2004, 48), there have been growing calls for some form of state intervention into the distribution of wealth. The state has the legal means to limit class disparities through the use of legal sanctions and taxation programs that would effect a redistribution of wealth in order to provide basic security, health, and social justice for a greater number of people. Such progressive legislation had been used in the past and there are increasing calls for its reintroduction. While it is true that this private wealth is private property, it is important to remember that the notion of private property is a human invention regulated by the nation-state. The inaction of nation-states in setting limits on the egregious disparities in access to wealth denies a major portion of humanity from a decent standard of living. This invites contempt for an unfeeling state apparatus and a questioning of the legitimacy of the status quo and those institutions that make it possible.
- The annual world military expenditure is some $975 billion. Lester Brown (2006, 255–260) argues that an annual expenditure of $68 billion is needed to meet basic social goals at the global level and that $93 billion is needed for earth restoration goals. This $161 billion would require the redirection of one-third of the U.S. military budget and one-sixth of the world's military budget. When the governments of the world invest in the death industry rather than the life-enhancing forms of human endeavour, can they really count on the continuing compliance of ordinary citizens to a rule of law that fails to protect the bulk of humanity from the excesses of the powerful few?

A pessimistic view of this situation suggests the possibility that at some time in the not-too-distant future, the growing concern about escalating ecological deterioration and the increasing misery caused by mounting social injustice may cross a threshold that will precipitate a massive challenge to the rule of law and spell the end of the social ordering principles of modernity.

The Dilemma and Challenge for the Modern State

In this chapter, the changing forms of social order have been traced from early small-scale societies to the complex arrangements of the modern era. Small communities based on self-restraint and mutual dependence were transformed into large industrial states in which social life is controlled by political and economic power. Societies that based their order on customary beliefs have been eclipsed by those that are organized according to differential access to surplus and the resultant stratification. These changing patterns of organization did not always happen as a result of historical developments within a single society. Important external forces often played an essential role in shaping the form and content of law. This is well illustrated by the case of Canada's legal inheritances in Box 2.4.

The nature of dispute settlement has undergone a dramatic transformation from the small-scale society in which every member had direct access to the process of redress, to the present era in which not everyone can afford the costs of seeking a remedy through the courts. Furthermore, some serious harms are not currently subsumed under the law and, without a crime, there are few alternatives available for victims to seek redress. The concentration of social power has seen the state come to play a central role in the dispute settlement process. Since **Tudor** times, the administration and control of the legal process have been the prerogative of the state. While the interests of all members formed the basis of customary practice in small-scale communities, the interests of the merchant class have been given a special place in law in Western industrial societies. The promotion and protection of the interests of this wealthy and increasingly powerful minority has increasingly put ordinary citizens at risk. The modern state has not extended protection to all interest groups under the law since the heterogeneous nature of contemporary society and inherent conflicts of interest of various groups make this impossible. Nevertheless, there is growing pressure on the state to regulate the business practices of transnational corporations when they cause serious harm to human beings and the natural environment. However, some argue convincingly that nation-states lack the ability, or the will, to regulate such powerful organizations, which have come to dominate the social landscape in the past 50 years. The very health of the economy in liberal democracies depends on the decisions made by those who privately own the "means of production." So the state needs to provide a "favourable climate for investment" in order to have those businesses operate in their country. And yet those very same companies are often involved in activities that are harmful to the ecosystems, employees, consumers, and the general health of the economy, activities for which they should be disciplined. It is because the liberal state has conjoined interests with the propertied class that it finds it difficult to regulate their harmful behaviour, even when there is strong public pressure from citizens to do so. It remains very much an open question whether the state and its legal system are up to the task of bringing these behemoths back under the rule of law. It is unrealistic to expect continuing compliance of the majority of humanity with the rule of law if it does not afford them some measure of security and social justice.

WWW

"The Harvard Negotiation Project
www.pon.harvard.edu/hnp/index.shtml

Tudor
Refers to the period of English history from 1485 to 1603, when the nation's monarchs were descended from Owen Tudor and Catherine (1401–1437), widow of Henry V.

Full Circle: Restorative Justice and a Return to Original Forms of Dispute Settlement?

WWW

Restorative Justice Online
www.restorativejustice.org/

While controlling modern corporations will require new and innovative legal methods, developments on other fronts bring this discussion of the evolution of law back to where we began. Many critics of the current justice system have advocated returning to a fundamentally different way of approaching criminal justice, to a system that is intended to restore social relationships rather than simply to punish. Advocates of restorative justice seek to return the focus of the

FOCUS

BOX 2.4 Canada's Legal Inheritances

Canada's Legal Inheritances is a collection of scholarly research reports that trace some of the key "threads in the tapestry that is Canada's current law. The weave is created from a complex of colonial, federal, provincial and local jurisdictions, ancient and recent, patterned from a multiplicity of statutes, judgments, behavioural rules and by-laws, some written and many oral, each coloured by religious values, private interests, moral maxims, public needs, and raw power."

While many people live out their lives close to the place of their birth and are guided by the culture of that place, many others move great distances, take their birth-culture with them and yet must learn the cultural expectations of their new residence. This phenomenon is part of the experience of many people in "an immigrant constructed country like Canada."

Canadian law is the product of several legal inheritances that include "indigenous laws and imported laws" reaching back to the 1620s when "the French were settling the northern St. Lawrence River valley and the English annually visiting Newfoundland, importing their respective legal inheritances; but, at least for that century, they applied their laws almost exclusively to themselves, as the Hudson's Bay Company would later in Rupert's Land. Aboriginal peoples, whether Algonquin or Huron, were repeatedly described . . . by the Jesuits as having and applying their own legal inheritances to themselves. . . . The French had their indigenous laws, now transplanted, and the First Nations had theirs with neither importing the other into their indigenous laws. Likewise for Newfoundland, so long as the fishing fleet English remained seasonal visitors, the Beothuk legal inheritance did not connect with English admiralty law, any more than it did with the laws of other regular fishing fleets from Spain and Portugal. . . .

"By the end of the eighteenth century, approximately nine generations of imported European laws, in Lower Canada (Quebec), the Maritimes, Newfoundland and Rupert's Land had begun a more deliberate extension westward. The French led as coureurs de bois, soon followed by the English and Scots for the fledgling Hudson's Bay Company after 1670 and its later Montreal-based competitors. Then came an even larger group, the Loyalist immigrants fleeing the thirteen southerly secessionist New England colonies after 1774, mainly into Upper Canada (Ontario). . . . The Loyalists imported after 1774 an English common law shaped by their New England experiences. By then, there was little European sensitivity left for recognition of Canada's first indigenous Aboriginal law, a century and a half after the first European settlements. By mid-century,

justice system to repairing the harm that has been done to the victim and the community. A key element of restorative justice is the involvement of the victim and other members of the community as active participants in the process. The focus of the restorative justice approach is to reconcile offenders with those they have harmed and to help communities *reintegrate* victims and offenders. The source of peace and order lies in a strong, active, and caring community, and proponents of restorative justice feel that a more humane and satisfying justice system can help to rebuild communities that may have been weakened by crime and other social ills.

WWW

"Aboriginal Corrections Publications" Public Safety Canada
www.publicsafety.gc.ca/res/cor/apc/apc-eng.aspx

Canada and New Zealand have led the way in the field of restorative justice. This is due at least in part to the influence of Aboriginal people in these two countries. Rupert Ross (1996) discusses some of the steps being undertaken in Aboriginal communities to place a renewed emphasis on healing as the community response to individual wrongdoing. Many community leaders view the

FOCUS

BOX 2.4 Canada's Legal Inheritances *(Continued)*

French and English laws had become the indigenous laws in their respective territories, awaiting the next wave of immigrants, largely from the newly formed United States. Nevertheless, Canada's three legal inheritances were in place: Aboriginal, French and English."

Significant changes came in 1763 when the "Treaty of Paris (3 September 1763) vested France's Lower Canada (Quebec), and lands east of the Mississippi River, in Great Britain's empire. Then Britain's Royal Proclamation of 1763 (7 October) played a double role in Canada's legal inheritances. It imposed the complete replacement of French civil law with the English common law in Lower Canada: '. . . as near as may be agreeable to the Laws of England.' The Proclamation had grown alongside events beginning with Quebec's capture in 1759 and become an instrument to neutralise Britain's expanded array of Aboriginal peoples. It did so by recognising their use of reserved lands, without mention of any rights, and only according to the English law based on royal prerogative, not on parliamentary or judge-made law, and not on any formal recognition of Aboriginal law. Defeating Old France had not translated into winning New France, and Britain soon had to restore French civil laws and procedures to Lower Canada (1774), albeit retaining the English criminal law." The British then set out to pacify "Aboriginal peoples without acknowledging their laws."

"Lord Durham's Report (1839), in the wake of Quebec's *patriote rebellion*, effectively imposed an English transplanted stability on the two territorial legal inheritances, which was institutionalised in the confederation created by the British North America Act (1867). Shortly thereafter the need to people the vast continent, at the expense of the Aboriginal birth and residence cultures, became too great to be limited to more English and French immigrants. The gates opened to Icelanders and Mennonites on the prairies, Irish in Newfoundland, Chinese in British Columbia." Each immigrant group brought its own "birth-culture laws and most kept them as their new residence-culture laws" to the extent possible. And so Canadian law emerged and continues to re-emerge from a multitude of local and imported legal inheritances that have continued to refashion the codes of conduct in the many locales of Canadian life.

Source: DeLloyd J. Guth. (2001). "Prologue to Law in Canada: Dynamics and Roots." In DeLloyd J. Guth and W. Wesley Pue (eds.), *Canada's Legal Inheritances*, Canadian Legal History Project, Faculty of Law, The University of Manitoba, Winnipeg, pp. xxx–xxxv. Reprinted with permission of the author.

restorative justice approach as a way to restore harmonious relationships and to foster the development of healthy communities.

The restorative approach is not just limited to Aboriginal communities. The Young Offenders Act and its successor, the Youth Criminal Justice Act, mandated youth courts to look for alternative measures to traditional punishment, and options such as restitution, alternative dispute resolution, victim–offender reconciliation, community group conferences, and sentencing panels are being used much more frequently for both juvenile and adult offenders. Braithwaite and Mugford (1994) have discussed some of the ways in which the traditional practices of shame, reintegration, and healing might be introduced into modern urban settings. As outlined earlier, there are important differences in the make-up of small-scale and modern communities. When an offence occurs within the intimacy of small-scale communities it typically involves a victim and an offender who have an already established bond. The trouble between

FOCUS

BOX 2.5 Restorative Justice: Present Prospects and Future Directions

There is a genuine difference of opinion about whether the restorative justice process can work in communities that do not have strong social ties prior to the commission of an offence. Elmar Weitekamp (2002, 325) sees it as follows:

> Looking at the newest developments of restorative justice within the context of existing justice systems, one finds that they resemble in fact very old and ancient forms of restorative justice as used in acephelous societies and other forms of humankind: family group conferences, family conferences, peace circles, community circles, or circle hearings as used by indigenous people such as the Aboriginals, Maori, Inuit, the Native Indians of North America and African peoples. The new concepts and models treat crime as an offence against human relationships, recognize that crime is wrong and when it happens can further alienate the community, the family of the victim and the offender and lead to damage, disrespect, disempowerment and feelings of insecurity. The chance of the restorative justice approach is to recognize the injustice, so that in some form, equity will be restored, thus leading the participants of this process to feel safer, more respected and more empowered. It is somewhat ironic that, at the beginning of the new millennium, we have to go back to methods and forms of conflict resolution which were practised some millennia ago by our ancestors.

In this view, we need to recover the restorative practice and apply it to our efforts to repair the damage done and restore peace between parties to a dispute. There is no call for a change in the overall make-up of social relationships or other social practices of modern society. This view may be overly optimistic about the ability of the restorative justice principle alone to restore peace between the offender, victims, and their respective communities of care. Barbara Gray and Pat Lauderdale (2007, 218) do not think that solely relying on restorative principles will be sufficient.

> Restorative justice is dependent on the foundational traditional preventative structures

them has weakened or shattered the bond, and the dispute settlement process seeks to restore the bond to the satisfaction of both parties and to reintegrate the offender into the community as a member in good standing. In modern communities, no such bond exists between many victims and offenders who are, more often than not, strangers to each other until the offense creates a connection between them. The goal of the restorative approach within this context is not to re-establish a nonexistent earlier bond; rather it is to intervene in such a way that the parties to the conflict can transform the negative ties they have to each other into positive ties. In this sense, conflict can actually create the opportunity for the establishment of positive bonds between former strangers whereas the normal adversarial court practice would solidify their interconnection into a permanent negative tie between them. In other respects, the similarities are worth noting. Not only are the offender and the victim touched by the offence, so too are their immediate circles of family and friends. To the extent that the restorative justice approach can mobilize these

FOCUS

BOX 2.5 Restorative Justice: Present Prospects and Future Directions *(Continued)*

> and practices that work together to create justice and prevent injustice. Focusing on the restorative aspects of justice without incorporating the preventative mechanisms creates injustice, for it breaks the Circle of Justice and leaves individuals and the community without the necessary cultural foundational structures to heal and prevent crime.

Their point is that the restorative principles are but a part of a much larger social fabric that has other ways to contribute to the achievement of a Circle of Justice within the community. "The preventative mechanisms are found within the traditional teachings—for example, in ceremonies, songs, dances, stories, kinship relations, and healing and warrior societies" (218). Teachings within traditional societies promote the development of the "good mind" in each member by implanting "the concepts of love, unity, peace, equity, coexistence, cooperation, power, respect, generosity, and reciprocity" (218). By using these concepts, each member of the community is encouraged to live in accordance with these teachings and to retain "balance by respecting and protecting each other and the rest of the natural order" (217). "The foundational narratives of many American Indian nations contain teachings about how humans are to live with each other and the rest of the natural world. They also provide the blueprints for societal structures: the political and spiritual form of governance, kinship relations, and specific duties and responsibilities in maintaining justice within the community. One has a duty to self and to the community to prevent injustice. . . . The duties and responsibilities of each person in the society are given and reaffirmed every time the people come together for ceremonies and social activities" (219). "The Great Law of Peace [of the Haudenosaunee], then, is a system of checks and balances that depends not only on people not wanting to commit a transgression, but on people understanding and having the will to prevent others from breaching the peace" (220). From this perspective, the attempt to use the restorative aspect without also providing the work necessary to build the larger set of preventative peace-keeping practices is unlikely to be adequate to the task.

"communities of care" (Johnstone, 2002, 51) in support of the healing process and involve them in the development of a solution that they also endorse, a larger community can be created where none existed previously. The restorative approach helps to empower the victims of crime in any community and increases their participation in the dispute resolution process rather than requiring them to surrender their voice to lawyers. While it is too soon to know the degree to which these practices will replace more punitive methods of justice, it is clear that these traditional ideas are being actively reconsidered.

It is enticing to imagine that the use of a limited set of restorative justice principles could help to repair the damage created by anonymity, excessive individualism and a heightened form of self-interest, the erosion of cohesive communities, the competitiveness and materialism of modern society, and the great inequalities of power and wealth. This is the attraction: we can repair the damage between people who are estranged from each other without repairing the social fabric which made them indifferent strangers to each other in the first place.

Summary

- For most of human history, we lived in small groups. Because individuals lacked the resources to live independently, such societies were coercive in their enforcement of codes of conduct.
- In small-scale societies, disputes were primarily settled by the parties to the dispute or by their kinship groups. The individual was expected to show a considerable degree of self-restraint because the survival of the group depended upon the cooperation of all its members.
- While people in small-scale societies were relatively equal to one another, changes in methods of production led to new social formations in which some families and individuals gained greater access to material surplus. This resulted in the growth of social power, the stratification of society, and the emergence of rulers. This process eventually gave rise to the development of the state.
- The rise of the central authority of the state undermined local kinship-based methods of resolving disputes. The harm was seen to be done to the ruler, who displaced the real victim of harm.
- As the merchant class grew, social life became increasingly regulated by contracts that were regulated and enforced by a strong central state. The interests of the capitalist class became central to the modern state, and the rule of law became the dominant means of regulating all aspects of human affairs.
- In democratic political structures, some laws reflect a broadly based consensus that certain behaviours need to be discouraged; however, other laws are passed because of the influence of groups with the power to have their interests reflected in legislation.
- The ineffectiveness of the nation-state system to provide peace, security, good government, and protection from harm to large portions of humanity threatens to undermine the very legitimacy of the rule of law. A loss of legitimacy will be very corrosive of the willingness to conform, which is the foundation of the modern legal order.
- In recent years, we have seen a return to restorative justice practices that are similar to those used in small-scale societies.

QUESTIONS FOR CRITICAL THINKING

1. Proponents of restorative justice are advocating that we move away from legalistic, punishment-oriented ways of dealing with social conflict. Do you think this will work in our contemporary society? Can you think of examples of restorative justice programs in your own community?
2. This chapter has discussed the role played by special interest groups in the passage and enforcement of particular laws. What are some of the laws that reflect the interests of some groups at the expense of others? What are some examples of laws that reflect the consensus of most members of society?

3. Assume you live in a small city. A local chemical company has been found to be improperly disposing of hazardous wastes by burying them underground. The wastes have leached into local wells and contaminated the water supply. Some say the company should be prosecuted and its operations shut down; however, the company is the largest employer in the community. Describe several ways in which the community might approach this problem. What sort of outcome is most likely?
4. Read the discussion of the history of vagrancy laws in Canada. What is the current Canadian law dealing with vagrancy? (Note: You can find the Criminal Code on the Internet at **http://www.efc.ca/pages/law/cc/cc.html**.) Why do you think the police can no longer arrest someone who has no place to live and no money?
5. One of the problems with dispute resolution systems based on intervention by the victims or their kinship groups is that such a system can lead to feuds or vendettas among groups that do not agree with the manner in which a conflict was resolved. How did small-scale societies avoid prolonging these disputes?

NET WORK

You have learned in this chapter that one of the major trends in criminal justice is the return to methods of restorative justice. To learn more about methods of restorative justice, go to the Correctional Service of Canada website at **http://www.csc-scc.gc.ca/text/pblct/satisfy/index_e.shtml**. This will give you access to a report written by the Church Council on Justice and Corrections. Using this report, answer the following questions:

1. What do the authors mean by "satisfying justice"? How can you use this concept to understand the dissatisfaction most Canadians seem to have with our current criminal justice system?
2. Describe four different types of restorative justice programs, and give an example of each.

KEY TERMS

acephalous society; pg. 31
bourgeois class; pg. 44
collective solidarity; pg. 31
common law; pg. 43
diffuseness of roles; pg. 32
feudalism; pg. 42
free trade zone; pg. 54
Gemeinschaft; pg. 34
Gesellschaft; pg. 45
hunting and gathering society; pg. 31
ideal type; pg. 31
mode of production; pg. 30
paramount chieftainship; pg. 41
sovereignty; pg. 43
state; pg. 30
stratification; pg. 31
surplus; pg. 34
transnational corporation; pg. 51
tribalism; pg. 37
Tudor; pg. 57

SUGGESTED READING

Braithwaite, John. (1989). *Crime, Shame, and Reintegration.* Cambridge: Cambridge University Press. The author reviews the dominant traditions in criminological theory and then suggests that we should seriously consider using the "family model of the criminal process: reintegrative shaming." His suggestion is that shaming is a powerful mechanism that should be used more deliberately to respond to deviance from core values in any good society. The intent should be to abhor the crime and not the person who commits it. The community should work to help the offender understand that harm has been caused, to feel shame, and then to seek and be granted reintegration into the community.

Chambliss, William, and Robert Seidman. (1982). *Law, Order, and Power.* (2nd ed.). Reading, Mass.: Addison-Wesley. Using a critical conflict perspective, the authors compare state and stateless societies with respect to dispute settlement. Primary emphasis is placed on the state system, the rule of law, and the role of social power in modern class-based social systems.

Friedman, Wolfgang. (1972). *Law in a Changing Society.* (2nd ed.). New York: Columbia University Press. This text traces legal change in a number of types of law, including contract, tort, insurance, criminal, family, and public law. The state, economic power, and corporate power are all examined for the part they have played in legal change. The changing place of the individual within modern law receives attention, as does the changing scope of international law.

Johnstone, Gerry. (2003) *A Restorative Justice Reader: Texts, Sources, Context.* Portland, Oregon: Willan Publishing. This sourcebook on the topic of restorative justice helps explain why the restorative justice movement is so important. The book offers extracts from important contributions to the restorative justice literature including its roots, emergent philosophy, and actual practice in community programs. It includes the work of some of the movement's proponents as well as its critics.

Perkins, John. (2004). *Confessions of an Economic Hitman.* San Francisco: Berrett-Koehler Publishers. John Perkins recounts his career as an "economic hitman" working for an international consulting firm. His job was to provide optimistic projections about the economic growth that would flow from various proposed mega-projects in many developing countries. These forecasts would help secure loans from international financial lending institutions that could never be paid back. In order to renegotiate the terms for these loans, these countries had to agree to "structural adjustment programs" that amounted to a loss of economic sovereignty. Perkins was well aware of the damage the corporate community with the aid of nation-states was inflicting on peoples around the world, but also found it hard to renounce the lifestyle it offered him as compensation. This autobiography provides a case-by-case exposition of the collusion between national governments, elites, and transnational corporations that has harmed the interests of hundreds of millions of people in order to amass wealth for a very few individuals and their families. (This book is also available in a paperback edition from Penguin Group.)

Ross, Rupert. (1992). *Dancing with a Ghost: Exploring Indian Reality.* Markham, Ont.: Octopus Publishing Group. Some of the author's work is featured in Box 2.1 and Box 2.2 in this chapter. This book compares Aboriginal and white culture within the framework of the justice system. The reader is provided a standpoint from which to appreciate the problems that members of these two cultures have in understanding the actions of others as they interact within the modern dispute settlement process in Canada.

Ross, Rupert. (1996). *Returning to the Teachings: Exploring Aboriginal Justice.* Toronto: Penguin. Ross continues his efforts to sensitize non-Aboriginal readers to the traditional Aboriginal values and processes that were used to settle disputes. This thought-provoking text discusses how the Hollow Water community has worked to revitalize the traditional healing approach, which was seriously undermined and eroded in the last 50 years, in order to help this Aboriginal community deal with the devastating effects of sexual abuse. Clearly, there are challenges in accommodating this approach within a judicial system that is based on a different set of organizing principles.

Synder, Francis. (1981). "Anthropology, Dispute Processes and Law: A Critical Introduction." *British Journal of Law and Society* 8(2) (Winter). This review article examines current anthropological studies of law and dispute processes. It provides an excellent overview of major work and attempts to assess the value of these contributions for the development of social theories of law. It is an excellent article that will help a newcomer get his or her bearings.

BIBLIOGRAPHY

Becker, Howard. (1963). "Moral Entrepreneurs." In Becker, *The Outsiders*. New York: Free Press.

Braithwaite, John, and S. Mugford. (1994). "Conditions of Successful Reintegration Ceremonies." *British Journal of Criminology* 34(2):139–71.

Brodeur, Paul. (1985). "The Asbestos Industry on Trial." In *The New Yorker* (June 10, June 17, June 24, July 1).

Broswimmer, Franz. (2002). *Ecocide: A Short History of the Mass Extinction of Species*. London: Pluto Press.

Brown, Lester R. (2006). *Plan B 2.0: Rescuing a Planet Under Stress and a Civilization in Trouble*. New York: W.W. Norton and Company.

Brownmiller, Susan. (1975). *Against Our Will: Men, Women and Rape*. New York: Simon and Schuster.

Cavanagh, John, and Jerry Mander (eds.). (2004). *Alternatives to Economic Globalization: A Better World Is Possible* (2nd. ed.). San Francisco: Berrett-Koehler Publishers.

Chambliss, William. (1969). "The Law of Vagrancy." In Chambliss (ed.), *Crime and the Legal Process* (pp. 51–63). New York: McGraw-Hill.

Clark, Lorenne, and Debra Lewis. (1977). *Rape: The Price of Coercive Sexuality*. Toronto: The Women's Press.

Colson, Elizabeth. (1974). *Tradition and Contract: The Problem of Order*. Chicago: Aldine Publishing.

Comack, Elizabeth. (1985). "The Origins of Canadian Drug Legislation: Labelling versus Class Analysis." In Thomas Fleming (ed.), *The New Criminologies in Canada: State, Crime and Control* (pp. 65–86). Toronto: Oxford University Press.

Dickson, Donald. (1968). "Bureaucracy and Morality: An Organizational Perspective on a Moral Crusade." *Social Problems* 16(2) (Fall):143–56.

Dowie, Mark. (1977). "Pinto Madness." *Mother Jones* 2(8) (Sept./Oct.).

Facts on File. (1991). 51 (August 8):2646.

———. (1993). 53 (March 25):2718.

———. (1997). 57 (June 26):2951.

———. (2000). 60 (December 31):1017.

———. (2001). 61 (December 31):1031.

———. (2002). 62 (December 31):1012.

———. (2004). 64 (June 3):403.

———. (2005). 65 (January 20):36.

Friedman, Lawrence, and Jack Ladinsky. (1980). "Social Change and the Law of Industrial Accidents." In William Evan (ed.), *The Sociology of Law* (pp. 395–414). New York: Free Press.

Goff, Colin, and Charles Reasons. (1978). *Corporate Crime in Canada*. Scarborough: Prentice Hall.

Graham, James. (1976). "Amphetamine Politics on Capital Hill." In William Chambliss (ed.), *Whose Law, What Order?* (pp. 107–22). New York: Wiley.

Gray, Barbara, and Pat Lauderdale. (2007). "The Great Circle of Justice: North American Indigenous Justice and Contemporary Restoration Programs." *Contemporary Justice Review* 10:2 (June):215–25.

Grossman, Richard L., and Frank T. Adams. (1993). *Taking Care of Business: Citizenship and the Charter of Incorporation*. http://www.ratical.org/corporations/TCoB.html.

Gulliver, P. H. (1979). *Disputes and Negotiations: A Cross-Cultural Perspective*. New York: Academic Press.

Guth, DeLloyd J., and W. Wesley Pue (eds.). (2001). *Canada's Legal Inheritances*. Canadian Legal History Project, Faculty of Law, The University of Manitoba, Winnipeg.

Hagan, John, and Jeffrey Leon. (1977). "Rediscovering Delinquency: Social History, Political Ideology and the Sociology of Law." *American Sociological Review* 42 (August):587–98.

Hall, Jerome. (1952). *Theft, Law, and Society*. (2nd ed.). Indianapolis: Bobbs-Merrill.

———. (1969a). "Theft, Law and Society: The Carrier's Case." In William Chambliss (ed.), *Crime and the Legal Process* (pp. 32–51). New York: McGraw-Hill.

———. (1969b). "Crime and the Commercial Revolution." In Donald Cressey and David Ward (eds.), *Delinquency, Crime and Social Process* (pp. 100–10). New York: Harper and Row.

Hoebel, E. Adamson. (1973). *The Law of Primitive Man*. New York: Atheneum Press.

Jeffery, Clarence Ray. (1969). "The Development of Crime in Early English Society." In William Chambliss (ed.), *Crime and the Legal Process* (pp. 12–32). New York: McGraw-Hill.

Johnstone, Gerry. (2002). *Restorative Justice: Ideas, Values, Debates*. Oregon: Willan Publishing.

Kennedy, Mark. (1976). "Beyond Incrimination: Some Neglected Facets of the Theory of Punishment." In William Chambliss (ed.), *Whose Law, What Order?* (pp. 34–65). New York: Wiley.

Kinnon, Dianne. (1981). *Report on Sexual Assault in Canada*. Report to the Canadian Advisory Council on the Status of Women.

Lenski, Gerhard. (1966). *Power and Privilege: A Theory of Social Stratification*. New York: McGraw-Hill.

Marchak, Patricia. (1991). *The Integrated Circus: The New Right and the Restructuring of Global Markets*. Montreal: McGill-Queen's University Press.

Michalowski, Raymond. (1985). *Law, Order and Crime*. New York: Random House.

Miliband, Ralph. (1969). *The State in Capitalist Society*. London: Quarter Books.

Newman, Katherine. (1983). *Law and Economic Organization: A Comparative Study of Preindustrial Societies*. London: Cambridge University Press.

Platt, Anthony. (1969). *The Child Savers: The Invention of Delinquency*. Chicago: University of Chicago Press.

Reasons, Charles, Lois Ross, and Craig Paterson. (1981). *Assault on the Worker*. Toronto: Butterworths.

Ross, Rupert. (1989). "Leaving Our White Eyes Behind: The Sentencing of Native Accused." 3 *Canadian Native Law Reporter* 1 at 4.

———. (1996). *Return to the Teachings: Exploring Aboriginal Justice.* Toronto: Penguin.

Rossi, Peter, and Emily Waite. (1974). "The Seriousness of Crimes: Normative Structure and Individual Differences." *American Sociological Review* 39 (April):224–37.

Sellin, Thorsten, and Marvin Wolfgang. (1964). *The Measurement of Delinquency.* New York: Wiley.

Small, Shirley. (1978). "Canadian Narcotics Legislation, 1908–1923: A Conflict Model Interpretation." In W. Greenaway and S. Brickey (eds.), *Law and Social Control in Canada* (pp. 28–42). Scarborough: Prentice Hall.

Smandych, Russell. (1985). "Marxism and the Creation of Law: Re-examining the Origins of Canadian Anti-Combines Legislation 1890–1910." In Thomas Fleming (ed.), *The New Criminologies in Canada: State, Crime and Control* (pp. 87–99). Toronto: Oxford University Press.

Snider, Laureen. (1980). "Corporate Crime in Canada." In Robert Silverman and James Teevan (eds.), *Crime in Canadian Society* (pp. 348–68). (2nd ed.). Toronto: Butterworths.

———. (1994). "The Regulatory Dance: Understanding Processes in Corporate Crime." In Ronald Hinch (ed.), *Readings in Critical Criminology* (pp. 276–305). Scarborough: Prentice Hall.

———. (1999). "Relocating Law: Making Corporate Crime Disappear." In Elizabeth Comack (ed.), *Locating Law: Race, Class/Gender Connections* (pp. 183–207). Halifax: Fernwood Publishing.

———. (2000). "The Sociology of Corporate Crime: An Obituary." *Theoretical Criminology* 4(2):169–206.

Stone, Christopher. (1975). *Where the Law Ends: Social Control of Corporate Behavior.* New York: Harper and Row.

Thompson, Edward P. (1976). *Whigs and Hunters: The Origin of the Black Act.* New York: Pantheon Books.

Tigar, Michael, and Madeleine Levy. (1977). *Law and the Rise of Capitalism.* New York: Monthly Review Press.

Tönnies, Ferdinand. (1887). *Community and Society.* New York: Harper Books.

UNICEF: *Progress for Children.* A Report Card on Immunization: Number 3, September 2005.

Walters, Vivienne. (1983). "Occupational Health and Safety Legislation in Ontario: An Analysis of Its Origins and Content." *Canadian Review of Sociology and Anthropology* 20(4) (November):138–69.

Weitekamp, Elmar G. M. (2002). "Restorative Justice: Present Prospects and Future Directions." In Elmar G.M. Weitekamp and Hans-Jürgen Kerner (eds.), *Restorative Justice: Theoretical Foundations.* Oregon: William Publishing.

West, Gordon, and Laureen Snider. (1985). "A Critical Perspective on Law in the Canadian State: Delinquency and Corporate Crime." In Thomas Fleming (ed.), The *New Criminologies in Canada: State, Crime and Control.* Toronto: Oxford University Press.

3 Criminal Law

Simon N. Verdun-Jones

SIMON FRASER UNIVERSITY

Criminology is concerned with crimes and those individuals who commit them. It is necessary for criminologists to acquire a basic understanding of the criminal law because it is this body of legal rules and principles that designates which types of behaviour should be prohibited and punished and also determines whether those persons who are accused of committing crimes should be convicted and officially labelled as criminals.

Learning Objectives

After reading this chapter, you should be able to

- Define a crime.
- Identify the sources of Canadian criminal law.
- Distinguish between regulatory offences and "true crimes."
- Analyze criminal offences in terms of the *actus reus* (physical) and *mens rea* (mental) elements.
- Understand the differences between subjective and objective *mens rea* requirements.
- Describe the different ways in which a person may become a party to a criminal offence.
- Identify the basic components of the inchoate crimes of counselling, attempt, and conspiracy.
- Describe the major defences that may be raised in response to a criminal charge: not criminally responsible on account of mental disorder; mistake of fact; mistake of law; intoxication; necessity; duress; provocation; and self-defence.

What Is a Crime?

crime
Conduct that is prohibited by law and that is subject to a penal sanction (such as imprisonment or a fine).

For a lawyer, the definition of a **crime** is remarkably simple: namely, the coupling of a *prohibition* against certain conduct with a *penal sanction* (such as imprisonment or a fine). In Canada, all crimes are the creatures of a legislative process and are contained in statutes such as the Criminal Code. Some crimes may reflect an almost universal social consensus that certain conduct is wrong and should be punished (for example, murder and sexual assault). Other crimes may not be based on such a general consensus and a significant proportion of Canadians may not consider them to be inherently wrong and deserving of

FOCUS

BOX 3.1 Conflict of Values: The Case of Euthanasia

If a person is suffering from a terminal illness, is in great pain, and wishes to end his or her life, should a physician be able to grant that wish by, for example, administering a lethal injection? In Canada, the Criminal Code (section 14) clearly prohibits anyone, including a physician, from killing another human being—even if that person has given an unequivocal consent to the taking of his or her life. As a consequence, in Canada, a so-called mercy killing constitutes murder under the Criminal Code. However, in both the Netherlands and Belgium, recent legislation has been passed that permits physicians to perform euthanasia on their patients in certain, strictly defined, circumstances. Does the existing criminal law in Canada reflect current values? What should the Parliament of Canada do if Canadians are profoundly divided on this issue?

In October 1993, Robert Latimer, a Saskatchewan farmer, killed his severely disabled daughter, Tracy. Although the 12-year-old Tracy was not capable of giving consent, the homicide was portrayed by many as a "mercy killing." Ultimately, Latimer was convicted of second-degree murder. Under the Criminal Code [section 745(c)], the minimum sentence that may be imposed for second-degree murder is life imprisonment with no possibility of parole for a period of 10 years. Some Canadians argued that this sentence should not apply to a father who had killed his daughter in order to spare her further pain and suffering. In fact, polls consistently indicated that most Canadians believed that the sentence was excessively harsh. On the other hand, other Canadians asserted that, if the courts were to impose a more lenient sentence on Latimer because his motive was that of compassion, they would be implicitly diminishing the value of the lives of persons with disabilities. After all, Tracy was not consulted as to her fate: her father made the decision for himself that her life was not worth living. In 2001, the Supreme Court of Canada ruled that the mandatory sentence in the Criminal Code did not contravene the Canadian Charter of Rights and Freedoms and that Latimer was not entitled to receive a so-called constitutional exemption that would relieve him of the penalty of life imprisonment. However, the Court did point out that the government of Canada has the power to exercise the "Royal Prerogative of Mercy" [Criminal Code, section 748(1)] and grant Latimer an early release. Was Latimer's sentence too harsh? Should Latimer be released before the 10-year period of ineligibility for parole has expired?

For further reading, see *R. v. Latimer*, [2001] 1 S.C.R. 3, available online at http://scc.lexum.umontreal.ca/en/2001/2001scc1/2001scc1.html and R. Malhotra. (2001). "Tracy Latimer, Disability Rights and the Left." *Canadian Dimension* (May/June 2001) 23–35.

punishment (for example, assisting a terminally ill patient to commit suicide when he or she is in great pain). While legislators need to wrestle with the ongoing task of trying to bring the criminal law into line with emerging community notions of crime and justice, the police and the judiciary are required to enforce the existing criminal law, regardless of their own private views as to whether particular conduct should or should not be defined as a crime (see Box 3.1). Therefore, while it is important to be aware of the intensely political nature of the process that results in the enactment of legislation dealing with crime and punishment, such considerations fall outside the scope of a chapter dealing with the contents of the existing criminal law.

What Is Criminal Law?

criminal law
A body of jurisprudence that includes the definition of various crimes, the specification of various penalties, a set of general principles concerning criminal responsibility, and a series of defences to a criminal charge.

The body of jurisprudence known as **criminal law** includes not only the definitions of the various crimes and the specification of the respective penalties but also a set of general principles concerning criminal responsibility and a series of defences to a criminal charge. In this chapter, the main focus will be on the general principles underlying Canadian criminal law and the major defences that have been developed both by the Parliament of Canada and by judges in the course of deciding specific cases that have come before them.

The Sources of Criminal Law

One of the most basic questions that might be asked about criminal law is "Where does it come from?" There are two primary sources of Canadian criminal law: (i) legislation and (ii) judicial decisions that either interpret such legislation or state the "common law."

Federal Legislation and Criminal Law

Since Canada is a federal state, legislation may be enacted both by the Parliament of Canada and by the legislatures of the various provinces and territories. However, under the terms of the Canadian Constitution, there is a distribution of specific legislative powers between the federal and provincial or territorial levels of government. Under the terms of the Constitution Act, 1867, the federal Parliament has the exclusive jurisdiction to enact "criminal law and the procedures relating to criminal matters." One might well think that it is relatively simple to define the term *criminal law* for the purpose of interpreting the scope of the federal criminal law power under the Constitution Act, 1867. However, this task is not quite as straightforward as it may appear at first glance. It was noted above that, for most purposes, a crime can be defined in terms of two basic elements: (i) a *prohibition* against certain conduct and (ii) a *penalty* for violating that prohibition. However, when the courts are required to decide whether Parliament has enacted legislation that legitimately falls within the scope of its criminal law power, a third element must be added to the definition of a crime. More specifically, the Supreme Court of Canada has ruled that the prohibition and penalty must be directed against a "public evil" or some form of behaviour that is having an injurious effect on the Canadian public. If any of these three elements is missing, the legislation concerned may not be considered to fall within the legitimate scope of the federal criminal law power; indeed, it may be ruled invalid insofar as it intrudes into areas of legislative authority that have been specifically allocated to the provincial and territorial legislatures. Consider the problem of environmental pollution. In the case of *Hydro-Québec* (1997), the Supreme Court of Canada held that the Parliament of Canada could use its criminal law power to enact legislation that imposes penalties on those individuals who engage in serious acts of pollution. The particular legislation in question in this case was the Canadian Environmental Protection Act, R.S.C.

1985, c. 16. In the words of Justice La Forest, "Pollution is an 'evil' that Parliament can legitimately seek to suppress." Therefore, the Canadian Environmental Protection Act was considered to constitute "criminal law" because the Parliament of Canada was unequivocally concerned with the need to safeguard public health from the devastating consequences of toxic pollution. If the Supreme Court had ruled that this statute was not a genuine exercise of the Parliament of Canada's criminal law power, then the Court would have ruled that the Act was invalid. Similarly, in *R. v. Malmo-Levine; R. v. Caine* (2003), the Supreme Court of Canada ruled that Parliament had the authority, by virtue of its criminal law power, to prohibit the simple possession of marijuana. Even though simple possession may be viewed as a "victimless crime," the criminal law power may nevertheless be used to protect the users of marijuana from self-inflicted harm. The "evil or injurious or undesirable effect" that Parliament sought to address is "the harm attributed to the non-medical use of marijuana." The Supreme Court, therefore, upheld the constitutional validity of the relevant provisions of the Narcotic Control Act, R.S.C. 1985, c. N-1.[1]

What important pieces of legislation has the Canadian Parliament enacted in the field of criminal law? Undoubtedly, the most significant federal statute, dealing with both the *substantive criminal law* and the *procedural* law relating to criminal matters, is the Criminal Code, R.S.C. 1985, c. C-46 (first enacted in 1892). "Substantive criminal law" refers to legislation that defines the nature of various criminal offences (such as murder, manslaughter, and theft) and specifies the various legal elements that must be present before a conviction can be entered against an accused person. The term also refers to the legislation that defines the nature and scope of such defences as provocation, duress, and self-defence.

The term **criminal procedure** refers to legislation that specifies the procedures to be followed in the prosecution of a criminal case and defines the nature and scope of the powers of criminal justice officials. For example, the procedural provisions of the Criminal Code classify offences into three categories: (i) *indictable offences*; (ii) offences punishable on *summary conviction*; and (iii) *"mixed" or "hybrid" offences* that may be tried either as indictable or as summary conviction offences. These provisions then specify the manner in which these different categories of offences may be tried within the system of criminal courts. For example, they spell out whether these offences may be tried by a judge sitting alone or by a judge and jury, and indicate whether they may be tried before a judge of the Superior Court or a judge of the Provincial (or Territorial) Court. Indictable offences carry the most serious penalties upon conviction of the accused. The procedural provisions of the Criminal Code are also concerned with defining the nature and scope of the powers of such officials as police officers. For example, these provisions stipulate the nature and scope of the powers of the police in relation to the arrest and detention of suspects. Likewise, the Criminal Code articulates the powers of judges in relation to the important task of sentencing convicted offenders.

criminal procedure
A body of legislation that specifies the procedures to be followed in the prosecution of a criminal case and defines the nature and scope of the powers of criminal justice officials.

[1] This Act was repealed in 1996. Possession of marijuana is now prohibited by section 4 of the Controlled Drugs and Substances Act, S.C. 1996, c. 19 (which came into force on May 14, 1997).

In addition to the Criminal Code, a number of other federal statutes unquestionably create "criminal law." These include the Controlled Drugs and Substances Act, S.C. 1996, c. 19, and the Youth Criminal Justice Act, S.C. 2002, c. 1.

Federal and Provincial or Territorial Regulatory Legislation: Quasi-Criminal Law

Under the Constitution Act, 1867, the provincial and territorial legislatures have been granted exclusive jurisdiction to enact legislation in relation to such issues as health, education, highways, liquor control, and hunting and fishing. This legislation may be enforced through the imposition of "a fine, penalty or imprisonment." At first blush, it may seem that the use of punishments of these types would persuade the courts to treat such legislation as criminal law—an area of legislative authority that is reserved exclusively for the Parliament of Canada. However, such regulatory legislation does not constitute "real" criminal law for the purpose of the distribution of powers under the Constitution because such legislation lacks the necessary element of "public evil" that was discussed earlier. Indeed, regulatory legislation is concerned with the orderly regulation of activities that are inherently legitimate (such as driving a vehicle or operating a business). Criminal law is directed toward the control of behaviour that is considered to be inherently wrong (namely, "**true crimes**" such as theft, assault, sexual assault, and wilful damage to property). **Regulatory offences**, therefore, are quite distinct from the "true crimes" that arise under the Criminal Code or the Controlled Drugs and Substances Act, and they are, therefore, classified as quasi-criminal law ("quasi" means seeming, not real, or halfway).

"true crime"
A "true crime" occurs when an individual engages in conduct that is not only prohibited but also constitutes a serious breach of community values; as such, it is perceived by Canadians as being inherently wrong and deserving of punishment. Only the Parliament of Canada, using its criminal law power under the Constitution Act, 1867, may enact a "true crime."

regulatory offences
Regulatory offences arise under legislation (either federal, provincial, or territorial) that regulates inherently legitimate activities connected with trade, commerce, and industry or with everyday living (driving, fishing, etc.). These offences are not considered to be serious in nature and usually carry only a relatively minor penalty upon conviction.

Regulatory offences are generally far less serious in nature than "true crimes." Indeed, the maximum penalties that may be imposed for violation of regulatory offences are generally no more than a fine or a maximum term of imprisonment of six months or both. Under the Criminal Code or the Controlled Drugs and Substances Act, however, the penalties may range as high as a life term of imprisonment.

Regulatory offences are also to be found in a broad range of federal statutes that regulate activities that fall within the jurisdiction of the Parliament of Canada: for example, the Competition Act, R.S.C. 1985, C. c-34; the Food and Drugs Act, R.S.C. 1985, F-27; the Hazardous Products Act, R.S.C. 1985, c. H-3; The Fisheries Act, R.S.C. 1985, c. F-14; and the Trade-Marks Act, R.S.C. 1985, c. T-13. Taken together with the quasi-criminal offences created under provincial and territorial legislation, these federal regulatory offences contribute to a vast pool of quasi-criminal law that has become increasingly complex as modern society has developed. Even the average lawyer is acquainted with only a fraction of the hundreds of thousands of regulatory offences that currently exist under both federal and provincial or territorial legislation. However, ignorance of the law is no excuse for those who commit regulatory offences.

Judge-Made Criminal Law

The second major source of criminal law in Canada is the large body of judicial decisions that either interpret criminal legislation or expound the "**common law**"—a term that refers to that body of judge-made law that evolved in areas that were not covered by legislation. Parliament cannot possibly provide for every possibility or provide comprehensive definitions of every term used in the legislation that it enacts; therefore, there is always great scope for judicial interpretation of the Criminal Code. For example, in section 380 of the Code, Parliament has created the offence of fraud. According to section 380, fraud may be committed by "deceit, falsehood, or other fraudulent means." However, the term "other fraudulent means" was left undefined and it was left to the Supreme Court of Canada to provide a working definition in the case of *R. v. Olan, Hudson and Hartnett* (1978), namely, "all other means which can properly be stigmatized as dishonest."

common law
The body of judge-made law that has evolved in areas not covered by legislation.

As far as the common law is concerned, it is important to recognize that, historically, much of the English criminal law, upon which the Criminal Code of 1892 was loosely based, was developed by judges who were required to deal with new situations and challenges that were not dealt with by the legislation of the day. In Canada, there is one common law offence that still exists—namely, contempt of court. However, with the exception of contempt of court, the Criminal Code (section 9) has, since 1954, made it clear that judges cannot create any new common law crimes. On the other hand, the judges have developed a number of common law defences that were not dealt with by legislation. For example, Canadian courts have developed a defence of necessity even though it is not mentioned in the Criminal Code; hence, necessity is known as a common law defence. Section 8(3) of the Criminal Code preserves any common law "justification," "excuse," or "defence" to a criminal charge "except in so far as they are altered by or are inconsistent with this act or any other act of the Parliament of Canada." This provision is particularly significant because it means that common law defences, such as necessity, may still be developed by Canadian judges.

Impact of the Canadian Charter of Rights and Freedoms on Criminal Law

The enactment of the Canadian Charter of Rights and Freedoms as part of the Constitution Act, 1982, heralded a dramatic new era in the relationship between judges and the elected members of the Parliament of Canada and the legislative assemblies of the various provinces and territories. As an entrenched bill of rights, the **Charter** empowers judges to declare any piece of legislation to be invalid—and of no force or effect—if the latter infringes on an individual's Charter rights (such as the presumption of innocence [section 11(d)] or the right not to be deprived of the right to life, liberty, and security of the person except in accordance with the principles of fundamental justice [section 7]). Canadian judges have demonstrated a willingness to use this awesome power where they believe it is necessary to do so. For example, in *R. v. Morgentaler, Smolig and Scott* (1988), the Supreme Court of Canada declared the controversial abortion provisions of the Criminal Code (section 287) to be invalid because they unjustifiably infringed the right of Canadian women to "security of the person" (protected by section 7 of the Charter). However, the

Charter
The Canadian Charter of Rights and Freedoms, enacted by the Canada Act 1982 (UK) c. 11 (see glossary for extended definition).

FOCUS

BOX 3.2 Terrorism and the Charter

Following the devastating attack on the twin towers of the World Trade Center in New York City, on September 11, 2001, there has been a widespread fear of terrorist acts in many countries, including Canada. This fear has prompted governments to enact legislation to enhance the security of their citizens. However, when governments move to protect their citizens from the perceived threat posed by terrorists, there is always a danger that they will sacrifice individual rights for what is perceived to be in the best interests of national security. In Canada, the courts have the task of ensuring that individual rights are not unjustifiably infringed in such circumstances and their authority for performing this role is derived from the Canadian Charter of Rights and Freedoms.

In the wake of the "9/11" attacks in New York, the Parliament of Canada swiftly responded to fears concerning the potential threat posed by terrorist activities by enacting a series of legislative measures, including the Anti-terrorism Act. The Act, which received royal assent on December 18, 2001, added a series of new sections to the Criminal Code that created specific terrorist offences (sections 83.01 to 83.32). The underlying rationale for these offences was the need to prevent terrorist attacks *before* they occur; therefore, an act, such as mere participation in a terrorist organization, now constitutes a specific offence. In addition, the Anti-terrorism Act automatically increased the maximum sentence for committing any indictable offence under the Criminal Code or any other Act of Parliament to one of life imprisonment if the offence in question was committed "for the benefit of, at the direction of or in association with a terrorist group."

While the Anti-terrorism Act creates specific offences that are based on terrorist activity, a major controversy has arisen in relation to the use of preventative measures that are available under provisions of the Immigration and Refugee Protection Act, S.C. 2001, c. 27 (the IRPA). This Act gives the ministers of citizenship and immigration and the minister of public safety and emergency preparedness the power to issue a "security certificate" (or "certificate of inadmissibility") that authorizes the detention of individuals who are not Canadian citizens (foreign nationals or permanent residents) if there are reasonable grounds to believe that they constitute a threat to the security of Canada. Allegations of involvement in terrorist activity may prompt the minister concerned to issue a certificate. The individual who is placed under such a certificate is considered "inadmissible" to Canada and may be removed from the country. If the individual may not be removed from Canada because his or her life may be at risk, the detention under the certificate may continue for a long period. An individual who is detained may obtain a judicial review of both the detention and the certificate; however, on the grounds of preserving national security, essential information that constitutes the very basis of the allegations of terrrorism may be kept secret from the detained person and his or her legal representative.

It might well be argued that, if there is evidence that a particular individual has been involved in terrorist activity, that person should be charged with one or more specific criminal

courts are bound to take into account the provisions of section 1 of the Charter, which permit Parliament or the provincial or territorial legislatures to impose "such reasonable limits [on Charter rights] as can be demonstrably justified in a free and democratic society." This provision requires Canadian courts to engage in an elaborate balancing act in which they must decide whether the infringement of an individual's Charter rights can be justified in the name of some "higher good." For example, in *R. v. Sharpe* (2001), the Supreme Court of

FOCUS

BOX 3.2 Terrorism and the Charter *(Continued)*

offences (including those offences added to the Criminal Code by the Anti-terrorism Act). It should be irrelevant that the individual concerned is a foreign national or a permanent resident rather than a citizen of Canada. Unfortunately, the perception has arisen that, although security certificates are not issued frequently, they are used primarily to target Arabs and Muslims, who may be detained for long periods. In light of the considerable discomfort that many Canadians have expressed in relation to the use of security certificates in cases of alleged terrorism, it is not surprising that a challenge was brought under the Charter.

In *Charkaoui v. Canada* (2007), the Supreme Court of Canada unanimously ruled that the secrecy surrounding the security certificate process denies those who are detained under such a certificate the right to make "full answer and defence" to the allegations made against them. The denial of the right to a fair hearing constitutes a violation of the fundamental principles of justice guaranteed by section 7 of the Charter, and the Supreme Court, therefore, declared that the IRPA's procedure for the judicial approval of security certificates was invalid under the Charter. The Court suspended this declaration for one year in order to give Parliament the opportunity to amend the Act in a manner that would provide detained persons with sufficient information to make a "full answer and defence" (for example, by appointing an independent lawyer who would provide a censored summary of the evidence to the detained person, thereby balancing the detained person's right to make full answer and defence with the need to preserve national security).

Chief Justice McLachlin said:

> One of the most fundamental responsibilities of a government is to ensure the security of its citizens. This may require it to act on information that it cannot disclose and to detain people who threaten national security. Yet in a constitutional democracy, governments must act accountably and in conformity with the Constitution and the rights and liberties it guarantees. These two propositions describe a tension that lies at the heart of modern democratic governance. It is a tension that must be resolved in a way that respects the imperatives both of security and of accountable constitutional governance. [at para. 1]

To what extent do you think that the rights of individual citizens should be subordinated to the interests of national security? Is it reasonable to detain individuals who are accused of terrorism on the basis that they represent a threat to national security rather than charging them with a specific crime and trying them with all the customary protections that are accorded to accused persons in a Canadian criminal trial? Is it fair to deny a detained individual access to all the evidence against him or her because of national security concerns? Do you agree with the ruling of the Supreme Court of Canada in the *Charkaoui* case? Does the Court's ruling, that an independent lawyer should be appointed to summarize the evidence for an individual detained under a security certificate, represent the most appropriate balance between the rights of the individual to a full and fair hearing and the interests of national security?

Canada ruled that certain aspects of the child pornography provisions of the Criminal Code (section 163.1) infringed the accused person's right to "freedom of thought, belief, opinion and expression"—a right that is guaranteed by section 2(b) of the Charter. However, the Court also ruled that the child pornography provisions constituted a "reasonable limitation" on the accused's section 2(b) right and were, therefore, justified under section 1 of the Charter. Some of the Charter issues raised by anti-terrorism legislation are discussed in Box 3.2.

The Basic Elements of a Crime: *Actus Reus* and *Mens Rea*

The study of criminal law invariably commences with the statement that every criminal offence can be analyzed in terms of two major elements: namely, *actus reus* and *mens rea*. These terms are derived from the Latin maxim, *actus non facit reum nisi mens sit rea* (which, translated literally, means that an act does not render a person guilty unless his or her mind is also guilty). Based on this principle, it can be stated that an accused person may not be convicted of a criminal offence unless the prosecution can prove the following beyond a reasonable doubt:

(a) that a particular event or state of affairs was "caused" by the accused person's conduct (*actus reus*); and
(b) that this conduct was simultaneously accompanied by a certain state of mind (*mens rea*).

In essence, the concept of *mens rea* refers to the mental elements of an offence while the term *actus reus* refers to all the other elements that must be proved by the Crown. However, there is an important gloss that must be placed on this seemingly simple formulation: namely, that the *actus reus* of a criminal offence includes an element of voluntariness. As Justice McLachlin said, in delivering the judgment of the majority of the justices of the Supreme Court of Canada in the case of *Théroux* (1993),

> The term *mens rea*, properly understood, does not encompass all of the mental elements of crime. The *actus reus* has its own mental element; the act must be the voluntary act of the accused for the *actus reus* to exist.

The *Actus Reus* Elements of a Crime

actus reus
All the elements contained in the definition of a criminal offence—other than the mental elements (*mens rea*).

In general, it is possible to divide the ***actus reus*** into three separate components:

(i) conduct (a voluntary act or omission constituting the central feature of the crime);
(ii) the surrounding or "material" circumstances; and
(iii) the consequences of the voluntary conduct.

For example, in order to prove that an accused person is guilty of the offence of assault causing bodily harm (section 267 of the Criminal Code), the Crown must establish that the accused applied force to the body of the victim (conduct); that the force was applied without the consent of the victim (circumstances); and that the application of force caused bodily harm (consequences). Bodily harm is defined in section 2 of the Criminal Code as meaning "any hurt or injury to a person that interferes with the health or comfort of the person and is more than merely transient or trifling in nature." For example, a swollen face and bleeding nose have been considered to constitute "bodily harm" and Canadian courts have also ruled that the term even includes psychological harm.

There are some significant exceptions to the division of the *actus reus* into three elements. For example, perjury (section 131 of the Criminal Code) is an offence that does not require proof of any consequences. Provided the accused person knowingly makes a false statement with intent to mislead a court, he or she will be guilty of perjury even though not a single person actually believed the false statement. However, consequences do constitute a crucial element of the *actus reus* of most criminal offences. Consider, by way of illustration, the offences of dangerous operation of a motor vehicle causing death or dangerous operation of a motor vehicle causing bodily harm (section 249 of the Criminal Code); these carry maximum penalties of 14 and 10 years, respectively. In contrast, the "simple" offence of dangerous operation of a motor vehicle (where the Crown does not have to prove the consequences of death or bodily harm) carries a maximum penalty of only five years. Occasionally, the *actus reus* of an offence does not contain the requirement that the accused engage in conduct of any kind; instead, the Crown must prove that the accused was found in a particular "condition" or "state." For example, it is an offence [section 351(1) of the Criminal Code] to be in possession of housebreaking instruments without a lawful excuse for having them. It is not necessary for the prosecution to establish that the accused person actually used the housebreaking instruments; it is enough that the accused person was found in possession of the instruments concerned. The rationale for this type of offence is that it is often necessary to use the criminal law in a preventative manner; it is undoubtedly preferable to stop the break-in before it occurs and it is only "guilty" possession that is the target of section 351(1) of the Criminal Code.

An important question that must be addressed is whether a mere failure to act (an omission) can qualify as the conduct element of the *actus reus* of an offence. The answer is that a failure to act can constitute a crime only if the accused was under a pre-existing legal duty to act. A good illustration is the duty owed by a parent to a small child to provide the latter with the "necessaries of life"—for example, by feeding the child and providing him or her with necessary medical care (section 215 of the Criminal Code). Under Canadian criminal law, there is no duty to rescue a stranger who is in serious danger. However, there is a duty to rescue when the person in danger is a child or spouse of the accused person or is in some other relationship that imposes a duty to act (for example, a prisoner is owed such a duty by the officer in charge of the jail in which the prisoner is being held). It has been argued that the criminal law is seriously deficient insofar as it does not require every adult citizen to take active steps to rescue a person who is in danger provided, of course, that the rescue may be undertaken without an unreasonable degree of danger to the rescuer. However, it may be very difficult to enforce such a duty in practice. For example, suppose a radio message is broadcast that informs listeners that volunteers are needed to help rescue children in a collapsed school building. Should everyone who hears that message be legally required to forsake what they are doing and rush to the scene of the disaster?

A final point that needs to be made about the *actus reus* component of an offence concerns the requirement that the accused's conduct be voluntary. If a driver is repeatedly stung by a swarm of bees and crashes his or her vehicle, the accident would be considered the consequence of a series of reflex actions that were beyond the driver's control; clearly, they did not flow from the free exercise of his or her will. Similarly, if an accused person's consciousness is impaired to such an extent that he or she is unable to control his or her actions, it may be concluded that there was no *actus reus* of any criminal offence because the accused acted involuntarily; when this situation occurs, the accused may raise the defence of automatism. In fact, automatism is a rare—and somewhat exotic—defence and may be successfully raised only in a very limited number of situations. For example, if an individual is hit on the head and immediately thereafter enters a state of impaired consciousness and assaults another person, he or she may claim the benefit of the defence of automatism—provided it is established that the assault constituted an involuntary action. In practice, automatism is a difficult defence to claim successfully because, in the *Stone* case (1999), the Supreme Court of Canada ruled that the burden of proving the defence is placed on the accused person who raises it (normally, the Crown is required to prove every element of the *actus reus* and *mens rea* components of an offence). Stone had been charged with the murder of his wife, following a series of provocative statements that she had directed at him. The accused had stabbed his wife 47 times but claimed that, at the time, he was in a state of dissociation following the shock of the "psychological blow" that had been inflicted on him by his spouse's hurtful words; more specifically, he stated that a "whoosh" sensation had swept over him and that he was unaware of what he was doing. Ultimately, the jury concluded that the claim of automatism had not been proved by Stone. However, Stone was convicted of manslaughter rather than murder because the jury concluded that there had been provocation (within the meaning of section 232 of the Criminal Code). Stone's conviction of manslaughter was later affirmed by the Supreme Court of Canada, where Justice Bastarache stated that the plausibility of a claim of automatism in such cases is significantly reduced if the victim is alleged to be the "trigger" of the violence directed at him or her. A successful defence of automatism presupposes that accused persons are plunged into such a state of impaired consciousness that they are barely aware of what is happening around them. In Stone's case, the accused responded directly to what he perceived to be insults and the jury evidently believed that his actions were those of a man who knew where he was and what he was doing.

The *Mens Rea* Elements of a Crime

mens rea
The mental elements (other than voluntariness) contained in the definition of a criminal offence.

Basically, ***mens rea*** refers to all the mental elements (other than voluntariness) that the Crown must prove (beyond a reasonable doubt) in order to obtain a conviction of a criminal offence. *Mens rea* is rather like a chameleon insofar as it changes its nature from one offence to another. Obviously, the *mens rea* for murder is very different from that required for theft. Furthermore, *mens rea* is not one mental state but rather a combination of mental states; indeed, it is necessary to analyze the *mens rea* required in relation to each of the three elements of the *actus reus* of any particular crime—that is, conduct, circumstances, and consequences.

The requirement that the prosecution prove *mens rea* reflects basic values that Canadians hold in relation to civil liberties. In essence, the *mens rea* requirement ensures that only those defendants who are morally blameworthy are convicted of "true crimes" under the Criminal Code. As Justice McLachlin said in the Supreme Court of Canada's decision in *Théroux* (1993),

> *Mens rea* . . . refers to the guilty mind, the wrongful intention, of the accused. Its function in the criminal law is to prevent the conviction of the morally innocent—those who do not understand or intend the consequences of their acts.

Subjective and Objective *Mens Rea*

There are two very distinct types of *mens rea* requirements in Canadian criminal law: (i) subjective and (ii) objective.

Subjective mens rea is based on the notion that accused persons may not be convicted of a criminal offence unless (a) they *deliberately intended* to bring about the consequences prohibited by the law; (b) *subjectively realized* that their conduct might bring about such prohibited consequences but recklessly continued with that conduct in spite of their knowledge of the risks involved; or (c) were *wilfully blind* in that they deliberately closed their minds to the obvious criminality of their actions. As Justice McLachlin explained in the Supreme Court of Canada's decision in *Creighton* (1993),

subjective *mens rea*
The *mens rea* elements of a criminal offence are considered to be subjective if they are based on a determination of "what actually went on in the accused person's mind." The forms of subjective *mens rea* are intention and knowledge; recklessness; and wilful blindness.

> The requisite intention or knowledge may be inferred from the act and its circumstances. Even in the latter case, however, it is concerned with "what was actually going on in the mind of this particular accused at the time in question."

Subjective *mens rea*, therefore, constitutes a requirement that the accused *deliberately chose to do something wrong*.

Objective mens rea is predicated on the principle that accused persons should be convicted of certain offences, not because they intended to bring about the prohibited consequences or acted recklessly, but rather because *reasonable* people, in the same situation, would have appreciated that their conduct created a risk of causing harm and would have taken action to avoid doing so. Here the fault of the accused does not lie in deliberately choosing to do something wrong; instead, the culpability lies in the fact that the accused person had the capacity to live up to the standard of care expected of a reasonable person and failed to do so. As Justice McLachlin said in *Creighton* (1993), "Objective *mens rea* is not concerned with what was actually in the accused's mind, but what should have been there if the accused proceeded reasonably." Who is the "reasonable person"? The answer to this question is simply that it is up to the judge or jury (if there is one) to decide what is reasonable in all the circumstances of the case and, no doubt, they call upon their own reservoir of life experience to determine what they think is reasonable. Nevertheless, this means that it is always difficult to predict whether a judge or jury will determine that a specific defendant in a criminal trial acted reasonably.

objective *mens rea*
The *mens rea* elements of a criminal offence are considered to be objective if they are based on a determination of whether a reasonable person, in the same circumstances and with the same knowledge as the accused, would have appreciated the risk involved in the accused's conduct and would have taken steps to avoid the commission of the *actus reus* elements of the crime in question.

In the *Creighton* case (1993), Justice McLachlin emphasized that the "moral fault of the offence must be proportionate to its gravity and penalty"; in other words, the most serious crimes, carrying the most severe penalties, should generally be based on a subjective *mens rea* requirement. Significantly, in the case of *Martineau* (1990), the Supreme Court of Canada ruled that the crime of murder is so serious and carries such a high degree of stigma that criminal responsibility for this offence must be based on subjective *mens rea*; indeed, the Court stated that the Charter requires that the Crown prove either that the accused deliberately intended to kill or, at the very least, subjectively foresaw that his or her conduct was likely to cause death. However, in *Creighton* (1993), the Supreme Court held that responsibility for manslaughter could be based on an objective *mens rea* requirement because the degree of stigma and the penalties attached to it were considerably less severe than is the case for murder. In Creighton's case, the accused had injected a quantity of cocaine into the arm of the victim. In order to convict Creighton of manslaughter, the Crown first had to prove that he had intentionally committed an unlawful act that had resulted in death. The unlawful act was the offence of trafficking in narcotics (trafficking includes the act of administering a drug) and there was no doubt that the victim died as a direct consequence of the injection. The *mens rea* for so-called unlawful act manslaughter is objective in nature. Therefore, the second task confronting the Crown was to prove that any reasonable person would have foreseen the risk of non-trivial bodily harm as a consequence of committing the unlawful act. The Supreme Court of Canada had no doubt that Creighton was correctly convicted of manslaughter because any reasonable person who administered a dangerous drug intravenously would foresee the risk of some degree of bodily harm.

There are three forms of subjective *mens rea* that the Crown may be required to prove in a criminal prosecution: intention and knowledge; recklessness; and wilful blindness.

Section 155(1) of the Criminal Code provides a typical example of the subjective *mens rea* requirement of intention and knowledge; indeed, it provides that an individual commits incest if, knowing that another person is "by blood relationship his or her parent, child, brother, sister, grandparent or grandchild," he or she intentionally has sexual intercourse with that person. Usually, the Criminal Code will require the Crown to prove a specific mental element in addition to intention and knowledge. Take, for example, the offence of first-degree murder. Section 231(2) of the Code states that this offence is committed when murder is both "planned and deliberate." In order to convict an accused person of murder, the Crown must establish that this person either intended to kill or intended to inflict bodily harm that he or she knew was likely to cause death and was reckless (did not care) whether death ensued or not [section 229(a)]. However, if the offender is to be convicted of first- as opposed to second-degree murder, then normally the Crown must also prove that the killing was planned and deliberate in the sense that the accused did not act impulsively and was following some pre-existing plan to kill someone. Intoxicated defendants who are found to have the necessary *mens rea* for murder will often be acquitted of first-degree murder because they acted on impulse or without thinking about what they were going to do ahead of time; these accused persons will instead be convicted of second-degree murder.

Recklessness is a form of subjective *mens rea* where the accused knows that his or her conduct could cause certain prohibited consequences but deliberately proceeds with that conduct because he or she does not care one way or the other. Take the case of arson. Section 434 of the Criminal Code states that a person who "intentionally or recklessly causes damage by fire or explosion to property that is not wholly owned by that person" is guilty of an indictable offence and may be sentenced to a maximum of 14 years in prison. If Nero throws a lighted cigarette onto a haystack, realizing that there is a good chance the haystack will catch fire, he will be convicted of arson even if he can demonstrate that he did not start the fire deliberately and that, in fact, he hoped very sincerely that there would not be any blaze as a consequence of his actions. Nero is guilty of arson because his recklessness constitutes one of the forms of *mens rea* that is necessary for conviction under the terms of section 434.

Wilful blindness is the final form of subjective *mens rea*. It exists where accused persons have every reason to make some kind of inquiry as to whether there are circumstances that would render their conduct criminal but deliberately choose to shut their eyes to the obvious because they wish to avoid being convicted of an offence. The most common example of wilful blindness occurs in relation to the crime of being in possession of stolen property [section 354(1) of the Criminal Code]. Suppose that an accused person pays for goods at a relatively small fraction of their known value but deliberately refrains from asking whether they are stolen because he or she wants to deny actual knowledge when subsequently confronted by the police. Such a person would be considered to have been wilfully blind as to the criminality of his or her actions and would be treated as though there had been actual knowledge that the goods were stolen.

Objective *mens rea* has been applied to a significant number of offences under the Criminal Code. For example, the following offences have all been characterized by the courts as requiring proof only of objective, rather than subjective, *mens rea*: manslaughter, dangerous operation of a motor vehicle, assault causing bodily harm, and criminal negligence causing death or bodily harm. However, it is important to bear in mind that the courts have consistently stated that accused persons may not be convicted of "true crimes" under the Criminal Code merely because they were "careless" in the sense that their conduct fell below the standard of care expected of a reasonable person acting prudently in the same circumstances as the accused. As Justice McLachlin said in the *Creighton* case (1993), "The law does not lightly brand a person as criminal." Therefore, for crimes that are based on objective *mens rea*, the Crown must prove that there was a *marked departure* from the standard of care expected of the reasonable person acting prudently. Furthermore, the Supreme Court of Canada has repeatedly stated that the courts should apply a "modified objective test" in such cases. This means that a judge or jury (if there is one) must ask what the accused person in the case before them actually knew about the circumstances surrounding their actions. The judge or jury must then decide whether the accused's behaviour constituted a marked departure from the standard of care expected of a reasonable person who faces the identical circumstances as the accused and who is armed with exactly the same knowledge of those circumstances. Suppose, for example, an accused person suffers an epileptic fit while driving a vehicle and he or she crosses over the centre of the road and causes a fatal collision with a car that is travelling in the opposite direction. On the face of it, straying over the centre line and causing a collision constitutes a marked departure from the standard of care expected of a reasonable person. However, if the accused did not know that he or she was likely to suffer from an epileptic fit, there would be no conviction on a charge of dangerous operation of a motor vehicle causing death [section 249(4) of the Criminal Code]. A reasonable driver, with no knowledge of the likelihood that he or she might suffer an epileptic fit, would have behaved in the same way as the accused. However, the situation would be very different if the accused person knew that he or she was suffering from epilepsy or subject to sudden fainting spells and, without first obtaining medical clearance, continued to drive a motor vehicle. Clearly, a reasonable person armed with this knowledge would never attempt to take a vehicle on the road; therefore, the accused's conduct would almost certainly be considered a marked departure from the standard of care expected of the reasonable person.

Although it may appear somewhat harsh to convict individuals of serious crimes on the basis of objective *mens rea*, it is clear that the courts have watered down the objective test of liability by requiring that the judge or jury take into account the subjective knowledge accused people have of the relevant circumstances surrounding their actions. Furthermore, if an accused person lacks the normal capacity of the reasonable person to appreciate that his or her conduct might create a risk of harm, that person may not be convicted of a crime, even if it is based on proof of objective *mens rea*. For example, suppose a 20-year-old man has a mental age of 10 and he hits a neighbour with a metal bar. Tragically, the neighbour dies from his injuries. In the case of an ordinary person who does not suffer from a severe disability, it would be relatively easy for the Crown to prove a charge of manslaughter. The *mens rea* requirements are objective in nature. The accused must be proved to have intentionally applied force to the victim and the Crown must then proceed to establish that a reasonable person would have foreseen the risk of non-trivial bodily harm. Any reasonable person would foresee the risk of fairly serious bodily harm if an attack is carried out with a metal bar; therefore, most accused persons would be routinely convicted of manslaughter in such circumstances. However, if the accused is so developmentally disabled that he or she cannot foresee that their actions may cause non-trivial bodily harm, then that individual may not be convicted of manslaughter. The essence of culpability in objective *mens rea* is the notion that the accused had the capacity to foresee—and avoid—the risk of physical harm but did not do so. If the accused lacks this basic capacity, to convict him or her of manslaughter would amount to punishing someone who lacks any blameworthiness. In *Creighton* (1993), the Supreme Court of Canada ruled that such an outcome would infringe the fundamental principles of justice that are enshrined in the Charter (section 7).

Mens Rea and Regulatory Offences

Earlier in this chapter, a distinction was drawn between regulatory offences ("quasi-criminal law") and "true crimes." Where "true crimes" are concerned, the Crown usually has to prove the required *mens rea* of the offence beyond a reasonable doubt. However, most regulatory offences are considered to be offences of strict liability. This means that the Crown only has to prove the *actus reus* elements of the offence; the onus is then on the accused to prove, on the balance of probabilities, that he or she was not negligent (or that he or she "acted with due diligence"). The rationale for strict liability is that it would be extremely difficult to conduct effective prosecutions of regulatory offences if the Crown were required to prove that accused persons were negligent. Usually, it is the accused person who has the best knowledge of the steps that he or she has taken to comply with the regulations that apply to his or her field of manufacturing or business activities, and so on; therefore, it is not unfair to require the accused to present this evidence and prove that he or she acted with the due diligence expected of a reasonable person in the same circumstances. Furthermore, the penalties for regulatory offences are comparatively lenient, since they rarely include imprisonment as a realistic sentencing alternative. In any event, strict liability is infinitely preferable to a regime of absolute liability, in which the accused is not permitted to claim a lack of *mens rea* as a defence. Prior to the decision of the Supreme Court of Canada in the case of *Sault Ste. Marie (City of)* in 1978, the majority of regulatory offences imposed absolute liability and accused persons were prevented from asserting that their actions were not blameworthy. However, since the *Sault Ste. Marie* case, by far the greatest proportion of regulatory offences have been considered to impose a regime of strict liability, leaving the accused with the opportunity to prove that he or she has done all that reasonably could be expected to be done in order to comply with the relevant regulations that apply to his or her business, occupation, industry, and so on.

In the *Wholesale Travel Group Inc.* case (1991), the accused had been charged with the regulatory offence of false or misleading advertising, under the federal Competition Act, R.S.C. 1970, c. C–23. The Act clearly imposed strict liability insofar as it permitted the accused to raise a defence of having acted "with due diligence." Essentially, the defence would be available where the accused proved that the "act or omission giving rise to the offence" was the "result of error" and that he or she "took reasonable precautions and exercised due diligence to prevent the occurrence of such error." It was contended before the Supreme Court of Canada that, because strict liability requires accused persons to prove their innocence, it infringed the presumption of innocence, enshrined in section 11(d) of the Charter, and was, therefore, invalid. However, the Supreme Court of Canada ultimately held that strict liability was not invalid under the provisions of the Charter. The *Wholesale Travel Group Inc.* case is, therefore, a decision of great importance since it has affirmed the legitimacy of the basic principles of liability that are at the heart of the vast network of regulatory legislation that governs the everyday lives of all Canadians.

Becoming a Party to a Criminal Offence

Individuals can be convicted of criminal offences even if they are not the persons who actually commit them. For example, section 21(1) of the Criminal Code provides that anyone is a party to an offence who (i) actually commits it;

(ii) aids another person to commit it; or (iii) abets (encourages) any person to commit it. In a homicide case, the person who actually commits the offence would be the individual who, for example, actually stabs a victim to death. However, the person who intentionally provides assistance and/or encouragement is liable to be convicted of murder on the same basis as the actual killer. In the *Thatcher* case (1987), which received wide publicity because the accused, Colin Thatcher, was the former leader of the Saskatchewan Liberal Party and the son of a former premier, the Crown contended that the accused either committed the murder of his ex-wife himself or aided and/or abetted another person to do it. The Supreme Court of Canada ruled that it was not necessary for the jury to be unanimous in its verdict as to whether Thatcher himself was the killer or he aided and/or abetted another party to do it on his behalf. As Justice Dickson noted, section 21 of the Code "has been designed to alleviate the necessity of choosing between the two different forms of participation in a criminal offence." Each form of participation in the murder was equally culpable and section 21 established "one single mode of incurring criminal liability." Similarly, a person who counsels ("procures," "solicits," or "incites") another to commit a crime becomes a **party to that crime** even if "the offence was committed in a way different from that which was counselled" (section 22 of the Criminal Code).

party to a crime
The Criminal Code specifies that one is a party to—and liable to conviction of—a criminal offence if one actually commits it; aids and/or abets it; becomes a party to it by virtue of having formed a common intention with others to commit a crime; or counsels the commission of an offence that is actually committed by another person.

An individual may also become a party to a criminal offence that has been committed by other people when he or she had previously formed a common intention with them to commit a crime. Section 21(2) of the Criminal Code deals with the situation in which two or more persons have agreed to commit a crime and to assist one another in carrying out this "common purpose." Each of these individuals is considered a party to any offence committed by the other person(s) who entered the original agreement provided (i) that this other offence was committed in order to carry out the "common purpose" and (ii) that these individuals either knew or ought to have known that the commission of this other offence "would be a probable consequence of carrying out the common purpose." Suppose that Arthur, Benedict, and Cassio agree to commit a robbery and to help one another in carrying out this "common intention." Cassio—without consulting his colleagues in crime—kills one of the robbery victims. In these circumstances, Arthur and Benedict would be convicted of manslaughter if they either knew or ought to have known that inflicting non-trivial bodily harm on the intended victim(s) would be a probable consequence of implementing their common intention to commit robbery. Since robbery necessarily involves an element of violence or threatened violence, any reasonable person would foresee the probability that someone may be seriously hurt; therefore, Arthur and Benedict would almost certainly be found guilty of manslaughter. The use of the phrase "or ought to have known" indicates that the *mens rea* elements are objective in nature and this means that the scope of potential liability under section 21(2) is remarkably broad. The only exception to this form of objective liability arises where the offence of murder is concerned. Since the Supreme Court of Canada has ruled [in *Martineau* (1990)] that an accused person may be convicted of murder only where there was an actual intention to kill or subjective foresight of the likelihood of death, Arthur and Benedict would be convicted of murder only if they subjectively realized that death was a probable consequence of carrying out their common intention to commit robbery.

One question that immediately springs to mind when discussing section 21(2) is whether an individual who agreed with others to commit a crime and to provide the necessary assistance to achieve his goal should be entitled to change his or her mind and withdraw from the common intention. The answer is that an individual may withdraw from the common intention, but may do so effectively only when he or she gives unequivocal notice to the other party or parties of his or her wish to abandon the criminal enterprise. Once effective notice has been given, the individual is no longer liable for any subsequent crimes committed by the other party or parties in pursuit of the common intention.

The Use of Criminal Law as a Preventative Tool: Inchoate Offences

Any system of criminal law will permit the police to intervene and arrest those who, in some way, demonstrate that they are about to embark upon the commission of a serious crime. If members of a gang of professional kidnappers agree to abduct a particular victim and to hold him or her to ransom, the police do not have to wait until the abduction is actually carried out before they intervene. Even though the kidnapping may exist only in the intentions of the members of the gang, it is undoubtedly legitimate for the state to punish them for having participated in a conspiracy to commit kidnapping. Conspiracy is an **inchoate crime** (literally, a crime "in embryo"); once their agreement to commit a crime has been reached, the accused may be convicted of the crime of conspiracy even though the offence that they originally planned to commit is never brought to fruition. Other inchoate crimes are criminal attempt and counselling an offence that is not committed.

inchoate crime
A criminal offence that is committed when the accused person seeks to bring about the commission of a particular crime but is not successful in doing so. The three inchoate offences in the Criminal Code are attempt, conspiracy, and counselling.

Inchoate crimes raise serious questions about the civil liberties of those who are charged with having committed them. In general, it is accepted that the criminal law should not punish people simply for entertaining evil thoughts. However, society does have the right to prevent individuals from translating their evil thoughts into criminal acts. The problem lies in defining the point at which the state is justified in laying a charge against someone who has not yet committed the crime that he or she has in mind. Basically, accused persons must take some form of action that manifests their intention to commit a crime; in counselling, the accused must importune another person to commit a crime; in attempt, the accused must take a substantial step toward completion of a crime; and, in conspiracy, the accused must enter into an agreement to commit a crime.

Counselling an Offence That Is Not Committed

According to section 22 of the Criminal Code, it is a crime to **counsel** another person to commit an offence that is not ultimately brought to fruition. Since the main focus of the offence is on the accused person's intentions, it does not

counselling
Procuring, soliciting, or inciting another person to commit a crime.

FOCUS

BOX 3.3 Counselling Crime over the Internet

Canadian courts are constantly faced with the need to adapt the criminal law to deal with the many opportunities that rapidly developing communication technologies create for novel methods of committing crimes. *R. v. Hamilton* (2005) furnishes a noteworthy example of a case in which the Supreme Court of Canada very cautiously adapted the existing principles of criminal law to deal with a situation in which it was alleged that the Internet was used to communicate information that was likely to incite other individuals to commit criminal offences.

Hamilton had used the Internet to sell computer files and documents to a number of individuals. These files contained detailed instructions for bomb making, burglary, and a program that generated credit card numbers that might be used for fraudulent purposes. Hamilton was charged with counselling the commission of four offences that were not in fact committed; namely, making explosive substances with intent, doing anything with intent to cause an explosion, break and enter with intent, and fraud. At his trial, Hamilton readily admitted that he had read a computer-generated list of the files concerned but denied that he had actually read the contents of those files. Although he had generated some credit card numbers, he had never used them and there had been no complaints from the bank concerning their misuse.

At his trial, the Judge acquitted Hamilton of all the charges against him because, in her view, Hamilton never intended that the persons to whom he sent the computer files should actually commit the offences described in them. The Crown took the case to the Supreme Court of Canada, which articulated the *mens rea* that must be proved before an accused person may be convicted of counselling an offence. According to Justice Fish,

> the *mens rea* consists in nothing less than an accompanying *intent* or *conscious disregard of the substantial and unjustified risk inherent in the counselling*: that is, it must be shown that the accused either intended that the offence counselled be committed, or knowingly counselled the commission of the offence while aware of the unjustified risk the offence counselled was in fact likely to be committed as a result of the accused's conduct. [at para. 29] [Emphasis in original]

Prior to the *Hamilton* case, the courts had always applied the principle that, in order to obtain a conviction for counselling,

matter that no one is actually influenced by the accused person's efforts to procure, solicit, or incite someone to commit a crime. Furthermore, once their counselling action is completed, accused persons cannot escape criminal conviction merely because they change their minds and renounce their criminal intent. Box 3.3 illustrates how technological change can affect the interpretation and application of the criminal law.

criminal attempt

A criminal attempt occurs when an individual does—or omits to do—anything for the purpose of carrying out a previously formed intention to commit a crime. The conduct in question must constitute a substantial step toward the completion of the crime that is intended.

Criminal Attempt

The offence of **criminal attempt** is focused on an accused person's intention to commit a crime that is never realized. Section 24(1) of the Criminal Code provides that "everyone who, having an intent to commit a crime, does or omits to do anything for the purpose of carrying out his intention is guilty of an attempt to commit the offence whether or not it was possible under the circumstances to commit the offence." Clearly, the *mens rea* of criminal attempt is

FOCUS

BOX 3.3 Counselling Crime over the Internet *(Continued)*

the Crown must prove that the accused person actually intended that the offence be committed. However, the Supreme Court ruled in *Hamilton* that an accused person may also be convicted if he or she was *extremely reckless* as to the likelihood that the offence would be committed. Nevertheless, even with this expanded definition of the necessary *mens rea*, the Supreme Court affirmed Hamilton's acquittal on all the counselling charges except the charge of counselling fraud. The Supreme Court ordered a new trial on the charge of counselling fraud because it took the view that the trial judge should have found that Hamilton had the necessary *mens rea* for this offence. The Supreme Court noted that Hamilton had sent an e-mail "teaser" to various individuals in which he advertised software that could generate "valid working credit card numbers." Justice Fish noted that Hamilton "sought to make "a quick buck" by encouraging the intended recipients of his Internet solicitation to purchase a device that generated credit card numbers easily put to fraudulent use." Furthermore, the Supreme Court emphasized that Hamilton knew very well that "the use of false credit card numbers is illegal." Therefore, even if Hamilton had not actually wanted the purchasers of the files to commit the offences described in them, he was at the very least extremely reckless as to the risk that the files were likely to incite the purchasers to commit the offence of fraud.

Do you agree with the Supreme Court of Canada's decision to expand the scope of the *mens rea* for counselling an offence to include extreme recklessness? Should this decision have been left to Parliament or was it appropriate for the Supreme Court to modify the existing law to meet the challenge posed by the use of the Internet to communicate information that is likely to incite individuals to commit potentially serious crimes? Do you think Parliament should amend the *Criminal Code* to make it easier to obtain convictions in such cases? For example, should individuals such as Hamilton be made criminally liable for the *negligent* transfer of files that turn out to contain information as to how to commit offences even though they may not have actually read the files in question?

nothing short of an actual intent to commit an offence. The *actus reus* of attempt is any step taken by the accused toward the completion of the offence, provided that this step goes beyond "mere preparation" and is not considered to be "too remote" from the completed offence. For example, buying a train ticket with a view to travelling to another city in order to rob a bank would be considered "mere preparation" and "too remote" from the completed robbery to justify convicting the accused of a criminal attempt. However, if the accused person actually reaches the front doors of the bank before being arrested by the police, it is clear that the *actus reus* of the offence of attempted robbery has been established. Unfortunately, it is often very difficult to predict exactly where the court will draw the line between mere preparation and an act that warrants conviction for a criminal attempt. It should also be emphasized that a criminal attempt may be committed even though it would be impossible for the accused to commit the complete offence that he or she has in mind.

For example, if someone tries to steal a motor vehicle that has been totally disabled by its owner, this person would be guilty of attempted theft even though it would have been impossible for that person to take the vehicle from the spot where it had been parked. Similarly, if an accused person mistakenly shoots a wax dummy, believing it is an enemy, that person will be guilty of attempted murder. What is important to recognize is that the accused person seriously intended to commit murder and that there is a very real likelihood that, having failed on this particular occasion, the accused will try again and, perhaps, be more successful on that subsequent occasion.

Conspiracy

conspiracy
An agreement by two or more persons to commit a criminal offence.

The crime of **conspiracy** is established when two or more individuals form a common intention to commit a crime. In addition, the Crown must prove that each individual who is charged with conspiracy actually intended to put the common design into effect. The *actus reus* of conspiracy is the agreement to engage in criminal conduct, while the *mens rea* component consists of the intent not only to enter into this agreement but also to implement it. Suppose two individuals apparently agree to kidnap a third party. However, it later turns out that one of these individuals was actually an undercover police officer who never had any intention to act on this supposed agreement. In this case, neither of the individuals may be convicted of conspiracy. The police officer lacks the necessary *mens rea* for conspiracy and the other individual cannot be convicted of this offence because the Crown must prove that there are at least two persons who seriously intended to implement the plan to commit murder. On the other hand, if there are two or more individuals who agree to commit murder and who fully intend to carry out their homicidal plans, they would be convicted of conspiracy even if an undercover officer is also part of this group. As long as there is a minimum number of two individuals who intend to carry out an agreement to commit a crime, there is a conspiracy. Conspiracy is a crime that provides the Crown with a number of distinct advantages. For example, certain types of evidence may be accepted at the joint trial of a group of alleged co-conspirators that would never be admitted against specific members of that group, had they been tried separately. In effect, there is always the danger of "guilt by association" in conspiracy trials.

Defences to a Criminal Charge

Conviction of a "true crime" should not occur unless the accused person is considered blameworthy. Merely because individuals engage in conduct that, from an objective point of view, is either actually or potentially harmful does not mean that they should be punished under the provisions of the criminal law. Indeed, the requirement of *mens rea* ensures that the Crown must first prove a culpable mental state or the prosecution will fail. However, in addition to the *mens rea* requirement, there are a number of distinct defences that may be raised by an accused person in a criminal trial. When analyzed carefully, some of these defences, such as mistake of fact, basically amount to a denial that the Crown has proved the necessary *mens rea,* but there are other defences, such as duress, that may be raised successfully even though the accused possessed the necessary *mens rea* for the offence that has been charged. Essentially, the patchwork of defences has evolved as a means of ensuring that those individuals who have a justification or excuse for their conduct are either acquitted of criminal charges or treated more leniently (for example, by conviction of a less serious offence).

Mental Disorder as a Defence to a Criminal Charge

In the Supreme Court of Canada's decision in the case of *Winko* (1999), Justice McLachlin said:

> In every society, there are those who commit criminal acts because of mental illness. The criminal law must find a way to deal with these people fairly, while protecting the public against further harms. The task is not an easy one.

In Canada, this difficult task is undertaken through the application by the courts of the special defence of **not criminally responsible on account of mental disorder** (NCRMD). The current test that must be used in deciding whether an accused should be found NCRMD is articulated in section 16(1) of the Criminal Code:

> No person is criminally responsible for an act committed or an omission made while suffering from a mental disorder that renders the person incapable of appreciating the nature and quality of the act or omission or of knowing that it was wrong.

NCRMD
The special verdict of "not criminally responsible on account of mental disorder." In order to be found NCRMD, it must be proved on the balance of probabilities that, because of mental disorder, the accused lacked the capacity to appreciate the nature and quality of the act or omission in question or of knowing that it would be considered morally wrong by the average Canadian.

The first requirement of the NCRMD defence is that the accused was suffering from a "mental disorder" at the time of the alleged offence(s). In fact, the Supreme Court of Canada has adopted an extremely broad definition of mental disorder but it is only those individuals who are suffering from very serious forms of mental disorder (such as schizophrenia) who will meet the other criteria specified in section 16(1), namely, that the accused has been rendered incapable either of appreciating the physical nature and quality of the act or omission in question or of knowing that the act or omission is considered morally wrong by the everyday standards of the ordinary Canadian. Most mentally disordered people understand the physical nature of their conduct (for example, do they realize stabbing someone in the heart will cause death?). Similarly, the majority of mentally disordered persons are capable of knowing that their conduct would be "morally condemned by reasonable members of society" [as Justice Arbour of the Supreme Court of Canada put it in the *Molodowic* case (2000)]. Significantly, section 16(1) does not extend the benefit of the NCRMD defence to mentally disordered persons who claim that—as a consequence of mental disorder—they succumbed to an irresistible impulse to commit a crime; provided such individuals were capable of understanding what they were doing and that it was wrong, they are not considered to be NCRMD in Canadian criminal law.

The very narrow scope of the NCRMD defence ensures that relatively few accused persons may raise it successfully at their trials. In addition, it is significant that section 16 places the burden of proving the NCRMD defence on the shoulders of the accused person if he or she raises it at trial; in this situation, the accused person has to prove the defence on the balance of probabilities. Although this provision infringes the presumption of innocence, enshrined in section 11(d) of the Charter, the Supreme Court of Canada ruled, in the *Chaulk* case (1990), that this infringement of the accused person's right was justified as a reasonable limitation under section 1. The Court took the view that it would be impractical to require the Crown to prove beyond a reasonable doubt that the accused was not mentally disordered—particularly, in light of the fact that an accused person may refuse to cooperate with a psychiatrist nominated by the Crown to report to the court on the accused's mental condition.

Accused persons who are found NCRMD are not acquitted in the technical sense of that word. Indeed, section 672.1 of the Criminal Code states that a verdict of NCRMD constitutes a finding that "the accused committed the act or omission that formed the basis of the offence with which the accused is charged but is not criminally responsible on account of mental disorder." NCR accused may be granted (i) an absolute discharge; (ii) a conditional discharge; (iii) an order holding them in custody in a psychiatric facility. Section 672.54(a) of the Criminal Code provides that, unless a court or review board determines that an NCR accused person constitutes a "significant threat to the safety of the public," then it *must* order an absolute discharge. In *Winko* (1999), the Supreme Court of Canada ruled that the threshold for justifying the imposition of restrictions on the liberty of a person who has been found NCRMD is very high:

> A "significant threat to the safety of the public" means a real risk of physical or psychological harm to members of the public that is serious in the sense of going beyond the merely trivial or annoying. The conduct giving rise to the harm must be criminal in nature.

General Defences to a Criminal Charge

mistake of fact
Mistake of fact may be a defence where the accused person acts under the influence of an honest mistake in relation to any of the elements of the *actus reus* of the offence charged.

Mistake of fact may constitute a defence to a criminal charge if it causes the accused to erroneously believe that the circumstances facing him or her did not render his or her actions criminal. For example, if a woman participates in a marriage ceremony with a man erroneously believing that her first husband is dead, she would not be guilty of the crime of bigamy. The central element of the *actus reus* of bigamy is that one of the parties to a marriage ceremony is already married. If the accused honestly believed that she was a widow, then—in the circumstances as she perceived them to be—she was not committing a prohibited act because she was no longer married to her first spouse. When the accused operates under a mistake of fact, he or she is really stating that the Crown has failed to prove the necessary *mens rea* of the offence. One of the most controversial uses of the defence of mistake of fact used to occur when an accused person who was charged with sexual assault claimed that he honestly believed in the complainant's consent, even though he was mistaken. However, section 273.2(b) of the Criminal Code (enacted in 1992) states that mistaken belief in consent will not be a valid defence to a charge of sexual assault unless the accused took "reasonable steps, in the circumstances known to the accused at the time, to ascertain that the complainant was consenting." By requiring the accused person to act reasonably, this amendment to the Code has considerably reduced the opportunities for abuse of the defence of honest belief in consent.

While honest mistake of fact constitutes a valid defence to a criminal charge, a mistake concerning the nature or scope of the criminal law does not absolve an accused person of criminal liability. Indeed, section 19 of the Criminal Code makes it very clear that ignorance of the law is no excuse. This is a harsh rule but an inevitable one since it would be impossible for the Crown to prove actual knowledge of the relevant legal principles. There are some exceptions to this rule. One of the more important exceptions arises when an official who is charged with the administration of certain types of regulatory legislation gives erroneous legal advice. If the accused person reasonably relies on this advice, he or she may take advantage of the defence of "officially induced error." For example, if a factory inspector tells a manufacturer that it is acceptable to modify a certain safety device, it would clearly be unfair to convict that manufacturer of a violation of the relevant occupational safety legislation. If the manufacturer reasonably relied on the advice of the factory inspector and committed what a court later concludes is a regulatory offence, then the defence of officially induced error will come to the rescue of the manufacturer.

intoxication
Intoxication caused by alcohol and/or other drugs may be a defence if it prevents the accused from forming the intent required for a specific intent offence, such as murder or robbery.

Intoxication is a complex, and highly problematic, defence. A high proportion of violent crimes are committed by individuals who have abused alcohol and/or other drugs, and the great majority of the inmates in Canada's prisons have been diagnosed as having suffered from a substance abuse disorder. If the scope of a defence of intoxication were drawn too broadly, many violent offenders would escape criminal liability even though they were considered to have ingested alcohol and/or other drugs voluntarily. One of the main effects of alcohol (and some other drugs) is to cause disinhibition—a condition in which the accused may be rendered less able to control his or her conduct. However, the courts have consistently ruled that intoxication may not be raised as a valid defence by accused persons who simply claim that alcohol and/or other drugs impaired their ability to control their conduct. Instead, the intoxication defence focuses on whether the accused's state of intoxication (from alcohol and/or other drugs) prevented him or her from forming the necessary *mens rea* for the crime in question.

The defence of intoxication is primarily a "common law" defence in the sense that it was developed by the courts in the absence of any legislation that defined its nature and scope. Traditionally, the defence has applied only to those offences that required proof of a complex form of *mens rea* known as "specific intent." Therefore, the defence of intoxication may reduce the severity of a charge (for example, from murder to manslaughter or from robbery to assault). On the other hand, it has been a longstanding principle that intoxication is not a valid defence to a charge of such "basic intent" offences as assault, sexual assault, or damage to property (mischief). The legal rationale for maintaining the distinction between crimes of specific and basic intent is that intoxication does not normally impair people to the extent that they do not even have the minimal degree of *mens rea* required to assault someone or to damage property. Even extremely intoxicated people have some degree of awareness of what they are doing and the acts of committing an assault or damaging property require only a very minimal degree of intent. On the other hand, assaulting someone with the specific intent to kill (murder) or forcefully taking something from another individual with the specific intent to steal (robbery) are acts that require a considerably more complex pattern of thought, and intoxication may well prevent the accused from forming the necessary specific intent that is required for conviction of these serious crimes.

In the case of *Daviault* (1994), the Supreme Court of Canada changed the traditional approach to the defence of intoxication. Daviault had been charged with sexual assault, a basic intent crime. He claimed that he had consumed seven or eight beers during the daytime and some 35 ounces of brandy on the evening of the alleged sexual assault. A pharmacologist who had been called by the defence to testify at the trial stated that Daviault's blood-alcohol content would have been in the region of 400 to 600 mg per 100 mL of blood. For most individuals, such a blood-alcohol level would cause a coma or death but, since Daviault was an alcoholic, he was "less susceptible to the effects of alcohol" and, according to the expert witness, the accused may have been suffering from a blackout during which he would not have been aware of his actions. Under the traditional approach, even such an extreme degree of intoxication as was claimed by Daviault could not be raised as a successful defence to a crime of basic intent such as sexual assault. However, in *Daviault*, the Supreme Court ruled that it would constitute an unjustifiable infringement of sections 7 and 11(d) of the Charter to convict accused persons of basic intent crimes if these persons were so severely intoxicated that they were in a "state akin to automatism or insanity." The Court ordered a new trial in Daviault's case and held that he would have to prove the defence of extreme intoxication on the balance of probabilities. Tragically, the complainant in this case died and a new trial could not be held. Although the Supreme Court had taken great care to emphasize that a "Daviault defence" could be raised successfully only in the most extreme—and rare—cases, there was nevertheless considerable public concern that the *Daviault* decision would be used by certain men to escape responsibility for the commission of crimes of violence against women and children. Parliament responded to this concern by enacting section 33.1 of the Criminal Code. Section 33.1 essentially states that accused persons who commit a basic intent offence that involves "an assault or any other interference with the bodily integrity of another person" will not be entitled to raise the defence of intoxication—even if they were "unaware of, or incapable of consciously controlling, (their) behaviour." Whether the Supreme Court of Canada will rule that section 33.1 of the Code should be ruled invalid, as an unjustified breach of an accused person's Charter rights, remains to be seen.

necessity
Necessity may be a defence to a criminal charge when the accused person commits the lesser evil of a crime in order to avoid the occurrence of a greater evil.

duress
Duress may be a defence to a criminal charge when the accused was forced to commit a crime as a consequence of threats of death or serious bodily harm made by another person.

The defences of **necessity** and **duress** are based on the notion that it would be unfair to convict individuals of a criminal offence if they did not have a genuine choice at the time that they committed it. These defences are conceptualized by the courts as being "excuses"; as Justice Dickson said, in the Supreme Court of Canada's decision in *Perka* (1984), "An 'excuse' concedes the wrongfulness of the action but asserts that the circumstances under which it was done are such that it ought not to be attributed to the actor." Necessity is a common-law defence that arises when the accused person can avoid some disaster or calamity only by breaking the law. In these circumstances, the accused person is considered to act involuntarily from a "moral or normative" point of view. As Justice Dickson stated in the *Perka* case (1984),

> The lost Alpinist who, on the point of freezing to death, breaks open an isolated mountain cabin is not literally behaving in an involuntary fashion. He has control over his actions to the extent of being physically capable of abstaining from the act. Realistically, however, his act is not a "voluntary" one. His "choice" to break the law is not true choice at all; it is remorselessly compelled by normal human instincts.

The "evil" that the accused person seeks to avoid must be greater than the "evil" involved in the breaking of the law, and the accused must have no reasonable legal alternative but to break the law. Take the case of a surgeon who is contemplating the surgical separation of conjoined twins who share vital organs, such as the heart or the lungs. Without an operation to separate the babies, both of them will ultimately die. However, the operation will save one of the twins, while inevitably killing the other. Is the surgeon justified in killing one twin in order to save the other? In these particular circumstances, one can assume that the defence of necessity would be available to the surgeon should he or she ever be charged with murder.

When claiming the defence of necessity, defendants may point to any circumstances that constitute a threat to life or limb; however, where the defence of duress is raised, defendants are really asserting that their power of choice is being overborne by another human being. In the *Hibbert* case (1995), the Supreme Court of Canada ruled that duress, like necessity, was a defence that was based on the concept of "normative involuntariness." Section 17 of the Criminal Code sets out the requirements for the defence of duress but, in the case of *Ruzic* (2001), the Supreme Court of Canada ruled that these requirements were so restrictive that they could result in the denial of the defence to an individual who was not blameworthy; therefore, the court struck down these requirements as being invalid under the Charter. The Supreme Court then held that the courts should apply the "common law" defence of duress. The main elements of this defence are that the accused had been subjected to a threat of death or serious bodily harm that is directed either toward the accused or toward another person (such as a child or spouse). The threat must be so serious that the accused believes it will be carried out and the court must also be satisfied that it would have caused a reasonable person, placed in exactly the same position as the accused, to act as he or she did. Finally, it should be established that the accused had no obvious "safe avenue of escape." After all, if the accused had the option to escape from the person who was making threats, he or she cannot now claim that he or she was acting involuntarily.

In the *Ruzic* case, for example, the accused was charged with importing a narcotic and use of a false passport. Two kilograms of heroin had been found strapped to her body when she arrived at Pearson Airport in Toronto. Ruzic admitted the offences but asserted that she had acted under duress. Her story was that she lived with her mother in Belgrade (in the former Yugoslavia) and that she had been persistently threatened by a "paramilitary" man who physically assaulted and sexually harassed her. The man had a reputation for extreme violence and he informed Ruzic that she must take a consignment of heroin to Toronto. When the accused protested, the man threatened to harm her mother. At the time of these threats, law and order had largely broken down in Belgrade, and Ruzic said that she did not inform the Belgrade police of the threats against her mother because they were "corrupt and would do nothing to assist her." The jury acquitted Ruzic on both charges and the Supreme Court of Canada ultimately upheld the acquittal. Ruzic had met all the requirements contained in the common-law defence of duress. She clearly believed that she had absolutely no alternative to bringing the heroin into Canada; if she had not done so, her mother might have been seriously harmed or killed, and seeking the assistance of the local police would have been a futile gesture given the particular circumstances that existed in Belgrade at that time.

provocation

Provocation may be a partial defence to a charge of murder (if successful, it reduces the offence from murder to manslaughter). The required elements of provocation are (i) that the accused responded to a wrongful act or insult that was of such a nature that an ordinary person would have been likely to lose the power of self-control and (ii) that the accused acted "on the sudden and before there was time for his (or her) passion to cool."

Other important defences are provocation and self-defence. **Provocation** is only a partial defence; it may be raised only when the accused is charged with murder. If provocation is raised successfully by the accused, he or she is convicted of manslaughter rather than murder. The defence is available even though the accused undoubtedly possessed the *mens rea* for murder. Under the terms of section 232 of the Criminal Code, murder may be reduced to manslaughter if the accused killed "in the heat of passion caused by sudden provocation." Before the defence may be raised successfully, it must be established that the provocation was of a kind that would be "sufficient to deprive an ordinary person of the power of self-control." This would appear to establish an objective test; however, the Supreme Court of Canada has effectively watered down the objective requirements of the defence by ruling that the issue is whether an ordinary person with the particular characteristics associated with the accused would have lost the power of self-control if confronted with the specific situation that confronted him or her. As Justice Cory stated in the *Thibert* case (1996), "If the test is to be applied sensibly and with sensitivity, then the ordinary person must be taken to be of the same age, and sex, and must share with the accused such other factors as would give the act or insult in question a particular significance." It also has to be established that the accused acted in the heat of the moment "before there was time for his or her passion to cool." The *Stone* case (1999), discussed earlier in connection with automatism, constitutes a typical case of provocation insofar as the accused killed the victim immediately following a series of hurtful insults (which included raising doubts about the paternity of his children and denigrating his sexual prowess). Clearly, the jury believed that an ordinary husband would be likely to lose the power of self-control in such circumstances and that Stone must be considered to have responded to sudden provocation before there had been time for his passion to cool.

self-defence

The Criminal Code permits the use of force in self-defence in certain circumstances where the individual concerned becomes the object of an unlawful assault. Where the individual acted in self-defence without intending to inflict death or grievous bodily harm on the assailant, it must be shown that no more force was used than was necessary in the circumstances. Where the individual concerned inflicted death or grievous bodily harm, then it must be shown that he or she acted under a reasonable apprehension of death or grievous bodily harm and under a reasonable belief that he or she had no alternative but to employ lethal force.

The **self-defence** provisions of the Criminal Code are extraordinarily complex and, in certain respects, contradictory. However, the central provision is section 34 of the Criminal Code. Section 34(1) applies where an accused person has used force in self-defence but did not do so with the intent to inflict death or grievous bodily harm. The accused must demonstrate that he or she was unlawfully assaulted and did not provoke the assault. In addition, it must be shown that the force used was "no more than is necessary to defend him(her) self"; this requirement is significant because it means that there must be a degree of objective proportionality between the force used by the assailant and the force used in self-defence in response to the assailant. This principle has been encapsulated in the phrase "One cannot use a tank against a chariot."

When an accused who has acted in self-defence has either killed the assailant or inflicted grievous bodily harm, he or she will rely on section 34(2) of the Criminal Code. Under this provision, an accused person who is unlawfully assaulted is justified in using lethal or potentially lethal force if

(a) he causes it under reasonable apprehension of death or grievous bodily harm from the violence with which the assault was originally made or with which the assailant pursues his purposes, and
(b) he believes, on reasonable grounds, that he cannot otherwise preserve himself from death or grievous bodily harm.

It would appear that Parliament intended to impose an objective test for self-defence in these circumstances; indeed, section 34(2) clearly refers to "reasonable apprehension" and belief "on reasonable grounds." However, the Supreme Court of Canada has consistently softened the objective nature of the requirements for self-defence under section 34(2) by emphasizing that the real question is whether the particular accused acted reasonably in the specific circumstances that faced him or her at the time of the assault upon him or her. For example, the Supreme Court of Canada has emphasized the need to ensure that women who are the victims of domestic violence are judged by the standards of "reasonable women" who face the same circumstances of ongoing abuse and not by the standards of "reasonable men" brawling in a bar. In the *Lavallee* case (1990), the accused had shot her abusive male partner (Rust) in the back of the head. Rust was leaving Lavallee's room just after he had physically assaulted her and threatened her with death. At Lavallee's trial for murder, a psychiatrist gave expert testimony concerning the so-called battered wife syndrome in order to help the members of the jury to determine whether the accused woman's beliefs and actions were reasonable in light of her experience of chronic abuse at the hands of her partner. The psychiatrist asserted that Lavallee "had been terrorized by Rust to the point of feeling trapped, vulnerable, worthless and unable to escape the relationship despite the violence." This witness concluded that Lavallee's shooting of Rust should be viewed as "a final desperate act by a woman who sincerely believed that she would be killed that night." The jury acquitted Lavallee. The Supreme Court of Canada later upheld the acquittal and ruled that the trial judge had acted appropriately in permitting an expert witness to testify about the "battered woman syndrome" as a means of assisting the members of the jury to assess the reasonableness of Lavallee's beliefs and actions.

In a later case, *Malott* (1998), the Supreme Court of Canada suggested that this type of evidence should be presented to the jury in order to assist them in understanding at least four separate issues: (i) why an abused woman might remain in an abusive relationship; (ii) the nature and extent of the violence that may exist in an abusive relationship; (iii) the woman's ability to perceive when her partner was dangerous; and (iv) whether she believed on reasonable grounds that she could not otherwise preserve herself from death or grievous bodily harm. Furthermore, the Supreme Court has held that there is no requirement in section 34(2) that the accused person must actually be under attack or even that the accused must be in imminent danger of such an assault. Indeed, in the *Pétel*

FOCUS

BOX 3.4 The International Criminal Court

Crimes may be committed not only against the laws of individual states, such as Canada, but also against international law. Indeed, serious crimes, such as genocide, crimes against humanity (including all forms of sexual violence and exploitation involving significant numbers of victims), and war crimes, may be prosecuted under the provisions of public international law. On March 11, 2003, the International Criminal Court (I.C.C.) was officially opened at The Hague, in the Netherlands. This Court is the first permanent tribunal to try cases under international criminal, and it has the power to order that reparations be paid to the victims of crimes that fall within its jurisdiction. Eighteen judges have been sworn in and will constitute the Judges' Chamber of the I.C.C. A Canadian, Philippe Kirsch, has been elected the first president of the Court.

The establishment of the I.C.C. was rendered possible when 60 nations ratified the Rome Statute, a treaty that was signed at the Rome Diplomatic Conference in 1998. To date, 104 countries, including Canada, have ratified the Rome Statute. The I.C.C. is a "court of last resort"; it will try cases involving grave crimes only when the national courts are unable or unwilling to do so themselves. For example, a country's court system may have collapsed following an armed conflict or a state may refuse to prosecute an individual who has the power or influence to escape justice within his or her own country. Canada played a major role in implementing the Rome Statute. However, the United States has refused to become a party to the Rome Statute and has indicated that it will not permit the Court to try an American citizen for a crime under international law. Similarly, Indonesia, China, and Russia have declined to submit to the jurisdiction of the I.C.C.

On June 26, 2007, the president of the Court stated that "today, the ICC is a fully-functioning judicial institution focused on its core activities of investigating and conducting trials of individuals accused of genocide, crimes against humanity or war crimes." Since 2004, the prosecutor has opened four investigations into "alleged grave crimes" in Uganda, the Democratic Republic of the Congo, Sudan (Darfur), and the Central African Republic. To date, the judges have issued eight arrest warrants in three different cases and the first trial before the I.C.C. was scheduled to take place later in 2007.

Do you think that there is a real need for a permanent international criminal court? In what circumstances, should an individual be brought before the I.C.C? Why has the United States insisted on remaining a non-party to the Rome Statute? Can the I.C.C. be truly effective when such major states as China, Indonesia, Russia, and the United States have not become parties to the Rome Statute? Can the I.C.C. achieve any tangible benefits for the victims of genocide, crimes against humanity, or war crimes? How should the I.C.C. use the funds that have been set aside for victims?

See Judge Philippe Kirsch. (2007). "ICC Marks Five Years since Entry into Force of Rome Statute." Online at: http://www.icc-cpi.int/library/organs/presidency/PK_20070627_en.pdf. For further information, see the website of the International Criminal Court: http://www.icc-cpi.int/home.html.

case (1994), the Supreme Court held that imminence is "only one of the factors which the jury should weigh in determining whether the accused had a reasonable apprehension of danger and a reasonable belief that she could not extricate herself otherwise than by killing the attacker." This means that a woman who is in acute fear for her life does not have to wait until she is actually being attacked or until such an assault is imminent, before she uses lethal force in self-defence. In *McConnell* (1996), the Supreme Court of Canada extended this notion to an entirely different context—namely, the highly charged atmosphere of a penitentiary. In this case, the Court indicated that it is possible to draw an analogy between the battered wife syndrome and the so-called prison environment syndrome. It was suggested by an expert witness, at the trial of two inmates for the murder of another prisoner, that—in an environment in which inmates had to "kill or be killed"—it might be reasonable for an inmate to believe that he or she was being assaulted (because of credible threats) even though the threatened violence was not imminent. Using section 34(2), it was argued that attacking another inmate from behind might constitute a reasonable action, from the point of view of the accused, if he believed that there was no other way of protecting himself from death or grievous bodily harm. It has certainly been suggested that the *McConnell* case has, perhaps, expanded self-defence far beyond the boundaries of the original defence that was envisaged by the legislators when Parliament first enacted section 34(2) of the Criminal Code. Does this case suggest that the "law of the jungle" might operate in certain penitentiaries?

While this concludes our brief survey of Canadian criminal law, it is important to recognize that one of the most significant developments in recent years has been the evolution of a body of international criminal law. The establishment in 2003 of the permanent International Criminal Court in The Hague, the Netherlands, heralds an age in which certain horrendous crimes may be tried outside of the courts and tribunals of individual nation-states (see Box 3.4). Significantly, Canada has been one of the foremost supporters and promoters of the International Criminal Court. The recent experience of "ethnic cleansing" in parts of the former Yugoslavia and of genocide in Rwanda suggests that the International Criminal Court is an institution that is sorely needed in the modern age.

Summary

- A crime consists of a prohibition against certain conduct and a penal sanction (such as imprisonment or a fine).
- The sources of criminal law are (i) legislation and (ii) judicial decisions.
- Under the terms of the Canadian Constitution, the Parliament of Canada has the exclusive authority to enact "criminal law and the procedures relating to criminal matters."
- There is a significant difference between "true crimes" that arise under the Criminal Code and regulatory offences that arise under regulatory legislation enacted both by the various provinces and territories and by the Parliament of Canada.
- The enactment of the Canadian Charter of Rights and Freedoms has given judges the power to invalidate criminal law that unjustifiably infringes on an accused person's Charter rights.
- Each criminal offence can be analyzed in terms of its *actus reus* and *mens rea* elements.
- The *actus reus* generally consists of three components: conduct, circumstances, and consequences.

- *Mens rea* may be subjective or objective.
- Subjective *mens rea* may consist of intention and knowledge; recklessness; or wilful blindness.
- Objective *mens rea* is based on the requirement that there be a marked departure from the standard expected of the reasonable person acting prudently.
- An individual may become a party to a criminal offence in a number of different ways: actually committing an offence; aiding and/or abetting an offence; becoming a party to an offence by way of common intention; and counselling an offence that is committed.
- There are three inchoate offences that permit the police to intervene before a particular crime is committed: counselling an offence that is not committed; criminal attempt; and conspiracy.
- A successful defence of not criminally responsible on account of mental disorder (NCRMD) is not an acquittal; instead, it is a finding that the accused person has committed the act or omission in question but may not be held criminally responsible on account of mental disorder.
- The most important defences to a criminal charge include mistake of fact; intoxication; necessity; duress; provocation; and self-defence.

QUESTIONS FOR CRITICAL THINKING

1. Why does Canadian criminal law place such importance on the requirement that the Crown prove the relevant *mens rea* elements of a criminal offence? Would it not make more sense for the state to intervene and deal with offenders solely on the basis of the fact that they have committed the *actus reus* of an offence (a harmful or potentially harmful act or omission)?
2. Pluto is driving his car down a steep hill in a large Canadian city. He discovers that his brakes are not functioning properly and the vehicle starts to gain speed. In the near distance, Pluto notices that there is a group of schoolchildren who are crossing the road. Worried that he may collide with these children, Pluto decides to steer his speeding car onto the sidewalk. Pluto is aware that there is an elderly man on the sidewalk but he is confident that he can avoid hitting him. Tragically, at that moment, Pluto suffers a fainting spell and, while he is unconscious, his car not only strikes and kills the man on the sidewalk but also returns to the road and injures five of the schoolchildren who are on the clearly marked crossing. There is some evidence that Pluto had experienced brief fainting spells before but he did not consider them to be serious. After the accident, it is discovered that Pluto probably suffers from a mild epileptic condition. Is Pluto guilty of dangerous driving causing death and dangerous driving causing bodily harm?
3. Should the criminal law be used as a preventative tool? Should the police be able to intervene and bring individuals to the criminal courts before those individuals have actually committed the crime(s) that they are planning to carry out? Do the existing inchoate offences in the Criminal Code strike

an acceptable balance between the demands of public security and the civil rights of accused persons?

4. It has been suggested that the defence of provocation should be abolished because it is frequently raised in the context of family violence [see, for example, the *Stone* case (1999) in this chapter]. Do you think that there is any place for a defence of provocation in a modern criminal code
5. Do you think self-induced intoxication should ever be a defence to a crime of violence? What are the arguments for and against permitting defendants to raise a defence of intoxication? For example, is it fair that an intoxicated person may kill someone and be sentenced to two years' imprisonment while a sober person who deliberately kills another will be convicted of first- or second-degree murder and be sentenced automatically to life imprisonment?
6. Daphne has lived with Apollo for 10 years, during which he has, on various occasions, subjected her to physical assaults, some of which have inflicted serious injuries (such as extensive bruising to the body, a broken nose, and concussion). One night, Daphne returns home late from an evening meeting and Apollo becomes furious with her. He yells that he is "going to fix her once and for all." However, Apollo is so drunk that he passes out on the couch. Daphne goes to the kitchen and picks up a sharp knife. She then returns to the room where Apollo is sleeping and stabs him to death. Would Daphne be able to raise a successful plea of self-defence if she were charged with murder or manslaughter?

NET WORK

Increasingly, basic legal research is being conducted online. The federal government and the governments of the various provinces and territories in Canada operate websites that offer swift access via the Internet to the full text of legislation and the decisions of the courts. In addition, a number of commercial electronic database services, such as Quicklaw, provide information concerning legislation, cases, and legal literature (journal articles and textbooks). You should be able to gain access to Quicklaw through your university or college. If you have access to Quicklaw, find Canadian cases in which the courts have discussed the defence of duress.

You can start to explore the powerful electronic tools that are available for research into Canadian criminal law by visiting the website of the Canadian Legal Information Institute. This website provides easy access to federal and provincial/territorial legislation and court decisions. In addition, the website provides access to the decisions of various federal and provincial/territorial boards and tribunals (such as the Canadian Human Rights Tribunal and the Human Rights Tribunal of Ontario) and it also contains links to various external websites that may be of particular value to students [for example, the debates of the House of Commons (Hansard) or the debates of the B.C. Legislative Assembly (Hansard)]. The website address for the Canadian legal Information Institute is **http://canlii.org/**. Using this website, find the report of the following case: *Truscott (Re),* 2007 ONCA 575, decided by the Ontario Court of Appeal on August 28, 2007.

Another general website that provides you with access to legislation and case law is the Access to Justice Network. It is of particular value as a means of searching federal and provincial legislation. In addition, it contains up-to-date news concerning law and justice issues and provides links to external websites that are of great value to researchers in the fields of criminal law and criminal justice. Log on to **acjnet.org/nahome/default.aspx**.

Another particularly useful website is operated by the Department of Justice Canada. This site provides not only detailed information about the activities of the Department of Justice and federal developments concerning criminal law but also access to all federal legislation and regulations. The website address for the Department of Justice Canada is **www.canada.justice.gc.ca.** In order to locate legislation and regulations, click onto "The Laws Site" on the home page.

Using the Department of Justice or the Access to Justice network websites, see what information is available concerning the Anti-Terrorism Act, which came into effect in December 2001.

Find the relevant website for the courts in your own province or territory (for example, in Ontario, log on to **www.ontariocourts.on.ca/english.htm**, or, in British Columbia, log on to **www.courts.gov.bc.ca**). It may be useful to know that both the Ontario and B.C. websites provide links to all of the other provincial and territorial court websites in Canada. As an exercise, find out if, during the period 2000 to 2007, your own provincial or territorial court of appeal decided any cases concerning the offence of fraud (section 380 of the Criminal Code).

KEY TERMS

actus reus; pg. 76
Charter; pg. 73
common law; pg. 73
conspiracy; pg. 88
counselling; pg. 85
crime; pg. 68
criminal attempt; pg. 86
criminal law; pg. 70
criminal procedure; pg. 71
duress; pg. 92
inchoate crime; pg. 85
intoxication; pg. 91
mens rea; pg. 78
mistake of fact; pg. 90
necessity; pg. 92
not criminally responsible on account of mental disorder (NCRMD); pg. 89
objective *mens rea*; pg. 79
party to a crime; pg. 84
provocation; pg. 94
regulatory offence; pg. 72
self-defence; pg. 94
subjective *mens rea*; pg. 79
"true crime"; pg. 72

SUGGESTED READING

The following texts provide an introduction to Canadian criminal law:

Roach, Kent. (2004). *Criminal Law.* (3rd ed.). Toronto: Irwin Law.

Verdun-Jones, Simon. (2007). *Criminal Law in Canada: Cases, Questions and the Code.* (4th ed.). Toronto: Thomson-Nelson.

Verdun-Jones, Simon, and David MacAlister. (2006). *Introduction to Criminal and Civil Law.* Toronto: Thomson-Nelson.

The following text is the leading authority on Canadian criminal law and is frequently cited by the courts:

Stuart, Don. (2007). *Canadian Criminal Law: A Treatise.* (5th ed.). Toronto: Thomson-Carswell.

The following books offer a selection of various cases, source materials, and commentaries in the field of Canadian criminal law:

Abell, Jennie, and Elizabeth Sheehy. (2002). *Criminal Law & Procedure: Cases, Context, Critique.* (3rd ed.). Concord, Ontario: Captus Press.

Stuart, Don, Ron Delisle, and Steve Coughlan. (2006). *Learning Canadian Criminal Law.* (10th ed.). Toronto: Carswell.

The following book provides an edited collection of leading Canadian criminal law cases, which were decided by the Supreme Court of Canada:

Verdun-Jones, Simon. (2007). *Canadian Criminal Cases: Selected Highlights.* (2nd ed.). Toronto: Thomson-Nelson.

The following Canadian texts cover issues that are closely related to criminal law:

Delisle, Ron, Don Stuart, and Justice Gary T. Trotter. (2005). *Learning Canadian Criminal Procedure.* (8th ed.). Toronto: Carswell.

Manson, Allan. (2001). *The Law of Sentencing.* Toronto: Irwin Law.

Quigley, Tim. (2005). *Procedure in Canadian Criminal Law.* (2nd ed.). Toronto: Carswell.

Salhany, Roger. (2002). *The Practical Guide to Evidence in Criminal Cases.* (6th ed.). Toronto: Carswell.

Stuart, Don. (2005). *Charter Justice in Canadian Criminal Law.* (4th ed.). Toronto: Carswell.

CASES CITED

Case of Pretty v. The United Kingdom, European Court of Human Rights, (Application no. 2346/02), Final judgment, 29 July 2002, available online at http://cmiskp.echr.coe.int/tkp197/view.asp?action=html&documentId=698325&portal=hbkm&source=externalbydocnumber&table=F69A27FD8FB86142BF01C1166DEA398649.

Charkaoui v. Canada, [2007] 1 S.C.R. 350. Available online at http://www.canlii.org/en/ca/scc/doc/2007/2007scc9/2007scc9.html.

Nancy B. v. Hôtel-Dieu de Québec (1992), 69 C.C.C. (3d) 450 (Quebec Sup. Ct.), available online through Quicklaw, [1992] Q.J. No.1.

R. v. Chaulk, [1990] 3 S.C.R. 1303. Available online at http://canlii.org/en/ca/scc/doc/1990/1990canlii34/1990canlii34.html.

R. v. Creighton, [1993] 3 S.C.R. 3. Available online at http://canlii.org/en/ca/scc/doc/1993/1993canlii61/1993canlii61.html.

R. v. Daviault, [1994] 3 S.C.R. 63. Available online at http://canlii.org/en/ca/scc/doc/1994/1994canlii61/1994canlii61.html.

R. v. Hamilton, [2005] 2 S.C.R. 432. Available online at http://www.canlii.org/en/ca/scc/doc/2005/2005scc47/2005scc47.html.

R. v. Hibbert, [1995] 2 S.C.R. 973. Available online at http://canlii.org/en/ca/scc/doc/1995/1995canlii110/1995canlii110.html.

R. v. Hydro-Quebec, [1997] 3 S.C.R. 213. Available online at http://canlii.org/en/ca/scc/doc/1997/1997canlii318/1997canlii318.html.

R. v. Lavallee, [1990] 1 S.C.R. 852. Available online at http://canlii.org/en/ca/scc/doc/1990/1990canlii95/1990canlii95.html.

R. v. Malmo-Levine; R. v. Caine, [2003] 3 S.C.R. 571. Available online at http://www.canlii.org/en/ca/scc/doc/2003/2003scc74/2003scc74.html.

R. v. Malott, [1998] 1 S.C.R. 123. Available online at http://canlii.org/en/ca/scc/doc/1998/1998canlii845/1998canlii845.html.

R. v. Martineau, [1990] 2 S.C.R. 633. Available online at http://canlii.org/en/ca/scc/doc/1990/1990canlii80/1990canlii80.html.

R. v. McConnell, [1996] 1 S.C.R. 1075. Available online at http://canlii.org/en/ca/scc/doc/1996/1996canlii189/1996canlii189.html.

R. v. Molodowic, [2000] 1 S.C.R. 420. Available online at http://canlii.org/en/ca/scc/doc/2000/2000scc16/2000scc16.html.

R. v. Morgentaler, Smolig and Scott, [1988] 1 S.C.R. 30. Available online at http://canlii.org/en/ca/scc/doc/1988/1988canlii90/1988canlii90.html.

R. v. Olan, Hudson and Hartnett, [1978] 2 S.C.R. 1175. Available online at http://canlii.org/en/ca/scc/doc/1978/1978canlii9/1978canlii9.html.

R. v. Perka, [1984] 2 S.C.R. 232. Available online at http://canlii.org/en/ca/scc/doc/1984/1984canlii23/1984canlii23.html.

R. v. Petel, [1994] 1 S.C.R. 3. Available online at http://canlii.org/en/ca/scc/doc/1994/1994canlii133/1994canlii133.html.

R. v. Ruzic, [2001] 1 S.C.R. 687. Available online at http://canlii.org/en/ca/scc/doc/1994/1994canlii133/1994canlii133.html.

R. Sault Ste. Marie (City of), [1978] 2 S.C.R. 1299. Available online through http://canlii.org/en/ca/scc/doc/1978/1978canlii11/1978canlii11.html.

R. v. Sharpe, [2001] 1 S.C.R. 45. Available online at http://canlii.org/en/ca/scc/doc/2001/2001scc2/2001scc2.html.

R. v. Stone, [1999] 2 S.C.R. 290. Available online at http://canlii.org/en/ca/scc/doc/1999/1999canlii688/1999canlii688.html.

R. v. Thatcher, [1987] 1 S.C.R. 652. Available online at http://canlii.org/en/ca/scc/doc/1987/1987canlii53/1987canlii53.html.

R. v. Theroux, [1993] 2 S.C.R. 5. Available online at http://canlii.org/en/ca/scc/doc/1993/1993canlii134/1993canlii134.html.

R. v. Thibert, [1996] 1 S.C.R. 37. Available online at http://canlii.org/en/ca/scc/doc/1993/1993canlii134/1993canlii134.html.

R. v. Wholesale Travel Group Inc., [1991] 3 S.C.R. 154. Available online at http://canlii.org/en/ca/scc/doc/1991/1991canlii39/1991canlii39.html.

Rodriguez v. British Columbia (Attorney General), [1993] 3 S.C.R. 519. Available online at http://canlii.org/en/ca/scc/doc/1993/1993canlii75/1993canlii75.html.

Wakeford v. Canada (Attorney General), [2001] O.J. No. 390 (Ont. S.C.J.); appeal dismissed, [2001] O.J. No. 4921 (C.A.); leave to appeal dismissed, [2002] S.C.C.A. No. 72. Available online through Quicklaw.

Winko v. British Columbia (Forensic Psychiatric Institute), [1999] 2 S.C.R. 625. Available online at http://canlii.org/en/ca/scc/doc/1999/1999canlii694/1999canlii694.html.

Counting Crime

4

John Evans

PRESIDENT, MANAGEMENT AND POLICY INTERNATIONAL, INC.

Alexander Himelfarb

FOREIGN AFFAIRS AND INTERNATIONAL TRADE, CANADA

This chapter is about statistics on crime and criminal justice. Those who have tried to understand crime have, over the past century, relied heavily on statistical descriptions of criminal behaviour, criminals, and the criminal justice response. What we know about crime, then, depends on the quality, coverage, reliability, and validity of our measures of crime.

This chapter describes how social scientists count crime. After discussing the problems of the validity and reliability of our measures of crime, we introduce the long-standing debate over whether crime statistics reflect accurately the amount of crime in Canada or whether they merely reflect the activities of the criminal justice system. To help you to understand the strengths and weaknesses of Canadian crime statistics, we describe how the administrative records of the police, courts, and prisons are turned into measures describing the amount of crime and the characteristics of offenders and victims. This process involves developing clear procedures concerning units of count, levels of data aggregation, definitions, data elements, and counting procedures. Particular attention will be paid to the most commonly used measure of crime: the Uniform Crime Report system (UCR). The UCR is based on crimes reported to the police across the country. Finally, the chapter describes victimization surveys and self-report studies. These provide data that are complementary to those produced by the UCR.

Learning Objectives

After reading this chapter, you should be able to

- Describe how the administrative records collected in the criminal justice system are turned into statistics about crime and the characteristics of offenders and victims.
- Understand the problems of the reliability and validity of our measures of crime and offenders.
- Understand the system that produces Canadian crime and criminal justice statistics.
- Describe the trends in Canadian crime rates over the past four decades.
- Describe the strengths and weaknesses of victimization and self-reported criminality surveys and understand how these two methods enhance our understanding of the problem of crime in Canada.

methodology
Methodology refers to the study or critique of methods. There are many philosophical issues about the use of a particular method or about positivism or measurement itself.

reliability
Identifies one of the standards (another being validity) against which the tools used to measure concepts are judged. Reliability refers to consistency of results over time. If a bathroom scale is used to measure the concept of weight, one must ask, is this tool (the bathroom scale) reliable? Does it provide consistent results? Notice that the bathroom scale or any other measure may be reliable and yet be inaccurate.

validity
The extent to which a tool or instrument (questionnaire, experiment) actually measures the concept the researcher claims to be interested in and not something else. For example, measuring people's feet to learn about the concept of intelligence, on the surface at least, does not seem valid.

crime rate
When studying crime, if a researcher wishes to compare the amount of crime over time or between communities of different sizes, it is not enough to just do a gross count of the amount of crime. To get around the problems involved with this, criminologists calculate crime rates (or rates of incarceration, conviction, or recidivism). This is done by dividing the amount of crime by the population size and multiplying by 100 000. This produces the standard rate per 100 000, but occasionally it is useful to calculate a rate per million or some other figure when looking at less frequently occurring offences.

Controversies over Counting Crime

The first concern of those who sought to measure crime was coverage—how can one obtain data about the amount and nature of crime in a society? As the official sources of statistics have increased, and as creative **methodologies** for data collection have advanced, the questions of **reliability** and **validity** have become the most pressing. In simple terms, are the methods and techniques involved in gathering statistics strong enough that anyone following the procedures would produce the same counts (reliability)? And do the statistics collected count what they purport to count (validity)?

Imagine a situation in which you wished to test a theory of crime causation. For example, what aspects of communities create pressures to greater criminality? Further, let us say that your theory predicts higher **crime rates** in big cities than in small towns. You are then going to need statistical data on the amount of crime in these two types of settings. How do you get these counts? You could consult police statistics. Police gather vast amounts of information on suspects, incidents, arrests, and charges. These are the data often used by criminologists to test their ideas. However, there have always been problems with police statistics. When police officers are dispatched to a call, each officer must use his or her own judgment to decide whether a crime has been committed or whether the call is unfounded. If the officer determines that there has been an offence, a report will be filled out by the officer and processed by police department staff. Most police departments then send the data from each incident to the Canadian Centre for Justice Statistics (CCJS), which is a division of Statistics Canada. Police are supposed to follow a uniform set of rules (the Uniform Crime Reporting Rules) in recording criminal incidents or calls for service. Yet it has been discovered that different police departments often use different rules for recording their information. In fact, individual police officers exercise a good deal of discretion in what they decide to record and how they record it. There may be doubts, then, about the reliability of the statistics derived from police records. However, there is perhaps an even more fundamental problem. Are suspects criminals? Are those arrested and charged criminals? Are all incidents that are recorded actual crimes, and are these incidents a complete count of crimes? Do the data provide a valid count of crime?

A particular difficulty arises in crime counts because as the reliability of a statistical measure increases, its validity as a count of crime frequently decreases. Thus, while the police certainly never detect or become aware of all crimes and despite enormous problems of reliability, their counts of crime are likely to be a far more valid reflection of the amount of criminal behaviour than are counts of convictions or counts of prisoners. The criminal justice system operates as a funnel: Only some fraction of incidents result in a police record of a criminal incident; only a portion of recorded incidents result in suspects identified; only a portion of suspects are arrested or charged; only a portion of charges result in conviction; and only a portion of convictions result in incarceration (see Figure 4.1). The farther you go into the system, the more confident you can be that the count is accurate and reliable and that it is a decreasingly valid representation of all criminal behaviour. Also, there are built-in biases

FIGURE 4.1 The Crime Funnel: Break-and-Enter Offences Processed through the Canadian Criminal Justice System, 2004

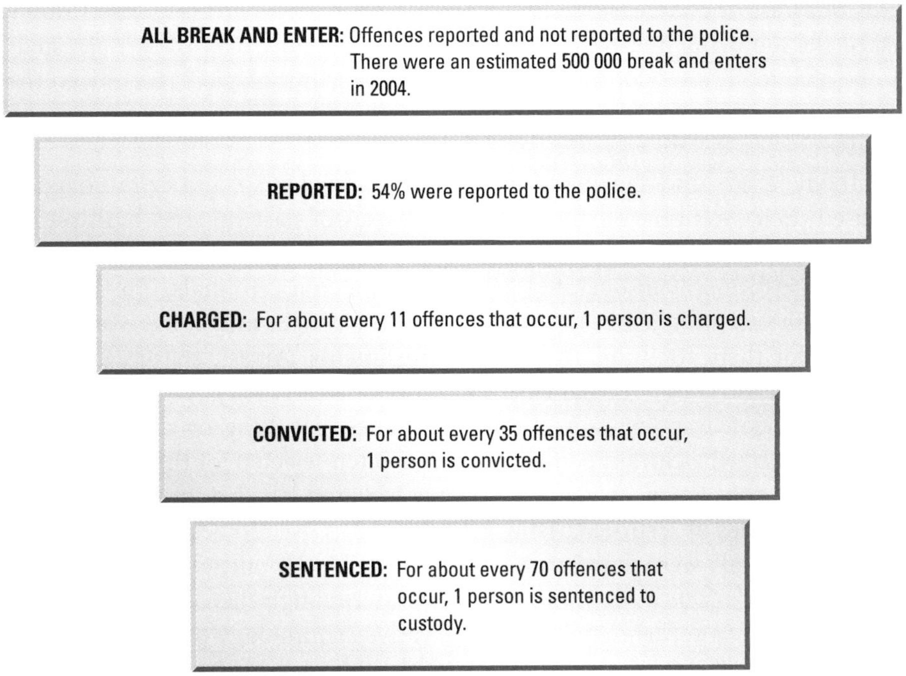

ALL BREAK AND ENTER: Offences reported and not reported to the police. There were an estimated 500 000 break and enters in 2004.
REPORTED: 54% were reported to the police.
CHARGED: For about every 11 offences that occur, 1 person is charged.
CONVICTED: For about every 35 offences that occur, 1 person is convicted.
SENTENCED: For about every 70 offences that occur, 1 person is sentenced to custody.

Note: This diagram illustrates the processing of break-and-enter offences through various stages in the criminal justice system. For cautions about these data, see Box 4.3, Summary and Cautions: Using Victimization Survey Data and Data from the UCR and the Court Surveys.

Sources: Statistics Canada, "Criminal Victimization in Canada, 2004," by Maire Gannon and Karen Mihorean. Catalogue no. 85-002-XPE, Vol. 25, no. 7. Uniform Crime Reporting Survey, 2004. The Court data are from custom data runs done by Statistics Canada.

in that some crimes (and some criminals) are more likely than others to be reported and to result in arrest, charge, conviction, and a sentence to incarceration. For example, murderers are more likely to be arrested and to go to jail than are corporate criminals or shoplifters. The farther you go into the system, the more obvious it becomes that you are counting something about how the system itself operates; you are counting official decisions about crime and criminals. To put this another way, statistical descriptions of the prison **population** may provide valid indicators of one way that a society and its criminal justice system respond to crime. These descriptions, however, do not provide a valid measure of the amount and the nature of crime.

How have criminologists handled these problems? For a long time, they acknowledged the problems and then, when they needed data, they pretended the problems away. Kaplan's "law of the hammer" holds that if you give a small child a hammer, he or she discovers that everything needs pounding. Similarly, social scientists have often been accused of letting their methods, or statistics that were most readily available, dictate their theories. Social scientists will often find out what they are able to discover most easily and build their theories around this limited information. Many of the early theories of criminology discussed elsewhere in this text were built upon a rather uncritical acceptance of

population
The term population refers to all members of a given class or set. For example, adult Canadians, teenagers, Canadian inmates, or criminal offenders can each be thought of as populations. Populations are difficult to study because we cannot find all the members (heroin addicts) or because there are too many in the population to address all of them. Social scientists avoid this problem by gathering a sample from the population and then generalizing from the sample to the population.

official sources of statistics. Many early criminologists used prisoners to study the differences between criminals and non-criminals. Some used police records of arrest or charge; some used court records. These criminologists rarely asked the following questions: Are all criminals equally likely to get arrested? To be charged? To be put in prison? Even when criminologists recognized the limits of the available information, they used these unreliable and often invalid measures because this was all they had.

In the 1960s and the 1970s, a number of sociologists and criminologists focused their attention on the systematic biases of past theories built on official records. New theories suggested that official records showed us how the criminal justice system operated to create crime and criminals. The statistics revealed information about the police, about the courts, and about whom they selected for their attention and worst punishments. Arrest, charge, and conviction were parts of a formal labelling process, a ceremony of degradation in which a person was formally stigmatized. These labelling or social reaction theories asked why certain people were more often selected for this process and studied the consequences for these people of being labelled and stigmatized. The same bodies of "crime statistics" that had been used to describe the behaviour of criminals were now being used to describe the official agents of social control. More recently, criminologists are increasingly becoming polarized. Many seem to be returning to the conservative criminology of the past, to the acceptance of official records as a reasonable indicator of crime, and focusing on explaining crime for the purpose of controlling it. Others, influenced by some variant of "critical" criminology, see crime statistics as simply part of the government's control mechanism, a way of characterizing the crime problem, a means of self-justification, and a reflection of more fundamental structural inequalities.

theory

All sciences use theory as a tool to explain. It is useful to think of theory as a conceptual model of some aspect of life. We may have a theory of mate selection, of the emergence of capitalist societies, of criminal behaviour, or of the content of dreams. In each case, the theory consists of a set of concepts and their nominal definition or assertions about the relationships between these concepts, assumptions, and knowledge claims.

ideology

A linked set of ideas and beliefs that act to uphold and justify an existing or desired situation in society. Ideologies offer explanations and justifications of features of society such as the distribution of wealth, status, and power.

Are crime statistics whatever one makes of them? Are statistics simply a resource to tell lies or support one's own favoured position? Yes, sometimes. But they need not be. **Theories** about crime and facts about crime are built simultaneously, are mutually dependent, and shape one another. Theory without facts is indistinguishable from **ideology**; facts without theory are often implicit ideology; statistical facts without theory are numerology, often bent to ideological ends. Theorists and policy-makers have often been guilty of using statistics to their own ideological ends, using crime counts to show that we are going through a crime wave, or using the same counts to show how we are living through a wave of repression. We live in an age when numerical values have a certain magic and a power to convince us, to make arguments seem true. Statistics can be dangerous if we do not have the tools to consider them critically.

For example, imagine that you read, in some credible source, that violence in Canadian society has risen by 100 percent over the past decade. Before you set off to explain this "fact," before you turn your home into a fortress, you should ask, just what is being counted as violence? Crimes? Some crimes? Political dissent? Violence by the state? Domestic violence? What theory or ideological assumptions have guided this choice of "fact"? And how good are the facts? How well and consistently have they been counted? Are they reliable and valid?

What have social scientists and policy-makers done about the lack of good crime information? Forty years ago, the American sociologist Ned Polsky

(1967) argued that our understanding of crime would never be significantly advanced if we relied on statistical data. He was concerned that sociologists and criminologists relied too heavily on remote sources of information. They remained too distant from the criminals they wished to understand. He advocated field research through which social scientists live among, and learn from, the criminals themselves. Not surprisingly, few have followed Polsky's lead. Rather, most have worked to improve the quality of statistics based on official sources, to specify the valid uses of these statistics, and to develop innovative methodologies to complement official data and to fill gaps. Despite the problems, criminological theory and criminal justice policy remain heavily dependent on statistics about crime and the criminal justice system. This is not to say that there are not many other ways to advance our understanding of crime. This, however, is not a methods chapter. Qualitative techniques and other methods of studying crime should be examined elsewhere.

One might distinguish three broad types of criminal justice statistics: statistics about crime and criminals, statistics about the criminal justice system and its response to crime, and statistics about perceptions of crime and criminal justice. Theory and policy require statistics about the decisions of those who break the law, about the decisions of those who maintain it, and about what people think of all of this.

administrative record
Collection of information about individual cases, such as statistics concerning what is common among individual cases. An administrative record contains information that can be the basis of statistics, provided that clear procedures are developed for handling the data and generating statistical descriptions.

Statistics on the Criminal Justice System

The criminal justice system produces an enormous amount of raw data in the form of police reports and records, the recorded decisions of prosecutors and judges, the **administrative records** of prisons and penitentiaries, and the recorded decisions of parole boards and probation and parole services. From these administrative records the Canadian Centre for Justice Statistics (CCJS) has developed a sophisticated system of statistics on the criminal justice system.

levels of aggregation
This refers to how data are to be combined. Do we want city-level, provincial, or national data? Among other things, data aggregation requires common rules, allowing confidence in the reliability and validity of the measures used.

From Records to Statistics

Administrative records are not statistics. Records are concerned with individual cases and are intended primarily to help practitioners make decisions about these individual cases. Statistics are aggregated; they are concerned with what is common among individual cases. Statistics are meant to provide information about larger questions: planning and evaluation, policy and program development, and theory building and testing. While good records are the base, the conversion of records into statistics requires a number of conceptual decisions. The potential clients or users of the statistics must decide what it is they want to know and how they plan to use the information. Statistical systems should be built to address the enduring theoretical and policy concerns.

Specifically, the following issues must be addressed before records can be converted into statistics: unit of count, **levels of aggregation**, definitions, **data elements**, and **counting procedures**.

data element
What, specifically, is to be collected? Operational issues may require more detail than the statistical system does. Also, statistical needs may require that operational agencies collect data that they do not need (or do not think that they need) for operational purposes. In any statistical system, there must be detailed agreements on exactly what is to be collected.

counting procedure
In any statistical system, there must be consensus on how to count units and data elements. This is not as easy an issue as it appears.

(A) Unit of count—consensus about what it is that we are counting.

In the course of their everyday activities, the police, for example, may count many different things: suspects, offences, charges, or calls for service. Typically, they work with occurrences. An occurrence may involve several offenders, several victims, and several offences. The unit we wish to count in a statistical system will depend on whether we are trying to learn something about police workload or productivity, or whether we are seeking to learn something about crime or victims. Recently, for example, there has been a growing awareness among policy-makers and criminologists that victims have been an ignored unit of count, and we know little about their characteristics. Some units of count are specific to a particular sector. For example, the prison sector can count inmates; the court sector, convictions; and the police, suspects.

(B) Levels of aggregation—consensus about how to combine data.

A crucial decision is the level at which we want our statistics. For example, do we want to combine police records for a city? Do we want to combine statistics for an entire province? Or region? Or the nation? To the extent that we want to generalize our theories or develop or evaluate national policies, we are likely to want national statistics. But several criminologists have warned that the further you move from those who produce the data and the more you try to combine data from different sources, the more questionable is the result. They prefer the richer and more detailed information available from local police to the abstracted, less complete data available about national policing.

(C) Definitions—consensus about how to define what is being counted.

While the Criminal Code provides a common set of definitions for counting crime, there remains a good deal of discretion about when an incident of crime is truly an incident, or even what, for example, constitutes "inmate." If one wishes to count inmates, should one count those who are temporarily absent, or those on remand, or those in community correctional facilities, or those assigned to mental institutions? Common definitions are essential. This is not merely a technical issue. Depending on how the terms are defined, you can inflate or deflate the statistics; you can make it appear that crime is higher or lower, or that there are more or fewer prisoners.

(D) Data elements—consensus about what specific information should be collected.

While the police will need certain kinds of information to help them in their investigative activities, this information will be far more detailed than, and sometimes quite different from, what is needed as aggregated statistics. Similarly, the police in one jurisdiction may, for their own good reasons, maintain records quite different from those of other police departments. As understandable as this is, it is extremely difficult to build aggregated statistics out of different types of records that may be incompatible.

(E) Counting procedures—consensus on how to count units and elements.

If an offender goes on a break-and-enter spree and hits a half-dozen houses in an evening, how many offences should be counted—six or one? Or, if, during a break and enter, an offender is confronted by the home owner and assaults him or her, is this one or two offences? If one, which offence should be counted? If we agree that the most serious should be counted, how do we determine seriousness?

Canadian Criminal Justice Statistics

The questions or issues of unit of count, levels of aggregation, definitions, data elements, and counting procedures are at the base of much of the technical and critical literature on criminal justice statistics. Within Canada, attempts to answer these questions have traditionally been the responsibility of our national statistical agency, Statistics Canada. More recently, the federal and provincial governments have created a national institute, the **Canadian Centre for Justice Statistics (CCJS)**, a division of Statistics Canada, governed by a board of directors of senior officials responsible for justice.

Canadian Centre for Justice Statistics
A division of Statistics Canada, formed in 1981, with a mandate to collect national data on crime and justice.

A major difficulty confronting the centre is getting agreement on priorities such as whose needs should be met. Crime statistics are used by different people and for different purposes: Criminologists and researchers want to build and test theories; policy-makers and analysts want to identify problems and develop and test solutions; and administrators and program managers want to plan and run their operations and to monitor and evaluate their programs. Most important, statistics serve the public interest by keeping people informed and by providing some measure of public accountability. Good statistics are important, but they are important in different ways for different users.

At the present time, Canada has reasonably good national data on criminal justice inputs such as resources and expenditures. The data are now far better when it comes to outputs such as incidents, arrests, charges, convictions, and dispositions. The CCJS had developed and improved the Adult Criminal Court Survey, a census of courts in Canada. As of 2007, the survey collects data from jurisdictions that represent about 90 percent of the national criminal court caseload. Correctional statistics are the most accurate since we can give a fairly accurate count of the number of prisoners in Canada and provide some information on their social characteristics. Despite some difference in counting from province to province, Canada can produce a reasonably accurate description of its inmate population. This can be quite useful for projecting future inmate populations and for planning future facilities and services. When linked to other data, it can also be useful for developing correctional policy. For example, how much are we using incarceration and are we doing so in the most useful and appropriate ways?

"Justice and Crime" Statistics Canada
www41.statcan.ca/2007/2693/ceb2693_000_e.htm

Data on prisoners, however, do not tell us much about crime and criminal behaviours. They tell us about the criminal justice system. The confusion comes when people equate "criminal" with "prisoner." Some people are more likely to be caught; some people are more likely to be charged; some people are more likely to be convicted; and some people are more likely to be sentenced to prison or to a penitentiary. We know too much about how people get selected for incarceration to assume that prison statistics tell us very much about crime.

But what can such data show? Figure 4.2 shows the growth in number of those incarcerated in Canada between 1950 and 2005. In this period, the inmate population increased approximately 2.5 times. Obviously, these figures are important for administrative and planning purposes. But do these figures tell us something about growing crime in Canada? No. Do they tell us something about harsher or more punitive sentencing practices? No. In fact, if we look at

FIGURE 4.2 Average Inmate Count, 1950–2005

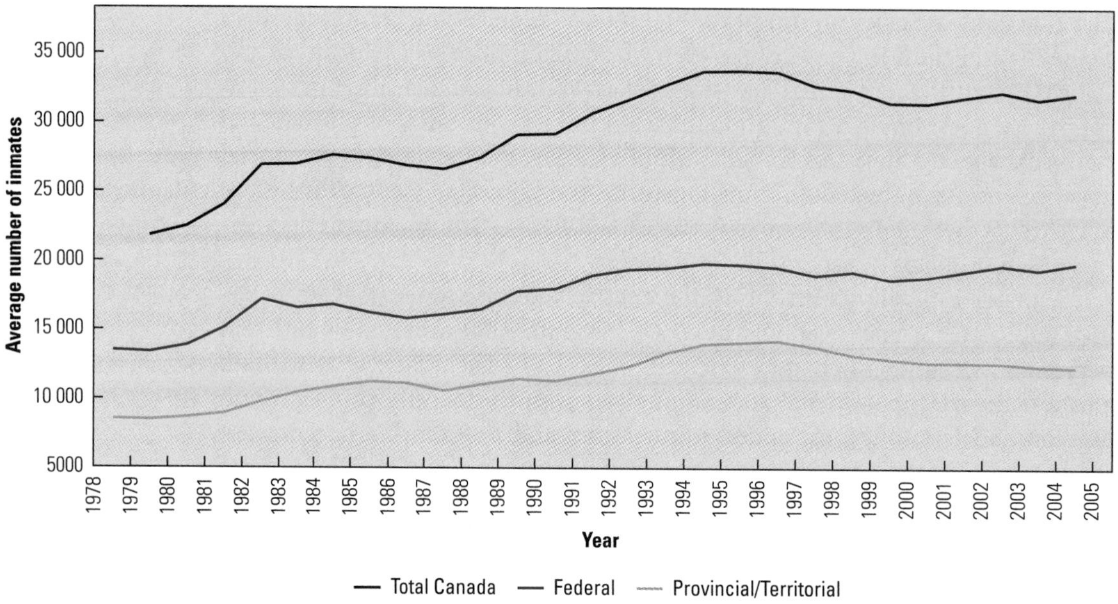

Source: Statistics Canada. Canadian Centre for Crime Statistics. Data derived from *Average Offender Counts for Canada, Fiscal Years 1950–51 to 1993–94, Corrections Key Indicator Report for Adults and Young Offenders*, 1996/97, Catalogue No. 85-222-XPE, *Adult Correctional Services in Canada 2000/01*, Catalogue No. 85-002-XIE, Vol. 22, No. 11 and Adult Correction Services Survey, CANSIM Table 251-0004.

the rate of incarceration (per 100 000 adult Canadians), we see that much of the growth in penitentiary population can be accounted for by the growth of the Canadian population (Figure 4.3). That is, the number of people incarcerated per 100 000 Canadians has not fluctuated markedly since 1950.

International comparisons are difficult and problematic, but they show Canada to be a nation that incarcerates at a much higher rate than most western European nations but at a much lower rate than the United States, where, in 2005, nearly 2.2 million people were incarcerated. This is an incarceration rate of 491 per 100 000 U. S. residents, up from 411 in 1995 (Bureau of Justice Statistics, 2006) and almost 4 times the Canadian rate of 129 per 100 000 in 2004–05. Some have argued that this is proof that Canada is too punitive, that too many people are being put behind bars and put there for too long. Others have argued that it simply means that Canada has more serious crime than many other nations. The debates flourish. Canadian statistics do not provide the answers; they indicate only where problems may exist.

How Much Crime?

It should come as no surprise that criminologists have had difficulty counting crime. By its very nature, crime is typically a secretive activity. When people commit crimes, they try to avoid becoming part of the count of criminals.

FIGURE 4.3 Incarceration Rate per 100 000 Adult Population, 1950–2005

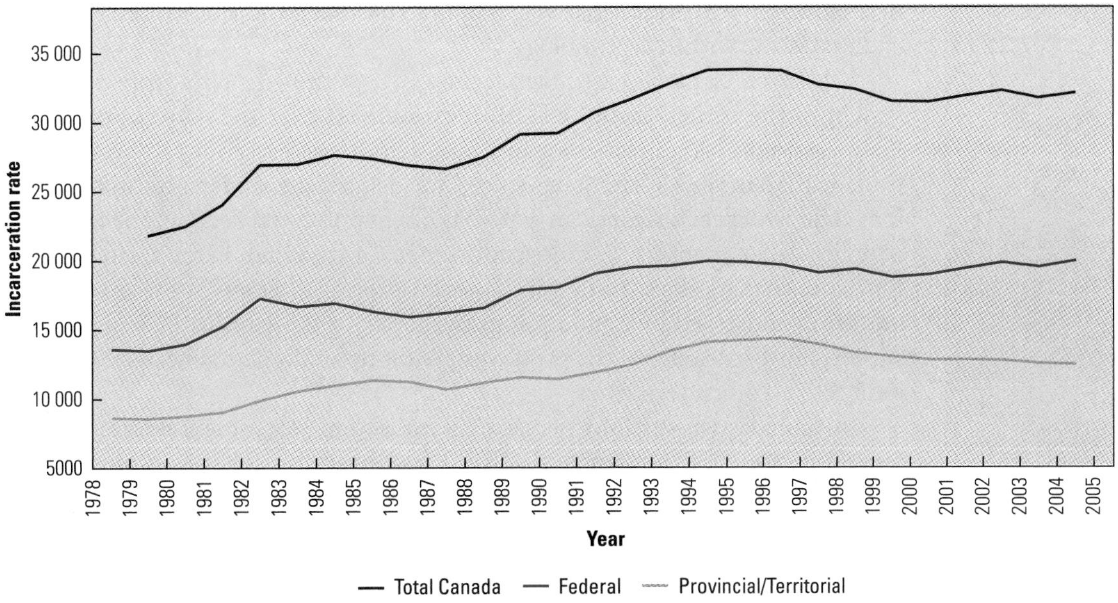

Source: Statistics Canada. Canadian Centre for Crime Statistics. Data derived from *Average Offender Counts for Canada, Fiscal Years 1950–51 to 1993–94, Corrections Key Indicators Report for Adults and Young Offenders*, 1996/97, Catalogue No. 85-222-XPE, *Adult Correctional Services in Canada 2000/01*, Catalogue No. 85-002-XIE, Vol. 22, No. 11, and Adult Correction Services Survey, CANSIM Table 251-0004.

(They do not want to become a statistic!) The "best" crime is one that no one knows about, and no criminal justice system will ever be able to ferret out all the crimes and criminals. Some crimes are harder to detect than others, and some criminals are harder to apprehend and convict. Criminologists have long recognized that the major problem of counting crime is the so-called **dark figure of crime** that remains unreported, unrecorded, and largely unknown. In response to the problem, criminologists have developed a variety of ways of counting crime, or at least to describe crime patterns and trends. They have tried to rationalize and improve official statistics, but they have also developed approaches that do not depend on official counts of crime. In the next section, we look at official records, victimization surveys, and self-report studies as sources of data about crime.

dark figure of crime
The amount of crime that is unreported or unknown. The total amount of crime in a community consists of crimes that are known or recorded and the dark figure of crime. Criminologists have used differing methods (such as victimization surveys) to try to decrease the amount of unknown or unrecorded crime.

Official Statistics: Canadian Uniform Crime Reports

Despite their problems, we rely heavily on official counts of the amount of crime. Until 45 years ago, we were dependent on local police records collected for police purposes and handled differently in each locale. For nearly five decades Canada has had in place a system called the Canadian **Uniform Crime**

Uniform Crime Reports (UCR)
Since 1962, Canada has had the Uniform Crime Reporting survey developed by Statistics Canada and the Canadian Association of Chiefs of Police. This system is designed to provide a measure of reliability for crime statistics through providing police agencies with a standardized set of procedures for collecting and reporting crime information.

Reports (UCR), designed to provide uniform, comparable, and national statistics. However, just what this system counts has been the subject of an almost endless debate within criminology.

While the Canadian Uniform Crime Report drew heavily from a similar system in the United States, it is an improvement over the American system. First, common crime classifications and definitions are easier to arrive at in Canada than in the United States since Canada operates under a common criminal code while each American state has a separate code. Second, the coverage of police departments is far more complete in Canada than in the United States. But both systems share some fundamental problems. Some of these problems are being addressed by ongoing improvements to the Uniform Crime Report survey; however, some of the problems are more fundamental because they are built into all official statistics.

In Canada two versions of the UCR collection instrument operate simultaneously: the UCR Aggregate (UCR1.0) Survey and the UCR2 Incident-based Survey, which is made up of two versions, UCR2.0 and UCR2.1. The UCR Aggregate Survey (UCR1.0) collects summary data for nearly 100 separate criminal offences and has been in place since 1962.*

The UCR2 Survey was developed in the mid-1980s as a method of collecting more detailed information on each incident, the victims, and the accused persons. This method of data collection, in which a separate statistical record is created for each criminal incident, is known as an incident-based reporting system. The first respondent reported incident-based data in 1988.

A revised version of the UCR2 survey, known as UCR2.1, was introduced in 1998. This survey introduced certain efficiencies for police services and lowered the response burden by eliminating or simplifying UCR2 variables (Statistics Canada, 2007).

Let us look more closely at the "seriousness rule." A number of studies (Nettler, 1974; Silverman and Teevan, 1975; Silverman, 1980; de Silva and Silverman, 1985) have documented some of the problems in the recording and scoring rules and how these rules are applied. Specifically, the studies have examined the implications of the "**seriousness rule**," which holds that only the most serious crime is scored in an incident involving several crimes. The concerns are threefold: First, this rule deflates the total crime count since less serious crimes are not counted separately; second, it inflates serious crimes as a proportion of the total; and third, the way in which seriousness is scored is problematic because not enough qualitative data about the crimes are recorded to use a sophisticated scale of seriousness. See Box 4.1 for a discussion of the main UCR categories and the most serious offence rule.

seriousness rule

If there are several crimes committed in one incident, only the most serious crime is counted. UCR1.0 uses the seriousness rule.

Concerns have also been expressed that the crime categories used are too general, allowing too many different kinds of acts to be recorded in the same

---

* The description of the UCR is based on the CCJS website: http://www.statcan.ca/cgi-bin/imdb/p2SV.pl?Function=getSurvey&SDDS=3302&lang=en&db=IMDB&dbg=f&adm=8&dis=2.

FOCUS

BOX 4.1 UCR Categories and the Most Serious Offence Rule

Violent incidents involve offences that deal with the application, or threat of application, of force to a person. These include homicide, attempted murder, various forms of sexual and non-sexual assault, robbery, and abduction. Traffic incidents that result in death or bodily harm are included under Criminal Code traffic incidents.

Property incidents involve unlawful acts with the intent of gaining property but do not involve the use or threat of violence against an individual. Theft, breaking and entering, fraud, and possession of stolen goods are examples of property crimes.

Other Criminal Code incidents involve the remaining Criminal Code offences that are not classified as violent or property incidents (excluding traffic). Examples are mischief, bail violations, disturbing the peace, arson, prostitution, and offensive weapons.

Total Criminal Code incidents is the tabulation of all violent, property, and other Criminal Code incidents reported for a given year.

Most Serious Offence

The UCR1.0 Survey classifies incidents according to the most serious offence (MSO) in the incident. In categorizing incidents, violent offences always take precedence over non-violent offences. Within violent and non-violent, offences are then sorted according to the maximum sentence under the Criminal Code. The UCR Survey scores violent incidents differently from other types of crime. For violent crimes, a separate incident is recorded for each victim (categorized according to the most serious offence against the victim). If, for example, one person assaults three people, then three incidents are recorded. If three people assault one person, only one incident is recorded. For non-violent crimes, one incident (categorized according to the most serious offence in the incident) is counted for every distinct or separate occurrence. Robbery is one exception to the above scoring rule. Robbery is categorized as a violent offence. Unlike all other violent offences, one occurrence of robbery is equal to one incident, regardless of the number of victims. The reason for this exception is that robbery can involve many people who could all be considered victims. In a bank robbery with 5 tellers and 20 customers present, 25 incidents of robbery would be counted if the normal scoring rule for violent incidents were applied. This would seriously overstate the occurrence of robbery. Thus, the total number of incidents recorded by the UCR Survey is not a census of all violations of the law that come to the attention of police. Rather, it is equal to the number of victims of violent (other than robbery) plus the number of separate occurrences of non-violent crimes (and robberies).

Actual Incidents

When a crime is reported to the police, the incident is recorded as a "reported" incident. Police then conduct a preliminary investigation to determine the validity of the report. Occasionally, crimes reported to the police prove to be unfounded. Unfounded incidents are subtracted from the number of reported incidents to produce the number of "actual incidents." Numbers and rates of crime are calculated on the basis of "actual incidents" categorized according to the most serious offence.

Source: Adapted from the Statistics Canada publication, "Canadian Crime Statistics," Catalogue No. 85-205-XIE, Canadian Centre for Justice Statistics, Ch. 6. Reprinted with permission of the Minister of Industry, 2003.

way. For example, thefts and attempted thefts are recorded under the same category.

Furthermore, as previously indicated, it is not always entirely clear just what it is we want to count. In Canada, the count of crimes includes violations of the Criminal Code, violations of other federal and provincial statutes, and violations of some municipal by-laws. Many of these criminal and quasi-criminal laws are not what most Canadians think of as crime. When most people think of crime, when they worry about or fear crime, they are thinking about particular offences. They are not thinking about the Criminal Code and the full range of behaviours legally defined as criminal. When we seek to count crime, we are invariably struck with a complex mix of these two sets of definitions. For this reason, **gross counts of crime** may be very misleading. For example, in 1969 the Ouimet report pointed out that total convictions for all criminal offences in Canada increased by an alarming 2500 percent between 1901 and 1965. The report added, however, that 98 percent of the increase was accounted for by summary convictions—less serious crime—particularly traffic offences. Thus much of the apparent increase in crime actually reflected the increased use of automobiles in Canada during this period. With the report of the gross crime counts alone, most people would no doubt have had horrific visions of violent predators preying on innocent victims, rather than the more accurate vision of careless motorists abusing one another and pedestrians. For these reasons, UCR programs count offences within particular offence categories so that each offence can be examined separately.

gross counts of crime
A count of the total amount of crime in a given community, making no distinction between crime categories.

Another often-cited problem is that the Canadian UCR treats property crimes and personal crimes differently. Several property crimes, even if they involve different victims, may be recorded as a single offence if they are considered to be part of the same incident. This is not the case for personal offences. However, even for personal offences, the UCR1 survey collects very little information about victims and offenders. The CCJS has sought to rectify this by developing the richer UCR, the UCR2, which as we saw above collects data on characteristics of the victim and the accused as well as characteristics of the incident itself. As a result of the most serious offence scoring rule, less serious offences are under-counted by the aggregate survey. However, the incident-based survey allows up to four violations per incident, permitting the identification of lesser offences.

In 2005, 122 police services that represent approximately 71 percent of the population of Canada supplied data for the complete year to the UCR2 survey. Thus, these data are not geographically representative at the national or provincial level. However, UCR2 data provide a rich source of information for the geographical areas covered. Continuity with the UCR aggregate survey data is maintained by a conversion of the incident-based data to aggregate counts at year-end.

The question remains, however, whether the new and improved Canadian UCR will provide us with an accurate count of crime or even a reasonable indicator of crime and crime trends. Can official statistics ever tell us about total crime? Are official statistics useful only for understanding the criminal justice system?

We might have discussed the Canadian UCR under the heading of criminal justice statistics because these official data may tell us more about police activities than about crime. "Official violations" statistics are, in part, a product of policy decisions within the criminal justice system, that is, decisions about which criminal infractions deserve the most police attention and resources.

Furthermore, crime statistics are the product of individual police decisions made in the exercise of police discretion about what crimes are serious enough to attend to, record, and pursue. In fact, the ways in which police and police departments apply crime recording and scoring procedures reflect, to some extent, the policing style and policy of the particular police department. Because combining or comparing statistics from different departments is highly problematic, the CCJS has developed elaborate rules and procedures for collecting and verifying data. It is worth going to the CCJS website and reading the full description of the UCR.

Police statistics are also shaped by public perceptions, concerns, and fears. The police are very much dependent on the accounts of victims and witnesses. In other words, victims and witnesses must recognize an act as a criminal justice matter, must believe it to be of sufficient seriousness to warrant a report to the police, and must believe that reporting the act is worthwhile—all this before the police make their decisions about how to respond to and record an act. (See, for example, Shearing, 1984.)

Official crime statistics, then, are shaped by both common-sense and legal definitions of what constitutes crime. These statistics reflect the decisions of many people, not simply the behaviours of criminals. Official counts of crime will change as legal definitions change, as common-sense definitions change, and as the priorities of agents of law enforcement change. For example, if Parliament made premarital sex illegal, we could well expect a rather sharp increase in crime. Would this be reflected in official crime counts? To the extent that there are no direct victims to bring these offences to police attention, the answer is probably no. Much would depend on the priority attached to enforcement of this offence.

Consider two less hypothetical examples. As official statistics reveal to us increasing rates of family violence, theoretical explanations of the crisis in the nuclear family abound. But has the incidence truly increased, or have Canadians, within and outside the criminal justice system, become increasingly intolerant of such behaviour and more willing to bring such incidents to police attention? Have police become more sensitive to the seriousness of the problem and more likely to record the incidents as crimes? In other words, has the incidence increased, or have the definitions and reporting and recording behaviours changed? For those students wanting more statistical and substantive information on this topic, the CCJS website has a wealth of excellent studies on family violence and victimization of women.

Now consider drug offences. During the period 1995 to 2005, total drug offences increased by 36 percent; cannabis offences were up by 24 percent; cocaine offences were up by 24 percent; heroin offences, by contrast, were down 38 percent. Other drugs, reflecting the increased popularity of ecstasy, methamphetamines, and other "designer drugs," were up 253 percent.

Why has there been such an increase in "other" drug offences? Has their use really increased that much or have the priorities of law enforcement agencies shifted as well? One factor contributing to the increase in cannabis offences may be the effort to shut down marijuana-growing operations across the country as hydroponics have enabled Canadian growers to supply an increasing

FIGURE 4.4 Total Criminal Code Offences Reported to Police by Most Serious Offence, Rate per 100 000 Canadians, 1962–2005

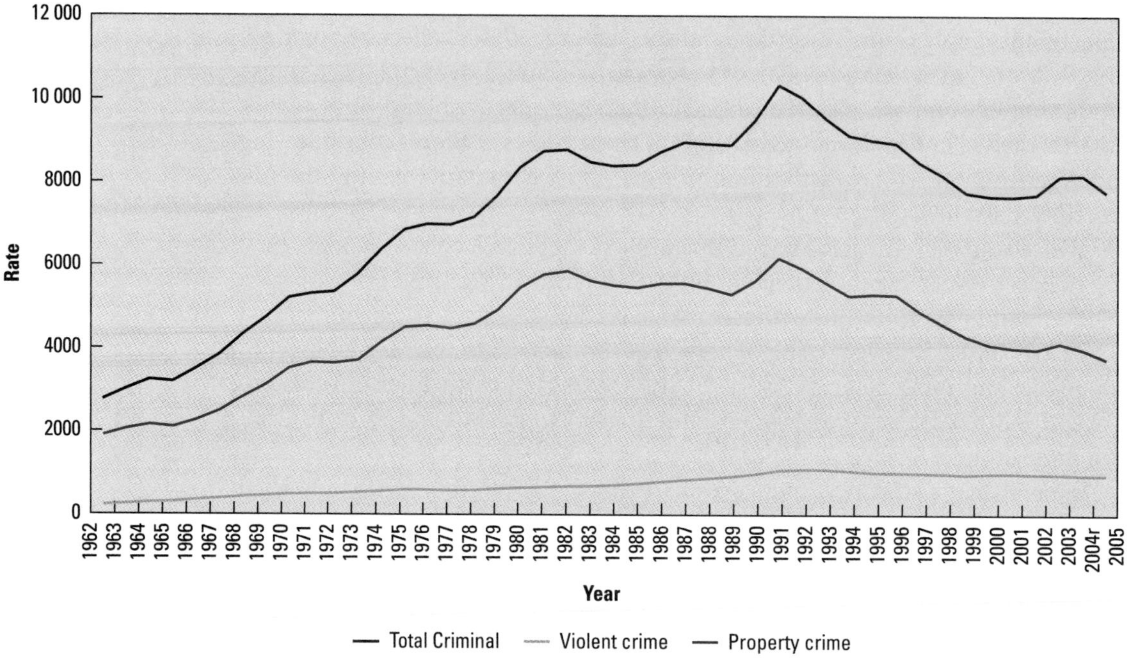

Source: Uniform Crime Reporting Survey, CCJS

share of the domestic market and to export to the United States, frequently in exchange for cocaine for the Canadian market. Because statistics for victimless crimes such as drug use are as much a result of police priorities and budgets as they are of the amount of criminal behaviour, official statistics leave much room for debate about the actual prevalence of these behaviours.

What, then, can the Canadian UCR tell us? From the inception of the Uniform Crime Reports in 1962, the total Criminal Code offence rate nearly tripled from 2771 offences per 100 000 Canadians to 7761 in 2005. Figure 4.4 shows the trend line during this period.

During this period, both violent and property crime rates increased steadily until 1992. They continued to decline or to be stable through 2005, with the 2005 decrease of 5 percent being offset by a 6 percent increase in 2003. Violent crimes, however, were consistently a small proportion of total crimes (943/100 000) as compared to the more frequent property crimes (3738/100 000) (see Figure 4.4). Those who work with crime statistics generally refer to crime rates when they wish to take into account the size of the population. The crime rate is simply the number of incidents for every 100 000 Canadians. Reference to rate, then, rather than incidence, makes sure that comparisons from jurisdiction to jurisdiction, or over time, do not reflect changes in population size rather than differences in criminal behaviour.

Violent crimes are relatively rare. In 2005 Canada had 661 homicides (first- and second-degree murder, manslaughter, and infanticide) and 772 attempted murders. Together these crimes account for less than half of 1 percent of reported violent incidents. The homicide rate remained stable in 2002 for the

FIGURE 4.5 **Homicide Rate per 100 000 Canadians, 1961–2005**

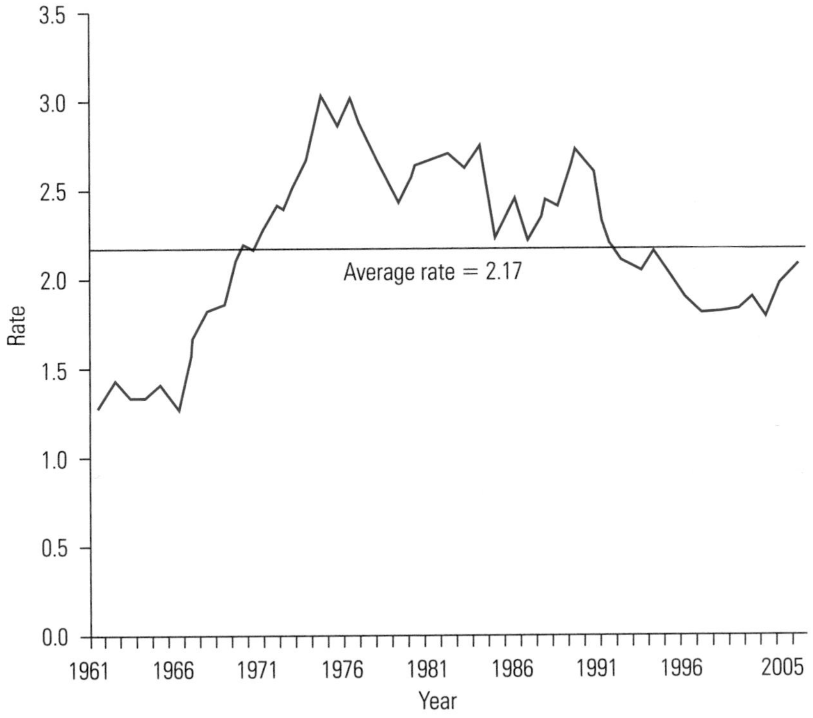

Source: http://www.statcan.ca/Daily/English/061108/d061108b.htm.

fourth consecutive year but in 2004 it increased by 14 percent and it increased by another 4 percent in 2005. The 2005 rate (2 homicides per 100 000 population) is about the same as during the late 1960s (see Figure 4.5).

The rate for attempted murder decreased 7 percent in 2002, following a similar decline in 2001 but it increased by 14 percent in 2005. Over the period 1995 to 2005 the attempted murder rate decreased by 20 percent.

Violent crimes continue to be about 13 percent of total offences. In fact, the category "violent offences" includes robberies, which are judged to have had the potential for violence even if no violence occurred. The presence of a weapon, even if the weapon was not used, and even if no injury occurred, would include the incident in the violent crime count.

The property crime rate declined by 14 percent from 1995 to 2005, continuing the downward trend in these offences seen since the early 1990s. The 2005 property crime rate was close to rates last seen in the late 1960s.

Crime seems to be declining during recent years. Although the crime rate rose from 1962 to 1991, it has generally declined or been stable since then. (See Table 4.1, which shows the levels of all recorded offences for the period 1999 to 2005.) The crime rate in 2005 was close to the 1979 level. Remember that all these data are based on reports to the police. But what can we say about crime rates given all the cautions with which we began this chapter? How much crime remains hidden to the police? Which crimes? How much do police recording practices shape the UCR figures? How much do these practices change over

TABLE 4.1 Federal Statute Incidents Reported to Police, by Most Serious Offence, Canada, 2001-2005

	1999		2001		2002		2003		2004r		2005		Percent change in rate*	Percent change in rate*
	Number	*Rate*[1]	*Number*	*Rate*[1]	*Number*	*Rate*[1]	*Number*	*Rate*[1]	*Number*	*Rate*[1]	*Number*	*Rate*[1]	*2004–2005*	*1995–2005*
Population	**30 403 878**		**31 021 251**		**31 372 587**		**31 669 150**		**31 974 363**		**32 270 508**			
Homicide[2]	538	2	553	2	582	2	549	2	624	2	661	2	5	2
Attempted murder	687	2	725	2	678	2	707	2	671	2	772	2	14	−20
Assault—Total	**221 348**	**728**	**236 957**	**764**	**235 710**	**751**	**236 802**	**748**	**234 259**	**733**	**234 729**	**727**	**−1**	**−2**
Level 1	181 330	596	191 147	616	189 185	603	188 667	596	184 883	578	182 049	564	−2	−8
Level 2—Weapon	37 501	123	43 094	139	43 793	140	45 222	143	46 643	146	49 653	154	5	25
Level 3—Aggravated	2 517	8	2 716	9	2 732	9	2 913	9	2 733	9	3 027	9	10	4
Other assaults	12 126	40	12 260	40	12 454	40	12 534	40	12 811	40	12 818	40	−1	−14
Sexual assault—Total	**23 859**	**78**	**24 044**	**78**	**24 499**	**78**	**23 514**	**74**	**23 036**	**72**	**23 303**	**72**	**0**	**−25**
Level 1	23 185	76	23 563	76	23 973	76	22 983	73	22 449	70	22 736	70	0	−24
Level 2—Weapon	461	2	320	1	373	1	359	1	397	1	396	1	−1	−39
Level 3—Aggravated	213	1	161	1	153	0	172	1	190	1	171	1	−11	−47
Other sexual offences	3 300	11	2 689	9	2 756	9	2 565	8	2 614	8	2 741	8	4	−29
Abduction	729	2	674	2	605	2	559	2	637	2	584	2	−9	−55
Robbery— Total	**28 740**	**95**	**27 284**	**88**	**26 662**	**85**	**28 437**	**90**	**27 495**	**86**	**28 669**	**89**	**−3**	**−15**
Firearms	5 122	17	3 818	12	3 483	11	3 856	12	3 645	11	3 505	11	−5	−53
Other Weapons	10 500	35	10 280	33	10 104	32	10 057	32	8 362	26	8 558	27	1	−24
No Weapons	13 118	43	13 186	43	13 075	42	14 524	46	15 488	48	16 606	51	6	12
Violent crime—Total	***291 327***	***958***	***305 186***	***984***	***303 946***	***969***	***305 667***	***965***	***302 147***	***945***	***304 277***	***943***	***0***	***−7***
Breaking & entering—Total	**318 054**	**1 046**	**279 461**	**901**	**275 573**	**878**	**284 925**	**900**	**275 869**	**863**	**259 521**	**804**	**−7**	**−40**
Residential	197 022	648	166 500	537	163 156	520	161 494	510	153 223	479	148 270	459	−4	−43
Business	83 971	276	80 264	259	81 162	259	86 842	274	86 226	270	79 722	247	−8	−33
Other	37 061	122	32 697	105	31 255	100	36 589	116	36 240	114	31 529	98	−14	−39
Motor vehicle theft	161 388	531	168 595	543	161 912	516	174 208	550	169 977	532	160 100	496	−7	−10
Theft over $5 000	22 493	74	20 845	67	19 816	63	19 416	61	16 968	53	17 491	54	2	−62
Theft $5 000 and under	678 367	2 231	659 589	2 126	667 312	2 127	700 605	2 212	673 999	2 108	640 714	1 985	−6	−29
Possession of stolen goods	29 308	96	26 960	87	30 056	96	33 151	105	35 743	112	33 848	105	−6	−2
Fraud	90 371	297	86 486	279	91 812	293	92 924	293	97 443	305	94 468	293	−4	−18
Property crime—Total	***1 299 981***	***4 276***	***1 241 936***	***4 004***	***1 246 481***	***3 973***	***1 305 229***	***4 121***	***1 269 999***	***3 972***	***1 206 142***	***3 738***	***−6***	***−29***
Mischief	312 266	1 027	333 136	1 074	333 334	1 063	357 568	1 129	353 518	1 106	353 955	1 097	−1	−15
Counterfelling currency[3]	36 265	119	38 674	125	79 790	255	139 267	440	201 108	629	163 323	506	−20	623
Ball violations	72 192	237	90 545	292	86 206	307	101 095	319	106 664	334	100 334	311	−7	36
Disturbing the peace	69 570	229	89 971	290	89 354	285	102 909	325	117 389	367	122 803	381	4	117
Offensive weapons	16 007	53	15 876	51	15 930	51	17 621	56	18 202	57	19 337	60	5	0
Prostitution	5 255	17	5 087	16	5 770	18	5 688	18	6 452	20	5 793	18	−11	−25
Arson	12 756	42	14 484	47	13 131	42	13 875	44	13 150	41	13 315	41	0	−8

Other	241 212	793	239 916	773	233 322	744	230 253	727	222 342	695	215 283	667	−4	−17
Other Criminal Code offences—Total	***765 523***	***2 518***	***827 689***	***2 668***	***867 017***	***2 764***	***968 276***	***3 057***	***1 038 825***	***3 249***	***994 143***	***3 081***	***−5***	***14***
CRIMINAL CODE WITHOUT TRAFFIC—TOTAL (CRIME RATE)	**2 356 831**	**7 752**	**2 374 811**	**7 655**	**2 417 444**	**7 706**	**2 579 172**	**8 144**	**2 610 971**	**8 166**	**2 504 562**	**7 761**	**−5**	**−14**
Impaired driving[4]	85 997	283	82 718	267	80 045	255	77 645	245	80 339	251	75 613	234	−7	−33
Fall to stop/remain	17 972	59	22 538	73	22 040	70	23 336	74	24 022	75	27 217	84	12	−54
Other—Criminal Code Traffic[6]	13 681	45	14 978	48	15 486	49	16 138	51	16 276	51	15 908	49	−3	−17
Criminal Code Traffic—Total	***117 650***	***387***	***120 234***	***388***	***117 571***	***375***	***117 119***	***370***	***120 637***	***377***	***118 738***	***368***	***−2***	***−38***
CRIMINAL CODE—TOTAL (INCL TRAFFIC)	**2 474 481**	**8 139**	**2 495 045**	**8 043**	**2 535 015**	**8 080**	**2 696 291**	**8 514**	**2 731 608**	**8 543**	**2 623 300**	**8 129**	**−5**	**−15**
DRUGS	**80 142**	**264**	**89 395**	**288**	**92 781**	**296**	**86 791**	**274**	**97 630**	**305**	**92 255**	**286**	**−6**	**36**
Cannabis	60 011	197	67 921	219	69 687	222	61 087	193	67 895	212	59 973	186	−12	24
Cocaine	11 963	39	12 145	39	12 737	41	14 225	45	16 974	53	18 951	59	11	51
Heroin	1 323	4	951	3	786	3	657	2	799	2	803	2	0	−38
Other drugs	6 845	23	8 378	27	9 571	31	10 822	34	11 962	37	12 528	39	4	253
OTHER FEDERAL STATUTES	**38 942**	**128**	**38 013**	**123**	**40 122**	**128**	**36 264**	**115**	**34 017**	**106**	**31 501**	**98**	**−8**	**−21**
TOTAL FEDERAL STATUTES (INCL. C.C.)	**2 593 565**	**8 530**	**2 622 453**	**8 454**	**2 667 918**	**8 504**	**2 819 346**	**8 902**	**2 863 255**	**8 955**	**2 747 056**	**8 513**	**−5**	**−14**

* Percent change based on unrounded rates.

[r]Revised figures.

1. Rates are calculated on the basis of 100, 000 population. The population estimates come from the Annual Demographic Statistics, 2005 report, produced by Statistics Canada, Demography Division. Population as of July 1st: final postcensal estimates for 2000 and 2006, and preliminary postcensal estimates for 2002.
2. As a result of ongoing investigations in Port Coquitlam, B.C. there were 15 homicides in 2002, 7 homicides in 2003 and 5 homicides in 2004 that occurred in previous years. Homicides are counted according to the year in which police file the report.
3. Due to an improved data collection methodology for counterfeiting introduced in 2005, numbers for certain police services, primarily in Ontario, were revised for 2004. Therefore, please use caution when comparing these data with prior years.
4. Includes impaired operation of a vehicle causing death, causing bodily harm, alcohol rate over 80mg, failure/refusal to provide a breath/blood sample. In 2001, the RCMP began reporting incidents in which a roadside suspension was issued, rather than a charge laid, to the CCJS. In 2002, most other police services began reporting this way as well. Previous to 2004, Vancouver Police only reported incidents of impaired driving when a charge had been laid. As of 2004, their data also include incidents where the driver was tested to be over .08 and received a roadside suspension. This resulted in 1,900 more impaired driving incidents being reported in 2004 than in 2003.
5. Includes dangerous operation offences and driving a motor vehicle while prohibited.

Source: Uniform Crime Reporting Survey, CCJS.

time? Are these data useless? The answer to the last question is no. For example, the homicide statistics collected by the Canadian Centre for Justice Statistics reflect the actual number of homicides fairly accurately. It is also probable that certain other offences that are of high priority within the criminal justice system, and which victims are likely to report, are relatively well captured by the UCR program. Motor vehicle theft is the best example of this type of offence. In sum, we can learn something about the incidence of crime from these data, but we are not sure how much.

We can be more confident that if police departments across Canada are recording and reporting crimes relatively consistently, then the UCR data give us a picture of what crimes the police are processing. For example, in the 1980s changes in policy limited police discretion in laying charges when handling domestic violence incidents. This policy has produced more official incidents of such assaults, reflecting changes in police practice if not changes in criminal behaviour. Some optimists would argue that the UCR gives an indication of trends in crime. The less optimistic say no, there is too much we do not know about victim reporting behaviour, about the exercise of police discretion in deciding what is criminal and what is not, about police recording and reporting practices, and about the nature and seriousness of the offences captured by the UCR. Out of these concerns have emerged attempts to develop other ways of counting crime. The most important of these is the victimization survey.

Victimization Surveys

victimization survey
A survey of a random sample of the population in which people are asked to recall and describe their own experience of being a victim of crime.

Victimization surveys are based on the idea of going directly to the people to ask them to indicate whether they have been victims of acts that the Criminal Code defines as criminal; to describe the nature and consequences of their victimization experiences; to describe the criminal justice response; to indicate whether victims or others brought the incidents to official attention, and, if not, why not; and to indicate their perceptions and attitudes about crime and criminal justice in Canada. The first large-scale victimization survey in Canada was carried out in 1982 by the Ministry of the Solicitor General of Canada and Statistics Canada. For those interested in the methodological developments for the first large-scale victimization surveys can read Catlin and Murray (1979), Solicitor General Canada (1983; 1984a; 1984b; 1985a; 1985b; 1985c; 1986), Evans and Leger (1978), and Skogan (1981).

Since 1988, Statistics Canada has conducted a victimization survey about every five years (1988, 1993, 1999, and 2004) as part of the General Social Survey.

sample
A group of elements (people, offenders, inmates) selected in a systematic manner from the population of interest.

For the 2004 survey, interviews were conducted by telephone with a random **sample** of approximately 24 000 people, aged 15 and older, living in the ten provinces. The three territories were included as part of a pilot test, but the territorial data are not included in the data presented for 2004. Those interviewed were asked for their opinions concerning the level of crime in their neighbourhood, their fear of crime, and their views concerning the performance of the justice system. They were also asked about their experiences with criminal victimization. Respondents who had been victims of a crime in the previous 12 months were asked for detailed information on each incident, including when and where it occurred; whether the incident was reported to the police; and how they were affected by the experience.

Not all crimes can be captured through this survey method. One need not be a methodologist to recognize that murder cannot be included in such a survey. Nor can consensual crimes for which there are no direct victims—drug use, gambling, and the like. These consensual crimes are not captured very well through official data or through victimization surveys. Similarly, those crimes designed to keep victims unaware that they have been victimized cannot be captured accurately in victimization surveys (or official data sources). Fraud, embezzlement, employee pilferage, price fixing, and the wide range of consumer, corporate, and white-collar crimes were not included in the survey. The eight categories of crime included were sexual assault, robbery, assault, break and enter, motor vehicle theft, theft of household property, theft of personal property, and vandalism. The major findings of the 2004 survey are reproduced below.

Highlights

- Results from the 2004 General Social Survey (GSS) indicate that 28% of Canadians aged 15 years and older reported being victimized one or more times in the 12 months preceding the survey. This is up slightly from 26% in 1999, when the victimization survey was last conducted.
- Increases in victimization rates were recorded for three of the eight offence types measured by the GSS: theft of personal property, theft of household property, and vandalism. There were no significant changes in rates of sexual assault, robbery, physical assault, and motor vehicle theft. The rate of break and enter declined.
- Household victimization offences were the most frequently occurring criminal incidents (34%), followed by violent victimization (29%) and thefts of personal property (25%). About 12% of incidents could not be classified within the eight offence types.
- Residents of western provinces generally reported higher rates of victimization than residents living east of the Manitoba-Ontario border. However, there were two exceptions to this regional pattern. Nova Scotia had the second highest rate of violent victimization, while Ontario's rate of personal property theft was comparable to rates recorded in the West.
- The risk of violent victimization (based on the number of incidents per 1,000 population) was highest among young Canadians (aged 15 to 24 years). Other factors, such as being single, living in an urban area, and having a low household income (under $15,000) also increased the likelihood of violent victimization.
- For household victimization, rates per 1,000 households were highest among renters, those living in semi-detached, row, or duplex homes, and urban dwellers. For both household victimization and personal property theft, higher household income made households and individuals more attractive targets for victimization.

- The GSS reveals that a large proportion of Canadians never reported criminal incidents to police. In all, only about 34% of criminal incidents came to the attention of police in 2004, down from 37% in 1999. Household victimization incidents were most likely to be reported (37%), while thefts of personal property were the least likely (31%).
- In 4% of all incidents, victims believed the act was hate-motivated. This is the same as the figure recorded in 1999. In 2004, among hate-motivated incidents, about two-thirds (65%) were believed to be motivated by the victim's race or ethnicity, 26% by the victim's sex, 14% by their religion, and 12% by their sexual orientation.
- Canadians who self-identified as being Aboriginal were three times as likely as the non-Aboriginal population to report being victims of violent victimization. There was no significant difference between rates for visible minorities and non-visible minorities, while rates were lower among immigrants than non-immigrants (68 versus 116 per 1,000 population).
- Although the proportion of violent incidents without a weapon has remained relatively stable since 1999 (69% in 2004 and 72% in 1999), violent incidents resulting in injury increased. In 2004, 25% of violent offences resulted in injury to the victim, compared to 18% in 1999.
- Most often, violent incidents took place in a commercial establishment or public institution (38%). Some form of workplace violence represented 43% of the incidents occurring in a commercial establishment or public institution. Source: Statistics Canada. "Criminal Victimization in Canada, 2004," by Maire Gannon and Karen Mihorean. Catalogue no. 85-002-XPE, Vol. 25, no. 7.

Note that of the incidents identified, just over one-third (34 percent) had been reported to the police or had otherwise come to police attention. Recognizing that the victimization survey cannot capture all of the "dark" figure missed by the UCR, the survey data do reveal that many more Canadians are victimized by crime than is revealed by official statistics.

As most would guess, a large proportion of the unreported crime is relatively trivial, the kinds of incidents that most of us would not expect the police to devote time or resources to. For example, a few dollars stolen by somebody within the household, a toy stolen from the porch, or an umbrella stolen from a restaurant are the kinds of common incidents that are rarely reported. Nonetheless, as Figure 4.6 shows, more serious incidents may often go unreported. For example, in the 2004 Victimization Survey, 92 percent of those who had been sexually assaulted did not report the incident to the police. Women assaulted by people they knew indicated that fear of revenge was one of the reasons they failed to report. Figure 4.7 presents the major reasons for failing to report to the police in the 2004 survey.

Where incidents produced great financial loss to the victim, reporting was far more likely, even more likely than for those incidents that resulted in pain or injury but no loss. Reporting property crimes, particularly when the loss was over $1000, is less an act of justice (or even revenge) than a far more utilitarian act—seeking redress, recompense, or recovery. On the other hand, 83 percent of

FIGURE 4.6 Incidents Reported to Police, 1993, 1999, and 2004

Incidents	*1993*	*1999*	*2004*
Theft personal property	42	35	31
Robbery	46	46	46
Physical assault	33	37	39
Break and enter	68	62	54
Motor vehicle/parts theft	50	60	49
Theft household property	43	32	29
Vandalism	46	34	31

Source: Statistics Canada, General Social Survey.

FIGURE 4.7 Reasons Given for Failure to Report to Police

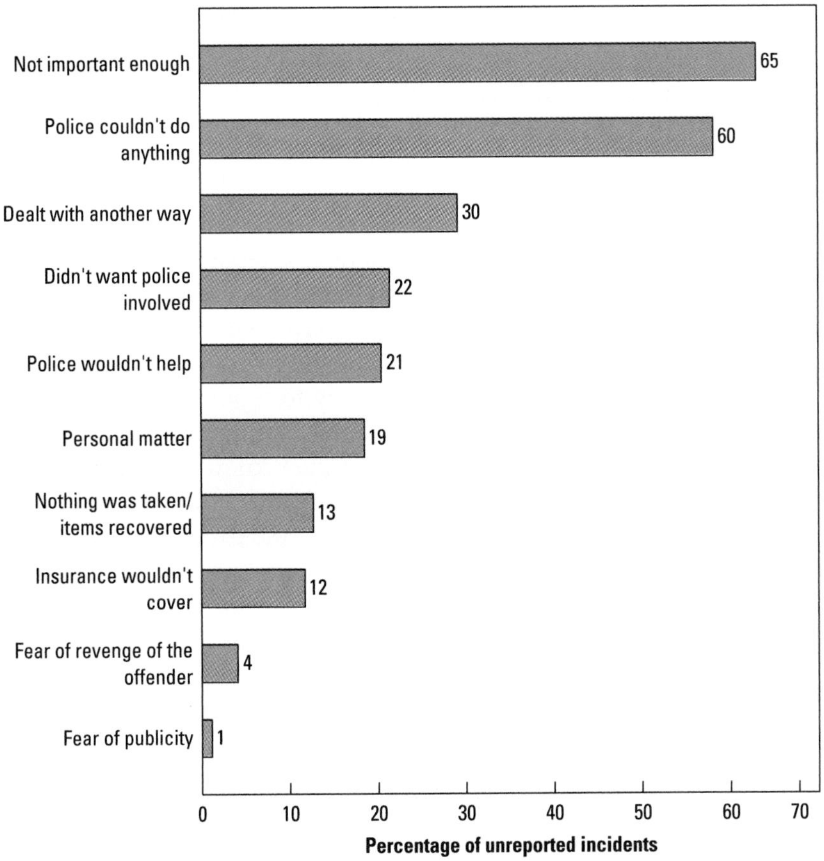

Source: Statistics Canada. Adapted from the Statistics Canada publication, *Criminal Victimization in Canada, 2004*. Catalogue No. 85-002-XPE Vol. 25, no. 17, p. 19. Reprinted with permission of the Minister of Industry, 2005.

FIGURE 4.8 Reasons Given for Reporting to Police

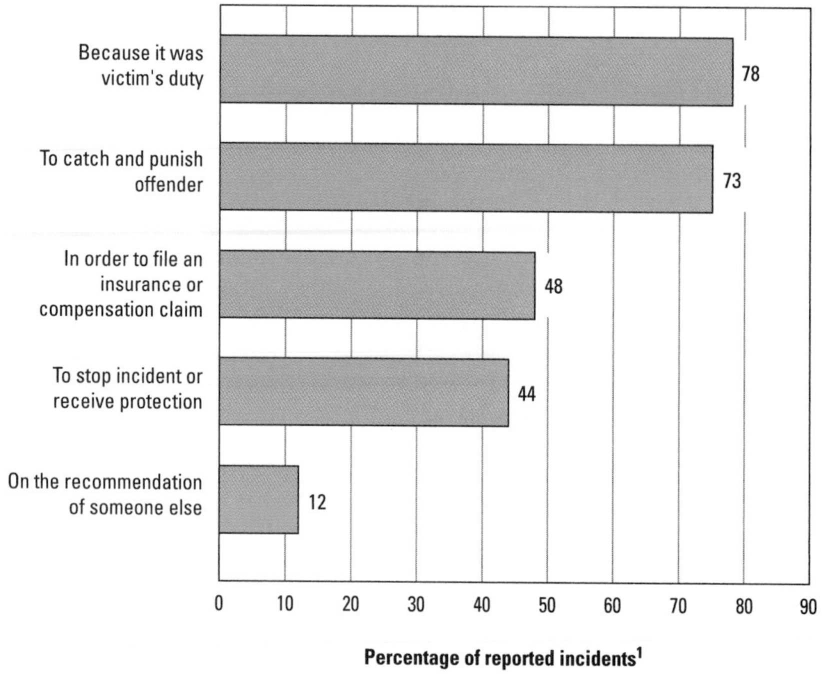

1 *Total exceeds 100% due to multiple responses. Excludes incidents that were not classified by crime type and incidents of spousal sexual and physical assault.*

Source: Statistics Canada. Adapted from the Statistics Canada publication, *Criminal Victimization in Canada*. Catalogue No. 85-002 Vol. 20, no. 10, p. 12. Reprinted with permission of the Minister of Industry, 2003.

victims of violent crime felt it was their duty to report to the police. Figure 4.8 displays the data on reasons for reporting from the 1999 survey.

The survey data confirm many of the concerns about official sources of crime data. Some crimes are more likely to come to police attention than others. Some categories of victims are more likely to report their victimizations, and some categories of offenders (for example, family members) are less likely to be reported. In general, it is only through such knowledge that we can begin to understand the UCR data and the dark figure of crime. Because victimization surveys are based on victims' perceptions and experiences, and because they collect information about the victims of crime, they are useful in identifying those categories of people most at risk of criminal victimization. For example, the 2004 survey shows that, contrary to the conventional wisdom, the risk of victimization is lowest for older Canadians, especially those 65 years of age or older. In fact, the victimization data provide a profile of the victim of crime that explodes many popular myths. The typical victim of crime is young, single, male, not employed full-time, and living an active social life. In particular, the number of evenings spent outside the home is one of the best predictors of whether one will have been victimized or not. Some of the reasons for these patterns of victimization are discussed in Chapter 14. Perhaps most important, victimization surveys allow us to go beyond merely counting incidents. They provide data on the costs of victimization, the financial losses,

FIGURE 4.9 **Crime Prevention Measures Routinely and Ever Taken to Protect Self or Property, 2004**

Measures routinely taken to protect self or property from crime	*% population aged 15 and over who have employed measures*
Lock car doors for safety when alone	59
Check back seat for intruders when returning to car alone	43
Plan route with safety in mind	43
Carry something to defend self or alert others	13
Stay home at night because afraid to go out alone	10
Measures ever taken in one's lifetime to protect self or property from crime	***% population aged 15 and over who have employed measures***
Changed activities or avoided certain places	35
Installed burglar alarms or motion detectors	34
Installed new locks or security bars	31
Took a self-defence course	13
Obtained a dog	9
Changed phone number	5
Changed residence or moved	4
Obtained a gun	1

Source: Statistics Canada. *Canadians' Use of Crime Prevention Measures* (85F0033MIE2006012, available as part of the *Canadian Centre for Justice Statistics Profile Series*. From the *Publications* module, under *Free Internet publications*, choose *Justice*.

the physical injuries, and the concern and fear victimization may produce. In addition, these data allow the exploration of various dimensions of seriousness. Clearly, victimization hits some harder than others. Nonetheless, and contrary to most people's expectations, women and men experience similar levels of violent victimization. Seniors have very low rates of victimization: "Households with only senior residents experienced household crimes (such as a break-in, property theft, motor vehicle theft or vandalism) at a rate of 87 incidents for every 1,000 senior households in Canada, nearly three times lower than the rate for all Canadian households (248 incidents per 1,000 households)"(Ogrodnick, 2007, 15). This is reflected in their perceptions of safety, as the survey also found that "seniors' satisfaction with their personal safety improved slightly between 1999 and 2004. The vast majority (92%) of seniors reported feeling satisfied with their overall level of safety from crime in 2004, compared to 89% reported in 1999. This increase closes the gap between seniors and younger Canadians, resulting in fairly consistent levels of satisfaction with their personal safety (92% compared to 94%)" (Ogrodnick, 2007, 17).

Victimization surveys can also gauge the kinds of activities people engage in to avoid victimization. As Figure 4.9 shows, about 35 percent of people changed activities or avoided certain places, and a third installed security hardware.

Victimization surveys cannot measure all crimes. They are dependent on the vagaries of human memory and are subject to the kinds of criticisms levelled against any survey, including the fact that some people may not tell interviewers the truth. Victimization surveys are dependent on respondents' ability not only to recall incidents and their details, but also to place the incidents correctly in time. We know that respondents are fallible. And, as Skogan (1978) suggests, well-educated, articulate respondents are more likely than others to talk to interviewers and to give rich and full accounts of their victimization experiences, thus perhaps biasing the data. There is reason as well to be cautious about interpreting data on domestic and sexual assaults that have been collected through surveys. Respondents may well be reluctant to discuss such experiences with an interviewer. Also, the methodology is still relatively young. Special methods will be needed to get data about rural victimization and victimization of Aboriginal Canadians. A good start was made in the 2004 survey. See the Box 4.2 "Violence Among Diverse Populations."

Special methodologies are also required to measure white-collar crime, consensual crime, and what has come to be called enterprise crime—organized crime and the crimes of organizations and the state. More information is also required on the psychological and emotional impact of victimization.

Despite the limitations, these data provide us with the opportunity to go beyond counting incidents and to gain some understanding of what it is we are counting. The data are an important, perhaps essential, complement to other sources of crime statistics.

Self-Report Studies

self-report study
A method for measuring crime involving the distribution of a detailed questionnaire to a sample of people, asking them whether they have committed a crime in a particular period of time. This has been a good method for criminologists to determine the social characteristics of offenders.

Yet another approach to generating data on the nature and distribution of crime is the **self-report study**. The people who know the most about crime are those who break the law. Rather than relying on police data that will inevitably be incomplete or on the knowledge of victims, why not just ask criminals what they do and how often they do it? Many sociologists have done this, most commonly through questionnaires given to students in junior and senior high schools. A classic study done by Travis Hirschi (1969) in the San Francisco area is typical of self-report studies (you will read about some of the results of this study in Chapter 13, "Social Control Theory"). Hirschi took a random sample of all the junior and senior high school students in Richmond, California, and administered questionnaires to 5545 students. The survey was a very lengthy one, and we will consider here only the questions measuring delinquent behaviour. The students were asked six questions about their illegal conduct and for each were asked to check off one of the following responses: A. No, never; B. More than a year ago; C. During the last year; and D. During the last year *and* more than a year ago. The delinquency questions were the following:

- Have you ever taken little things (worth less than $2) that did not belong to you?
- Have you ever taken things of some value (between $2 and $50) that did not belong to you?

FOCUS

BOX 4.2 Violence Among Diverse Populations

Through the 2004 GSS, it is possible to examine rates of violent victimization experienced by visible minorities, immigrants, including recent immigrants, and Aboriginal people, and to assess whether these segments of the population are at increased risk of being victimized.

Overall, Aboriginal people reported the highest rates of violent victimization compared to the other minority populations and the non-Aboriginal population. Those who self-identified as being Aboriginal were three times more likely than the non-Aboriginal population to be the victim of a violent incident (319 people per 1,000 versus 101 per 1,000). Even when controlling for other factors such as age, sex, and income, Aboriginal people remained at greater risk of violent victimization.

Aboriginal women appeared particularly at risk of victimization. Rates for Aboriginal women were 3.5 times higher than the rates recorded for non-Aboriginal women, while rates for Aboriginal men were 2.7 times higher than those for non-Aboriginal men.

In the case of visible minorities, it was found that the risk of violent victimization did not differ significantly from their non-visible minority counterparts (98 versus 107 per 1,000 population). (See the accompanying figure.) This was true for both men and women. However, in the case of immigrants, overall rates were lower than that of non-immigrants (68 versus 116 per 1,000 population). The reduced likelihood of victimization was even more pronounced when only those who had immigrated to Canada since 1999 were excluded. For example, 71 per 1,000 population of those who immigrated prior to 1999 were the victims of a violent crime, compared to 53 per 1,000 population of those who had immigrated in the past 5 years. Again, these patterns were similar for immigrant women and men.

Aboriginal people have highest rates of violent victimization, 2004

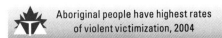

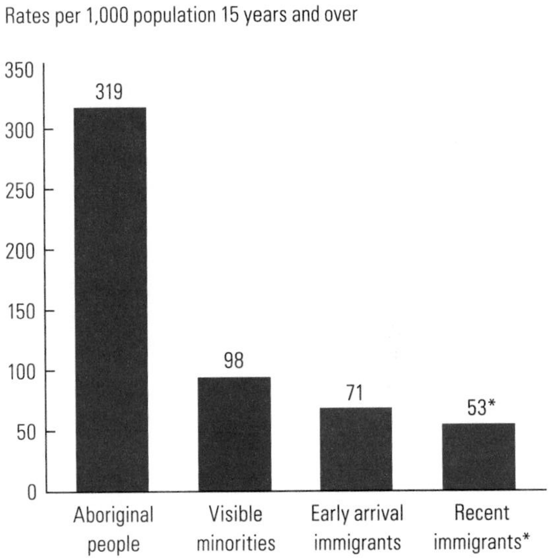

Notes: Includes incidents of spousal sexual and physical assault.
[E]Use with caution.
1. Included are immigrants arriving between 1999 and 2004.
Source: Statistics Canada, General Social Survey, 2004.

One possible explanation for lower rates within the immigrant population may be due to the fact that the immigrant population tends to be older, a factor which reduces risk of victimization. According to the Census of the Population, compared to immigrants, a higher proportion of non-immigrants were under the age of 25 years, the most at-risk group for violent victimization.

FOCUS

BOX 4.3 Summary and Cautions: Using Victimization Survey Data and Data from the UCR and the Court Surveys

Victimization Surveys

These surveys provide rich data but remember that they collect information on a limited set of crimes—eight in the Statistics Canada surveys. The Uniform Crime Survey covers more than 100 offence types. When considering these data use caution. Refer back to Figure 4.1, The Crime Funnel. The 2004 victimization survey estimated that there were 505 000 break and enters in Canada. Note that these are break and enters of households. Break-and-enter offences against businesses are not included. Thousands of break and enters are therefore excluded from the victimization survey but they will be included in police and court data. This in turn affects each subsequent item in the funnel. The figure is an illustration only.

Defining Courts-Based Data and Police Incident-Based Data

Police

The Canadian Centre for Justice Statistics conducts the Uniform Crime Reporting (UCR) survey. This survey collects data on the crimes reported to the police. Coverage of the UCR Survey in 2005 was at 99.9 percent of the caseload of all police services in Canada. Currently there exists both an aggregate UCR survey and an incident-based UCR2 survey. The latter replaces the former as respondent police services become capable of providing the level of detail required by the incident-based survey.

Counting Procedures

The basic unit of count selected to report crimes to the incident-based UCR survey is the "criminal incident." The fundamental characteristic of an incident is that it may involve several victims, several accused persons, and several different violations of the law. All these different elements will be grouped together into one incident if they meet specified conditions (or rules). These rules are outlined in the *Uniform Crime Reporting Incident-Based Survey, Reporting Manual, March 2006,* Canadian Centre for Justice Statistics, Statistics Canada.

Most Serious Offence and Scoring Rules

The UCR survey classifies incidents according to the most serious offence in the incident. Generally, this is the offence that carries the longest maximum sentence under the Criminal Code. However, in categorizing or ranking incidents, violent offences always take precedence over non-violent offences.

Furthermore, for violent crime, a separate incident is recorded for each victim. For example, if one person assaults three people, then three incidents are recorded. For non-violent crime, one incident is counted for every distinct or separate occurrence. For example, a fraudulent offence involving three victims would only result in one incident being recorded.

"Persons cleared by charge" refers to persons who have been formally charged or recommended to be charged by police.

Courts

The purpose of the Adult Criminal Court Survey (ACCS) and the Youth Court Survey is to provide a national database of statistical information on the processing of cases through the adult and

(Continued)

- Have you ever taken things of large value (worth over $50) that did not belong to you?
- Have you ever taken a car for a ride without the owner's permission?
- Have you ever banged up something that did not belong to you on purpose?

FOCUS

BOX 4.3 Summary and Cautions: Using Victimization Survey Data and Data from the UCR and the Court Surveys *(Continued)*

youth criminal court systems. The surveys consist of a census of Criminal Code and other federal statute charges dealt with in adult criminal courts and youth courts. In 2003–04, the ACCS represented approximately 90 percent of the national adult criminal court caseload. The Youth Court Survey has 100 percent coverage.

Counting Procedures

The basic unit of count for the Court Surveys is a case. A case is one or more charges against an accused person or corporation, where the charges receive a final disposition on the same date. Charges are linked to a case on the basis of the accused identifier and the date of the last court appearance.

Most Serious Offence and Decision Rules

When a case has more than one charge, it is necessary to decide which charge will be used to represent the case (since a case is identified by a single charge). In such multiple-charge cases, the "most serious decision" rule is applied. Decisions are ranked from the most to the least serious as follows: 1) guilty, 2) guilty of a lesser offence, 3) acquitted, 4) stay of proceeding, 5) withdrawn, dismissed, and discharged, 6) not criminally responsible, 7) other, and 8) transfer of court jurisdiction.

In cases where two or more offences have resulted in the same decision (e.g., guilty), the "most serious offence" rule is applied. All charges are ranked according to an offence seriousness scale, which is based on the average length of prison sentence and rate of incarceration. If two charges are tied according to this criterion, information about the sentence type (e.g., prison, probation, and fine) is considered. If a tie still exists, the magnitude of the sentence is considered.

Comparisons Between Courts and Police UCR Survey Data

Counts from the UCR survey for offences cleared by charge are not comparable to the Adult Criminal Court Survey (ACCS) figures for charges disposed of. There are many reasons for this. In part, it is the result of scoring rules used by the UCR survey. The UCR survey counts violent offences by the number of victims in the incident; non-violent offences are counted by the number of separate incidents.

For example, two persons break into a house and subsequently commit vandalism and theft. This would be considered as one police incident. Assuming the charges were laid and the matter proceeded to court, there would be a minimum of six charges—three charges for each accused.

In addition, the differences in the "most serious offence" rule between the courts and police surveys can result in court cases and police incidents being represented by different offences even though they may have been part of the same crime.

Furthermore, the published UCR figures include offences involving youths, while the ACCS case counts include only the very few youth offences that have been transferred to adult court (<100 per year).

Moreover, information is captured in the UCR with the laying of a charge, while in the ACCS information is captured upon the court rendering a decision. This time lag in data collection between the two surveys further affects comparability.

- Not counting fights that you may have had with a brother or sister, have you ever beaten up on anyone or hurt someone on purpose?

Hirschi looked at responses to these delinquency questions and compared them with other measures, including such things as students' reports of their friends' behaviour, and their family and school relationships, in order to try

FOCUS

BOX 4.4 "If It Bleeds, It Leads": The Media and Public Perceptions of Crime

Most Canadians learn about crime through the media rather than from first-hand experience. As a result, the stories portrayed on television and radio, and in newspapers, magazines, and books, shape our views about crime and criminals. But the media do not always simply "report" the news. In fact, editors and reporters select the crime news that they wish to run and construct the ways in which that news is presented to us. Unfortunately, the picture of crime we receive from the media is not always accurate. For example, while most actual crime consists of property crime, most of the stories about crime in the media deal with violent crime. Thomas Gabor reviewed all the crime-related stories reported over two months in an Ottawa newspaper (Gabor, 1994). Over half the stories focused on violent crimes, particularly murders; however, violent crimes made up only 7 percent of reported crimes in Ottawa, and the city averaged just six murders per year. While violent crimes were over-reported, property crimes received little attention, and white-collar and political crimes were almost never discussed.

Why do the media misrepresent crime? The truth is that stories that attract viewers or readers boost ratings and circulation. The informal media rule "if it bleeds, it leads" reflects the fact that the public is fascinated by sensationalized, bloody stories. Commenting on his experience with the media, the executive director of the Nova Scotia Bar Society said, "If there's no blood and gore, or there's no sex, it's not newsworthy. And if it falls into the category of being newsworthy, then they have to show the dead body. They've got to show the corpse" (McCormick, 1995, 182).

The media's misrepresentation of crime has several consequences. First, Canadians greatly over-estimate the prevalence of violent crime and have a fear of crime that is disproportionate to the real risk of victimization. One survey found that the vast majority of Canadians (75 percent) felt that more than half of all crimes are accompanied by violence. The true figure is less than 10 percent (Doob and Roberts, 1983). Crime stories lead us to see Canada as a violent and dangerous place.

The media also provide us with a distorted stereotype of offenders. Violent crimes are often committed by relatives, friends, and acquaintances (51 percent in 2004), and not by the anonymous stranger that so many of us fear. The trouble is that our fear of crime and our image of the criminal have an impact on government policy toward crime. Actual crime trends are irrelevant—if the public feels crime is out of control, it will demand that government do something about it. While crime rates are in reality on the decline, a combination of increasing media coverage of crime and pressure from a variety of interest groups has led the federal government to tighten several laws, including those concerning immigration, young offenders, and firearms.

to shed some light on what caused some students to become delinquent while others did not. Like victimization surveys, self-report studies were used to try to overcome some of the weaknesses of police data. In most cases the results have supported the view that there are systematic biases.

Because self-report studies supposedly avoid these biases, they have been particularly important in research and theory on the causes of crime and delinquency, especially the relationship between social class and crime. For a long time, these studies were not very carefully scrutinized. They were perceived as such a significant breakthrough that few questions were asked. A major work to determine the reliability of self-report studies was carried out by Hindelang, Hirschi, and Weis (1981). They concluded that the self-report method does demonstrate that people are willing to report crimes, both those known and not known to officials, and that respondents' reports are internally consistent. A difficulty arises in that it appears that different populations answer self-report questions in different ways. Lower-class males and black males, in the United States study, are more likely to underreport their own criminal behaviour than are middle-class white males. Similarly, in Canada, Fréchette and LeBlanc (1979; 1980) confirm that while self-report studies do uncover much hidden delinquency and raise questions about the biases in official statistics that show the preponderance of lower-class crime, previous self-report studies have also masked the fact that lower-class crime is typically more serious and persistent.

There are two related problems here. First, it would appear that those who are typically law abiding are more likely to report completely their occasional infractions than are the more committed delinquents to report their more serious and frequent infractions. Second, differences between official statistics of delinquent behaviour and self-report data may reflect not simply biases in official data, but biases in the self-report method as well. The official data are likely to include more serious offences, and self-report data are more likely to include more minor infractions, as you can see from the items used in Hirschi's studies.

A number of other more technical problems regarding, for example, sampling—the difficulty in getting "hard-core criminals" in a sample, disagreements about which offences to select and which produce the most reliable and valid data, and which scoring procedures best suit the uses of the data—are given full discussion in Hindelang, Hirschi, and Weis (1981), and in Thornberry and Krohn (2000). Although self-report studies are never likely to be an instrument for counting crimes, recent methodological refinements have enhanced their potential for addressing fundamental questions about crime and the correlates of crime.

Self-report data can be used for other purposes as well. By using formal self-report surveys such as Hirschi's or by interviewing criminals in prison or in other, less restrictive situations we can learn a great deal about their motivations for committing crimes and the techniques they use to commit crimes. This information is invaluable for understanding the causes of crime and for helping to prevent it. Since this chapter is about counting crime, these issues will not be considered here, but in later chapters of the book you will read about many of the lessons that criminologists have learned from talking to criminals.

The Future of Crime and Criminal Justice Statistics

The importance of good statistics for planning, policy-making, and administration has long been recognized within the criminal justice system. Out of this recognition and concern emerged, in 1981, the Canadian Centre for Justice Statistics, with a mandate to collect national statistics. The existence of the Canadian Centre for Justice Statistics is a recognition—in a country with shared jurisdiction for criminal justice—of the importance of developing national commitment and national strategies for producing and sharing criminal statistics.

The new information technology holds great promise for improving the official records that form the basis of most criminal justice statistics on prisons, courts, and police. It is only through a nationally coordinated effort that we can avoid the danger of developing incompatible systems in each province (or worse, municipality) that feed many different criminal justice systems and inhibit the continued development of a coordinated national system of justice.

The methods for counting crimes are still in their formative stages. Some, like the UCR, will be derived from official records (designed in accordance with UCR rules) and will, therefore, suffer the limitations of all such official statistics. Nevertheless, recent advances in police management information systems and crime classification systems hold great promise for providing us with a measure of calls for police service, police caseloads, and police activity. The richer information from the UCR2 will help here. Other methods, like victimization surveys, will draw on people's experiences and will, therefore, suffer the limitations of all such surveys. Significant progress has been achieved in Canada in the development and refinement of victimization surveys and self-report studies.

How much crime is there in Canada, and what are the trends? Is it bad and getting worse? Do we have cause for alarm? Are things good and getting better? Do we have cause for complacency? Depending on your bias and prejudices, the state of the art allows you to find some evidence and numbers to justify either extreme. But with the improvements in our knowledge about crime and the development of new methods, we are coming to recognize the complexity of the questions. When taken together, the UCR and the victimization surveys encourage neither alarm nor complacency. Overall, there is certainly less serious crime than most Canadians assume based on media accounts and the high visibility of sensational incidents. At the same time, we are starting to uncover some particular kinds of serious incidents that have, for too long, remained hidden. Sexual assault and family violence are two important examples. Much more work is needed. Only through an integrated program of criminal justice statistics, recognizing the limits of any one source of information, will we be able to build powerful theories of crime and sound policies and programs for crime prevention and control.

Summary

- Statistics can help us to better understand the nature and extent of crime in Canada. However, in order to interpret these crime statistics properly, we must understand their strengths and weaknesses.
- The quality of official statistics varies depending on their sources. Corrections data are the most reliable and valid because the task of counting prisoners can be done accurately. On the other hand, crimes known to the police, the most commonly used statistics, will always be biased by inconsistencies in reporting and recording, although the CCJS is very stringent about verifying data.

- Administrative records can be the basis of statistics if clear procedures are developed about units of count, levels of data aggregation, definitions, data elements, and counting procedures.
- The Canadian Uniform Crime Report (UCR) system is designed to provide uniform and compatible national statistics. There is much debate about just what is counted. Some hold that the UCR provides a reasonable estimate of crime rates. Others hold that what is being measured is criminal justice processing.
- The crime rates provided by the UCR, based on crimes reported to the police, have declined since the peak year of 1991. Both violent and property crimes have declined. The overall decline from 1995 to 2005 is about 14 percent.
- Victimization surveys provide an alternative and complementary method of measuring crime. These surveys ask random samples of the population about their victimization experiences. They also provide data on such important issues as reasons for reporting and not reporting crimes to the police.
- Self-report studies are not serious rivals of either the UCR or victimization surveys as a method of measuring crime. However, they do have a useful place in answering specific questions related to understanding the causes and correlates of crime.
- Developing Canada's national statistics will take continued effort and commitment from all the actors in the system. The CCJS has made great progress and the statistics now available are much better than they were 10 or 20 years ago.

QUESTIONS FOR CRITICAL THINKING

1. Crime rates in Canada declined between 1995 and 2005. How would you account for this decline? You might wish to read ahead in Chapter 5 to help you find some possible answers to this question.
2. The media do not provide an accurate portrayal of the nature and extent of crime in Canada. Can you find examples in your own community of media distortions of crime? Why do the media behave in this way? What are the consequences of these distortions?
3. Victimization surveys reveal that many crimes, including serious violent crimes, are not reported to the police. Why not? What is the significance of this for society?
4. To what extent do official statistics measure the amount of crime in society? What are the major biases in official statistics?
5. How are self-report studies used in criminology? Can you find examples of the use of self-report data in later chapters of this book?

NET WORK

Canadian crime statistics are compiled by the Canadian Centre for Justice Statistics, which reports the annual number of crimes reported to the police. Go to the Statistics Canada website at **www41.statcan.ca/2007/2693/ceb2693_000_e .htm**.

Using the information on "Crimes, by type of offence," identify the trends in the crimes reported in Figure 4.4 of this text. Look at the information on "Homicide offences, number and rate." Have homicide rates gone up or down in the past five years? Which provinces and territories have the highest rate of homicide? Do the actual crime figures reported by Statistics Canada correspond with your perception of crime rates reported by the mass media?

KEY TERMS

administrative record; pg. 107
Canadian Centre for Justice Statistics; pg. 109
counting procedure; pg. 107
crime rate; pg. 104
dark figure of crime; pg. 111
data element; pg. 107
gross counts of crime; pg. 114
ideology; pg. 106
levels of aggregation; pg. 107
methodology; pg. 104
population; pg. 105
reliability; pg. 104
sample; pg. 120
self-report study; pg. 126
seriousness rule; pg. 112
theory; pg. 106
Uniform Crime Reports (UCR); pg. 111
validity; pg. 104
victimization survey; pg. 120

SUGGESTED READING

Alvazzi del Frate, Anna, Ugljesa Zvekic, and Jan J.M. van Dijk (eds.). (1993). *Understanding Crime: Experiences of Crime and Crime Control.* Rome: United Nations Interregional Crime and Justice Research Institute. This is a good source for international insights and comparisons.

Fréchette, M., and Marc LeBlanc. (1980). "Pour une pratique de la criminologie: configurations de conduites délinquantes et portraits de délinquants." *Inadaptation juvénile* Cahier 5. Montréal: Université de Montréal. Fréchette and LeBlanc's monograph provides not only rich data and insights on delinquency but also a good illustration of the use of self-report studies.

Miller, Jerome G. (1996). *Search and Destroy: African-American Males in the Criminal Justice System.* Cambridge, UK: Cambridge University Press. This book examines the vast overrepresentation of African Americans in the United States justice system. It is an object lesson for those who think that accurate counts are not important.

Skogan, W. (1981). "Issues in the Measurement of Victimization." Washington, DC: U.S. Department of Justice, Bureau of Justice Statistics. Skogan's monograph on victimization surveys, one of many he has written in this area, is the most readable and exhaustive account of the potential and limits of this approach to counting crime. His discussion is based largely on the American experience.

Solicitor General Canada. (1983). "Victims of Crime." Canadian Urban Victimization Survey. Ottawa: Solicitor General Canada. This, the first in a series of bulletins, provides a brief overview of the major findings and methodology of the first large-scale Canadian victimization survey, conducted in 1982.

Statistics Canada. (1997). "An Overview of the Differences between Police-Reported and Victim-Reported Crime." Ottawa. This report reduces the level of confusion arising from the use of crime data originating from two very different sources—the Uniform Crime Report (UCR) system and the General Social Survey (GSS)—and informs discussions about which is the better measure of crime. It explains why the findings based on these data sources diverge and summarizes the major differences between the two sources.

Statistics Canada. (2006). "Family Violence in Canada: A Statistical Profile. (85-224-XIE)." Ottawa. This series provides the most up-to-date data on the nature and extent of family violence in Canada and monitors trends over time. Each year, the report has a special focus or theme.

Statistics Canada. (2002). "National Trends in Intimate Partner Homicides, 1974–2000." *Juristat* 22(5). Catalogue no. 85-002-XIE. This *Juristat* documents trends in spousal homicides as well as subgroup variations (e.g., common-law, separated and divorced partners, age group variations), and it identifies factors that may be associated with the decline in spousal homicide over the past 25 years.

Statistics Canada. (2002). "Criminal Victimization: An International Perspective—Results of the 2000 International Crime Victimization Survey." *Juristat* 22(4). Catalogue no. 85-002-XPE. This *Juristat* presents results from the 2000 victimization survey of 17 industrialized countries.

Statistics Canada. *Juristat.* Ottawa. The Canadian Centre for Justice Statistics at Statistics Canada produces Canadian Crime Statistics. The *Juristat* series of reports provides detailed statistics and analysis on a variety of topics and issues concerning Canada's justice system. Annual *Juristats* are produced in the following areas: crime statistics, homicide, impaired driving, justice system resources and expenditures, youth court statistics, youth custody and probation, and corrections statistics. Additional *Juristats* are also produced each year on current topics of interest to the justice community. This is a unique periodical, of great interest to those who have to plan, establish, administer, and evaluate justice programs and projects, or anyone who has an interest in Canada's justice system. These publications are available from Statistics Canada in print or online.

BIBLIOGRAPHY

Bureau of Justice Statistics. (2006). "Prison Statistics." Washington: Department of Justice. http://www.ojp.usdoj.gov/bjs/prisons.htm. Accessed 25 September, 2007.

Catlin, G., and S. Murray. (1979). "Report on Canadian Victimization Survey Methodological Pretests." Ottawa: Statistics Canada.

de Silva, S., and R. A. Silverman. (1985). "New Approaches to Uniform Crime Reporting in Canada." Paper presented at the annual meeting of the American Society of Criminology, San Diego (November).

Doob, A., and J. V. Roberts. (1983). *An Analysis of the Public's View of Sentence.* Ottawa: Department of Justice Canada.

Evans, J., and G. Leger. (1978). "The Development of Victimization Surveys in Canada." *Public Data Use* 6 (November).

Fréchette, M., and Marc LeBlanc. (1979). "La délinquance cachée à l'adolescence." *Inadaptation juvénile* Cahier 1. Montreal: Université de Montréal.

———. (1980). "Pour une pratique de la criminologie: configurations de conduites délinquantes et portraits de délinquants." *Inadaptation juvénile* Cahier 5. Montreal: Université de Montréal.

Gabor, T. (1994). *Everybody Does It: Crime by the Public.* Toronto: University of Toronto Press.

Hindelang, M. J., T. Hirschi, and J. G. Weis. (1981). *Measuring Delinquency.* Beverly Hills: Sage.

Hirschi, Travis. (1969). *Causes of Delinquency.* Berkeley: University of California Press.

McCormick, C. (1995). *Constructing Danger: The Misrepresentation of Crime in the News.* Halifax: Fernwood Publishing.

Nettler, G. (1974). *Explaining Crime.* New York: McGraw-Hill.

Ogrodnick, Lucie. (2007). "Seniors as Victims of Crime, 2004 and 2005." Statistics Canada Catalogue Number 85F0033MIE20-014. http://www.statcan.ca/english/research/85F0033MIE/85F0033MIE2007014.pdf. Accessed 29 September, 2007.

Polsky, Ned. (1967). *Hustlers, Beats, and Others.* Chicago: Aldine.

Shearing, Clifford D. (1984). "Dial-A-Cop: A Study of Police Mobilization." Report for the Centre of Criminology, University of Toronto.

Silverman, R. A. (1980). "Measuring Crime: More Problems." *Journal of Police Science and Administration* 8(3):265–74.

Silverman, R. A., and J. Teevan. (1975). *Crime in Canadian Society.* Toronto: Butterworths.

Skogan, W. (1978). "Review of Surveying Crime." *Journal of Criminal Law and Criminology* 69: 139–40.

———. (1981). "Issues in the Measurement of Victimization." Washington, D.C.: U.S. Department of Justice, Bureau of Justice Statistics.

Solicitor General Canada. (1983). "Victims of Crime." Canadian Urban Victimization Survey. Ottawa: Solicitor General Canada.

———. (1984a). "Reported and Unreported Crimes." Canadian Urban Victimization Survey. Ottawa: Solicitor General Canada.

———. (1984b). "Crime Prevention: Awareness and Practice." Canadian Urban Victimization Survey. Ottawa: Solicitor General Canada.

———. (1985a). "Female Victims of Crime." Canadian Urban Victimization Survey. Ottawa: Solicitor General Canada.

———. (1985b). "Cost of Crime to Victims." Canadian Urban Victimization Survey. Ottawa: Solicitor General Canada.

———. (1985c). "Criminal Victimizations of Elderly Canadians." Canadian Urban Victimization Survey. Ottawa: Solicitor General Canada.

———. (1986). "Household Property Crimes." Canadian Urban Victimization Survey. Ottawa: Solicitor General Canada.

Statistics Canada. (1999). "Illicit Drugs and Crime in Canada." *Juristat* 19(1). Catalogue No. 85-002-XPE.

———. (2000). "Criminal Victimization in Canada, 1999." *Juristat* 20(10). Catalogue No. 85-002-XIE.

———. (2001). "Canadian Crime Statistics, 2000." Catalogue No. 85-002-XIE.

———. (2002a). "Adult Correctional Services in Canada, 2000/01." *Juristat* 22(10). Catalogue No. 85-002-XIE.

———. (2002b). "Canadian Crime Statistics, 2001." *Juristat* 22(6). Catalogue No. 85-002.

———. (2007). "Uniform Crime Reporting Survey (UCR). Ottawa: Statistics Canada. http://www.statcan.ca/cgi-bin/imdb/p2SV.pl?Function=getSurvey&SDDS=3302&lang=en&db=IMDB&dbg=f&adm=8&dis=2. Accessed 25 September, 2007.

Thornberry, Terence P., and Marvin D. Krohn. (2000). "The Self-Report Method for Measuring Delinquency and Crime." *Criminal Justice 2000,* Vol. 4. National Institute of Justice, Washington, D.C.

Correlates of Criminal Behaviour

5

Timothy F. Hartnagel

UNIVERSITY OF ALBERTA

Which Canadians are most likely to commit crimes? Are older people more likely to commit crimes than younger people? Are men more likely to commit crimes than women? Are upper-class people more or less likely to break the law than their lower-class counterparts? Which provinces have the highest rate of crime? Each of these questions asks about a correlate of crime. A correlate is a phenomenon that accompanies another phenomenon and is related in some way to it. **Correlates** of crime are those phenomena that are associated with criminal activity. While a list of such phenomena would include any number of conditions, the discussion in this chapter will be limited to some of the social conditions that are correlated with crime. We will describe and discuss the relationship between criminal behaviour and age, sex, race, drug abuse, social class, and region.

correlate
Any variable that is related to another variable. Age and sex are the two strongest correlates of crime.

Learning Objectives

After reading this chapter, you should be able to

- Distinguish between correlates and causes of criminal behaviour.
- Identify and describe the major social correlates of criminal behaviour in Canada.
- Describe and explain trends in the age and sex distribution of criminal behaviour.
- Describe the relationship between race and criminal behaviour and explain the over-representation of Aboriginal people in the Canadian criminal justice system.
- Understand the relationship between drug misuse and criminal behaviour.
- Discuss and reconcile the apparently conflicting evidence regarding the correlation between social class and criminal behaviour.
- Describe how crime rates vary by geographic region.

Correlates Defined

Before turning to the details of these specific correlates, the concept of correlation itself should be considered briefly. **Correlation** refers to a relationship between at least two phenomena that are related, or occur, or vary together. For

correlation
A relationship that exists when two or more variables, such as age and crime, are associated or related to one another.

example, some criminologists have claimed that delinquent behaviour is correlated with physique or body type. They claim that adolescent males with an athletic, muscular body build commit more delinquent acts than those whose physique is lean and fragile. Other criminologists have shown that some types of crime occur more frequently in larger cities than in smaller towns and rural areas. They argue that city size and crime vary together. These examples give measurements on two variables (for example, city size and crime) for a number of individuals or aggregates (for example, cities). The task is to determine whether and how these two sets of measurements go together—that is, whether and how they're correlated. When we analyze the relationship between two variables, we may find that they are positively correlated, negatively correlated, or unrelated to each other. A positive relationship means that as one variable increases, the other also increases. For example, the more deviant friends we have, the more likely we are to be deviant ourselves. A negative relationship means that as one variable increases, the other decreases. For example, as we get older, we are less likely to be involved in criminal behaviour. Discovering such correlations or relationships is an important first step for any scientific discipline such as criminology. Thus, a good deal of the early work in criminology was devoted to the task of identifying and describing the correlates of crime.

Having identified and described a correlate of crime—a relationship—it is natural to want to know why it exists. How might this relationship be explained? What might have produced it?

One explanation for a correlation or relationship between two variables is causal. The concept of causation has been debated by philosophers and social scientists. At the very least, the idea of causation has proven to be a useful way of thinking about the natural and social world. A causal explanation refers to the inference that a change in one variable results from or is produced by change in another variable. A common mistake is to confuse correlation with causation and so to infer that one variable causes another from the fact that they are correlated. However, correlation means only that two variables are related. They are associated or go together, but change in one does not necessarily produce a change in the other. Criminologists are frequently interested in establishing causal explanations. They are not usually satisfied, for example, with knowing that poverty and crime are correlated; they want to know if crime results from poverty, and if it does, how? However, it would be a mistake to conclude from their correlation alone that poverty causes crime. So correlation between two variables is a necessary first step toward causal explanation but is not in itself sufficient for inferring such an explanation.

The second element of a causal explanation is a *theory* linking the variables. Events may occur together, but one will not be viewed as causing the other unless we have some explanation of how they are linked. We look for correlates of crime to help us to explain criminal behaviour, and our explanatory theories must be tested against what we know about crime. For example, we may have a theory that the movement of the planets causes criminality. However, when we test this explanation, we find that there is no correlation between planetary movements and crime rates. Thus, we will reject the theory, at least until some evidence supporting it can be found. Much of the attention of criminologists has been devoted to developing and testing theories of crime, and these theories must explain the facts about crime. Therefore, the correlates discussed in this chapter set the stage for the theories that follow.

Human beings have a tendency to simplify their perceptions of the world. This tendency can lead to a distortion of the understanding of correlates and causes. There is a temptation to assume that an effect can have only one cause that is both necessary and sufficient. There is also the temptation to assume that causes must be perfectly correlated with their effects and that no other variables are necessary for interpreting how the cause operates or for specifying the particular conditions or circumstances under which it has its effect(s) (Hirschi and Selvin, 1966). But reality is substantially more complicated than this, and it would be wise to develop the habit of thinking of crime as the consequence of multiple causes that combine in complicated ways to produce their effects. Nettler (1982) uses the image of a dense web to communicate the meaning of this view of causation. He describes this as a multiplicity of tightly packed causes that interact strongly and non-uniformly. As selected correlates of crime are examined, then, the urge to reach hasty conclusions concerning the causal character and significance of these correlations should be resisted.

Age

Peak Ages for Crime

Without much exaggeration, crime can be said to be a young man's game. To put this into more technical terms, age and sex are strong correlates of criminal behaviour. Any number of criminologists has singled out these two variables for their strong relationship with crime. For example, Sutherland and Cressey (1978) state that sex status is of greater importance in differentiating criminals from non-criminals than any other trait, and that statistics from a variety of years and jurisdictions uniformly indicate a higher prevalence of crime among young persons compared with other age groups.

Figure 5.1 shows the distribution of persons accused of property and violent crimes by age for 2003. While the percentage of persons accused of crime increases from early adolescence to young adulthood and then generally declines, this pattern is stronger for property crimes. Although in 2003 persons aged 15 to 24 represented 14 percent of the total population, they accounted for 45 percent of persons accused of property crimes and 32 percent of persons accused of violent crimes (Bunge et al., 2005).

WWW

"Youth Court Statistics, 2003/04." 2005. Jennifer Thomas. *Juristat* 25(4).
To find this and other interesting research papers, go to
www.statcan.ca/bsolc/english/bsolc?catno=85-002-XIE

Data for 2003–04 from the Adult Criminal Court Survey (Thomas, 2004) also show that younger adults are over-represented among accused persons when comparing the age distribution of offenders to the age distribution of the general adult population. For example, 18-to-24-year-olds made up 12 percent of the adult population but accounted for 31 percent of all cases in adult criminal court in 2003–04. In contrast, persons 55 or older represented 30 percent of the adult population but only 5 percent of the adult criminal court cases. This age distribution is stronger for property crimes (36 percent of accused were 18 to 24) than for violent crimes (25 percent were 18 to 24).

FIGURE 5.1 Persons Accused of Property Crimes and Violent Crimes by Age, per 100 000 Population, Canada, 2003

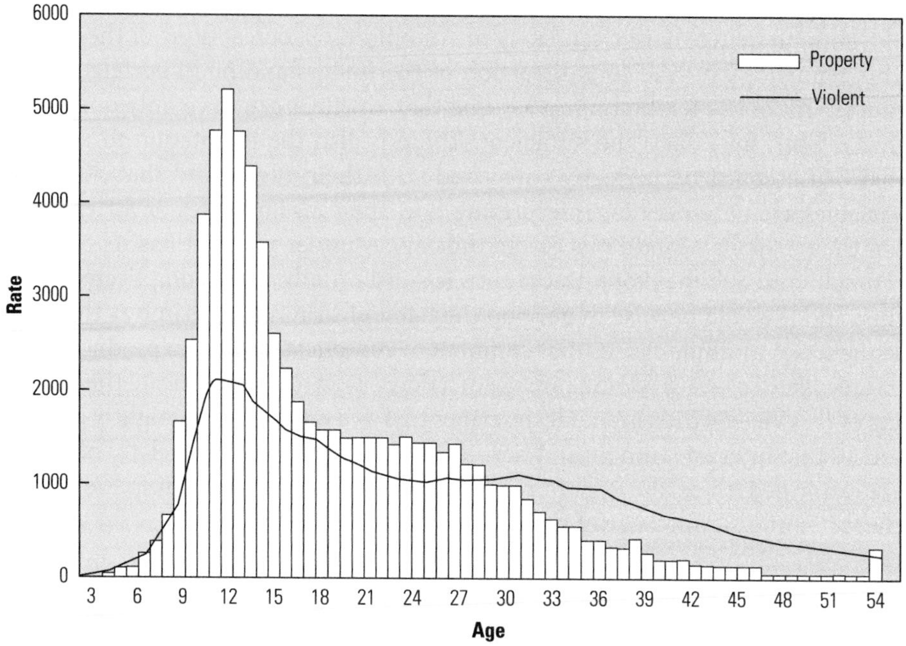

Source: Statistics Canada. "Crime Statistics in Canada, 2003." *Juristat*, Catalogue 85-002, Vol. 24, no. 6.

Different crimes peak at different ages, and rates of some types of crime decline much more slowly with increasing age (Steffensmeier et al., 1989). Some crimes, including embezzlement, fraud, and gambling, do not conform to the general pattern and peak later in the life cycle (Steffensmeier and Allan, 1995). Braithwaite (1989) has pointed out that white-collar crimes, which are committed by persons of respectability and high status in the course of their occupation, peak later in life because these crimes require the opportunities provided by occupations that most people under 25 have yet to attain.

Self-report data also support the age–crime relationship, though such research has generally limited its attention to juveniles and is, therefore, of only limited usefulness for examining the full range of the age–crime relationship. The self-report results from a national survey of adolescents in the United States by Ageton and Elliott (1978) only partially agree with the official data concerning age and crime. Their results suggest that the peak ages for youthful crime are somewhat younger than the official data indicate, with the highest incidence for many property and violent offences occurring between the ages of 13 and 15. Juvenile diversion programs and hesitancy to formally process adolescents through the criminal justice system may play some role in explaining the higher peak ages in official data on arrests and convictions. Osgood et al. (1989) compared offence rates based on arrests and on self-reports and found that both methods show substantial declines from ages 17 through 23 for virtually all offences, with the major exception of arrests for assault.

Canadian self-report research in Montreal by LeBlanc (1983) found that in a sample of adolescents aged 12 to 18, self-reported delinquency increased progressively until age 16 or 17 and then diminished, though this pattern varied with the nature of the delinquency. Serious delinquency tended to diminish with increasing age, while drug and status offences increased. Similarly, Fréchette (1983) found delinquency to be closely linked with age in his sample of male wards of the Montreal Social Welfare Court. Seventy-five to 80 percent of his respondents reduced or stopped their delinquency during the second half of their adolescence. However, he found an abrupt and substantial rise in criminal activity with the onset of adulthood. Fifteen to 20 percent of his initial sample of respondents had an adult record for serious crime.

Since younger age categories are over-represented among criminal offenders, it's quite likely that changes over time in the crime rate reflect, at least in part, changes in the age composition of the total population. Several researchers have shown that a significant amount of the rise and fall of U.S. crime rates can be explained by the changing age composition of the American population, primarily the aging of the "baby boomers" (Cohen and Land, 1987; Sagi and Wellford, 1968; Steffensmeier and Harer, 1991; Wellford, 1973). Overall crime rates rose as this group reached their late teens in the 1960s and then fell as they began to reach their 30s a decade later (Carrington, 2001). Similarly in Canada, baby boomers—those born between 1947 and 1966—reached 15 years of age in the 1960s and 1970s, a time when violent and property crime rates were rising. Figure 5.2 shows the trend in overall crime and in the number of 15-to-24-year-olds as rates per 100 000 population. The rate of 15-to-24-year-olds began dropping in the early 1980s. The general decline in crime rates since the early 1990s coincided with a decrease in the proportion of persons aged 15 to 24 during the

FIGURE 5.2 Crime Rate and Population Aged 15–24, per 100 000 Population, Canada 1962–2003[1]

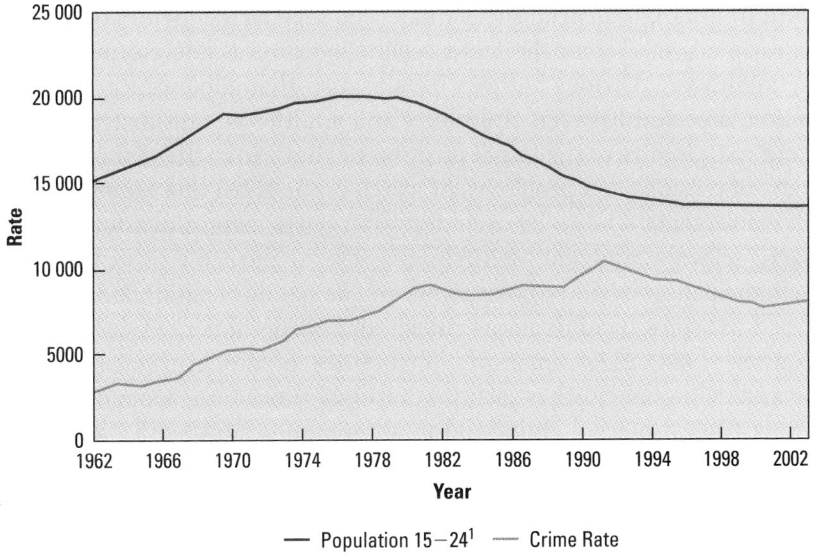

[1] Note that the population 15–24 refers to changes in the population for these age groups and not changes in crime rates.

Source: Statistics Canada. Adapted from the Statistics Canada publication, "Crime Statistics in Canada, 2003." *Juristat*, Catalogue 85-002, Vol. 24, no. 6.

same time period (Savoie, 2002). Ouimet (2002) examined the drop in crime in the 1990s in both the United States and Canada and attributed it primarily to these shifts in the age composition of the population, as well as improved employment opportunities. Carrington (2001) has forecast that all types of crime in Canada should decline to the year 2041 because of the continuing aging of the population, ignoring all other factors that might affect crime rates.

However, other researchers have found the changing age structure of the population to have only a limited impact on crime rates (Levitt, 1999; Steffensmeier and Harer, 1991). This may depend on the type of crime. For example, two Canadian studies reported the changing age composition had a significant impact on the decline in Canadian homicide rates (Leenaars and Lester, 2004; Sprott and Cesaroni, 2002). But an examination of the relationships between changes in crime rates for the four major crime types of homicide, robbery, break and enter, and motor vehicle theft and a number of socio-demographic and economic trends during the period 1962 to 2003 found only a positive relationship between the proportion of the population aged 15 to 24 and rates of break and enter (Bunge et al., 2005). These authors conclude that shifts in the age composition of the population are only one of many factors contributing to crime rate changes.

Maturational Reform

To conclude this discussion on age and its relation to crime, the ways in which criminologists have attempted to explain this correlation should be briefly noted. Factors such as bias in the criminal justice system in favour of the very young or the much older offender, increased skill in avoiding detection with advancing age, and the decline in physical strength and agility associated with aging have all been mentioned as possible causes. However, the social position of youth in urban, industrial society has been seen as the major contributor to "**maturational reform**" or the rapid decline in crime as adolescents move into young adulthood. Various authors have argued that adolescence is a time of transition, a period between childhood and adulthood, and that the ambiguities and marginality of the social position of youth in modern societies create a variety of tensions and problems, of which crime is but one example (Nettler, 1984). Adolescents tend to be excluded from participation in adult roles such as marriage, work, and adult leisure activities. At the same time, they experience emancipation from the constraints and demands of childhood and are encouraged to aspire to adult status (Bloch and Niederhoffer, 1958; West, 1984). As Nettler (1984, 217) remarks, "[S]tructures of modern states encourage crime and delinquency. They lack institutional procedures for moving people smoothly from protected childhood to autonomous adulthood." But as youth move into the adult ages and their social status and integration increase, the personal costs of crime to the individual also increase—they now have more to lose—while at the same time, crime becomes somewhat redundant to their improved social position. Youth acquire added stakes in conforming behaviour (see Chapter 13) as they occupy social roles and acquire material goods that would be jeopardized by criminal behaviour. They become more socially integrated into relationships, groups, and organizations and, therefore, more

maturational reform
The observation that involvement in crime tends to decrease as people age.

dependent on the social rewards of conformity (Rowe and Tittle, 1977). New rewards and costs associated with their new adult status replace those that sustained delinquency in adolescence; new satisfactions replace those previously provided by delinquency (Trasler, 1980).

Greenberg (1979) has offered the most elaborate version of this type of explanation. He argues that adolescents in North American society are particularly vulnerable to the expectations and evaluations of their peers because of the increased age segregation resulting from the exclusion of young people from adult work and leisure activity. At the same time, money is necessary for participation in this youth culture, but the deterioration of the teenage labour market has resulted in adolescents being less able to finance their costly social life. Greenberg regards theft as a way of financing participation in activities with peers in the absence of legitimate sources of income. With increasing age, both the dependence on peers and the lack of legitimate sources of funds are reduced for many of these young people; consequently, theft declines. Greenberg also discusses how the extended requirements for schooling restrict adolescent autonomy and how public humiliation of some students by teachers undermines self-esteem and produces embarrassment before peers. This can result in non-utilitarian crime, such as vandalism and violence, as an attempt to assert independence and enhance self-esteem before a sympathetic audience of peers. These motivations to crime are removed when young people leave the restrictive and sometimes degrading school setting. Greenberg also claims that the cost of crime for youth through legal penalties increases as they progress from early to later adolescence, as do opportunities for establishing stakes in conforming behaviour, particularly employment. These social controls, or costs, increase with age and, therefore, also contribute to the decline in crime.

Hirschi and Gottfredson (1983) present evidence that the relationship of age to crime has been similar in earlier historical times and in other types of society, thus challenging the premise that the nature of modern, urban, industrialized society is crucial for explaining this age–crime correlation. Hirschi and Gottfredson cite research suggesting that the effects of age on crime do not depend on such life-course events as leaving school, finding gainful employment, getting married, and so forth: "Age affects crime whether or not these events occur" (1983, 580). Some recent research (Tittle and Ward, 1993) also supports the Hirschi–Gottfredson hypothesis that the correlates and causes of crime do not significantly vary by age. Furthermore, Tanner and Krahn (1991) report a small *positive* effect of part-time work on illegal behaviour among Canadian high school seniors, although other variables were more strongly linked to this self-reported delinquency. Teenagers with part-time jobs while in school were more likely than those not working to report illegal behaviour, a finding somewhat at odds with Greenberg's (1979) argument. These findings undermine the maturational reform type of explanation, though other research questions this interpretation.

Recent research examining crime over the life course suggests that such salient life events as leaving school, entering the labour market, and getting married influence the likelihood of criminal behaviour (Loeber and LeBlanc, 1990; Sampson and Laub, 1990, 1992). Maturational reform among males may be accelerated by such events as completion of education, marriage, and parenthood, and delayed by events such as joining a gang or experiencing unemployment (Rand, 1987). A longitudinal study of Canadian high school graduates, which followed them during the transition into young adulthood, found that those who had delinquent friends reported more criminal behaviour (Hartnagel, 1998). Furthermore, the combination of longer amounts of unemployment and having delinquent peers during this time of transition also led to increased crime. So despite evidence of continuity in deviant behaviour over the life course, certain social transitions help explain the decline in crime in young adulthood. Finally, Warr (1993) has recently shown that the age–crime relationship is modified by the amount of exposure to delinquent peers, casting additional doubt on Hirschi and Gottfredson's claim that the age distribution of crime cannot be explained by social variables. Although the correlation of age with crime is one of the most undisputed facts of criminology, its interpretation and explanation still remain open to a good deal of debate.

Sex

Sex Differences and Crime Trends

"Correlates of Delinquency: A Look at Gender Differences" Linda Simourd and D. A. Andrews, Correctional Service of Canada
www.csc-scc.gc.ca/text/pblct/forum/e06/e061g_e.shtml

As has already been indicated, sex is strongly correlated with crime. The crime rate for men greatly exceeds the rate for women. In Canada, in 2003, adult males constituted 81 percent of adults charged with Criminal Code offences, while 70 percent of youths charged with Criminal Code offences were male (Wallace, 2004).

This sex difference in crime varies somewhat by type of crime. Table 5.1 shows that males made up 84 percent of the adults charged with violent crimes in 2003 and 78 percent of those charged for property crime. Females, in contrast, constituted only 16 percent and 22 percent of those charged for violent and property crimes, respectively. Violent crime, in particular, then, is correlated with being male, although this sex difference is reduced among youth.

Data from victim surveys parallel arrest statistics in demonstrating that offenders are disproportionately male (Bureau of Justice Statistics, 1993). Victimization data from the 2004 General Social Survey in Canada (Gannon and Mihorean, 2005) estimated that males represented 87 percent of the perpetrators of all violent crime, 91 percent of sexual assault, 88 percent of robbery, and 86 percent of physical assault—figures reasonably similar to those provided by the official data on males charged with these offences.

Self-report research with juveniles has generally substantiated this sex difference in delinquency, though the gap is not as great as in the official data on adults. Hagan (1985) noted that the sex ratio in a number of self-report surveys conducted in the United States in the 1970s showed males exceeding females in self-reported delinquency by more than 2 to 1, compared to the 1975 official arrest ratio of 3.72 to 1 for those younger than 18. Yet LeBlanc's (1983) research in Montreal showed a much smaller gap between male and female delinquency (3 to 1) than the official statistics indicated (8 or 10 to 1). This may, at least in part, reflect differences in police handling of juvenile offenders. Furthermore, Hindelang et al. (1979) have argued sex differences found in self-report studies are highly

TABLE 5.1 Persons Accused by Age Group and Sex, Selected Incidents, 2003

	Age Group by Sex					
	Adult (18 and over)		*Youth (12 to 17)*		*Total by Age Group*	
	Male	*Female*	*Male*	*Female*	*Adult*	*Youth*
	%		%		%	
Homicide	90	10	79	21	86	14
Attempted Murder	85	15	94	6	88	12
Assaults	82	18	71	29	81	19
Sexual assaults	98	2	97	3	79	21
Other sexual offences	97	3	94	6	75	25
Abduction	42	58	100	0	98	2
Robbery	91	9	86	14	65	35
Violent crime—Total	84	16	74	26	82	18
Break and enter	93	7	91	9	67	33
Motor vehicle theft	91	9	84	16	61	39
Fraud	71	29	66	34	93	7
Theft over $5,000	82	18	84	16	81	19
Theft $5,000 and under	70	30	61	39	67	33
Property crime—Total	78	22	75	25	69	31
Mischief	87	13	90	10	56	44
Arson	83	17	91	9	45	55
Prostitution	51	49	23	77	99	1
Offensive weapons	82	18	92	8	98	2
Criminal code—Total (excluding Traffic)	81	19	70	30	83	17
Impaired driving[1]	87	13	84	16	99	1
Cannabis Offences	88	12	85	15	72	28
Cocaine Offences	82	18	79	21	95	5
Other Drug Offences	84	16	83	17	80	20

[1] Includes impaired operation of a vehicle causing death, causing body harm, alcohol rate over 80 mg., failure/refusal to provide a breath/blood sample.

Source: Statistics Canada. Adapted from the Statistics Canada publication, *Crime Statistics in Canada, 2003. Juristat* 24(6). Catalogue No. 85-002-XIE, 2004.

contingent upon the content of the specific items asked. They concluded that once the typically limited seriousness of these items is taken into account, apparent discrepancies between self-report and official data prove to be illusory; they don't measure the same domain of behaviour. Fitzgerald (2003) examined sex differences in delinquency among Canadian youth aged 12–15 surveyed in the National Longitudinal Survey of Children and Youth. As expected, the females reported lower rates of delinquency than did the males for each of the property and violent acts. While 29 percent of males reported committing violent and property-related delinquency, only 19 percent of females said they committed property crimes and 10 percent reported involvement in violent acts. The ratio of male to female delinquency was greater for the more serious acts.

TABLE 5.2 Rate of Adults Charged[1] by Sex per 100 000 Population[2] for Selected Criminal Code Offences, Canada, 1968, 2000

	1968		*2000*	
	Males	*Females*	*Males*	*Females*
Homicide	2.4	0.3	2.7	0.3
Robbery	26.6	1.6	38.3	3.5
Crimes of violence	270.5	15.0	652.7	112.7
Break and enter	157.6	3.4	130.0	9.8
Theft over[3]	82.4	8.5	9.7	2.9
Theft under[4]	175.0	49.7	253.4	100.7
Frauds	105.0	12.8	103.9	43.9
Property crimes	639.7	79.2	636.1	176.7
Criminal Code	1443.4	152.0	2059.7	432.4

[1] Source: Statistics Canada. (1968). *Crime Statistics, 1968*, Catalogue No. 85-205; Canadian Centre for Justice Statistics. (2001). *Canadian Crime Statistics, 2000*, Catalogue No. 85-205.
[2] Sources of population estimates: Statistics Canada. (1970). *Estimates of Population by Marital Status, Age and Sex, Canada and Provinces, 1968*. Catalogue No. 91-203; Statistics Canada. (2002). E-STAT, Table 051-0001, Estimates of population, by age group and sex, Canada, provinces and territories, annual (persons). 1968 males = 10 409 900; females = 10 334 100; 2000 males = 15 234 321; females = 15 535 348.
[3] 1968—Theft over $50; 2000—Theft over $5000.
[4] 1968—Theft $50 and under; 2000—Theft $5000 and under.

These official statistics and self-report studies are static and don't give any indication of historical trends. For instance, it is *possible* that sex differences in crime have varied over the years such that at certain times, females may have approached equality with males in a broad spectrum of offences. In fact, some criminologists have argued that a new female criminal has arisen in the past few years (Adler, 1975). She argues that not only has the participation of women in crime increased, but they have moved into areas of lawbreaking that were formerly the exclusive domain of men. The data on trends through time in the criminality of men and women should be considered, then, to see whether the gap between them has expanded and/or narrowed over the years.

Table 5.2 presents the rate of adults charged in Canada, by sex, for the years 1968 and 2000. Over the 32 years, the rate for all Criminal Code offences for males increased by 43 percent, while for females, the increase was 184 percent. The percentage of females increased from 9 percent to 18 percent of adults charged with Criminal Code offences. For violent crime, the rate at which males were charged increased by 141 percent and for females, 652 percent. For property crime, the male rate declined slightly (–5 percent) while the female rate increased by 123 percent. So the increases for females have greatly exceeded those for males over this 32-year period. However, a quick glance down the two columns of rates for 2000 will reveal that large absolute differences remain, with the male rates greatly exceeding those for females, particularly for crimes of violence. In 1968, only 10 percent of all women charged were charged for violent crimes, while 52 percent were charged for property crimes. By 2000, the number of women charged for violence had increased to 26 percent of all women charged, but 41 percent were charged with property crime. However, the highest rates for women charged continue to be for less serious thefts of property.

A number of researchers have examined and attempted to interpret trends in male and female contributions to crime in the United States (Simon, 1975; Hagan, 1985; Steffensmeier, 1978; Steffensmeier et al., 1979; Austin, 1993). The general consensus of this research is that the gender gap in crime, particularly serious and violent crime, remains substantial. O'Brien (1999) examined the trends in selected arrest rates for males and females in the United States over a longer time period (1960 to 1995). He reported that the rates appeared to be converging for robbery, burglary, and auto theft and diverging for homicide, with no significant overall trends in either direction for aggravated assaults or larceny. This shows the importance of examining male and female trends in specific crimes, some of which appear to be converging. In Canada there has been a definite narrowing of the gender gap in crime overall, and for both violent and property offences (Campbell, 1990). But the speed of convergence has not been constant, depending upon the time period examined, and most Canadian female crime still consists of petty property offences such as shoplifting (Boritch, 1997).

Fisher (1986) replicated Steffensmeier's U.S. research with Canadian data on trends in persons charged by sex between 1962 and 1978. Like Steffensmeier, she found a narrowing of the relative gap between males and females in property crime charge rates, with the greatest increases in the rate at which females are charged with petty property crime—the crimes with which women have traditionally been associated. However, the absolute gap widened for all property crimes except for theft over $200, such that female property crime levels continue to lag behind those of males despite large increases in the rate at which females are charged for property crime. The relative gap between the sexes in violent crime remained about the same, while the absolute gap widened. Violent crime remained predominantly the domain of males. Fisher also documented the much lower base rates from 1962 for females. Therefore, large percentage increases resulted from relatively small absolute increases in female crime. Fisher's Canadian results are generally quite comparable to those of Steffensmeier for the United States, though the Canadian crime rates for both men and women are lower, particularly for violent crime.

Conclusions about trends in female crime that are based on official data sources, such as arrest rates or charge rates, are vulnerable to the claim that such official data reflect changes in the response to female crime by the criminal justice system as much as or more than they do real changes in criminal behaviour. Therefore, it would be desirable to have trend data from alternative sources such as self-report research. But self-report data are generally very time-bound, having been conducted in a particular location at a given point in time, and they are, therefore, limited in their usefulness for examining trends in crime. However, Smith and Visher (1980) analyzed 44 different self-report and official data studies that reported on the relationship between sex and deviance and found that the year the data were gathered was an important factor in explaining the magnitude of the sex-deviant behaviour correlation. They found that this correlation has been decreasing in size over time—meaning less gender disparity in deviant behaviour—and has declined more rapidly according to self-report studies than to research based on official sources of data. This narrowing of the gap is mainly for minor acts of deviance rather than for serious criminal behaviour and more for youths than for adults.

These various data on sex differences and crime trends lead to the conclusion that sex, like age, remains strongly correlated with criminal behaviour. Males are much more involved in criminal acts than females. Women have increased their participation in crime, including violent crime, although the increase has been greatest for minor property crimes such as theft and fraud. These two categories include offences such as shoplifting, credit card fraud, and passing bad cheques that women have commonly committed in the past. While the gender gap in crime has narrowed somewhat, it remains substantial, particularly for the most serious offences.

Role Convergence?

Criminologists have offered various explanations for the sex difference in criminal involvement, as well as for the changes in female participation in crime through time. Early theories of female criminality emphasized biological and psychological factors (Smart, 1976). Some claimed that sex differences in criminality were illusory and resulted from the greater cunning and deceitfulness of women, as well as from their preferential treatment by the police and the courts (Pollak, 1950). More recently, greater emphasis has been placed on the importance of socially structured differences in gender roles. This line of reasoning argues that males and females are subjected to differing expectations and demands regarding appropriate behaviour, as well as being subject to different mechanisms of social control. Boys are socialized to greater independence and risk taking and are, therefore, freer to experiment with deviant conduct (Hagan et al., 1979). Girls, on the other hand, are rewarded for compliance and dependence and so have fewer opportunities to experiment with delinquency. The traditional division of labour between the sexes, with women facing greater restriction to the private sphere in the domestic roles of wife and mother, further limited women's opportunities to engage in many forms of criminal conduct. The more public role of men, on the other hand, not only provided more opportunities for certain crimes; it also exposed them, to a much greater extent, to the formal social controls of the criminal justice system (Hagan et al., 1979).

Changes in gender role expectations should have consequences on the actual behaviour of males and females, including their criminal behaviour. More specifically, the convergence hypothesis suggests that as the social roles of the sexes become more equal or begin to converge, differences in their criminal behaviour should diminish (Nettler, 1984; Fox and Hartnagel, 1979). In one version of this thesis, Simon (1975) suggested that increases in property crimes committed by women could be attributed to the expansion of employment opportunities for women. This apparent emancipation of women from domestic roles may bring with it increased opportunities to commit property crime as well as subjecting women to greater pressures for achievement, which may create pressures or strains toward crime (Merton, 1938). Fox and Hartnagel (1979) tested the **role convergence** hypothesis by examining the relationship between changes in the Canadian conviction rate for females from 1931 to 1968

role convergence
Explanation for the rising crime rate among women has been that their roles have become similar to (converged with) those of men.

and three measures of women's changing gender role. Women's participation in the labour force over these same years and the rate at which females were granted post-secondary degrees were used as measures of the convergence of gender roles, while the total fertility rate indicated the degree of persistence of women's domestic role. The convergence hypothesis was generally supported by this analysis, particularly for the female conviction rate for theft. As the female labour force participation rate and the rate at which females were granted post-secondary degrees increased and the fertility rate declined, the female conviction rate for theft increased. However, the authors note that they were unable to introduce measures to control for an alternative hypothesis. Changes in the treatment of females by the police or courts may better account for any changes in the female conviction rate. Less preferential treatment for women by the criminal justice system could explain rising female crime rates.

Other criminologists have questioned the role convergence hypothesis. Steffensmeier (1980), for example, has argued that most of the increase in female property crime is for the traditional female crimes of petty theft and fraud. These crimes are more related to the traditional female domestic roles of shopper and consumer. He questioned the degree to which gender roles have really changed by pointing to women's restricted labour market participation. Most women work in jobs with limited access to illegitimate opportunities. Furthermore, women still have primary responsibility for home and child care. "Female experiences are not moving beyond traditional roles, either legitimate or illegitimate" (1980, 1102). As Holly Johnson (1987) has reminded us, the high proportion of women offenders charged with theft or fraud (54 percent of all Criminal Code charges against women in 1988) is consistent with women's traditional role as consumers and, increasingly, as low-income, semi-skilled, single parents. Female offenders tend to be young, poor, undereducated, and unskilled, suggesting that female crime is at least partly the product of women's subordinate socio-economic position (Boritch, 1997; Johnson, 1987). The typical crimes of women may be symptomatic of their economic deprivation and marginality. Box and Hale (1984) found some limited evidence in their British data that deteriorating economic conditions experienced by women, rather than female emancipation, were related to increases in female crime. Steffensmeier and Streifel (1992) tested alternative explanations for changes in the female share of property crime arrests in the United States. Their findings did not support the gender equality–role convergence argument. Instead, increases in the female share of property crime were largely a function of more formal, bureaucratic policing and, to a lesser extent, the greater economic marginality of women. Further research on this topic should include attention to the relation between gender roles and patterns of social control.

Race

Race and Crime

While not as strongly related to crime and delinquency as age and sex, race has been found to be a good predictor of criminality, at least in the United States

FIGURE 5.3 Racial Distribution of Offenders in Federal Correctional System, Canada, November, 2002

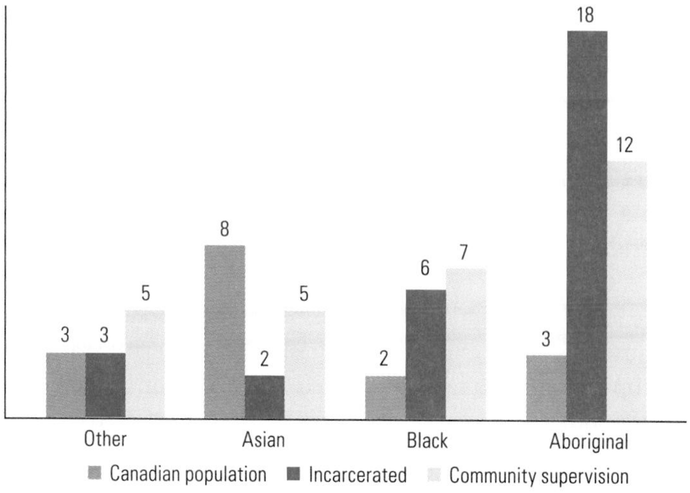

Source: Shelly Trevethan and Christopher Rastin. *A Profile of Visible Minority Offenders in the Federal Canadian Correctional System*. 2004. Ottawa: Correctional Services Canada.

(Tonry, 1995). However, Canadian research on race and crime is much more limited since such information is generally not collected by the criminal justice system. The question of whether race and crime data should be routinely collected in Canada has been the subject of some debate (Johnston, 1994; Roberts, 1994). In 1990, Statistics Canada decided to collect police data on the race of crime suspects on a trial basis but had to reverse this decision when only a minority of police forces were willing or able to provide such data and because of criticism from various minority organizations and academics (Roberts and Doob, 1997). Thus our information on the relationship between race and crime in Canada is very limited.

The information that is available suggests that certain racial minorities are over-represented in the Canadian correctional system.

Specifically, the data in Figure 5.3 reveal that in combination visible minorities account for approximately 11 percent of those incarcerated and 16 percent of those serving time in the community. Since they constituted 13 percent of the total population in 2001, visible minorities as a category are not over-represented among incarcerated offenders although they are slightly over-represented among those serving time in the community. But differences emerge when specific groups are examined. While they make up only about 2 percent of the population, Blacks represent 6 percent of the federally incarcerated and 7 percent of those serving time in the community. Asian offenders, on the other hand, are under-represented relative to their share of the Canadian population; "other" minorities are not over-represented among the incarcerated but are slightly over-represented among those serving time in the community. Caucasians are under-represented among both categories of offenders. Aboriginal offenders, on the other hand, are significantly over-represented among both categories: while they made up approximately 3 percent of the population in 2001, they accounted for 18 percent of offenders in federal prisons in 2002 and

12 percent of those under community supervision. Despite apparent increased attention on the "problem" of crime committed by immigrants, Thomas (1993) concluded that the foreign-born were highly under-represented among those incarcerated for violent crimes.

Controversy has surfaced in recent years on the topic of alleged racial profiling by police. Much of this debate has been focused on the Toronto police due in part to a series of articles by the *Toronto Star* newspaper and subsequent discussion in academic journals (see, for example, Melchers, 2003; Wortley and Tanner, 2003; 2005; Gold, 2003; Gabor, 2004). The focus of this discussion has been on the Black population in Toronto and their treatment by the Toronto Police Service. The series of *Toronto Star* articles alleging the racial profiling of Blacks was based on the newspaper's analysis of arrest data obtained under a freedom of information request and interviews with Black community leaders and advocates. The Toronto Police Service denied these claims and commissioned an independent review of the *Star*'s analysis that concluded that the conclusions of the *Star*'s articles were completely unjustified and irresponsible (quoted in Melchers, 2003:347). But the bases for this conclusion have, in turn, been severely critiqued on methodological and interpretive grounds (Melchers, 2003; Wortley and Tanner, 2003). Since police in Canada are not required to report on the race of the people they target for field investigations (Wortley, 2003), it is difficult for Canadian researchers to determine whether racial minorities received greater police surveillance than people from other racial backgrounds, although there is some evidence from field studies suggesting this is the case (James, 1998; Neugebaur, 2000). If racial minorities are subject to greater police surveillance, they are also more likely to be caught when they break the law than are white people who engage in the same forms of criminal behaviour. So arrest statistics, particularly for certain crimes, may have more to do with police surveillance practices than actual racial differences in criminal behaviour. Thus racial profiling may help explain the over-representation of minorities in arrest statistics (Wortley, 2003), as well as contributing to their over-representation in subsequent stages of the criminal justice system.

Social surveys are an alternative method for gathering data to address this issue. As part of their response to the controversy in Toronto, Wortley and Tanner (2005) reported on some results from their Toronto Youth Crime and Victimization Survey conducted in 2000 in the Toronto school systems with a random sample of 3393 high school students. Students who self-identified as black were much more likely to self-report being stopped and searched by the police than students from other racial backgrounds, with white students more likely to report being stopped and searched than Asians, South Asians, or West Asians. Black students also scored significantly higher on a self-report deviant behaviour scale than white or Asian students. Black youths were also more likely to report gang membership while white students reported the highest levels of drug and alcohol use. These authors also conducted a multivariate analysis to estimate the impact of race on self-reported police stops and searches while controlling for deviant activity, leisure routines, and demographic variables. While the results suggested that youths who reported more deviant activity and those who reported more public leisure activities such as riding in cars with friends and partying and hanging out in public spaces were more likely to report being stopped and searched by the police, black racial identity was the strongest predictor of being stopped and searched. In additional analyses these racial differences in self-reported police stop-and-search experiences were greatest among the low-deviance youths. Wortley and Tanner concede that research on racial profiling in Canada is still in its infancy. Additional work on race, crime, and criminal justice should focus, among other things, on how race intersects with other important identity markers such as social class, gender, age, immigration status, religion, language, and sexual orientation (Wortley, 2003).

While the circumstances of Aboriginal Canadians in the criminal justice system—particularly in correctional institutions—have received a fair amount of attention, this is much less so in the case of the black population and other visible minorities. Therefore, the remainder of this section will focus on Aboriginal over-representation in the criminal justice system.

Over-Representation of Canadian Aboriginal People in the Criminal Justice System

As early as 1967, the report *Indians and the Law* (Canadian Corrections Association, 1967) showed the disproportionate presence of Aboriginal people in the Canadian criminal justice system (Nielsen, 1992). Subsequently, a number of commissions and task forces have recognized this **over-representation** and made numerous recommendations to respond to it (see, for example, LaPrairie, 1996; Manitoba Public Inquiry into the Administration of Justice and Aboriginal People, 1991; Task Force on the Criminal Justice System and Its Impact on the Indian and Métis People of Alberta, 1991). Although the over-representation of Aboriginal people is widely recognized (LaPrairie, 1983), implementation of recommendations to change this situation has been slow (Blackburn, 1993), and the over-representation persists.

over-representation
A group that has a number of its members in some condition in greater numbers than their population would suggest. If a group makes up 20 percent of the population, then a researcher might predict, other things being equal, that they would represent 20 percent of offenders.

Currently, the only available data on offenders in the Canadian criminal justice system are in correctional statistics. Additional data concerning Aboriginal offenders can be found in various reports and special studies and in the homicide database. These data sources document various aspects of the disproportionate involvement of Aboriginal offenders in the criminal justice system. For example, while Statistics Canada projected the Aboriginal population at approximately 3 percent of the total Canadian population, Aboriginal offenders accounted for 21 percent of all sentenced admissions to provincial custody in 2003–04, 16 percent of all intakes to provincial probation, 18 percent of admissions to remand, 19 percent of conditional sentence admissions, and 18 percent of admissions to federal prisons (Beattie, 2005). The sentenced admission data probably even underestimate the extent of Aboriginal over-representation (Task Force on Aboriginal Peoples in Federal Corrections, 1989).

While Aboriginal people are generally over-represented in admissions to correctional services throughout Canada, Table 5.3 demonstrates that there are considerable differences across the country. For example, in 2003–04 Aboriginal people made up 80 percent of those admitted to adult custodial facilities in Saskatchewan, compared to their representation of 10 percent of the adult population. In Manitoba, Aboriginal people represented 68 percent of admissions to provincial custody compared to their makeup of 11 percent of

WWW
Indian and Northern Affairs Canada
www.ainc-inac.gc.ca

TABLE 5.3 Percentage of Adult Admissions to Remand, Provincial/Territorial Sentenced Custody, Probation, and Conditional Sentence Accounted for by Aboriginal People by Jurisdiction, 2003–04

	Percent Aboriginal				
	Remand	*Provincial/ Territorial Sentenced Custody*	*Probation*	*Conditional Sentence*	*Total Adult Population*[1]
Newfoundland and Labrador[2]	—	—	—	—	3.2
Prince Edward Island	4.8	2.0	—	—	0.8
Nova Scotia	7.4	7.3	6.7	7.0	1.5
New Brunswick	8.5	8.9	7.4	8.3	2.0
Quebec	3.8	2.4	7.2	5.8	0.9
Ontario	8.6	8.8	6.5	8.4	1.5
Manitoba	62.1	68.2	50.4	44.4	10.6
Saskatchewan	77.5	80.2	66.6	71.8	9.9
Alberta	27.9	38.7	23.6	16.5	4.2
British Columbia	22.2	19.8	19.0	16.9	3.6
Yukon	77.9	72.9	61.3	65.6	19.9
Northwest Territories	85.3	87.5	—	—	44.7
Nunavut	97.4	97.1	98.9	97.9	78.5
Total (all available data)	17.6	21.2	15.7	18.5	—
Adjusted total[2]	17.5	20.8	15.7	18.5	2.6

Not available for a reference period.
1. Indicates the percentage of the total adult population who are Aboriginal per Jurisdiction as of the 2001 Census.
2. Due to missing data for some categories Newfoundland and Labrador, Prince Edward Island and Northwest Territories data were excluded.

Source: Statistics Canada. *Victimization and Offending Among the Aboriginal Population in Canada. Juristat* 26(3). Catalogue No. 85-002-XIE. 2006.

the population; and in Alberta 39 percent of admissions to provincial facilities were Aboriginal persons compared to their 4 percent makeup of the adult population. Similar patterns exist for community correctional services such as probation and conditional sentences (Brzozowski et al., 2006).

For all custody admissions, the proportion of Aboriginal admissions increased over the ten-year period between 1994–95 and 2003–04 while the Aboriginal adult admissions to community supervision remained stable. Although the number of admissions to sentenced custody has generally decreased over time, admissions to remand have been increasing (34 percent for Aboriginal adults compared to 3 percent for non-Aboriginals) (Beattie, 2005). Similar to their representation in the general population, Aboriginal adults in correctional services were younger, had lower levels of education, and were less likely to have been employed compared to their non-Aboriginal counterparts (Brzozowski et al., 2006).

Previous research indicates that this prison over-representation has persisted for some time (Indian and Northern Affairs Canada, 1980). The report of the Task Force on Aboriginal Peoples in Federal Corrections (1989) concluded that the rate of growth of the Aboriginal offender population has exceeded that of the general inmate population since at least 1982–83.

LaPrairie's (1996) review of various surveys and research studies dealing with Aboriginal inmates also indicates that they are generally younger, have more prior contact with the criminal justice and correctional systems, and come from more dysfunctional backgrounds than non-Aboriginal offenders. Proportionately, more Aboriginal than non-Aboriginal offenders are serving time for fine defaults, and Aboriginal women are particularly over-represented in correctional institutions. While use of incarceration as a sentence is greater for federal Aboriginal offenders after controlling for type of offence (but without information on prior record), they also receive shorter sentences on average than non-Aboriginal offenders in both federal and provincial institutions (LaPrairie, 1996). Aboriginal persons are also more likely than non-Aboriginals to be readmitted to the correctional system after being released (Johnson, 2005).

There is only limited evidence concerning the over-representation of Aboriginal peoples at earlier stages of the criminal justice system. Two studies of urban Aboriginal crime (in Calgary, Regina, Saskatoon, and Vancouver) concluded that for those offences with an identified accused, Aboriginal persons were more likely than non-Aboriginals to be accused of a property or violent offence or to have been the victim of a violent crime (Griffiths et al., 1994; Trevethan, 1993). In these four cities, Aboriginals constituted from 2 to 6 percent of the population but represented from 9 to 43 percent of those accused of a crime, depending on the type of crime and on the city.

For homicides in which Aboriginal status of the accused is known, Aboriginal persons represented 23 percent of all those accused of committing a homicide between 1997 and 2004. Aboriginal people were ten times more likely to be accused of homicide than were non-Aboriginal people, with Aboriginal males particularly highly over-represented (Brzozowski et al., 2006). One factor that may contribute to this over-representation is the age composition of the Aboriginal population. The high-risk age group for homicide and other violent crime is 15 to 24, and this age group accounted for 17 percent of the Aboriginal population in 2001 compared to 13 percent for the rest of the population. A detailed analysis of homicides involving Aboriginal people in Ontario between 1980 and 1990 revealed that the rate of homicides among Aboriginal people on reserves was approximately the same as the rate off reserve, although in both settings, the suspect and victim rates were considerably higher than the rates for non-Aboriginal people (Doob et al., 1994). On most comparisons, on- and off-reserve Aboriginal homicides and homicides involving Aboriginal victims were more likely to have occurred after a non-violent social encounter, a verbal argument, or a fight that escalated. This pattern of results suggests that the causes of Aboriginal homicides are likely to be different from those of non-Aboriginal homicides (Doob et al., 1994).

Crime rates on reserves are higher than those outside reserves, and the nature and extent of crime on reserves differ compared to crimes committed elsewhere in Canada. On-reserve crime rates were about three times higher in 2004 than crime rates elsewhere. For certain types of offences, the differences were greater still. Just over half (55 percent) of on-reserve incidents were classified as "Other Criminal Code" offences, such as mischief and disturbing the peace, while 25 percent were violent and 21 percent were property offences. In off-reserve areas, in contrast, property crimes were the most frequently recorded (51 percent), followed by "Other Criminal Code" (38 percent) and violent offences (11 percent) (Brzozowski et al., 2006).

Although the level of crime among Aboriginal people, particularly violent crime, is considerably higher than that for non-Aboriginals, there is still a great deal of variation in the rates of both violent and property crimes among Aboriginal communities and Aboriginal populations across Canada (Wood and Griffiths, 1996). This variation in recorded crime is probably at least partly due to differences in the nature of policing in these communities and jurisdictions, as well as differences in the likelihood of the police recording incidents reported to them (Roberts and Doob, 1997). A comparison of several research studies conducted in different jurisdictions revealed that the mean of the rates for violent crimes varied between 19 and 70 per 1000 population, while for property crime the rates ranged from 22 to 108 per 1000 population (Wood and Griffiths, 1996). This means that at least some Aboriginal communities have rates of crime below the average for Canada.

Explanations of Aboriginal Over-Representation

There are a number of potential explanations for this over-representation of Aboriginal people in the Canadian criminal justice system. These include the following: conflict between the values of Aboriginal culture and the dominant Canadian culture; the social and economic deprivation experienced by many Aboriginal peoples stemming from their colonization and oppression and resulting in higher Aboriginal offending rates and/or their discriminatory treatment by the criminal justice system; the commission by Aboriginals of types of offences more likely to result in a justice system response; and a decline in interdependency in Aboriginal communities, resulting in cultural dislocation and the decline of informal mechanisms of social control (see, for example, LaPrairie, 1983; 1996).

Verdun-Jones and Muirhead (1979–80) distinguish between cultural and structural explanations. **Cultural explanations** emphasize the lack of certain traits in Aboriginal culture that are valued by the dominant white culture. James (1979), while claiming that the core values of Aboriginal and white cultures may be essentially the same, argues that there is conflict in the ways in which these values are expressed behaviourally in society. "Native values are placed under stress by the pressures of expressing them acceptably in a complex urban society" (1979, 455). For example, James suggests that the sharing of material possessions among Aboriginal people implies a potentially reciprocal action rather than a permanent transfer of ownership. However, when such sharing of belongings is practised without permission in the dominant culture, it is called theft. The Native Counselling Services of Alberta (1982) has identified a number of areas of conflict between Aboriginal and non-Aboriginal cultures related to the legal system and has suggested that many Aboriginal people have only a limited understanding of the dominant Canadian legal and justice system. Similarly, Dumont (1993) describes a number of conflicts between

cultural explanation
An explanation for crime that is phrased in terms of the values and beliefs of a society or its component subgroups.

Aboriginal responses to the law and the expectations of the Canadian legal system. For example, while Aboriginal culture emphasizes mediation and negotiation to resolve disputes and reconcile offenders with victims, the Canadian legal system is based on retributive justice with punishment set by legislation. Furthermore, Aboriginal defendants are reluctant to testify and often plead guilty on the basis of honesty or the avoidance of confrontation; in contrast, the Canadian system is adversarial and assumes innocence until proven guilty. So cultural explanations emphasize conflicting values. The over-representation of Aboriginals results from the imposition of a somewhat alien set of values and rules on Aboriginal culture, as well as from the higher rate of commission by Aboriginals of acts called crime by Canadian law but regarded as normative or expected behaviour in the context of Aboriginal culture.

structural explanation
An explanation for crime that focuses on social structure (usually this refers to inequality, poverty, or power differentials). For example, the patriarchal structure of the family might help explain the abuse of women and children within the family.

Structural explanations of Aboriginal over-representation emphasize the economically and socially dependent position of Aboriginals in Canadian society. Thus Hylton (1982) claims that the over-representation of Aboriginal people is a symptom of the underlying social and economic inequality of Canadian society, while LaPrairie (1983) states that the suggestion of a link between the living conditions of Aboriginals and their over-representation in the criminal justice system is compelling. She views over-representation as an effect of structural disadvantage. She documents examples of such disadvantage with comparisons between Aboriginals and non-Aboriginals in federal penitentiaries. Only 12 percent of Aboriginal inmates compared to 26 percent of non-Aboriginal inmates had more than a Grade 9 education; 31 percent of Aboriginal inmates but only 19 percent of non-Aboriginal inmates had either no education or education of only Grade 6 or less. The Métis and Non-Status Indian Crime and Justice Commission (1978) report also attributed the high rate of Aboriginal imprisonment to their deprived social situation, illustrated by the report's findings from a survey of Aboriginal inmates in federal penitentiaries. Fifty-seven percent of the inmates said they were unemployed at the time of their offence; 49 percent had spent time in skid row areas of cities; and 49 percent had less than a Grade 9 education. The final report of the Task Force on Aboriginal Peoples in Federal Corrections (1989) concluded that any reduction in Aboriginal crime must address the correlated socio-economic conditions among Aboriginals—conditions that, compared to those of other Canadians, are discouraging. Generally, Aboriginals continue to have a lower average level of education, fewer marketable skills, a higher rate of unemployment, an infant mortality rate twice the national rate, a higher degree of family instability, and a rate of violent death three times the national average. Aboriginal inmates, then, are even more disadvantaged in some respects than other inmates.

LaPrairie (2002) explored the impact of socio-demographic characteristics of Aboriginal populations living in nine Canadian cities and found regional disparities with higher levels of social disadvantage in the Prairie cities of Saskatoon, Regina, and Winnipeg and in Thunder Bay, compared to cities in British Columbia, Ontario, and Nova Scotia. These disadvantaged populations live predominantly in the regions with the highest levels of over-representation of Aboriginal people in the criminal justice system. Furthermore, the three Prairie cities had three to four times as many Aboriginal people living in extremely poor neighbourhoods of these cities. LaPrairie suggests that this concentration of poor, single parent, and poorly educated Aboriginal people in the inner core of cities weakens social cohesion and informal social controls, resulting in more disorder and crime. An earlier study of Aboriginal residents of the inner-city areas of four Canadian cities (Edmonton, Regina, Toronto, and Montreal) explained the over-representation of Aboriginal people by their marginalization and alienation resulting from unstable and violent childhoods, as well as their lack of opportunity and dependency on alcohol (LaPrairie, 1995).

Verdun-Jones and Muirhead (1979–80), moreover, argue that the structurally deprived position of Aboriginals in contemporary Canadian society is rooted in a history of exploitation by the dominant white society through what was, in essence, a colonial system based on the fur trade. From this perspective, the criminal justice system functions today primarily to control subjugated groups such as Aboriginals—to keep them in their dominated, powerless position—in order to protect the interests of the dominant, powerful segment of society. This dominant segment of society is made up of the white majority generally and, more particularly, its leading, economically powerful segments. The criminal justice system, and the state generally, is seen by these authors as agents of the economically powerful who control the underclasses. The criminal justice system mirrors the socio-economic organization and operation of society. Hence, over-representation of Aboriginals within the criminal justice system is merely a reproduction of the basic socio-economic inequalities present in the surrounding society. Furthermore, the criminal justice system functions to support and maintain that structure of inequality. Thus the Canadian justice system has been seen as the central institution that reinforces colonial relationships against Aboriginal people, with over-representation a systemic problem of a society structured on discriminatory values, beliefs, and practices (Monture-Angus, 1996).

LaPrairie (1996) has argued that a decline in traditional interdependency in Aboriginal communities has resulted from their colonization and the creation of the reserve system, as well as their cultural dislocation and the decline of informal mechanisms of social control. "The end result is socially stratified communities where limited resources and resource distribution create large groups of disadvantaged people, a growing youth sub-culture with few legitimate outlets or opportunities, decontextualized exposure to the mass media, and the lack of cultural and social resources to assist in identity formation which support pro-social values" (LaPrairie, 1996, 63). The result is a large group of marginalized and nonintegrated people in many Aboriginal communities who have few tools for survival or integration into mainstream society when they leave reserves for urban areas. Their lack of skills, coupled with substance abuse problems and dysfunctional family life, leads to negative peer associations and the adoption of pro-criminal attitudes. Structural explanations, then, regard higher Aboriginal crime rates as a product of the social and economic oppression of Aboriginals by the dominant white society. The majority of Aboriginals are kept poor and dependent, and this breeds crime, violence, and other social disorders to which the criminal justice system responds, thereby furthering Aboriginals' exploitation by the existing system of inequality.

Discriminatory treatment of Aboriginal people by the criminal justice system has also been offered as an explanation of over-representation by several task forces (Manitoba Public Inquiry, 1991; Task Force on the Criminal Justice System, 1991) and some criminologists (Havemann et al., 1985; Monture-Angus, 1996). The Manitoba inquiry, for example, pointed out that Aboriginal people were more likely to face multiple charges, to be held in jail before their court appearance, to spend a longer time in custody before their trials, to see their lawyers less frequently and for less time, to enter guilty pleas, to be sentenced to jail terms, to receive longer sentences, and to receive absolute or conditional discharges less frequently.

Several Canadian research studies that investigated this hypothesis of differential treatment by the criminal justice system included race as a variable in their analysis. The most relevant of these studies for the present discussion is no doubt Hagan's (1974) early research in five Alberta correctional institutions. He examined the sentences received by Indian and Métis inmates, who were represented at least four times as often among newly incarcerated offenders as among the general population. Hagan discovered that Aboriginals were primarily charged with minor offences and, as a result, received shorter sentences. Incarceration resulting from failure to pay a fine was nearly twice as common for Aboriginals as for non-Aboriginals. Almost two-thirds of Aboriginal inmates were serving sentences resulting from such default. Race, therefore, played no *direct* role in influencing the over-representation of Aboriginals in these institutions. The sentences imposed conformed to legal requirements and reflected the disproportionate involvement of Aboriginals in minor offences, particularly involving alcohol abuse, for which they received a fine. However, because of their poverty, many were unable to pay these fines and ended up serving time in jail for minor offences. In a subsequent analysis, Hagan (1977) found that Aboriginals were more likely to be sent to jail in default of fine payments in rural than in urban Alberta communities, a finding he attributed to the trend toward greater uniformity of treatment in the more bureaucratic urban criminal justice system. Other research has suggested that limited sentencing options in remote Aboriginal communities may explain some of the disproportionate use of incarceration for convicted Aboriginals (LaPrairie, 1990).

Several other studies have examined the hypothesis of selective enforcement against Aboriginal people in different parts of the criminal justice system. Hagan (1977), for example, found that probation officers in rural jurisdictions in Alberta were more likely to recommend more severe sentences for Aboriginal offenders in their presentence reports, without the justification of legally relevant considerations such as prior record, seriousness of offence, or number of charges. But Boldt et al. (1983) found no racial effect on presentence recommendations in the Yukon. In general, Hagan (1975a; 1975b) failed to discover evidence of differential treatment due to race itself in presentence recommendations or sentencing, though probation officers took a dimmer view of Aboriginal defendants' prospects for success on probation, which in turn affected their sentence recommendations and the final disposition of the case by the judge. But those judges characterized by Hagan as less concerned about the maintenance of a conservative notion of "law and order" used part of their discretion to sentence Aboriginal defendants more *leniently* (Hagan, 1975c). Since there is evidence that Aboriginal offenders sentenced to incarceration receive shorter sentences for certain offences than comparable non-Aboriginal offenders, over-representation of Aboriginals in prisons cannot be simply explained by racial discrimination (LaPrairie, 1990). Research on parole decision making by Demers (1978) supported Hagan's conclusion that Aboriginal candidates were less likely to receive favourable recommendations from parole officers. This was probably due to a variety of factors, but indirectly produced racial inequality in parole release decisions made by the Parole Board, which is dependent on parole officers for information and advice. Wynne and Hartnagel (1975) found evidence from a study of Crown prosecutors' files that Aboriginals were less likely than whites to successfully engage in plea bargaining, though this depended on certain conditions, such as being represented by defence counsel and the presence of repetitious counts and/or multiple charges in the indictment.

Unfortunately, there is little evidence on how the police exercise their discretion with respect to Aboriginal people. It has been suggested that in cities, Aboriginal people may tend to attract police attention by their physical appearance and/or location in run-down, skid row areas (Canadian Corrections Association, 1967). Aboriginals may have a greater public visibility, particularly when drinking, and this may result in more frequent arrests (Bienvenue and Latif, 1974). Some criminologists (Giffen, 1966; Greenaway, 1980; Frideres, 1988) have even argued that the police "find" crime where they look for it, at least with respect to public-order offences such as public drunkenness. Therefore, police initiative and discretion in seeking out the poor and disadvantaged may be implicated to some extent in the higher frequency of Aboriginal arrests for certain types of crime. But there is also some evidence that the police may be called by Aboriginal people in some communities to deal with problems that would not be seen as police business in non-Aboriginal communities, due in part to the fact that the police may be the only service available in the community to deal with such problems (Roberts and Doob, 1997).

While it is clear that Aboriginal people are over-represented in the criminal justice system, the explanation for this over-representation remains somewhat in doubt. Furthermore, little research has been done in Canada on the ways in which crime may be produced by the relations between indigenous Aboriginal society and culture and the dominant white society and its culture. However, the disproportionately high rates of Aboriginal crime and violence suggest "a serious rupture of traditional control mechanisms in contemporary aboriginal communities" (LaPrairie, 1992:285).

Drug Misuse and Criminal Behaviour

The 2004 Canadian Addiction Survey (Canadian Centre on Substance Abuse, 2004) of how Canadians aged 15 years and older use alcohol, cannabis, and other drugs indicates that while nearly 80 percent drink, most drink in moderation. Seventeen percent of past-year drinkers are considered high-risk drinkers; they are predominantly male and under the age of 25. While 45 percent reported using cannabis at least once, only 14 percent reported use in the past year; males and younger people are again more likely to be past-year users. Among past-year users, 16 percent report use monthly, 20 percent weekly, and

18 percent daily. Although about 1 in 6 Canadians had used an illicit drug other than cannabis in their lifetime, few (1 percent or less, except 1.9 percent for cocaine use) have used these drugs during the past year; both lifetime and past-year use was highest among males and those aged 18 to 24. This survey suggests that while alcohol and other drug use is fairly widespread, misuse or serious abuse in the general population is limited to a smaller proportion.

Canadian Centre on Substance Abuse CCSA
www.ccsa.ca

The picture is quite different when we examine the offender population. The misuse of serious drugs is particularly widespread in the criminal population (Bennett and Holloway, 2005). This suggests that misuse/abuse of drugs and crime are linked in some fashion. The concept of drug-related crime includes a number of crime types, including drug offences such as possession of illegal substances; crimes committed as part of the functioning of drug markets (e.g., trafficking, money laundering, violent crime to "protect" markets); and crimes committed as a result of drug use, or drugs consumed as a result of crime (Bennett and Holloway, 2005). The link between drug abuse and crime refers to this latter type. Research from a number of countries indicates a strong association or correlation between crime and the use and abuse of alcohol and illicit drugs: There are high rates of prevalence of drug use among offenders, and a large number of drug abusers are involved in criminal activities (Pernanen, et al., 2002; see also the literature reviews in Bennett and Holloway, 2005, and Bean, 2004).

While drug abuse and crime may be related to one another, they may not be causally linked but merely occur together among some individuals or groups. For example, crime and drug abuse may both be part of a deviant street lifestyle but not be causally linked. Furthermore, they may both be effects of a common cause or causes. There is some evidence, for example, that drug effects may be confounded with pre-addiction psychiatric conditions; in such cases this could be a common factor to explain both the abuse of alcohol/drugs and the criminal behaviour (Pernanen, et al., 2002). Social circumstances of disadvantage and exclusion could lead to both drug abuse and crime. Of course, misuse of alcohol/drugs may cause some criminal conduct, although this would likely depend on the type of drug, frequency and extent of the drug misuse, ability to support a drug habit through conventional means, and specific crime types. The most common drugs investigated in the drugs-crime relationship are heroin, crack, and cocaine, and the most common offences are burglary, theft, and robbery (Bennett and Holloway, 2005). So, for example, heavy dependence on heroin may lead to acquisitive crimes such as theft, shoplifting, or burglary to pay for further drug use. Criminal behaviour may also act as a cause of alcohol/drug abuse when, for example, prior involvement in criminal activity results in economic proceeds that are used to finance a lifestyle involving heavy use of alcohol and other drugs.

While it is clear, then, that alcohol/drug misuse is correlated with criminal behaviour, their relationship is complex and contingent on a number of factors. At a minimum, it is necessary to determine two things before assuming a causal link between them: which came first, the alcohol/drug (mis)use or the criminal behaviour; and whether both are merely effects of a common cause that results in their correlation. In the case of recreational drugs like cannabis, the majority of research findings indicates the drug use preceded any crime; for the more serious drugs (typically heroin, crack, or cocaine), the majority of findings show that crime preceded drug use (Bennett and Holloway, 2005).

The Canadian Centre on Substance Abuse (Pernanen et al., 2002) conducted a series of studies to estimate the strength of the association between different types of crime and the use and abuse of drugs, and the share of crimes in Canada that can be attributed to the use and abuse of alcohol and drugs. Data were obtained from self-report surveys and interviews of federal and provincial prison inmates and from the observations of arresting police officers in 14 cities. A large proportion of inmates reported using illicit drugs while free. Many used frequently, with 30 percent reporting use at least a few times a week. Inmates scored higher on psychometric scales measuring alcohol and drug dependency when compared to the general population. Alcohol-dependent federal inmates were much more likely to have committed a violent crime than were drug-dependent inmates, while the latter were more likely to have committed a gainful crime. The inmates who were dependent upon drugs and/or alcohol committed the most crimes—averaging about 7 crimes per week. Slightly more than half (54 percent) of offenders entering federal custody reported having been under the influence of a psychoactive substance when they committed the most serious crime on their current sentence, with alcohol intoxication more common than drug intoxication (24 percent vs. 19 percent). The arresting police reported 51 percent of arrestees were under the influence of a psychoactive substance at the time of arrest, with alcohol indicated more often than illicit drugs. A significant proportion of crimes were reported to have been committed in order to obtain psychoactive substances for personal use. The authors estimated that between 40 and 50 percent of the crimes committed by federal and provincial inmates were attributable to the use of alcohol and/or illicit drugs in Canada. Between 10 and 15 percent were attributed to illicit drugs only, between 15 and 20 percent to alcohol only, and 10 to 20 percent to both alcohol and illicit drugs.

Fischer et al. (2001) conducted a survey of a cohort of untreated illicit opiate drug users in Toronto. Self-report interview data illustrated that criminal involvement is a prevalent and frequent occurrence in this sample, with very few reporting no involvement in illegal activities. The majority of crimes were non-violent income-generating offences to obtain the substantial funds required to finance their addiction. A large part of the sample also participated in illicit drug market activities, engaging in small-scale dealing.

There is strong evidence for an association between alcohol use and crime—particularly aggression and violent crime—although it is unclear whether this correlation also implies a causal relationship (Mosher and Jernigan, 2001; Parker and Auerhahn, 1998). A sizeable presence of alcohol is found in almost all studies of assaults and homicides, with 40 to 45 percent of perpetrators in Canadian studies drinking (Pernanen et al., 2002). Fagan's (1990) review of a large amount of research shows that people who become aggressive after consumption of intoxicants often have a long history of aggression; there is only limited evidence that ingestion of intoxicants is a direct pharmacological cause either stimulating or disinhibiting aggression. Although intoxication may not directly cause aggression, there is evidence that in situations that become violent, substance use may increase the severity of the violence (Wolff and Reingold, 1994). Immediate situational influences as well as various social and cultural variables are likely important mediating factors in the alcohol–violent crime link.

Alcohol abuse has had a severe impact on Aboriginal people. The survey *Indian Conditions* (Indian and Northern Affairs Canada, 1980) estimated that between 50 and 60 percent of Indian illnesses and deaths were alcohol related. Alcohol also plays a major role in Native American criminal behaviour (Lester, 1999). Havemann et al. (1985) have reviewed a number of Canadian studies that identify alcohol as a major contributor to the crimes Aboriginal people commit. This contribution can be direct, through the violation of liquor laws, as well as indirect, as when other crimes are committed under the influence of alcohol. Surveys of Aboriginal inmates (Irvine, 1978; Metis and Non-Status Indian Crime and Justice Commission, 1978) found that a large percentage admitted alcohol played a role in the commission of their crimes. According to data from the Homicide Survey, between 1997 and 2004, while the consumption of an intoxicating substance was common among many accused persons, it was much more prevalent among Aboriginal accused; in incidents where it was known that intoxicants were involved, 89 percent of Aboriginals had consumed an intoxicant at the time of the homicide compared to 61 percent of non-Aboriginal accused. Furthermore, while substance abuse was assessed to be at a medium or high level for a majority of adults involved in correctional services, it was particularly prevalent among Aboriginal persons (9 in 10 compared to 7 in 10 non-Aboriginals) (Brzozowski et al., 2006).

However, the link between alcohol abuse and Aboriginal criminality is not well understood or agreed on. Some have suggested that heavy drinking has become a regular, normal occurrence within some Aboriginal communities, associated with family and group activities and, therefore, accorded a good deal of tolerance (Brody, 1971; Jensen et al., 1977). Highly visible group drinking may be socially accepted and expected, without the development of corresponding informal social controls to regulate or limit the extent of such drinking. An additional possibility is that alcohol abuse and its associated criminal consequences may be a response to, or reaction against, the poverty and deprivation experienced by so many Aboriginal people. Alcohol may provide some respite, however temporary, from their oppressive life circumstances, whether on reserves, in impoverished rural areas, or in the city slums. Havemann et al. (1985) expand on this argument by linking alcohol and involvement with the criminal justice system with the social impact of the underdevelopment of Aboriginal communities. They argue that alcohol is used as a means to modify moods and escape real-life situations and that it is a way for Aboriginal people to manage the alienation created by the destruction of their culture and the economic exploitation of their land resources for the benefit of southern Canada and the corporate structure. Thus these authors locate the use of alcohol by Aboriginal people and their consequent over-representation in the criminal justice system in the structure of socio-economic relations between Aboriginal people and the dominant white society, rather than in some disease model or other individualistic-type explanation that ends up blaming the victim.

Social Class

Conflicting Evidence?

Few issues have been in greater dispute among criminologists in recent years than the correlation between social class and criminal behaviour. Thus Gordon (1976), for example, regards the crime or delinquency relationship with social class status as one of the most thoroughly documented, while Tittle and Villemez (1977) conclude that the purported relationship between class and criminality is problematic; Tittle et al. (1978) refer to such a relationship as a myth. Hindelang et al. (1979) state that illusions of discrepancies in the research evidence abound, while Braithwaite (1981) concludes from his review of over 100 studies that class is one of the very few correlates of criminality, a conclusion persuasively supported by a large body of empirical evidence. Clearly, this is a controversial question among criminologists, and there are disagreements over what the research literature reveals.

Official data appear to support an inverse or negative relationship. Those arrested, convicted, and/or incarcerated are more likely to come from lower socio-economic categories of the population as indexed by such variables as income, education, and occupational status. Tittle and Villemez (1977) report that of the 23 studies on this relationship they could locate that used official police or court data, 65 percent found a negative relationship, while another 8 percent detected class variation in crime but only for some subcategories of individuals. Twenty-six percent of these studies found no consistent class variation. Of course, these official records may underestimate the amount of crime committed by those in the higher socio-economic positions. Nettler (1984) states that official statistics on serious crimes from a variety of countries show that people with less money, lower occupational status, and less schooling are disproportionately represented. But it could be immediately asked: what qualifies as a serious crime? Some would argue that bank embezzlement, for example, is at least as serious as bank robbery or that corporate crimes are more seriously harmful than many of the crimes typically committed by lower-class individuals.

Additional evidence, using official crime statistics, on the class–crime relationship comes from the long history of research on poverty, economic inequality, and crime. While the argument that crime is one of a number of undesirable consequences of poverty can be traced far back into antiquity, the first empirical research examining the relationship between poverty and crime can be found in the mid-19th-century work of Guerry and of Quetelet in Europe (Vold and Bernard, 1986). Anticipating later developments, this early work showed that wealthier provinces had higher property crime rates and suggested that the greater opportunities for theft and other property offences offered by these wealthier regions might explain this unexpected pattern. Quetelet also suggested that great inequality between wealth and poverty in the same place, rather than absolute poverty, might be a critical factor. While poverty refers to the lack of that level of income necessary for mere survival, economic inequality signifies the size of the income gap between those who have the least income and those who have the most income (Vold and Bernard, 1986).

Since this early research, criminologists have continued to analyze and interpret various data relating economic conditions and crime at different levels of ecological aggregation ranging from city neighbourhoods to nation-states. Summarizing this large body of research is complicated by this variation in units of analysis, as well as by such factors as varying measurement of poverty and inequality, the inclusion of a variety of crime types, and the use of differing sets of control variables. However, there appears to be some consensus that the degree of economic inequality rather than the amount of poverty is the more important variable (Braithwaite, 1979; Box, 1987; Vold and Bernard, 1986). More specifically, nations with greater economic inequality have higher homicide rates, particularly under conditions of political democracy (Krahn et al., 1986). Cross-national comparisons of property crime rates are more inconsistent, perhaps as a result of the effect of varying opportunities for property crime in different nations (Stack, 1984). Economic inequality and crime rates, with the possible exception of homicide, are fairly strongly and consistently related in studies of U.S. cities and Standard Metropolitan Statistical Areas, but less so at the level of states. Daly et al. (2001) reported a strong, positive relationship between the income inequality and homicide rates of the ten Canadian provinces, averaged across a period of 15 years, a relationship that persisted when controlling for provincial median household income levels. So this body of work suggests that the degree of contrast between economic classes—poverty amid affluence—is more strongly correlated with rates of crime than the proportion of the population in the poorest class. The limited Canadian research on this topic also supports this interpretation (Kennedy et al., 1991).

Evidence from self-report research seems to challenge this conclusion of a negative relationship between class and criminal behaviour. It was Short and Nye's (1957) use of the self-report measurement of delinquency that stimulated much of the later debate concerning the class and delinquency correlation, since they reported no relationship between self-reports of delinquency and parental socio-economic status. However, they did find a moderately strong relation between social class and incarceration in a training school. Fifty percent of the institutionalized boys studied came from the lowest socio-economic status category, compared to only 13 percent of the high school boys. But Hindelang et al. (1979) have shown how Short and Nye over-estimated the strength of the relationship between official delinquency and socio-economic status, since the institutionalized boys did not constitute a representative sample.

Tittle et al. (1978) examined 35 studies in which the relationship between a measure of individual class position and a measure of crime or delinquency was reported and found, on average, only a very slight, negative correlation (−.09). Moreover, this conclusion didn't appear to vary in the presence of different conditions such as type of offence, age, sex, or race; the specific indicator of socio-economic status used; and so forth. The two exceptions to this, however, were type of data (official or self-report) and the decade in which the study was conducted. Tittle et al. (1978) claim that studies using official data show a more marked negative correlation (average of −.25) than do those based on self-report data (−.06). They argue that the average correlation between class and crime or delinquency showed a steady decline in strength from the 1940s (−.73) to the 1970s (−.03), a trend they believe is largely the result of a decline in the relationship between class and official measures of crime, since the correlation for self-report measures remained relatively constant and low. However, others (Clelland and Carter, 1980) have pointed out that none of the 1970s research reviewed by Tittle et al. (1978) involved adults. In fact, prior to the 1970s, only six studies of adult crime and social class were included in their review. In any event, Tittle et al. interpret these findings as a reflection of changes in the way in which criminal justice agencies deal with members of the various social classes. Their interpretation implies that the true correlation between class and crime "has remained consistently near zero and has only appeared to be greater because official data reflected biases in the law enforcement process which have now been ameliorated" (1978, 652).

Of course, any number of researchers have attempted to account for the apparent discrepancy between self-report and official measures of delinquency in their relationship to socio-economic status by examining the hypothesis of official discrimination against lower-class adolescents in the enforcement of the law (see Nettler, 1984, for a review of many of these studies). However, once legally relevant factors such as seriousness of the offence and prior record of the suspect or accused are taken into account, the evidence for such class bias in law enforcement is weak and is, therefore, unlikely to substantially affect the official statistics.

Two other studies that used the self-report technique found a negative relationship between class and crime once certain refinements in measurement and analysis were introduced. Elliott and Ageton's (1980) research, which involved a national sample with a fairly large number of respondents and a self-report measure covering the full range of delinquent and criminal acts with a true measure of frequency, discovered class differences on an overall delinquency scale as well as for predatory crimes against persons, but not for other types of offences. Lower-class respondents reported close to four times as many predatory crimes against persons (for example, assault and robbery) as did middle-class respondents. But these differences were largely the result of the high-frequency offenders. Lower-class youths were found disproportionately among high-frequency offenders; they reported more than one and a half times as many offences overall as middle-class youths in the high-frequency category, and nearly three times as many predatory crimes against persons. So Elliott and Ageton seem to have demonstrated a behavioural basis for the class differences observed in the official data since the more frequent and serious offenders are more likely to be arrested and the class differences in self-reported delinquency are greater at the high end of the frequency continuum and for serious, predatory crimes.

In the second study, Farnworth et al. (1994) argued that criminological theories imply that it is the sustained experience of deprivation and poverty among the underclass that creates a greater risk of crime and delinquency. Furthermore, these authors claimed that most theories that incorporate class as an important predictor of delinquency are concerned with explaining a serious, frequent, and persistent pattern of offending. Therefore, measures of class and crime should be consistent with these theoretical concerns. In this study, the strongest and most consistent class–crime relationships were found between measures of continuing underclass membership and sustained involvement in street crimes.

These two studies, then, support the conclusion of a negative correlation between social class and crime under certain conditions, specifically for more serious offences and among more frequent and adult offenders, particularly those most disadvantaged educationally, racially (Blacks), and in employment status.

There is comparatively little Canadian research on the class and crime relationship. The studies that do exist illustrate some of the same problems and apparently conflicting conclusions as discussed. Bell-Rowbotham and Boydell (1972) looked at the official data concerning the characteristics of persons convicted of indictable offences and found both educational and occupational status were related to such convictions. Those with no schooling had much higher rates of conviction for virtually all of the more serious offences, while those with some education beyond high school had the lowest rates, except for homicide. However, there were some crimes—fraud is an example (Giffen, 1965)—for which those with more education had the highest rates, probably as a result of the opportunities available to those with white-collar occupations. But to the extent that educational attainment can be taken as a measure of socio-economic status, these official data generally support the negative correlation between class and crime. West (1984) has noted that a study by Byles in Toronto found that working-class juveniles were five times more likely to be arrested than middle-class juveniles and that about 90 percent of Ontario training school inmates were from working-class backgrounds. West goes on to argue that, although official delinquency is largely a working-class phenomenon, officially defined delinquents are not representative of all those who commit delinquencies.

Canadian self-report studies raise the same issues as the U.S. studies discussed. LeBlanc (1975) found no difference in the self-reported delinquency of adolescents from working-class areas compared to those from upper-class neighbourhoods, using a standard set of self-report delinquency items, even though adolescents from the working-class neighbourhoods were more likely to be officially labelled as delinquent by the police. Gomme's (1985) analysis of self-reported delinquency among younger adolescents (Grades 7 to 10) in a small urban centre in southern Ontario found no direct relationship between socio-economic status, measured by father's occupation, and participation in delinquent behaviour. But in a study in New Brunswick, Tribble (1972) concluded that the higher the status of the father's occupation, the lower was the probability that the son would be involved in delinquency. Furthermore, among the delinquents, the higher the status, the fewer the number of offences reported. Statistics Canada's Violence Against Women Survey supported the view that domestic violence is greatest in the lower class (Johnson, 1996). The study found that men who were out of work committed assaults at twice the rate of men who were employed and that men who earned less than $15 000 per year assaulted their wives at twice the rate of men with higher incomes. Above this $15 000 level, there was no relationship between income and wife assault. This again suggests that the highest crime rates can be found at the very bottom of the economic ladder.

Reconciling the Apparent Conflicts

There are several methodological and substantive issues in the research on class and crime that, once understood, should help clarify and, one hopes, reconcile the apparently conflicting conclusions of different studies. First, most of these studies of the relationship between class and crime are not very representative of the population at large, and this severely limits the degree to which one can generalize from them. Almost all of this research has focused on juveniles rather than adults and, more specifically, on white male adolescents in small towns to medium-sized cities (Elliott and Ageton, 1980; Tittle et al., 1978). Poor adults in large cities—precisely those whom many criminologists would expect to have higher crime rates—have been very under-represented in the research on socio-economic status and crime (Clelland and Carter, 1980). Research by Hagan and McCarthy (1990) has suggested that the use of self-report surveys administered for convenience to school populations has diverted attention from street youths who experience current class conditions that are more likely to cause serious delinquency. Baron (1994) has shown that living on the street detaches youths from conventional society as they come to blame society for their predicament and immerses them in a lifestyle centred on drugs, alcohol, and criminal behaviour. Street youths develop the view that the legitimate labour market is closed to them and turn to crime since it pays them better than conventional jobs, provides structure to their day, brings excitement to their lives, and funds drug habits. Their illegal behaviour also offers them a sense of being in control of their lives, which the experience of unemployment and poverty tends to strip away. Baron interviewed 200 western Canadian street youths and found that they reported committing an average of 1673 crimes in a year, 72 percent of which were drug offences. Many of the remaining offences were serious crimes such as robbery, break and enter, and assault, showing that these lower-class youths represented a major source of crime in that community. Because these youths were not in school, their offences would not be represented in typical self-reported delinquency surveys.

Second, serious crime is a relatively rare event, so rare that the victimization surveys in the United States spend a large amount of money to draw a sample of the general population large enough to identify sufficient numbers of crime victims to make comparisons with the official data. The typically small sample sizes, restricted time frame, and crude measurement of frequency of crime commission in self-report studies make it extremely difficult to identify class differences in serious crime, given its low prevalence in the general or adolescent population (Hindelang et al., 1979).

Third, it is inappropriate to compare most self-reports with official data on crime since they only rarely refer to the same domain of conduct (Hindelang et al., 1979). The usual set of self-report items is weighted in favour of less serious acts, particularly those trivial acts for which middle-class adolescents report higher prevalence (Elliott and Ageton, 1980). So the typical self-report delinquency scale overlaps only in part with the crimes in official statistics, particularly those predatory, interpersonal crimes most often officially reported. Therefore, one should be cautious about generalizing from the failure to find class differences in the self-reports of the less serious forms of delinquency to *any* conclusion concerning predatory criminal acts by adults (Farnworth et al., 1994).

Fourth, it should be recognized that official statistics are limited and give only a partial picture of the class distribution of crime. In particular, official data are notorious for understating the frequency of certain crimes, some of which are characteristically committed with greater frequency by members of the middle class (for example, occupationally related theft) and representatives of the powerful segments of society (such as consumer fraud). So official statistics distort the true relationship between class and crime since the crimes of higher-status persons may be less visible (Nettler, 1984) and, therefore, less likely to come to the attention of the official agents of social control. And, of course, class position may also influence the likelihood of official intervention (Tittle and Villemez, 1977), particularly for those crimes more typically committed by those higher in status.

Criminologists have not paid sufficient attention to the many meanings and measures of class. Class position has most often been equated by criminologists with occupational status or prestige, at least for purposes of measurement. Class is thereby reduced to a handful of occupational categories, such as blue-collar, white-collar, or professional/managerial. These categories lump together some quite diverse positions in the labour market on questionable grounds, while at the same time excluding those not in the labour force, such as the unemployed.

Some criminologists have questioned these conventions (Clelland and Carter, 1980), and others have proposed alternative conceptualizations. For example, Quinney (1977) argues for the adoption of a Marxist orientation, with a focus on the relative surplus population of a capitalist economy as the locus for much of the conventional personal and property crime. Those most marginal to the labour market—rather than those in less skilled occupations, with less education or fewer financial resources—are, from this perspective, most at risk for turning to conventional, predatory crime. This is precisely the population segment typically ignored in criminological research on class and crime, partly because this segment is difficult for researchers to locate and survey (Clelland and Carter, 1980), and partly on account of the fuzzy thinking that has characterized much of the empirical research on this topic. Quinney also identifies a second category of crime in capitalist society: the crimes of domination. These include offences committed by members of the so-called ruling class, such as violations of human rights not currently defined as crimes, as well as illegal acts engaged in by government authorities and law enforcement officials. These crimes of domination most often go undetected and/or unpunished, and hence rarely appear in official statistics. Quinney and others argue that the negative correlation between class and crime found in such statistics applies only to the crimes of the underclass or marginalized segment of the population. So class position may be related to crime in something of a curvilinear fashion—high crime at both the bottom and the top of the class hierarchy—depending on how one defines and measures both class position and criminal behaviour. In fact, Tittle et al. (1978) have gone so far as to suggest that it is *only* at the extremes of the class hierarchy that class is a significant factor in crime in a mass society with a mass culture such as that found in North America. It's a bit paradoxical, then, that these same authors conclude their paper by stating that criminology should shift away from class-based theories. Rather, what seem to be required "are class-based theories which explain why certain types of crime are perpetrated almost disproportionately by the powerless, while other forms of crime are almost exclusively the prerogative of the powerful" (Braithwaite, 1981, 49).

Region

Criminal behaviour is correlated with geographic region. That is, crime rates are higher in certain nations of the world, regions within a country, communities, and urban neighbourhoods (Brantingham and Brantingham, 1984).

It is difficult to compare the crime rates of different countries. There are major differences in criminal codes, in police practices, in the willingness of citizens to report crime, and in record keeping that make most international comparisons meaningless. The only figures that can be compared with any degree of confidence are homicide statistics, and even these are not completely reliable for many countries. Table 5.4 shows the homicide rates for selected countries in 2005. Although Canada's homicide rate is about three times lower than the U.S. rate, it is still higher than rates in many European countries, such as England and Wales, Germany, and Denmark (Dauvergne and Li, 2006). The highest rates of murder are generally found in the less economically developed countries. This conclusion is consistent with the pattern of high levels of violent crime in the less-developed nations and high levels of property crime in the economically more developed nations evident in Interpol statistics for several decades. While a number of variables are no doubt involved in the explanation of this pattern, income inequality and economic opportunity seem particularly relevant. Countries with greater inequality in the distribution of income have higher homicide rates (Krahn et al., 1986), but economic development creates

WWW

UNCJIN (United Nations Crime and Justice Information Network)
www.uncjin.org

TABLE 5.4 Homicide Rates for Selected Countries, 2005

Country	*Homicide Rate per 100 000*
Ukraine	7.04
Turkey	6.23
United States	5.63
Scotland	2.69*
Sweden	2.64
Finland	2.17
Canada	2.04
New Zealand	2.00
Armenia	1.71
N. Ireland	1.68**
Hungary	1.64
France	1.59
Australia	1.45
Engl. & Wales	1.43**
Germany	0.98
Denmark	0.98
Japan	0.64
Hong Kong	0.49
Singapore	0.48

* Figures reflect 2004–05 data
** Figures reflect 2005–06 data

Source: Statistics Canada. Adapted from the Statistics Canada publication, "Homicide in Canada—2005." *Juristat*, Catalogue 85-002-XIE, Vol. 26, No. 6, November 2006.

many more opportunities for property crime (Brantingham and Brantingham, 1984; Hartnagel, 1982).

Crime rates show a definite regional pattern within Canada, with the highest provincial rates in the west (see Figure 5.4). While prior to 2002 both violent and property crime rates generally increased from east to west, Ontario and Quebec have recently recorded lower rates than most Atlantic provinces. Rates in the three territories far surpassed those recorded by the provinces, although the territorial crimes rates can have large year-over-year fluctuations due to their relatively small populations. In 2006 provincial crime rates varied from a low of 5780 in Ontario to a high of 14 320. Saskatchewan reported the highest violent crime rate (2039) for the ninth year in a row, about 28 percent higher than Manitoba (1598), the next highest province. Quebec and Ontario had the lowest rates of violent crime (both at 756). Consistent with previous years, Newfoundland and Labrador had the lowest property crime rate (2363) in the country. Western provinces had the highest rates, with British Columbia highest at 5685 per 100 000 population (Statistics Canada, 2007) Victim survey data for 2004 indicate that residents of Western provinces generally reported higher rates of victimization than those living east of Manitoba, although comparisons with police-recorded crime are limited by crime coverage and definition (Gannon and Mihorean, 2005).

These regional differences have not received much research attention to date. Provincial differences in the age and sex composition of populations and degree of urbanization may contribute to these crime rate differences. Provinces with a higher proportion of young males and urban residents could be expected to have higher crime rates, but the evidence does not suggest that these variables are of major importance (Hartnagel, 1978; Giffen, 1965; 1976). A recent examination of trends in unemployment rates, age composition, and education levels did not reveal any discernable pattern that would distinguish Manitoba, Saskatchewan, and the Yukon Territory from eastern Canada. Rates of inflation, on the other hand, tended to be somewhat higher in Manitoba and Saskatchewan. Saskatchewan and Manitoba are also home to a larger proportion of Aboriginal people who have higher levels of social disadvantage than Aboriginal people in other parts of the country (LaPrairie, 2002). Kennedy et al. (1991) attributed regional variation in homicide rates to differences in economic inequality and social disorganization. They found a convergence of murder rates among eastern, central, and western Canada in Census Metropolitan Areas where there were higher levels of inequality and disorganization. Provincial differences in crime rates are at least partly a function of differences in the amount of geographic mobility experienced in different provinces (Hartnagel, 1997). Provinces with higher amounts of migration of population from other provinces have higher rates of both violent and property crime, controlling for urbanization, age composition, police per capita, and percentage of the provincial population with low income.

Crime rates also vary by community size: rates of many crimes are higher in larger-sized communities than in smaller towns and rural areas. The correlation between community size and crime is stronger for property crime than violent crime (Hartnagel and Lee, 1990). However, crime is not necessarily a large urban phenomenon: overall crime rates as well as total violent and total

FIGURE 5.4 Crime Rates per 100 000 Population, Canada, Provinces, 2006

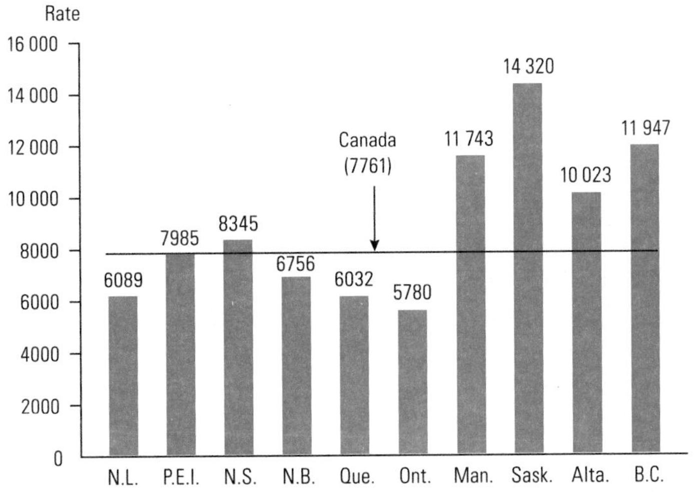

Source: Statistics Canada. Adapted from Statistics Canada, 2007. "Crime Statistics, 2006." *The Daily*, 18 July, 2007. Ottawa: Statistics Canada.

property crime rates in Canada in 2005 were highest in small urban areas. Smaller cities like Winnipeg, Saskatoon, and Regina had higher total, violent, and property crime rates than the larger cities of Toronto and Montreal. Rural areas had the lowest overall and property crime rates but reported higher violent crime rates than large urban areas (Francisco and Chenier, 2007). Urban residents continue to report higher rates of both personal and, in particular, household victimization than do rural residents. Overall in 1999, 27 percent of the urban population and 18 percent of the rural population reported being the victim of at least one crime in the preceding 12 months (Mihorean et al., 2001).

Research examining differences in crime rates by community size has a long history. However, several potential explanations for these differences can be summarized (Hartnagel and Lee, 1990). Social disorganization theory (see Chapter 13) proposes that urbanization—the increasing size, density, and heterogeneity of a community—leads to a weakening of community cohesiveness and normative consensus, thereby undermining informal mechanisms of social control and increasing crime (Wirth, 1938; Skogan, 1977). Economic deprivation arguments locate the causes of urban crime in poverty and/or the degree of inequality in the distribution of income (Braithwaite, 1979; Blau and Blau, 1982). Routine activities theory (see Chapter 14) (Cohen and Felson, 1979) suggests that features of urban locations, such as the density of potential targets, increased potential for social interaction, greater anonymity, and ease of transportation, are particularly conducive to crime. Finally, the demographic composition of cities may affect their crime rates. Since urban populations are disproportionately young and childless, behaviours such as crime to which they are especially at risk should be more evident in urban areas (Fischer, 1976). Hartnagel and Lee (1990) tested these arguments with data from 88 Canadian cities with a population of 25 000 and over. The results provided strong support for routine activities theory, although the authors qualify this conclusion by noting some of the study's limitations. Cities with a greater dispersal of work and leisure activities away from households offer more opportunities for direct contact, predatory crimes of violence, and crimes against property. The structure of urban opportunities for crime deserves further investigation as an explanation for differences in community crime rates.

Within urban centres, crime rates vary by neighbourhood (Brantingham and Brantingham, 1984; Bursik and Grasmick, 1993). Criminal areas where many criminals reside exist in most cities and persist for long time periods (Brantingham and Brantingham, 1984). These areas tend to be located adjacent to the central business district, although this can vary depending upon local land-use patterns (Shaw and McKay, 1969). The early research of Shaw and McKay (1942) in Chicago found these areas to be characterized by physical deterioration, low income, a heterogeneous population, high density, population mobility, and the presence of many renters in multiple-family dwellings. Later studies have generally replicated these findings (Kornhauser, 1978; Stark, 1987; Byrne and Sampson, 1986). There has been virtually no Canadian research on urban neighbourhoods and crime, although Jarvis and Messinger (1974) examined delinquency rates in the census tracts of London, Ontario. Their findings were consistent with the U.S. research. The 1985 survey of crime victims in Edmonton found that reports of violent victimization were twice as high for residents of the downtown area as for residents of suburban areas (Solicitor General Canada, 1987). However, reports of property crime victimization were not greatly different in the two areas (Solicitor General Canada, 1988).

Neighbourhood variation in crime rates has most often been interpreted from a social disorganization perspective. Neighbourhoods of low economic status, ethnic heterogeneity, and residential mobility experience a disruption of local social organization and informal control since residents have few stakes in the local area and experience difficulty in forming primary relationships and groups to solve common problems (Kornhauser, 1978). Although Shaw and McKay (1942) and early replications of their work did not directly test this model of social disorganization, more recent research has examined indicators of neighbourhood structure and control with generally favourable results (Sampson and Groves, 1989; Bursik and Grasmick, 1993). However, the neighbourhood distribution of criminal opportunities may also affect the distribution of criminal acts within cities (Bursik and Grasmick, 1993). For example, Sampson and Wooldredge (1987) discovered that high levels of target attractiveness were related to neighbourhood burglary rates, and individuals were most at risk of personal theft in areas with high levels of street activity. Ouimet (2000) tested the ability of the social disorganization and criminal opportunities perspectives to explain juvenile offender rates (where delinquents live) and juvenile crime rates (where crimes are committed) at both the census tract (495) and neighbourhood (84) levels of aggregation in the city of Montreal. Social disorganization variables predicted offender rates fairly well while opportunity variables were generally unimportant. On the other hand, opportunity variables helped explain juvenile crime rates, along with the social disorganization variables. More of the variation in both offender rates and crime rates was explained at the neighbourhood rather than the census tract level. As yet, however, there has been little investigation of the dynamics involved in the convergence of offenders and suitable targets at the neighbourhood level (Bursik and Grasmick, 1993).

Summary

- Correlates of crime are those phenomena that are associated with, or related to, criminal behaviour. Among the most important correlates of crime are age, sex, race, drug abuse, social class, and region.
- Crime is strongly associated with age. After peaking in late adolescence/early adulthood, crime decreases with age.
- Sex is also strongly associated with crime. Males are much more likely to be involved in criminal behaviour than females, particularly for violent crimes and for serious property offences. However, in the past three decades, women have increased their involvement in both violent and property crime, although their highest rates continue to be found among the less serious property crimes.
- Blacks and particularly Aboriginal people are greatly over-represented in our criminal justice system. This is most evident when looking at the population of jails and prisons. Alcohol plays a major role in the crimes of Aboriginal people and, directly or indirectly, contributes to this over-representation. Both cultural and structural explanations have been given for the disproportionate involvement of Aboriginal people in crime, as has the possibility of biased enforcement of the law.
- There is a strong correlation between criminal behaviour and the use and abuse of alcohol and illicit drugs. However, their relationship may not be causal but is complex and contingent on a number of other factors.
- Finally, crime varies by region. Violent crime rates are higher in less economically developed countries, while property crime is higher in more developed nations. Crime in Canada varies by region, with the highest rates occurring in the west and the north. Crime rates are also correlated with community size. Larger communities generally have higher crime rates, particularly for property crime, than do small towns and rural areas, although small urban areas had the highest rates in 2005. Neighbourhoods within cities differ in their rates of crime, with high-rate neighbourhoods tending to be located near the city centre. A combination of theories stressing economic inequality, social disorganization, and opportunities for crime has been used to explain these regional patterns.

QUESTIONS FOR CRITICAL THINKING

1. Define correlation, distinguish it from causation, and illustrate the difference with a criminological example.
2. Describe maturational reform, and discuss its application to the age distribution of criminal behaviour.
3. Summarize the trends in the sex differences in criminal behaviour, and discuss the concept of role convergence as applied to these trends.
4. Should data on the race of criminal offenders be routinely collected by criminal justice agencies in Canada?

5. Discuss and evaluate several possible explanations of Aboriginal over-representation in the Canadian criminal justice system.
6. Discuss the ways in which the correlation between drug abuse and crime could be explained.
7. Describe and evaluate the evidence concerning the relationship between social class and criminal behaviour.
8. Discuss how provincial variation in crime rates could be explained.

NET WORK

Statistics Canada provides a great deal of information about crime and its correlates over the Internet. To learn more about correlates of crime, first go to the Statistics Canada home page at **www.statcan.ca/start.html**. Under "Statistics by Subject," click on "Crime and Justice," then "Crimes and Offences," then "Summary Tables in Canadian Statistics." Then click on the table "Crimes by Offences, by Province and Territory." Using the data in this table, answer the following question:

1. How do the provincial and territorial crime rates vary across the country when you compare all Criminal Code offences, crimes of violence, and property crimes? How do drug offences vary across the country?

Then click on the table "Homicide Offences, Number and Rate, by Province and Territories." Using the data in this table, answer the following question:

2. How do the provinces rank in terms of the number of homicide offences in 2005? Does their rank vary depending on the year?

Then click on the table "Victims and Persons Accused of Homicide, by Age and Sex." Using the data in this table, answer the following question:

3. Look at homicide victims; what is the five-year trend for male and female victimization? Is the trend the same for male and female victims under the age of 12? What about for male and female victims ages 18 to 24?

KEY TERMS

correlate; pg. 137
correlation; pg. 137
cultural explanation; pg. 155
maturational reform; pg. 142
over-representation; pg. 152
role convergence; pg. 148
structural explanation; pg. 156

SUGGESTED READING

Boritch, Helen. (1997). *Fallen Women: Female Crime and Criminal Justice in Canada*. Toronto: ITP Nelson. A text reviewing the patterns and trends in female offending and victimization, as well as the theoretical perspectives on female criminality and the response of the criminal justice system to it.

Braithwaite, John. (1981). "The Myth of Social Class and Criminality Reconsidered." *American Sociological Review* 46:36–57. A comprehensive survey of the evidence concerning the relationship between social class and criminality, which concludes that the evidence for such a relationship is persuasive.

Farrington, David P. (1986). "Age and Crime." In Michael Tonry and Norval Morris (eds.), *Crime and Justice* (pp. 189–250). Chicago: University of Chicago Press. A detailed analysis of the age–crime relationship.

Hartnagel, Timothy F., and G. W. Lee. (1990). "Urban Crime in Canada." *Canadian Journal of Criminology* 32:591–606. A research article testing several alternative explanations of the variation in urban crime rates in Canada.

LaPrairie, Carol. (1996). *Examining Aboriginal Corrections in Canada*. Ottawa: Supply and Services Canada. A discussion and evaluation of the evidence concerning the disproportionate involvement of Aboriginal peoples in the Canadian justice system, with a review of policy options and recommendations for responding to this over-representation.

BIBLIOGRAPHY

Adler, F. (1975). *Sisters in Crime*. New York: McGraw-Hill.

Ageton, Suzanne S., and Delbert S. Elliott. (1978). *The Incidence of Delinquent Behavior in a National Probability Sample of Adolescents*. Boulder, Colorado: Behavioral Research Institute.

Austin, R. L. (1993). "Recent Trends in Official Male and Female Crime Rates." *Journal of Criminal* Justice 21:447–66.

Baron, S. W. (1994). "Street Youth and Crime: The Role of Labour Market Experiences." Unpublished Ph.D. dissertation, Department of Sociology, University of Alberta.

Bean, Philip. (2004). *Drugs and Crime*. Portland, Oregon: Willan Publishing.

Beattie, K. (2005). "Adult Correctional Services in Canada, 2003/04." *Juristat* 25(8).

Bell-Rowbotham, B., and C. L. Boydell. (1972). "Crime in Canada: A Distributional Analysis." In C. L. Boydell, C. F. Grindstaff, and P. C. Whitehead (eds.), *Deviant Behavior and Societal Reaction* (pp. 93–116). Toronto: Holt, Rinehart and Winston.

Bennett, Trevor, and Katy Holloway. (2005). *Understanding Drugs, Alcohol and Crime*. Maidenhead, Berkshire UK: Open University Press.

Bienvenue, R. M., and A. H. Latif. (1974). "Arrests, Disposition and Recidivism: A Comparison of Indians and Whites." *Canadian Journal of Criminology and Corrections* 16(2):105–16.

Blackburn, C. (1993). "Aboriginal Justice Inquiries, Task Forces and Commissions: An Update." In *Royal Commission on Aboriginal Peoples, Aboriginal Peoples and the Justice System* (pp. 15–41). Ottawa: Minister of Supply and Services Canada.

Blau, J. R., and P. M. Blau. (1982). "The Cost of Inequality." *American Sociological Review* 47:114–29.

Bloch, H. A., and A. Niederhoffer. (1958). *The Gang*. New York: Philosophical Library.

Boldt, E. D., L. E. Hursh, S. D. Johnson, and K. W. Taylor. (1983). "Presentence Reports and the Incarceration of Natives." *Canadian Journal of Criminology* 25:269–76.

Boritch, H. (1997). *Fallen Women*. Toronto: ITP Nelson.

Box, S. (1987). *Recession, Crime and Punishment*. London: Macmillan Education.

Box, S., and C. Hale. (1984). "Liberation/Emancipation, Economic Marginalization, or Less Chivalry." *Criminology* 22(4):473–97.

Braithwaite, J. (1979). *Inequality, Crime, and Public Policy.* London: Routledge.

———. (1981). "The Myth of Social Class and Criminality Reconsidered." *American Sociological Review* 46:36–57.

———. (1989). *Crime, Shame and Reintegration.* New York: Cambridge University Press.

Brantingham, P., and P. Brantingham. (1984). *Patterns in Crime.* New York: Macmillan.

Brody, H. (1971). *Indians on Skid Row.* Ottawa: Information Canada.

Brzozowski, Jodi-Anne, Andrea Taylor-Butts, and Sara Johnson. (2006). "Victimization and Offending among the Aboriginal Population in Canada." *Juristat* 26(3).

Bunge, Valerie Pottie, Holly Johnson, and Thierno A. Balde. (2005). *Exploring Crime Patterns in Canada.* Ottawa: Statistics Canada.

Bureau of Justice Statistics. (1993). *Highlights from 20 Years of Surveying Crime Victims.* Washington, D.C.: U.S. Department of Justice.

Bursik, R. J., and H. G. Grasmick. (1993). *Neighborhoods and Crime.* Toronto: Maxwell Macmillan.

Byrne, J. M., and R. J. Sampson (eds.). (1986). *The Social Ecology of Crime.* New York: Springer-Verlag.

Campbell, G. (1990). "Women and Crime." *Juristat* 10(20):1–14.

Canadian Centre on Substance Abuse. (2004). *Canadian Addiction Survey.* Ottawa: Canadian Centre on Substance Abuse.

Canadian Corrections Association. (1967). *Indians and the Law.* Ottawa: Canadian Corrections Association.

Carrington, P. J. (2001). "Population Aging and Crime in Canada, 2000–2041." *Canadian Journal of Criminology* 43:331–56.

Clelland, D., and T. J. Carter. (1980). "The New Myth of Class and Crime." *Criminology* 18(3):319–36.

Cohen, L. E., and M. Felson. (1979). "Social Change and Crime Rate Trends." *American Sociological Review* 44:588–608.

Cohen, L. E., and K. C. Land. (1987). "Age Structure and Crime." *American Sociological Review* 52:170–83.

Daly, M., M. Wilson, and S. Vasdev. (2001). "Income Inequality and Homicide Rates in Canada and the United States." *Canadian Journal of Criminology* 43:219–36.

Dauvergne, Mia, and Geoffrey Li. (2006). "Homicide in Canada, 2005." *Juristat* 26(6).

Demers, D. J. (1978). "Discretion, Disparity and the Parole Process." Unpublished Ph.D. dissertation, University of Alberta.

Doob, A. N., M. G. Grossman, and R. P. Auger. (1994). "Aboriginal Homicides in Ontario." *Canadian Journal of Criminology* 36(1):29–62.

Dumont, J. (1993). "Justice and Aboriginal People." In *Royal Commission on Aboriginal Peoples, Aboriginal Peoples and the Justice System* (pp. 42–85). Ottawa: Minister of Supply and Services Canada.

Elliott, D. S., and S. Ageton. (1980). "Reconciling Differences in Estimates of Delinquency." *American Sociological Review* 45(1):95–110.

Fagan, J. (1990). "Intoxication and Aggression." In M. Tonry and J. Q. Wilson (eds.), *Drugs and Crime* (pp. 241–320). Chicago: University of Chicago Press.

Farnworth, M., T. P. Thornberry, M. D. Krohn, and A. J. Lizotte. (1994). "Measurement in the Study of Class and Delinquency." *Journal of Research in Crime and Delinquency* 31:32–61.

Fischer, Benedikt, Wendy Medved, Maritt Kirst, Jurgen Rehm, and Louis Gliksman. (2001). "Illicit Opiates and Crime: Results of an Untreated User Cohort Study in Toronto." *Canadian Journal of Criminology* 43(2):197–217.

Fischer, C. S. (1976). *The Urban Experience*. New York: Harcourt Brace Jovanovich.

Fisher, J. (1986). "Canadian Trends in Selected Female Crimes." Unpublished M.A. thesis, University of Alberta.

Fitzgerald, Robin. (2003). "An Examination of Sex Differences in Delinquency." Ottawa: Statistics Canada.

Fox, J., and T. Hartnagel. (1979). "Changing Social Roles and Female Crime in Canada." *Canadian Review of Sociology and Anthropology* 16(1):96–104.

Francisco, Joycelyn, and Christian Chenier. (2007). "A Comparison of Large Urban, Small Urban and Rural Crime Rates, 2005." *Juristat* 27(3).

Fréchette, M. (1983). "Delinquency and Delinquents." In R. R. Corrado et al. (eds.), *Current Issues in Juvenile Justice* (pp. 49–60). Toronto: Butterworths.

Frideres, J.S. (1988). *Native Peoples in Canada*. Scarborough: Prentice Hall.

Gabor, Thomas. (2004). "Inflammatory Rhetoric on Racial Profiling Can Undermine Police Services." *Canadian Journal of Criminology and Criminal Justice* 46:457–66.

Gannon, Maire, and Karen Mihorean. (2005). "Criminal Victimization in Canada, 2004." *Juristat* 25(7).

Giffen, P. J. (1965). "Rates of Crime and Delinquency." In W. T. McGrath (ed.), *Crime and Its Treatment in Canada*. Toronto: Macmillan.

———. (1966). "The Revolving Door." *Canadian Review of Sociology and Anthropology* 3(3):154–66.

———. (1976). "Official Rates of Crime and Delinquency." In W. T. McGrath (ed.), *Crime and Its Treatment in Canada* (pp. 66–110). Toronto: Macmillan.

Gold, Alan D. (2003). "Media Hype, Racial Profiling, and Good Science." *Canadian Journal of Criminology and Criminal Justice* 45(3):391–399.

Gomme, I. M. (1985). "Predictors of Status and Criminal Offences among Male and Female Adolescents in an Ontario Community." *Canadian Journal of Criminology* 27(2):147–59.

Gordon, R. A. (1976). "Prevalence: The Rare Datum in Delinquency Measurement and Its Implications for the Theory of Delinquency." In M. W. Klein (ed.), *The Juvenile Justice System* (pp. 201–84). Beverly Hills: Sage.

Greenaway, W. K. (1980). "Crime and Class: Unequal Before the Law." In J. Harp and J. R. Hofley (eds.), *Structured Inequality in Canada* (pp. 247–65). Scarborough: Prentice Hall.

Greenberg, D. (1979). "Delinquency and the Age Structure of Society." In S. L. Messinger and E. Bittner (eds.), *Criminology Review Yearbook* (pp. 586–620). Beverly Hills: Sage.

Griffiths, C. T., D. S. Wood, E. Zellerer, and J. Simon. (1994). *Aboriginal Policing in British Columbia*. Victoria: Ministry of Attorney General.

Hagan, J. (1974). "Criminal Justice and Native People." *Canadian Review of Sociology and Anthropology* Special Issue (August):220–36.

———. (1975a). "The Social and Legal Constitution of Criminal Justice." *Social Problems* 22(5):620–37.

———. (1975b). "Parameters of Criminal Prosecution." *Journal of Criminal Law and Criminology* 65(4):536–44.

———. (1975c). "Law, Order and Sentencing." *Sociometry* 38(2):374–84.

———. (1977). "Criminal Justice in Rural and Urban Communities." *Social Forces* 55(3):597–612.

——. (1985). *Modern Criminology: Crime, Criminal Behavior, and Its Control.* New York: McGraw-Hill.

Hagan, J., and B. McCarthy. (1990). "Streetlife and Delinquency." Paper presented to American Society of Criminology.

Hagan, J., J. Simpson, and A. R. Gillis. (1979). "The Sexual Stratification of Social Control." *British Journal of Sociology* 30:25–38.

Hartnagel, T. F. (1978). "The Effect of Age and Sex Compositions of Provincial Populations on Provincial Crime Rates." *Canadian Journal of Criminology* 20(1):28–33.

——. (1982). "Modernization, Female Social Roles, and Female Crime." *Sociological Quarterly* 23:477–90.

——. (1997). "Crime Among the Provinces: The Effect of Geographic Mobility." *Canadian Journal of Criminology* 39(4):387–402.

——. (1998). "Labour Market Problems and Crime in the Transition from School to Work." *Canadian Review of Sociology and Anthropology* 35(4):435–59.

Hartnagel, T. F., and G. W. Lee. (1990). "Urban Crime in Canada." *Canadian Journal of Criminology* 32:591–606.

Havemann, P., K. Couse, L. Foster, and R. Matonovich. (1985). *Law and Order for Canada's Indigenous People.* Regina: Prairie Justice Research, School of Human Justice, University of Regina.

Hindelang, M. J., T. Hirschi, and J. G. Weis. (1979). "Correlates of Delinquency." *American Sociological Review* 44(6):995–1014.

Hirschi, T., and M. Gottfredson. (1983). "Age and the Explanation of Crime." *American Journal of Sociology* 89(3):552–84.

Hirschi, T., and H. Selvin. (1966). "False Criteria of Causality in Delinquency Research." *Social Problems* 13(3):254–68.

Hylton, J. H. (1982). "The Native Offender in Saskatchewan." *Canadian Journal of Criminology* 24(2):121–31.

Indian and Northern Affairs Canada. (1980). *Indian Conditions.* Ottawa: Minister of Indian Affairs and Northern Development.

Irvine, M. J. (1978). *The Native Inmate in Ontario.* Toronto: Ministry of Correctional Services, Province of Ontario.

James, C. (1998). "Up to No Good: Black on the Streets and Encountering Police." In V. Satzewich (ed.), *Racism and Social Inequality in Canada* (pp. 157–76). Toronto: Thompson.

James, J. T. L. (1979). "Toward a Cultural Understanding of the Native Offender." *Canadian Journal of Criminology* 21(4):453–62.

Jarvis, G. K., and H. B. Messinger. (1974). "Social and Economic Correlates of Juvenile Delinquency Rates." *Canadian Journal of Criminology and Corrections* 16:361–72.

Jensen, G. F., J. H. Stauss, and V. W. Harris. (1977). "Crime, Delinquency, and the American Indian." *Human Organization* 36(3):252–57.

Johnson, H. (1987). "Getting the Facts Straight." In E. Adelberg and C. Currie (eds.), *Too Few to Count* (pp. 23–46). Vancouver: Press Gang Publishers.

——. (1996). *Dangerous Domains: Violence Against Women in Canada.* Scarborough: Nelson Canada.

Johnson, S. (2005). "Returning to Correctional Services After Release: A Profile of Aboriginal and non-Aboriginal Adults Involved in Saskatchewan Corrections from 1999/00 to 2003/04." *Juristat* 25(2).

Johnston, P. (1994). "Academic Approaches to Race-Crime Statistics Do Not Justify Their Collection." *Canadian Journal of Criminology* 36:166–73.

Kennedy, L. W., R. A. Silverman, and D. R. Forde. (1991). "Homicide in Urban Canada." *Canadian Journal of Sociology* 16:397–410.

Kornhauser, R. (1978). *Social Sources of Delinquency.* Chicago: University of Chicago Press.

Krahn, H., T. F. Hartnagel, and J. W. Gartrell. (1986). "Income Inequality and Homicide Rates." *Criminology* 24:269–95.

LaPrairie, C. P. (1983). "Native Juveniles in Court." In T. Fleming and L. A. Visano (eds.), *Deviant Designations* (pp. 337–50). Toronto: Butterworths.

———. (1990). "The Role of Sentencing in the Overrepresentation of Aboriginal People in Correctional Institutions." *Canadian Journal of Criminology* 32:429–40.

———. (1992). "Aboriginal Crime and Justice." *Canadian Journal of Criminology* 34:281–97.

———. (1995). *Seen But Not Heard: Native People in the Inner City.* Ottawa: Minister of Public Works and Government Services Canada.

———. (1996). *Examining Aboriginal Corrections in Canada.* Ottawa: Supply and Services Canada.

———. (2002). "Aboriginal Over-representation in the Criminal Justice System: A Tale of Nine Cities." *Canadian Journal of Criminology* 44(2):181–208.

LeBlanc, M. (1975). "Upper Class vs. Working Class Delinquency." In R. A. Silverman and J. J. Teevan Jr., *Crime in Canadian Society* (pp. 102–18). Toronto: Butterworths.

———. (1983). "Delinquency as an Epiphenomenon of Adolescence." In R. R. Corrado et al. (eds.), *Current Issues in Juvenile Justice* (pp. 31–48). Toronto: Butterworths.

Leenaars, A., and D. Lester. (2004). "Understanding the Declining Canadian Homicide Rate: A Test of Holinger's Relative Cohort Size Hypothesis." *Death Studies* 28:263–65.

Lester, D. (1999). *Crime and the Native American.* Springfield, Ill.: Charles Thomas.

Levitt, S. (1999). "The Limited Role of Changing Age Structure in Explaining Aggregate Crime Rates." *Criminology* 37(3):581–97.

Loeber, R., and M. LeBlanc. (1990). "Toward a Developmental Criminology." In M. Tonry and N. Morris (eds.), *Crime and Justice*, Vol 12. Chicago: University of Chicago Press.

Manitoba Public Inquiry into the Administration of Justice and Aboriginal People. (1991). *Report of the Aboriginal Justice Inquiry of Manitoba.* Winnipeg: The Inquiry.

Melchers, Ron. (2003). "Do Toronto Police Engage in Racial Profiling?" *Canadian Journal of Criminology and Criminal Justice* 45(3):347–66.

Merton, R. (1938). "Social Structure and Anomie." *American Sociological Review* 3:672–82.

Métis and Non-Status Indian Crime and Justice Commission. (1978). *Report.* Ottawa: Minister of Supply and Services.

Mihorean, K., S. Besserer, D. Hendrick, J. A. Brzozowski, C. Trainor, and S. Ogg. (2001). *A Profile of Criminal Victimization: Results of the 1999 General Social Survey.* Ottawa: Minister of Industry.

Monture-Angus, P. A. (1996). "Lessons in Decolonization." In D. A. Long and O. P. Dickason (eds.), *Visions of the Heart* (pp. 335–54). Toronto: Harcourt Brace and Company.

Mosher, J., and D. Jernigan. (2001). "Making the Link: A Public Health Approach to Preventing Alcohol-Related Violence and Crime." *Journal of Substance Use* 6:273–89.

Native Counselling Services of Alberta. (1982). "Native People and the Criminal Justice System." *Canadian Legal Aid Bulletin* 5(1):55–63.

Nettler, G. (1982). *Explaining Criminals*. Cincinnati: Anderson Publishing.

———. (1984). *Explaining Crime*. New York: McGraw-Hill.

Neugebauer, R. (2000). "Kids, Cops and Colour." In R. Neugebauer (ed.), *Criminal Injustice: Racism in the Criminal Justice System* (pp. 46–59). Toronto: Canadian Scholars' Press.

Nielsen, M. O. (1992). "Introduction." In R. A. Silverman and M. O. Nielsen (eds.), *Aboriginal Peoples and Canadian Criminal Justice*. Toronto: Butterworths.

O'Brien, R. M. (1999). "Measuring the Convergence/Divergence of 'Serious Crime' Arrest Rates for Males and Females: 1960–1995." *Journal of Quantitative Criminology* 15:97–114.

Osgood, D. W., P. M. O'Malley, J. G. Backman, and L. D. Johnston. (1989). "Time Trends and Age Trends in Arrests and Self-Reported Illegal Behaviour." *Criminology* 27:389–417.

Ouimet, M. (2000). "Aggregation Bias in Ecological Research." *Canadian Journal of Criminology* 42:135–56.

———. (2002). "Explaining the American and Canadian Crime 'Drop' in the 1990s." *Canadian Journal of Criminology* 44:33–50.

Parker, R. N., and K. Auerhahn. (1998). "Alcohol, Drugs, and Violence." *Annual Review of Sociology* 24:291–311.

Pernanen, Kai, Marie-Marthe Cousineau, Serge Brochu, and Fu Sun. (2002). *Proportions of Crimes Associated with Alcohol and Other Drugs in Canada*. Ottawa: Canadian Centre on Substance Abuse.

Pollak, O. (1950). *The Criminality of Women*. Philadelphia: University of Pennsylvania Press.

Quinney, R. (1977). *Class, State and Crime*. New York: David McKay Company.

Rand, A. (1987). "Transitional Life Events and Desistance from Delinquency and Crime." In M. E. Wolfgang and T. P. Thornberry (eds.), *From Boy to Man: From Delinquency to Crime* (pp. 134–62). Chicago: University of Chicago Press.

Roberts, J. (1994). "Crime and Race Statistics: Toward a Canadian Solution." *Canadian Journal of Criminology* 36:175–85.

Roberts, J. V., and A. N. Doob. (1997). "Race, Ethnicity, and Criminal Justice in Canada." In M. Tonry (ed.), *Ethnicity, Crime, and Immigration* Vol. 21 (pp. 469–522). Chicago: University of Chicago Press.

Rowe, A. R., and C. R. Tittle. (1977). "Life Cycle Changes and Criminal Propensity." *The Sociological Quarterly* 18:223–36.

Sagi, P. C., and C. F. Wellford. (1968). "Age Composition and Patterns of Change in Criminal Statistics." *Journal of Criminal Law, Criminology and Police Science* 59:29–36.

Sampson, R. J., and W. B. Groves. (1989). "Community Structure and Crime." *American Journal of Sociology* 94:774–802.

Sampson, R. J., and J. H. Laub. (1990). "Crime and Deviance over the Life Course." *American Sociological Review* 55:609–27.

———. (1992). "Crime and Deviance in the Life Course." *Annual Review of Sociology* 18:63–84.

Sampson, R. J., and J. Wooldredge. (1987). "Linking the Micro- and Macro-Level Dimensions of Lifestyle-Routine Activity and Opportunity Models of Predatory Victimization." *Journal of Quantitative Criminology* 3:371–93.

Savoie, J. (2002). "Crime Statistics in Canada, 2001." *Juristat* 22 (6):1–22.

Shaw, C. R., and H. D. McKay. (1942). *Juvenile Delinquency and Urban Areas.* Chicago: University of Chicago Press.

———. (1969). *Juvenile Delinquency and Urban Areas*, 2nd ed. Chicago: University of Chicago Press.

Short, J .F., Jr., and F. I. Nye. (1957). "Reported Behavior as a Criterion of Deviant Behavior." *Social Problems* 5:207–13.

Simon, R. J. (1975). *Women and Crime.* Lexington, Mass.: D.C. Heath.

Skogan, W. G. (1977). "The Changing Distribution of Big-City Crime." *Urban Affairs Quarterly* 13:33–48.

Smart, C. (1976). *Women, Crime and Criminology.* London: Routledge and Kegan Paul.

Smith, D. A., and C. A. Visher. (1980). "Sex and Involvement in Deviance/Crime." *American Sociological Review* 45 (4):691–701.

Solicitor General Canada. (1987). *Patterns in Violent Crime: Canadian Urban Victimization Survey*, Bulletin No. 8. Ottawa: Ministry of Solicitor General.

———. (1988). *Patterns in Property Crime: Canadian Urban Victimization Survey*, Bulletin No. 9. Ottawa: Ministry of Solicitor General.

Sprott, Jane, and C. Cesaroni. (2002). "Similarities in Homicide Trends in the United States and Canada: Guns, Crack, or Simple Demographics?" Homicide Studies 6(4):348–359.

Stack, S. (1984). "Income Inequality and Property Crime." *Criminology* 22:229–57.

Stark, R. (1987). "Deviant Places." *Criminology* 25:893–909.

Statistics Canada. (2007). "Crime Statistics, 2006." *The Daily*, 18 July, 2007. Ottawa: Statistics Canada.

Steffensmeier, D. (1978). "Crime and the Contemporary Woman." *Social Forces* 57(2):566–83.

———. (1980). "Sex Differences in Patterns of Adult Crime, 1965–77." *Social Forces* 58(4):1080–1108.

Steffensmeier, D., and E. Allan. (1995). "Criminal Behavior: Gender and Crime." In J. F. Sheley (ed.), *Criminology: A Contemporary Handbook*, 2nd ed. (pp. 83–113). Belmont, Calif.: Wadsworth.

Steffensmeier, D. F., E. A. Allan, M. D. Harer, and C. Streifel. (1989). "Age and the Distribution of Crime." *American Journal of Sociology* 94:803–31.

Steffensmeier, D. J., and M. D. Harer. (1991). "Did Crime Rise or Fall During the Regan Presidency?" *Journal of Research in Crime and Delinquency* 28:330–59.

Steffensmeier, D., and C. Streifel. (1992). "Time-series Analysis of the Female Percentage of Arrests for Property Crimes, 1960–1985." *Justice Quarterly* 9(1):77–103.

Steffensmeier, D., R. H. Steffensmeier, and A. S. Rosenthal. (1979). "Trends in Female Violence, 1960–1977." *Sociological Focus* 12(3):217–27.

Sutherland, E., and D. Cressey. (1978). *Criminology.* New York: J.P. Lippincott.

Tanner, J., and H. Krahn. (1991). "Part-Time Work and Deviance among High-School Seniors." *Canadian Journal of Sociology* 16:281–302.

Task Force on Aboriginal Peoples in Federal Corrections. (1989). *Final Report.* Ottawa: Minister of Supply and Services.

Task Force on the Criminal Justice System and Its Impact on the Indian and Métis People of Alberta. (1991). *Report of the Task Force on the Criminal Justice System and Its Impact on the Indian and Métis.* Edmonton: The Task Force.

Thomas, D. (1993). "The Foreign Born in the Federal Prison Population." Canadian Law and Society Association Conference, Ottawa, June 8.

Thomas, M. (2004). "Adult Criminal Court Statistics, 2003/04." *Juristat* 24(12).

Tittle, C. R., and W. J. Villemez. (1977). "Social Class and Criminality." *Social Forces* 56 (2):474–502.

Tittle, C. R., W. J. Villemez, and D. A. Smith. (1978). "The Myth of Social Class and Criminality." *American Sociological Review* 43(5):643–56.

Tittle, C. R., and D. A. Ward. (1993). "The Interaction of Age with the Correlates and Causes of Crime." *Journal of Quantitative Criminology* 9:3–53.

Tonry, M. (1995). *Malign Neglect: Race, Crime and Punishment in America.* New York: Oxford University Press.

Trasler, G. (1980). "Aspects of Causality, Culture, and Crime." Paper presented at the 4th International Seminar at the International Centre of Sociological, Penal and Penitentiary Research and Studies, Messina, Sicily.

Trevethan, S. (1993). *Police-Reported Aboriginal Crime in Calgary, Regina and Saskatoon.* Ottawa: Canadian Centre for Justice Statistics.

Tribble, S. (1972). "Socio-Economic Status and Self-Reported Juvenile Delinquency." *Canadian Journal of Criminology and Corrections* 14:409–15.

Verdun-Jones, S. N., and G. K. Muirhead. (1979–80). "Natives in the Canadian Criminal Justice System." *Crime and Justice* 7/8(1):3–21.

Vold, G. B., and T. J. Bernard. (1986). *Theoretical Criminology.* New York: Oxford University Press.

Wallace, M. (2004). "Crime Statistics in Canada, 2003." *Juristat* 24(6).

Warr, M. (1993). "Age, Peers, and Delinquency." *Criminology* 31:17–40.

Wellford, C. F. (1973). "Age Composition and the Increase in Recorded Crime." *Criminology* 11:61–70.

West, W. G. (1984). *Young Offenders and the State.* Toronto: Butterworths.

Wirth, L. (1938). "Urbanism as a Way of Life." *American Journal of Sociology* 44:3–24.

Wolff, L., and B. Reingold. (1994). "Drug Use and Crime." *Juristat* 14(6):1–19.

Wood, D. S., and C. T. Griffiths. (1996). "Patterns of Aboriginal Crime." In R. A. Silverman, J. J. Teevan, and V. F. Sacco (eds.), *Crime in Canadian Society,* 5th ed. (pp. 222–33). Toronto: Harcourt Brace and Company.

Wortley, Scot. (2003). "Hidden Intersections: Research on Race, Crime and Criminal Justice." *Canadian Ethnic Studies* 35(3):99–117.

Wortley, Scot, and Julian Tanner. (2003). "Data, Denials, and Confusion: The Racial Profiling Debate in Toronto." *Canadian Journal of Criminology and Criminal Justice* 45(3):367–91.

———. (2005). "Inflammatory Rhetoric? Baseless Accusations? A Response to Gabor's Critique of Racial Profiling Research in Canada." *Canadian Journal of Criminology and Criminal Justice* 47(3):581–609.

Wynne, D. F., and T. F. Hartnagel. (1975). "Race and Plea Negotiation." *Canadian Journal of Sociology* 1(2):147–55.

Feminism and Criminology

6

Elizabeth Comack

UNIVERSITY OF MANITOBA

Like other academic disciplines, criminology has been a male-centred enterprise. Despite the use of generic terms such as "criminals," "defendants," and "delinquents," most of criminology has really been about what *men* do. As a consequence, women have been rendered invisible in much criminological inquiry. When women are looked at as offenders, their small numbers relative to men have typically been used to justify or rationalize this neglect. In 2003, for instance, females constituted only 19 percent of adults charged with Criminal Code offences in Canada (Wallace, 2004). When women were looked at as victims, violence against them was traditionally not a major area of concern. Official statistics on crime indicated that offences such as rape were relatively infrequent, and victim surveys reported young males to be the group most at risk from crime. Perhaps even more significant is that even though the subject matter of criminology has been men, criminologists have done very little work on men *as* men. In short, they have neglected to consider the "maleness" of their subjects. Over the past three decades, there has been a growing awareness of the implications that these omissions hold for the discipline. This has come about largely through the feminist engagement with criminology: the efforts of feminist criminologists to move women—and an analysis of gender—from the periphery to the centre of criminological inquiry. The purpose of this chapter is to recount this history with a view to clarifying the kinds of issues and questions that are now commanding criminologists' attention.

Learning Objectives

After reading this chapter, you should be able to

- Explain the various theories that have been developed to understand women's involvement in crime.
- Understand the social, cultural, and legal factors that pertain to the issue of male violence against women.
- Appreciate some of the connections between a woman's law violations and her history of abuse.
- Evaluate the claim that women are "men's equals" in violence and some of the problems raised with the use of the Conflict Tactics Scale for researching violence between intimate partners.

The Invisibility of Women

The feminist engagement with criminology began over 30 years ago, when pioneers in the discipline, such as Marie-Andrée Bertrand (1967) and Frances Heidensohn (1968), first called attention to criminology's amnesia when it came to women. Heidensohn (1968, 171), for instance, described the analysis of women and crime as "lonely uncharted seas" and suggested that what was needed was a "crash programme of research which telescopes decades of comparable studies of males." In its initial phases, however, the feminist engagement with criminology consisted of a critique of the existing approaches to explaining crime. This critique took two paths. Initially, writers like Dorie Klein (1973) and Carol Smart (1976, 1977) focused attention on the **sexism** of the small body of theories that had been developed to explain women's crime. Other writers soon broadened the focus to include the invisibility of women in the mainstream theories within the discipline.

sexism
Attributing to women socially undesirable characteristics that are assumed to be intrinsic characteristics of that sex.

Theories of Women's Crime

The Conservative Approach

Historically, a particular pathway can be followed when tracing the initial attempts to explain women's criminality. It begins with the publication of Cesare Lombroso and William Ferrero's *The Female Offender* in 1895 and is followed by W. I. Thomas's *The Unadjusted Girl* in 1923, Sheldon and Eleanor Glueck's *Five Hundred Delinquent Women* in 1934, and Otto Pollak's *The Criminality of Women* in 1950. Each of these works reflects a **conservative approach** to understanding differences between men and women. Specifically, "difference" is rooted in biology. Women are viewed as "naturally" inferior to men, and it is this inferiority that is used to explain women's criminality.

conservative approach
An approach that understands "difference" between men and women as biologically based sex differences. Women are viewed as "naturally" inferior or unequal to men.

For example, in applying the concepts of atavism and social Darwinism (see Chapter 7, "Early Theories of Criminology"), Lombroso and Ferrero suggested that women possessed limited intelligence. They were also less sensitive to pain than men, full of revenge and jealousy, and naturally passive and conservative. Women's natural passivity, for instance, was caused by the "immobility of the ovule compared to the zoosperm" (Lombroso and Ferrero, 1895, 109). Atavistically, women were seen as displaying fewer signs of degeneration than men. The reason, according to Lombroso and Ferrero, was that women (and nonwhite males) had not advanced as far along the evolutionary continuum as (white) males and so could not degenerate as far. Given that women were relatively "primitive," the criminals among them would not be highly visible. However, those women who were criminal were cast as excessively vile and cruel in their crimes. They combined the qualities of the criminal male with the worst characteristics of the female: cunning, spite, and deceitfulness. Lacking the "maternal instinct" and "ladylike qualities," criminal women were seen as genetically more male than female.

First published in 1923, W.I. Thomas's (1967) work on female delinquency was premised on a similar kind of biological determinism. Thomas suggested that human behaviour was based on four "wishes": for adventure, security, response, and recognition. These wishes corresponded to features in the nervous system, which were expressed as biological instincts of anger, fear, love, and the will to gain status and power respectively. However, Thomas asserted that men's and women's instincts differed both in quantity and quality. Since women had more varieties of love in their nervous systems, their desire for response was greater than men's. According to Thomas, it was the need to feel loved that accounted for women's criminality, and especially prostitution.

Sheldon and Eleanor Glueck (1934) continued in this same tradition with *500 Delinquent Women*. The Gluecks described the women in their study as a "sorry lot. Burdened with feeblemindedness, psychopathic personality, and marked emotional instability, a large proportion of them found it difficult to survive by legitimate means" (299). The view of criminal women as "Other" is clearly evident in the Gluecks' work: "This swarm of defective, diseased, antisocial misfits . . . comprises the human material which a reformatory and a parole system are required by society to transform into wholesome, decent, law-abiding citizens! Is it not a miracle that a proportion of them were actually rehabilitated?" (303).

Otto Pollak's (1961) work attempted to account for what he described as the "masked" nature of women's crime. Sceptical of the official data on sex differences in crime, Pollak suggested that women's crime was vastly undercounted. He put forward the view that female criminality was more likely to be hidden and undetected. Women were more often the instigators than perpetrators of crime. Like Eve in the Garden of Eden, they manipulated men into committing offences. Women were also inherently deceptive and vengeful: they engaged in prostitution, blackmailed their lovers, as domestics they stole from their employers, and as homemakers they carried out horrendous acts on their families (like poisoning the sick and abusing children). According to Pollak, woman's devious nature was rooted in her physiology. While a man must achieve erection in order to perform the sex act, and hence will not be able to conceal orgasm, a woman can fake orgasm (10). This ability to conceal orgasm gave women practice at deception. Pollak also suggested that female crime was caused by the vengefulness, irritability, and depression women encountered as a result of their generative phases. For example, menstruation drove women to acts of revenge by reminding women of their inferior status (and their ultimate failure to become men) (see Box 6.1). The concealed nature of their crimes, the vulnerability of their victims, and their chivalrous treatment by men who could not bear to prosecute or punish them, all combined to "mask" women's offences. When these factors are taken into account, according to Pollak, women's crimes are equal in severity and number to those of men.

As Heidensohn (1985, 122) notes, these early approaches to explaining women's crime lent an aura of intellectual respectability to many of the old folk tales about women and their behaviours. They reflected the widely held assumptions about "women's nature," including the good girl/bad girl duality and a double standard that viewed sexual promiscuity as a sign of "amorality" in women but "normality" in men. Relying on "common-sense," anecdotal evidence, and circular reasoning—that is, "things are as they are because they are natural, and they are natural because that is the way things are" (Smart, 1976,

FOCUS

BOX 6.1 The "Women Problem"

In the following passage, Otto Pollak offers us an illustration of a male-centred view of what has been traditionally referred to as the "woman problem" and its relationship to female criminality.

The student of female criminality cannot afford to overlook the generally known and recognized fact that [women's] generative phases are frequently accompanied by psychological disturbances which may upset the need satisfaction balance of the individual or weaken her internal inhibitions, and thus become causative factors in female crime. Particularly because of the social meaning attached to them in our culture, the generative phases of women are bound to present many stumbling blocks for the law-abiding behaviour of women. Menstruation with its appearance of injury must confirm feelings of guilt which individuals may have about sex activities which they have learned to consider as forbidden. As a symbol of womanhood, it must also, because of its recurrent nature, aggravate any feeling of irritation and protest which women may have regarding their sex in a society in which women have had, and still have, to submit to social inequality with men. In both instances, it must lead to a disturbance of the emotional balance of the individual and this becomes potentially crime-promoting. Pregnancy in a culture which frowns upon illegitimacy and fosters in large sectors of society limitation in the number of children or even childlessness must become a source of irritation, anxiety, and emotional upheaval in many instances. The menopause in a society which makes romance and emotional gratification the supreme value in a monogamous marriage system must be experienced, at least by married women, frequently as a threat to the basis of their emotional security if not to their general marital existence. In view of these cultural implications of the generative phases and their psychological consequences, it is difficult to understand why the existing literature contains so little discussion of their possible crime-promoting influence.

Source: Otto Pollak. (1961). *The Criminality of Women*. New York: A. S. Barnes, pp. 157–58. Originally published by University of Pennsylvania Press (Philadelphia) in 1950.

36)—the early theorists failed to call into question the structural features of their society and the gendered nature of the roles of men and women. Instead, sex (a biological difference) and gender (a cultural prescription) were equated as one and the same, with the "ladylike qualities" of the middle- and upper-class white woman used as the measuring rod for what was inherently female. In the process, the theories constructed were not only sexist, but classist and racist as well.

While we can look back on these early theories of women's crime with some amusement, it bears noting that the kinds of assumptions and beliefs reflected in them have not disappeared. As Klein (1973, 7) comments, "The road from Lombroso to the present is surprisingly straight." Throughout the 1960s, researchers continued to rely on the assumptions and premises of the earlier approaches (see, for example, Cowie et al., 1968; Konopka, 1966). Following in the footsteps of Otto Pollak, a more contemporary version of this conservative approach to understanding the difference between men and women links hormonal changes associated with women's menstrual cycles to their involvement in crime.

Premenstrual syndrome or PMS has been described as a condition of "irritability, indescribable tension" and a "desire to find relief by foolish and ill-considered actions" that is thought to occur during the preceding week or two prior to the onset of menstruation (Frank cited in Osborne, 1989, 168). There have been some 150 different symptoms (behavioural, psychological, and physiological) associated with PMS, and estimates of its incidence vary from 20 to 95 percent of the female population. There are no biomedical tests for determining the existence of PMS; it is the only "disease" not dependent on a specific type of symptom for its diagnosis. Nevertheless, premenstrual syndrome has been argued to be a cause of violent behaviour in women who suffer from it. It gained popularity as a cause of women's criminality in the 1980s, when PMS was introduced in two British court cases as a mitigating factor in homicide (Luckhaus, 1985).

While research linking PMS to women's criminality has been criticized for its methodological deficiencies (Morris, 1987), feminist criminologists have questioned the validity of framing explanations for women's criminality that isolate the source of the problem in women's bodies, thereby ignoring the cultural meanings (especially with regard to menstruation) and social contexts that are at play (Kendall, 1991; 1992). So long as women are pathologized as "sick" or "diseased," the broader structural factors that impinge upon women's lives—and are thereby implicated in their offending behaviours—will be ignored.

The Liberal Approach

In the 1970s, theories of women's crime began to shift toward a more sociological orientation. Rather than focusing on biology, attention shifted to culture. In this **liberal approach**, differences between men and women are not necessarily innate or inborn, but are learned by individuals through the process of socialization. It is the culture that marks off the differences between men and women by proscribing certain roles and behaviours as "male appropriate" and "female appropriate." "Gender" was therefore separated from "sex" and made the key focus of inquiry. This liberal approach to understanding difference took the form of role theory as an explanation for female criminality. Dale Hoffman-Bustamante (1973), for example, suggested that the lower rate of delinquency of girls can be accounted for by differential socialization and child-rearing practices. Whereas boys are encouraged to be aggressive, outgoing, and ambitious and are allowed greater freedom, girls are taught to be passive and domesticated and are more closely supervised. Since girls are taught to be non-violent, they do not acquire the skills, technical ability, or physical strength to engage in violent acts such as gang fighting. When women do engage in violent behaviour, their actions reflect their greater domesticity. For example, women who murder are more likely to use kitchen knives than guns. The finding that women are more likely to be charged with shoplifting offences was similarly explained with reference to their gender roles and socialization. Women are traditionally the consumers in society and, when they steal, girls are more likely to take small items like make-up. Role theory, then, offered an explanation in terms of the differential gender socialization for both the types and nature of offences that females commit.

liberal approach
Distinguishes sex (biological) from gender (cultural) and sees differences between men and women as resulting from gender roles and socialization patterns.

Another version of role theory was put forward by John Hagan and his colleagues (Hagan et al., 1979; 1987; Hagan et al., 1985) in the form of a power-control theory of sex and delinquency. Power-control theory is designed to explain the sex differences in delinquency by drawing linkages between the variations in parental control and the delinquent behaviour of boys and girls. More specifically, Hagan and his colleagues suggest that parental control and adolescents' subsequent attitudes toward risk-taking behaviour are affected by family class relations. They distinguish two ideal types of family: the *patriarchal family* in which the husband is employed in an authority position in the workforce and the wife is not employed outside the home, and the *egalitarian family* in which both husband and wife are employed in authority positions outside the home. Hagan and his colleagues suggest that in the former, a traditional gender division exists, whereby fathers and especially mothers are expected to control their daughters more than their sons. Given the presence of a "cult of domesticity," girls are socialized to focus their futures on domestic labour and consumption activities, while boys are prepared for their participation in production activities. In the latter form, parents redistribute their control efforts so that girls are subject to controls more like those imposed on boys. "In other words, in egalitarian families, as mothers gain power relative to husbands, daughters gain freedom relative to sons" (1987, 792). As such, the authors predict that these different family forms will produce differing levels of delinquency in girls: "Patriarchal families will be characterized by large gender differences in common delinquent behaviours, while egalitarian families will be characterized by smaller gender differences in delinquency" (1987, 793).

Carol Smart (1976) has commented that role theory can offer only a partial explanation of women's crime. Because of a failure to situate the discussion of gender roles in broader structural terms, little attention is devoted to *why* socialization patterns are gender differentiated and *how* they have come to be that way. In the absence of a structural analysis, it is too easy to fall back on explanations that view such differences as biological, and not social, in their origins: "role is destiny" can therefore act as a ready substitute for "biology is destiny" (Morris, 1987, 64). While Hagan and his colleagues endeavour to place role theory in a broader structural context (by attending to the labour force participation of parents), they make an important assumption: if a woman is working for wages, there will be "equality" within the household. Their formulation does not pay enough attention to the nature of women's paid work and to other variables that might be in operation (such as how power and control may be exercised between males and females within the household).

In addition to engaging in critical evaluations of the specific theories that had been developed to explain women's involvement in crime, feminist criminologists drew attention to the invisibility of women in the mainstream approaches within the discipline.

The Mainstream Theories of Crime

Since the 1970s, mainstream approaches to explaining crime have come under increasing scrutiny. Writers such as Eileen Leonard (1982), Frances Heidensohn (1985), Allison Morris (1987), and Ngaire Naffine (1987) have highlighted the general failure of mainstream theories in criminology to adequately explain or account for women's involvement in crime; "mainstream" was, in effect, "malestream."

For example, in explaining crime in relation to the strain that results from the disjunction between culture goals (like monetary success) and institutionalized means (education, jobs), Robert Merton's anomie theory (see Chapter 9, "Strain Theories") reflected a sensitivity to the class inequalities that exist in society. The same could not be said, however, with regard to an awareness of gender inequalities. If lower-class individuals were more likely to engage in crime because of a lack of access to the institutionalized means for achieving monetary success, then it follows that women—who as a group experience a similar lack of access—should also be found to commit crime as a consequence of this strain. This is not the case.

Like strain theory, Edwin Sutherland's differential association theory is presented as a general theory of crime (see Chapter 12, "Interactionist Theories"). In focusing on the processes by which individuals learn definitions of the legal codes as either favourable or unfavourable, Sutherland posited the existence of a "cultural homogeneity" in society with regard to pro- and anti-criminal associations. While this cultural heterogeneity accounted for men's involvement in crime, women were the anomaly or exception in that they displayed a "cultural homogeneity." In Sutherland's view, women were more altruistic and compliant than men. As Naffine (1987) has noted, Sutherland missed a great opportunity when he neglected to explore this apparent cultural homogeneity in females. Given his critical outlook on the individualism and competition that he felt characterized American society, an examination of women's conformity could have provided Sutherland with clues to better understand crime and its causes.

Travis Hirschi's work on social control theory is also characterized by a neglect of the female (see Chapter 13, "Social Control Theory"). While other criminologists focused their attention on explaining deviance, Hirschi set out to explain conformity. In this regard, since women appear to be more conformist than men, it would have made sense to treat women as central to his analysis. Nevertheless, despite having collected data on female subjects, Hirschi set these data aside and—like his colleagues—concentrated on males.

With the advent of the labelling and conflict theories during the 1960s and 1970s, the potential for a more inclusive approach to crime increased. Yet, while Howard Becker's labelling perspective raised the question of "Whose side are we on?" and advocated an approach to deviance that gave a voice to those who were subject to the labelling process, it was never fully realized in the case of women. Similarly, Ian Taylor, Paul Walton, and Jock Young's *The New Criminology* (1973), which offered up a devastating critique of the traditional criminological theories, failed to give any mention to women.

In general, when sex differentials in crime are considered by the mainstream theorists, the tendency has been to rely on stereotypical constructions of masculinity and femininity: men are aggressive, independent, daring, and adventurous; women are submissive, dependent, and compliant. In the process, female law violators are classed as a rather "dull lot." Even in their deviance, they are less interesting than men. Moreover, such stereotypical depictions of women have been considered "so obvious" that they require no further discussion (see, for example, Cohen, 1955, 142)—let alone theoretical or empirical concern.

We have seen in Chapter 5 that females commit less serious offences, in smaller numbers, and with less frequency than males. Criminologists have typically responded to these findings by formulating their theories to account for only male crime and delinquency. The ramifications of this tendency have been spelled out by Lorraine Gelsthorpe and Allison Morris:

> Theories are weak if they do not apply to half of the potential criminal population; women, after all, experience the same deprivations, family structures and so on that men do. Theories of crime should be able to take account of both men's and women's behaviour and to highlight those factors which operate differently on men and women. Whether or not a particular theory helps us to understand women's crime is of *fundamental*, not marginal importance for criminology. (Gelsthorpe and Morris, 1988, 103; emphasis added)

The Generalizability Problem

generalizability problem
Raises the issue of whether mainstream theories of crime—which have largely been developed with men in mind—can be made to "fit" women.

One issue raised by this critique of the mainstream theories is referred to by Kathleen Daly and Meda Chesney-Lind (1988) as the **generalizability problem**: can theories generated to explain male offending be modified to apply to women? Several criminologists responded to this problem by attempting to make the mainstream theories of crime "fit" women. Eileen Leonard (1982), for example, in a reformulation of Merton's strain theory, suggested that females may be socialized to aspire to different culture goals than males, in particular, relational ones concerning marriage and having children. If this is the case, then women's low rate of criminality would be explained by the relatively easy manner in which females can realize their goals. Nevertheless, as Morris (1987) notes, such a formulation relies on an idealized and romanticized version of women's lives. Not only does it display an insensitivity to the strains and frustrations associated with women's familial role, but it also fails to acknowledge the economic concerns that women confront. Such efforts to revise mainstream theories of crime to include women have been referred to as the "add women and stir" approach. Part of the difficulty with this endeavour is that women are presented as afterthoughts, not as integral to the arguments being developed (Gelsthorpe and Morris, 1988). A more significant problem with this effort is captured by Naffine (1997, 32): "The point of these exercises has been to adapt to the female case, theories of crime which purported to be gender-neutral but were in fact always highly gender specific. Not surprisingly, the results have been varied and generally inconclusive."

The Gender-Ratio Problem

gender-ratio problem
Poses the question of why are there sex differences in rates of arrest and types of criminal activity between men and women.

A second issue raised by the feminist critique of mainstream criminology is one which Daly and Chesney-Lind (1988, 119) refer to as the **gender-ratio problem**. Why are women less likely than men to be involved in crime? What explains the sex difference in rates of arrest and in the variable types of criminal activity between men and women? Attention to the gender-ratio problem sparked a plethora of studies in the 1970s and 1980s on the processing of men and women by the criminal justice system (see, for example, Scutt, 1979; Kruttschnitt, 1980–81 and 1982; Steffensmeier and Kramer, 1982; Zingraff and Thomson, 1984; Daly, 1987 and 1989). The main question that guided much of this research stemmed from Pollak's assertion of the "chivalry" on the part of criminal justice officials: are women treated more leniently than men? Like the generalizability problem, the results have been mixed. For instance, research that supports the chivalry hypothesis indicates that when it does exist, chivalry benefits some women more than others, in particular, the few white middle- or upper-class women who come into conflict with the law. It also appears to apply only to those female suspects who behave in a stereotypical fashion, that is, "crying, pleading for release for the sake of their children, claiming men have led them astray" (Rafter and Natalizia, 1981, 92). In this regard, Nicole Rafter and Elena Natalizia have argued that chivalrous behaviour should be seen as a means of preserving women's subordinate position in society, not as a benign effort to treat women with some special kindness. Naffine (1997, 36), however, points to a larger problem with this research. By turning on the question of whether women were treated the same as or different than men, the chivalry thesis (and its rebuttal) took men to be the norm: "Men were thus granted the status of universal subjects, the population of people with whom the rest of the world (women) were compared."

The Women's Liberation Thesis

While research on the chivalry thesis drew the attention of criminologists in the 1970s and 1980s, another thesis was attracting considerable attention. The women's liberation thesis posits that women's involvement in crime will come to more closely resemble men's as differences between men and women are diminished by women's greater participation and equality in society. As reflected in the work of Rita Simon (1975) and Freda Adler (1975), the thesis suggests that changes in women's gender roles will be reflected in their rates of criminal involvement. Simon suggested that the increased employment opportunities that accompanied the women's movement would also bring an increase in opportunities to commit crime (such as embezzlement from employers). Adler linked the apparent increase in women's crime statistics to the influence of the women's movement and suggested that a "new female criminal" was emerging: women were becoming more violent and aggressive, just like their male counterparts.

Naffine (1997, 32) refers to the thesis that "women's liberation" causes crime in women as "perhaps the most time-consuming and fruitless exercise" in criminology. The numerous empirical difficulties with the thesis have already been discussed at some length in Chapter 5. For feminist criminologists, the main difficulty with the women's liberation thesis—similar to the chivalry thesis—was that it posed a question that took males to be the norm: were women becoming more "liberated" and thus more like men, even in their offending?

Given the difficulties encountered in the efforts to respond to the generalizability and gender-ratio problems, many feminist criminologists saw the need to "bracket" these issues for the time being in order to understand better the social worlds of women and girls (Daly and Chesney-Lind, 1988, 121). Maureen Cain (1990) took this suggestion further. She noted that while feminist criminologists needed to understand women's experiences, there were no tools in existing criminological theory with which to do this. Cain therefore advocated a "transgressive" approach, one that started from outside the boundaries of criminological discourse.

Criminalized Women

For many feminist criminologists, starting from outside criminology has meant resisting the temptation to fashion theories of women's involvement in crime that take crime categories (such as crimes against the person or crimes against property) as their starting point. As writers such as Carol Smart (1989), Danielle Laberge (1991), and Karlene Faith (1993) have pointed out, "crime" is not a homogenous category. There are notable differences between women in the nature and extent of both their criminal involvement and their contacts with the criminal justice system. As well, crime categories are legal constructions, the end result of a lengthy process of detection, apprehension, accusation, judgment, and conviction. They represent one way of ordering or making sense of social life. Crime categories are also premised on a dualism between "the criminal" and "the law-abiding," which reinforces the view of criminal women as "Other" and thereby misses the similarities that exist between women. In this respect, criminal women are in very many ways no different from the rest of us. They are mothers, daughters, sisters, girlfriends, and wives, and they share many of the experiences of women collectively in society. Since crime is the outcome of interactions between individuals and the criminal justice system, writers like Laberge (1991) have proposed that we think not in terms of "criminal women" but "criminalized women."

In these terms, women may commit a variety of crimes for a variety of reasons; there is no single or special theory for their criminality. As Pat Carlen (1985, 10) has emphasized, "The essential criminal woman does not exist." In contrast to the conservative and liberal approaches that have dominated criminologists' thinking about the "difference" between men and women, a **feminist approach** understands "difference" as rooted in the structure of society. More specifically, the lives of criminalized women are located within a broader social context characterized by inequalities of class, race, and gender.

feminist approach
Understands "difference" between men and women as structurally produced by inequalities of class, race, and gender that condition and constrain women's lives.

With regard to their class location, criminalized women tend to be young, poor, undereducated, and unskilled. They are most likely to be involved in property crimes. Holly Johnson and Karen Rodgers (1993, 98) suggest that "women's participation in property offences is consistent with their traditional roles as consumers and, increasingly, as low income, semi-skilled, sole support providers for their families. In keeping with the rapid increase in female-headed households and the stresses associated with poverty, greater numbers of women are being charged with shoplifting, cheque forging and welfare fraud."

In contrast to the women's liberation thesis, feminist criminologists have suggested that increases in women's involvement in crime are more directly connected with the "feminization of poverty" than with women's emancipation. Indeed, several writers have called attention to how government cutbacks to social assistance have left increasing numbers of women and children at risk (Chunn and Gavigan, 2006; Mosher, 2006). In the province of Ontario, for example, social assistance payments were cut by 21.6 percent in 1995, "workfare" programs were implemented, and a zero-tolerance policy on welfare fraud was put in place. The feminization of poverty has been accompanied by the "criminalization of poverty." Next to homicide, individuals convicted of welfare fraud now have the greatest likelihood of receiving a sentence of incarceration. A 1997 study of 50 cases of welfare fraud convictions found that 80 percent were sentenced to time in prison (Martin, 1999). One individual caught up in this process was Kimberly Rogers (see Box 6.2).

WWW

Justice with Dignity—includes articles and information on the inquest on the death of Kimberly Rogers
http://dawn.thot.net/Kimberly_Rogers/

FOCUS

BOX 6.2 We've Learned Little from Kimberly Rogers's Death

By JoAnne Frenschkowski

It was sweltering hot this time last year when Kimberly Rogers, 40 years old and eight months pregnant, died in her Sudbury apartment. She was serving a six-month sentence of house arrest after pleading guilty to defrauding the Ontario Works program (she'd collected welfare while receiving student loans to cover her studies in the social services program at Cambrian College).

What have Canadians learned since she died? The B.C. government has actually reduced welfare benefits and tightened eligibility criteria; single parents' cheques have been trimmed along with allowances for clothing and school supplies. Ontario has continued to ban other people convicted of fraud from collecting welfare benefits, and some of those bans are for life (three cases are being challenged in court). Could Kimberly Rogers's tragedy happen again? Yes.

Under the Ontario Works Act, student loans are considered income, despite the fact that the primary goal is to cover the cost of tuition and books, and are to be repaid. Never mind that Ms. Rogers had taken the initiative to change the direction of her life, had graduated near the top of her college class and had excellent prospects for moving into the workforce.

Her sentence was strict. She was only allowed to leave her house for three hours a week. A restitution order also required her to pay back the excess amount she had received. And she was placed on probation for 18 months.

Her guilty plea also triggered a newly enacted section of the Ontario Works Act, which banned her from receiving welfare for three months. This left her with no income—at a time when she was prohibited from leaving her house to work or look for work. Along with the ban on welfare benefits, she lost her drug card and could no longer afford the medications prescribed for her migraines, insomnia, anxiety and depression (the Elizabeth Fry Society was able to get the card reinstated).

Pregnant and desperate, Ms. Rogers found only a few charities willing to help. Had she gone to jail, she and her unborn child would have at least had the necessities of life.

On May 31, 2001, as a part of a constitutional challenge, a judge temporarily lifted the ban, reasoning that the act of forcing a pregnant woman into destitution would harm both Ms. Rogers and the public at large. Ms. Rogers began to receive benefits again. But because she had to repay welfare, her debt was deducted off each monthly cheque, reducing $520 to $468. Her rent cost $450 a month, leaving $18 a month for food and other expenses.

A year ago she was found dead in her apartment.

What has society learned?

Ontario's welfare rates remain as low as they have been since they were cut by 21.6 per cent in 1995 (there hasn't even been a cost of living adjustment). A single person still receives a maximum of $520 per month.

(Continued)

FOCUS

BOX 6.2 We've Learned Little from Kimberly Rogers's Death *(Continued)*

Just months before Kimberly's death, Ontario introduced further amendments to its social assistance laws. Now, for anyone convicted of welfare fraud committed after April 2000, there is a lifetime ban. Those convicted can never receive welfare again. Ever. Not even if they need it to survive. The fiscal savings that result from clamping down on welfare remain a greater political priority to government than the lives of citizens who are left without shelter and food.

And the Ontario government is still crowing about the success of "workfare" in helping welfare recipients return to work. But the reality is different: Instead of integrating people into the new, knowledge-based economy, workfare is geared toward pushing people into low-paying, insecure jobs.

Still, some things have changed.

Opposition to the province's treatment of welfare recipients is growing. To date, 10 Ontario municipalities have passed resolutions to oppose the lifetime ban. Recently, the Court of Appeal determined that the province can't discriminate against welfare recipients simply because they are welfare recipients and dependent on government programs for support—in other words, a government does not have carte blanche to impose stricter conditions on welfare recipients than any other citizen. And later this year the Ontario Superior Court will consider the cases of three people who are appealing their lifetime welfare-benefit bans.

What the government did to Kimberly Rogers, it did in the name of Ontario's citizens. So her case forces all citizens to think about what kind of society we want. One that truly gives us all opportunities to participate in all aspects of society? Or one that condemns the most vulnerable to die alone? We cannot ignore these questions even if we wish to: An inquest into Kimberly Rogers's death is set to begin Oct. 7.

Source: JoAnne Frenschkowski. (August 9, 2002). "We've Learned Little from Kimberly Rogers's Death," *The Globe and Mail*. Reprinted by permission of the author.

Locating women's involvement in crime in its broader social context also involves attending to racial inequality. Aboriginal people in Canada are disproportionately represented in crime statistics, but the over-representation of Aboriginal women in Canadian prisons is even greater than that of Aboriginal men (Finn et al., 1999; Correctional Service of Canada, 2006). Aboriginal women are incarcerated for more violent crimes than non-Aboriginal women. And alcohol has played a role in the offences of twice as many Aboriginal women in prison than Aboriginal men (La Prairie, 1993; Comack, 1996). The historical forces that have shaped Aboriginal communities—the processes of colonization, of economic and political marginalization, and of forced dependency on the state—have culminated in a situation where violence and drugging and drinking have reached epidemic proportions in many Aboriginal centres (Hamilton and Sinclair, 1991; Royal Commission on Aboriginal Peoples, 1996). As Patricia Monture Angus (1999, 27) has noted, "Aboriginal people do not belong to communities that are functional and healthy (and colonialism is significantly responsible for this fact)."

Attention to gender inequality—and its interconnections with race and class—assists in explaining prostitution or sex trade work (Brock, 1998; Bruckert and Parent, 2006). According to Johnson and Rodgers, women's involvement in prostitution is a reflection of their subordinate social and economic position in society: "Prostitution thrives in a society which values women more for their sexuality than for their skilled labour, and which puts women in a class of commodity to be bought and sold. Research has shown one of the major causes of prostitution to be the economic plight of women, particularly young, poorly educated women who have limited *legitimate* employment records" (Johnson and Rodgers, 1993, 101, emphasis in original).

The structured inequalities in society that contour and constrain the lives of criminalized women provide an important backdrop for understanding their involvement in crime. As Carlen (1988, 14) notes, women set about making their lives within conditions that have certainly not been of their own choosing. Indeed, in their efforts to transgress criminology, feminist criminologists have become increasingly aware that to understand women's lives we must bring into view women's experiences of violence at the hands of men. This violence needs to be understood as a manifestation of **patriarchy** or the systemic and individual power that men exercise over women (Brownmiller, 1975; Kelly, 1988).

patriarchy
A system of male domination that includes both a structure and an ideology that privileges men over women. For example, men exercise control over women both overtly by objectifying women's bodies in pornography and covertly in the form of a "monogamous heterosexuality" that legitimates male control over women and children and reinforces the ideology that women are dependent on men for both their economic and sexual needs.

Violence Against Women

At the same time that feminist criminologists were criticizing criminology for its neglect of women, feminists in the women's movement were raising the issue of male violence against women. This is an issue that historically has not been a matter of societal, legal, or academic concern.

The Cultural Construction of Rape

With regard to the lack of societal concern about male violence against women, feminists questioned the kinds of assumptions and beliefs that have dominated the public's understanding of sexual violence. The **cultural construction** of rape, for example, was riddled with certain myths or misconceptions about the nature of the act itself, and with stereotypical images of "true" rape victims and offenders. These myths and stereotypes—and their limitations—include the following:

cultural construction
A perspective on a subject that is shaped by cultural assumptions rather than having a natural or objective basis. For example, concepts of "masculine" and "feminine" suggest how men and women should behave, but very few of these gender differences are determined by biological sex.

- *Women "ask for it" by their dress or their behaviour.* The absurdity of this claim is revealed when we apply the same logic to victims of robbery (see Box 6.3).
- *Rape is a sexual act brought on by a man's uncontrollable sexual urges that cannot be halted once a woman has "turned him on."* Such a view not only depicts male sexuality in a distorted way, it ignores the element of physical coercion and the effects of fear and threats on the woman.
- *When women say no they really mean yes.* This belief suggests that women are expected to be coy and flirtatious, and men are encouraged *not* to take no for an answer. In these terms, it legitimates the act of rape.

FOCUS

BOX 6.3 Was He Asking for It?

In 1975, Harper's Weekly *carried the following response to an American Bar Association finding that few rapists are punished for their crime. The article asks us to imagine a male complainant in a robbery case undergoing the same sort of cross-examination that a female complainant in a rape case does.*

"Mr. Smith, you were held up at gunpoint on the corner of First and Main?"

"Yes."

"Did you struggle with the robber?"

"No."

"Why not?"

"He was armed."

"Then you made a conscious decision to comply with his demands rather than resist?"

"Yes."

"Did you scream? Cry out?"

"No. I was afraid."

"I see. Have you ever been held up before?"

"No."

"Have you ever given money away?"

"Yes, of course."

"And you did so willingly?"

"What are you getting at?"

"Well, let's put it like this, Mr. Smith. You've given money away in the past. In fact, you have quite the reputation for philanthropy. How can we be sure you weren't contriving to have your money taken by force?"

"Listen, if I wanted—"

"Never mind. What time did this holdup take place?"

"About 11 p.m."

"You were out in the street at 11 p.m.? Doing what?"

"Just walking."

"Just walking? You know it's dangerous being out on the street that late at night. Weren't you aware that you could have been held up?"

"I hadn't thought about it."

"What were you wearing?"

"Let's see—a suit. Yes, a suit."

"An expensive suit?"

"Well—yes. I'm a successful lawyer, you know."

"In other words, Mr. Smith, you were walking around the streets late at night in a suit that practically advertised the fact that you might be a good target for some easy money, isn't that so? I mean, if we didn't know better, Mr. Smith, we might even think that you were asking for this to happen, mightn't we?"

Source: *Harper's Weekly*. (1975).

- *If a woman has had sexual relations in the past, she will be less credible when she says she didn't consent to sex.* This myth suggests that "bad girls" or "loose women" deserve to be raped.
- *Women cannot be trusted.* For instance, they will make false accusations against innocent men. Casting all women as inherently untrustworthy acts to silence survivors and exonerate rapists.
- *The act of rape really has little long-term impact on the woman.* So long as the harm of rape is denied, society can continue to ignore the issue and its effects on women's lives.
- *Men who commit "real" rape are an "abnormal" group in society.* Attributing rape to the actions of a small, disturbed minority in society effectively lets men as a group off the hook. Rape is thus cast as an isolated problem

for psychologists and psychiatrists to deal with or is narrowly defined as a "women's issue"—not an issue that *all* of us need to confront.

Carol Smart (1989, 28) has described this cultural construction of rape as "phallocentric," by which she means "the prevailing dominance of the masculine experience of, and meaning of, sexuality. Sexuality is comprehended as the pleasure of the Phallus, and by extension the pleasures of penetration and intercourse—for men." Clearly, the more prevalent such phallocentric myths and stereotypes about sexual violence are in society, the more far-reaching will be their consequences. For perpetrators of sexual violence, they can translate into less chance of detection, higher acquittal rates, and lighter sentences. Studies show, for example, that most rapists do not even believe that they have done anything wrong (Clark and Lewis, 1977; Scully and Marolla, 1985; Messerschmidt, 1986). For survivors of sexual violence, rape myths can mean a "double victimization." Survivors not only endure the humiliation and degradation inherent in the act itself, but may experience further humiliation if they choose to report the case to the authorities. Also, since phallocentric cultural beliefs suggest that rape is the woman's fault, survivors may feel responsible for their own victimization. As Smart (1989, 35) has argued, "The whole rape trial is a process of disqualification (of women) and celebration (of phallocentrism)." For women generally, the cultural construction of rape can produce feelings of fear and vulnerability that impose restrictions on their daily activities. One study, for example, reported that 24 percent of women (compared with only 3 percent of men) stay at home at night because they are afraid to go out alone (Johnson, 1996). Another study (Statistics Canada, 2005) found that 27 percent of women worried for their personal safety when they were home alone at night, compared with only 12 percent of men. And twice the proportion of female as compared to male night-time transit users worried when taking it alone at night (58 percent versus 29 percent).

The Law's Role in Condoning Male Violence Against Women

Recognition of the pervasiveness of these phallocentric myths and stereotypes led to a questioning of the role that law has played in condoning male violence against women. Feminists noted, for example, that women have historically been viewed as the "property" of men. The law upheld this view by granting husbands certain legal rights, in particular, the "right to consortium" and the "right to chastise" their wives.

Consortium generally refers to the companionship, affection, and assistance that one spouse in a marriage is entitled to receive from the other. According only husbands the right to consortium meant that wives had a legal obligation with respect to the "consummation of marriage, cohabitation, maintenance of conjugal rights, sexual fidelity, and general obedience and respect for his wishes" (Dobash and Dobash, 1979, 60). The husband's right to consortium was reflected in Canadian law until 1983. Under the old rape law, a rape was defined to have occurred when "[a] male person has sexual intercourse with a female person *who is not his wife*, (a) without her consent, or (b) with her consent if the consent (i) is extorted by threats or fear of bodily harm, (ii) is obtained by impersonating her husband, or (iii) is obtained by false and fraudulent representations as to the nature and quality of the act" (s. 143, emphasis added). It made no sense, under law's logic, to prevent men from "consorting" with their own property; wives did not have the legal right to say no.

In addition to granting a husband's immunity from rape charges, the rape law also reinforced the cultural construction of rape. For instance, reflecting the belief that "women cannot be trusted" when they claim they have been raped, the legislation included a corroboration requirement, whereby the accused could not be found guilty in the absence of corroborating evidence (such as cuts and bruises) that would support the testimony of the complainant. As well, under the doctrine of recent complaint, it was assumed that a woman who complained at the first reasonable opportunity was more credible or believable than one who complained some time after the rape had taken place. Because the key element in establishing the guilt of the accused in rape cases was consent, the focus of the trial rested on the credibility of the woman. Her moral character came under the scrutiny of the court in the attempt to determine whether she could be believed when she said she did not consent. Defence lawyers were permitted to ask questions about the past sexual history of the complainant, reinforcing the belief that women who have had sexual relations in the past are "less credible" when they say they didn't consent to sex.

With regard to the right to chastise, law historically has given a husband the authority to use force in order to ensure that his wife fulfilled her obligations. The only restraint law placed upon a husband was that he did so in a moderate manner. As English jurist Sir William Blackstone explained in 1765, since the husband was obliged under law to answer for his wife's misbehaviour (as she was his property), "the law thought it reasonable to intrust him with his power of restraining her, by domestic chastisement, in the same moderation that a man is allowed to correct his apprentices and children, for whom the master or parent is also liable in some cases to answer" (Blackstone cited in Dobash and Dobash, 1979, 61). When husbands went too far, and their wives died as a result, the British courts were inclined to leniency. On the other hand, if a wife killed her husband, it was considered a "species of treason" akin to killing the king, as she was going against his authority (Edwards, 1985). Law, in essence, reflected and reinforced patriarchal relations between men and women. This view continued to inform legal practice into the latter part of the 20th century. Because police officers were inclined to view violence in the home between intimate partners as a "private trouble" that was not the law's business, they were reluctant to intervene or to define the situation as a criminal matter.

Criminology's Complicity

Within criminology, male violence against women was similarly not seen as a social problem. Official statistics suggested that crimes like rape were relatively infrequent in their occurrence. Victim surveys—which asked respondents whether they had been victimized by crime—indicated that the group most at risk of victimization was young males, and not women. When criminologists' attention did turn to crimes like rape, the focus was on the small group of men who had been convicted and incarcerated for the offence, and these men were typically understood as an abnormal and pathological group. Much of traditional criminology, then, tended to mirror the cultural construction of rape. In his "classic" study of rape, for example, Menachem Amir (1971) introduced the notion of "victim precipitation." The concept suggests that some women are "rape prone" or invite rape, and Amir's work essentially blamed the woman for the violence she encountered.

Breaking the Silence

In combination, the absence of societal, legal, and academic concern about the issue of male violence against women had the effect of silencing women. One of the main goals of the women's movement, as it gained momentum in the 1970s, was to break this silence. As women came together to share their stories, and with increasing efforts devoted to providing support and services to women (such as rape crisis centres, crisis lines, and shelters for abused women), it soon became evident that the incidence of sexual violence far exceeded what was reported in the official crime statistics. In 1980, for example, the Canadian Advisory Council on the Status of Women (CACSW) estimated that one in every five Canadian women will be sexually assaulted at some point in her life, and one in every seventeen will be subjected to forced sexual intercourse. Yet only one in ten sexual assaults was ever reported to the police (Kinnon, 1981). That same year, the CACSW released its report, *Wife Battering in Canada: The Vicious Circle*. Linda MacLeod (1980), the author of the report, estimated that every year, one in ten Canadian women who is married or in a relationship with a live-in partner is battered. Yet when this finding was reported in the House of Commons (on May 12, 1982), it was met with laughter from members of Parliament. Public outrage ensued and, over the next decade, wife abuse was gradually transformed from a "private trouble" into a "public issue."

WWW
Canadian Association of Sexual Assault Centres
www.casac.ca

The growing awareness of male violence against women led to pressures for legislative reform. Two major changes occurred in 1983. First, the old rape law was repealed and three new categories were added to the offence of assault: sexual assault (s. 246.1); sexual assault with a weapon, threats to a third party, and bodily harm (s. 246.2); and aggravated sexual assault (s. 246.3). Under this new legislation, husbands could now be charged with sexually assaulting their wives, limitations were placed on the ability of the defence to ask questions about the past sexual history of the complainant, the corroboration requirement was dropped, the doctrine of recent complaint was formally removed, and there was provision for a publication ban on any disclosure of the identity of the complainant. These changes were designed to redress the apparent gender inequities in the law and to reduce the trauma experienced by the complainant during the trial in an attempt to encourage the reporting of cases. Second, a national directive was issued to encourage police to lay charges in wife assault cases (previously, the decision was left to the wishes of the complainant) and police training was upgraded to stress sensitive interventions in cases of wife assault. These reforms led to increases in the number of charges for domestic assaults. In Winnipeg, for instance, there were 629 domestic assault charges laid in 1983; by 1989, the number had increased to 1137 charges laid (Ursel, 1994).

The Montreal Massacre

The reality of violence against women was made most evident on December 6, 1989, when a gunman entered a classroom at the École Polytechnique in Montreal, separated the men from the women students, proclaimed, "You're all a bunch of feminists," and proceeded to gun them down. Fourteen women were killed that day and thirteen others wounded. The gunman's suicide letter explicitly identified his action as politically motivated: he blamed "feminists" for the major disappointments in his life. Police also found a "hit list" containing the names of prominent women (see Box 6.4). The Montreal Massacre served to reinforce what women's groups across the country had been arguing for decades: that violence against women is a widespread and pervasive feature of our

FOCUS

BOX 6.4 A Time for Grief and Pain

Montreal

Fourteen women are dead for one reason: they are women. Their male classmates are still alive for one reason: they are men. While gender divides us in thousands of ways every day, rarely are the consequences of misogyny so tragic.

I found out about the murders early yesterday morning. I came home from dinner with friends about 1 a.m., and listened as usual to my answering machine. It was the last message that gave me a jolt. It was a good friend telling me that there would be a vigil last night for the 14 women who had been killed at the University of Montreal.

Not believing my ears and desperate for news, I turned on the radio. I ended up listening to an open-line show. The talk was about relationships between young men and women these days.

Most of the callers were men. They blamed the murders on everything from drugs and condom distributors in high schools to women who have made men feel insecure. Many callers said they did not understand what had happened. It's all very well and fine to be misogynous, said one caller, but you can't lose your head.

I realized, as I was listening to this show, that I was trembling. So were the voices of the female callers. I felt something I had not experienced in a long time: fear of being alone in my apartment. There were sounds at the window I would normally ignore. Now I could not. Immobilized, I was afraid to stay alone and afraid to go out.

It does not matter that the man who decided to kill 14 women—and he clearly did decide to do that—killed himself afterward; it is not of him I am afraid. I am afraid of what he represents, of all the unspoken hatred, the pent-up anger that he expressed. Hatred and anger that is shared by every husband who beats his wife, every man who rapes his date, every father who abuses his child, and by many more who would not dare.

It happened at the École Polytechnique in Montreal but it could have been anywhere.

It would be a great mistake, I think, to see this incident as some kind of freak accident, the act of a madman that has nothing to do with the society in which we live. The killer was angry at women, at feminism, at his own loss of power. He yelled: "You're all a bunch of feminists" on his way to killing 14 women.

Now there is little that is comforting to say to women. It is a time for grief for all of us; grief for those who have died, and pain at being reminded of how deep misogyny still runs in our society.

Source: Diana Bronson. "A Time for Grief and Pain." *The Globe and Mail* (8 December 1989), A7. Reprinted with permission of the author.

society. It takes many forms, including sexual harassment in the workplace, date rape, violent sexual assaults, incest, and wife abuse.

While the murder of 14 women in Montreal has understandably received the attention it deserves, it is also noteworthy that the violence that women encounter at the hands of men has become "routine." In 1993, Statistics Canada released the findings of the Violence Against Women Survey (VAWS). The first national survey of its kind anywhere in the world, the VAWS included responses from 12 300 women (see Johnson, 1996). Using definitions of physical and sexual assault consistent with the Canadian Criminal Code, the survey found that one-half (51 percent) of Canadian women have experienced at least one incident of physical or sexual violence since the age of 16. The survey also confirmed the results of other research in finding that women face the greatest risk of violence from men they know. "Almost one-half (45%) of all women experienced violence by men known to them (dates, boyfriends, marital partners, friends, family, neighbours, etc.), while 23% of women experienced violence by a stranger (17% reported violence by both strangers and known men)" (Statistics Canada, 1993, 2). The VAWS also found that 29 percent (or 3 in 10) of ever-married women had been assaulted by a spouse. Findings such as these confirm that male violence against women continues to be a serious social problem in Canadian society. They also raise concerns about the effectiveness of the criminal justice system in responding to this pressing problem.

Recent Developments in Law's Response to Violence Against Women

As the 1990s unfolded, many feminists became uncertain as to whether engaging with the criminal justice system to combat male violence against women was having the desired outcome. With respect to sexual assault, it appeared that the phallocentric myths and stereotypes surrounding rape were continuing to invade the practice of law. Some judges, for instance, were making statements in court that suggested their decisions were being influenced by these myths. In a British Columbia case heard in 1991, the judge made the following statement in his written decision: "The mating practice, if I may call it that, is less than a precise relationship. At times no may mean maybe, or wait awhile" (*Letendre* cited in Boyle, 1994, 141). In June of 1998, an Alberta Court of Appeal judge upheld a lower court's acquittal of a man charged with sexually assaulting a 17-year-old girl. In his decision, the judge commented on the clothing worn by the young woman (a T-shirt and shorts), noting, "It must be pointed out that the complainant did not present herself to [the accused] in a bonnet and crinolines" (Laghi, 1998). Several decisions by the Supreme Court of Canada also raised concerns over the law's treatment of sexual assault cases.

In a 1991 ruling on the cases of *Seaboyer* and *Gayme*, the Supreme Court struck down section 276 of the Criminal Code. Known as the "rape shield" provision, section 276 was included in the 1983 sexual assault law with the aim of preventing a woman's sexual conduct from being used to discredit her testimony. The Supreme Court ruled that, while laudable in its intent, the provision went too far and could deny the accused the right to a fair trial. Critics took exception to this decision, as it left the question of whether evidence of the complainant's past sexual history would be admissible in court to the discretion of the trial judge. In response, Parliament introduced Bill C-49 in 1992, which was designed to amend the 1983 sexual assault legislation.

Under this new legislation, rules of evidence now state that evidence that the complainant has engaged in sexual activity, whether with the accused or with any other person, is not admissible to support an inference that the complainant is either more likely to have consented to the sexual activity in question or is less worthy of belief. A new test for judges is also provided for determining whether a complainant's sexual history may be admitted at trial. Bill C-49 also provided a definition of "consent" as it applies to sexual assault cases—"the voluntary agreement of the complainant to engage in the sexual activity in question" [s. 243.1 (1)]—and specified the conditions under which "no consent" is obtained (for instance, where the complainant is incapable of consenting to the activity by reason of intoxication or where the complainant expresses, by words or conduct, a lack of agreement to engage in the activity). As well, restrictions were placed on the defences available to men accused of sexual assault; the onus was now on the accused to show that he took "reasonable steps" in the circumstances to ascertain that the woman was consenting [s. 273.2 (b)].

The Supreme Court's ruling in the *O'Connor* case in 1995 had even more profound implications for survivors of sexual assault. Bishop O'Connor was a priest and principal at a residential school near Williams Lake, British Columbia, where four Aboriginal women attended and worked. In 1991, the women laid charges of rape and indecent assault against O'Connor for incidents that occurred at the school between 1961 and 1967. The charges were stayed by the trial judge in 1992 when the Crown failed to release to the defence counsel the women's residential school records and all therapy and medical records since the time they had left the school (none of these records were in the Crown's possession). When the case reached the Supreme Court, the Court overturned the stay and ordered a new trial for O'Connor, but gave exceptionally large scope to defence access to complainants' records held by third parties. Subsequent to the Court's decision, women's shelters and rape crisis centres were being subpoenaed to turn over all files and counselling records relating to cases before the courts, and criminal defence lawyers were being advised by their association that they would be "negligent" if they did not subpoena complainant's files (Busby, 1997).

The Supreme Court's ruling in *O'Connor* meant that confidential records as well as personal diaries, letters, and the like could now all be accessed. The ruling also had special implications for the work of therapists and rape crisis counsellors, as they could now be required to hand over any and all records or notes relating to a complainant in a sexual assault case. Critics noted that such materials are not designed to be a written record of allegations; they are maintained for therapeutic, not evidentiary, purposes. For example, one of the issues regularly dealt with in therapy sessions is the need to explore feelings of guilt or shame that a woman may experience after a rape. In the hands of the court, this could be taken as evidence of "consent" or "complicity" on the part of the woman. To this extent, the *O'Connor* decision supports the old rape myths: that women lie or make false allegations, and that they cannot be trusted. One of the main effects of the ruling was the silencing of women. Women who were sexually assaulted had to decide whether they would seek counselling or initiate criminal prosecution of their assailant (Busby, 1997, 2006).

In response to concerns raised over the *O'Connor* decision, Parliament passed Bill C-46 in May of 1997 to limit the access of defendants to confidential records of complainants in sexual assault cases. The bill established more restrictive grounds for access, required that the defence establish that the records are relevant to the case at hand, and restricted the disclosure only to those parts that are important to the case.

This recent history of the law's treatment of sexual assault highlights a number of tensions. For one, there appears to be tension between the courts—whose decisions become binding as case law—and Parliament—which, in passing statute law, has endeavoured to be sensitive to the concerns raised from women's constituencies across the country. For another, there is a tension within the law with regard to competing rights, in particular, the right of a defendant to a fair trial compared with the right of a complainant to privacy. Clearly, the extent to which the legal system will be able to resolve these tensions and thereby offer both women and men equal protection and treatment under the law is a matter of ongoing debate.

Although the national directive to police forces in 1983 resulted in increasing numbers of domestic assault charges entering the criminal justice system, several provinces took further steps to respond to the problem of wife assault. In the city of Winnipeg, for example, a specialized Family Violence Court was established in 1990. The number of spousal assault cases dealt with by this court rose from 1302 in 1990–91 to 3543 in 1993–94, a 172 percent increase (Ursel, 1998). A large part of this increase can be attributed to the implementation of a zero-tolerance policy on domestic violence by the Winnipeg Police Service in 1993. Under this policy, police are instructed to lay a charge when there are reasonable grounds to believe that a domestic assault has occurred, whether or not the victim wishes to proceed with the matter and even in circumstances where there are no visible injuries or independent witnesses. The zero-tolerance policy resulted in increasing numbers of men—and women—being charged. Nevertheless, a large proportion of charges were resulting in a dismissal or stay of proceedings. One Winnipeg study, for instance, found that 80 percent of charges against women and 51 percent of those against men were subsequently stayed by the Crown (Comack et al., 2000). While the underlying intent of this more rigorous charging protocol was to assist victims of domestic violence (who are predominantly women), zero tolerance opened the way for "double-charging" to occur, whereby both partners end up being charged with an offence when police are called to the scene. Elizabeth Comack, Vanessa Chopyk, and Linda Wood (2000) found that double-charging occurred in 55 percent of the cases they studied involving women accused and in 10 percent of those cases involving men. Stays of proceedings were even higher in these cases (88 percent and 70 percent respectively). In sum, while the changes that have occurred within the criminal justice system have a symbolic value—they carry a strong message of society's unwillingness to tolerate wife abuse—feminists have questioned whether the traditionally punitive and adversarial nature of the system is the most effective means for combating the problem (see, for example, Snider, 1991; 1994).

Blurred Boundaries: Women as Victims and Offenders

Breaking the silence around male violence against women has had an impact on how feminist criminologists understand the lives of criminalized women. Violence against women is clearly a gender-related factor; it both reflects and reinforces women's inequality in society in relation to men. As the *War Against Women* report (1991, 9) noted, "The vulnerability of women to violence is integrally linked to the social, economic and political inequalities women experience as part of their daily lives." How, then, does this gender-based violence figure in the lives of criminalized women?

Canadian Association of Elizabeth Fry Societies
www.elizabethfry.ca

Several studies carried out in the 1990s revealed the extent of abuse experienced by criminalized women. Research conducted for the Task Force on Federally Sentenced Women, for instance, found that 68 percent of women serving a federal term of imprisonment in Canada had been physically abused as children or adults, and 53 percent were sexually abused at some point in their lives. Among Aboriginal women, the figures were considerably higher: 90 percent said that they had been physically abused and 61 percent reported sexual abuse (Shaw et al., 1991, vii and 31). Another study of women in a provincial jail found that 78 percent of the women admitted over a six-year period reported histories of physical and sexual abuse (Comack, 1993).

Qualitative research conducted by feminist criminologists explored women's accounts of their law breaking and its connections to abuse. *Women in Trouble* (Comack, 1996), for instance, was built around the stories of 24 women who were incarcerated in a provincial jail (see also, Gilfus, 1992; Adelberg and Currie, 1993; Sommers, 1995; Ritchie, 1996). The women's stories revealed the connections between a woman's law violations and her history of abuse to be complex. Sometimes the connections are direct, as in the case of women who are criminalized for resisting their abusers. Janice, for instance, was serving a sentence for manslaughter. The offence occurred at a party:

> I was at a party, and this guy, older guy, came, came on to me. He tried telling me, "Why don't you go to bed with me. I'm getting some money, you know." And I said, "No." And then he started hitting me. And then he raped me. And then [pause] I lost it. Like, I just, I went, I got very angry and I snapped. And I started hitting him. I threw a coffee table on top of his head and then I stabbed him. (Janice cited in Comack, 1996, 96)

Sometimes the connections become discernable only once a woman's law violations are located in the context of her struggle to cope with the abuse and its effects. Merideth, for example, had a long history of abuse that began with her father sexually assaulting her as a young child, and extended to several violent relationships with the men in her life. She was imprisoned for writing cheques on her bank account when she didn't have the money to cover them. The cheques were used to purchase "new things to keep her mind off the abuse":

> I've never had any kind of conflict with the law. [long pause] When I started dealing with all these different things, then I started having problems. And then I took it out in the form of fraud. (Merideth cited in Comack, 1996, 86)

Sometimes the connections are even more entangled, as in the case of women who end up on the street, where abuse and law violation become enmeshed in their ongoing, everyday struggle to survive. Brenda had this to say about street life:

> Street life is a, it's a power game, you know? Street life? You have to show you're tough. You have to beat up this broad or you have to shank this person, or, you know, you're always carrying guns, you always have blow on you, you always have drugs on you, and you're always working the streets with the pimps and the bikers, you know? That, that alone, you know, it has so much fucking abuse, it has more abuse than what you were brought up with! . . . I find living on the street I went through more abuse than I did at home. (Brenda cited in Comack, 1996, 105–6)

In seeing the connections between a woman's law violations and her history of abuse, the traditional boundaries that divide "offenders" from "victims" become blurred. Nevertheless, this dichotomy of "offender versus victim" came under a different kind of scrutiny as the 20th century drew to a close. Increasingly, media and academic attention became focused on the issue of women's violence.

Gendered Violence

In breaking the silence around male violence against women, feminists tended to cast men as the "offenders" and women as the "victims." This typification has been challenged in recent years. One publication that received considerable media attention was Patricia Pearson's (1997) book, *When She Was Bad: Violent Women and the Myth of Innocence.* Pearson argues not only that "women are violent, too" but also that their violence can be just as "nasty" as men's. Following in the tradition of Otto Pollak, she suggests that women's violence is more masked and underhanded than men's violence: women kill their babies, arrange for their husbands' murders, beat up on their lovers, and commit serial murders in hospitals and boarding houses (Pearson, 1997, 20–21). Yet, argues Pearson (1997, 61), when their crimes are discovered, women are more likely to receive lenient treatment from a chivalrous criminal justice system.

Pearson drew support for her analysis from studies that utilize the Conflict Tactics Scale (CTS) to measure abuse in intimate relationships. Developed by U.S. researcher Murray Straus and his colleagues (Straus et al., 1980), the scale is a quantitative instrument that consists of eighteen items and measures three different ways of handling interpersonal conflict in intimate relationships: reasoning, verbal aggression, and physical violence. The scale categorizes items on a continuum from least to most severe (for example, "discussed an issue calmly" and "cried" to "threw something," "hit with a fist," and "used a knife or a gun"). Respondents in a survey are asked how frequently they perpetrated each act in the course of conflicts or disagreements with their partners within the past year, and how frequently they had been on the receiving end. These self-reports of perpetration and victimization are then used to construct estimates of the rate of violence used by male and female partners. Most researchers who have employed the CTS have found equivalent rates for women and men on both minor and severe types of violence (Straus and Gelles, 1986; Steinmetz, 1981; Brinkerhoff and Lupri, 1988; Kennedy and Dutton, 1989). Such findings have led to the conclusion that there is a sexual symmetry in intimate violence; that is, that women are just as violent as men.

Despite its popularity, the CTS has not been without its critics (see, for example, DeKeseredy and Hinch, 1991; Dobash et al., 1992; Schwartz and DeKeseredy, 1993; and Johnson, 1996). Criminologists have noted that the CTS is an incomplete measure of intimate violence because

- it measures only incidents of violence and thus ignores the social context of the violence (such as whether a woman is acting in self-defence);
- it situates items only in the context of settling quarrels or disputes and thus misses assaults that "come out of the blue" or are motivated by the desire to control another person;
- it relies on self-reports of violence and may thereby underestimate the incidence of violence by males (who, it has been found, are more likely to underreport);
- it fails to make adequate distinctions between the severity of different forms of violence (for example, "tried to hit with something" is defined as "severe" while "slapped" is defined as "minor"); and
- it does not capture the outcome of the violence (for example, the degree of injury incurred by the participants).

Pearson, however, argues that these methodological concerns amount to unwarranted attacks by battered women's supporters who are invested in a gender dichotomy of "men as evil" and "women as good." In her view, violence is gendered only to the extent that women and men differ in the methods they use and the vocabulary of motives that accompany their actions. The problem, according to Pearson (1997, 32, 243), is that under the sway of feminists, we have failed to acknowledge that women, like men, possess a "will to power"; there are "dimensions of power that have nothing to do with formal structures of patriarchy" and to ignore women's violence is to promote a "culture of victimhood" that denies women's agency and responsibility.

The claims made by writers like Pearson, in combination with the difficulties encountered with using the CTS as a measure of violence between intimate partners, have led feminist criminologists to seek alternative strategies for determining whether, in fact, women are "men's equals" in violence. Comack and her colleagues (2002), for instance, drew a random sample of 1002 cases from police incident reports involving men and women charged with violent crime in the city of Winnipeg over a five-year period (1991 to 1995). Women represented only 15 percent of the 23 090 violent crime charges laid against adults during that period. The aim of the study, however, was to determine whether qualitative differences exist between men's and women's violence.

One of the findings of the research was that over half (53 percent) of the cases studied involved violence between intimate partners. The large number of cases involving partner violence is, in large part, a reflection of the impact of the zero-tolerance policy on domestic violence implemented by the Winnipeg Police Service in 1993. In this respect, the policy has opened a window into the violence that occurs between intimate partners. Unlike the CTS, which approaches the issue of intimate violence from the vantage point of "settling disputes" in marital relationships, police incident reports are governed by the requirement to establish evidence (physical or otherwise) that a criminal act has occurred. As such, police officers include fairly detailed accounts in their reports of "who did what to whom." Also, because criminal law distinguishes between violent offences on the basis of their "seriousness" (for example, assault, assault with a weapon, assault causing bodily harm), police incident reports are a good source of information for measuring the degree of injury incurred by participants in a violent event—a variable that has been missing in most CTS research.

Studies that utilize the CTS have concluded that a sexual symmetry exists in intimate violence: men are as likely as women to be victims of abuse, and women are as likely as men to be perpetrators of both minor and serious acts of violence. Comack and her colleagues, however, found a different picture emerged from studying police incident reports. First, the violence tactics used by men and women differed on the basis of their seriousness. Men were more likely to use their physical strength or force against their female partners, while women were more likely to resort to the use of objects or weapons during the course of a violent event. Second, female partners of men accused of violence used violence themselves in only 23 percent of the cases, while male partners of women accused used violence in 65 percent of the cases, which suggests that the violence that occurs between intimate partners is not "mutual combat." Third, almost one-half (48 percent) of the women accused—as opposed to only 7 percent of the men accused—in partner events were injured during the course of the event, which adds weight to the conclusion that violent events between men and women are not symmetrical. Finally, in incidents involving partners, it was the accused woman who called the police in 35 percent of the cases involving a female accused (compared with only 7 percent in those involving a male accused). If calls to the police are interpreted as a form of "help-seeking behaviour" on the part of someone in trouble, this finding would suggest that in more than one-third of the cases involving a woman accused, she was the one who perceived the need for police intervention. Nevertheless, she ended up being charged with a criminal offence. In combination, these four indicators suggest that partner violence is asymmetrical.

Comack, Chopyk, and Wood's findings are supported by data from the General Social Survey (Statistics Canada, 2000), which show that the nature and consequences of spousal violence are more severe for women than for men. For instance, women were more likely to report severe forms of violence (25 percent of women compared with 10 percent of men reported having been beaten on at least one occasion during the five years prior to the survey) and some form

TABLE 6.1 Theories of Women's Crime

Theory	*Theorists*	*Key Elements*
Early theorists	Lombroso/Ferrero, Thomas, Glueck/Glueck, Pollak	Women's "inherent nature" and their natural inferiority to men account for the nature and extent of their criminality.
Sex role socialization	Hoffman-Bustamante	Differential socialization of females is reflected in the types of offences they commit and the nature of their participation in crime.
Power-control theory	Hagan/Simpson/Gillis	Gender differences in delinquency can be explained by variations in parental control. Girls in patriarchal families will be less free to deviate than those in egalitarian families.
Women's liberation thesis	Adler, Simon	Women's changing gender roles are reflected in the nature and extent of their criminal involvement. Women are becoming "more like men"—more aggressive and violent—and have greater opportunities to commit crime.
Feminist theories	Carlen, Chesney-Lind, Comack, Daly, Gilfus, Morris, Naffine	Structured inequalities of class, race, and gender (including experiences of male violence) condition and constrain the lives of criminalized women.

of physical injury (40 percent of women compared with 13 percent of men). While a similar percentage of women and men who were married or living in a common-law relationship during the previous five-year period experienced some type of violence by their partner, the frequency of violence directed at women by their partners was significantly greater than the frequency of violence directed at men by their partners.

While women are certainly capable of violence, these findings suggest that they are not "men's equals." Writers like Pearson are to be credited for pointing to the "culture of victimhood" that is produced when feminists rest their understandings on dualistic constructions such as "victim versus offender." Yet, in her efforts to call attention to women's capacity for violence, Pearson goes to the other extreme. By casting women as scheming, underhanded manipulators who engage in violence "to defend their aspirations, their identity and their place on the stage" (Pearson, 1997, 20), she effectively replaces the "men as evil" image that she so roundly criticizes feminists for with a "woman as evil" imagery.

Violence is "gendered." Its manifestations are tied to social and cultural distinctions attributed to men and women in our society. In these terms, the concept of patriarchy—a system of male domination—allows us to understand some of the pervasive patterns of male violence in society. This does not mean, however, that women are without agency or bereft of power. Indeed, there is no reason to believe that women are not influenced by the cultural messages that permeate our society—especially when those messages herald violence as a means of "getting your way." So long as violence is held up as a resource to be used when someone is confronted with problems and conflicts in life, we should not be surprised when women act out violently.

Summary

- One of the primary aims of the feminist engagement with criminology has been to bring women into view. This has involved a re-evaluation of the accumulated knowledge about criminalized women, the nature of their offending, and the claims made about their "differences" from males. In the process, mainstream criminologists have been forced to consider how their traditional subject matter—men and male criminality—has influenced their theories and research.
- Feminist criminologists have argued that understanding women's involvement in crime requires an awareness of the larger social context, specifically, the structured inequalities of class, race, and gender that condition and constrain the lives of criminalized women.
- Breaking the silence around male violence against women has meant questioning the ways in which societal and legal responses reinforce and reproduce the problem.
- Making women more visible in criminology requires not simply letting women into the mainstream of the discipline but developing alternative ways of conceptualizing and studying the social world so that the interests and concerns of *both* men and women are included. In the process, the criminological enterprise is itself transformed.

QUESTIONS FOR CRITICAL THINKING

1. How does the way in which the "difference" between men and women is understood influence our understanding of women's involvement in crime?
2. To what extent is the "cultural construction of rape" evident in films, music videos, advertising, and other aspects of Canadian culture? To what extent does it influence your own thinking about sexual violence?
3. In what ways have rape myths and stereotypes been evident in law and legal practice?
4. Is the criminal justice system the most effective strategy for responding to the problem of domestic violence?
5. How would making gender a central focus of criminological inquiry affect the ways in which criminologists study men's involvement in crime?

NET WORK

Are you interested in finding more information about the issues of domestic violence and sexual assault? To find a variety of sites that deal with these issues, first visit the Womennet.ca (The Canadian Women's Virtual Information Centre) home page at **www.womennet.ca**. Here you will find various links to domestic violence sites and sites dealing with sexual assault.

Using these links or any of the links found throughout this chapter, answer the following questions:

1. Describe some of the programs that are offered in Canada to serve survivors of domestic violence and sexual assault.
2. Identify some of the controversies concerning domestic violence. Can you find sites on the Internet that present different perspectives on this problem? How can you assess the validity of the information presented on different websites?

KEY TERMS

conservative approach; pg. 184
cultural construction; pg. 195
feminist approach; pg. 192
gender-ratio problem; pg. 190
generalizability problem; pg. 190
liberal approach; pg. 187
patriarchy; pg. 195
sexism; pg. 184

SUGGESTED READING

Alarid, Leanne, and Paul Cromwell. (2006). *In Her Own Words: Women Offenders' Views on Crime and Victimization.* Los Angeles, Calif.: Roxbury Publishing Company. A collection of articles that utilize in-depth and life history interviews to explore the lives of women lawbreakers, including their family origins, relations with men, roles in subcultures, victimization, and economic marginalization,

Balfour, Gillian, and Elizabeth Comack (eds.). (2006). *Criminalizing Women: Gender and (In)justice in Neo-liberal Times.* Halifax: Fernwood Publishing. In this book feminist academics and activists explore issues relating to the conditions of criminalized women's lives, the forms of regulation used to discipline and punish them, and the various feminist strategies that have been adopted to address the conditions in women's prisons and the systemic abuses against poor and racialized women.

Daly, Kathleen, and Lisa Maher (eds.). (1998). *Criminology at the Crossroads: Feminist Readings in Crime and Justice.* New York: Open University Press. A compilation of 14 articles that raise some of the key issues and unresolved problems for feminist work in criminology.

McKenna, Kate, and June Larkin (eds.). (2002). *Violence Against Women: New Canadian Perspectives.* Toronto: Ianna Publications. This collection presents some of the most recent Canadian research and policy initiatives on violence against women.

Smart, Carol. (1989). *Feminism and the Power of Law.* London: Routledge. In her classic work, Smart approaches law as a discourse and a claim to power capable of disqualifying alternative worldviews such as feminism. Smart challenges us to think about law and the prospects of law reform in an entirely new way.

BIBLIOGRAPHY

Adelberg, Ellen, and Claudia Currie. (1993). "In Their Own Words: Seven Women's Stories." In E. Adelberg and C. Currie (eds.), *In Conflict with the Law: Women and the Canadian Justice System.* Vancouver: Press Gang.

Adler, Freda. (1975). *Sisters in Crime.* New York: McGraw-Hill.

Amir, Menachem. (1971). *The Patterns of Forcible Rape.* Chicago: University of Chicago Press.

Bertrand, Marie-Andrée. (1967). "The Myth of Sexual Equality Before the Law." Fifth Research Conference on Delinquency and Criminality. Montreal, Centre de Psychologies et de Pédagogie (pp. 129–61).

Boyle, Christine. (1994). "The Judicial Construction of Sexual Assault Offences." In J. Roberts and R. Mohr (eds.), *Confronting Sexual Assault: A Decade of Social and Legal Change.* Toronto: University of Toronto Press.

Brinkerhoff, Merlin, and Eugen Lupri. (1988). "Interspousal Violence." *Canadian Journal of Sociology* 13(4):407–34.

Brock, Deborah. (1998). *Making Work, Making Trouble: Prostitution as a Social Problem.* Toronto: University of Toronto Press.

Brownmiller, Susan. (1975). *Against Our Will: Men, Women and Rape.* New York: Bantam Books.

Bruckert, Chris, and Colette Parent. (2006). "The In-Call Sex Industry: Reflections on Classed and Gendered Labour on the Margins." In G. Balfour and E. Comack (eds.), *Criminalizing Women: Gender and (In)justice in Neo-liberal Times.* Halifax: Fernwood Publishing.

Busby, Karen. (1997). "Discriminatory Uses of Personal Records in Sexual Violence Cases." *Canadian Journal of Women and the Law* 9(1):149–77.

———. (2006). " 'Not a Victim Until a Conviction Is Entered': Sexual Violence Prosecutions and Legal Truth." In E. Comack (ed.), *Locating Law: Race/Class/Gender/Sexuality Connections* (2nd ed.) Halifax: Fernwood Publishing.

Cain, Maureen. (1990). "Towards Transgression: New Directions in Feminist Criminology." *International Journal of the Sociology of Law* 18:1–18.

Carlen, Pat (ed.). (1985). *Criminal Women.* Cambridge: Polity Press.

———. (1988). *Women, Crime and Poverty.* Milton Keynes: Open University Press.

Chunn, Dorothy E., and Shelley A. M. Gavigan. (2006). "From Welfare Fraud To Welfare As Fraud: The Criminalization of Poverty." In G. Balfour and E. Comack (eds.), *Criminalizing Women: Gender and (In)justice in Neo-liberal Times.* Halifax: Fernwood Publishing.

Clark, Lorenne, and Debra Lewis. (1977). *Rape: The Price of Coercive Sexuality.* Toronto: Women's Press.

Cohen, Albert. (1955). *Delinquent Boys.* Glencoe, Ill.: The Free Press.

Comack, Elizabeth. (1993). "Women Offenders' Experiences with Physical and Sexual Abuse: A Preliminary Report." Criminology Research Centre, University of Manitoba.

———. (1996). *Women in Trouble: Connecting Women's Law Violations to Their Histories of Abuse.* Halifax: Fernwood Publishing.

Comack, Elizabeth, Vanessa Chopyk, and Linda Wood. (2000). "Mean Streets? The Social Locations, Gender Dynamics and Patterns of Violent Crime in Winnipeg." Winnipeg: Canadian Centre for Policy Alternatives (Manitoba) (*www.policyalternatives.ca*).

———. (2002). "Aren't Women Violent Too? The Gendered Nature of Violence." In B. Schissel and C. Brooks (eds.), *Marginality and Condemnation: An Introduction to Critical Criminology.* Halifax: Fernwood Publishing.

Correctional Service of Canada. (2006). *Ten-Year Status Report on Women's Corrections, 1996–2006.* Ottawa: Correctional Service of Canada.

Cowie, John, Valerie Cowie, and Eliot Slater. (1968). *Delinquency in Girls.* London: Heinemann.

Daly, Kathleen. (1987). "Discrimination in the Criminal Courts: Family, Gender, and the Problem of Equal Treatment." *Social Forces* 66(1):152–75.

———. (1989). "Rethinking Judicial Paternalism: Gender, Work-Family Relations, and Sentencing." *Gender and Society* 3(1):9–36.

Daly, Kathleen, and Meda Chesney-Lind. (1988). "Feminism and Criminology." *Justice Quarterly* 5(4):101–43.

DeKeseredy, Walter, and Ronald Hinch. (1991). *Woman Abuse: Sociological Perspectives.* Toronto: Thompson.

Dobash, R. Emerson, and Russell Dobash. (1979). *Violence Against Wives: A Case against Patriarchy.* New York: Free Press.

Dobash, Russell, R. Emerson Dobash, Margo Wilson, and Martin Daly. (1992). "The Myth of Sexual Symmetry in Marital Violence." *Social Problems* 39(1)(February):71–91.

Edwards, Susan. (1985). "Gender Justice? Defending Defendants and Mitigating Sentence." In S. Edwards (ed.), *Gender, Sex and the Law.* Kent: Croom Helm: (pp. 129–54).

Faith, Karlene. (1993). *Unruly Women: The Politics of Confinement and Resistance.* Vancouver: Press Gang Publishers.

Finn, Anne, Shelley Trevethan, Gisele Carriere, and Melanie Kowalski. (1999). "Female Inmates, Aboriginal Inmates, and Inmates Serving Life Sentences: A One Day Snapshot." *Juristat* 19: 5.

Frenschkowski, JoAnne. (2002). "We've Learned Little from Kimberly Rogers's Death." *Globe and Mail* (August 9:A13).

Gelsthorpe, Lorraine, and Allison Morris. (1988). "Feminism and Criminology in Britain." *British Journal of Criminology* 23:93–110.

Gilfus, Mary. (1992). "From Victims to Survivors to Offenders: Women's Routes of Entry and Immersion into Street Crime." *Women and Criminal Justice* 4(1): 63–89.

Glueck, Eleanor, and Sheldon Glueck. (1934). *Five Hundred Delinquent Women.* New York: Alfred A. Knopf.

Hagan, J., A. R. Gillis, and J. Simpson. (1985). "The Class Structure of Gender and Delinquency: Toward a Power-Control Theory of Common Delinquent Behavior." *American Journal of Sociology* 90:1151–78.

Hagan, J., J. Simpson, and A. R. Gillis. (1979). "The Sexual Stratification of Social Control: A Gender-Based Perspective on Crime and Delinquency." *British Journal of Sociology* 30:25–38.

———. (1987). "Class in the Household: A Power-Control Theory of Gender and Delinquency." *American Journal of Sociology* 92(4)(January):788–816.

Hamilton, A. C., and C. M. Sinclair. (1991). *The Justice System and Aboriginal People: Report of the Aboriginal Justice Inquiry of Manitoba.* Vol. 1. Winnipeg: Queen's Printer.

Heidensohn, Frances. (1968). "The Deviance of Women: A Critique and an Enquiry." *British Journal of Sociology* 19(2):160–75.

———. (1985). *Women and Crime.* London: Macmillan.

Hoffman-Bustamante, Dale. (1973). "The Nature of Female Criminality." *Issues in Criminology* 8:117–36.

Johnson, Holly. (1996). *Dangerous Domains.* Toronto: Nelson.

Johnson, Holly, and Karen Rodgers. (1993). "A Statistical Overview of Women in Crime in Canada." In Ellen Adelberg and Claudia Currie (eds.), *In Conflict with the Law: Women and the Canadian Justice System* (pp. 95–116). Vancouver: Press Gang.

Kelly, Liz. (1988). *Surviving Sexual Violence.* Minneapolis: University of Minnesota Press.

Kendall, Kathleen. (1991). "The Politics of Premenstrual Syndrome: Implications for Feminist Justice." *Journal of Human Justice* 2(2)(Spring):77–98.

———. (1992). "Dangerous Bodies." In D. Farrington and S. Walklate (eds.), *Offenders and Victims: Theory and Policy.* British Society of Criminology: (pp. 45–61).

Kennedy, Leslie, and Donald Dutton. (1989). "The Incidence of Wife Assault in Alberta." *Canadian Journal of Behavioural Science* 21:40–54.

Kinnon, Dianne. (1981). *Report on Sexual Assault in Canada.* Ottawa: CACSW.

Klein, Dorie (1973). "The Etiology of Female Crime: A Review of the Literature." *Issues in Criminology* 8(3).

Konopka, Gisella. (1966). *The Adolescent Girl in Conflict.* Englewood Cliffs, N.J.: Prentice Hall.

Kruttschnitt, Candace. (1980–81). "Social Status and Sentences of Female Offenders." *Law and Society Review* 15(2):247–65.

———. (1982). "Women, Crime and Dependancy." *Criminology* 195:495–513.

Laberge, Danielle. (1991). "Women's Criminality, Criminal Women, Criminalized Women?: Questions in and for a Feminist Perspective." *Journal of Human Justice* 2(2):37–56.

Laghi, Brian. (1998). "Alberta Judge Stirs Outrage in Sex Case." *The Globe and Mail* (February 23): A1, A11.

La Prairie, Carol. (1993). "Aboriginal Women and Crime in Canada: Identifying the Issues." In Ellen Adelberg and Claudia Currie (eds.), *In Conflict with the Law: Women and the Canadian Justice System* (pp. 235–46). Vancouver: Press Gang.

Leonard, Eileen. (1982). *Women, Crime and Society: A Critique of Theoretical Criminology.* New York: Longman.

Lombroso, C., and W. Ferrero. (1895). *The Female Offender.* London: Fischer Unwin.

Luckhaus, Linda. (1985). "A Plea for PMT in the Criminal Law." In S. Edwards (ed.), *Gender, Sex and the Law.* Kent: Croom Helm (pp. 159–81).

MacLeod, Linda. (1980). *Wife Battering in Canada: The Vicious Circle.* Ottawa: CACSW.

Martin, Dianne. (1999). "Punishing Female Offenders and Perpetuating Gender Stereotypes." In Julian V. Roberts and David P. Cole (eds.), *Making Sense of Sentencing.* Toronto: University of Toronto Press.

Messerschmidt, James. (1986). *Capitalism, Patriarchy and Crime: Toward a Socialist Feminist Criminology.* Totowa, N.J.: Rowman and Littlefield.

Monture Angus, Patricia. (1999). "Women and Risk: Aboriginal Women, Colonialism, and Correctional Practice." *Canadian Women's Studies* 19(1)(Spring/Summer):24–29.

Morris, Allison. (1987). *Women, Crime and Criminal Justice.* Oxford: Basil Blackwell.

Mosher, Janet E. 2006. "The Construction of 'Welfare Fraud' and the Wielding of the State's Iron Fist." In E. Comack (ed.), *Locating Law: Race/Class/Gender/Sexuality Connections.* (2nd ed.) (pp. 207–29). Halifax: Fernwood Publishing.

Naffine, Ngaire. (1987). *Female Crime: The Construction of Women in Criminology.* Sydney: Allen and Unwin.

———. (1997). *Feminism and Criminology.* Sydney: Allen and Unwin.

Osborne, Judith. (1989). "Perspectives on Premenstrual Syndrome: Women, Law and Medicine." *Canadian Journal of Family Law* 8:165–84.

Pearson, Patricia. (1997). *When She Was Bad: Violent Women and the Myth of Innocence.* Toronto: Random House.

Pollak, Otto. (1961). *The Criminality of Women.* New York: A. S. Barnes.

Rafter, N. H., and E. M. Natalizia. (1981). "Marxist Feminism: Implications for Criminal Justice." *Crime and Delinquency* 27(January):81–98.

Ritchie, Beth. (1996). *Compelled to Crime: The Gender Entrapment of Battered Black Women*. New York: Routledge.

Royal Commission on Aboriginal Peoples. (1996). *Report of the Royal Commission on Aboriginal Peoples*. Ottawa: Department of Indian and Northern Affairs.

Schwartz, Martin, and Walter DeKeseredy. (1993). "The Return of the 'Battered Husband Syndrome' Through the Typification of Women as Violent." *Crime, Law and Social Change* 20:249–65.

Scully, D., and J. Marolla. (1985). "'Riding the Bull at Gilly's': Convicted Rapists Describe the Rewards of Rape." *Social Problems* 32:251–63.

Scutt, Jocelyn. (1979). "The Myth of the 'Chivalry Factor' in Female Crime." *Australian Journal of Social Issues* 14(1):3–20.

Shaw, Margaret, Karen Rogers, Johannes Blanchette, Tina Hattem, Lee Seto Thomas, and Lada Tamarack. (1991). *Survey of Federally Sentenced Women: Report on the Task Force on Federally Sentenced Women: The Prison Survey*. Ottawa: Ministry of the Solicitor General of Canada. User Report No. 1991-4.

Simon, Rita. (1975). *Women and Crime*. Lexington, Mass.: D. C. Heath.

Smart, Carol. (1976). *Women, Crime and Criminology: A Feminist Critique*. London: Routledge and Kegan Paul.

———. (1977). "Criminological Theory: Its Ideology and Implications Concerning Women." *British Journal of Sociology* 28(1):89–100.

———. (1989). *Feminism and the Power of Law*. London: Routledge.

Snider, Laureen. (1991). "The Potential of the Criminal Justice System to Promote Feminist Concerns." In E. Comack and S. Brickey (eds.), *The Social Bias of Law: Critical Readings in the Sociology of Law* (2nd ed.) (pp. 238–60). Halifax: Fernwood Publishing.

———. (1994). "Feminism, Punishment and the Potential of Empowerment." *Canadian Journal of Law and Society* 9(1):74–104.

Sommers, Evelyn. (1995). *Voices from Within: Women Who Have Broken the Law*. Toronto: University of Toronto Press.

Statistics Canada. (1993). "The Violence Against Women Survey." *The Daily* (18 November).

———. (2000). "Family Violence." *The Daily*. (25 July). www.statcan.ca/Daily/English/000725/d000725b.htm.

Statistics Canada. (2005). "General Social Survey: Victimization." *The Daily* (Thursday, July 7). Available at: http://www.statcan.ca/Daily/English/050707/d050707b/htm (accessed February 2, 2007).

Steffensmeier, Darryl, and J. Kramer. (1982). "Sex-based Differences in the Sentencing of Adult Criminal Defendants." *Sociology and Social Research* 663:289–304.

Steinmetz, Suzanne. (1981). "A Cross-cultural Comparison of Marital Abuse." *Journal of Sociology and Social Welfare* 8:404–14.

Straus, Murray, and Richard Gelles. (1986). "Societal Changes and Change in Family Violence from 1975 to 1985 as Revealed by Two National Surveys." *Journal of Marriage and the Family* 48:465–80.

Straus, Murray, Richard Gelles, and Suzanne Steinmetz. (1980). *Behind Closed Doors: Violence in the American Family*. New York: Doubleday.

Taylor, I., P. Walton, and J. Young. (1973). *The New Criminology*. London: Routledge and Kegan Paul.

Thomas, W. I. (1967). *The Unadjusted Girl*. New York: Harper and Row.

Ursel, Jane. (1994). "The Winnipeg Family Violence Court." *Juristat,* Canadian Centre for Justice Statistics 14:12.

———. (1998). "Eliminating Violence Against Women: Reform or Co-optation in State Institutions." In L. Samuelson and W. Antony (eds.), *Power and Resistance: Critical Thinking About Canadian Social Issues* (2nd ed.). Halifax: Fernwood Publishing.

Wallace, Marnie. (2004). "Crime Statistics in Canada, 2003." *Juristat,* Canadian Centre for Justice Statistics 24:6.

The War Against Women. (1991). Report of the Standing Committee on Health and Welfare. Social Affairs, Seniors and the Status of Women. (June) Ottawa.

Zingraff, M., and R. Thomson. (1984). "Differential Sentencing of Women and Men in the U.S.A." *International Journal of the Sociology of Law* 12:401–13.

PART

II

Explanations of Crime

The field of criminology is multidisciplinary. Lawyers, sociologists, political scientists, psychologists, biologists, physicians, historians, and philosophers all may consider the study of crime as part of their discipline. Nowhere is this diversity more apparent than in the development theories of the causes of crime. Why some people commit crime while others do not has been addressed from each of these perspectives.

Part 2 covers many of the most popular explanations of crime. The debate over which of these explanations is "best" has often become heated, and no attempt is made to resolve this issue here. It would be premature to impose such a judgment on a field that has been described as consisting of "a number of fitful leads from one partially examined thesis to another." * Instead, each theory is presented by an author who has had experience (and some sympathy) with it, and who presents the theory's strengths and weaknesses. A number of researchers are now trying to synthesize several of the different approaches, and some of the authors discuss this integrative work.

Part 2 illustrates how theories of crime causation have developed over time. In Chapter 7, several of the earliest approaches to the explanation of crime are discussed. The most important point made in this chapter is that explanations of crime arise from particular historical milieus and reflect the social and intellectual fashions of the day. Chapter 8 presents theories that focus on the traits of individuals. The psychological perspective has been with us for many years and is still popular today. Chapters 9 to 13 are concerned with the sociological explanations of crime. They illustrate the diverse ways in which social structure and social processes may promote or restrain criminal behaviour.

---

* Paul Rock. (1980). "Has Deviance a Future?" In Hubert M. Blalock (ed.), *Sociological Theory and Research* (pp. 290–303). New York: Free Press.

Early Theories of Criminology

7

Tullio Caputo

CARLETON UNIVERSITY

Rick Linden

UNIVERSITY OF MANITOBA

We begin this chapter by exploring the context within which modern criminology developed. Societal beliefs relating crime to superstition and sin were slowly replaced during the Enlightenment by naturalistic explanations based on the idea that people are free and rational beings. This development was consistent with the struggle for individual rights and freedoms that was gaining prominence during this period and the view that the social order reflected a social contract between the individual and the state. These changes were based on the growing power of the rising merchant classes and the reduced influence of the feudal aristocracy, whose power rested on the ownership of the land and the loyalty of the peasants who lived and worked on it.

Next we discuss the rise of the Classical School of criminology during this era. The principle of "let the punishment fit the crime" represents the core of the philosophy of the Classical School and its belief in people's ability to reason and to act rationally. Although this reform provided the basis for our modern Criminal Code, it was found to be too inflexible in practice. The argument of later Positive criminologists that mitigating circumstances had to be considered when dealing with crime and criminals led to further reforms in the manner in which we dealt with criminals. The chapter concludes with an examination of the early theories that searched for the causes of crime in the biological make-up of individual offenders.

Learning Objectives

After reading this chapter, you should be able to

- Discuss the context within which modern explanations of crime and criminality were developed.
- Identify the founders of the Classical School of criminology, the key principles of this approach, and the impact of this school on our legal system.
- Outline the criticisms of the Classical approach and the changes in the legal process that were influenced by the Positive criminologists.
- Describe the basic features of the Positive School of criminology, and outline their approach and key principles.

- Show how the ideas advanced by the Positive School influenced other researchers to search for the biological causes of crime.
- Discuss how biological explanations of criminality influenced the development of this field at the beginning of the 20th century.

Prior to the 18th century, theories about crime were inspired primarily by religious beliefs and superstition. As Zilborg (1969, 11) notes,

> [F]rom the most primitive beginnings of human history, man [*sic*] believed in the existence of spirits and magic, and . . . from the earliest days of his existence on earth, he began to ascribe various unusual phenomena of nature to the activities of evil spirits. This naturally led him to believe that any pathology in human behavior must be due to an evil spirit.

The link between evil spirits and wrongdoing is an important one for many religions. For example, Judeo-Christian teachings provide two powerful explanations outlining the role of evil spirits in sinful behaviour: temptation and possession. The idea of temptation is based on the belief that people exercise their free will and choose to act in particular ways, even ways they know to be wrong. Indeed, the Devil is thought to be at work tempting people. Of course, righteous believers can resist the Devil's powerful allure by drawing strength from their faith. They are encouraged to do this by religious leaders who employ images of hell-fire and threats of eternal damnation to help steel the spines of the faithful who might otherwise waver. These images and beliefs about temptation imply that people who succumb are weak and morally inferior beings. In this way, the poor, the destitute, and other unfortunate members of society have been held responsible for their situations throughout much of history. Their misfortunes are seen as the result of their own moral failures. These beliefs also provide the basis for our ideas about deterrence. Thus most people believe that the threat of severe punishment should be enough to persuade people to avoid engaging in misdeeds.

The second, and equally powerful, Judeo-Christian imagery linking sin to evil spirits is that of possession. Wrongdoers were often suspected of being possessed by the Devil or some other malevolent spirit. These unfortunate individuals were thought to have little hope of recovering and were treated quite harshly. A host of horrifying tortures were used to drive the evil spirits from their bodies, and evidence of guilt was determined through a series of trials designed to differentiate between the righteous and the sinner. These included trial by battle, trial by ordeal, trial by fire, and trial by water. In most cases, the accused had little to look forward to, whether innocent or guilty, since these trials were extremely severe and often fatal.

These practices reflect a belief in the power of supernatural forces. They reached their zenith during the Middle Ages with the introduction of the notorious Inquisition and the witch craze it spawned. This was a period marked by tremendous social upheaval and rapid social change. Western Europe was in the midst of the transition from feudalism to capitalism. Confusion and fear followed the revolution that was underway in the material and intellectual worlds of the day. Those in power—the political and religious elites—used every means at their disposal to protect their positions and privileges. They sought to preserve the status quo and maintain the existing order. This included using both religious and civil laws. As Angell (1965, 118) notes,

> The development of a common criminal law was aided by the close connection between crime and sin. . . . [P]unishment meant expiation. It is only one step from the fear of gods' displeasure to the desire for reassurance concerning the integrity of the moral order.

Medieval society was forced to change because existing social arrangements did not meet the needs of a growing European population. Poverty, misery, wars, and sickness ravaged the masses. These problems led people to question and even to challenge longstanding practices and beliefs, including those related to civil and religious authority. For example, the Protestant Reformation shook the foundations of the Christian world by challenging the power and authority of the Catholic Church. Throughout Europe, those in power were increasingly being held to account for deteriorating material conditions and social problems. It is in this context that the Inquisition and the witch craze found fertile ground. The religious and political elites began to seek ways of diverting attention from themselves and of silencing the rebellious members of society. Blaming the existing social problems on the influence of the Devil and other evil spirits provided a means of meeting both objectives. First, this diverted the public's attention from the elites and helped to place blame for social problems on individuals who were identified as being possessed or otherwise in league with the Devil. Second, those in power made themselves indispensable by arguing that they alone had the knowledge and ability to deal with the threat of the Devil on earth (Harris, 1974).

Importantly, these developments helped to blur the distinctions between sin and crime and provided ideal conditions for the confluence of civil and religious authority. In medieval England, for example, there existed

> an almost paranoid concern for order in society, and a close association between crime and sin. The Reformation and the increased power of the Puritans changed perceptions of crime and justice both in government and in the popular mind. Religion and morality became matters of state law and potential sources of rebellion; although sin and crime were usually dealt with by different courts (crime by the civil court, sin by the ecclesiastical court), they were in some ways almost indistinguishable. (Best, 1998)

By linking morality to rebellion, the authorities were effectively preventing anyone from challenging the status quo. Those who did were likely to be accused of heresy and as a result, subjected to extremely harsh punishments, including death. This is precisely what happened to those accused of witchcraft and offers a partial explanation of how more than half a million people could be put to death during the 300 years in which the witch craze flourished. Indeed, the plight of those accused of being witches illustrates how charges of heresy were used to silence critics and quash any rebellious inclinations in the population.

Witches had been active in Western Europe for centuries, although they were never prosecuted. This changed as a result of the growing challenge to both religious and civil authorities during the 15th century. Witches provided a convenient scapegoat against whom the masses could vent their anger. Importantly, it was usually the less powerful members of a community who were most susceptible to accusations of witchcraft. Although this group included the elderly, the infirm, and children, the witch craze mainly victimized women. As Pfohl (1985) points out, women made up 85 percent of the people executed for witchcraft throughout history. He suggests that "it is hardly surprising that during times in which the great male mastery over nature seemed least secure, times of economic hardship and political instability, the priestly finger of men often found bewitching women to blame" (39). He goes on to note that this led to horrific ritual punishments, including "baths in boiling water, crushing by heavy weights, tearing the flesh from the breasts with searing-hot pincers, and torture of the female sex organs" (39).

Economically independent women and women who lived alone and outside the protection of men were most susceptible to charges of witchcraft. Their presence in a community disrupted and threatened the male-dominated power structures. Charges of witchcraft and public executions served to reassert the authority of male leaders and remind community members of their subordinate positions in the social hierarchy. At the same time, however, the cruelty and sheer barbarism of the courts and their punishments fuelled the cries for reform across Western Europe.

Early theorizing about crime and the beginnings of our modern system of criminal justice began to emerge during this tumultuous period of European history. "It was an era of racing industrial revolution, enclosure movements, growing capitalism and growing cities" (Sylvester, 1972). These developments were hastened by a rapidly expanding population and by the growth of trade and manufacturing.

The feudal economy was based on agricultural production, with clearly established relations between the aristocracy, who owned the land, and the peasants, who worked it. A system of mutual rights and obligations bound these two classes together, and when this relationship was challenged, the entire system was threatened. Increasingly, feudalism was unable to meet the needs of the growing population. It is estimated that England's population soared from 2.8 million in 1500 to 8.9 million in 1800. Similar increases were reported for the rest of Europe (Pfohl, 1985). This surge in population fuelled a period of colonial expansion as European monarchs sought havens for their surplus population and access to the markets and raw materials that colonies could provide. Europe's merchant classes gained considerable power during this period, as their economic activities offset the mounting economic shortfall (see Chapter 2).

Changes in the economy were mirrored by changes throughout the society. Revolutionary developments had taken place in philosophy, art, music, literature, and other intellectual pursuits. Progressive thinkers of the day fought to usher Europe into a new era—"the age of reason" emerged during the period known as the Enlightenment (see Box 7.1). The Enlightenment thinkers argued against fanaticism and religious superstition, advocating "naturalistic" explanations of the world based on people's ability to reason.

The Enlightenment philosophers believed that people were free and rational beings. This belief led them to call for the establishment of individual rights

FOCUS

BOX 7.1 The European Enlightenment

Of all the changes that swept over Europe in the seventeenth and eighteenth centuries, the most widely influential was an epistemological transformation that we call the "scientific revolution." In the popular mind, we associate this revolution with natural science and technological change, but the scientific revolution was, in reality, a series of changes in the structure of European thought itself: systematic doubt, empirical and sensory verification, the abstraction of human knowledge into separate sciences, and the view that the world functions like a machine. These changes greatly changed the human experience of every other aspect of life, from individual life to the life of the group. This modification in world view can also be charted in painting, sculpture and architecture; you can see that people of the seventeenth and eighteenth centuries are *looking* at the world very differently . . .

It's hard to pinpoint the shift in these attitudes. The introduction of humanism in the fourteenth century was in large part based on the idea that human intellect and creativity were trustworthy, and human experience was, to some extent, a reliable base on which to hang knowledge. But the humanist revolution didn't happen all at once; the dichotomy between "experience" and "authority" was a vexed question throughout the fourteenth and fifteenth centuries. What should you believe? What your experience shows you? Or what authorities, including the church and the bible, tell you to believe?

While it's hard to pinpoint the shift in European attitudes, the first, unambiguous statement of this shift in values comes in Leonardo da Vinci's treatise on painting:

> Here, right here, in the eye, here forms, here colors, right here the character of every part and every thing of the universe, are concentrated to a single point. How marvelous that point is! . . . In this small space, the universe can be completely reproduced and rearranged in its entire vastness! . . .

This new perspective expressed by Leonardo was a profound shift in the European world view. In a fundamental way, it postulated that human experience was and should be the central concern of human beings. It also postulated that human sensory experience, especially vision, was not only a valid way of understanding the universe, it also made it possible for humans to understand anything whatsoever about the universe.

Source: Richard Hooker. The European Enlightenment. World Civilizations. Washington State University. http://www.wsu.edu/~dee/ENLIGHT/ENLIGHT.HTM.

and freedoms. In their view, society was based on a social contract under which people chose to relinquish a small portion of their individual autonomy in order to ensure their own safety and the well-being of the entire group. These ideas were clearly contrary to the collectivist orientation of feudalism and the notion of noble privilege held by its rulers. If realized, a system based on rights and freedoms could seriously undermine the bonds of fealty, which held feudalism together. At the same time, the feudal bonds restricted the availability of labour and hampered the development of manufacturing and industry. Herein lies the essence of the conflict between the aristocracy and the merchants. What was useful for one was detrimental to the other. Each group fought to advance its own interests.

The merchant classes enjoyed little political influence despite their growing economic power because participation in the legislatures of the day was restricted to landowners. Importantly, land was not considered a commodity that could be bought and sold. Rather, it was held primarily for its immediate use in agricultural and other pursuits. So, even though they were financially wealthy, the merchants owned little land and were prevented from acquiring any more since they could not buy land. As a result, they were barred from gaining political power through landownership. In response, the merchants turned to the legal arena to have their interests served.

In an ironic twist, the merchant classes found an opportunity to strengthen their position in society by financing the costly wars being fought by European monarchs over new colonies. The European aristocracy was forced to turn to the merchants for funds as their own resources were depleted. In exchange for their financial assistance, the merchants were able to gain significant legal concessions. While many of these concessions were aimed specifically at enhancing mercantile activities, a number of important legal principles were established, which reflected the ideals of the Enlightenment philosophers. It was within this milieu that the **Classical School** of criminology made its most significant contributions to the establishment of our modern criminal justice system.

WWW

"Cesare Beccaria (1738–1794)" The Internet Encyclopedia of Philosophy
www.iep.utm.edu/b/beccaria.htm

Classical School
Considered to be the first formal school of criminology, Classical criminology is associated with 18th and early 19th century reforms to the administration of justice and the prison system. Associated with authors such as Cesare Beccaria (1738–1794), Jeremy Bentham (1748–1832), Samuel Romilly (1757–1818), and others, this school brought the emerging philosophy of liberalism and utilitarianism to the justice system, advocating principles of rights, fairness, and due process in place of retribution, arbitrariness, and brutality.

The Classical School

In 1764, Cesare Beccaria published his major work, *An Essay on Crimes and Punishments*. Although this work contained little that was novel, "it captivated the attention of Europe, much more than did the voluminous lucubrations of theologians and publicists . . . for it summed up in a masterly, unanswerable manner the conceptions and aspirations of the progressive minds of the age" (Phillipson, 1970). Beccaria provided a focus for the humanitarian reform movement that was gaining momentum throughout Europe with his criticism of the cruelty and inhumanity that characterized the criminal justice system of his day.

Abuses in the administration of justice were routine. Practices established in the notorious Court of Star Chamber and the institutionalized terror of the Inquisition had become commonplace. "The existence of criminal law of eighteenth-century Europe was, in general, repressive, uncertain, and barbaric. Its administration encouraged incredibly arbitrary and abusive practices" (Mannheim, 1972). Few safeguards existed for the accused, and judicial torture was a routine method of securing confessions and discovering the identities of accomplices (Langbein, 1976). "A great many crimes were punished by death not infrequently preceded by inhuman atrocities" (Mannheim, 1972). This was particularly evident in the fanatical attack against heresy and witchcraft that swept across Europe.

The more popular forms of torture for these crimes included the rack, the ducking stool, thumbscrews, and other mechanical devices designed to inflict severe pain. The death penalty was administered in a number of ways, including burning at the stake, hanging, decapitation, and drawing and quartering.

In 18th-century England, as many as 350 offences were punishable by death. About 70 percent of death sentences were given for robbery and burglary (Newman, 1978). Practices in the colonies were similar in the early 1800s. The first person executed in Toronto was hanged for passing a bad cheque.

FOCUS

BOX 7.2 Witchcraft and Torture

It is estimated that five hundred thousand people were convicted of witchcraft and burned to death in Europe between the fifteenth and seventeenth centuries. Their crimes: a pact with the Devil; journeys through the air over vast distances mounted on broomsticks; unlawful assembly at sabbats; worship of the Devil; kissing the Devil under the tail; copulation with incubi, male devils equipped with ice-cold penises; copulation with succubi, female devils.

Other more mundane charges were often added: killing the neighbor's cow; causing hailstorms; ruining the crops; stealing and eating babies. But many a witch was executed for no crime other than flying through the air to attend a sabbat. . . .

Torture was routinely applied until the witch confessed to having made a pact with the Devil and having flown to a sabbat. It was continued until the witch named other people who were present at the sabbat. If a witch attempted to retract a confession, torture was applied even more intensely until the original confession was reconfirmed. This left the person accused of witchcraft with the choice between dying once and for all at the stake or being returned repeatedly to the torture chambers. Most people opted for the stake. As a reward for their cooperative attitude, penitent witches could look forward to being strangled before the fire was lit.

Source: Marvin Harris. (1974). *Cows, Pigs, Wars and Witches*. New York: Vintage Books. Copyright © by Marvin Harris. Reprinted by permission of Random House, Inc.

Clamour for the reform of such practices had started long before Beccaria's book was published. Humanitarian appeals were heard from jurists, writers, and philosophers of the era, including Hobbes, Locke, Montesquieu, and Voltaire. The administration of the criminal law, in particular, embodied practices that were in direct contrast to many of the principles advocated by the Classical theorists. It was contrary to the ideals of the social contract, as it denied the average citizen fair and impartial treatment at the hands of the state. European society was ripe for the liberating ideas of the Classical theorists and their humanitarian reforms. Beccaria's book served as a catalyst for these sentiments. The reform of a barbaric system of justice provided an excellent vehicle through which the ideas of the Classical theorists could be focused.

The Classical Theory of Crime

The roots of Classical criminology lie in the philosophy of the Enlightenment. Social contract theory represented a new way of looking at the relationship between people and the state. To avoid living in a state of nature that was, to use Hobbes's famous description, "solitary, poor, nasty, brutish, and short" (1958, 107), people voluntarily entered into a social contract with the state. This involved giving up some of their freedom to the state. In return, the state agreed to protect the citizen's right to live in security. The social contract was made with the consent of both parties, and neither had the right to break it. The state had to provide protection but could not violate the rights of citizens. The citizen had to obey the rules or face punishment from the state. In the opening chapter of his book, Beccaria writes:

> Laws are the conditions whereby free and independent men unite to form society. Weary of living in a state of war, and of enjoying a freedom rendered useless by the uncertainty of its perpetuation, men will willingly sacrifice a part of this freedom in order to enjoy that which is left in security and tranquility. (quoted in Monachesi, 1972)

The reforms proposed by the Classical theorists were based on a very well-developed theory of the causes of crime, a theory that represented a significant break with earlier theories. The Classical theorists had a simple explanation for crime. People broke the law because they thought that doing so would advance their own interests. In other words, deviance is the natural result of our rational self-interest. If it suits us, and if we think we can get away with it, we will break the law. Crime was understood to be a rationally calculated activity and not the result of some supernatural force or demonic possession.

Having addressed the causes of crime, the Classical theorists turned to the problem of finding ways to control it. The solution was to set up a system of punishment that would deter people from breaking the law. The Classical theorists believed that humans were rational beings who carefully calculated the consequences of their behaviour. Thus a person who might be tempted to break the law would consider the positive and negative consequences of his or her actions. A well-crafted criminal code would ensure that most people would choose to be good rather than evil. One might think that the extremely brutal justice system of the time should have been an effective deterrent, but its excessive harshness was contrary to the Enlightenment view that citizens should not be treated unfairly by the state. Instead, Beccaria proposed that the punishment should fit the crime, that is, it should be proportional to the harm done to society. Beccaria argued this on two grounds: that this amount of punishment would be the most effective deterrent; and that this was the fairest way to punish those who were not deterred and who chose to break the law. Unfair punishment would be a violation of the social contract and would be perceived as unjust by the individual and by other members of society. In the following quotation, Beccaria describes how this would affect the social contract and reduce the deterrent effect of law:

> In proportion as torments become more cruel, the spirits of men, which are like fluids that always rise to the level of surrounding objects, become callous, and the ever lively force of the passions brings it to pass that after a hundred years of cruel torments the wheel inspires no greater fear than imprisonment once did. . . . The countries and times most notorious for severity of penalties have always been those in which the bloodiest and most inhumane of deeds were committed, for the same spirit of ferocity that guided the hand of the legislators also ruled that of parricide and assassin. (1963, 43–44)

Crime would be reduced if these reforms were implemented in law because calculating criminals would see that they would not profit from their actions. The punishment would cost them more than they could gain from their criminal behaviour. Beccaria also proposed that punishment should be swift and certain. If punishment followed too long after the act, or if it was unlikely to happen at all, then the law would not be an effective deterrent to crime. Finally, the law would be most effective in preventing crime if it was clear and simple enough that people could understand it.

With regard to specific reforms, Beccaria felt that the brutality of torture and the practice of executing people for minor offences must be abolished, as they were abuses of state power. Criminal matters should be dealt with in public according to the dictates of the law. Beccaria wanted to restrict the power of judges, which had been exercised in an arbitrary manner, in private, and generally without recourse for the defendant. He sought to restrict this power by separating the lawmaking power of the legislature from the activities of the judges. In his view, the law should be determined by the legislature; it should be accessible to all; trials should be public; and the role of the judiciary should be restricted to the determination of guilt and the administration of punishment set out in law.

The reforms suggested by Beccaria represented a call for equality and for the establishment of due-process safeguards. The creation of graded punishments effectively restricted the arbitrariness and inequality that characterized the existing system. By arguing that the punishment should "fit the crime," Beccaria shifted the focus away from the actor and onto the act. In this way, both noble and peasant would be judged on the basis of what they did and not who they were. Moreover, the judiciary was stripped of its discretion in sentencing since judges were bound to give punishments that were fixed by law. This was a powerful directive for equality since the preferential treatment formerly accorded to those of wealth and power could no longer be granted. However, as you have read in Chapter 2, those with wealth and power had the most influence in shaping the law, so the reforms in the justice system did little to alter the fundamental inequalities based on ownership of property.

Assessing the Contributions of the Classical School

The Classical School and Legal Reform

The ideals of the social contract theorists were translated into progressive criminal justice policy in the reforms promoted by the Classical School. In the process, the excesses and injustices that existed were attacked, and the foundations of our modern legal system were established. The due-process safeguards, which are taken for granted today, as well as reforms such as the guarantee of individual rights, equality before the law, the separation of judicial and legislative functions, and the establishment of fixed penalties, remain as the legacy of the Classical School of criminology. Canada's Criminal Code and our modern criminal justice system still reflect the work of the Classical theorists.

Limitations of the Classical School

Despite this success, the influence of the Classical School was not all positive. A serious problem with Classical theory was Beccaria's insistence that the degree of punishment must be proportional to the degree of harm that was done to society. While at first glance this proposal seemed reasonable, it meant that the personal characteristics of the offender and the circumstances of the offence could not be considered when courts determined punishments (Roshier, 1989). Also, by removing the flexibility of judicial discretion, the reforms actually gave more power to the state, which was responsible for passing very specific sentencing laws (Newman and Marongiu, 1990).

Although punishments could be rationally determined on paper, their application in real life often resulted in gross injustices. The courts were bound to follow the letter of the law and could not use discretion to temper the justice being meted out. For example, the hardship that results from having to pay a $1000 fine varies dramatically depending on whether a person is wealthy or poor. The courts, however, could not take this into account. Further, they were unable to consider mitigating circumstances or factors such as motive or mental competence, which would alter the responsibility of the convicted person. In this way, attempts to enforce equality resulted in a system that produced a great deal of injustice.

Changing this rigid system was one of the goals of Neoclassical criminologists, including the French magistrate Gabriel Tarde. Tarde contributed a number of ideas to criminology, most notably his "laws of imitation," but his main contribution came from his criticism of the legal system established by proponents of the Classical School (Beirne, 1993). Tarde rejected the notion of free will and proposed a modification of the system of punishment to recognize that there must be some individual treatment of offenders. As a result of the work of Tarde and other Neoclassical writers, courts began to take into account factors such as age (children were held less accountable), mental competence, motive, and mitigating circumstances. For example, in France, the Penal Code of 1791, which reflected the views of the Classical School, was revised in 1810 and again in 1819. With each revision, the rigid nature of the code was modified to include more discretion for judges as well as consideration of extenuating circumstances.

deterrence

As used in criminal justice, it refers to crime prevention achieved through the fear of punishment.

Another problem with the Classical School is its emphasis on **deterrence**. The approach the Classical School advocated was based more on a theory of deterrence than on a theory of crime, and it can be assessed on these grounds. The issue of deterrence continues to be an important element of this approach as modern-day Classical theorists emphasize its message. The work of James Q. Wilson, for example, is a current example of Classical thinking. "He argues that penalties need not be long and severe as long as they are swift and certain" (Pfohl, 1985). However, for most offences, the likelihood of punishment is so small, and the time between the criminal event and any punishment that is given is so great, that the Classical theorists' hopes of reducing crime by changing the legal codes have not been met.

An additional problem with the Classical School is its overly simplified view of human nature and the theory of human behaviour that this supports (Thomas and Hepburn, 1983). The Classical theorists wholly accepted the image of the free and rational human being. This view completely ignores the objective realities faced by different individuals as they make their choices, the inequalities they experience, the state of their knowledge at any given time, and a multitude of other factors that may influence their decisions.

Finally, the emphasis on the rational dimension of human behaviour did not stem from the collection of empirical evidence but was based mostly on philosophical speculation. Little effort was made to examine these theoretical ideas in the real world. The notion of deterrence based on a rationally calculated set of punishments was assumed to work because it was felt that most reasonable people would follow the same logic.

In spite of the problems with the ideas of the Classical School, their contribution to our modern criminal justice system cannot be denied. Legal principles such as due process and equality before the law are fundamental to our legal system. Beccaria's work had a direct influence on the drafting of the legal code of France following the French Revolution and on the U.S. Bill of Rights, and Classical principles remain as part of the legal systems of many countries. For example, in section 15 of our Charter of Rights and Freedoms, Canadians are guaranteed the right to equal treatment before and under the law. We are protected from cruel and unusual punishment by section 12. In sections 7 through 11, a whole array of procedural safeguards are outlined that guarantee Canadians the right to due process of law. Clearly, modern criminal justice owes a great debt to the Classical theorists and the reforms that they introduced. However, our legal system also incorporates the changes suggested by the Neoclassical reformers.

WWW

"Canadian Charter of Rights and Freedoms" Department of Justice Canada
http://laws.justice.gc.ca/en/charter/

The Statistical School: Social Structure and Crime

The first half of the 19th century saw the emergence of an approach to criminology that differed markedly from that of the Classical School. This was evident in the work of André-Michel Guerry (1802–1866) in France, Adolphe Quetelet (1796–1874) in Belgium, and Henry Mayhew (1812–1887) in England. These researchers believed that crime, like other human behaviour, was the result of natural causes. Once discovered, these causes could be altered through the application of scientifically derived knowledge. Guerry, Quetelet, and Mayhew's reliance on objective empirical data, as opposed to philosophical conjecture or speculation, identified them as positivists.

Members of the **Statistical School** did not share the image of the rational individual held by the Classical theorists. Instead, they saw behaviour as the product of a whole host of factors. They systematically analyzed the statistical information available to them and tried to find a relationship between this information and crime. They analyzed such things as population density, education, and poverty (Thomas and Hepburn, 1983). A great deal of their work was based on geographical or cartographic analysis, which involved the plotting of various crime rates onto maps.

Statistical School
Associated with early social scientists such as Adolphe Quetelet (1795–1874) and André-Michel Guerry (1802–1866), who began to explore the structure of emerging European societies with the assistance of statistical methods. While their early use of statistics is important, they also developed a structural explanation of crime and other social problems.

These theorists went far beyond simply describing what they learned from their maps and graphs. Many of their ideas anticipated the work of modern sociologists as they addressed issues related to criminal careers, delinquent subcultures, and social learning theory. They provided a critical and insightful

FOCUS

BOX 7.3 What happens to Old Theories? Classical Theory Today

Beccaria's book *Dei Delitti E Delle Pene* was written in 1764. You have learned that the work of Beccaria and the other Enlightenment writers had a lasting impact on our legal system, but what other elements of the theory remain? While many of the other early theories have deservedly disappeared, the work of the Classical School continues to guide two related streams of criminological theory and research. The first is deterrence theory, the second is rational choice theory.

You will recall that the heart of Classical theory was the belief that humans were rational beings who carefully calculated the consequences of their behaviour. Crime would be prevented if the potential criminal realized that the costs of committing the crime would be greater than the potential rewards. Classical theorists had great faith in the ability of a well-designed criminal code to deter criminal behaviour.

How effective is the law as a deterrent? Because our legal system operates in large part on the basis of its ability to deter, one might think there was a large body of research on this topic. In fact, because the Classical School quickly fell out of fashion among academics and was replaced by a succession of positivist theories that minimized the importance of rational choice, we know surprisingly little about deterrence, though the rebirth of classical thinking in recent years has begun to change this. Research has focused on two different types of deterrence—specific deterrence and general deterrence.

Specific deterrence refers to the impact of deterrence on the individual. For example, a judge may sentence a burglar to six months in jail to teach him not to repeat his offence. Will punishment of a person who breaks the law actually deter him or her from breaking the law again in the future? The research on specific deterrence has been ambiguous. The fact that most people in prison have long prior records and that most people released from prison continue to reoffend tells us that deterrence is far from perfect. One reason for this is that most crimes do not result in punishment, so offenders correctly assume that their chances of getting away with a particular offence are good. Also, you may be surprised to learn that some research suggests that those who are more severely punished are more likely to reoffend than those who receive milder punishment for the same offences (Gibbs, 1975). Labelling theorists (see Chapter 12) would suggest that this is because punishment may stigmatize people so that their opportunities for a life in the non-criminal world may be reduced.

perspective, as well as a thorough statistical analysis of criminal behaviour in their work.

Perhaps the most significant contribution of these theorists is their discovery of the remarkable regularity of phenomena such as crime. Countries, provinces, cities, and towns all had rates of crime that were remarkably stable from one year to the next. Even murder, a highly individualistic act, varied little over time. They attributed this stability to elements of the social structure. Quetelet, for example, argued that "rather than being the result of our individual free wills, [our behaviour] is the product of many forces that are external to us" (Thomas and Hepburn, 1983). The fact that these forces appeared in regular and recurring patterns prompted these theorists to believe that human behaviour was governed by certain laws akin to those found in the natural or physical sciences.

FOCUS

BOX 7.3 What happens to Old Theories? Classical Theory Today *(Continued)*

General deterrence refers to the effect of punishment on the public at large. The existence of a system of punishment will deter most of us from committing crimes. Thus a judge may decide that burglaries are getting out of hand and give one burglar a severe sentence to set an example for others. We do know that at one level, general deterrence is effective. You do not deliberately park where you know your car will be towed away and you do not speed if you see a police car behind you. Further, when the police have gone on strike, crime has risen dramatically. In one notable police strike in Montreal, armed robberies began to occur within minutes of the strike and on several occasions huge mobs of people ran through the shopping district, breaking windows and stealing whatever they could get their hands on. However, such strikes are rare and the more important question is not whether the law deters, but whether we can change our current system to make it more effective as a deterrent.

The research that has been done on this issue suggests that certainty of punishment is more important than the severity of punishment, a finding that would have been predicted by the Classical theorists. A simple example is that obscene and harassing telephone calls declined dramatically after the introduction of caller ID because this new technology made it much easier to identify the offending caller. Unfortunately, it is difficult to increase the certainty of punishment for most offences so policy-makers have turned their attention to severity. "Get tough" politicians regularly assure us that cracking down on crime by increasing the penalties will enable us to solve our crime problems. The evidence suggests otherwise, probably because the likelihood of being arrested, convicted, and punished for any offence is so low that tinkering with the level of punishment makes no difference. Also, it may be the case that the existing level of punishment is severe enough for most of us. To cite just one example, there is no evidence that capital punishment is any greater deterrent to crime than lengthy terms of imprisonment. In fact, one international study found that homicide rates actually went down after capital punishment was abolished (Archer et al., 1983).

The second area where the concerns of the Classical School are enjoying a resurgence is in the growing popularity of the rational choice theory of crime. (You can learn more about this theory in the Net Work exercise at the end of this chapter and in Chapter 14.)

In a style that anticipated much of our contemporary thinking about crime, these theorists focused on inequalities and other structural features of their society. People in unfavourable social circumstances were seen to have few options open to them. In Quetelet's words, "The crimes which are annually committed seem to be a necessary result of our social organization . . . the society prepares the crime and the guilty are only the instruments by which it is executed" (Bierne, 1993, 88).

The influence of the Statistical School was, unfortunately, limited. This was not the result of any shortcomings on their part; rather, it reflected the wider appeal of the biological theories of Cesare Lombroso and his colleagues. Nevertheless, these early pioneers of statistical analysis of criminology provided a uniquely sociological contribution to this emerging field of inquiry and demonstrated the value of testing theoretical formulations with empirical observations.

Lombroso and the Positive School

Positive School
The first scientific school consisting of the Italian criminologists Cesare Lombroso (1836–1909), Raffaelo Garofalo (1852–1934), and Enrico Ferri (1856–1929). They supported the assumptions of positivism and argued that criminality is determined—the effect in a cause–effect sequence—and that the mandate of criminology should be to search for these causes. It was believed that with the exception of those deemed to be born criminals, the discovery of the causes of crime would allow for effective treatment.

WWW

"Cesare Lombroso" Museo Criminologico
www.museocriminologico.it/lombroso_3_uk.htm

The **Positive School** of criminology is also known as the Italian School because its most influential members were the Italian criminal anthropologist Cesare Lombroso (1836–1909) and his students Enrico Ferri (1856–1929) and Raffaelo Garofolo (1852–1934). Lombroso was influenced by the evolutionary theories of Charles Darwin, by the positivist sociology of Auguste Comte, and by the work of the sociologist Herbert Spencer, who attempted to adapt Darwin's theory to the social world.

Like the members of the Statistical School, Lombroso brought the methods of controlled observation to the study of criminals, comparing them with non-criminals in order to isolate the factors that caused criminality. His own research was badly flawed, and his work is remembered because of his use of the scientific method rather than because of the specific findings he reported. Despite their flaws, Lombroso's ideas were widely accepted at the end of the 19th century. Their popularity was partly due to the growing influence of science, particularly to the awareness of Darwin's theory of evolution. It was likely also due to the comfort of the ruling classes with the view that criminals were not produced by society's flaws, as Quetelet and his colleagues had shown; rather, criminals were genetic misfits who were born to break the rules that governed the lives of civilized people (Radzinowicz, 1966).

The impact of Darwin's ideas on the Positive School cannot be overstated. As Lilly et al. (2007, 28) note,

> Darwin's evolutionary thesis represents one of the most profound theories of all times. It not only offered revolutionary new knowledge for the sciences but also helped to shatter many philosophies and practices in other areas. It commanded so much attention and prestige that the entire literate community felt "obligated to bring his world outlook into harmony with their findings" (Hofstadter, 1955b, p3). According to Hofstadter, (1955b) Darwin's impact is comparable in its magnitude to the work of Nicolaus Copernicus 1473–1543) the European astronomer; Isaac Newton (1642–1727), the English mathematician and physicist; and Freud, the Austrian psychoanalyst. In effect, all of the Western world had to come to grips with Darwin's evolutionary scheme.

The main ideas in Darwin's theory—"the struggle for survival" and "the survival of the fittest" found fertile ground in the minds of the Positive School criminologists who incorporated these ideas into their thinking about criminals and the way society should deal with them. Identifying criminals became a matter of searching for those physical and moral traits that differentiated more developed human beings from those who were less advanced in evolutionary terms. Dealing with criminals became a matter of incapacitating them since little could be done for them because their criminality was based on their genetic make-up. As you will see, however, some interpretations of these ideas led to a far more drastic approach called "eugenics," which promoted the sterilization and even elimination of those deemed to be inferior.

Lombroso had worked as an army doctor and as a prison physician. He was interested in psychology and at one stage of his career was a teacher of psychiatry. These diverse interests are reflected in his theory of criminality. Lombroso's interest in physiology led him to note certain distinct physical differences between the criminals and soldiers with whom he worked. His thoughts on the subject came together during an autopsy he was performing on the notorious thief Vilella. He noted that many of the characteristics of Vilella's skull were similar to those of lower animals. In a remarkable description of the moment of discovery, Lombroso recalled:

> This was not merely an idea, but a revelation. At the sight of that skull, I seemed to see all of a sudden, lighted up as a vast plain under a flaming sky, the problem of the nature of the criminal—an atavistic being who reproduces in his person the ferocious instincts of primary humanity and the inferior animals. Thus were explained anatomically the enormous jaws, high cheek-bones, prominent superciliary arches, solitary lines in the palms, extreme size of the orbits, handle-shaped or sessile ears found in criminals, savages, and apes, insensibility to pain, extremely acute sight, tattooing, excessive idleness, love of orgies, and the irresistible craving for evil for its own sake, the desire not only to extinguish life in the victim, but to mutilate the corpse, tear its flesh, and drink its blood. (Wolfgang, 1972)

This discovery led Lombroso to believe that criminals were throwbacks to an earlier stage of evolution, or **atavisms.** His theory has been succinctly described by Gould (1981):

atavism

Cesare Lombroso (1836–1909) believed that some criminals were born criminals; they were atavistic. This suggested that they were throwbacks to an earlier stage of human evolution and that this limited evolutionary development meant that they were morally inferior. This inferiority could be identified through a series of physical stigmata.

> These people are innately driven to act as a normal ape or savage would but such behaviour is deemed criminal in our civilized society. Fortunately, we may identify born criminals because they bear anatomical signs of their apishness. Their atavism is both physical and mental, but the physical signs, or stigmata as Lombroso called them, are decisive. Criminal *behaviour* can also arise in normal men, but we know the "born criminal" by his anatomy. Anatomy, indeed, is destiny, and born criminals cannot escape their inherited taint.

The contrast between the primitive nature of the criminal and the more completely evolved contemporary man is shown in Lombroso's explanation of the use of professional slang, or argot, by criminals. Born criminals talk differently because they experience the world differently. "They talk like savages because they are veritable savages in the midst of this brilliant European civilization" (Parmelee, 1912).

To support his theory, Lombroso had to show that organisms lower on the evolutionary ladder were naturally criminal. Thus primitive humans were described as "savages." Even when evidence of their savagery was absent, Lombroso was able to save his theory by speculating that among honourable

stigmata

Physical signs of some special moral position. Cesare Lombroso (1836–1909) used the term to refer to physical signs of the state of atavism (a morally and evolutionary inferior person).

primitives, the conditions for criminality simply did not yet exist. For example, "it is not possible . . . to steal when property does not exist or to swindle when there is no trade" (Lombroso, 1912). Once these supposed savages take on a little civilization, their criminality is inevitable. Lombroso went even further down the evolutionary ladder, finding evidence of criminality in the behaviour of animals, insects, and even insectivorous plants.

Lombroso tested his ideas by observing many imprisoned criminals. In one study, he compared the physical characteristics of a group of criminals with those of a group of soldiers and found that the criminals had many more of the atavistic **stigmata** than did the soldiers. In another piece of research, he found that stigmata were present in 30 to 40 percent of anarchists, but in less than 12 percent of members of other extremist movements (Taylor et al., 1973). He also concluded that different types of offenders were characterized by different physiological characteristics. For example, "robbers have . . . small, shifting, quick-moving eyes; bushy connecting eyebrows; twisted or snub noses, thin beards . . . and foreheads almost receding," while "habitual homicides have glassy, cold, motionless eyes, sometimes bloodshot and injected. The nose is often aquiline, or rather hawklike, and always voluminous" (Lombroso, 1972). Lombroso felt that women had fewer stigmata and lower crime rates than males because women were closer to their primitive origins. Although he concluded that women were vengeful, deceitful, and jealous, he said that their crime rates were relatively low because these negative traits were neutralized by their maternal instinct, piety, and lack of passion.

Lombroso initially postulated two types of offenders—born criminals and occasional criminals. However, in response to his critics, he later added several more categories, including the following:

1. *Epileptics.* In addition to their disability, epileptics also had the atavistic characteristics of criminals.
2. *Criminal insane.* This is the category of those whose insanity has led to their involvement in crime.
3. *Criminals of passion.* These are criminals who contrast completely with born criminals in that they lack any of the criminal stigmata. They commit crimes because of "noble and powerful" motives such as love or politics.
4. *Criminaloids.* This is a grab-bag category, which includes anyone who commits a crime but does not fall into one of the other classifications. Lombroso felt that precipitating factors other than biological ones caused criminality among this group.

Some have interpreted this expansion of categories as a softening of Lombroso's commitment to his biological theory. This view seems to be supported by his last major work, *Crime: Its Causes and Remedies*, in which he discusses social and environmental causes of crime along with biological causes. However, examination of these modifications suggests that this change was more apparent than real. While there were differences between atavistic criminals, the insane, and the epileptics, all three categories had elements of degeneration that stemmed from epilepsy, which he called the "kernel of crime" (Lombroso, 1912). Criminaloids may lack some of the stigmata, but they differ from born criminals only in degree, not in kind. After long periods in prison, criminaloids may

FOCUS

BOX 7.4 A "Novel" Theory

Criminal anthropology reached the attention of novelists as well as theorists. Bram Stoker and Lombroso were contemporaries, but Stoker's *Dracula* was published almost 20 years after Lombroso's most famous work. Compare Stoker's description of Count Dracula with Lombroso's description of the born criminal:

Dracula: "His face was . . . aquiline, like the beak of a bird of prey."

Lombroso: "[The criminal's] nose on the contrary is often aquiline like the beak of a bird of prey."

Dracula: "His eyebrows were very massive, almost meeting over the nose . . ."

Lombroso: "The eyebrows are bushy and tend to meet across the nose."

Dracula: ". . . his ears were pale and at the tops extremely pointed . . ."

Lombroso: "with a protuberance on the upper part of the posterior margin . . . a relic of the pointed ear. . . ."

Source: Leonard Wolf. (1981). In Stephen Jay Gould, *The Mismeasure of Man*. New York: W.W. Norton.

even come to resemble born criminals. While those who commit crimes out of passion do not show any of the stigmata, they show some points of resemblance with epileptics. The only category that has no connection with atavism or epilepsy is that of the occasional criminals. Even these pose no threat to Lombroso's theory, however, for he suggests that they should not be called criminals at all.

The Contribution of the Positive School

In its day, Lombroso's work attracted a large following among those interested in studying the causes of criminality. The stigmata were used as indicators of criminality in many trials, and Lombroso himself appeared as an expert witness on several occasions. In one case, the court had to decide which of two brothers had killed their stepmother. Lombroso's testimony that one of the men had the features of a born criminal helped secure the man's conviction.

However, Lombroso's theory of criminal anthropology has not stood up to empirical test. Lombroso's research was poorly done by today's standards. His comparison groups were chosen unsystematically, his statistical techniques were crude, his measurements were often sloppy, and he assumed that those in prison were criminals and those out of prison were non-criminals. Many of the stigmata he mentioned in his research, such as tattooing, were social factors that could not possibly have been inherited. Yet despite these weaknesses, his work did represent an attempt at providing a scientific explanation of the causes of criminality.

Perhaps the most lasting contribution of Lombroso was his discussion of the criminal justice system. The Classical theorists felt that crime could be controlled if society could design punishments to fit the crime. Positive theorists, on the other hand, felt that the punishment should fit the *criminal*. Radzinowicz and King (1977) have nicely outlined the difference between the two perspectives: "The Classical School exhorts men to study justice, the Positivist School exhorts justice to study men."

Because Lombroso believed that people became involved in criminality for different reasons, he felt that they should be treated differently by the criminal justice system. If a respectable man committed murder because of passion, honour, or political belief, no punishment was needed as that man would never repeat the crime. For other offenders, indeterminate sentences would best ensure rehabilitation. Born criminals should not be held responsible for their actions, though they needed to be incarcerated for the protection of society. However, this was to be done in a humane way. He recommended that "sentences should show a decrease in infamy and ferocity proportionate to their increase in length and social safety" (Lombroso-Ferrero, 1972).

Some born criminals could be channelled in a socially useful direction. For example, banishment and transportation to one of the colonies might allow their tendencies to be redirected toward the difficult business of building settlements in a hostile environment. For others, more severe sanctions were required. "There exists, it is true, a group of criminals, born for evil, against whom all social cures break as against a rock—a fact which compels us to eliminate them completely, even by death" (Lombroso, 1912).

A number of features of our current criminal justice system stem from the concern of Lombroso and his followers with individualizing the treatment of offenders. Probation, parole, indeterminate sentences, and the consideration of mitigating circumstances by the court were all influenced by Lombroso's work as well as by the work of Neoclassical criminologists. The rational person of Classical theory now had a past and a future.

Biological Theories in the Early 20th Century

Crime and Physical Characteristics

During his lifetime, Lombroso's theories came under frequent attack. In 1889, he responded to his critics by challenging them to compare 100 born criminals, 100 people with criminal tendencies, and 100 normal people. He promised to retract his theories if the criminals did not turn out to be different from the other groups. His challenge was ultimately taken up by an English prison medical officer, Dr. G. B. Griffiths, and completed by his successor, Dr. Charles Goring, who succeeded Griffiths in 1903 shortly after the project began.

Goring carefully measured and compared the physical and mental characteristics of 3000 English convicts with those of diverse samples of "normals," including British university students, schoolboys, university professors, insane Scots, German Army recruits, and British Army soldiers (Goring, 1972). Based on his comparison of these groups on 37 physical and 6 mental traits, Goring concluded that there was no evidence of a distinct physical type of criminal. Lombroso's "anthropological monster has no existence in fact" (Goring, 1913). Criminals were no more or less likely to possess stigmata than were members of the control groups. Goring did find that criminals were physically inferior to normals, but attributed this fact to social selection processes.

Goring's most important finding was the high correlation between criminality and low intelligence. This led to his own explanation that crime was inherited and that the most important constitutional mechanism through which crime was genetically transmitted was mental inferiority. Unlike Lombroso, Goring did feel that hereditary predispositions could be modified by social factors such as education. However, he also supported eugenic measures, which would restrict the reproduction of the constitutional factors leading to crime.

In some respects, Goring's research represented a major advance over the work of Lombroso. His measurement was far more precise, and he had access to statistical tools that were not available to Lombroso. However, his work also contained a number of serious methodological flaws. Among them was the fact that he was comparing officially labelled criminals, who were not a representative sample of all criminals, with diverse groups of other people who did not represent the non-criminal population. While many of the other criticisms of Goring's research are quite technical, they are serious enough to cause doubt both about his own theories and about his refutation of Lombroso (Driver, 1972).

The search for individual differences as the cause of crime did not end with Goring. This theme was picked up again in the 1930s by Ernest A. Hooton, a Harvard anthropologist. He compared more than 13 000 criminals with a sample of non-criminals drawn from groups of college students, firemen, hospital out-patients, militiamen, mental hospital patients, people using the change house at a public beach, and others. On the basis of this comparison, Hooton concluded that "criminals as a group represent an aggregate of sociologically and biologically inferior individuals" (1939). Among the new stigmata he attributed to criminals were such characteristics as "low foreheads, high pinched nasal roots, nasal bridges and tips varying to both extremes of breadth and narrowness," and "very small ears" (1939).

While Hooton was not as concerned as some of his predecessors with the policy implications of his research, he did not hesitate to draw the obvious conclusion. Since "crime is the resultant of the impact of environment upon low grade human organisms . . . it follows that the elimination of crime can be effected only by the expiration of the physically, mentally, and morally unfit, or by their complete segregation in a socially aseptic environment" (1939). These ideas formed the basis of the "eugenics" movement that developed in the United States at the turn of the 20th century (see Box 7.5).

Hooton's work stirred up a great deal of controversy, and his findings were challenged on a variety of grounds. He was accused of using poor scientific methods and circular reasoning. For example, he used conviction of a crime as a method of separating criminals from non-criminals; he then examined the convicted groups and concluded they were inferior; finally, he used this finding of inferiority to account for their criminality (Empey, 1982). Only in this way could a trait such as thin lips be turned into an indicator of criminality.

There are several other criticisms of Hooton's methods worth considering. His control group did not represent the general population. Students, firefighters, and mental patients have particular characteristics that distinguish them from the rest of the population. Furthermore, his findings show tremendous differences within the various control groups he used. In fact, the differences between his control groups drawn from Boston and Nashville were actually greater than between prisoners and controls (Pfohl, 1985). As in the case of

FOCUS

BOX 7.5 Criminology and Eugenics

The term "eugenics". . . . simply means "well born" and it connotes a sense of contributing to or improving the stock of the race or the nation. The term became one of some suspicion when the goal of genetics was embraced by various political regimes and enforced through the state's coercive power as an effective instrument for social engineering. In modern times, the first extended programs in state-sponsored eugenics were developed in the United States in the late nineteenth and early twentieth century. These eugenics programs grew from a constellation of ideas derived from evolutionary theory which embraced Social Darwinism, from contemporaneous criminology encouraged by a scientific hypothesis supported by post-mortem studies of brains of criminals and the findings of the famous Juke Report (1875) on inheritance and criminal behaviour, from demographic concerns about dysgenics—the growth of criminal population and the growth of the feeble-minded population because of their unrestrained breeding patterns—and from surgical advances, such as vasectomy and salpingectomy [female sterilization], in the practice of medicine. Involuntary sterilization became the instrument of this modern attempt at eugenics. The idea of genetic sterilization, the pursuit of this end as a national goal, and the procurement of means to attain their desired result were pressed by some of the most influential families, by some of the most prestigious societies and foundations, by some powerful lawyers, judges, scientists, and physicians, and by some of the most elite universities in the United States. This central notion and clearest articulation of the goals of this movement are best recorded in the words of Mr. Justice Oliver Wendell Holmes who, writing for the majority in a 1927 United States Supreme Court decision, *Buck v. Bell*, found involuntary sterilization to be compatible with the guarantees found in the U.S. Constitution. Holmes concluded:

> We have seen more than once that the public welfare may call upon the best citizens for their lives. It would be strange if it could not call upon those who already sap the strength of the state for lesser sacrifices, often not felt to be such by those concerned, in order to prevent our being swamped with incompetence. It is better for all the world, if instead of waiting to execute degenerative offspring for crime, or to let them starve for their imbecility, society can prevent those who are manifestly unfit from continuing their kind. The principle that sustains compulsory vaccination is broad enough to cover cutting the Fallopian tubes (*Jacobson v. Massachusetts*, 197 U.S. 11). Three generations of imbeciles are enough (*Buck v. Bell*. United States Supreme Court. Report 274, 1927). [Canada also practised involuntary sterilization and the practice remained legal in Alberta until 1972.]

Source: Margaret Monahan Hogan, "Medical Ethics: The New Eugenics: Therapy—Enhancement—Screening—Testing." International Catholic University. http://home.comcast.net/~icuweb/c04106.htm.

Lombroso, Hooton's attempt to link criminal behaviour to physical types was thoroughly discredited.

This kind of research has made periodic appearances in a variety of forms since the days of Lombroso and Hooton. In the 1950s, William Sheldon attempted to re-establish the link between body type and criminality in his elaboration of a "somatotype" theory. He described three basic body types, which, he argued, were related to particular types of personalities and temperament. These consisted of endomorphs, with fat, round bodies and easygoing personalities; ectomorphs, who are tall and lean individuals with introverted personalities and nervous dispositions; and mesomorphs, who have well-built, muscular bodies with aggressive personalities and who are quick to act and insensitive to pain. Sheldon related each of these types to particular kinds of criminal behaviour. He found that the muscular mesomorphs were the type most likely to become involved in delinquent or criminal behaviour.

Sheldon fared no better than his predecessors, however, when his work was subjected to scrutiny. It was found that he had done an extremely poor job of measuring delinquency among the young people he had studied. He had used vague and inconsistent categories that have been described as scientifically meaningless.

These criticisms could not be levelled at the Gluecks, who followed up on Sheldon's ideas. They applied his somatotype theory to a study of 500 juvenile delinquents. In their study, they compared the bodies of 500 adjudicated delinquents with a matched sample of non-delinquents. The Gluecks concluded from their work that delinquents were more likely to be mesomorphs. However, this finding may have raised more questions than it answered. Putting aside a whole host of methodological criticisms levelled at the Gluecks, it may be that mesomorphs actually look more like stereotypical delinquents than either endomorphs or ectomorphs. As a result, people may respond to mesomorphs differently and they may be more likely to be labelled delinquent than those who are non-mesomorphs. Also, other social selection factors may have been involved. Youths who are athletic, muscular, and active may be better candidates for Little League baseball, hockey, or delinquency than their less athletic peers.

Crime and Intelligence

Other examples of a biological approach have focused on a variety of factors that have been associated with individual differences. Goring proposed one such point of view when he suggested that instead of looking for defective body types, the focus should be on genetic weaknesses demonstrated by low intelligence.

In one famous study of family and heredity, the American psychologist Henry Goddard traced the legitimate and illegitimate offspring of an army lieutenant, Martin Kallikak. Young Martin fathered an illegitimate son with a feeble-minded barmaid before he settled down and married a "respectable" woman. The study compared the family trees of the descendants of Kallikak's feeble-minded mate to those of his "normal" wife. The offspring of the feeble-minded barmaid produced a collection of deviants and feeble-minded degenerates. By contrast, the family of his wife showed no such weakness (Goddard, 1912).

Even if the enormous methodological weaknesses of Goddard's study are ignored (Gould [1981] has shown that even the photographs showing the "depraved" Kallikaks had been retouched to make them look like defectives), little is left of scientific consequence. It is hardly surprising that children raised under difficult and impoverished circumstances should be less than model citizens. In fact, a requirement for life under these conditions may be that an individual learns a great deal of undesirable behaviour simply to survive. The absence of any consideration of the social factors involved in this comparison clearly undermines the findings of Goddard's research.

Goddard continued his work using the Binet-Simon intelligence test, which had recently been developed in France. This IQ test was based on the notion of "mental age." Goddard studied the residents of a New Jersey mental institution and, on the basis of this work, established the mental age of 12 as the cutoff point for determining feeble-mindedness. Goddard then applied this IQ test to the inmates of jails and prisons throughout the New Jersey area. He found that in approximately half of the institutions, 70 percent of the inmate population was at or below the mental age of 12. From these findings, he concluded that IQ was an important determinant of criminal behaviour. He also concluded that feeble-mindedness was directly inherited and could only be eliminated by denying those he called "morons" the right to reproduce (1914). Goddard also argued that "criminal imbeciles" should not be held criminally responsible for their actions. His expert testimony helped to acquit at least one murderer on grounds of criminal imbecility (Rafter, 1997).

The acceptance of Goddard's position was short-lived. In 1926, Murchinson published the results of a study in which he compared IQ data from World War I army recruits with that of a group of inmates (Pfohl, 1985). He found that 47 percent of the recruits, compared with only 30 percent of the prisoners, had IQ scores that fell below the mental age of 12. This startling finding implied that almost half of a very large sample of normal American men could be considered mentally feeble. The absurdity of these findings forced Goddard to lower his cutoff point for feeble-mindedness from 12 years to 9. This reduction resulted in the disappearance of any significant differences between inmates and soldiers, or anyone else for that matter (Pfohl, 1985).

Despite evidence so convincing that even Goddard disavowed his earlier work, governments responded to their fear of those with low IQs by passing legislation controlling their behaviour. These laws resulted in thousands of mentally retarded people in North America being forced into institutions and, in many cases, being involuntarily sterilized.

In Canada, sterilization laws were passed in Alberta in 1929 and in British Columbia in 1933. The Alberta law was not repealed until 1972. As a child growing up in Alberta, Leilani Muir was incorrectly labelled as mentally retarded. She was kept in an institution and was sterilized without her knowledge or consent. In 1995 Muir, who actually had normal intelligence, successfully sued the Alberta government and was awarded substantial damages. This case shows the problems with developing policies based on notions of individual inferiority.

The controversy over IQ tests has continued. A number of serious flaws in the assumptions behind this approach have been realized. For example, it has been suggested that high scores on these tests may have more to say about test-taking ability than they do about intelligence. Furthermore, the composition of these tests has been found to be biased in favour of the cultural groups of the designers of the tests. In a dramatic demonstration, Adrian Dove, a black sociologist, devised an IQ test based on the cultural referents and language of the black ghetto (Pfohl, 1985). Black respondents who were familiar with this culture did well on the tests, but white middle-class respondents did poorly. The validity of IQ tests remains suspect, and their use has often been linked with racist ideology and propaganda.

FOCUS

BOX 7.6 Bad Science or Bad Politics? Criminology in Nazi Germany

Throughout this chapter, we have tried to link the developments in criminology to the wider social, political, and intellectual contexts from which they emerged. For example, we noted the impact of the Enlightenment and humanistic thinking on the development of the Classical School and the reforms they struggled to make to the criminal justice system of the day. We also noted how Social Darwinism had a far-ranging influence on the type of thinking that began to gain prominence in a number of fields after Charles Darwin published his famous treatise on evolution. This included the field of criminology and the ideas promoted by the Positive School.

What happens to these ideas and theories once they become popularized depends in large part on how they are used to further particular agendas or views of the world. In the case of the eugenics movement, criminological-biological research was used to justify forced sterilizations, executions of habitual criminals, and even genocide as was the case in Nazi Germany. "Hitler himself, in a speech to the 1929 Nazi Party Congress in Nuremburg, called it outrageous that 'criminals are allowed to procreate' and demanded drastic eugenic measures" (Wetzell, 2000, 180). This pronouncement eerily foreshadowed what was to come. As Rosenhaft (2001) notes, "From 1935 on, certain categories of criminals were officially treated as racially undesirable. Prostitutes, vagrants, and other so-called asocials, including Roma, or Gypsies, were taken off the streets and sent to prisons or camps indefinitely and without the right to appeal. Homosexuals, whose lifestyle contradicted both criminal law and the racial duty to produce children, were hounded and arrested. . . . It was from managing these thousands of ordinary captives that the concentration camp system was set up right at the beginning of the regime in 1933."

However unconscionable the horrors perpetrated by the Nazis were, they could be attributed to the vicious and racist ideology of the Nazi regime. Their use of science and biological-criminological research to justify their actions, however, should serve as a cautionary tale to us all. The conclusions drawn by Richard Wetzell (2000) after his extensive investigation of German criminology during the Nazi era provide a sobering view on the role of "science." He states:

> A more complex picture of science under the Third Reich also diminishes the distance that we often perceive between "Nazi science" and our own science. Contemporary scientists as well as the general public often assume that science under Nazism was "bad" or "perverted" science. This view is reassuring because it suggests that our own, more "advanced" science does not have the same dangerous implications that "Nazi science" had. But if science under the Nazis was in fact more sophisticated, the distance between "Nazi science" and science in our own day is diminished, and we are forced to ask ourselves whether the role of science and medicine under the Nazi regime might point to dangers inherent in scientific research in the present. My point here is not to suggest that research on the genetic causes of crime, for instance, is intrinsically evil and dangerous and will necessarily lead to inhumane and murderous state policies. Rather, my point is that much of the scientific research conducted during the Nazi years was not as different from current scientific research as we would like to think. Like science before and after the Third Reich, scientific research in Nazi Germany was characterized by continual tension between the internal dynamics of science and the intellectual and political biases of the scientists and their society. This argument should make us uncomfortable in salutary ways. For it makes us realize that the connection between scientific research and the Nazi regime was more complicated than we might have thought, and it gives us a more critical view of science in our own time.

TABLE 7.1 Early Theories of Crime

Theory	*Theorists*	*Key Elements*
Classical theory	Beccaria Glueck/Glueck, Pollak	Humans were rational thinkers. Those who contemplated breaking the law considered the positive and negative consequences of their actions. A measured system of punishments was needed to deter crime.
Neoclassical theory	Tarde	Helped to develop a more individualized system of criminal justice.
Statistical School	Guerry, Quetelet, Mayhew	Explored the social causes of crime. Related structural factors such as inequality to crime.
Positive School	Lombroso	Criminals were born, not made. They were atavisms who were less evolved than the law-abiding.
Early 20th-century biological	Goring, Hooton, Sheldon, Goddard	Related criminality to several types of theories of biological inferiority including intelligence and body shape.

A number of other recent formulations have sought to re-establish a link between individual characteristics and criminal behaviour. These include a focus on such things as chromosomes, unusual EEG results, hypoglycemic disorders, and premenstrual tension. The results in many of these cases are similar. While it would be foolhardy to deny the biological or psychological dimensions of human behaviour, the evidence supporting a link between pathology and criminal behaviour is weak. Moreover, this approach ignores the essentially political nature of social control, for what one society praises and rewards, another may condemn. Given this variability in what we define as crime, an assessment of the underlying social and political context is indispensable.

The continued search for individual differences and the erroneous identification of a normal "us" and a criminal "them" carries with it distinct political overtones as was the case in Nazi Germany (see Box 7.6). The emergence of a positive science coincided with the rise of a powerful capitalist class and expanded colonial activity. Both of these developments welcomed the ideological justification contained within the Darwinian notion of survival of the fittest. Social Darwinism and positive criminology flourished in this environment.

This biological-criminological approach of the Positive School offered a ready-made and "humane" way of dealing with the problems of social control. This was extremely important at a time when the population was being transformed into a disciplined industrial labour force. Rather than applying the harsh and barbaric punishments of the past, a scientifically designed technology of control could be used to "treat" troublesome individuals. This focus on the pathologies of individuals also serves to conveniently remove one's gaze from the social structure. If it is certain that problems like crime are the result of individual deficiencies, then it is not necessary to be concerned with the social structure. If, on the other hand, the structural sources of inequality, such as racism, sexism, and other social ills, are examined, the very nature of the society may be called into question.

Summary

- Early theories of crime were based on superstition and religious beliefs.
- This view of crime changed when the Classical School of criminology became popular. Members of this school argued that people were free and rational actors and proposed that the key to preventing crime was the establishment of a criminal code based on the principle that the punishment should fit the crime.
- The Classical School had a major impact on legal systems in many countries. However, the resulting legal codes were rigid and inflexible. Other scholars proposed a series of Neoclassical reforms that have now been incorporated in the legal systems of many countries.
- Lombroso and other members of the Positive School brought scientific methods to the study of crime. While Lombroso's biological theory has not stood up to scientific scrutiny, the application of science to criminology represented a major shift in the discipline.
- Lombroso's work was followed by a number of other researchers who sought to blame crime on the biological inferiority of criminals. As with Lombroso's theory, research has not supported these early 20th-century biological theories. However, they did have a major impact on the legal system, as measures such as involuntary sterilization and lengthy incarceration for "defectives" were passed in many jurisdictions.

QUESTIONS FOR CRITICAL THINKING

1. How did the development of the Classical School of criminology reflect the wider changes taking place in European society at the time? Consider how the social, economic, and ideological forces influenced the founders of the Classical School.
2. What changes did the Positive School of criminology introduce? How did these alter the existing explanations of crime and criminality? What are the implications of the Positive School for the way we treat people who break the law today?
3. What were the major biological explanations of criminality that emerged early in this century? How were these explanations received by social scientists?
4. Discuss the social policy implications of the early biological theories. In other words, if the theories were correct, what should societies do to deal with crime?
5. In general, what have you learned in this chapter about the relationship between theories of criminality and social policy concerning the treatment of criminals?

NET WORK

In Box 7.2 you learned about contemporary work that is in the tradition of the Classical School. Rational choice theory (discussed in detail in Chapter 14) is based on the assumption that criminal behaviour is the result of a rational choice between good and evil. Prior to committing the offence, the potential offender calculates the probability of being caught and the likely penalty and weighs these against the potential rewards of committing the offence. Crime-prevention specialists have used this theory as the basis for a wide variety of prevention programs directed at increasing the cost of crime or at decreasing its rewards. This has been called situational crime prevention.

To learn more about this approach, visit **http://www.ncjrs.gov/works/**.

This site contains a major report on crime prevention— "Preventing Crime: What Works, What Doesn't, What's Promising."

Go to Chapter 7: "Preventing Crime at Places" to answer the following questions:

1. What does the author of this chapter tell us about the relationship between place and crime? How can we use our knowledge of this relationship to prevent crime? Can you think of any places in your own community that have high rates of crime?
2. Find three different types of situational crime prevention programs. For each of these programs, describe one study that measures the program's success or lack of success.
3. Read the section on crime and public transportation. Based on the research cited in the report, list three recommendations you would make to reduce crime on the public transportation system in your community.
4. Many of our politicians suggest that the best way to deal with crime is to toughen up the Young Offenders Act and increase the penalties for crime. After reading this report on situational crime prevention, do you think these politicians are correct?

KEY TERMS

atavism; pg. 233
Classical School; pg. 224
deterrence; pg. 228
Positive School; pg. 232
Statistical School; pg. 229
stigmata; pg. 234

SUGGESTED READING

Beccaria, Cesare Bonesana, Marquis. (1819). *An Essay on Crimes and Punishments.* Philadelphia: Philip H. Nicklion Publishers. This is Beccaria's major work. It is important to read the original text since it contains the ideas that inspired many of the criminal justice reforms of the period.

Lombroso-Ferrero, Gina. (1972). *Criminal Man According to the Classification of Cesare Lombroso.* Montclair, N.J.: Patterson Smith. Lombroso's daughter Gina compiled this work, which contains the major ideas developed by her father. First published in 1911, it provides a number of vivid examples of how Lombroso applied his theory to a whole range of offenders.

Maestro, Marcello T. (1942). *Voltaire and Beccaria as Reformers of Criminal Law*. New York: Columbia University Press. An excellent source for delineating the ideas of Beccaria in relation to the intellectual developments of the era. Maestro presents a clear and thorough treatment of Beccaria's work in light of both social contract and Classical theories.

Monachesi, Elio. (1972). "Cesare Beccaria." In Hermann Mannheim (ed.), *Pioneers in Criminology* (pp. 36–50). Montclair, N.J.: Patterson Smith. A useful introduction to Beccaria and his ideas. This article is informative and concise and helps the reader to appreciate the conditions that existed when Beccaria was writing.

Phillipson, Coleman. (1970). *Three Criminal Law Reformers*. Montclair, N.J.: Patterson Smith. An excellent source on the contributions of Beccaria. It presents a thorough discussion of his work and the conditions surrounding the rise of the Classical School.

Sylvester, F. Sawyer, Jr. (1972). *The Heritage of Modern Criminology*. Cambridge, Mass.: Schenkman Publishing Company. This book contains short selections from the major works of such early criminologists as Beccaria, Lombroso, Quetelet, and Mayhew.

Vold, George B. (1979). *Theoretical Criminology*. New York: Oxford University Press. In this classic text in criminology, Vold presents a colourful description of Lombroso and the development of the Positive School of criminology.

BIBLIOGRAPHY

Angell, Robert. (1965). *Free Society and Moral Crisis*. Ann Arbor: University of Michigan Press.

Archer, Dane, Rosemary Gartner, and Marc Beittel. (1983). "Homicide and the Death Penalty: A Cross-National Test of a Deterrence Hypothesis." *Journal of Criminal Law and Criminology* 74:991–1014.

Beccaria, Cesare. (1963). *On Crimes and Punishments*. Translated by H. Paolucci. Indianapolis: Bobbs-Merrill. (First published as *Dei Delitti E Delle Pene* in 1764.)

Beirne, Piers. (1993). *Inventing Criminology*. Albany: State University of New York.

Best, Michael. (1998). "What Did Elizabethans Consider a Crime?" Shakespeare's Life and Times Home Page. Internet Shakespeare Editions 2001. web.uvic.ca/shakespeare/Library/SLTnoframes/history/crime.html. Accessed July 14, 2003.

Driver, Edwin D. (1972). "Charles Buckman Goring." In Hermann Mannheim (ed.), *Pioneers in Criminology* (pp. 429–42). Montclair, N.J.: Patterson Smith.

Empey, LaMar T. (1982). *American Delinquency: Its Meaning and Construction*. Homewood, Ill.: The Dorsey Press.

Gibbs, Jack R. (1975). *Crime, Punishment, and Deterrence*. New York: Elsevier.

Goddard, H. H. (1912). *The Kallikak Family: A Study in the Heredity of Feeble-Mindedness*. New York: Macmillan.

———. (1914). *Feeble-Mindedness: Its Causes and Consequences*. New York: Macmillan.

Goring, Charles. (1913). *The English Convict*. London: His Majesty's Stationery Office.

———. (1972). *The English Convict*. Montclair, N.J.: Patterson Smith.

Gould, Stephen Jay. (1981). *The Mismeasure of Man*. New York: W.W. Norton.

Harris, Marvin. (1974). *Cows, Pigs, Wars and Witches*. New York: Vintage Books.

Hobbes, Thomas. (1958). *Leviathan, Parts I and II*. Indianapolis: Bobbs-Merrill. (First published in 1651.)

Hogan, Margaret Monahan. (n.d.). "Medical Ethics: The New Eugenics: Therapy—Enhancement—Screening—Testing." International Catholic University. http://home.comcast.net/~icuweb/c04106.htm.

Hooton, Ernest Albert. (1939). *The American Criminal: An Anthropological Study.* Cambridge, Mass.: Harvard University Press.

Langbein, John H. (1976). *Torture and the Law of Proof.* Chicago: University of Chicago Press.

Lilly, J. Robert, Frances T. Cullen, and Richard A. Ball. (2007). *Criminological Theory: Context and Consequences.* (4th ed.). Thousand Oaks, Calif.: Sage Publications.

Lombroso, Cesare. (1912). *Crime: Its Causes and Remedies.* Boston: Little, Brown and Company.

———. (1972). "Criminal Man." In S. F. Sylvester (ed.), *The Heritage of Modern Criminology* (pp. 67–78). Cambridge, Mass.: Schenkman.

Lombroso-Ferrero, Gina. (1972). *Criminal Man According to the Classification of Cesare Lombroso.* Montclair, N.J.: Patterson Smith.

Mannheim, Hermann (ed.). (1972). *Pioneers in Criminology* (pp. 36–50). (2nd ed.). Montclair, N.J.: Patterson Smith.

Monachesi, Elio. (1972). "Cesare Beccaria." In Hermann Mannheim (ed.), *Pioneers in Criminology.* Montclair, N.J.: Patterson Smith.

Newman, Graeme. (1978). *The Punishment Response.* New York: J.B. Lippincott.

Newman, Graeme, and Pietro Marongiu. (1990). "Penological Reform and the Myth of Beccaria." *Criminology* (May):325–46.

Parmelee, Maurice. (1912). "Introduction to the English Version." In Cesare Lombroso, *Crime: Its Causes and Remedies* (pp. xi–xxxii). Boston: Little, Brown and Company.

Pfohl, Stephen J. (1985). *Images of Deviance and Social Control.* New York: McGraw-Hill.

Phillipson, Coleman. (1970). *Three Criminal Law Reformers.* Montclair, N.J.: Patterson Smith.

Radzinowicz, Sir Leon. (1966). *Ideology and Crime.* London: Heinemann.

Radzinowicz, Sir Leon, and Joan King. (1977). *The Growth of Crime.* London: Pelican Books.

Rafter, Nicole Hahn. (1997). *Creating Born Criminals.* Urbana: University of Illinois Press.

Rosenhaft, Eve. "The Nazi Persecution of Deaf People." Panel Presentation, United States Holocaust Memorial Museum, Tuesday, August 14, 2001. http://www.ushmm.org/research/center/presentations/discussions/details/2001-08-14/details/.

Roshier, Bob. (1989). *Controlling Crime: The Classical Perspective in Criminology.* Philadelphia: Open University Press.

Sylvester, F. Sawyer, Jr. (1972). *The Heritage of Modern Criminology.* Cambridge, Mass.: Schenkman.

Taylor, Ian, Paul Walton, and Jock Young. (1973). *The New Criminology: For a Social Theory of Deviance.* London: Routledge and Kegan Paul.

Thomas, Charles W., and John R. Hepburn. (1983). *Crime, Criminal Law and Criminology.* Dubuque, Iowa: Wm. C. Brown Company Publishers.

Wetzell, Richard. (2000). *Inventing the Criminal: A History of German Criminology: 1880-1945.* Chapel Hill: The University of North Carolina Press.

Wolfgang, Marvin E. (1972). "Cesare Lombroso." In Hermann Mannheim (ed.), *Pioneers in Criminology* (pp. 232–91). Montclair, N.J.: Patterson Smith.

Zilborg, Gregory. (1969). *The Medical Man and the Witch During the Renaissance.* New York: Cooper Square Publishers.

Psychological Perspectives on Criminality

8

Patricia A. Zapf

JOHN JAY COLLEGE OF CRIMINAL JUSTICE

Nathalie C. Gagnon

KWANTLEN UNIVERSITY COLLEGE

David N. Cox

SIMON FRASER UNIVERSITY

Ronald Roesch

SIMON FRASER UNIVERSITY

Many theories have been proposed to explain why people commit criminal acts. This chapter reviews different psychological perspectives on criminality. We begin with a discussion of the characteristics of psychological theories and then review various psychological theories that have been proposed to explain criminality. Next, antisocial personality and psychopathy are described, and the differences between the two are illustrated through the use of three case studies—Charles Manson, Ted Bundy, and Canada's most notorious criminal, Clifford Olson. We conclude with a discussion of crime and mental illness, including a review of research in this area and a discussion of the prevalence of mental illness in jail and prison populations.

Learning Objectives

After reading this chapter, you should be able to

- Describe and critique the different psychological theories that have been used to explain criminal behaviour, including psychoanalytic theory, moral development theory, Eysenck's theory, social learning theory, and operant conditioning theory.
- Understand what is meant by the term "antisocial personality."
- Describe the difference between Antisocial Personality Disorder and psychopathy.
- Describe the most current theories linking crime and mental illness.

Psychological Theories of Crime

assumption of offender deficit
The view that offenders who break the law have some psychological deficit that distinguishes them from normal law-abiding citizens.

assumption of discriminating traits
The view that offenders are distinguished from non-offenders by, for example, their high levels of impulsiveness and aggression.

There has been considerable debate over psychological explanations of criminal behaviour. Psychologists typically approach the problem of understanding, explaining, and predicting criminality by developing theories of personality or learning that account for an individual's behaviour in a specific situation. One extensive review of a decade of published research on offenders (Reppucci and Clingempeel, 1978) found that nearly all the research could be characterized as reflecting one of two value assumptions. The first is the **assumption of offender deficit**, which asserts that theories and interventions are premised on the notion that there is something psychologically wrong with offenders. The second is the **assumption of discriminating traits**, which holds that criminals differ from non-criminals, particularly in such traits as impulsivity and aggression. Research based on this assumption would involve studies of offender and non-offender populations and would utilize a number of personality tests in an attempt to find traits that differentiate the two groups.

Critics have taken issue with psychology's reliance on these two assumptions. Reppucci and Clingempeel (1978) point to two major omissions in psychological research. One is that there is typically very little emphasis placed on studies of the strengths of offenders. Most of the research and interventions focus on the deficits rather than on the positive characteristics of individuals. While this continues to be true today, the field is currently undergoing a transition with recent research and theory increasingly recognizing the importance of offender strengths (Webster et al., 2006). A second omission identified by Reppucci and Clingempeel is that psychological research tends to ignore the potential importance of situational and environmental factors on individual behaviour. Others, such as Reid (2003), have been critical of psychological theories of crime that are founded on the expectation that it is possible to classify individuals as criminals and non-criminals, arguing that this classification cannot be done reliably. Rather, evidence suggests that criminal behaviour is pervasive as indicated by studies of self-reported delinquency, white-collar crime, and corporate crime (Thornberry and Krohn, 2000).

Conversely, the work of David Farrington (1978, 1979, 2002) illustrates the importance of understanding individual differences. Farrington views criminal behaviour as the outcome of several different social and psychological factors (see also Loeber et al., 2001a, 2001b). According to him, the motivation to commit delinquent acts arises primarily out of a desire for material goods or a need for excitement. If these desires cannot be satisfied in a socially approved manner, an illegal act may be chosen. The motivation to commit delinquent acts will be influenced by psychological variables, including the individual's learning history and the beliefs he or she may have internalized regarding criminal behaviour. Eysenck and Gudjonsson (1989) support this position, suggesting that "psychological factors and individual differences related to the personality are of central importance in relation to both the causes of crime and its control." They contend that psychology, with its focus on individual differences, is the central discipline in the study of criminal behaviour and that "no system of criminology has any meaning that disregards this central feature of all criminology: the individual person whom we are trying to influence."

While the individual perspective is clearly the dominant one in psychology, there are other psychological perspectives, such as those of **community psychology** (Roesch, 1988), that are quite closely akin to sociological perspectives. Commonly, such psychologists view social problems from what Rappaport (1977) has termed a "levels of analysis" perspective. Briefly, the four levels are (1) *individual level*, in which social problems are defined in terms of individual deficit; (2) *small-group level*, which suggests that social problems are created by problems in group functioning, essentially problems in interpersonal communication and understanding; (3) *organizational level*, in which the organizations of society have not accomplished what they have been designed to accomplish; and (4) *institutional or community level*, in which it is suggested that social problems are created by institutions rather than by persons, groups, or organizations. At this level the emphasis is on the values and policies underlying institutional functioning.

community psychology
A perspective that analyzes social problems, including crime, as largely a product of organizational and institutional characteristics of society. It is closely related to sociology.

An example that cuts across these four levels would be the way in which "victimless" crimes, such as drug abuse and prostitution, are defined. If the problem is defined at the first level, individuals would be examined to determine what psychological problems they have. Once this has been determined, direct interventions could be employed in changing these individuals so that they might fit into society better and conform to the existing laws. At the small-group level, the influence of peers, such as drug-abusing friends, could be viewed as influencing the individual's behaviour. At the next level, organizations such as law enforcement agencies would be seen as having insufficient resources to prevent or deter individuals from engaging in criminal behaviour. Finally, if this problem is defined at the institutional level, it might be said that the problems that individuals face are caused by the laws their society has created. Therefore, the focus would be on changing the laws so that they do not affect people negatively. If the problem is defined at the institutional level, therapy for an individual would be inappropriate if the cause of the problem was, for example, related to socio-economic factors (Seidman and Rabkin, 1983). Community psychologists tend to define social problems at the organizational and institutional levels and have a theoretical perspective that has much in common with that of sociologists.

These concerns and alternative perspectives should be kept in mind as different psychological theories of criminal behaviour are considered. These theories focus, for the most part, on individual-level variables and explanations. The remainder of this chapter will review psychological theories that can be directly related to understanding criminal behaviour.

Psychoanalytic Theory

Sigmund Freud is the figure most associated with psychoanalytic theory, but he did not make any significant attempts to relate his theory specifically to criminal behaviour. Other psychoanalysts have, however, attempted to explain criminal behaviour with psychoanalytic concepts (Alexander and Healey, 1935; Bowlby, 1953; Friedlander, 1947; Polansky et al., 1950; Redl, 1966).

id

A psychoanalytical term that denotes the most inaccessible and primitive part of the mind. It is a reservoir of biological urges that strive continually for gratification. The ego mediates between the *id* and the *superego*.

ego

A psychoanalytical term that denotes the rational part of the personality. It mediates between the *id* and the *superego* and is responsible for dealing with reality and making decisions.

superego

A psychoanalytical term that denotes the ethical and moral dimensions of personality; an individual's conscience. The *ego* mediates between the *superego* and the *id*.

WWW

"Freud Net" The Abraham A. Brill Library of The New York Psychoanalytic Institute
www.psychoanalysis.org/resources-library.html

socialization

The interactive process whereby individuals come to learn and internalize the culture of their society or group.

A basic premise of psychoanalytic theory is that people progress through five overlapping stages of development. These are the oral, anal, phallic, latency, and genital stages. Freud believed that personality is composed of three forces: the **id** (biological drives); the **ego** (which screens, controls, and directs the impulses of the id and acts as a reality tester); and the **superego** (conscience). Psychoanalytic theory holds that the ego and superego are developed through the successful resolution of conflicts presented at each stage of development. It is believed that both biological and social factors are involved in the resolution of each stage. (See Figure 8.1.)

Psychoanalytic theory presents an elaborate, comprehensive view of the psychological functioning of individuals. It deals with all aspects of human behaviour, but the discussion here will be limited to its impact on the study of criminal behaviour. Briefly, this theory suggests that criminal behaviour occurs when "internal (ego and superego) controls are unable to restrain the primitive, aggressive, antisocial instincts of the id" (Nietzel, 1979). Criminal behaviour is the consequence of an individual's failure to progress through the early stages of development, which leaves the superego inadequately developed or deficient. The individual is left susceptible to antisocial behaviour (Martin et al., 1981).

Warren and Hindelang (1979) have summarized five other interpretations of criminal behaviour that can be derived from psychoanalytic theory:

> (1) criminal behavior is a form of neurosis which does not differ in any fundamental way from other forms of neuroses (e.g., while some neurotics work too hard, others set fires); (2) the criminal often suffers from a compulsive need for punishment in order to alleviate guilt feelings and anxiety stemming from unconscious strivings; (3) criminal activity may be a means of obtaining substitute gratification of needs and desires not met inside the family; (4) delinquent behavior is often due to traumatic events whose memory has been repressed; and (5) delinquent behavior may be an expression of displaced hostility.

Schoenfeld (1971) offered a theory of juvenile delinquency that illustrates psychoanalytic theory. Schoenfeld proposed that delinquent behaviour reflects a weak, defective, or incomplete superego that is unable to control the oral, anal, and phallic impulses that are resurrected at puberty. Schoenfeld believes that parental deprivation and lack of affection, especially during the first few years of a child's life, is the cause of a weak superego. Boys raised in a fatherless home, he adds, will be especially prone to deviant behaviour as they attempt to establish their male identity.

A number of studies support the view that family life is important in the process of **socialization**. Bowlby (1953) stressed that a stable attachment to a mother in the first few years of life allows the child to show affection toward others and to care for them. If this attachment does not occur, the child will be unable to show affection and, thus, may damage others without remorse through various forms of victimization.

One of the difficulties in assessing psychoanalytic theory is that many aspects of it are untestable because they rely on unobservable underlying constructs. As Ewen (1988, p. 55) has observed, "Psychoanalytic theory pre-

FIGURE 8.1 **Freud's Theory of Personality**

This illustration shows how Freud might picture a person's internal conflict over whether to commit an antisocial act such as stealing a candy bar. In addition to dividing personality into three components, Freud theorized that our personalities are largely unconscious—hidden away outside our normal awareness. To dramatize this point, Freud compared conscious awareness (portions of the ego and superego) to the visible tip of an iceberg. Most of our personality—including all of the id, with its raw desires and impulses—lies submerged in our subconscious.

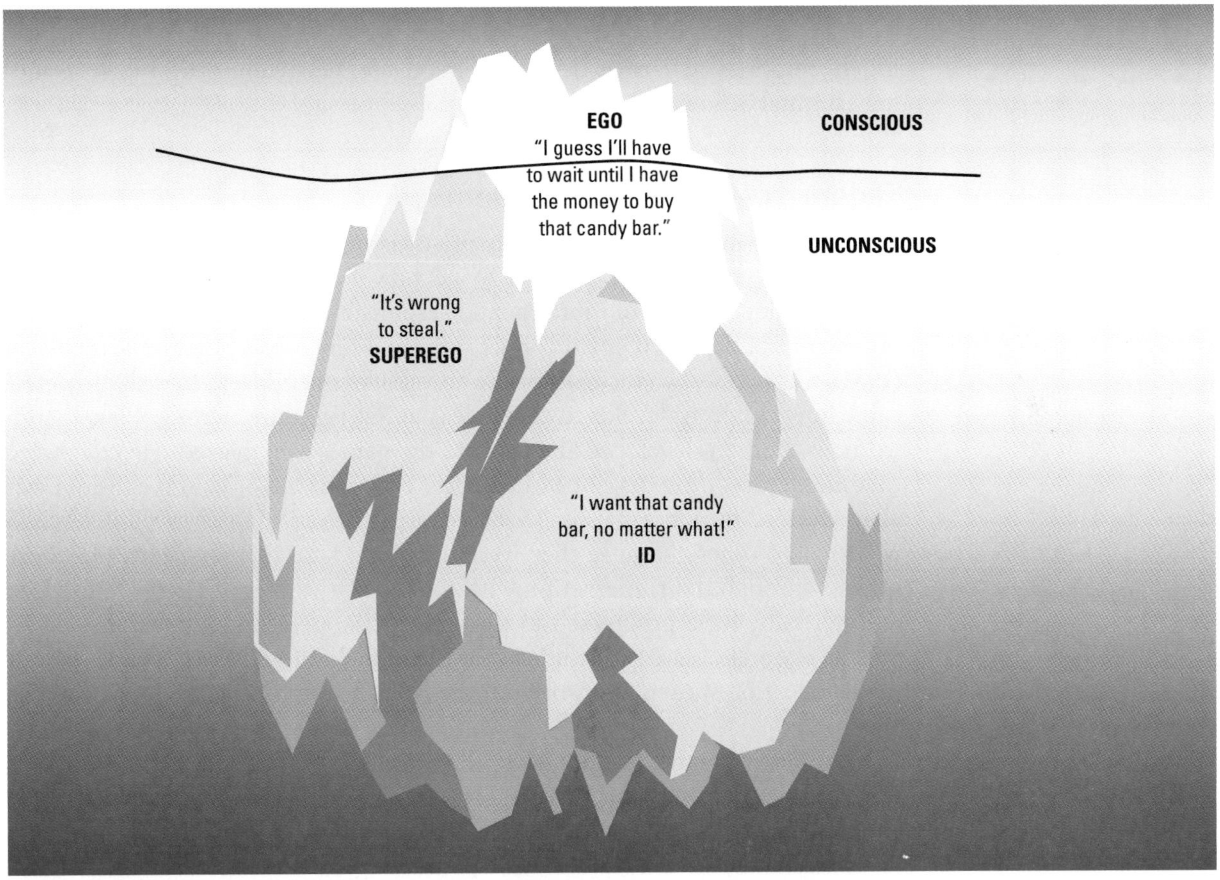

Source: Diana Kendall, Rick Linden, and Jane Lothian Murray. (1998). *Sociology in Our Times: The Essentials* (with InfoTrac), 2nd ed., p. 81. Reprinted with permission of Wadsworth, a division of Thomson Learning. www. thomsonrights.com. Fax 800-730-2215.

sents a formidable difficulty: the most important part of the personality, the unconscious, is also the most inaccessible." It is therefore the psychoanalyst who interprets the offender's behaviours and actions. Any attempt by the offender to refute the interpretation is seen as resistance and further evidence of its truth.

As Cohen (1966) points out, "Aggressive or acquisitive acts are often explained by underlying aggressive or acquisitive impulses." This explanation is a tautology in that aggressive acts are explained by aggressive impulses, but the only evidence of the aggressive impulses is the occurrence of aggressive acts. Many have suggested that psychoanalytic theory is empirically unverifiable, a necessary criteria for any scientific theory.

Another criticism of psychoanalytic theory is that studies have failed to demonstrate that criminals desire to be punished or suffer from guilt or anxiety, as one psychoanalyst (Abrahamsen, 1944) suggested. In fact, as Nietzel (1979) asserts, "criminals are very successful in their efforts to prevent detection or if detected, elude official prosecution and conviction. Most offenders do not appear unduly frustrated or further guilt-ridden by the fact that their 'crime pays' at least some of the time." Despite these problems, psychoanalytic theory is regarded by some as a useful conceptual framework for understanding the importance of early development on later behaviour of all types, including criminal behaviour.

Theories of Moral Development

According to moral development theorists, if we wish to understand criminal and delinquent behaviour, we need to ask how it is that individuals develop, or fail to develop, a sense of morality and responsibility. One of the first contemporary moral development theorists was the French psychologist Jean Piaget (1932), whose research focused on the moral lives of children. In order to determine how children developed their ideas about right and wrong, Piaget studied how children developed the rules to the games they played. He concluded that moral reasoning developed in stages. The thinking of young children was characterized by egocentrism. That is, they projected their own thoughts and wishes onto others because they were unable to take the perspective of those others. Through their interaction with others, by the ages of 11 or 12, children will normally have progressed to the stage of cooperation with others. Based on this research, Piaget concluded that the schools should teach moral reasoning by allowing students to work out the rules through problem solving in the classroom.

Kohlberg, expanding on Piaget's theory, has hypothesized that there are six stages of moral development (see Table 8.1). The stages are age related, and progression through the stages occurs as "the developing child becomes better able to understand and integrate diverse points of view on a moral-conflict situation and to take more of the relevant situational factors into account" (Jennings et al., 1983). Kohlberg believes that all individuals go through the same sequence of stages, although the pace may vary and some individuals may never progress beyond the first few stages.

Kohlberg categorizes the six stages into three levels of moral judgment development, each with two stages of moral reasoning.

The first is the *preconventional* level, characteristic of children under age 11 and of many adolescent and adult offenders. At this level, the morals and values of society are understood as "do's" and "don'ts" and are associated with punishment. The preconventional person is one for whom roles and social expectations are something external to the self.

The *conventional* level reflects the average adolescent and adult in our society and others. He or she understands, accepts, and attempts to uphold the values and rules of society. For a conventional person, the self is identified with or has internalized the rules and expectations of others, especially those of authorities.

TABLE 8.1 Kohlberg's Theory of Moral Development

Level	*Stage*	*Description*	
I.	Preconventional	1. Punishment 2. Instrumental hedonism	Egocentric (What happens to me?)
II.	Conventional	3. Approval of others 4. Authority maintaining morality	Social expectations (What do others expect of me?)
III.	Postconventional	5. Democratically accepted law 6. Principles of conscience	Universality (What is best for all?)

Source: D. A. Andrews and James Bonta. (1994). *The Psychology of Criminal Conduct.* Cincinnati: Anderson Publishing.

The *postconventional* level is the one at which customs are critically examined with regard to universal rights, duties, and moral principles. It is characteristic of a minority of adults after the age of 20. The postconventional person has differentiated his or her self from the rules and expectations of others and defined his or her value by means of self-chosen principles (Jennings et al., 1983).

Carol Gilligan (1982) has criticized Kohlberg's theory of moral development, stating that it is biased in favour of males. Gilligan argues that there is variation in moral standards by gender, with females taking a more care-oriented approach to morality, while males typically use a more justice-oriented approach. She believes that Kohlberg's theory does not take into consideration the more care-oriented approach of females, and that as a result females rarely obtain the higher stages of moral development in Kohlberg's theory. To support her argument, she points out that females were not taken into consideration when Kohlberg was developing his theory, as the development of moral judgment was based on an empirical study of 84 males whom Kohlberg followed for a 20-year period. Gilligan states that females typically reach only the second level (third stage) in Kohlberg's theory, which is characterized by goodness being equated with helping and pleasing others and is consistent with the care-oriented approach of females to morality. She argues that Kohlberg and Kramer (1969) have looked at this concept of goodness and concluded that this level of moral reasoning would be adequate for women whose lives will take place in the home. They indicate that only when women enter the "traditional arena of male activity" do they realize that this level of moral reasoning is not sufficient, and therefore go on to progress toward the higher stages as men do. Gilligan points out that "herein lies a paradox, for the very traits that traditionally have defined the 'goodness' of women, their care for and sensitivity to the needs of others, are those that mark them as deficient in moral development" (1982, 18).

Considerable research has been done on the relationship between moral development and delinquency. Kohlberg believes that people with high moral development are more likely to make individual choices and be less influenced by friends or by consequences of actions. Thus there should be an inverse relationship between moral development and delinquency. Jennings et al. (1983) reviewed a large number of studies on this relationship and concluded that "the overwhelming weight of the empirical data reviewed here supports the notion that juvenile delinquents' moral judgement is at a less advanced level than that of non-delinquent controls matched on a variety of variables." But they are careful to point out that a cause–effect relationship has not been established. Individuals at the same level of moral development may or may not become delinquent. They add that

> these studies lend support to the more modest claims that moral reasoning of increased maturity has an insulating effect against delinquency. Advanced stages of moral judgment cause one's moral orientation to be more integrated, stable and consistent. Higher reasoning makes one a more reliable moral agent and thus better able to withstand some incentives to illegal conduct postulated by a variety of sociological and psychological theories of the etiology of delinquency.

moral development theory
Refers generally to theories of individual psychology that investigate how moral reasoning emerges in the individual and develops as the individual matures.

This last statement suggests that **moral development theory** has considerable relevance for a sociological explanation of criminal behaviour. Indeed, Morash (1983) has discussed at length the possible integration of moral development and sociological theories, suggesting that it may be more fruitful to study the interaction of personal and situational variables. She concludes:

> Most serious delinquency would result from social conditions, primarily those that are enduring, that impinge on youths who possess the personality factors and the pre-conventional reasoning conducive to serious delinquent behavior. An advantage of this explanation is that it allows for the many pre-conventional individuals who do not break the law regularly or not at all, and it accounts for different patterns in delinquency—that is, the repeated serious delinquency and sporadic and/or less serious delinquency.

More recent research has supported the link between moral development and crime. In a study examining the moral development of 72 adult male sex offenders participating in a community-based treatment, Buttell (2002) found that sex offenders employed a level of moral reasoning that was two standard deviations lower than the national norm. In addition, theories of moral development have important implications for offender rehabilitation programs (Blasi, 1980). Evidence suggests that education programs that focus on moral development have positive effects on inmates' moral judgments (MacPhail, 1989). However, future research will need to examine whether this increased morality leads to lower rates of criminal behaviour and recidivism.

In conclusion, there is evidence to suggest that level of moral reasoning is related to behaviour (see also Hogan, 1973). However, the correlations reported in many studies are often quite low. Moral development may affect how an individual behaves in a given context, but it is clear that other characteristics of the individual, as well as the situation, will also be important determinants of behaviour.

Eysenck's Theory of Crime and Personality

Hans Eysenck, a noted British psychologist, has developed an elaborate theory of how personality characteristics are related to criminal behaviour (Eysenck, 1977). This theory has generated considerable research, in large part because it lends itself quite readily to the identification of groups of offenders and to predictions about their behaviour.

WWW

"Hans Eysenck and Other Temperament Theorists"
C. George Boeree, Shippensburg University of Pennsylvania
www.ship.edu/~cgboeree/eysenck.html

Eysenck believes that illegal, selfish, or immoral behaviour is simple to explain. These behaviours are inherently reinforcing and, hence, it is more fruitful to try to explain why people do *not* commit crimes. Eysenck claims that children will naturally engage in such acts and only refrain from doing so if they are punished. Eysenck's theory is based on **classical conditioning**. Each time a child is punished, he or she may experience pain and fear. This pain and fear may be associated with the act itself. Thus whenever the child contemplates the act, he or she will experience fear, which will tend to inhibit the response. Eysenck equates this conditioned fear with conscience. Delinquents and criminals do not readily develop this conditioned response, either because of lack of exposure to effective conditioning practices by parents and others, or because they are less susceptible to conditioning. Eysenck (1990) states:

classical conditioning
A basic form of learning whereby a neutral stimulus is paired with another stimulus that naturally elicits a certain response; the neutral stimulus comes to elicit the same response as the stimulus that automatically elicits the response.

> Depending on the frequency of pairings between the conditioned and unconditioned stimulus in the field of social behavior, and on the precise content of the conditioning program, children will grow up to develop appropriate types of behavior. Conditionability is a crucial factor on the social or environmental side. In a permissive society where parents, teachers, and magistrates do not take seriously the task of imposing a "conscience" which would lead them to behave in a socialized manner, a large number of individuals with poor or average conditionability will acquire a "conscience" too weak to prevent them from indulging in criminal activities, although had they been subjected to a stricter regime of conditioning, they might have grown up to be perfectly respectable and law-abiding citizens.

As Eysenck points out, the concept of "strictness" is not a function of excessive strength of the conditioning process, but a result of the certainty and frequency of pairings of the conditioned and unconditioned stimulus.

There are three dimensions of personality, according to Eysenck. **Extraversion** is a personality characteristic with highly sociable, impulsive, and aggressive people at one extreme of the continuum. Highly introverted, introspective, and inhibited people are the other extreme. *Neuroticism* is linked to the psychiatric concept of neurosis. People who are high on this dimension are characterized by such symptoms as anxiety, restlessness, and other emotional responses. The opposite extreme of neuroticism is referred to as stability. The third dimension, *psychoticism*, is a recent addition. According to Eysenck and Eysenck (1976), a person who is high on this dimension is "cold, impersonal, hostile, lacking in sympathy, unfriendly, untrustful, odd, unemotional, unhelpful, antisocial, lacking in human feelings, inhumane, generally bloodyminded, lacking in insight, strange, with paranoid ideas that people are against him."

extraversion
A personality characteristic associated with sociability, impulsiveness, and aggression.

A number of hypotheses have been generated about the relationship of these dimensions to criminal behaviour. Extraverts, because of their high need for excitement, their impulsivity, and relatively weak conscience, are believed to be more prone to criminal behaviour. In addition, persons high on both neuroticism and extraversion would be predicted to be delinquents or criminals. Persons high on psychoticism would tend to be more serious offenders, with a propensity for violence. Hare (1982) investigated the relationship between these three dimensions and psychopathy. While neuroticism and extraversion did not correlate with measures of psychopathy, psychoticism did. It is concluded that this may be because each taps a common element of psychopathy (criminal and antisocial tendencies) rather than those psychological features that are assumed in the diagnosis of psychopathy (for example, lack of remorse, lack of empathy).

Eysenck and others have developed psychological measures of each of these dimensions. Research in testing predictions about offenders has produced mixed results. In their extensive and excellent review of Eysenck's theory, Farrington et al. (1982) summarized data from 16 studies, most of which were conducted in Great Britain, and found that while some studies support the predictions of Eysenck's theory, other studies do not. Bartol (1980) comes to a similar conclusion.

Like other theories, personality theories such as Eysenck's have problems with tautology or circular reasoning. That is, in many measures of personality, the sub-scale that differentiates delinquents from non-delinquents includes items asking about antisocial behavior (e.g., have you been in trouble with the law)—the very thing it proposes to explain. In addition, some have criticized personality theories for failing to adequately define its terms (Einstadter & Henry, 1995).

Eysenck's theory is important because it shows how psychological and social variables can be interrelated. Individuals who may have a psychological propensity to commit crime may be effectively socialized if they grow up in an environment that provides effective conditioning. Similarly, individuals with a low propensity for criminality may become criminal if their environment is too permissive. Although Eysenck argues strongly for the importance of individual differences, he recognizes the importance of societal influences: "Crime . . . is essentially a function of the ethos of the society in which we live; it reflects the practices of positive and negative reinforcement, of reward and punishment, of teaching and conditioning, which are prevalent, and these in turn are mirrored and reflected by the types of films we see, television programs we watch, books and newspapers we read, and teaching and examples we receive at school." In the next section, it will be seen that social learning theory reflects this perspective more explicitly.

Social Learning Theory

Another theory that lends itself to an integration of sociology and psychology is social learning theory. Although this theory focuses on individual behaviour, it takes into account the influence of the environment and of social conditions on the individual. Cognitive functioning, the ability to think and make choices, is central to social learning theory.

modelling
A form of learning that occurs as a result of watching and imitating others.

An important element of social learning theory is the role of **modelling**. Individuals can learn new behaviours through direct experience or by observing the behaviour of others. The latter, also referred to as vicarious learning, can be a most effective and efficient way to acquire new behaviours. Albert Bandura, a Stanford University professor of psychology, is a leading social learning theorist. He suggests that "virtually all learning phenomena resulting from direct experiences can occur on a vicarious basis through observation of other persons' behavior and its consequences for them" (Bandura, 1979).

Social learning theory has been used to explain how aggression is learned. Since this is of great concern to criminology theory, aggression will be used as an example of an application of social learning theory.

Bandura (1979) suggests that aggressive behaviour can be learned from three sources. The *family* is one source, with a number of studies showing that children of parents who respond aggressively to problems will tend to use similar tactics. Bandura also points to research on child abuse, which shows that many children who have been abused will later become abusers themselves. Another source of aggressive behaviour can be referred to as *subcultural influences*, or the influence of social models and peers. Bandura suggests that "the highest incidence of aggression is found in communities in which aggressive models abound and fighting prowess is regarded as a valued attribute." The third source of learned aggressive behaviour is through *symbolic modelling*. An example of this is violence on television, which provides models of aggressive behaviour (Skoler et al., 1994).

WWW

"Albert Bandura (1925–present)" C. George Boeree, Shippensburg University of Pennsylvania
www.ship.edu/~cgboeree/bandura.html

Bandura's research on the role of film models reinforced existing concerns about the effects of television on aggressive behaviour. Geen (1983) reviewed the research on the relationship between viewing television violence and aggression. He first looked at the vast number of correlational studies, the majority of which support the conclusion that there is a positive relationship between viewing violence and aggressive behaviour. A typical study is the one by Teevan and Hartnagel (1976), which showed that high school students who described their favourite television shows as violent also reported committing more aggressive acts than students whose favourite shows were non-violent.

The problem with correlational research, as Geen points out, is that the direction of causation is unknown. It is possible that people who are more likely to behave aggressively simply prefer more violent television shows. Thus it cannot be concluded through correlational studies alone that viewing violence is the cause of aggressive behaviour. Cook et al. (1983) re-analyzed data from several large-scale studies of the effects of television violence. They concluded that an association between television viewing and aggression by children can be found regularly, but the level of association is typically quite small and often not statistically significant. Nevertheless, they conclude that the association is most probably a causal one, that watching violence on television does have an effect on children's aggressive behaviour. The same can be said for violence in music videos (Smith and Boyson, 2002).

WWW

"Television Violence: A Review of the Effects on Children of Different Ages" Child and Family Canada
www.cfc-efc.ca/docs/mnet/00001068.htm

In addition to its direct effect on aggressive behaviour, it is also possible that exposure to television violence increases one's tolerance toward violence and decreases one's sensitivity to acts of violence. Thomas et al. (1979) found that both adult and child subjects showed less **autonomic reactivity** to a scene of real-life interpersonal aggression if they had first watched a violent scene from a television show. Malamuth and Check (1981) reported similar results

autonomic reactivity
A measurement of the extent to which an individual's physical organism reacts to external stimuli.

in their study of the effects of film violence on attitudes toward violence. Male and female university students were randomly assigned to view either a violent-sexual or a control feature-length film. The films were shown as part of the regular campus film program, and subjects believed they were viewing the films as a film-rating task. Several days later, they were asked to respond to a number of attitude measures, but were unaware of any relationship between the film and the questionnaire. Malamuth and Check found that exposure to the film portraying violent sexuality was associated with a greater acceptance of interpersonal violence against women. This finding was true only for male subjects. Female subjects had a nonsignificant tendency in the opposite direction, as women exposed to violence tended to be less accepting of interpersonal violence than control females. It is important to realize, however, that this study does not provide any data on whether males exposed to violence would actually behave differently toward women. But the study does demonstrate that such exposure may have a significant effect on attitudes.

In his analysis of antisocial behaviour, Bandura (1986) suggests that the best deterrent to such activity is the provision of more attractive pro-social alternatives. However, he acknowledges that "when inducements to criminal acts are strong, when personal sanctions against such conduct are weak, and when people lack socially acceptable means of getting what they want, fear of punishment serves as a major deterrent to transgressive conduct." Deterrence may take two forms—direct or vicarious. In the former, punishment is used to discourage current transgressors of such activity in the future. In the latter, punishment serves as a general deterrent to others. Bandura identifies three major sources of deterrence against criminal activity: legal sanction, social sanction, and self-sanction. Legal sanctions derive from the belief that there are legal consequences to transgressions despite the reality that most crime goes unpunished. Bandura cites research by Clastner (1967) in stating that "people who are not in the habit of breaking the law share a distorted perception of legal threats, in which they greatly overestimate the risks of getting caught and punished for unlawful acts. In contrast, offenders judge personal risks to be lower and more in line with the actual probabilities." Social sanctions reflect the negative social consequences that criminal stigmatization can have for an individual and the powerful deterrent effect this risk has. Self-sanctions are self-imposed moral standards; they are seen as the most effective deterrent as they are operative even when there is no risk of detection involved. Bandura (1986) states, "In the absence of self-sanctions rooted in societal standards, whenever personal desires conflict with societal codes, external threats in the form of legal and social sanctions, and extensive social surveillance are needed to insure that the rights and welfare of others are not completely disregarded."

The empirical status of social learning theory has recently been summarized by Akers and Jensen (2006):

> Indeed, it is reasonable to propose that the theory has been tested in relation to a wider range of forms of deviance, in a wider range of settings and samples, in more different languages, and by more different people, has survived more "crucial tests" against other theories, and is the most strongly and consistently supported by empirical data than any other social psychological explanation of crime and deviance.

Operant Conditioning

Another learning theory is based on the principle of **operant conditioning**. This involves the use of rewards and punishments to increase the probability or frequency of a given response. B. F. Skinner is the psychologist most identified with this theory, and his research forms the basis for both the theoretical and the applied applications of operant conditioning.

operant conditioning
The basic process by which an individual's behaviour is shaped by reinforcement or by punishment.

One way a response can be learned is through a process referred to as shaping. This involves rewarding approximations of some target behaviour until the behaviour gradually progresses to the desired response. Behaviour can also be learned through punishment, which can be either a withdrawal of a positive reinforcer or the introduction of a negative stimulus such as an electric shock. There have been a number of attempts to use operant conditioning theory to account for the acquisition of criminal behaviour. Notable among this work is that of Jeffery (1965) and that of Burgess and Akers (1966).

Burgess and Akers (1966) and Akers (1990) conceptualize criminal behaviour in terms of operant conditioning and imitation. The main component in Akers's (1990) social learning theory is differential reinforcement. This refers to the balance of rewards and punishments that govern behaviour. In this theory, operant conditioning is the basic process by which an individual's behaviour is shaped, and this can occur through both reinforcement and punishment. Reinforcement refers to any process that strengthens a behaviour, while punishment is any process that weakens a behaviour. As applied to deviance and crime, Akers (1990) states that

WWW
"Operant (Instrumental) Conditioning" Bill Huitt, Valdosta State University
http://chiron.valdosta.edu/whuitt/col/behsys/operant.html

> social learning is a behavioral approach to socialization which includes individuals' responses to rewards and punishments in the current situation, the learned patterns of responses they bring to that situation, and the anticipated consequences of actions taken now and in the future in the initiation, continuation, and cessation of those actions. It is a "soft behaviorism" that allows for choice and cognitive processes. It views the individual's behavior as responding to and being conditioned by environmental feedback and consequences. It does not view the individual as unreasoning and only passively conditioned.

Considerable research has been conducted on the application of learning theory to the treatment of delinquents. The "teaching-family" group-home model begun in the late 1960s has been at the centre of group-home development. The approach

> rests on the view that an adolescent's behavior patterns, behavior discriminations, and skills are functions of past behavior-environment interactions (learning history), currently ongoing behavior-environment interactions, and genetic organismic variables (Braukman et al., 1980). In this conceptualization, inherited characteristics and environmental features in childhood, particularly parenting practices (relationship development, teaching, supervision, and discipline) affect later development. In adolescence, earlier developed antisocial patterns tend to persevere (indeed, are self-perpetuating) and can be maintained further by ongoing behavior-environment interactions associated with

> inappropriate parenting, deviant peers, and school failure. (Braukman and Wolf, 1987)

The group home provides the reinforcing environment designed to change existing behavioural interactions in the direction of functional and pro-social skills. The emphasis is on learning social and family life skills. The best known of these programs is Achievement Place, a program first implemented in a cottage-style treatment facility for delinquent youths in Lawrence, Kansas. (The name of the treatment facility was Achievement Place, hence the name of the program.) Youths in Achievement Place programs live in a residence with trained "house-parents." The heart of the program is a **token economy** system in which points can be earned (or lost). For example, residents can earn points for being at class on time, cleaning their bedroom, and engaging in other positive behaviours. Disruptive behaviour in the classroom, making aggressive statements or fighting, and being late for class can result in a loss of points. The points can be used to purchase privileges and material goods. Research on Achievement Place has demonstrated that "contingent token consequences could both establish behaviors basic to participation in lawful, productive intra- and extra-treatment activities, and eliminate behaviors likely to get the participants in further trouble" (Braukman and Wolf, 1987). A comprehensive outcome study on the teaching-family program (Braukman et al., 1985) indicates that this approach has considerable short-term positive effects. However, the long-term implications are less positive since it is very difficult to control reinforcement following release from the institution. Because of this, increased emphasis has been placed on systematic aftercare to help maintain treatment effects.

token economy
A behaviour therapy procedure based on operant learning principles. Individuals are rewarded (reinforced) for positive or appropriate behaviour and are disciplined (punished) for negative or inappropriate behaviour.

Antisocial Personality

The study of antisocial personality provides a good example of how psychological theory can be applied to criminal populations. Some confusion has resulted from the variety of terms used to describe basically the same set of behaviours: sociopathy, psychopathy, moral insanity, antisocial personality, and **Antisocial Personality Disorder**. There has also been a tendency for some to use the term very loosely as a "wastebasket" category for antisocial individuals generally. There is, however, strong empirical evidence that the traits underlying this disorder form a valid and clinically meaningful cluster (Hare and Cox, 1978; Skilling et al., 2002). For many, this term is associated with images of violent and sadistic murderers as portrayed countless times on television or, all too often, demonstrated in real life. The brutal murders committed by Ted Bundy (see Box 8.1), Clifford Olson (see Box 8.3), and Charles Manson and his followers in California are frequently cited examples of psychopathy. Indeed, while there is some debate over the most appropriate diagnosis for Manson, many would argue that his behaviour best fits the clinical picture of psychopathy. As Nathan and Harris (1975) point out:

Antisocial Personality Disorder
A personality disorder that involves disregard for the rights of others, as well as impulsive, irresponsible, and aggressive behaviour.

> Charles Manson acted upon society in an unbelievable variety of antisocial ways. At one time or another he robbed, deceived, assaulted, exploited, seduced—and murdered. But despite the extraordinary

range of antisocial acts for which he had been responsible, perhaps his most surprising characteristic was that at no time did he show guilt or remorse about anything he had done. During his trial for the Tate murders, he said, "I've considered innocence and guilt and I know the difference between them and I have no guilt" (quoted from the *New York Times*, Dec. 25, 1969). A man who could be charming and captivating, brutal and ruthless, Manson could not be guilty, at least in his own eyes. What kind of human being feels no remorse over murder?

FOCUS

BOX 8.1 Ted Bundy—Why?

Born in 1946, Theodore Robert Bundy seemed destined for a charmed life; he was intelligent, attractive, and articulate (Holmes and DeBurger, 1988). A Boy Scout as a youth and then an honour student and a psychology major at the University of Washington, he was at one time a work-study student at the Seattle Crisis Clinic. Later he became assistant to the chairman of the Washington State Republican Party. It is likely that about this time he claimed his first victim; a college-age woman was viciously attacked while sleeping, left alive but brain-damaged. During the years from 1974 through 1978, Bundy stalked, attacked, killed, and then sexually assaulted as many as 36 victims in Washington, Oregon, Utah, Colorado, and Florida. Apparently some of the women were distracted when the good-looking casual Bundy approached, seeming helpless because of being on crutches or with an apparent broken arm. He usually choked them to death and then sexually abused and mutilated them before disposing of their bodies in remote areas (Nordheimer, 1989).

It is characteristic of the psychopathic personality or sociopath to maintain a facade of charm, so that acquaintances will describe him (as they did Bundy) as "fascinating," "charismatic," and "compassionate." At his trial for the murder of two Chi Omega sorority sisters in their bedrooms at Florida State University, he served as his own attorney (Bundy had attended two law schools). But he was convicted; he was also found guilty of the kidnapping, murder, and mutilation of a Lake City, Florida, girl who was 12 years old.

Bundy was sentenced to death. Shortly before he was executed on January 24, 1989, Bundy gave a television interview to California evangelist James Dobson in which he attributed the cause of his problems to pornography. He said: "Those of us who are . . . so much influenced by violence in the media, in particular pornographic violence, are not some kind of inherent monsters. We are your husbands, and we grew up in regular families" (quoted by Lamar, 1989, p. 34). Bundy claimed that he spent his formative ages with a grandfather who had an insatiable craving for pornography.

He told Dr. Dobson, "People will accuse me of being self-serving but I am just telling you how I feel. Through God's help, I have been able to come to the point where I much too late, but better late than never, feel the hurt and the pain that I am responsible for" (quoted by Kleinberg, 1989, p. 5A).

The tape of Bundy's last interview, produced by Dobson and titled "Fatal Addiction," has been widely disseminated, especially by those who seek to eliminate all pornography. (Dr. Dobson served on a federal pornography commission during the Reagan administration.) But Bundy's claim that pornography was the "fuel for his fantasies" has been received skeptically by others, who saw it as one last manipulative ploy to gain further time. Even his mother stated that no evidence existed in her son's first 28 years (before he became a murder suspect for the first time) that hinted at any aberrant behaviour (Nordheimer, 1989). In none of his previous interviews, including

(*Continued*)

FOCUS

BOX 8.1 Ted Bundy—Why? *(Continued)*

extensive conversations in 1986 with Dorothy Lewis, a psychiatrist he had come to trust, did he ever cite "a pornographic preamble to his grotesqueries" (Nobile, 1989, p. 41). Bundy had decided at that time that he needed psychiatric testimony in order to escape the electric chair—that is, by being diagnosed as not competent to stand trial because he was supposedly too confused and irrational to assist in his own murder defense. Despite Dr. Lewis's testimony in 1986, the judge would not declare Bundy incompetent. Thus perhaps at that time he decided to portray himself as a normal youth who had been corrupted by pornography (Nobile, 1989).

According to psychiatrist Park Dietz, most serial sexual killers have two distinct qualities: sexual sadism and psychopathy, or the lack of normal inhibitions about acting on that desire (quoted by Nobile, 1989). This classification seems a succinct summary of Ted Bundy.

Source: Adapted from L. S. Wrightsman, M. T. Nietzel, and W. H. Fortune. (1991). *Psychology and the Legal System*, 2nd ed. Copyright © 1991. Reprinted with permission of Wadsworth Publishing, a division of Thomson Learning: www.thomsonrights.com. Fax 800-730-2215.

Why would a person keep committing crimes despite repeated punishment? How can a man charm so many people and yet never relate with genuine feeling to anyone?

These questions are difficult to answer because the crimes Manson, Olson, and Bundy committed seem so senseless to society. However disturbing they may be, it is possible for most people to understand murders motivated by greed or passion, but the murder of Sharon Tate and others by Manson cannot be explained by either of these motivations.

Similarly, it is difficult to understand the motivations of "Canada's Ken and Barbie Killers"—Paul Bernardo and Karla Homolka—who were responsible for the grotesque rape and murder of three young women, including Karla Homolka's own sister. Although the prevalence of female psychopaths is lower than that of males, we are especially intrigued by these women. In recent parole board reports, Karla Homolka has been deemed a psychopath (see Box 8.2), though the motivation for her actions remains unclear.

This section began with a discussion of Charles Manson because it is this image that best fits the common conception of persons with an antisocial personality. It is a misleading picture, however, because many individuals with diagnoses of antisocial personality do not have a history of violence and, even among those who do, very few would exhibit the extreme forms that Manson did. The term *sociopath* was later used instead of the term *psychopath* to convey this less violent picture. More recently, the use of the term *Antisocial Personality Disorder* has become common.

The current edition of the American Psychiatric Association's *Diagnostic and Statistical Manual of Mental Disorder* (DSM-IV-TR) defines Antisocial Personality Disorder in the following manner:

> The essential feature of Antisocial Personality Disorder is a pervasive pattern of disregard for, and violation of, the rights of others that begins in childhood or early adolescence and continues into adulthood.

Lying, stealing, fighting, truancy, and resisting authority are typical early childhood signs. In adolescence, unusually early or aggressive sexual behaviour, excessive drinking, and use of illicit drugs are frequent. In adulthood, those kinds of behaviour continue, with the addition of inability to sustain consistent work performance or to function as a responsible parent and failure to accept social norms with respect to lawful behaviour. After age 30, the more flagrant aspects may diminish, particularly sexual promiscuity, fighting, criminality, and vagrancy. It is estimated that between 15 and 30 percent of the inmate population in Canadian prisons could be considered psychopathic (Ogloff et al., 1990).

In his book *The Mask of Sanity*, Cleckley (1976) provided a clinical description of the antisocial personality and described the psychopath using the following criteria: unreliability; insincerity; pathological lying and deception; egocentricity; poor judgment; impulsivity; a lack of remorse, guilt, or shame; an inability to experience empathy or concern for others and to maintain warm, affectionate attachments; an impersonal and poorly integrated sex life; and an unstable life plan with no long-term commitments.

Since the 1960s, Hare and his colleagues have devoted considerable attention to the development of a reliable and valid procedure for the assessment of psychopathy. This program has culminated in the Revised Psychopathy Checklist (PCL-R) (Hare, 1991), a 20-item checklist of traits and behaviours associated with psychopathy (see Table 8.2). Research has continued to support

TABLE 8.2 **The 20 Items of the Psychopathy Checklist**

1. Glibness/superficial charm[p]	11. Promiscuous sexual behaviour
2. Grandiose sense of self-worth[p]	12. Early behavioural problems[ab]
3. Need for stimulation/proneness to boredom[ab]	13. Lack of realistic, long-term goals[ab]
4. Pathological lying[p]	14. Impulsivity[ab]
5. Conning/manipulative[p]	15. Irresponsibility[ab]
6. Lack of remorse or guilt[p]	16. Failure to accept responsibility for own actions[ab]
7. Shallow affect[p]	17. Many short-term marital relationships
8. Callous/lack of empathy[p]	18. Juvenile delinquency[ab]
9. Parasitic lifestyle[ab]	19. Revocation of conditional release[ab]
10. Poor behavioural controls[ab]	20. Criminal versatility

The checklist is composed of two factors: [p] identifies the items that define personality traits, and [ab] identifies items descriptive of antisocial behaviour.

Source: R.D. Hare. (1991). "The Hare Psychopathy Checklist—Revised." Multi-Health Systems, Inc. Adapted from R.D. Hare. (1980). "A Research Scale for the Assessment of Psychopathy in Criminal Populations." *Personality and Individual Differences* 1:111–19. Oxford: Pergamon Press. © 1990 R.D. Hare. Reprinted with permission from Elsevier Science Ltd.

FOCUS

BOX 8.2 Psychologists Suggest Bernardo and Homolka Are Psychopaths

TORONTO—Prosecutors painted a picture of a battered woman and a controlling, abusive husband who forced her to take part in unspeakable crimes. But some experts suspect that both Karla Homolka and Paul Bernardo are psychopaths—people who aren't mentally ill but lack any conscience and single-mindedly pursue their own pleasure.

In Bernardo, they suggest, psychopathic qualities combined with sexual sadism to form an explosive mix. Some psychologists who have followed the Bernardo trial say the crimes Homolka and Bernardo admitted to committing, and their almost total lack of emotion in the witness box, suggest psychopathic tendencies.

"What bothers me about him, and her, too, is the casual way these horrific things are described on the witness stand," said psychologist Robert Hare of the University of British Columbia, one of the world's leading experts on psychopaths.

"When a psychopath commits a violent act, they're not doing it because they're malicious or malevolent or evil. They're doing it because they don't give a damn."

Bernardo was "such a good psychopath" that he found a woman who had a penchant for submissive sex that complemented his urge to dominate, said psychologist Marnie Rice of Ontario's Penetanguishene Mental Health Centre. Homolka may not have got into trouble with another man. But hooked up with Bernardo, it's possible she agreed to take part in three-way sex with kidnapped teenage girls as part of a willingly subservient role, said Rice, whose hospital houses some of the province's most dangerous offenders.

"It appears the two found each other."

Homolka testified Bernardo beat her into submission and blackmailed her over her role in the death of her sister, who was drugged and raped by the couple. Two psychologists called by the Crown suggested Homolka suffered from battered women's syndrome. Rendered helpless and hopeless by repeated beatings, someone in her shoes could feel obliged to take part in the most heinous crimes, they said. Hare is skeptical.

"We look for very simple explanations for complex behavior," he said. "To me, battered women's syndrome does not explain what she did."

Even a psychiatrist retained by the prosecution—but not called as a witness at Bernardo's trial—said Homolka's role in the horrific crimes

the use of this scale in prison populations. An excellent review of the use, and misuse, of the PCL-R has been provided by Hare. In discussing the PCL-R and its screening version, the PCL-SV (Hart et al., 1995), he concludes that these checklists "provide reliable and valid assessments of the traditional construct of psychopathy. They are used widely for research purposes and for making decisions in the mental health and criminal justice systems. They are strong predictors of violence and recidivism in offenders and psychiatric patients, form a key part of current risk assessment procedures, and play an important role in many judicial decisions" (Hare, 1998c, 99).

DSM-IV estimates that the prevalence of Antisocial Personality Disorder is 3 percent for men and less than 1 percent for women. However, estimates of this diagnostic classification in prison populations are, not surprisingly, considerably higher. Indeed, depending on how one interprets the diagnostic criteria, virtually all inmates could be so classified. The differences in interpretation may partly account for the large disparity in prison studies of this disorder, reflecting, in part, changes in diagnostic procedures and criteria. In a Canadian

FOCUS

BOX 8.2 Psychologists Suggest Bernardo and Homolka Are Psychopaths *(Continued)*

can't be fully explained by the abuse she suffered.

"Karla Homolka remains something of a diagnostic mystery," Dr. Angus McDonald wrote in his report, which the Bernardo jury never saw.

"Despite her ability to present herself very well, there is a moral vacuity in her which is difficult, if not impossible, to explain."

In Bernardo's case, it appears there were no ethical restraints to hold him back from sex that inflicted pain, terror and humiliation on his partner, psychologists say. Among evidence ruled inadmissible at his trail was a statement the Crown says Bernardo made to two witnesses.

"I have no conscience," prosecutors quoted him as saying. "I could kill anybody."

Experts also say his videotaping of the sexual assaults is typical of many rapists and sex killers, who keep souvenirs of their victims such as jewelry, clothing or hair. Serial killer Harvey Murray Glatman used photographs of the women he murdered in Los Angeles during the 1950s to relive his sexual fantasies.

"They're like stamp collectors," said psychologist Vern Quinsey of Queen's University in Kingston. "They look at them and think about them and try to do better next time."

Psychopaths tend to be egocentric, lack remorse or guilt and constantly seek excitement, said Hare. They're also unable to empathize with others and tend to be deceitful and emotionally shallow. Only a small percentage are physically violent, he said.

"They are predators—emotional and physical and sexual predators."

Bernardo's cool, confident and sometimes condescending demeanor in the witness box was typical, Hare said.

"A psychopath who has committed a crime and is caught is now on stage. He doesn't see himself as any sort of pariah, he sees himself as a victim of the system. . . . He's on stage, he's enjoying it, he's loving it.

"What these people do is confuse fame and infamy."

Source: Tom Blackwell. (n.d.) "Psychologists Suggest Bernardo and Homolka Are Psychopaths." Printed with permission of The Canadian Press.

study of the prevalence of Antisocial Personality Disorder, Hare (1983) had two clinicians examine a provincial and a federal prison inmate sample. The clinicians found that approximately one-third of the provincial sample and 42 percent of the federal sample met the criteria for Antisocial Personality Disorder. Overall, 39 percent of the total prison sample received this diagnosis. However, in a previous study described in the same paper, Hare, using the initial criteria proposed in a draft of DSM-III-R, found that 76 percent of a sample of 145 white male criminals met the criteria for Antisocial Personality Disorder. The reason for the difference is that the published version of DSM-III-R required that more stringent criteria be met before a diagnosis of Antisocial Personality Disorder could be made. Hare's work was influential in the decision to change the criteria. The two studies provide a clear illustration of how changes in diagnostic criteria and procedures can influence the perceived prevalence of antisocial personality.

A leading theory about antisocial personality is that these individuals do not learn from negative experiences because they do not become anxious in circumstances that should elicit anxiety. Also, they do not have sufficient fear of the consequences of their behaviour (Brodsky, 1977; Hare, 1970). Applying Eysenck's model, reviewed earlier in this chapter, the psychopath can be viewed as an extravert who does not easily acquire conditioned responses or, if he or she acquires them, extinguishes them very rapidly. Given these characteristics, particularly the inability to learn from punishment or to experience fear or anxiety, it is understandable that Brodsky (1977) concludes that imprisonment is unlikely to have much effect on the post-release behaviour of such individuals. Newman (1998) reviews a position suggesting that psychopaths exhibit deficits in information processing that limit their ability to use contextual cues appropriately in the implementation of goal-directed behaviour and interfere with effective self-regulation. Hare (1998b) suggests that while a great deal remains to be done, there is a convergence emerging with regard to etiologic bases of psychopathy, which forms "a reasonably coherent conceptual/empirical package that helps us understand how and why psychopaths differ from others in the processing and use of semantic and affective information, and in their capacity for callous, predatory behaviour" (1998b, 131).

Heilbrun (1979) conducted an interesting study of the influence of intelligence on the relationships between psychopathy, violence, and impulsiveness. His sample of 76 white male prisoners was divided into psychopathic and nonpsychopathic groups ($n = 38$). Two personality measures were used (one of which, incidentally, was validated in a study by Craddick [1962] using a Canadian prison sample). He further divided the groups into high-intelligence and low-intelligence subgroups. Heilbrun found that intelligence level does indeed have an influence on violence and impulsiveness among psychopaths. The more intelligent psychopaths were neither violent nor impulsive and were more likely to have attained educational goals. This study points to the importance of viewing persons with the label of psychopath, or antisocial personality, in multidimensional ways. Not all such individuals should be expected to be violent or impulsive.

The Heilbrun study should also serve as a reminder that studies of prison populations may present a misleading picture of antisocial personality. Most of the research on antisocial personality has used samples obtained from institutional populations. This may give a distorted view because the impressions one has about people with antisocial personalities are, thus, based on people who committed criminal acts but were not able to avoid apprehension. Furthermore, it is certainly true that not all persons with this label are criminals (Cleckley, 1976). An exception to the focus on institutionalized populations is the work of Cathy Spatz Widom (Widom, 1977; Widom and Newman, 1985). In one study, Widom placed an advertisement in a local newspaper asking for "charming, aggressive, carefree people who are impulsively irresponsible but are good at handling people and at looking after number one." Twenty-nine applicants were interviewed. The demographic and personality test data applied to these people revealed some interesting information about this noninstitutionalized population. Only two subjects had not finished high school, and most had some college. Nearly two-thirds had at least one arrest, but the conviction rate was quite low (18 percent), even though many of the charges were felonies. While 50 percent had been incarcerated, most had been in jail less than two weeks.

The subjects scored high on the extraversion and neuroticism scale of Eysenck Personality Inventory, consistent with Eysenck's (1977) notions of psychopathy. Scores on the Minnesota Multiphasic Personality Inventory (MMPI), an objective personality test, fit the classic profile of psychopathy (high scores on the psychopathic deviate and manic scales). Subjects had low scores on the measure of socialization, and most also had low scores on the empathy scale.

While many of the results of Widom's study were similar to those found in institutional populations, it presents a picture of somewhat more successful antisocial persons. That is, they are better educated and more successful at avoiding conviction and lengthy incarceration. These results support the conclusion of Widom and Newman (1985) that research on the antisocial personality must avoid a primary focus on the incarcerated criminal. Her methodology seems to have been successful in drawing a sample of noninstitutionalized persons who meet the antisocial personality criteria. This is important as it is vital for us to become more aware of the prevalence of psychopathy within the general population and to begin to understand better the non-criminal manifestations of this personality. However, at this time, the fascination with such individuals continues to be mostly a consequence of the overwhelmingly antisocial nature of their acts. In *Without Conscience*, Hare (1998a) captures the essence of this in his description of Clifford Olson (see Box 8.3).

WWW

"MMPI-2 Workshops and Symposia" Department of Psychology, University of Minnesota
Click on "Current Newsletter" and "Past Editions."
www1.umn.edu/mmpi/

As theories of crime, antisocial personality disorder and psychopathy do not completely avoid the tautology that results from failing to distinguish between the criterion (antisocial personality disorder) and the outcome (crime). However, as previously discussed, psychopathy not only identifies those that have committed past offences but also predicts *future* criminality—both general and violent recidivism (Hare, 1998c). The construct of psychopathy has also been criticized for its oversimplicity and disregard for the dynamic nature of human behaviour (Walter, 2004). Nonetheless many consider psychopathy to be "the single most important clinical construct in the criminal justice system" (Hare, 1998c, p.99).

A final note on treatment seems appropriate. Losel (1998) reviews a position taken by Suedfeld and Landon (1978) that no effective treatments exist for this disorder. While acknowledging that our understanding of issues related to concerns such as assessment, etiology, prediction, and the biological, cognitive, emotional, and behavioural correlates has advanced greatly in the past 20 years, he indicates that treatment of such individuals remains an area of uncertainty.

Crime and Mental Illness

We begin this discussion of crime and mental illness with a most extreme statement: all crime is symptomatic of mental illness. While this may seem a preposterous statement to some, many mental health professionals have held this belief. Hakeem (1958) has summarized these views:

> So powerful is the conviction of some psychiatrists that crime stems from mental disease, that they have held that the commission of crime in itself constitutes evidence of the presence of mental disease. Again,

FOCUS

BOX 8.3 Clifford Olson—The Prototypical Psychopath

Canada's most notorious and reviled criminal is Clifford Olson, a serial murderer sentenced in January 1982 to life imprisonment for the torture and killing of eleven boys and girls. These crimes were the latest and most despicable in a string of antisocial and criminal acts extending back to his early childhood. Although some psychopaths are not violent and few are as brutal as he, Olson is the prototypical psychopath.

Consider the following quotation from a newspaper article written around the time of his trial: "He was a braggart and a bully, a liar and thief. He was a violent man with a hairtrigger temper. But he could also be charming and smooth-tongued when trying to impress people. . . . Olson was a compulsive talker. . . . He's a real smooth talker, he has the gift of gab. . . . He was always telling whoppers. . . . The man was just an out-and-out liar. . . . He always wanted to test you to the limits. He wanted to see how far he could go before you had to step on him. . . . He was a manipulator. . . . Olson was a blabbermouth. . . . We learned after a while not to believe anything he said because he told so many lies" (Farrow, 1982). A reporter who talked with Olson said, "He talked fast, staccato. . . . He jumped from topic to topic. He sounded glib, slick, like a con trying to prove he's tough and important" (Ouston, 1982).

These reports by people who knew him are important, for they give us a clue to why he was able to get his young, trusting victims alone with him. They may also help to explain the Crown's decision to pay him $100 000 to tell them where he hid the bodies of seven of the eleven young people he had killed. Not surprisingly, public outrage greeted disclosure of the payment. Some typical headlines were: KILLER WAS PAID TO LOCATE BODIES; MONEY-FOR-GRAVES PAYMENT TO CHILD KILLER GREETED WITH DISGUST.

In the years since his imprisonment Olson has continued to bring grief to the families of his victims by sending them letters with comments about the murders of their children. He has never shown any guilt or remorse for his depredations; on the contrary, he continually complains about his treatment by the press, the prison system, and society. During his trial he preened and postured whenever a camera was present, apparently considering himself an important celebrity rather than a man who had committed a series of atrocities. On January 15, 1983, the *Vancouver Sun* reported, "Mass killer Clifford Olson has written to the *Sun* newsroom to say he does not approve of the picture of him we have been using . . . and will shortly be sending us newer, more attractive pictures of himself." (Quotes are from articles by R. Ouston, *Vancouver Sun*, January 15, 1982; and M. Farrow, *Vancouver Sun*, January 14, 1982.)

At this writing Olson has written to several criminology departments in Canada offering to help them establish a course devoted to studying him.

Source: Robert D. Hare. (1998). *Without Conscience: The Disturbing World of the Psychopaths Among Us.* New York: Guilford Press, pp. 132–34. Reprinted with permission of the author.

this aspect of the ideology usually draws on the medical analogy. The thesis runs as follows: just as fever is a symptom of physical disease, so crime is a symptom of mental disease.

Today, most would disagree with this position. Indeed, the current view is that while many criminals exhibit symptoms of mental illness, many do not (Corrado et al., 2000; Freeman and Roesch, 1989). In the remainder of this section, some of the current theories of crime and mental illness will be reviewed. In particular, the extent to which persons charged with crimes are in need of mental health intervention will be examined.

WWW

"Mental Disorders and Crime: The Connection Is Real"
Crime Times
www.crimetimes.org/96c/w96cp1.htm

Studies over the past 20 years have shown that many men and women involved in the criminal justice system suffer from serious mental illness such as schizophrenia, bipolar disorder, and major depressions (Abram & Teplin, 1991; Abram et al., 2003; Human Rights Watch, 2003). Rates of mental illness can differ between studies in part because of methodological differences. Substance use disorders may be included in some studies and excluded in others, for example. The diversity of research findings have made the prevalence of mental illness in jail and prison populations difficult to assess.

Teplin (1991) reported the prevalence rates of mental disorder among jail detainees range from about 5 to 12 percent for severe mental disorders and from 16 to 67 percent for any mental illness. Silber (1974) argues that the rate of severe mental illness is quite low, as do Brodsky (1972) and Guze (1976). Monahan and Steadman (1983) reviewed a number of studies addressing the issue of prevalence and concluded that the rates of mental illness in jails or prisons are no higher than the rates in the general population, controlling for social class. A more recent review of the literature found that the prevalence of mental illness among inmates was high and specifically that "prisons have higher rates of mentally ill offenders than jails, and jails have higher rates of mental illness than the nonincarcerated community" (Diamond et al., 2001). In addition, a recent study suggests that many individuals have co-occurring disorders, that is suffer from a serious mental illness such as schizophrenia and also suffer from a substance use disorder (Abram et al., 2003).

The prevalence of mental illness in jails has prompted the American Psychiatric Association (2000) and the National Commission on Correctional Health Care (2003) to recommend, in their standards and guidelines for the delivery of mental health services in jails, that all institutions adopt a systematic program for screening individuals upon detention, a recommendation echoed by health-care providers and researchers (Birmingham et al. 2000; Nicholls et al., 2005; Osher, Steadman & Barr, 2003; Roesch, 1995). Specialized screening tools, devised specifically for mental health screening in jails, have started to emerge in the literature. For example, in Canada, Nicholls and her colleagues (2005) developed the Jail Screening Assessment Tool, a semi-structured interview used to screen inmates for mental health concerns, risk of suicide and self-harm, and risk of violence and victimization. In the same year, researchers in the United States created the Brief Jail Mental Health Screen (Steadman et al., 2005), a screening tool for serious mental illness comprising eight yes or no questions.

There have been only a few studies in Canada on the extent of mental health problems in jail populations. Allodi et al. (1977) reported that increases in referrals of jail inmates to a jail psychiatric unit were associated with decreases in mental hospital populations in the Toronto area. Statistics Canada data on the number of admissions to psychiatric units within correctional facilities also support the view that the referral rate has increased (see Borzecki and Wormith, 1985, for a review of this issue). A study by Hodgins and Côté (1990) of 650 inmates in Quebec prisons revealed a high rate of mental disorder. Indeed, these researchers report that "the prevalence of schizophrenic disorders . . . is about seven times that observed in samples of non-incarcerated adult males." Hodgins and Côté also commented on the fact that most of the inmates diagnosed with a major mental disorder did not receive any mental health treat-

WWW

"The Prison Careers of Offenders with Mental Disorders" Correctional Service of Canada
www.csc-scc.gc.ca/text/rsrch/reports/r33/r33e_e.shtml

ment during their confinement in prison (see Steadman et al., 1988, for similar conclusions based on a national survey of American jails). In a study using a pretrial population, Roesch (1995) found that the prevalence of major mental disorders was 15.6 percent. As well, the prevalence of substance use disorders was exceptionally high, with over 77 percent considered to have alcohol use or dependence disorders, and over 63 percent with drug use disorders. Many of these individuals had co-occurring disorders (e.g., schizophrenia and substance abuse), further compounding the mental health and social problems these individuals experience. This finding is consistent with the results of a study by Abram and Teplin (1991), which found considerable overlap between mental disorders and drug or alcohol abuse in jail populations. This has been referred to as co-occurring disorders. The high rate of individuals with co-occurring disorders suggests the need for treatment programs both within the jail and after release. Abram and Teplin suggested that these individuals might be particularly appropriate for alternatives to prosecution, such as pretrial diversion programs.

There is little question that individuals with mental health problems are increasingly involved with the legal system. The first contact is usually by police officers. These officers have considerable discretion in responding to the mentally ill, although changes in the civil commitment laws have placed some limits on them. Jacobsen et al. (1973) found that police rarely arrested persons they suspected of being mentally ill, indicating that they believed that hospitalization was more helpful than jail. The police officers frequently looked for alternatives to jail, such as contacting a responsible person, family counselling, or not taking any action at all.

The training provided to police officers on mental health related issues and the use of specialized responses for calls involving people with mental illnesses varies widely between departments (Hails and Borum, 2006). In their recent study, Hails and Borum found that some police agencies provided zero hours of training in handling calls involving people with mental illnesses while others provided as many as 41 hours of training. Most of the agencies provided no post-academy in-service training hours dealing with the topic of mental illness. Hails and Borum also found that only 21 percent of agencies had a special unit or bureau within the department to assist police in handling people with mental illness. This percentage is disappointing given findings that specialized teams composed of a police officer and a mental health professional have helped avoid the criminalization of the mentally ill in some jurisdictions (Lamb et al., 1995).

There is some evidence that the discretionary powers of the police in dealing with the mentally ill have been affected by the deinstitutionalization movement. This movement resulted in the release of large numbers of patients from mental hospitals. At the same time, the civil commitment laws were changed so that commitment had to be based on findings of mental illness and dangerousness. As a consequence, police could no longer use the mental hospital as an alternative disposition to jail and were often forced to arrest a mentally ill person.

If this is true, does it suggest that there is a significant relationship between crime and mental disorder? In his study of the rates of mental disorder in prisons, Gunn (1977) answers this question with a note of caution, suggesting that, as other alternatives for the placement of mentally ill persons were blocked off, it would be expected that a greater number of persons previously detained in mental hospitals would now end up in prisons. As Roesch and Golding (1985) point out, the increased rate of mental disorder in prisons is the result of "institutional and public policy practices that have nothing to do with individual deviance *per se*. In fact, the individual behavior may not have changed at all. What has changed, however, is the manner in which institutions of our society react to that individual behavior."

With these cautions in mind, it will be instructive to review some studies on the extent to which persons considered to be mentally ill are arrested for criminal offences. Most of the research on arrest rates of the mentally ill has relied on police or court records. Such research is limited by the availability of information in the files, which are often incomplete and inaccurate. One of the few researchers to actually observe how the police dealt with the mentally ill was Linda Teplin (1984). She was interested in examining the probability of arrest for mentally ill persons as compared to persons who were not mentally ill.

Teplin's sample was 1382 police–citizen encounters involving 2555 citizens. Overall, the probability of arrest was low, occurring in only 12 percent of 884 encounters (traffic-offence and public-service incidents were deleted from the total). In individual terms, 506 of the 1798 citizens involved were considered suspect, but only 29 percent were arrested.

Does the presence of symptoms of mental illness affect the probability of arrest? Teplin's data suggest that it does. Of 506 suspects, 30 were considered by observers to be mentally ill. Nearly one-half (14) were arrested, compared to an arrest percentage of 27.9 percent for those not mentally ill. Furthermore, this difference was not accounted for by differences in type of charge. In other words, mentally ill suspects were not arrested more often because they were suspected of committing more serious crimes. The difference held up across types of crime.

Lamb (1982) also examined police arrests of mentally ill persons. The sample was 102 inmates who had been referred to a forensic unit within a county jail. Ninety percent had a history of prior hospitalization, and 92 percent had prior arrests. Lamb was interested in why the police chose to arrest rather than hospitalize these individuals. About one-half were arrested for felonies, so police had little choice since persons who have allegedly committed serious crimes are almost uniformly arrested, regardless of mental condition. Lamb argues that police have become reluctant to take persons charged with less serious crimes to mental health treatment centres, as they have learned through experience that the centres frequently release such people because of bed shortages or because they do not meet the criteria for civil commitment. Lamb concluded that "the police may well book the person into jail—which is less time-consuming and ensures the person's removal from the community pending further evaluation—rather than take him to the hospital."

Once arrested, do mentally disordered offenders recidivate at a high level? In a recent meta-analysis of a large number of empirical studies, Bonta et al. (1998) found that mentally disordered offenders on average showed lower recidivism rates than other offenders. A diagnosis of Antisocial Personal-

TABLE 8.3 Psychological Theories

Theory	*Theorists*	*Key Elements*
Psychoanalytic theory	Freud	Crime results when the ego and superego cannot control the antisocial instincts of the id. This occurs because the individual has not been adequately socialized in early childhood.
Moral development theory	Piaget Kohlberg	Each individual must go through a sequence of moral development. Those with a high level of moral development will be more likely to make responsible choices when faced with the opportunity to get involved in criminal behaviour.
Personality theory	Eysenck	Law-abiding people must develop a conditioned fear of deviance. Those who become delinquents and criminals do not develop this fear because of poor conditioning by parents or because they are less susceptible to conditioning.
Social learning theory	Bandura	Deviant behaviour such as aggression can be learned through direct experience or through modelling the behaviour of others.
Operant conditioning theory	Skinner	Individual behaviour is shaped through both reinforcement and punishment. Behaviour that is rewarded will tend to be continued; behaviour that is punished will cease.
Psychopathy	Cleckley Hare	Psychopaths seem to lack empathy for their victims and do not feel guilty about their crimes. They do not learn from their experience or fear the consequences of their behaviour.

ity Disorder was found to be a more potent predictor than any other clinical diagnosis. However, with respect to violence after release from custody, Borum (1996) notes that mental disorder is now considered a robust and significant risk factor for predicting violent recidivism, as mentally disordered offenders have a greater probability of committing violent offences after release. But Borum adds that most persons with mental disorders are not violent, so it is a relative rather than an absolute risk factor. It is important to keep in mind that most mentally disordered offenders are not violent and may have a decreased risk of general recidivism.

In conclusion, it is likely that theories of criminal behaviour that rely on models of mental illness will not account for the behaviour of most criminals. It is certainly true that some people who commit crimes can be considered mentally ill, but these individuals make up only a small percentage of the total criminal population. In a legal sense, most criminals are responsible for their actions in that they are aware of their behaviour and can distinguish between right and wrong.

Each of the psychological theories reviewed in this chapter makes a contribution to the understanding of criminal behaviour. However, there is a need for greater integration of sociological and psychological perspectives so that both situational determinants and individual differences can be taken into account in attempts to explain criminal behaviour (Monahan and Splane, 1980). A study by Conger (1976) provides an excellent example of an attempt to integrate the two approaches. Conger examined the relationship between two models of delinquent behaviour: the social control model (which is discussed in Chapter 13) and a social learning model. Based on data collected from a sample of Grade 7 boys, Conger demonstrated how social learning theory, particularly the effects of differential reinforcement and punishment, can be used to explain how an individual's bonds to society can be strengthened or weakened. Conger argued that the combination of the two theories can provide a more comprehensive theory of delinquent behaviour than can either theory by itself. It is likely that the same arguments can be made for any of the theories reviewed in this chapter.

Summary

- Psychological theory is primarily concerned with explanations of behaviour at the level of the individual. Some psychological theories have been criticized for relying too much on trying to explain crime at the level of the individual and for not placing enough emphasis on environmental and situational factors.
- Certain psychological perspectives, such as community psychology, view social problems from a "level of analysis" perspective. Such levels include individual, small-group, organizational, and institutional or community levels.
- The premise for psychoanalytic theory is a series of five stages of development (oral, anal, phallic, latency, and genital) and three components of personality (id, ego, and superego). Psychoanalytic interpretations of criminality suggest that criminal behaviour occurs when the ego and superego are unable to restrain the id.
- Kohlberg has proposed a six-stage theory of moral development, with two stages occurring at each of three levels (preconventional, conventional, and postconventional). This theory has been criticized from a feminist perspective for not adequately considering the different approaches of males (more justice-oriented) and females (more care-oriented) to morality.
- Eysenck's theory of crime and personality is based on the premise of classical conditioning. He has proposed three dimensions of personality (extraversion, neuroticism, and psychoticism), has developed measures of each of the three dimensions, and has generated a number of hypotheses about the relationship of these dimensions of personality to criminal behaviour. Eysenck's work offers a comprehensive model or theory of criminal behaviour that remains to be validated.
- Social learning theory integrates sociology and psychology in explaining criminal behaviour. Modelling is an important aspect of social learning

theory. Family, subcultural influences, and symbolic modelling are all important sources from which an individual can learn aggressive behaviour. Deterrence, on the other hand, can occur through legal sanction, social sanction, and self-sanction.

- Operant conditioning is a subset of learning theory that has been proposed to explain criminal behaviour. Reinforcement and punishment are theorized to play a large part in strengthening or weakening criminal behaviours. A token economy is one method that has been used to change existing behavioural interactions of individuals.
- Antisocial Personality Disorder is a diagnostic label that refers to a cluster of traits that underlie a pervasive pattern of disregard for the rights of others. Such traits include lying, stealing, fighting, and truancy. Behaviours that may be characteristic of this disorder include excessive drinking or the use of illicit substances, aggressive sexual behaviour, inconsistent work performance, and a failure to accept social norms with respect to lawful behaviour.
- Psychopathy is a term that is often confused with antisocial personality. Psychopathy refers to a pattern of behavioural features that are similar to those associated with Antisocial Personality Disorder. However, in addition to these behavioural features, psychopathic individuals also display certain attitudinal features such as grandiosity, glib and superficial charm, lack of empathy, and a lack of remorse, guilt, or shame.
- The majority of criminals do not display any symptoms of mental illness. The prevalence of mental illness in jails and prisons is difficult to assess. However, some studies have estimated it to be between 5 and 12 percent for severe disorders and between 16 and 67 percent for any mental disorder.

QUESTIONS FOR CRITICAL THINKING

1. Describe how each of the major psychological theories would explain criminal behaviour (i.e., psychoanalytic theory, theories of moral development, Eysenck's theory of crime and personality, social learning theory, and operant conditioning). What are the social policy implications of each of these theories?
2. Describe what is meant by Antisocial Personality Disorder and psychopathy, and discuss how these two disorders differ from each other.
3. Discuss the relationship between crime and mental illness, and describe the prevalence of mental illness in criminal populations. Is prison the most appropriate place to deal with people with mental illness?

NET WORK

In this chapter, you have learned about theories of moral development. You can read more about these theories at **http://tigger.uic.edu/~lnucci/MoralEd/overview.html.**

Go to the "Overview" section of this website to read more about the work of Piaget, Kohlberg, and Gilligan. Then do the following:

1. Go to the "Classroom Practices" section of the website. Describe one of the programs that has been used to teach moral development in the schools. How does this differ from the teaching program that you experienced when you were in school?
2. In the same section, you will see a link to a site called "Leading Moral Discussions." Can you think of a moral dilemma from fiction or from real life that would be suitable if you were doing a moral development session with first-year university students?
3. Go to the "Articles of the Month" section of the website. Using the articles for this month as well as the "Archives," can you find two different contexts to which proponents feel moral development should be applied? Do you think moral development training would be useful in these contexts?

KEY TERMS

Antisocial Personality Disorder; pg. 260
assumption of discriminating traits; pg. 248
assumption of offender deficit; pg. 248
autonomic reactivity; pg. 257
classical conditioning; pg. 255
community psychology; pg. 249
ego; pg. 250
extraversion; pg. 255
id; pg. 250
modelling; pg. 256
moral development theory; pg. 254
operant conditioning; pg. 259
socialization; pg. 250
superego; pg. 250
token economy; pg. 260

SUGGESTED READING

Akers, R. L., and G. F. Jensen (2002). *Social Learning Theory and the Explanation of Crime.* New Brunswick, N. J.: Transaction Publishers. A text that examines social learning theory as it applies to crime and deviance.

Andrews, D. A., and J. Bonta. (2007). *The Psychology of Criminal Conduct.* Cincinnati: Anderson Publishing. A text by two Canadian psychologists that presents an interdisciplinary general psychology of criminal conduct.

Bartol, C. R., and A. M. Bartol. (2004). *Criminal Behavior: A Psychosocial Approach.* Englewood Cliffs, N.J.: Prentice Hall. An overview of the contributions of psychology to the field of criminology. The emphasis is on the interactionist approach in which criminal behaviour is viewed as the interaction of dispositional and learning factors with social and environmental factors.

Hervé, H., and J. C. Yuille. (2007). *The Psychopath: Theory, Research, and Practice.* Mahwah, N. J.: Lawrence Erlbaum Associates. Edited by two Canadian researchers, each chapter in this text is devoted to a particular issue that has relevance to the study of psychopathy.

Hilton, N. Z., M. A. Jackson, and C. D. Webster (eds.). (1990). *Clinical Criminology: Theory, Research and Practice.* Toronto: Canadian Scholar's Press. This is an edited text that brings together papers and articles representing a decade (the 1980s) of work by influential theorists in the field of forensic psychiatry and psychology. The exception is a 1953 paper by the late B. F. Skinner that outlines the basic principles of operant conditioning.

Hollin, C. R. (1989). *Psychology and Crime.* London and New York: Routledge. Topics include reviews of psychological approaches to criminal behaviour, mental disorder and crime, psychology in the courtroom, psychology and the police, and crime prevention.

Jacks, I., and S. G. Cox (eds.). (1984). *Psychological Approaches to Crime and Its Correction: Theory, Research, Practice.* Chicago: Nelson-Hall. This is an edited volume with contributions by well-known theorists (Eysenck, Rosenthal, Eron, Quay, and Rosenhan, among others) on aggression, heredity, and television and violence, as well as sections on treatment approaches.

Laufer, W. S., and J. M. Day. (1983). *Personality Theory, Moral Development, and Criminal Behavior.* Lexington, Mass.: Lexington Books. This is an edited volume with a chapter on interpersonal maturity theory, one by Eysenck on antisocial personality, and several chapters on moral development theory.

McGuire, J. (2004). *Understanding Psychology and Crime.* Open University Press. The author examines some of the contributions psychology has made to theories of crime including chapters on the psychological processes in crime and preventing and reducing crime.

Roesch, R., J. R. P. Ogloff, P. A. Zapf, S. D. Hart, and R. Otto. (1998). "Mental Health Issues for Jail and Prison Inmates: A Review of Prevalence, Assessment, and Treatment." In N. N. Singh (ed.), *Comprehensive Clinical Psychology: Applications in Diverse Populations.* Oxford: Elsevier. The authors provide a comprehensive review of the literature and the research on mental health issues with respect to offender populations, including a section on female offenders.

BIBLIOGRAPHY

Abrahamsen, D. (1944). *Crime and the Human Mind.* New York: Columbia University Press.

Abram, K. M., and L. A. Teplin. (1991). "Co-Occurring Disorders Among Mentally Ill Jail Detainees: Implications for Public Policy." *American Psychologist* 46:1036–45.

Abram, K. M., L. A. Teplin, and G. M. McClelland. (2003). "Comorbidity of Severe Psychiatric Disorders and Substance Use Disorders among Women in Jail." *American Journal of Psychiatry* 160:1007–1010.

Akers, R. (1990). "Rational Choice, Deterrence, and Social Learning Theories in Criminology: The Path Not Taken." *Journal of Criminal Law and Criminology* 81:653–76.

Akers, R. L., and G. F. Jensen. (2006). "Empirical Status of Social Learning Theory of Crime and Deviance: The Past, Present, and Future." In K. Blevins, F. Cullen, and J. Wright (eds)., *Taking Stock: The Status of Criminological Theory.* Beverly Hills, Calif.: Sage.

Alexander, F., and M. Healey. (1935). *Roots of Crime.* New York: Knopf.

Allodi, F., H. Kedward, and M. Robertson. (1977). "Insane But Guilty: Psychiatric Patients in Jail." *Canada's Mental Health* 25:3–7.

American Psychiatric Association. (1994). *Diagnostic and Statistical Manual of Mental Disorders* (4th ed.). Washington, D.C.: American Psychiatric Association.

American Psychiatric Association. (2000). *Psychiatric Services in Jails and Prisons, 2nd ed.* Washington, D.C.: American Psychiatric Association.

Bandura, A. (1979). "The Social Learning Perspective: Mechanisms of Aggression." In H. Toch (ed.), *Psychology of Crime and Criminal Justice* (pp. 198–236). New York: Holt, Rinehart and Winston.

———. (1986). *Social Foundations of Thought and Action: A Social Cognitive Theory.* Englewood Cliffs, N.J.: Prentice Hall.

Bartol, C. R. (1980). *Criminal Behavior: A Psychosocial Approach.* Englewood Cliffs, N.J.: Prentice Hall.

Birmingham, L., J. Gray, D. Mason, and D. Grubin. (2000). "Mental Illness at Reception into Prison." *Criminal Behaviour and Mental Health,* 10:77–87.

Blasi, A. (1980). "Bridging Moral Cognition and Moral Action: A Critical Review of the Literature." *Psychological Bulletin* 88:1–45.

Bonta, J., M. Law, and K. Hanson. (1998). "The Prediction of Criminal and Violent Recidivism Among Mentally Disorders Offenders: A Meta-Analysis." *Psychological Bulletin* 123:123–42.

Borum, R. (1996). "Improving the Clinical Practice of Violence Risk Assessment: Technology Guidelines and Training." *American Psychologist* 51:945–46.

Borzecki, M., and J. S. Wormith. (1985). "The Criminalization of Psychiatrically Ill People: A Review with a Canadian Perspective." *Psychiatric Journal of the University of Ottawa* 10:241–47.

Bowlby, J. (1953). *Child Care and the Growth of Love.* Baltimore: Penguin Books.

Braukman, C. J., K. A. Kirigin, and M. M. Wolf. (1980). "Group Homes Treatment Research: Social Learning and Social Control Perspectives." In T. Hirschi and M. Gottfredson (eds.), *Understanding Crime: Current Theory and Research.* Beverly Hills, Calif.: Sage.

Braukman, C. J., and M. M. Wolf. (1987). "Behaviorally Based Group Homes for Juvenile Offenders." In C.J. Braukman and M.M. Wolf (eds.), *Behavioral Approaches to Crime and Delinquency.* New York: Plenum Press.

Braukman, C. J., M. M. Wolf, and K. K. Ramp. (1985). "Follow-Up of Group Home Youths into Young Adulthood." (Progress Report, Grant MA 20030). Achievement Place Research Project. Lawrence, Kan.: The University of Kansas.

Brodsky, S. L. (1972). *Psychologists in the Criminal Justice system.* Urbana, Ill.: University of Illinois Press.

———. (1977). "Crime and Dangerous Behavior." In D. C. Rimm and J. W. Somervill (eds.), *Abnormal Psychology.* New York: Academic Press.

Burgess, R. L., and R. L. Akers. (1966). "A Differential Association Reinforcement Theory of Criminal Behavior." *Social Problems* 14:128–47.

Buttell, F. P. (2002). "Exploring Levels of Moral Development Among Sex Offenders Participating in Community-based Treatment." *Journal of Offender Rehabilitation* 34: 85–95.

Clastner, D. S. (1967). "Comparison of Risk Perception Between Delinquents and Nondelinquents." *The Journal of Criminal Law, Criminology and Police Science* 58:80–86.

Cleckley, H. (1976). *The Mask of Sanity.* St. Louis: Mosby.

Cohen, A. K. (1966). *Deviance and Control.* Englewood Cliffs, N.J.: Prentice Hall.

Conger, R. D. (1976). "Social Control and Social Learning Models of Delinquent Behavior: A Synthesis." *Criminology* 14:17–40.

Cook, T. D., D. A. Kendzierski, and S. V. Thomas. (1983). "The Implicit Assumptions of Television Research: An Analysis of the 1982 NIMH Report on Television and Behavior." *Public Opinion Quarterly* 47:161–201.

Corrado, R. R., I. Cohen, S. D. Hart, and R. Roesch. (2000). "Comparative Examination of the Prevalence of Mental Disorders among Jailed Inmates in Canada and the United States." *International Journal of Law and Psychiatry* 23:633–47.

Craddick, R. (1962). "Selection of Psychopathic from Non-Psychopathic Prisoners Within a Canadian Prison." *Psychological Reports* 10:495–99.

Diamond, P. M., W. W. Eugene, C. E. Holzer, C. Thomas, and D. A. Cruser. (2001). "The Prevalence of Mental Illness in Prison." *Administration and Policy in Mental Health* 29:21–40.

Einstadter, W., and S. Henry. (1995). *Criminological Theory: An Analysis of Its Underlying Assumptions.* Fort Worth: Harcourt Brace College Publishers.

Ewen, R. B. (1988). *An Introduction to Theories of Personality.* Hillside, NJ: Lawrence Erlbaum Associates.

Eysenck, H. J. (1977). *Crime and Personality.* London: Routledge and Kegan Paul.

———. (1990). "Crime and Personality." In N. Z. Hilton, M. A. Jackson, and C. D. Webster (eds.), *Clinical Criminology: Theory Research and Practice* (pp. 85–99). Toronto: Canadian Scholars' Press.

Eysenck, H. J., and S. B. Eysenck. (1976). *Psychoticism as a Dimension of Personality.* London: Hodder and Stoughton.

Eysenck, H. J., and G. H. Gudjonsson. (1989). *The Causes and Cures of Criminality.* New York and London: Plenum Press.

Farrington, D. P. (1978). "The Family Background of Aggressive Youths." In L. A. Hersov, M. Berger, and D. Shaffer (eds.), *Aggression and Antisocial Behavior in Childhood and Adolescence.* Oxford: Pergamon.

———. (1979). "Environmental Stress, Delinquent Behavior, and Conviction." In I. G. Sarason and C. D. Spielberger, (eds.), *Stress and Anxiety,* vol. 6. Washington, D.C.: Hemisphere.

———. (2002). "Multiple Risk Factors for Multiple Problem Violent Boys." In R. R. Corrado, R. Roesch, S. D. Hart, and J. K. Gierowski (eds.), *Multi-problem Violent Youth: A Foundation for Comparative Research on Needs, Interventions and Outcomes* (pp. 23–34). Amsterdam, Netherlands Antilles: IOS Press.

Farrington, D. P., L. Biron, and M. LeBlanc. (1982). "Personality and Delinquency in London and Montreal." In J. Gunn and D. P. Farrington (eds.), *Abnormal Offenders, Delinquency, and the Criminal Justice System.* Chichester, U.K.: Wiley.

Freeman, R. J., and R. Roesch. (1989). "Mental Disorder and the Criminal Justice System: A Review." *International Journal of Law and Psychiatry* 12:105–15.

Friedlander, K. (1947). *The Psychoanalytic Approach to Juvenile Delinquency.* New York: International Universities Press.

Geen, R. G. (1983). "Aggression and Television Violence." In R. G. Geen and E. I. Donnerstein (eds.), *Aggression: Theoretical and Empirical Reviews.* New York: Academic Press.

Gilligan, C. (1982). *In a Different Voice: Psychological Theory and Women's Development.* Cambridge, Ma.: Harvard University Press.

Gunn, J. (1977). "Criminal Behaviour and Mental Disorder." *British Journal of Psychiatry* 130:317–29.

Guze, S. (1976). *Criminality and Psychiatric Disorders.* New York: Oxford University Press.

Hails, J., and R. Borum. (2006). "Police Training and Specialized Approaches to Respond to People With Mental Illnesses." *Crime and Delinquency* 49:52–61.

Hakeem, M. (1958). "A Critique of the Psychiatric Approach to Crime and Correction." *Law and Contemporary Problems* 23:650–82.

Hare, R. D. (1970). *Psychopathy: Theory and Research.* New York: Wiley.

———. (1982). "Psychopathy and the Personality Dimensions of Psychoticism, Extraversion and Neuroticism." *Personality and Individual Differences* 3:35–42.

———. (1983). "Diagnosis of Antisocial Personality Disorder in Two Prison Populations." *American Journal of Psychiatry* 140:887–90.

———. (1991). *The Hare Psychopathy Checklist—Revised.* Toronto: Multi-Health Systems.

———. (1998a). *Without Conscience: The Disturbing World of the Psychopaths Among Us.* New York: Guilford Press.

———. (1998b). "Psychopathy, Affect and Behavior." In D. J. Cooke, A. E. Forth, and R. Hare (eds.), *Psychopathy: Theory, Research and Implications for Society* (pp. 105–37). Dordrecht, The Netherlands: Kluwer Academic Publishers.

———. (1998c). "The Hare PCL-R: Some Issues Concerning Its Use and Misuse." *Legal and Criminological Psychology* 3:101–19.

Hare, R. D., and D. N. Cox. (1978). "Clinical and Empirical Conceptions of Psychopathy, and the Selection of Subjects for Research." In R. D. Hare and D. Schalling (eds.), *Psychopathic Behavior: Approaches to Research.* Chichester, England: Wiley.

Hart, S. D., D. N. Cox, and R. D. Hare. (1995). *The Hare Psychopathy Checklist: Screening Version.* Toronto: Multi-Health Systems.

Heilbrun, A. B., Jr. (1979). "Psychopathy and Violent Crime." *Journal of Consulting and Clinical Psychology* 47:509–16.

Hodgins, S., and G. Côté. (1990). "Prevalence of Mental Disorders among Penitentiary Inmates in Quebec." *Canada's Mental Health* (March):1–4.

Hogan, R. (1973). "Moral Conduct and Moral Character: A Psychological Perspective." *Psychological Bulletin* 79:217–32.

Human Rights Watch. (2003). *Ill-Equipped: U.S. Prisons and Offenders with Mental Illness.* New York: Human Rights Watch.

Jacobsen, D., W. Craven, and S. Kushner. (1973). "A Study of Police Referral of Allegedly Mentally Ill Persons to a Psychiatric Unit." In J. R. Snibbe and H. M. Snibbe (eds.), *The Urban Policeman in Transition: A Psychological and Sociological Review.* Springfield, Ill.: C. C. Thomas.

Jeffery, C. R. (1965). "Criminal Behavior and Learning Theory." *Journal of Criminal Law and Criminology* 56:294–300.

Jennings, W. S., R. Kilkenny, and L. Kohlberg. (1983). "Moral-Development Theory and Practice for Youthful and Adult Offenders." In W. S. Laufer and S. M. Day (eds.), *Personality Theory, Moral Development, and Criminal Behavior.* Lexington, Mass.: Lexington Books.

Kohlberg, L., and R. Kramer. (1969). "Continuities and Discontinuities in Child and Adult Moral Development." *Human Development* 12:93–120.

Lamb, H. R. (1982). *Treating the Long-Term Mentally Ill.* San Francisco: Jossey-Bass.

Lamb, H. R., R. Shaner, D. M. Elliott, W. J. DeCuir, and J. T. Foltz. (1995). "Outcome for Psychiatric Emergency Patients Seen by an Outreach Police—Mental Health Team." *Psychiatric Services* 46: 1267–1271.

Loeber, R., D. P. Farrington, and M. Stouthamer-Loeber. (2001a). "Male Mental Health Problems, Psychopathy, and Personality Traits: Key Findings from the First 14 years of the Pittsburgh Youth Study." *Clinical Child and Family Psychology Review* 4:273–97.

———. (2001b). "The Development of Male Offending: Key Findings from the First Decade of the Pittsburgh Youth Study." In R. Bull (ed.), *Children and the Law: The Essential Readings* (pp. 336–78). Malden, Mass.: Blackwell Publishers.

Losel, F. (1998). "Treatment and Management of Psychopaths." In D. J. Cooke, A. E. Forth, and R. Hare. (eds.), *Psychopathy: Theory, Research and Implications for Society* (pp. 303–54). Dordrecht, The Netherlands: Kluwer Academic Publishers.

MacPhail, D. D. (1989). "The Moral Education Approach in Treating Adult Inmates." *Criminal Justice and Behavior* 16:81–97.

Malamuth, N. M., and J. V. P. Check. (1981). "The Effects of Mass Media Exposure on Acceptance of Violence Against Women: A Field Experiment." *Journal of Research in Personality* 15:436–46.

Martin, S. E., L. E. Sechrest, and R. Redner (eds.). (1981). *New Directions in the Rehabilitation of Criminal Offenders.* Washington, D.C.: National Press Academy.

Monahan, J., and S. Splane. (1980). "Psychological Approaches to Criminal Behavior." In E. Bittner and S. Messinger (eds.), *Criminology Review Yearbook.* Beverly Hills, Calif.: Sage.

Monahan, J., and H. J. Steadman. (1983). "Crime and Mental Disorder: An Epidemiological Approach." In M. Tonry and N. Morris (eds.), *Crime and Justice: An Annual Review of Research.* Chicago: University of Chicago Press.

Morash, M. (1983). "An Explanation of Juvenile Delinquency: The Integration of Moral-Reasoning, Theory and Social Knowledge." In W. S. Laufer and J. M. Day (eds.), *Personality Theory, Moral Development, and Criminal Behavior.* Lexington, Mass.: Lexington Books.

Nathan, P. E., and S. L. Harris. (1975). *Psychopathology and Society.* New York: McGraw-Hill.

National Commission on Correctional Health Care (2003). *Standards for Health Services in Jails.* Chicago: National Commission on Correctional Health Care.

Newman, J. P. (1998). "Psychopathic Behavior: An Information Processing Perspective." In D. J. Cooke, A. E. Forth, and R. Hare (eds.). *Psychopathy: Theory, Research and Implications for Society* (pp. 81–104). Dordrecht, The Netherlands: Kluwer Academic Publishers.

Nicholls, T. L., R. Roesch, M. C. Olley, J. R. P. Ogloff, and J. F. Hemphill. (2005). *Jail Screening Assessment Tool (JSAT): Guidelines for Mental Health Screening in Jails.* Burnaby, B.C.: Mental Health, Law and Policy Institute, Simon Fraser University.

Nietzel, M. T. (1979). *Crime and Its Modification: A Social Learning Perspective.* New York: Pergamon.

Ogloff, J. R. P., S. Wong, and A. Greenwood. (1990). "Treating Criminal Psychopaths in a Therapeutic Community Program." *Behavioral Sciences and the Law* 8:181–90.

Osher, F., H. J. Steadman, and H. Barr. (2003). "A Best Practice Approach to Community Reentry from Jails for Inmates with Co-occurring Disorders: The APIC Model." *Crime & Delinquency* 49: 79–96.

Piaget, J. (1932). *The Moral Judgment of the Child.* New York: Free Press.

Polansky, N., R. Lippitt, and F. Redl. (1950). "An Investigation of Behavioral Contagion in Groups." *Human Relations* 3:319–48.

Rappaport, J. (1977). *Community Psychology: Values, Research, and Action.* New York: Holt, Rinehart and Winston.

Reid, C. L. (2003). "Do Minority and Female Offenders Have Distinct 'Criminal Personalities'?: A Critique of Yochelson-Samenow's Theory of Criminality." *Criminal Justice Studies* 16:233-44.

Redl, F. (ed.). (1966). *When We Deal With Children: Selected Writings.* New York: Free Press.

Reppucci, N. D., and W. G. Clingempeel. (1978). "Methodological Issues in Research with Correctional Populations." *Journal of Consulting and Clinical Psychology* 46:727–46.

Roesch, R. (1988). "Community Psychology and the Law." *American Journal of Community Psychology* 16:451–63.

———. (1995). "Mental Health Interventions in Pretrial Jails." In G. M. Davies, S. Lloyd-Bostock, M. McMurran, and C. Wilson (eds.). *Psychology and Law: Advances in Research* (pp. 520–31). Berlin: De Greuter.

Roesch, R., and S. L. Golding. (1985). "The Impact of Deinstitutionalization." In D. P. Farrington and J. Gunn (eds.), *Aggression and Dangerousness*. New York: Wiley.

Schoenfeld, C. G. (1971). "A Psychoanalytic Theory of Juvenile Delinquency." *Crime and Delinquency* 19:469–80.

Seidman, E., and B. Rabkin. (1983). "Economics and Psychosocial Dysfunction: Toward a Conceptual Framework and Prevention Strategies." In R. D. Felner et al. (eds.), *Preventive Psychology* (pp. 175–98). Elmsford, N.Y.: Pergamon.

Silber, D. E. (1974). "Controversy Concerning the Criminal Justice System and Its Implications for the Role of Mental Health Workers." *American Psychologist* 29:239–44.

Skilling, T. A., G. T. Harris, M. E. Rice, and V. L. Quinsey. (2002). "Identifying Persistently Antisocial Offenders Using the Hare Psychopathy Checklist and DSM Antisocial Personality Disorder Criteria." *Psychological Assessment* 14:27–38.

Skoler, G. D., A. Bandura, and D. Ross. (1994). "Aggression." In W.A. Lesko (ed.), *Readings in Social Psychology: General, Classic, and Contemporary Selections* (2nd ed., pp. 296–326). Boston, Mass.: Allyn & Bacon.

Smith, S. L., and A. R. Boyson. (2002). "Violence in Music Videos: Examining the Prevalence and Context of Physical Aggression." *Journal of Communication* 52:61–83.

Steadman, H. J., D. W. McCarty, and J. P. Morrissey. (1988). *The Mentally Ill in Jail: Planning for Essential Services*. New York: Guilford.

Steadman, H. J., J. E. Scott, F. Osher, F., T. K. Agnese, and P. C. Robbins. (2005). "Validation of the Brief Jail Mental Health Screen." *Psychiatric Services* 56:816–22.

Suedfeld, P., and P. B. Landon. (1978). "Approaches to Treatment." In R. D. Hare and D. Schalling (eds.), *Psychopathic Behaviour: Approaches to Research* (pp. 347–76). Chichester, England: Wiley.

Teevan, J. J., and T. F. Hartnagel. (1976). "The Effects of Television Violence on the Perceptions of Crime by Adolescents." *Sociology and Social Research* 60:337–48.

———. (1984). "Criminalizing Mental Disorder: The Comparative Arrest Rate of the Mentally Ill." *American Psychologist* 7:794–803.

———. (1991). "The Criminalization Hypothesis: Myth, Misnomer, or Management Strategy." In S. A. Shah and B. D. Sales (eds.), *Law and Mental Health: Major Developments and Research Needs* (pp. 149–83). Rockville, Md.: U.S. Department of Health and Human Services.

Thomas, M. H., R. W. Horton, E. C. Lippincott, and R. S. Drabman. (1979). "Desensitization to Portrayals of Real-Life Aggression as a Function of Exposure to Television Violence." *Journal of Personality and Social Psychology* 35:450–58.

Thornberry, T. P., and M. D. Krohn. (2000). "The Self-report Method for Measuring Delinquency and Crime." *Criminal Justice* 4: 33–83.

Walter, G. D. (2004). "The Trouble with Psychopathy as a General Theory of Crime." *International Journal of Offender Therapy and Comparative Criminology* 48:133–48.

Warren, M. Q., and M. J. Hindelang. (1979). "Current Explanations of Offender Behavior." In H. Toch (ed.), *Psychology of Crime and Criminal Justice* (pp. 166–82). New York: Holt, Rinehart and Winston.

Webster, C. D., T. L. Nicholls, M-L. Martin, S. L. Desmarais, and J. Brink. (2006). "Short-Term Assessment of Risk and Treatability (START): The Case for a New Structured Professional Judgment Scheme." *Behavioral Sciences and the Law* 24: 747–66.

Widom, C. (1977). "A Methodology for Studying Non-Institutionalized Psychopaths." *Clinical Psychology* 45:674–83.

Widom, C., and J. P. Newman. (1985). "Characteristics of Non-Institutionalized Psychopaths." In D. P. Farrington and J. Gunn (eds.), *Aggression and Dangerousness* (pp. 57–80). New York: Wiley.

9

Strain Theories

James C. Hackler

UNIVERSITY OF VICTORIA

consensus perspective
Also known as *functionalism*, the foundation of this perspective is the assumption that societies have an inherent tendency to maintain themselves in a state of relative equilibrium through the mutually adjustive and supportive interaction of their principal institutions. The approach also assumes that effective maintenance of a particular form of society is in the common interest of all its members.

conflict perspective
Sociological perspectives that focus on the inherent divisions of societies based on social inequality and the way these social divisions give rise to different and competing interests. The central assumption is that social structures and cultural ideas tend to reflect the interests of only some members of society rather than society as a whole. This contrasts with consensus or functionalist perspectives that assume a foundation of common interest among all members of society. Marxism and feminism are examples of conflict perspectives.

strain theory
The proposition that people feel strain when they are exposed to cultural goals that they are unable to obtain because they do not have access to culturally approved means of achieving those goals.

Societies have long attempted to explain the criminality of individuals. With the growth of sociology, scholars began to look at the wider relationship between crime and social structure. Two broad theoretical perspectives have guided this work. The older tradition can be called the **consensus perspective.** This approach maintains that the vast majority of the population shares similar values regarding right and wrong. Morality is universal, and important values are shared by all members of society. Customs persist, and the law represents a codification of societal values.

The **conflict perspective** questions such assumptions and argues that the criminal law does not necessarily represent the moral values of the majority but rather reflects the interests of the groups that are in a position to create and enforce those laws. The character of laws, the kinds of conduct they prohibit, and the types of sanctions depend on the nature of the powerful groups that influence legislation. The social values that receive the protection of the criminal law are ultimately those that are treasured by the dominant interest groups. It is not the *majority*, but rather the most *powerful*, whose values and concerns will be represented in the justice system. Some of these ideas are discussed in the next chapter. This chapter reviews some historical traditions that reflect the consensus perspective. While authors differ in their use of terms, recent discussions of **strain theory** fit this general orientation.

Consensus theorists assume a reasonable degree of agreement on things that matter in society. They also assume that social institutions such as the family, education, government, religion, and the economy normally all contribute to the smooth running of society. Crime occurs when something unusual happens that affects some or all of these institutions. This results in strains, stresses, or frustrations that affect people's behaviour.

It is convenient to separate the consensus and conflict perspectives, but this arbitrary classification oversimplifies reality. It may be more appropriate to think of particular crimes as being of the conflict or consensus type. In most societies, there is a high level of agreement that robbing someone and doing them bodily harm is a crime. Other crimes, such as smoking marijuana and gambling, will lead to less agreement regarding the need for criminalization. Laws regarding homosexuality illustrate not only varying attitudes but changes in attitudes and laws over time. Thus elements of consensus and conflict are always present in modern societies.

Learning Objectives

After reading this chapter, you should be able to

- Understand the differences between conflict and consensus perspectives of crime.
- Describe Durkheim's pioneering work dealing with the relationship between crime and social structure. Of particular importance is his conception of anomie or normlessness.
- Discuss how Robert Merton modified Durkheim so that anomie theory became a theory of relative deprivation rather than a theory of a lack of social regulation.
- Note that strains can arise from features in the society or from situations surrounding individuals.
- Outline the role played by community opportunities in the theories of Kobrin and Cloward.
- Explain the role played by the school and by peers in Cohen's theory of lower-class delinquency.
- Note how a *Code of the Streets* can evolve from strains arising in inner cities.
- Understand the strengths and weaknesses of strain theories.
- Describe the social policy implications of strain theories.

Durkheim: The Functions of Crime and Anomie

WWW

The Emile Durkheim Archive
L. Joe Dunham
http://durkheim.itgo.com/main.html

In his book *Division of Labor in Society*, first published in France in 1893, Émile Durkheim argued that social solidarity—social groups working together toward agreed-upon goals—was an essential characteristic of human societies (1933). These agreed-upon goals led to a set of shared norms. Without norms to guide them, societies function poorly. Such "normlessness," or anomie, occurs during periods of rapid change when social solidarity or social cohesion is reduced. The lack of a sense of community and a collective conscience leads to a breakdown in society and increases in suicide and crime.

Although some crime is normal, even necessary, to define the boundaries of acceptable behaviour, there must be a balance between the functional and dysfunctional aspects of deviance. Excessive crime and deviance would destroy a society, but if there were none at all, society would almost be compelled to create some. Even in a society of saints, someone would have to be defined as pushing the limits of proper behaviour. Behaviour may be restrained, but someone will violate the rules. For Durkheim, every society needs its quota of deviants.

Anomie and Normlessness

Durkheim popularized the concept of **anomie** to explain crime in more advanced and differentiated urban societies. Heterogeneity and increased division of labour weakened traditional societal norms. The resultant changes loosened the social controls on people, allowing a greater materialism and individualism. When social cohesion breaks down in society and social isolation is great,

anomie
A concept developed by Émile Durkheim (1858–1917) to describe an absence of clear societal norms and values. Individuals lack a sense of social regulation: people feel unguided in the choices they have to make. American sociologist Robert Merton (1910–2003) used the term more narrowly to refer to a situation in which people's goals—what they wanted to achieve—were beyond their means. Their commitment to the goal was so strong that they would adopt deviant means to achieve it.

society loses its traditional social control mechanisms and eventually suffers from a high rate of crime.

Anomie is often defined as a "sense of normlessness," but in Durkheim's *Suicide* (1897/1951) he also refers to anomie as a condition in which individual desires, or self-interests, are no longer governed and controlled by society. In other words, self-interest, rather than norms control behaviour.

Merton: The Gap Between Aspirations and Means

social structure
The patterned and relatively stable arrangement of roles and statuses found within societies and social institutions. The idea of social structure points out the way in which societies, and institutions within them, exhibit predictable patterns of organization, activity, and social interaction.

culturally prescribed aspiration
A rejection of the notion that aspirations are entirely self-created; rather, they are defined by culture and transmitted by other members of the society.

Merton applied this idea to crime by linking **social structure** and anomie (1938). If there is too much emphasis on the pursuit of self-interested goals and not enough on "legitimate means" to achieve those goals, the society is left "normless" or anomic. People then use illegitimate, or criminal, means to achieve their desires. For Durkheim and Merton an anomic society places a higher priority on self-interested values like the acquisition of wealth, status, and power, but gives a lower priority to collective values like fairness, equality, and justice.

Crime is a symptom of the gap between **culturally prescribed aspirations** and the socially structured means for realizing those aspirations. The culturally prescribed aspirations are the goals that are held up for all members of society. Merton argues that in America, the accumulation of money, and the status that results from material wealth, is a universal goal.

Socially structured avenues such as schooling are the accepted institutionalized means of reaching such goals. The socially structured avenues to achieve these goals may not be a problem for certain members of the society. If one comes from a family in which the father is a medical doctor, it may be realistic for the son or daughter to aspire to the same occupation and social status. The family may live in a nice neighbourhood, the children may attend schools that condition students toward thinking about a university or college education, and there may be a home environment that encourages reading and getting good grades. Although certain individual characteristics, such as a certain level of intelligence, may be required, the means to achieve culturally prescribed aspirations may be available to many middle-class youths.

By contrast, the child of a poor family, especially a racial minority family, could find things a bit more difficult. If the father has abandoned the family, if an older sibling has already been in trouble with the law, and if the mother has been on welfare, the means to achieve success may not be readily available. A youth coming from such an environment may not respect the school system and may have poor grades and minimal likelihood of entering university or college. However, he or she might aspire to become a doctor and to have both the material and social rewards that accrue to that occupation.

The gap between goals and means is small for certain portions of the society but large for others. The strain resulting from the gap between goals and means to achieve those goals could result in some sort of innovation, usually

FOCUS

BOX 9.1 Durkheim's General Model of Deviance

In his classic work on suicide, Durkheim argues that in contrast to community-oriented or collective thinking, individualism leads to a lack of social cohesion. Suicide, crime, and general deviance are inhibited in cohesive communities. His research showed that Protestant communities, which are more individualistic, had higher suicide rates than Catholic communities, which are more oriented toward collective thinking. From this, Durkheim concluded that individualism can cause deviant behaviour by reducing the strength of communities. One can generalize the argument from the specific act of suicide to deviance and crime in general, as illustrated in the sequence below:

An Oversimplified Model of Durkheim's Explanation of Suicide as a General Explanation of Crime

Greater Individualism —> Lack of Social Cohesion —> Suicide and Crime

deviant in nature. In simpler terms, when society encourages people to want things but makes it difficult for certain groups to get them, members of these groups are more likely to steal or go into prostitution.

Not only is the society anomic but the individual is as well. This is the condition known as *microanomie*—where an individual places more value on self-interest than on collective values. An individual with these values is then motivated to seek out self-interested desires and not think or care of the effect such a pursuit has on the group. This is what Konty (2005) found in a sample of college students. Those favouring "self-enhancing" values over "self-transcending" values were more likely to report criminal and deviant acts. The effect of these values on self-reported behaviour was stronger than the effects of other sociological variables like race and social class. Surprisingly, Konty found that the gap between male and female offending was mostly explained by these different values. Males were more likely to have microanomie than females. But simply having self-enhancing values did not produce crime and deviance if the self-transcending values were also strong. It was when self-transcending, or collective, values were weak that crime and deviance became more likely.

These arguments also seem to fit many forms of lower-class crime, particularly among marginally employed people. Robert Crutchfield (1995) points out that the lack of work influences crime. In addition, if these marginally employed people reside in concentrations of similarly underemployed people, the propensity to engage in crime is greater. This description fits certain ethnic groups in the United States and Canada.

The argument also fits certain upper-class crimes in which people in business, and others, aspire to great wealth. The legitimate avenues to success may not be sufficient because of severe competition; others may be "cutting corners" in a variety of ways. Political situations also create opportunities for diverting money illegally. When the Liberal Party of Canada provided funds for advertising, some of that money was evidently diverted by certain advertising executives (see Chapter 16). Thus if there is a gap between the desired goals and the means, innovation or illegitimate tactics are more likely.

Strain as a Feature of Society (Rather Than of Individuals)

Debates have arisen over what Merton meant. Were his ideas intended to explain the behaviour of individuals or, as Thomas Bernard (1987) argued, the behaviour of aggregates or groups? Bernard argued that it was not correct to interpret strain or anomie in psychological or social psychological terms; rather, these were properties of social structures. According to Bernard, Merton's theory would predict that societies whose cultures overemphasized the goal of monetary success and underemphasized adherence to legitimate means would have high rates of instrumental crime. If legitimate opportunities to achieve those monetary goals were unevenly distributed, instrumental crime would be unevenly distributed.

One must note the distinction between *cultural* factors and *structural* factors in society. In societies in which structural features create an uneven distribution of legitimate opportunities—that is, where there are many blocked opportunities—there will be pockets of instrumental crime, regardless of cultural values. When a culture emphasizes the ruthless pursuit of wealth, even if there is equal opportunity, crime will be widespread, and such a society will have a high rate of crime. One could argue that the United States, and perhaps to a slightly lesser extent, Canada, fit this pattern. Other wealthy countries, like Denmark, Norway, and Sweden, seem to be less concerned with the pursuit of wealth.

Steven Messner and Richard Rosenfeld (2007) extend this argument with their institutional-anomie theory. American culture emphasizes monetary success, but places less emphasis on *legitimate* means of achieving that success. This combination of strong pressures to succeed monetarily and *weak restraints on the means* is intrinsic to the "American Dream." It contributes to crime *directly* by encouraging people to use illegal means to achieve culturally approved goals, especially monetary goals. It also exerts an *indirect* effect on crime through its links with, and impact on, the institutional structure, or "the institutional balance of power." One institution—the economy—dominates all others. Such an emphasis has created a greater potential for crime.

The modern corporation may increase this tendency toward crime by splitting the production aspects from the financing. In the past, many companies were created by individuals who were primarily concerned with producing a product or service. Of course, they hoped to make a profit. Today, one can make money trading shares while disregarding the productive activities of a company. Shareholders play no part in daily operations. Nor are they committed to the reputation of the product or the long-term success of the company. They are simply entitled to a share of the profits. In fact, investors who "buy low and sell high" are admired. Northern Telecom, which became Nortel, illustrated this mentality when it was dominating business news in 2000 and 2001. A person selling Nortel stock at $125 in 2000 would have been congratulated. However, if one bought Nortel at its peak only to watch it drop to $1 in 2002, such an investor might be seen as stupid and greedy. Concern for the many people who lost their jobs, as well as genuine interest in the production of fibre optics, was secondary to the interest in the financial bubble that expanded and then burst.

The Enron and Worldcom trials (see Chapter 16, Corporate and White-Collar Crime) were unique in that top leaders were actually punished for their criminal behaviour. These cases illustrate a pattern by those at the top that can be described as a *subculture of power abuse*. In addition to being criminogenic, such behaviour is generally antisocial and tears at the very fabric of society (Hackler, 2006, Chapter 20).

Stock markets also create a new potential criminal—the inside trader. Those with intimate knowledge of a company are not supposed to profit from that insider knowledge. Terry Hungle, chief financial officer of Nortel, traded shares of the company just before the corporation announced some bad news, including the layoff of 15 000 employees (*Globe and Mail*, February 12, 2002). Similarly, Bill Bennett, former premier of British Columbia, had close relations with the forestry company Doman Industries. He unloaded his shares in Doman, thus reaping a $6-million windfall, minutes before those shares plummeted in value when a previously announced sale of the company was called off by the buyer. Bennett testified that the owner of Doman Industries never called him (even though phone records show that someone called him from Doman's office) just before he sold the stock.

Robber barons of the past might ruthlessly exploit others to build a railway, oil company, or steel mill; modern entrepreneurs with deviant tendencies might find fraudulent stock deals a faster way of achieving monetary goals. At age 32, Mark Valentine had achieved wealth and social standing. He came from a privileged family. Valentine could draw enough friends and sports celebrities, such as hockey star Eric Lindros, to a Valentine Golf Invitational to raise $800 000 in one year for the Children's Wish Foundation. His father, a former ambassador, was director of the World Trade Centre in Toronto. In August 2002 he was accused of conspiring to sell $29.4 million (U.S.) of stock at inflated prices to an FBI agent posing as a corrupt mutual fund manager (*Globe and Mail*, August 24, 2002).

Garth Drabinsky surrendered to police to face 19 counts of fraud, totalling half a billion dollars, for allegedly cooking the books at Livent Inc., his defunct live-theatre company (*Maclean's*, November 4, 2002). Drabinsky illustrates the weak restraints on the means to achieve wealth described by Messner and Rosenfeld (2007). Today there are new opportunities to manipulate finances. Bernie Ebbers, a former Edmonton milkman, was able to steal from his company, WorldCom, much faster than Leland Stanford and his railway could pillage California in the 19th century. Enron was able to use new strategies to manipulate the sale of energy in a manner that was not possible previously.

Similarly, cultural factors, such as the nature of our mass media, may minimize the impact of public opinion. Fraud at Enron was very much in the news for a short time. The coverage dwindled rapidly after the 9/11 attack on the World Trade Center. One must be wary of conflict theories that suggest the "war on Iraq" was designed to distract the public from corporate wrongdoing, but Vice-President Dick Cheney has been accused of being aware of accounting irregularities while he was CEO of Halliburton. George W. Bush was a director of Harken Energy and sold stock worth $850 000 just before the company released bad news. The company was also accused of hiding $10 million in debt to make the balance sheet look good. Is it also a coincidence that the accounting firm of Arthur Andersen, which has been charged with encouraging unethical practices, was advising Enron, WorldCom, Halliburton, Harken Energy, and many other well-known companies (*Maclean's*, July 22, 2002)? If world leaders and lawmakers are part of a *subculture of power* abuse that condones or at least tolerates these activities, is it likely that corrective action will be taken in Canada or the United States? Is it any wonder that George W. Bush's claims that he wants to clean up corporate wrongdoing have been met with skepticism? At any rate, the 9/11 attack on the World Trade Center and the Iraq war pushed the wrongdoing of corporations out of the public eye and off of government agendas for reform.

Responding to Opportunistic Crimes of the Powerful

Assuming that North America wishes to reduce the crime that arises out of the abuse of power by corporate leaders, traditional enforcement measures can be successful. Our judicial system may not be particularly effective against family violence or juvenile delinquency, but courts and watchdog agencies can deter powerful people who break the law. While long sentences for corporate criminals have become common in the United States, Canadian investigators have not been nearly as aggressive as their U.S. counterparts, and Canadian sentences have remained light.

The publicity arising out of prosecution might make corporate leaders rethink certain behaviour. In 2003 the Canadian Imperial Bank of Commerce (CIBC) paid a fine of $80 million to the Securities Exchange Commission for assisting Enron to commit fraud. In 2005 CIBC paid an additional $125 million to U. S. regulatory agencies. Later CIBC paid $2.4 billion in a lawsuit from the University of California alleging that CIBC "participated in an elaborate scheme to defraud investors." While this did not have much of a negative impact on the price of CIBC shares, bad publicity may have an impact in a competitive banking environment.

The watchdog role of government can deter without actually going to trial. The Ontario government under Mike Harris cut the resources to those who are supposed to investigate and prosecute corporate wrong doing (Snider, 2000, 2003). This sends a clear message to potential criminals. Since there are already weak restraints on the means to achieve monetary success, the inability of watchdog agencies and our justice system to respond effectively increases the likelihood of white collar and corporate crime.

Compared with other societies in the past, economic institutions dominate North America. Other important institutions—the family, education, and the political system—are relegated to secondary roles. Although these other institutions traditionally curbed criminal tendencies and imposed controls over the conduct of individuals, economic factors overwhelm those institutions that socialize people into pro-social behaviour. In other nations, such as Japan and India, the family appears to rank higher on the hierarchy of institutions and to be more influential relative to economics. Thus North America produces higher levels of serious crime than those countries in which the institutional balance of power leans toward non-economic institutions.

Strain as a Feature of Individuals

Perhaps Bernard is correct in arguing that Merton was applying his ideas to structures, but many of us find it useful to apply his ideas to individuals. As one applies strain theory to individuals, one can see a convergence with differential association (Chapter 12) and control theory (Chapter 13). An attempt in this direction, using strain theory as a base, is offered by Robert Agnew (1992). Strain triggers negative emotions, which in turn require that the individual cope with those emotions. Usually we are able to deal with our stresses. For example, strain could result from failing an exam. A legitimate coping strategy might be to accept the fact that one should have studied more. Another illustration: a boy develops a crush on a girl. She ignores him, so he works extra hard to become a top athlete. But if legitimate coping strategies are ineffective or unavailable, one may adopt illegitimate coping strategies.

Adolescents located in unpleasant environments, such as school, from which they cannot escape are more likely to be delinquent. Parental rejection, unfair or inconsistent discipline, parental conflict, and unsatisfactory relations with peers can be sources of strain. Often adolescents have few means to cope. If the coercive treatment is perceived as unjust or arbitrary, the resulting anger can lead to the defiance of authority.

Agnew and others (Brezina, 1998; Mazerolle and Piquero, 1997, 1998) call attention to the intervening role of anger in the relationship between strain and delinquency. If the strain doesn't make you mad, you may simply endure it rather than search for illegitimate alternatives. If the strain does lead to anger that cannot be handled legitimately, because opportunities are not available or are ineffective, crime becomes more likely.

Strain has usually been defined in the past in terms of blocked opportunities in education and jobs, but Agnew reminds us that other negative experiences also lead to stress and hence a search for illegitimate alternatives. In addition, different types of strain are more relevant to different subgroups (1991, 1992). There is also empirical support for the interaction of strain variables and social psychological ones, such as having delinquent friends (Agnew and White, 1992). Bonds with both delinquent and non-delinquent friends can lead to other stresses.

As more sophisticated measures of strain/anomie are developed, these ideas are being applied to different populations (Agnew et al., 1996). Recent empirical studies suggest that strain, or anomie, theory is more complex than the simplified versions presented here. We are learning more about the sources of individual strain and the macro-level determinants of such strain (Agnew, 1997; Jensen, 1995). The nature of the relationships among these variables is probably more complex than even the elaboration of strain theory offered by Agnew. This chapter, however, will simplify these arguments.

Coercion and Strain

Colvin et. al (2002) point out that coercive forces, such as economic pressures, can produce strains that in turn produce desperation and anger. Hagan and McCarthy (1997b) noted such forces among homeless youth in Canada. These coercive forces can be consistent or erratic as well as varying in strength (Colvin, 2000). Erratic coercion teaches individuals that they cannot control consequences because the strain is not predictable. Thus there is no pattern and no incentive to learn self-control. Erratic coercion is particularly conducive to chronic predatory crime.

One might argue that consistent coercion produces conformity. Dictatorships may be able to produce temporary conformity. Or the successful indoctrination of a social philosophy, such as communism, may result in a low crime rate. East Germany seemed to have a low crime rate, but with reunification the former East Germany has experienced a growing crime rate. The reunified eastern Germany may provide more erratic coercion, fewer legitimate opportunities, and less social support for legitimate activities.

Women in Afghanistan under the Taliban may have conformed under consistent coercion, but in a democracy, it is difficult to constantly monitor people to detect non-compliance. Thus consistent but mild coercion that is seen as fair, coupled with legitimate coping opportunities, combined with social support that reduces strain and anger, would lead to less crime.

Let us oversimplify by suggesting that some consistent coercion produces anger that is directed toward the self (Colvin, 2000). This could produce depression. Outward expressions of anger are likely to be met with a painful reprisal. Erratic coercion, which heightens the sense of injustice, produces anger directed against others. Since stresses are influenced by different settings, let us turn to the nature of opportunity structures.

The Shift from Control to Opportunity Structures

opportunity structure
Opportunity is shaped by the way the society or an institution is organized or structured.

relative deprivation
Relative deprivation and absolute deprivation are often contrasted. Absolute deprivation refers to the inability to sustain oneself physically and materially. However, in relative terms, deprivation is not judged against some absolute standard of sustainability but against deprivation in relation to others around you. You may have sufficient money to meet your needs and even meet them adequately, but you may feel relatively deprived because others around you have more.

Durkheim argued that human aspirations had to be regulated and channelled. Since human aspirations were boundless, and people could not always have what they want, they had to be persuaded to accept what they received. When people were not persuaded, the society became anomic. The moral guidelines were unclear. Social control broke down, and some people violated the norms established by those in power.

While Durkheim emphasized the restraints that control crime, Merton focused on **opportunity structures**. He suggested that American society had an overriding dominant goal—material success—but the guidelines for achieving that success were not always clear. If this type of anomie was so widespread, however, why wasn't crime distributed evenly through society? Merton accepted the argument that crime was distributed unevenly—that it was higher in the urban slums, for instance. To explain this social-class-specific crime by anomie, he redefined anomie as the disjuncture between the cultural goal of success and the opportunity structures by which this goal might be achieved. Anomie was shifted from normlessness to **relative deprivation**, whereby it was not the entire community that was anomic but rather specific individuals who were committed to the goal of wealth while being barred from the means that

TABLE 9.1 Typology of Community Opportunity Structures Implicit in Kobrin (1951)

	I	*II*	*III*	*IV*
Type of Community	*"Stable Slum"*	*"Transitory Slum"*	*"Suburbia"*	*Unlikely*
Legitimate opportunities	Yes	No	Yes	No
Illegitimate opportunities	Yes	No	No	Yes

Source: Adapted from Sol Kobrin. (1951). "The Conflict of Values in Delinquency Areas." *American Sociological Review* 16:653–61.

would realize that goal. However, different opportunity structures may facilitate breaking the law. Some communities, or some situations, may not provide opportunities for crime even though individuals are discontented. In one of the seminal articles in criminology, Sol Kobrin (1951) argues that opportunities differ in various types of communities.

Kobrin: Opportunities in the Community

In a seminal, but often forgotten article, Sol Kobrin points out that we live in communities that offer a variety of opportunities, both legitimate and illegitimate. Although globalization and the outsourcing of many jobs to countries that pay lower wages has impoverished many U.S. cities (Anderson, 1999), no community entirely lacks legitimate opportunities for its inhabitants to attain their aspirations or entirely lacks illegitimate opportunities. All communities offer a mixture of possibilities. Table 9.1 oversimplifies those possibilities to make its point. If communities have legitimate opportunities and/or illegitimate opportunities, four types of communities are possible. This typology oversimplifies reality; there will always be a gradation in opportunities. Nonetheless, it is useful to think in terms of ideal types.

In Type I communities, there are illegitimate opportunities as well as legitimate ones. One might call this type of community a "stable slum," where prostitution, gambling, and a variety of other illegal activities are well organized. The organized criminal element may concentrate on certain activities and avoid, or even discourage, violence and other types of crime that would upset the community and the forces of control. In such stable lower-class neighbourhoods, one would expect to find a number of legitimate opportunities that reflect the normal ongoing activities of a city. These would include restaurants, stores, repair shops, and all the other normal economic functions that arise to meet the needs of any urban society.

The Type II community might be called a "transitory slum," as typified by a decaying housing project. In such a disorganized community, there is extensive unemployment. No business dares to establish a store in the neighbourhood because of the fear of robbery. Paper carriers do not deliver in the area because customers would probably lose their papers, the deliverers might be attacked, and the newspaper would find it unprofitable. Restaurants are not established; thus there are few opportunities for servers, dishwashers, or cooks. In other words, it is an area with very few legitimate opportunities for earning money. Even the illegitimate opportunities are minimal because the neighbourhood is poorly organized. Prostitutes find it dangerous to work there, those who wish to gamble go to the more stable slum areas, and although the residents may occasionally attack one another, the pickings are rather slim. In these disorganized areas, there is little sense of community life, and families tend to be poorly integrated. Minimal opportunities exist for either legitimate or illegitimate enterprise.

The Type III community has legitimate opportunities but practically no illegitimate ones. Perhaps "suburbia" fits this description. A teenager can find work mowing lawns, especially if the neighbours know that the teenager comes from a good, solid family. Paper routes are available, and through their contacts in the community, juveniles may learn of opportunities for summer work and other part-time jobs. Adults and adolescents are involved in economic activities that create opportunities for work and the anticipation of future work. Illegitimate opportunities are rare. A would-be suburban prostitute might find difficulty in approaching customers out peacefully walking their dogs. A university or college student may not find much success trying to sell an armful of stolen hubcaps door-to-door in his or her suburban neighbourhood. Such a community can be expected to be lacking in illegitimate opportunities.

What about the Type IV community? Although such a combination is theoretically possible, it is probably unlikely that any neighbourhood could develop a wide range of illegitimate opportunities without also spawning some legitimate ones. If the illegitimate opportunities were well organized, we would expect restaurants, stores, laundries, and other facilities to develop to provide those stable lower-class communities with normal services. If either organized crime or the citizenry had things fairly well under control, the community could become viable. While the control mechanisms may differ in such neighbourhoods, the suggestion is that it would be very unlikely to find a community with well-organized illegitimate opportunities alone.

Kobrin (1951) emphasizes the *dual* characteristics of lower-class communities. Both legitimate and illegitimate opportunities exist together in greater or lesser degree. Questions regarding how these two structures interact and what draws people to one rather than another have generated considerable debate among sociologically oriented criminologists. Policy-makers must take community characteristics into account and be aware that a uniform strategy is unlikely to work because all communities are different.

Richard Cloward: Illegitimate Opportunity Structures

Just as there are differences between legitimate and illegitimate opportunities, there are different types of illegitimate opportunities. Cullen (1984) points out the importance of "structuring variables." Cloward (1959) asserts that simply being subjected to socially generated strain does not enable a person to deviate in any way he or she chooses. People can participate in a given adaptation only if they have access to the means to do so (Cullen, 1984, 40). Even though members of the lower class may be under a great deal of strain, they are unlikely to engage in violations of financial trust, political corruption, and other white-collar crimes in order to achieve their goals. In an article (1959) and then in a book with Lloyd Ohlin entitled *Delinquency and Opportunity* (1960), Cloward extended the ideas of Merton by combining them with themes found in Sutherland's "differential association" (see Chapter 12). Sutherland argued that criminal behaviour is learned through associations with others who define criminal activity favourably. While Merton emphasized legitimate means, Sutherland concentrated on illegitimate means (Cullen, 1988). People under strain cannot become any kind of criminal they choose; they are limited by the opportunities available to them. Dealing in drugs is not automatically available to a "square" college or university professor as a means of supplementing her income; she probably lacks the skills and contacts to obtain a source of illegal drugs. In other words, illegitimate means are not readily available to people simply because they lack legitimate means. While Durkheim and Merton developed plausible theories of structurally induced pressures, it remained to Cloward to try to explain the resulting adaptive behaviour.

Merton appreciated Cloward's insights and extension of his ideas, as was apparent in the commentary Merton wrote in the *American Sociological Review*, which appeared immediately after Cloward's article. Merton noted that some earlier research showed that there were five times as many fraud convictions in Texas as in Massachusetts. Perhaps, he went on, it was more difficult to sell someone a dry oil well in Massachusetts than in Texas. Illegal opportunities for certain types of fraud are more available in some areas than others.

Opportunity theory fits many different types of deviance, but Cloward and Ohlin are best known for the application of these ideas to juvenile delinquency. Although undergoing strain, juveniles face different barriers to resolving that strain than adults do. The way they respond to social barriers for achieving goals could lead to three different types of gangs or **subcultures**: *criminal*, *conflict*, and *retreatist* gangs. Herbert Costner, in lectures at the University of Washington, used the diagram shown in Figure 9.1 to explain how these gangs are formed.

subculture
A group of people who share a distinctive set of cultural beliefs and behaviours that differs in some significant way from that of the larger society.

There are pressures toward conventional goals and there are pressures toward achieving middle-class values, such as respectability and conventional success. When juveniles overcome those barriers, as most middle-class juveniles do, they commit little crime. However, lower-class males may actually have different goals. Instead of respectability, they may be more interested in money, a car, and showing off for their girlfriends. Under certain economic conditions, this might be achieved by working in areas in which their skills are scarce, working in a hazardous occupation, or possibly being fortunate as an athlete. In other words, it is possible to be successful in a working-class style of life. These ideas differ somewhat from Merton's in that aspirations are not universal, as Merton has argued. Striving for success can mean different things to different people.

However, Cloward emphasizes the barriers to lower-class as well as middle-class goals. Not only is there an opportunity structure for the goals of the lower class, but crime also has an opportunity structure of its own. If legitimate opportunities are blocked, the next step may be to search for illegal success, but even here there are barriers. Without certain contacts, it may be difficult to get into illegal gambling or learn the skills of a successful safecracker. Many juveniles will have difficulty learning the skills necessary to succeed in these areas. However, if there are barriers to profitable property crime, juveniles can still turn to conflict as a means of attaining status, at least among their peers.

FIGURE 9.1 Barriers to Legal and Illegal Opportunities Implicit in the Work of Cloward and Ohlin (1960)

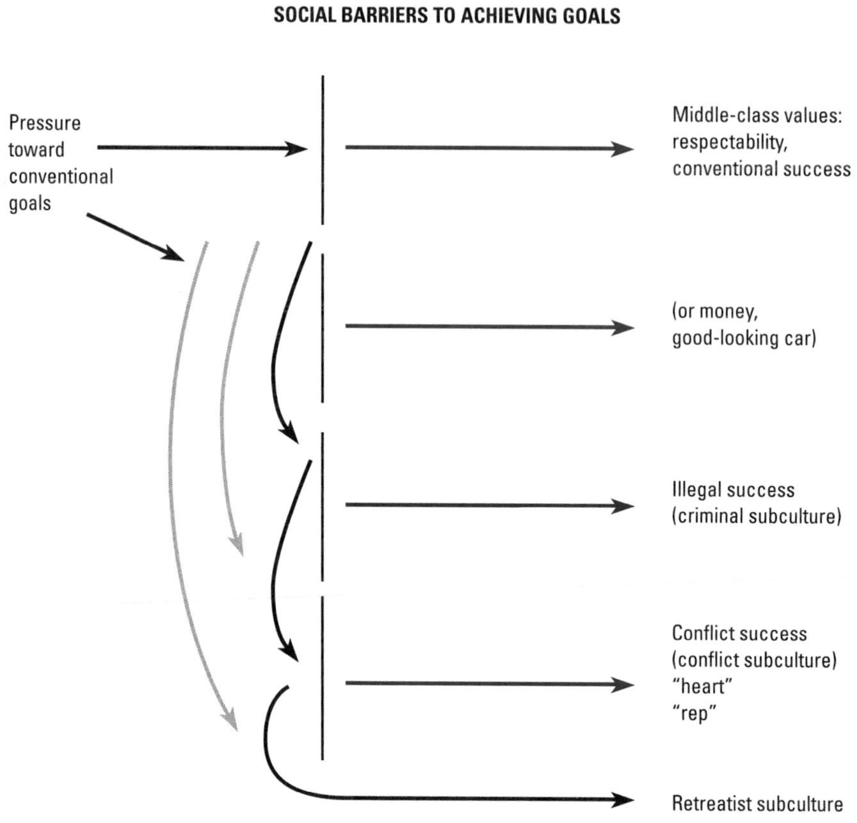

Juveniles who are unskilled as thieves can show their bravery by fighting for their "turf." This will show others that they have "heart"; their courageous behaviour will give them a "rep." But even conflict success has barriers. Not every juvenile is keen on wielding a bicycle chain in a gang war. Some may lack strength or courage or both. These juveniles may employ a third delinquent alternative: the use of drugs. In the drug or retreatist subculture there are practically no barriers.

Individual characteristics, such as race, will be related to some of these barriers. Thus Asian youths in Vancouver may have opportunities to work with Asian gangs who extort money from restaurant owners. Blacks who have lived in Nova Scotia since the American Revolution, Jamaican youths in Toronto, and Haitian immigrants in Montreal probably have a realistic view of the barriers to legitimate and illegitimate success. Violence and drugs may be the only things left. In Canada, the abuse of alcohol by First Nations people may also be influenced by barriers to both legitimate and illegitimate opportunities.

Marginal Opportunity Structures

Francis Cullen (1988) believes that many scholars have not fully appreciated the contributions made by Cloward because they are focused primarily on the gap between aspirations and perceived opportunities. In fact, other deviant styles of adaptation to illegitimate opportunities become apparent when one looks beyond traditional types of crime and at different settings. Fred Desroches describes the way some men adapt to pressures related to homosexual activity in public restrooms in Ontario (1995). The "tearoom," a public washroom where homosexual activity takes place, provides an opportunity structure for those under certain types of strain. Alternatives do not seem to fill the need; thus, this marginal opportunity structure is used with the risk that police action will create additional problems in their lives.

Street life offers another type of marginal or illegitimate opportunity structure (Hagan and McCarthy, 1997a, 1997b). Youths in families that are functioning well do better in school as well as in finding work. Negative family experiences increase the likelihood of "hanging out" on the street. The interactions among parental employment, weakened marital ties, neglect, and abuse increase the likelihood of crime directly, but they also expose such youths to additional new stresses when they leave one negative environment for another. Seeking food and shelter on the street, these vulnerable youths meet seasoned offenders, who coach the newcomers in criminal activities. The police will also view them as criminally inclined.

Street life increases exposure to networks of seasoned offenders who offer tutelage in offending and a means of acquiring "criminal capital"—that is, information (e.g., where to sell stolen goods) and skills (e.g., how to use burglary tools). Physical and sexual abuse, the erratic coercion suggested by Colvin (2000), has conditioned them to respond to police confrontations with defiance and rage. Hagan and McCarthy show how employment, a source of social and **human capital**, in contrast to criminal capital, can reduce involvement in crime and street life. (See Chapter 13.)

human capital
The talents and capabilities that individuals contribute to the process of production. Companies, governments, and individuals can invest in this capital, just as they can invest in technology and buildings or in finances.

Cloward's work may also offer an explanation of certain marginal activities, such as being an oil company spy. In Alberta, where many oil companies drill wells in the wilderness and try to keep their findings secret, spies from rival companies sometimes pose as hunters or wilderness trekkers to observe drilling operations without being detected. This often-hazardous activity highlights the presence of particular opportunities and barriers to potentially profitable tasks. Kobrin and Cloward have applied these ideas to conventional crime, but there may be a much wider range of marginal behaviours that would fit these models.

In Figure 9.1, one can see that there are a number of barriers or "structuring variables" that influence the choice of activities. If all opportunities are blocked, skid row may be the alternative. P. J. Giffen (1966) describes the "revolving door" in Toronto where skid row alcoholics went in and out of jail on a regular basis. If the retreatist subculture is the end of the line for certain types of delinquents, we might argue that skid row represents a similar situation for those who find other barriers insurmountable.

The question of opportunity structures, including illegitimate ones, poses an interesting policy question for society. Which is more desirable: having skid row alcoholics with no opportunities, or having prostitutes and gamblers engaging in activities that are seen as deviant by society? While legitimate opportunities are clearly preferable to illegitimate ones, is it possible that the integration of some borderline, or even obvious, deviance would be better than the total breakdown represented by some of society's rejects? In a society that must sometimes choose between levels of evils, would policy-makers be wise to consider the nature of different opportunity structures and assess the impact of selected illegitimate opportunities on society?

From Albert K. Cohen: The Middle-Class Measuring Rod to Elijah Anderson: The Code of the Street

middle-class measuring rod
A phrase suggesting that children and young people from the lower class often find themselves in situations in which they are measured against middle-class standards.

Can strain theories help us explain violent crime? About half a century ago Albert Cohen, in his very influential book *Delinquent Boys: The Culture of the Gang* (1955), focused our attention on the way situations develop. Cohen differs from Cloward in that he feels that lower-class boys aspire to middle-class goals when they enter the education system. Cloward's work tends to neglect the opportunity structure of schools and the ways in which schools block opportunity. According to Cohen, schools are dominated by the **middle-class measuring rod**, which sets up a certain set of standards: sophistication, good appearance, selling oneself, controlling aggression, respect for authority, deferred gratification, and those general characteristics that make young boys and girls a success in the middle-class world. If a student follows these standards, he or she is likely to have success in school. The clear implication is that this will lead to success in the larger society. This process begins early. The lower-class child begins school with desires and goals that are similar to those of other young children. The difference is that the lower-class child may have difficulty meeting the standards set by the middle-class measuring rod. While middle-class children are taught to respect books and be polite, the lower-class child may have been taught to stand up for her rights and not let people push her around. The middle-class child has been taught to "save for a rainy day," but the lower-class child has learned that men who win money gambling spend it quickly and treat their friends.

Other strain theorists have attempted to identify sources of stress but have spent less time explaining the dynamics of how an individual adapts to that stress. A lower-class student could make an effort to change his or her behaviour to please the teacher, but there may be little support from home and from peers. A second alternative is to withdraw from the contest and lead an isolated existence. Cohen argues that male juveniles who fail in the educational system when they cannot meet middle-class standards can gain status by reversing those standards. In this third alternative, juveniles try to modify the goals and begin looking for others who are in the same predicament. If the goals have been turned upside down, "good" boys become "squares" and teachers' pets. Instead of respecting authority, one challenges it. "Tough" guys gain prestige. Fighting becomes important; "rep" and "heart" are important to show that a boy is capable of participating in a gang rumble. The juvenile strives for higher prestige among the gang. Instead of saving money and developing economical habits, one shares with fellow gang members. Destroying property shows

TABLE 9.2 Strain Theories

Theory	*Theorists*	*Key Elements*
Anomie: weak social regulation	Durkheim	When social cohesion breaks down, society loses its traditional mechanisms of social control and eventually suffers from a high rate of crime.
Anomie: the gap between aspirations and means	Merton	Crime occurs when there is a gap between culturally prescribed aspirations and socially structured means for realizing those aspirations.
Institutional-Anomie	Messner, Rosenfeld	Strong pressures to succeed monetarily and weak restraints on the means to succeed in a society emphasizing economics leads to crime.
General strain	Agnew	Adolescents in unavoidable unpleasant environments face strain leading to anger and delinquency.
Coercion and strain	Colvin	Erratic coercion heightens a sense of injustice, produces anger against others and destroys social bonds.
Opportunity structures	Kobrin, Cloward	In addition to strains that create a pressure toward criminal behaviour, there are also different opportunity structures that may facilitate breaking the law. These structures are both legitimate and illegitimate.
The middle class	Cohen measuring rod	Lower-class youths are unable to meet the middle-class standards of the school. As a result, they collectively build a new set of values and standards that are the opposite of those of the middle class.
Code of the Street	Anderson	Lack of employment opportunities leads to alternative ways of achieving respect: displaying toughness, taking another person's possessions, pulling a trigger. It helps build a reputation that prevents future challenges. But it also creates other problems.

contempt for those whose goals one has rejected. Instead of being courteous, the gang member emphasizes discourtesy and dresses in a manner to provoke middle-class teachers.

Reaction formation is a psychological mechanism for redefining goals when the individual cannot meet the standards expected of him or her. However, reversing middle-class standards cannot be done by one individual alone. This is a collective process brought about through **mutual conversion**. In relations with others, people generally explore the nature of the response from others before they commit themselves too far. The juvenile who is doing poorly in school notices that there are others who are not succeeding in school. While walking home together, two boys might explore their feelings about school. "What do you think about the teacher?" The other responds cautiously, "I dunno, do you like him?" Response: "Not much, how about you?" "I don't like him at all."

The mutual conversion continues. Each boy commits himself a bit more until they have mutually agreed that the teacher is unfair, the teacher's pet is a

reaction formation
In Freudian terms, it is an adaptation in which the ego unconsciously develops attitudes and interests the direct opposite of those in the id striving for expression. In Albert Cohen's theory, lower-class children who cannot succeed when measured by middle-class criteria collectively reverse these values and obtain status by doing the opposite.

mutual conversion
A phrase suggesting that conversion to deviance (and perhaps to other lifestyles) is not a solitary activity but is achieved through a process of interaction with others.

creep, and so is the boy who gets good grades. As the process continues, they can rebuild a new set of values and different standards, which they can meet more easily than middle-class standards.

It is important to note that as these boys achieve new status among gang members, such status is limited to the inner group. Outside of the gang, their status is low and becomes even lower. As a result, they turn more to the gang for gratification and become even more separated from the middle-class orientation of the school.

Many studies of gang dynamics followed Cohen's work. Skipping several decades of research, we can use Elijah Anderson's *Code of the Street: Decency, Violence, and the Moral Life of the Inner City* (1999) to describe the cumulative effects of structural changes in inner cities.

But how does strain theory explain violence in the inner city? During and after World War II, manufacturing jobs in the cities utilized many unskilled and semi-skilled workers. Many blacks, Hispanics, and other ethnic groups benefited from these opportunities. At the same time, more minorities were moving into middle-class jobs. However, with the exporting of manufacturing to countries paying low wages, the loss of these unionized jobs that paid reasonably well had a serious impact on those at the bottom of the social scale.

Barriers to participate in mainstream society persist for young blacks. Employers prefer white women and new immigrants to young blacks. The resulting strains led to what might be described as full-blown *reaction formation. The Code of the Street* requires young males, and often females, to let others know how tough they are, how hard it would be for someone else to "roll on" them, how much "mess" they will take before they respond with a fist in the mouth.

The most effective way of gaining respect is to manifest nerve. A man shows this by taking another person's possessions, messing with someone's woman, throwing the first punch, "getting in someone's face," pulling a trigger. It helps build a reputation that prevents future challenges (Anderson, 92).

Many young blacks actively live their lives in opposition to whites and middle-class blacks. Lacking trust in mainstream institutions, many turn to "hustling" in the underground economy (Anderson, 108). To be self-respecting, young men and women must exhibit contempt for a system they are sure has contempt for them.

The drug trade offers economic opportunity, is organized around the code of the streets that employs violence for social control, and thus contributes significantly to the violence of inner-city neighbourhoods. For those with minimal success in the legal job market, illegal activities provide alternatives: the drug trade, prostitution, welfare scams, and other rackets.

Even though the majority of youths in school may be "decent," the street element dominates. It victimizes those who show weakness. Thus decent kids must take on the code of the street if they are to avoid being victimized.

This chapter will not dwell on the dynamics of inner-city crime but simply point out that the lack of opportunity for legitimate employment leads to strain. To achieve respect, and the money that enhances respect, young people must display a willingness to use violence. The drug trade also provides significant economic opportunities.

Assessing Strain Theories

When Durkheim introduced his ideas, scholars were still explaining crime primarily by genetics and inner psychological forces. Durkheim focused attention on social forces, a radical idea at the time, but now the dominant methodology for explaining crime. His attempts to explain the link between crime and modernization may or may not be accurate, but it seems that the basic patterns of crime that have evolved in western Europe have also occurred in eastern European countries and in the emerging nations of Asia, Africa, and Latin America as they move toward modernization (Shelley, 1981).

Durkheim was less accurate in his description of premodern nations as stable, crime-free societies. In fact, many had high levels of violence. Furthermore, Western countries seem to have experienced a long-term decline in crime over the past few centuries (Gurr, 1981). Despite the continual complaints we hear today, during the 17th century, the average citizen in most cities in western Europe would rarely leave the security of a locked home after dark.

Gwynne Nettler feels that the concept of "opportunity" is vague. Is there a difference between perceived opportunities and real ones? "Opportunities are by their nature much easier to see after they have passed than before they are grasped" (1984, 209). If people do not end up equally happy and rich, is this due to differences in opportunities? We must avoid the circular argument of explaining the cause by using the outcome.

Merton's strain theory does not help us explain the lower crime rates of women. Merton takes into account differences in opportunity that arise out of social class, but he does not apply the same reasoning to blocked opportunities based on gender (Comack, 1992). Women, like disadvantaged lower-class males, might be expected to be more criminal as a means to achieve universal goals. While many conventional theorists have assumed that women experience less strain than men in the struggle to achieve through institutionalized means, many feminist scholars reject these statements as assumptions and biases rather than fact (Morris, 1987; Naffine, 1987). Although the strains women are subject to may differ from those experienced by men, they may be just as severe. Unless one assumes women have more modest goals, strain theory does not explain why women are less criminal.

Strain theories that link coercion with social support may be more compatible with less female crime (Colvin et al., 2002). Females may get more social support from families and from one another, which may help them cope and may lead to less anger. In one sense, women have had considerable experience coping with injustice.

The Static State of Strain Theories

With the exception of Cohen, Agnew, Colvin, Anderson, and some recent authors, the traditional strain theorists offer rather static explanations without taking into account the dynamic nature of social interaction. Cohen moved the thinking in that direction and Anderson applied it to the urban ghetto, but most strain theories tend to ignore group dynamics, making them inadequate for explaining certain types of crime. Imagine, for example, that a group of boys have gained entry to a feed-mill warehouse to play tag among the stacks of feedbags.

> Soon the motorized fork-lift trucks were discovered, and the boys began having fun driving them. They didn't *deliberately* drive them into the feed bags, but they were unskilled pilots of the fork-lift trucks. The first time the grain sacks were damaged, the boys may have hesitated, perhaps a bit anxious about what they had done; but they may have also wondered how deeply you could drive the forks on the trucks into a bag of grain if you really took a run at it. The challenge, the dare, the competition, and the perverse pleasure in the destruction stimulated others to go further than they had earlier planned. This is *mutual excitation.* (Hackler, 2006, 79)

In earlier studies of collective behaviour, Blumer (1951) suggested the term *circular reaction.* This is the type of interstimulation in which the actions of one individual stimulate another, which in turn is reflected back to the first person, providing reinforcement. Soon there is *group contagion.* Andrew Wade (1967) provides an explanatory argument for vandalism that is quite compatible with these ideas.

Traditional strain theory is clearly lacking in its power to incorporate the dynamic elements of social interaction. While some of the static variables may have been relevant at the beginning, the interstimulation, the dynamics of the events seem to play a much more powerful role. These factors may also provide tools for preventing crime. What are the conditions that lead to a potential participant refusing to take part right from the beginning and possibly changing the entire direction of the process? While Albert Cohen takes some of these interactive factors into account with *reaction formation* and *mutual conversion*, these dynamic elements are lacking in most structural–functional explanations of crime, which may be their greatest weakness. Explanations that do consider these elements are presented in Chapter 12, which discusses interactionist theories.

The Convergence of Strain Theory and Other Perspectives

Despite the criticisms of strain theory, these ideas have been of considerable interest to criminologists. More recent elaborations of strain theory (Agnew, 1992; Colvin et al., 2002) have led to some convergence with other theories, including control theory and differential association theory. There is considerable agreement that the contributions emerging from Merton, Kobrin, and Cloward are still useful (Bernard, 1987; Agnew, 1997; Agnew et al., 1996; Menard, 1997; Messner and Rosenfeld, 2007; Vaughan, 1997; Cullen, 1988; Farnworth and Leiber, 1989). Nor do traditional theoretical perspectives have to be seen as distinct and competing explanations. There has been a convergence of ideas that permits strain theory, differential association, and control theory to complement one another. In addition, the policy implications of the different theories can be similar. For example, enabling the disenfranchised to participate more fully in what society has to offer is probably related to greater social bonding with others and a stronger belief in the rules that guide the larger society. However, if social bonds are primarily with people who condone or rationalize criminal behaviour, and with those who face similar blocked opportunities, criminal behaviour is likely. In such situations, control theory, differential association, and strain theory complement one another.

There is similar logic in the work of Robert Agnew (1992; 1997). He argues that adolescents located in unpleasant environments, such as school, from which they cannot escape are more likely to be delinquent. Although strain has usually been defined in the past in terms of blocked opportunities in education and jobs, Agnew reminds us that there are other negative experiences that lead to stress. This can lead to the search for illegitimate alternatives. In addition, different types of strain are more relevant to different subgroups. Furthermore, there is empirical support for the interaction of strain variables and social psychological ones, such as having delinquent friends (Agnew and White, 1992). Differential association emphasizes ties with delinquents (Chapter 12). Social control theory (Chapter 13) focuses on the lack of social bonds juveniles have with non-deviant members of society. Agnew and White note that some of these bonds could lead to strain. Furthermore, some criminologists have measured reciprocal effects (Thornberry, 1987). One variable affects another, which in turn has a further impact on the previous variable.

A vast oversimplification of these ideas might be as follows: (1) learning theories (Chapter 12), such as differential association, explain delinquency by *positive* relations with deviant others; (2) social control theories (Chapter 13) argue that delinquency occurs when juveniles have *little or no* attachment or social bonds to others; (3) Agnew's elaboration of strain theory emphasizes that *negative* relations and experiences in situations beyond their control lead juveniles to delinquency; (4) all three conditions can reinforce one another and can have a reciprocal impact, increasing the likelihood of criminal behaviour.

Uses of Strain Theory

Modern society creates many illegitimate opportunities for those wishing to take advantage of them. Credit cards, computers, and the flow of information across borders make new forms of theft possible. The terrorist attacks of September 11, 2001, on the World Trade Center created opportunities for fraud. More than 200 people have been arrested for defrauding agencies that were trying to help victims and relatives. A lawyer stole $78 000 from several agencies. A morgue manager was accused of stealing coffins and reselling them. However, most normal people do not avail themselves of the vast opportunities for theft in complex societies. Strain theories may be less adequate in explaining non-deviance.

Messner and Rosenfeld (2007) argue that the emphasis on material wealth in North America encourages crime, but other countries may have a different value structure. In one informal study done by *Reader's Digest*, 1100 wallets were "lost" in about a dozen countries. Each wallet contained $50 in local currency and the name and phone number of the owner. About 44 percent of the wallets disappeared. However, in Norway and Denmark, every single wallet was returned. Do some societies create a climate that produces more good Samaritans and where illegitimate opportunities are ignored?

John Braithwaite: Greater Class Mix and the Reduction of Crime

Braithwaite (1979) argues that one must look at the interaction between the social class of individuals and the social class of the neighbourhood in order to answer the question of whether an increase in class heterogeneity in neighbourhoods would reduce crime. He offers two propositions. The first is that crime is most likely when both exposure to illegitimate opportunities is high and exposure to legitimate opportunities is low. The second states that crime is unlikely either when legitimate opportunities are high or when illegitimate opportunities are low. In other words, in three out of the four possible combinations, there are factors that would inhibit crime. Only when both illegitimate opportunities and a lack of legitimate opportunities exist would there be a marked increase in crime.

Braithwaite also argues that belonging to the lower class has more effect on delinquency for youth in lower-class areas than for youth in middle-class areas. Consequently, cities with relatively large numbers of lower-class people living in predominantly middle-class areas and relatively large numbers of middle-class people living in predominantly lower-class areas have relatively low crime rates. That is, greater class mix results in less crime.

This implies that if the middle classes could keep together, they would be better off; on the other hand, if the lower classes stay together, they will be even worse off. Hence, it may be to the advantage of those with power and influence to keep themselves segregated. The quality of life for the society as a whole, however, would be improved if residential heterogeneity characterized the society.

Braithwaite's ideas seem more applicable to property crime, but another study shows that if there is a culture of violence, its roots are to be found in racial and economic inequalities (Blau and Blau, 1982). Spatial mixing in neighbourhoods would be more easily achieved with a reduction of racial and economic inequalities. Some observers have suggested that Canada has a lower crime rate than the United States in part because our housing policies have been less likely to "ghettoize" the poor in areas that could develop very high crime rates.

Reducing Upper-Class Crime

Braithwaite also offers an interesting idea about crime among the upper classes. He argues that "too little power and wealth creates problems of living, and this produces crime of one type; too much power corrupts, and this produces crime of another type" (1979, 200). This does not mean that upper-class people are more criminal than lower-class people. If lower-class people were exposed to the same vast opportunities as white-collar criminals, they, too, would engage in large-scale "power" crimes. Powerful people abuse their occupational power. Lawyers, business owners, pharmacists, and medical doctors all have unique opportunities to commit crimes with very little risk. It makes little sense to ask which social class commits more crime. Rather, opportunities differ by social class. However, the class-mix logic described above applies to the upper class as well. If we reduced the power of these people, that is, reduced their opportunities for crime, white-collar crime would also be reduced. If lower-class people commit crimes because of a lack of power and wealth, increasing their influence and well-being might help. Braithwaite (who admits a socialistic bias) argues that greater economic equality and a greater distribution of influence among people would modify to some extent those factors that lead to crime.

Lower-class crime may be caused by the failure to achieve success goals. By contrast, upper-class crimes arise from an unprincipled overcommitment to success goals. One study of college students found that those most dedicated to monetary success were those most likely to argue that they "can't afford to be squeamish about the means." Similarly, certain occupational structures can increase commitment to illegitimate success. Richard Quinney (1963) found that retail pharmacists tended to fall into two divergent categories with different role expectations: professional and business. Those who were oriented toward the professional role were bound by guidelines for compounding and dispensing prescriptions. Those oriented toward the business role subscribed to the popular belief that self-employment carries with it independence and freedom from control. For them, professional norms exercised less control. Prescription violations occurred more frequently among the business-oriented pharmacists. As both Quinney and Braithwaite would argue, the mutual support of like-minded individuals insulated from the broader society, and from their professional colleagues, increased the likelihood of crime.

Policy Implications

Four decades ago, crime-prevention projects utilized strain theories to change opportunity structures. In hindsight, the narrow focus of these projects made it difficult to obtain significant impacts, but they illustrate attempts to apply some of the ideas reviewed in this chapter.

In the 1960s, the Mobilization for Youth Project was launched in New York City following the principles outlined by Cloward and Ohlin. This project attempted to improve education, create work opportunities, organize lower-class communities, and provide a variety of social services. There is little evidence to suggest that the project was successful in an overall sense (Helfgot, 1981). It is extremely difficult to alter the social-structural arrangements that create barriers to opportunity. Moreover, the programs were later taken over by traditional social service bureaucracies that normally act to protect and enhance their own interests. Under their jurisdiction, actual implementation involved attempts to change individuals instead of making basic changes in the structure of society. In his book *The Betrayal of the Poor*, Rose (1972) argues that the War on Poverty in the United States failed because it was transformed to serve the interests of poverty-serving agencies.

Opportunities for Youth (OFY) in Seattle was another attempt to use work opportunities to reduce delinquency that met with little success (Hackler, 1966). One might argue that temporary job programs do not have a meaningful impact on the larger community. However, this same project had an impact on the attitudes of the adults living in the four communities in which the project was conducted (Hackler and Linden, 1970). Furthermore, parents of black children seemed particularly responsive to the idea of job opportunities for their children. Like so many programs launched during the 1960s, OFY attempted to utilize strain theories. Lower-class populations did respond and became involved. Although evidence of crime reduction in the short term is lacking, the opportunity structure was altered for some lower-class families. We should not be overly cynical or skeptical. Early childhood education programs implemented in the 1960s have demonstrated that they can have a significant effect on later school achievement and, eventually, success in the adult world (Schweinhart et al., 1993).

Unfortunately, opportunities for the lower classes may have decreased in North America in the past decade. While there has been a dramatic increase in the wealth of the upper classes, the frequent display of a luxurious lifestyle, especially on television, creates all the more strain for those who aspire to a share of that material wealth.

It may be difficult to alter the structure of society, but governments could support those institutions that ease some of the strains that arise from blocked opportunities. Public policies could provide visiting nurses, training and support for disadvantaged mothers, paid family leave, and universal health care. The work done by Richard Tremblay and his colleagues at the Université de Montréal on early childhood development is consistent with preschool "head start" programs that help reduce the strains caused by the challenges of education (Tremblay and Craig, 1995). Young people could be involved in national service programs, such as the Peace Corps, which lead to government funding for higher education or training in skilled occupations. Workplaces could offer continuing training and upgrading. In other words, some of the strains experienced in the family, school, and workplace do not have to lead to anger and attacks on society if institutions provide alternatives.

Other strains are created by the criminal justice system itself, which is based largely on coercion (Colvin et al., 2002). Disintegrative shaming pervades our current coercive criminal justice operations (Braithwaite, 1989). Social support is the key ingredient in "reintegrative shaming." Andrews and Bonta (1998) show that individuals can control their behaviour with rehabilitation programs that use cognitive and behavioural therapies. Given the right setting, this can lead to positive outcomes and legitimate ways of coping. In fact, most current crime control measures produce an erratic coercive cycle, which increases strain and anger. Unfortunately, moving toward a noncoercive, socially supportive criminal justice system does not seem likely at the present time.

Scholars do not have to be in complete agreement regarding strain theory before applying many of its principles to public policy in the important pursuit of reducing the gap between rich and poor. Nor should we ignore the warning Merton voiced in his 1938 article: *The ruthless pursuit of profit creates a criminogenic society.* Increasing opportunities for the less privileged members of society makes a great deal more sense than rewarding the wealthy to encourage them to invest (for a profit, of course) so that some of the wealth will trickle down to the poor. The self-serving policies advocated by many powerful people in North America in recent years should, according to any version of strain theory, lead to more crime.

Summary

- Two broad theoretical perspectives have guided sociological theories of crime. The consensus perspective maintains that the vast majority of the population share similar values regarding right and wrong. The law represents a codification of societal values. The conflict perspective questions such assumptions and argues that the criminal law does not necessarily represent the moral values of the majority but rather reflects the interests of the groups that are in a position to create and enforce those laws.
- Strain theory is part of the consensus tradition. Strain theorists assume that social institutions such as the family, education, government, religion, and the economy normally all contribute to the smooth running of society. Crime occurs when something unusual happens that affects some or all of these institutions. This results in strains, stresses, or frustrations that affect people's behaviour.
- Durkheim saw crime and other deviance as a consequence of modernity. Changes associated with modernity led to a weakening of social controls, and consequently rates of deviance increased.
- Merton began with Durkheim's concept of anomie but modified Durkheim's theory to account for what he felt were the realities of American society. In Merton's anomie theory, crime resulted from the gap between culturally prescribed aspirations and the socially structured means for realizing those aspirations.
- Messner and Rosenfeld argued that American culture emphasizes monetary success. When combined with weak restraints on illegitimate means this encourages economic crimes.
- Agnew suggests that adolescents located in unpleasant and stressful environments, such as school, from which they cannot escape become frustrated and angry. If legitimate coping alternatives are not available, violent outbursts and delinquency are likely.
- Kobrin extended Merton's theory by introducing the idea of community opportunity structures. Some communities provide more legitimate opportunities than do others. Cloward pointed out that illegitimate opportunities were also not equally accessible to all. As a result, he hypothesized that there would be three different types of delinquent subcultures: criminal, conflict, and retreatist.
- Albert Cohen took a more dynamic approach to the problems created by strain. Lower-class youth are unable to meet the middle-class standards of the school. As a result, they collectively build a new set of values and standards that are the opposite of those of the middle class. This inversion of middle-class standards often results in delinquency.
- Elijah Anderson notes that exporting manufacturing jobs overseas has made a bad situation worse in inner cities. With respect through traditional work not being available, young people have adopted a code of the street. One gains status by being tough and willing to use violence.

- While most strain theorists have looked exclusively at crime committed by members of the lower class, the theory can also be used to explain white-collar and corporate crime. Upper-class crimes can arise from an unprincipled overcommitment to success goals. Even successful people may feel pressure to make more money and may choose to break the law in order to achieve these financial goals.

QUESTIONS FOR CRITICAL THINKING

1. In this chapter, you have read about the consensus and conflict perspectives to crime. Think of three different laws that prohibit behaviour that most people would agree is wrong. Can you think of any circumstances under which these acts might be permissible? Now think of three different laws that prohibit behaviour that a significant number of Canadians think should be tolerated. Why do these behaviours remain against the law?
2. How would Merton's anomie theory explain the higher rates of deviance and crime among Canada's Aboriginal people? Does the theory help you to think of any possible solutions to this problem?
3. Researchers who have studied delinquent gangs have failed to find the three distinct criminal, conflict, and retreatist subcultures predicted by Cloward and Ohlin. Why do you think these distinct types of gangs do not exist?
4. Discuss some of the strengths and weaknesses of strain theory.
5. Merton, and those who followed him, developed strain theory to explain lower-class crime and delinquency. However, some might argue that strain theory actually provides a better explanation of white-collar and corporate crime. Describe how strain theory can be used to explain the crimes of the rich and powerful.

NET WORK

Go to this website:

http://www.safecanada.ca/link_e.asp?category=2&topic=14.

Look at the list of programs designed to prevent crime and delinquency and select a few. Which of these programs address issues raised by strain theorists? How likely do you think it is that these programs will have an impact on crime? Why?

KEY TERMS

anomie; pg. 283
conflict perspective; pg. 282
consensus perspective; pg. 282
culturally prescribed aspiration; pg. 284
human capital; pg. 295
middle-class measuring rod; pg. 296
mutual conversion; pg. 297
opportunity structure; pg. 290
reaction formation; pg. 297
relative deprivation; pg. 290
social structure; pg. 284
strain theory; pg. 282
subculture; pg. 293

SUGGESTED READING

Agnew, Robert. 1997. "The Nature and Determinants of Strain." In Nikos Passas and Robert Agnew (eds.), *The Future of Anomie Theory*. Boston: Northeastern University Press. This essay broadens the traditional discussion of anomie.

Anderson, Elijah. (1999). *Code of the Street: Decency, Violence, and the Moral Life of the Inner City*. New York: W. W. Norton. Lack of employment opportunities leads to alternative ways of achieving respect by displaying toughness, taking another person's possessions. This helps build a reputation that prevents future challenges. But it creates other problems.

Bernard, Thomas. (1987). "Testing Structural Strain Theories." *Journal of Research in Crime and Delinquency* 24:262–80. This article debates the application of strain theory to individuals or groups.

Cohen, Albert K. (1955). *Delinquent Boys: The Culture of the Gang*. Glencoe, Ill.: Free Press. One of the classic studies of delinquency that linked ideas of opportunity structure to the subculture of gang delinquency. Extensively influenced later studies of delinquency.

Cohen, Deborah. (1995). "Ethics and Crime in Business Firms: Organizational Culture and the Impact of Anomie." In Freda Adler and William S. Laufer (eds.), *Advances in Criminological Theory. Vol. 6: The Legacy of Anomie*. New Brunswick, N.J.: Transaction. Strain theory applied to the business world.

Hagan, John, and Bill McCarthy. (1997). *Mean Streets: Youth Homelessness and Crime*. New York: Cambridge University Press. Being on the street leads to a variety of illegitimate and dangerous opportunities.

Merton, Robert. (1968). *Social Theory and Social Structure*. (2nd ed.). New York: Free Press. The third revision of Merton's classic anomie theory of crime.

Messner, Steven F., and Richard Rosenfeld. (2007). *Crime and the American Dream*. (4th ed.). Belmont, Calif.: Wadsworth. Economic factors are pervasive in North America, and there are only weak restraints on ethical behaviour.

BIBLIOGRAPHY

Agnew, Robert. (1991). "A Longitudinal Test of Social Control Theory and Delinquency." *Journal of Research in Crime and Delinquency* 28:126–56.

———. (1992). "Foundation for a General Strain Theory of Crime and Delinquency." *Criminology* 30:47–87.

———. (1997). "The Nature and Determinants of Strain." In Nikos Passas and Robert Agnew (eds.), *The Future of Anomie Theory*. Boston: Northeastern University Press.

Agnew, Robert, and Helene Raskin White. (1992). "An Empirical Test of General Strain Theory." *Criminology* 30:475–99.

Agnew, Robert, Francis T. Cullen, Velmer S. Burton Jr., T. David Evans, and R. Gregory Dunaway. (1996). "A New Test of Class Strain Theory." *Justice Quarterly* 13:681–704.

Anderson, Elijah. (1999). *Code of the Street: Decency, Violence, and the Moral Life of the Inner City*. New York: W. W. Norton.

Andrews, Donald A., and James Bonta. (1998). *The Psychology of Criminal Conduct* (2nd ed.). Cincinnati, Oh.: Anderson.

Bernard, Thomas. (1987). "Testing Structural Strain Theories." *Journal of Research in Crime and Delinquency* 24:262–80.

Blau, Judith, and Peter Blau. (1982). "Metropolitan Structure and Violent Crime." *American Sociological Review* 47 (February):114–29.

Blumer, Herbert. (1951). "Collective Behaviour." In A. M. Lee (ed.), *Principles of Sociology.* New York: Barnes and Noble.

Braithwaite, John. (1979). *Inequality, Crime and Public Policy.* London: Routledge and Kegan Paul.

Braithwaite, John. (1989). *Crime, Shame, and Reintegration.* Cambridge: Cambridge University Press.

Brezina, Timothy. (1998). "Adolescent Maltreatment and Delinquency: The Question of Intervening Processes." *Journal of Research in Crime and Delinquency* 35:71–99.

Cloward, Richard. (1959). "Illegitimate Means, Anomie, and Deviant Behavior." *American Sociological Review* 24 (April):164–76.

Cloward, Richard, and Lloyd Ohlin. (1960). *Delinquency and Opportunity.* Glencoe, Ill.: Free Press.

Cohen, Albert K. (1955). *Delinquent Boys: The Culture of the Gang.* Glencoe, Ill.: Free Press.

Colvin, Mark. (2000). *Crime and Coercion: An Integrated Theory of Chronic Criminality.* New York: St. Martin's Press.

Colvin, Mark, Francis T. Cullen, and Thomas Vander Ven. (2002). "Coercion, Social Support and Crime: An Emerging Theoretical Consensus." *Criminology* 40:19–42.

Comack, Elizabeth. (1992). "Women and Crime." In Rick Linden (ed.), *Criminology: A Canadian Perspective* (2nd ed.). Toronto: Harcourt Brace.

Crutchfield, Robert D. (1995). "Ethnicity, Labor Markets and Crime." In Darnell F. Hawkins (ed.), *Ethnicity, Race and Crime: Perspectives Across Time and Place.* Albany: State University of New York Press.

Cullen, Francis. (1984). *Rethinking Crime and Deviance Theory: The Emergence of a Structuring Tradition.* Totowa, N.J.: Rowman and Allanheld.

———. (1988). "Were Cloward and Ohlin Strain Theorists? Delinquency and Opportunity Revisited." *Journal of Research in Crime and Delinquency* 25:214–41.

Desroches, Fred. (1995). "Tearoom Trade: A Law Enforcement Problem." *Canadian Journal of Criminology* 33(1):1–21.

Durkheim, Émile. (1893/1933). *The Division of Labor in Society.* New York: Free Press.

———. (1897/1951) *Suicide.* New York: The Free Press.

Farnworth, Margaret, and Michael Leiber. (1989). "Strain Theory Revisited." *American Sociological Review* 54:263–74.

Giffen, P.J. (1966). "The Revolving Door: A Functional Interpretation." *Canadian Review of Sociology and Anthropology* 3 (August):154–66.

Gurr, Ted. (1981). "Historical Forces in Violent Crime." In Michael Tonry and Norval Morris (eds.), *Crime and Justice*, Vol. 3 (pp. 295–353). Chicago: University of Chicago Press.

Hackler, James C. (1966). "Boys, Blisters, and Behavior." *Journal of Research in Crime and Delinquency* 3 (July):155–64.

———. (2006). *Canadian Criminology: Strategies and Perspectives* (4th. ed.). Toronto: Prentice Hall Canada.

Hackler, James C., and Eric Linden. (1970). "The Response of Adults to Delinquency Prevention Programs: The Race Factor." *Journal of Research in Crime and Delinquency* 7 (January):31–45.

Hagan, John, and Bill McCarthy. (1997a). *Mean Streets: Youth Homelessness and Crime.* New York: Cambridge University Press.

———. (1997b). "Anomie, Social Capital, and Street Criminology." In Nikos Passas and Robert Agnew (eds.), *The Future of Anomie Theory.* Boston: Northeastern University Press.

Helfgot, Joseph. (1981). *Professional Reforming: Mobilization for Youth and the Failure of Social Science*. Lexington, Mass.: Heath.

Jensen, Gary F. (1995). "Salvaging Structure Through Strain: A Theoretical and Empirical Critique." In Freda Adler and William S. Laufer (eds.), *Advances in Criminological Theory, Vol. 6: The Legacy of Anomie*. New Brunswick, N.J.: Transaction.

Kobrin, Sol. (1951). "The Conflict of Values in Delinquency Areas." *American Sociological Review* 16 (October):653–61.

Konty, Mark. (2005). "Microanomie: The Cognitive Foundations of the Relationship between Anomie and Deviance." *Criminology* 43 (February):107–31.

Mazerolle, Paul, and Alex Piquero. (1997). "Violent Responses to Strain: An Examination of Conditioning Influences." *Violence and Victims* 12:323–43.

———. (1998). "Linking Exposure to Strain with Anger: Investigation of Deviant Adaptations." *Journal of Criminal Justice* 26:195–211.

Menard, Scott. (1997). "A Developmental Test of Cloward's Differential Opportunity Theory." In Nikos Passas and Robert Agnew (eds.), *The Future of Anomie Theory*. Boston: Northeastern University Press.

Merton, Robert K. (1938). "Social Structure and Anomie." *American Sociological Review* 3 (October):672–82.

Messner, Steven F., and Richard Rosenfeld. (2007). *Crime and the American Dream* (4th ed.). Belmont, Calif.: Thomson Wadsworth.

Morris, Alison. (1987). *Women, Crime, and Criminal Justice*. Oxford: Basil Blackwell.

Naffine, Ngaire. (1987). *Female Crime: The Construction of Women in Criminology*. Sydney: Allen and Unwin.

Nettler, Gwynne. (1984). *Explaining Crime*. New York: McGraw-Hill.

Quinney, Richard. (1963). "Occupational Structure and Criminal Behavior: Prescription Violation by Retail Pharmacists." *Social Problems* 11 (Fall):179–95.

Rose, Stephen. (1972). *The Betrayal of the Poor: The Transformation of Community Action*. Cambridge, Mass.: Shenkman.

Schweinhart, L. L., H. V. Barnes, and D. P. Weikart. (1993). *Significant Benefits: The High/Scope Perry Preschool Study through Age 27*. Ypsilanti, Mich.: High/Scope Press.

Shelley, Louise. (1981). *Crime and Modernization*. Carbondale, Ill.: Southern Illinois Press.

Snider, Laureen. (2000). "The Sociology of Corporate Crime: An Obituary." *Theoretical Criminology* 4 (May):169–206.

———. (2003). "Resisting Neo-Liberalism: The Poisoned Water Disaster in Walkerton, Ontario." *Social and Legal Studies* 5 (2):27–47 .

Sutherland, Edwin. (1949). *White Collar Crime*. New York: Dryden.

Thornberry, Terence P. (1987). "Toward an Interactional Theory of Delinquency." *Criminology* 25:863–91.

Tremblay, Richard E., and Wendy M. Craig. (1995). "Developmental Crime Prevention." In M. Tonry and D. P. Farrington (eds.), *Building a Safer Society: Strategic Approaches to Crime Prevention*. Vol. 19. Chicago: University of Chicago Press.

Vaughan, Diane. (1997). "Anomie Theory and Organizations: Culture and the Normalization of Deviance." In Nikos Passas and Robert Agnew (eds.), *The Future of Anomie Theory*. Boston: Northeastern University Press.

Wade, Andrew L. (1967). "Social Processes in the Act of Juvenile Vandalism." In Marshall B. Clinard and Richard Quinney, *Criminal Behavior Systems: A Typology*. New York: Holt, Rinehart, and Winston.

10 Conflict Theories

Danica Dupont

In this chapter we will explore a number of conflict theories, including cultural conflict theory, group conflict theory, instrumental and structuralist Marxism, socialist feminism, and left realism. The conflict perspective assumes that societies are more divided by conflict than they are integrated by consensus. Whereas consensus theorists (see Chapter 9) view the law as the codification of mutually agreed upon societal norms and values, conflict theorists question the assumption that our laws represent the interests of society as a whole. Instead, the conflict perspective argues that the social norms and values that receive the protection of the law are those endorsed by the more powerful or dominant groups in society.

Learning Objectives

After reading this chapter, you should be able to

- Understand the differences between Sellin's culture group conflict theory and Vold's interest group conflict theory.
- Describe how Quinney's (1970) group conflict theory differs from both Vold and Sellin's conflict theories.
- Know the basic elements of Marx's mode of production, and what is meant by the economic base and the superstructure.
- Understand the differences between instrumental Marxism and structural Marxism, and the meaning of relative autonomy.
- Know how socialist feminism modified radical feminism and Marxism to arrive at a theory of capitalist patriarchy.
- Describe the basic elements of the left realist position.

Cultural Conflict Theory

Thorsten Sellin

conduct norms
Specification of rules or norms of appropriate behaviour generally agreed upon by members of the social group to whom the behavioural norms apply.

Thorsten Sellin was one of the first criminologists to propose a conflict perspective for the analysis of crime. In his 1938 book, *Culture Conflict and Crime*, Sellin presented a criminological theory that focused on the role of "**conduct norms**" in explaining crime. For Sellin, modern society is composed of various and diverse cultural groups, each maintaining its own distinct "conduct norms," or cultural rules, governing appropriate conduct. Sellin suggests that in culturally homogeneous elementary societies, the values and norms to which people subscribe will be fairly similar, so the conduct norms of the broader social group will tend to reflect a societal consensus. However, in more complex societies that are characterized by cultural heterogeneity, urbanization, and industrialization, an overall societal consensus is less likely, and it is more likely that there will be conflict between the conduct norms of different cultural groups. In other words, the more complex a society becomes, the greater the probability that there will be culture conflict.

According to Sellin, **cultural conflict** can arise when conduct norms clash on the border areas between distinct cultures; as a result of colonization, migration, or immigration; or when the laws of one cultural group are extended to cover the territory of another. Sellin was particularly interested in the way in which the conduct norms of immigrant cultures could potentially come into conflict with the conduct norms of the established or dominant culture. For example, the genital mutilation of young girls is an approved practice in some cultures, but is illegal in Canada. One sphere where culture conflict appears is in the legal sphere, especially criminal law. While there are various ways in which social groups secure conformity of their members, the criminal law stands out because "its norms are binding upon all who live within the political boundaries of the state and are enforced through the coercive power of the state" (Sellin, 1938, 21). Thus when immigrants seek to continue the practice of female genital mutilation in Canada, they come into conflict with the law.

cultural conflict
A theory that attempts to explain certain types of criminal behaviour as resulting from a conflict between the conduct norms of divergent cultural groups.

Sellin felt that the criminal law "depends upon the character and interests of those groups in the population which influence legislation" (1938, 21). Ultimately, the social values that receive the protection of the criminal law are those treasured by dominant interest groups. Sellin uses the term *criminal norms* to describe the "conduct norms" embodied in the criminal law that represent the values of the dominant group. The criminal law will generally reflect the social values and the conduct norms of the dominant cultural group. According to Sellin, then, crime can be viewed as an expression of culture conflict when individuals who act based on the conduct norms of their own cultural group find themselves in violation of the conduct norms that the dominant group has enacted into law. Box 10.1 describes a conduct norm in the outports of Newfoundland that local custom does not view as a crime, but which is considered illegal under the law.

Group Conflict Theory

George Vold

In his 1958 text, *Theoretical Criminology*, George Vold outlined his formulation of **group conflict** theory as an explanation for certain types of criminal behaviour. Much like Sellin, Vold is interested in examining crime as it relates to conflict between groups. Unlike Sellin's explanation of crime as resulting from a conflict between the conduct norms of divergent cultural groups, Vold primarily focuses on crime that occurs as a result of conflict between diverse "interest" groups. Vold begins with the assumption that men and women are always "group-involved" beings, whose lives are oriented toward group associations. Groups are formed when members have common interests that can best be furthered through collective action. Groups will come into contact with one

group conflict
A theory that attempts to explain certain types of criminal behaviour as resulting from a conflict between the interests of divergent groups.

FOCUS

BOX 10.1 Patterns of Outport Big Game Poaching in Newfoundland

Big game poaching as a crime in the outports is of particular significance because it is perhaps the most visible manifestation of the process of cultural conflict and change that is occurring with alarming speed in fishing and forestry-based communities in Newfoundland and other parts of Atlantic Canada. [For Newfoundlanders], hunting for the table was a necessary economic activity that was part of the traditional way of life in outport communities. Because of this and because the economic situation for most outport citizens still requires a flexible optimization of sources of economic support, community cultural norms still support subsistence hunting. Hunting, legal or not, is an activity which a great number of able-bodied men of the outports engage in. However, government rules and regulations concerning the hunt have proliferated and have been implemented through a sophisticated law enforcement effort and increasingly severe punishment meted out to those caught. The conflict between community norms and state regulations has made poaching an important regional crime issue. . . .

Brymer (1990) has produced a typology of hunting that is relevant to outport poaching. His category of "local rural hunter" represents a group of traditional hunters who are hold-overs from a pre-industrial agrarian communal/familial network. With the imposition of game laws, their activities became illegal, thus producing a deviant subculture among those who continued hunting. This subculture is marked by perceptions of a traditional right to hunt in the hunting "territory," the use of game for food or other instrumental purposes, and the sharing of game within social networks. . . .

Given the long history of exploitation, impoverishment, and subsistence survival in the outports of Newfoundland, it should be no surprise that community norms and mores in regard to hunting emphasize its importance as a food source more than its illegality. The isolation of the outports has long placed a premium on the ability to support one's family without outside help. . . .

The penalties for violations of big game regulations can be quite severe, especially considering the low income and high unemployment in the region. The minimum penalty for violations under the Wildlife Act during the period of fieldwork was a $1,000 fine or thirty days in jail for the first offence and a jail sentence of at least thirty days *and* a minimum $3,000 fine for a second offence if it occurred within five years of the first. In addition, hunting privileges may be suspended for up to five years, and guns, hunting equipment, boats, vehicles, and practically anything else in the possession of the charged individual capable of being used to kill, store, or transport wildlife can be seized and forfeited.

Source: Norman Okihiro. (1997). *Mounties, Moose, and Moonshine: The Patterns and Context of Outport Crime.* Toronto: University of Toronto Press, 72–73, 79, 83.

another as their interests begin to overlap and become competitive. Vold sees society as a collection of groups existing in a constantly shifting, but more or less stable, equilibrium of opposing group interests.

Vold is interested in the process of law creation as it relates to the activities of antagonistic interest groups in the broader community. One interest group may seek the assistance of the state to enact a new law while an opposing interest group tries to resist the proposed legislation. The interest group that can marshal the greater number of votes will have the most influence in determining whether the new law is enacted. Therefore Vold (1958, 209) argues that

> the whole political process of law making, law breaking and law enforcement becomes a direct reflection of deep-seated and fundamental conflicts between interest groups and their more general struggles for the control of the police power of the state. Those who produce legislative majorities win control over the police power and dominate the policies that decide who is likely to be involved in violation of the law.

For Vold, conflict between interest groups is a normal social process, and one of the fundamental principles of organized political society.

Vold explains two general classes of group conflict that can result in criminal behaviour. These are crimes that arise as a result of minority group behaviour, and crimes that result from direct contact between groups struggling for the control of power in the political and cultural organization of society. As an example of crime that is associated with minority group behaviour, Vold argues that the delinquent gang can be understood as a minority group whose interests are in opposition to the rules of the dominant majority—the adult world of regulations established in law and enforced by the police. A second example of a minority group whose interests are in opposition to the dominant majority is that of "conscientious objectors" during wartime who opt to serve prison sentences rather than participate in any form of compulsory wartime service. Vold's broader point is that group conflict theory is helpful in explaining crime that results from a conflict between the behaviour of minority groups and the legal norms, rules, and regulations of the dominant majority, which are established in law.

Educational Resource for Criminology
www.crimetheory.com

Vold argues that group conflict theory is also helpful in explaining crime that results from a conflict between interest groups who are vying for power. Vold offers several examples of intergroup conflict that can result in criminal behaviour. First, many crimes are the result of political revolution or protest movements whose aim is direct political reform. "A successful revolution," as Vold argues, "makes criminals out of government officials previously in power, and an unsuccessful revolution makes its leaders into traitors subject to immediate execution" (Vold, 1958, 215). Second, crime may directly result from the conflict of group interests of management and labour unions. In the case of strikes or lockouts, escalating tensions between management and striking workers may result in violence, property damage, or other crimes. Third, crimes may be committed as a result of jurisdictional disputes between different labour unions, who are each attempting to organize the same group of workers. These disputes may involve intimidation and personal violence as each union attempts to gain support for its position.

Vold argues that criminological theories that focus on notions of individual choice and responsibility are not necessarily relevant in understanding criminal behaviour that occurs as a result of conflict between interest groups. This is because individual criminal behaviour that results from intergroup conflict for the control of power represents, for that same individual, a type of "loyal service" to the interest group struggling to maintain or improve its position. Group conflict theory is strictly limited to instances where individual criminal behaviour arises from the conflict between interest groups and does not try to explain other kinds of criminal acts.

Conflict theory has been criticized for its narrow scope of explanation. That is, critics argue that it applies to only a narrow range of crimes, of which perhaps only politically or ideologically motivated crimes can be said to fit the model well. In addition, others point out that most crime is intra-group, that is, committed by one member of a group against another member, rather than the intergroup crime that Vold focuses on.

Richard Quinney

Although Richard Quinney's theoretical perspective changed significantly in his later work, his 1970 book, *The Social Reality of Crime,* was widely viewed as an important contribution to group conflict theory. Like both Sellin and Vold, Quinney's theory of crime explains criminality as the result of conflict between groups. Whereas Sellin focused on cultural group conflict, and Vold on interest group conflict, Quinney's formulation of group conflict theory focused on the more broadly defined notion of "segments" of society, which he defined as types of "social groupings." For Quinney, the more powerful segments or social groups are able to secure and protect their own interests by influencing the formulation, enforcement, and administration of criminal law. Although both Sellin and Vold viewed the criminal law as being generally reflective of the values and norms of the dominant groups in society, Quinney places a much greater emphasis than either Sellin or Vold on the unequal distribution of power in society, especially as it relates to the formation of public policy. While Vold would view society as existing in a more or less stable equilibrium of opposing group interests where all groups are able to make themselves heard in policy decision making, Quinney argues that only some interest groups are sufficiently powerful to influence policy, and that this power is "unequally distributed because of the structural arrangements of the political state" (1970, 12).

Quinney outlines his conflict theory of crime in six propositions:

1. *Crime is a definition of human conduct that is created by authorized agents in a politically organized society.* Quinney's major point here is that crime is not inherent in behaviour, but rather is the product of legal definitions; it is a *definition* of behaviour conferred on some persons by others.
2. *Criminal definitions describe behaviours that conflict with the interests of the segments of society that have the power to shape public policy.* Here Quinney argues that the more powerful segments of society are able to incorporate their interests, values, and norms into the criminal law, so these powerful segments are able to regulate the formulation of criminal definitions. These definitions are formulated because less powerful segments of society are in conflict with other more powerful segments.
3. *Criminal definitions are applied by the segments of society that have the power to shape the enforcement and administration of criminal law.* The interests of powerful segments are not only represented in the formulation of criminal law, but also in its application. The enforcement and administration of the law has been delegated to legal agents (e.g., police, prosecutors, judges) who are said to represent the interests of these powerful segments.

4. *Behavioural patterns are structured in segmentally organized society in relation to criminal definitions, and within this context persons engage in actions that have relative probabilities of being defined as criminal.* For Quinney, it is not the quality of the behaviour that makes it criminal, but rather the action taken against the behaviour. The decision as to which acts are defined as criminal is made by the more powerful segments of society who formulate and apply criminal definitions. Thus persons in less powerful social segments are more likely to have their behaviours defined as criminal, because their interests are not represented in the formulation and application of criminal definitions.
5. *Conceptions of crime are constructed and diffused in the segments of society by various means of communication.* Quinney argues that one of the most important agents involved in the diffusion of criminal conceptions throughout society is the mass media. The mass media portray a conception of crime that is diffused throughout society and subsequently "becomes the basis for the public's view of reality" (Quinney, 1970, 285). The more powerful segments of society are able to influence the mass media's portrayal of crime.
6. *The social reality of crime is constructed by the formulation and application of criminal definitions, the development of behavioural patterns related to criminal definitions, and the construction of criminal conceptions.* The sixth proposition is essentially a summation of propositions 2 to 5, and thus Quinney's model posits that the "social reality of crime" is a function of (2) the formulation of criminal definitions; (3) the application of criminal definitions; (4) the development of behaviour patterns in relation to criminal definitions; and (5) the construction of criminal conceptions. Note that Quinney views the first proposition as a definition, thus the body of the theory comprises the middle four propositions.

Marxist Conflict Perspectives in Criminology

Beginning in the 1970s, Marxist theories began to gain prominence in the socio-legal and criminological literature. While Marx himself had very little to say about crime, many criminologists believed that aspects of Marx's work could help to analyze the relationship between crime and the broader social world. Similar to the conflict theories of Sellin, Vold, and Quinney, Marxist theories of crime and deviance do not look to the individual offender for explanations of crime. Criminal behaviour is not viewed in isolation as an individual pathology. As Greenberg points out, Marxist criminology takes the position that crime "must be analyzed in the context of its relationship to the character of the society as a whole" (1993, 17). Marxists take the position that crime should be understood in relation to the social, political, and economic structures of the society in which it occurs.

You will recall that group conflict theorists, broadly speaking, view conflict as arising from opposing group interests, and crime as resulting from the ability of more powerful or dominant groups to criminalize the behaviour of other less powerful groups who find themselves in violation of the criminal norms and standards of the dominant majority. Marxist criminologists, on the other hand, view conflict as rooted in the very structure of capitalist society, and especially capitalist economic relations. The political and economic structures under capitalism promote conflict, in turn providing the precipitating conditions (such as unemployment) for crime to occur. Marxist criminologists focus their attention on the relations between crime and the social arrangements of society, particularly the way in which societies organize their political, legal, and economic structures (Bohm, 1982). Generally speaking, Marxist criminologists take the position that the way in which capitalist society is organized—both its way of producing material goods and its organization of political, legal, and economic structures—has important implications for the study of the amount and types of crime present in society (Greenberg, 1993).

Marxist Internet Archive
www.marxists.org

For Marx, the history of the development of human societies can be best understood through the fundamental role played by production. Through production, we are able to satisfy our basic needs, such as the need for food, clothing, and shelter. Marx is interested in examining the history of societies from the perspective of how production is organized, or what is described as the *mode of production*. The mode of production essentially refers to the economic system whereby goods are produced, exchanged, and distributed in society. Marx identifies several different modes of production throughout history, including the slave economies of ancient Greece and Rome, the agrarian economy of feudalism, and the wage-labour economy of capitalism.

The mode of production, in turn, is composed of the *forces of production* and the *social relations of production*. The forces of production refers to the tools, techniques, raw materials, and labour power used in production, while the social relations of production refers to the relationships that exist among humans with respect to the ownership of the means of production. For Marx, the social relations of production under capitalism—that is, under the capitalist mode of production—give rise to two major groups or classes. The bourgeoisie are the economically dominant class who own the means of production (the land, machinery, and factories), and the proletariat are the economically subordinate class who are propertyless. Because they neither own nor control the means of production, they have only their labour power to sell in exchange for their livelihood in the form of wages. It is important to note that class is *not* an attribute or characteristic of an individual or group in Marxist thought; rather it refers to a position in a relationship (Greenberg, 1993). For Marx, capitalist society, like earlier societies, is based on class exploitation. The relationship between the capitalist class and the working class is exploitative because the capitalist is able to extract the surplus labour of the worker in the form of profits. This surplus is based on the difference between the value the workers produce and what is received by the worker in wages.

In his *Contribution to the Critique of Political Economy*, Marx argues that because societies are always organized around the dominant mode of production "the mode of production of material life conditions the social, political, and intellectual life process in general" (Marx in Cain and Hunt, 1979, 54). Marx makes use of the metaphor of a building to describe the relationship between the mode of production and other aspects of society:

> The sum total of these relations of production constitutes the economic structure of society, the real foundation, on which rises a legal and political superstructure and to which correspond definite forms of social consciousness. (Marx in Cain and Hunt, 1979, 54)

According to Marx, in Western societies the economic base of capitalism is the foundation upon which the various superstructural institutions of society are built, including political and legal institutions. Another way Marxists put this is that the economic base of capitalism has a *determining influence* on the superstructural institutions of society. Where one class is in a position of dominance over the other class (based on its ownership of the means of production) in the economic sphere, the other social institutions in society will be organized according to the interests of the dominant class (Comack, 1999a). The implication for Marxist approaches to law, crime, and criminology is that both the law and crime should not be studied in isolation, but rather in relation to the whole of society and particularly the economic sphere (Greenberg, 1993).

The Marxist approach provides criminologists and legal scholars with a theoretical framework that allows them to study the interrelationships between the capitalist mode of production, the state, law, crime control, and crime (Bohm, 1982). In addition, Marxist analysis typically involves a critical element (see also Chapter 11). It is a critique of the logic of the existing capitalist social order. In critiquing the existing society or social order, Marxian thought often begins with an analysis of the state. While Marx himself did not develop a systematic theory of the state, Marxist theorists have made use of aspects of Marx's writings to attempt to theorize the relationships between the state in capitalist society and class relations, law, crime, and crime control. It has become conventional in the criminological and socio-legal literature to distinguish between *instrumental* and *structural* Marxist accounts of the state, law, and crime.

Instrumental Marxism

Instrumental Marxists generally begin with the assumption that the state in capitalist societies broadly serves the interests of the ruling or capitalist class. A well-known passage from Marx and Engels' work, *The Communist Manifesto*, is often cited in support of this position: "The executive of the modern State is but a committee for managing the common affairs of the whole bourgeoisie" (Marx and Engels, 1992, 5). We saw earlier that Marx implied that the economic base determines the processes of the superstructure. Instrumentalist Marxists interpret Marx's statement quite literally and argue that both the state, and the legal and political institutions within the state, are a direct reflection of the interests of the capitalist class. Law, then, is equated with class rule, where the ruling class controls the formation of law, and where the focus is on the coercive nature of the law. As Tierney (1996) points out, this approach was based upon an instrumentalist school of thought in political theory (Miliband, 1969; Domhoff, 1970), which argued that those who occupied powerful positions in the state apparatus were either capitalists themselves or they strongly identified with the interests of the capitalist class.

instrumental Marxism
In this perspective, the state is viewed as the direct instrument of the ruling or capitalist class. Instrumentalism is based on the notion that the processes of the superstructure are determined by the economic base.

Instrumental Marxists viewed the state and the legal system as instruments that could be directly manipulated by the capitalist class. For example, Miliband (1969, 22) argued that because the ruling class of capitalist society owns and controls the means of production, it is able to "use the state as its instrument for the domination of society." Early studies tended to focus on how the economic power of the capitalist class afforded the opportunity to influence law and law formation. A good example of an instrumental Marxist position is found in Richard Quinney's book, *Critique of the Legal Order* (1974). We might recall that in Quinney's earlier work, he was endorsing a conflict perspective on crime. Many theorists change their views over time as their perspectives widen, narrow, shift, or completely alter. In the *Critique of the Legal Order*, Quinney (1974, 16) offers six propositions that summarize his critical Marxist theory of crime control, and that are somewhat different from his earlier position:

1. American society is based on an advanced capitalist economy.
2. The State is organized to serve the interests of the dominant economic class.
3. Criminal law is an instrument of the state and ruling class to maintain and perpetuate the existing social and economic order.
4. The contradictions of advanced capitalism . . . require that the subordinate classes remain oppressed by whatever means necessary, especially through the coercion and violence of the legal system.
5. Only with the collapse of capitalist society and the creation of a new society, based on socialist principles, will there be a solution to the crime problem.

While the instrumentalist Marxist position offers some useful insights into the sociology of the capitalist class, the relationship between class power and state power, and the place of law in capitalist society, it has been criticized on a number of fronts. For example, instrumental Marxism has been critiqued for portraying the ruling class as a unified and largely homogeneous group, thus ignoring the factions that may exist within the capitalist class itself. Second, instrumentalist accounts have been critiqued for the lack of any systematic analysis as to how the actions of ruling class members may be shaped or constrained by structural causes. For example, are there limits to any particular ruling class member's sphere of influence, such as shifting affiliations with the current party in power in a parliamentary democracy, the deep fluctuations of the stock market, political exigencies, and so on? Third, the instrumentalist position has been critiqued for the argument that the law represents only the interests of the ruling class, and thus is unable to account for legislation that is not in the immediate interest of the ruling class, such as health and safety legislation, employment standards, and so on. Fourth, it is also argued that instrumentalism draws upon an overly rigid interpretation of the base/superstructure metaphor. That is, the Marxist argument that the economic base is the foundation of the superstructure is said to be deterministic. By deterministic, we mean there is a form of causality where the superstructure is a necessary consequence of the economic base. In other words, the economic base under capitalism more or less wholly determines the political, economic, ideological, and cultural superstructure. This is why the instrumentalist position argues that the legal and political institutions in the state are a direct reflection of the capitalist class.

Structural Marxism

Toward the middle of the 1970s and throughout the 1980s, Marxist theorists began to develop structuralist Marxist accounts of the state, law, and crime. Structuralist Marxism disputes the instrumentalist view that the state can be viewed as the direct servant of the capitalist or ruling class. Whereas the instrumentalist position argues that the institutions of the state are under the direct control of those members of the capitalist class in positions of state power, the structuralist perspective takes the position that the institutions of the state must function in such a way as to ensure the ongoing viability of capitalism more generally. Another way that Marxists put this is that the institutions of the state must function so as to reproduce capitalist society as a whole (Gold et al., 1975). Structuralists view the state in a capitalist mode of production as taking a specifically capitalist form, not because particular individuals are in powerful positions, but because the state reproduces the logic of capitalist structure in its economic, legal, and political institutions. We might say that a structuralist perspective would argue that the institutions of the state (including its legal institutions) function in the long-term interests of capital and capitalism, rather than in the short-term interests of members of the capitalist class. Structuralists would thus argue that the state and its institutions have a certain degree of *independence* from specific elites in the ruling or capitalist class.

structural Marxism
In this perspective, the state is viewed as acting in the long-term interests of capitalism as a whole, rather than in the short-term interests of the capitalist class. Structuralism rejects the belief that law is an instrument of the capitalist class.

The idea that the state is—to a certain degree—independent of the ruling class is known as **relative autonomy.** In this regard structural Marxists have drawn from the work of Poulantzas (1975) and Althusser (1969) to argue that the relative autonomy of the state functions to preserve the long-term interests of capital, and the long-run stability of the capitalist structure as a whole. To begin with, we cannot assume the capitalist class is united in its interests and homogeneous in its beliefs. The state must therefore have the relative autonomy to mediate between divergent capitalist class factions in order to preserve the long-term interests of the capitalist class as a whole (Poulantzas, 1975). The relative autonomy of the state, therefore, provides a state structure "capable of transcending the parochial, individualized interests of specific capitalists and capitalist class factions" (Gold et al., 1975, 38). In addition, structural Marxists point to the relative autonomy of the state and its institutions to explain why many laws are enacted that do not represent the immediate interests of the capitalist class. That is, an instrumentalist Marxist position cannot account for the existence of minimum wage laws, laws against discrimination in employment, consumer protection laws, rent control, anti-trust legislation, and welfare legislation, in that these laws are not in the immediate interests of the capitalist class.

relative autonomy
A term used in the structural Marxist perspective to indicate that the state has a certain amount of independence from the capitalist class and is therefore able to enact laws that are not in the immediate interests of the capitalist class.

An interesting area that Canadian researchers have explored, with respect to law creation that does not seem to represent the immediate interests of the capitalist class as a whole, has been the development of anti-combines legislation in Canada (Goff and Reasons, 1978; Snider, 1979; Smandych, 1985). The aim of this legislation was to prevent corporations from monopolizing or cornering the supply of certain commodities or markets, and to fix prices. Goff and Reasons (1978) argue that Canada's first anti-combines legislation—the Combines Investigation Act of 1889—came about less from the desire to protect the general populace than from the complaints of small businessmen who "felt their firms were at the mercy of big business interests" (1978, 42). For the first decade, this legislation was unenforceable because of the weak wording of the act, which stipulated that combines had to be engaged in behaviour that *unlawfully* as well as *unduly* restricted trade. Snider (1979) examined the later revisions and amendments to the act in 1923, 1935, 1952, and 1960 and concluded that "at each stage proposals were weakened or eliminated in the face of business opposition" (1979, 110). Both Snider and Goff and Reasons concluded that while reforms do occur, the state "is susceptible to the interests of powerful economic groups" (Goff and Reasons, 1978, 114), and thus reforms tend to be "resisted for as long as possible by the corporate elite" (Snider, 1979, 118).

Smandych (1985) has argued that anti-combines legislation in Canada must also be considered in relation to the increasingly vocal trade unions of the late 19th century and the growing confrontations between capital and labour. He points out that the rise of militant trade unions in the late 1800s, such as the Knights of Labour in Toronto, "owed as much to labour's hatred of monopolistic companies as it did to labour's desire to improve working conditions" (1985, 45). In addition, the Knights of Labour and other trade unions had a great deal of influence on the working man's vote. Thus Smandych argues that the emergence of Canadian anti-combines legislation can be viewed as a pragmatic attempt by the government to find a "symbolic" solution to the confrontation between capital and labour, given the political influence of the more prominent trade unions. The solution was symbolic because the immense economic and political power of the monopolistic companies of the period influenced the state to enact what was ultimately an "ineffectual law that served only to foster the reproduction of combines activity in the late 19th century" (1985, 47). As Chambliss and Siedman (1982, 312) point out, "A great deal of state action concerns not the enhancement of profit for a particular faction of the ruling class, but the maintenance of relations of production that make capitalism possible." Thus the state ensures the reproduction of capitalism as a whole. In some instances, the state enacts laws that are ostensibly meant to curb the excesses of capital, yet are ineffective in their design and implementation.

In the structuralist perspective, then, the law cannot be said to exclusively represent the instrumental interests of the dominant capitalist class. Rather, structural Marxists argue that enacted laws that benefit the less powerful reflect an ideological need to develop a widespread *consent* for the existing social order (Einstadter and Henry, 2006). On this view, consensus is generated for the established order by promoting law as an impartial system that protects the public rather than private interests, and where all are equal before the law. Structuralists argue that this notion of "equality before the law," also described as "the rule of law," masks or otherwise obscures the substantive inequalities of class, race, and gender that may exist between individuals who are nevertheless considered equal before the law. Stated differently, the formal equality of each individual in the legal sphere does not extend to the economic sphere (Brickey and Comack, 1989). Thus, for example, corporations and labour are treated in collective bargaining law as being on an equal footing, despite the structural inequalities between them, including the corporation's greater material and organizational resources (Bartholomew and Boyd, 1989). Structuralists therefore argue that law functions as an ideological means of domination. Ideological domination, as Hunt argues, "consists of those processes that produce and

FOCUS

BOX 10.2 Law, Ideology, and the Struggle for the Vote by Canadian Women

The ideological character of the law, that is, the way in which the law produces and reaffirms the existing social order, can sometimes be easier to view from a distance, in times other than our own.

The struggle for the vote by Canadian women in the early 1900s is an example that helps to illustrate how the law served to reaffirm and legitimate the existing social order. As Hunt (1993, 25) has argued, "The most pervasive ideological effect of law is to be found in the fact that legal rules and their application give effect to existing social relations. The rules of law affirm the social and economic relations that exist within capitalist society."

Consider, for example, the following excerpt from a 1914 essay by Andrew Macphail, where he argues against the vote for women:

Vote for Women—An Argument Against, 1914

> The first equipment they demand is the right to vote. On the part of the gentler [sex], it is an appeal rather than a demand. They ask that they be allowed . . . to assume the privilege and undertake the duty of casting a ballot, so that they may work side by side with men, as comrades in social service for the uplift of humanity, if one may be permitted again to employ those flamboyant terms with which constant iteration has made us all so familiar. There is something pathetic in the appeal, and none but the most hardened can be insensible to it. If men have shown little alacrity in welcoming these volunteers to their ranks, it is because they are not convinced of the value of the work which is proposed to be done. . . .
>
> What complicates the situation is that persons who are appealing for the vote are of higher intelligence, but with shallower instincts, than the average of the sex to which they apparently belong. They are not typical. They belong to a higher, a more masculine type. . . .
>
> And this hesitancy to advocate so revolutionary a measure [as the vote] is increased by a lack of agreement amongst women themselves. It is a matter of common knowledge that the feminist propaganda is confined to a small number of persons. (Macphail, 1914/1976, 301, 304)

For those who were against the enfranchisement of women, one argument that was typically used was that women did not belong in public life; rather, as wives and mothers the proper sphere of women was the "domestic circle." For example, in 1916 Canadian economist and humorist Stephen Leacock expressed his opinion against the right of women to vote by arguing that a woman's only role was motherhood: "Women need not more freedom but less. Social policy should proceed from the fundamental truth that women are and must be dependent" (Leacock, quoted in Prentice et al., 1996, 222).

Hunt has also argued that "law is ideological in that it conveys or transmits a complex set of attitudes, values, and theories about aspects of society. Its ideological content forms parts of the dominant ideology because these attitudes, values, etc. are ones that reinforce and legitimize the existing social order" (Hunt, 1993, 25). In one sense, we can say that the laws that prevented women from having the legal right to vote also served to legitimate the existing social order of the early 20th century that understood the proper place of women to be in the home.

A similar position is taken in an even earlier article written in the *Queen's College Journal* in 1876, which argues that women should not be allowed to take a university degree, because a degree only has value for those in public life:

> The degrees of a University we consider inappropriate to ladies for this reason—that

(*Continued*)

FOCUS

BOX 10.2 Law, Ideology, and the Struggle for the Vote by Canadian Women *(Continued)*

[degrees] have reference solely to public life. Their conferment implies that the objects of it are to go forth to push their way in the outside world, and there acquire *ipso facto* a certain acknowledged position. They only have value when considered with reference to public life, and their bestowal upon women would be a great step towards effectuating the views of the advocates to Women's Rights, and opening to them the professions and employments of public life, a consummation devoutly to be deprecated. If the conclusion arrived at be admitted, we are confident that among people who appreciate the delicate grace and beauty of women's character too much to expose it to the rude influences, the bitterness and strife of the world, few will be found to advocate her admission to universities. . . .

Their proper sphere of action is the domestic circle. Their highest duties they owe to the family, which also calls forth their most shining virtues. Therefore her education should be practical, fitting her to govern her household with wisdom and prudence. For her own sake, her mind should be cultivated, but her mental culture should not be what is regarded as distinctively intellectual. ("Sweet Girl Graduates," 1876, in Cook and Mitchinson, 1976, 123)

As laws change, so too do our attitudes, values, and beliefs. As our attitudes and beliefs change, so too do our laws. The struggle for the enfranchisement of women gives us a window into an earlier time when the social order was very different, and the laws both reflected and legitimized this difference.

In 1916, Manitoba granted women the right to vote, the first province in Canada to do so. Later that same year, women were enfranchised in Alberta and Saskatchewan, with British Columbia and Ontario following in 1917. Women in Nova Scotia, New Brunswick, Prince Edward Island, Newfoundland, and Quebec were granted the right to vote in 1918, 1919, 1922, 1925, and 1940, respectively (Prentice et al., 1996, 234). Women were given the right to vote in federal elections in 1918.

Source: Andrew Macphail, "On Certain Aspects of Feminism," *University Magazine*, Feb. 1914, in Cook and Mitchinson (1976) (eds.) *The Proper Sphere: Women's Place in Canadian Society.* Toronto: Oxford University Press, pp. 301, 304.

"Sweet Girl Graduates," *Queen's College Journal*, December 16, 1876, in Cook and Mitchinson (1976) (eds.) *The Proper Sphere: Women's Place in Canadian Society*, Toronto: Oxford University Press, pp. 123.

reaffirm the existing social order, and thereby legitimate class domination" (1993, 17). Law may be said to function as an ideological means of domination to the extent that it acts to legitimate the existing capitalist social order. Box 10.2 explores the relationship between law and ideology by using the example of the struggle for the vote by Canadian women.

By the end of the 1980s, a large body of critical work had been produced by Marxist scholars that examined the relationships between the capitalist state, the economy, and the legal and political institutions of the state. Canadian Marxist theorists, in particular, contributed to a rich literature that explored the relationship between the Canadian state, its laws, and its legal institutions, as well as the relationship between the state and the criminal justice system (Brickey and Comack, 1989; Mandel, 1987; Pearce, 1985; West and Snider, 1985; Snider 1987, 1989; Hinch, 1983). In addition, Canadian Marxist criminologists have also explored the broader area of corporate crime and social harm (Pearce, 1976; Sargent, 1991; McMullan, 1992; Snider, 1993). We will examine two further areas of Marxist research to illustrate some of the work undertaken in Marxist criminology: first, research that focuses on the crimes of the powerless, and second, research that investigates the crimes of the powerful.

Crimes of the Powerless

Stephen Spitzer

Spitzer (1975) made use of the Marxian notion of "surplus population" to formulate his "Marxian theory of deviance." Essentially Spitzer argued that the criminalization of much behaviour is directed toward those problem populations who are surplus to the labour market. These problem populations are created in two ways. First, they are created *directly* through the contradictions in the capitalist mode of production. For example, a surplus population is generated in capitalist economies as new technologies replace workers with machines, or when work is outsourced to other countries. Second, problem populations are created *indirectly* through contradictions in the institutions that help to reproduce capitalism, such as the schools. For example, Spitzer argues that while mass education of youths provides a means of training future wage labourers, this schooling also provides youths with critical insight into the alienating and oppressive character of capitalist institutions. This, in turn, can lead to problem populations in the form of dropouts and student radicals. Finally Spitzer argues that problem populations become candidates for deviance processing when they disturb, hinder, or call into question any of the following (Spitzer, 1975, 642):

1. Capitalist modes of appropriating the product of human labour (for example, when the poor "steal" from the rich).
2. The social conditions under which capitalist production takes place (for example, those who refuse or are unable to perform wage labour).
3. Patterns of distribution and consumption in capitalist society (for example, those who use drugs for escape and transcendence rather than sociability and adjustment).
4. The process of socialization for productive and nonproductive roles (for example, youths who refuse to be schooled or those who deny the validity of family life).
5. The ideology that supports the functioning of capitalist society (for example, proponents of alternative forms of social organization).

David Greenberg

Another theorist who makes use of the Marxian notion of surplus population is Greenberg (1993). Greenberg is interested in explaining juvenile delinquency from a Marxist perspective and has argued that juveniles can be described as forming a class of their own because they share a common relationship to the means of production. That is, young people are excluded from economically productive activity in a capitalist society, but are required to undergo training for their future productive role in the capitalist system. Juveniles can thus be considered a part of the surplus population, because they are excluded from lawful sources of income. In turn, this creates motivation toward delinquency, because juveniles' exclusion from the labour market means they cannot finance their leisure and social activities. If their parents are unable or unwilling to finance their social life to the required level, juveniles must seek out other sources of funding. Adolescent theft then occurs because of a conflict between the desire to participate in activities valued by peer culture and the lack of legitimate sources of funding to finance these activities (Greenberg, 1993).

Crimes of the Powerful

Whereas researchers who focus on the Marxian notion of "surplus population" are interested in the relationship between crime and those who are *outside* the sphere of production, Marxist research on corporate crime focuses on the socially harmful conduct of those who are *inside* the sphere of production in capitalist economies. Focus Box 10.3 explores one instance of socially harmful conduct from a Marxist perspective by examining the tainted dog and cat food produced by Menu Foods Income Fund, a pet food manufacturing facility headquartered in southern Ontario. Canadian Marxist scholars argue that the study of corporate crime is important because the losses incurred as a result of corporate malfeasance—whether it is the total dollar amount, or the number of deaths, injuries, and illnesses—are far in excess of the losses incurred as a result of street crime (Pearce, 1976; Snider, 1993; McMullan, 1992). In an early Marxist analysis of illegal activity of U.S. corporations, Pearce (1976) demonstrated that the dollar amount of corporate crime was much greater than the aggregate dollar amount of conventional crime. Similarly, both Snider (1993) and McMullan (1992) draw upon statistical evidence to argue that the total number of workers who die each year from both work-related accidents and occupationally induced diseases is far in excess of death rate statistics for homicide and manslaughter.

Generally speaking, this branch of Marxist criminology attempts to situate law, the state, corporate crime, and social harm within the logic of the mode of production under capitalism. Marxist theorists argue that the structure of capitalist economies and the imperative of profit maximization create strong motivation for corporations to engage in criminal activities or other socially harmful behaviours (Snider, 1993; Pearce, 2001; Pearce and Tombs, 1997; Henry, 1986). Accordingly, Marxist studies attempt to document both the nature and extent of corporate crime, and to analyze the relationship of corporate criminality to the capitalist mode of production (Goff and Reasons, 1978; Snider, 1999; Pearce and Tombs, 1998; Pearce and Snider, 1995; Henry, 1986; Glasbeek, 1989). At the same time, Marxist criminologists are also interested in examining the contradictory role of the state in capitalist economies, where the state must both create laws and regulate the criminal activities of corporations, but must also protect the overall interests of the capitalist economy as a whole by reproducing the conditions necessary for capitalism to continue (Gordon and Coneybeer, 1999; McMullan, 1992; Snider, 1993; Sargent, 1991).

Structural Marxism criminology has been criticized for its tautological character. This means that critics feel that it presents a circular argument. The

FOCUS

BOX 10.3 Is it a Corporate Crime? The Menu Foods Pet Food Recall

In Wudi, in eastern China, "a few companies tried to save money by slipping the industrial chemical melamine into pet food ingredients as a cheap protein enhancer, helping to incite one of the largest pet food recalls ever" (NYT, June 5, 2007).

In Mississauga, Ontario, on March 16, 2007, Menu Foods Income Fund, a pet food manufacturing facility, recalled 60 million cans of dog and cat food sold under 98 brands including Iams, Nutro and Eukanuba. The Menu Foods products are sold in Canada, the United States, and Mexico. The FDA (Food and Drug Administration) report that at least 16 animals died of kidney failure from eating tainted pet food, although some veterinarians believe the number to be far higher (NYT, April 13, 2007).

The U.S. Food and Drug Administration said on Friday, March 30, 2007 that melamine, a chemical used in fertilizers, had been discovered in some of the wheat gluten used by the Mississauga, Ontario based company Menu Foods Income Fund. The FDA confirmed that the wheat gluten came from a company based in China.

As the largest wet pet food manufacturer in North America, Menu Foods produces dog and cat food for many different companies, including Nutro, President's Choice, Price Chopper, Science Diet, Medi-Cal, Eukanuba, among others. Pet owners may have been surprised to discover that so many different brands of dog and cat food are produced by just one company. A Marxist analysis would point to the structure of capitalist economies and the pressure to extract ever-increasing amounts of surplus value in the form of profits. This, in turn, creates a tendency toward centralization and concentration of capital, as corporations attempt to increase in size and power through mergers, acquisitions, takeovers, and vertical and horizontal integration (McMullan, 1992). For example, many more efficiencies can be exploited from a large manufacturing facility producing 98 brands of pet food than from many manufacturing facilities producing just one or a few brands of dog or cat food each.

Pet owners may have also been shocked to discover that a toxic substance like melamine could enter into the food supply as a form of wheat gluten and could subsequently remain undetected in the pet food manufacturing process. A further way that corporations attempt to maximize profits is by cutting costs—for example, by attempting to source cheaper suppliers offshore, where regulations may be lax or nonexistent. The *New York Times* reports that the practice of doctoring animal and fish feed with melamine is widespread in China. "This is cut-throat market capitalism," said Wenran Jiang, a specialist on China who teaches at the University of Alberta (June 5, 2007).

Pearce (2001, 45) offers a Marxist explanation for this type of cut-throat market capitalism: "The limited-liability corporation has a strong proclivity to engage in anti-social, illegal, and criminal conduct. As a capitalist business, it is essentially dedicated to making continuous, and, if possible, ever-increasing profits. It is intrinsically indifferent to what commodities it produces as long as there is a market for them. . . . Company executives are also fundamentally concerned with profitability, and with 'wilful blindness' are again often distanced from production, conceive of it abstractly and, in turn, pressure managers to produce as much and as cheaply as possible. This creates a form of structural irresponsibility where it is often difficult to identify how decisions are made and how well or poorly they relate together."

Michalowski (1985, 314) offers the following definition for crimes of capital: "Crimes of capital are socially injurious acts that arise from the ownership or management of capital or from occupancy of positions of trust in institutions designed to facilitate the accumulation of capital."

Has a crime of capital occurred in the case of Menu Foods Income Fund?

theory begins with the assumption of class exploitation under capitalism in order to demonstrate that crime, in turn, is caused by capitalist class exploitation. Structural Marxism has also been critiqued for emphasizing structure at the expense of human agency, that is, at the expense of human action and ability to shape and direct the social world. A further critique has been that the exclusive focus on class relations has precluded other considerations from entering into analysis, such as gender oppression and race oppression. Socialist feminism, as we shall see below, represents one endeavour to incorporate Marxist analysis into a framework that considers the relationship between class exploitation and gender oppression in capitalist societies.

Socialist Feminism

Socialist feminist perspectives on the law, state, and crime began to emerge in the late 1970s and early 1980s and can be considered as both a critique and an extension of traditional Marxist categories of analysis. In addition, socialist feminism can also be considered as a critique and extension of the radical feminist position. **Radical feminism** itself emerged in the early 1970s as a critique of the liberal feminist focus on rectifying gender inequality through legal reforms to the existing system. The liberal feminist concern with providing equal opportunities to women by altering aspects of existing social systems was critiqued by radical feminists, who argued that simply concentrating on "equal opportunities" for women would not address the fundamental structural inequalities between men and women. Instead, radical feminists locate the fundamental conditions of women's oppression in the institution of **patriarchy**, defined as "a systematic expression of male domination and control over women which permeates all social, political and economic institutions" (Boyd and Sheehy, 1989, 260).

radical feminism
A perspective that views the problem of gender inequality and of women's subordination in society as rooted in the institution of patriarchy.

patriarchy
A system of male domination and control whereby the structure of society privileges men over women. Stresses the systemic nature of the oppression of women.

While radical feminist theorists have made important contributions to the feminist literature, particularly in the critical analysis of laws governing sexual assault, pornography, and reproduction, this perspective was itself subsequently critiqued for assuming a universality of women's subordination, and thus failing to recognize power differentials among women themselves, particularly working class women and women of colour. In addition, the radical feminist position was also critiqued for its tendency to give primacy to gender oppression under patriarchy, at the expense of class oppression under capitalism. In other words, radical feminism replaced capitalism with patriarchy as the primary system of oppression.

Zillah Eisenstein (1979) was one of the first to articulate a socialist feminist position. Eisenstein argued that Marxist analysis, by priorizing class relations, does not adequately explain the unique position of women in relation to the capitalist mode of production, while radical feminist analysis, by giving priority to patriarchy, does not adequately explain women's relationship to the economic class structure. Thus Eisenstein makes the argument that women's economic exploitation under capitalism and sexual oppression under patriarchy cannot be considered separately. These two systems support each other, and therefore they must be understood as "mutually dependent." What is needed, therefore, is a theory that integrates both Marxism and radical feminism (Eisenstein, 1979, 21). Socialist feminism, as Danner (1991, 52) points out, unites the major concepts in Marxism and radical feminism "to identify women's oppression as based in capitalist patriarchy."

In this understanding of **socialist feminism**, the interconnections between capitalism (class) and patriarchy (gender) are examined, with a particular emphasis on the relationship between productive and reproductive labour. Marx was interested in examining society from the perspective of how production is organized and viewed the mode of production under capitalism as giving rise to exploitative class relations, because the capitalist class is able to extract surplus value or profit from the worker's labour. The worker's labour is also described as *productive labour*, or wage labour, because a wage is received. Socialist feminists are interested in examining society from the perspective of both productive labour and reproductive labour, also described as domestic labour because a wage is not received and because this labour takes place in the home (Comack, 1999a). While socialist feminists disagree on the exact composition of reproductive labour, it is often thought to include the reproduction of the next generation of workers (childbirth and childrearing), and the work required to transform the labour wage received into a consumable form (cooking, cleaning, shopping) (Armstrong and Armstrong, 1985). The socialist feminist position is sometimes, but not always, described as a synthesis of certain aspects of Marxism and radical feminism that does not give priority to either production (capitalism) or reproduction (patriarchy), but views them as equivalent concepts (Messerschmidt, 1986).

socialist feminism
A perspective that views women's exploitation under capitalism and oppression under patriarchy as interconnected. Neither the class structure of capitalism nor patriarchal gender relations are given priority in socialist feminism, rather gender and class relations are viewed as mutually dependent.

Canadian socialist feminist scholars have more broadly contributed to a rich literature, particularly in the area of the state, law, and crime (Comack, 1999a; Gavigan, 1999; Snider, 1991, 1998; Ursel, 1991). Feminist criminology in Canada dates back to the late 1960s and has endeavoured, among other things, to make the concerns of women more visible within the "criminological enterprise." One of the major issues that Canadian feminist criminologists have studied has been violence against women. These scholars have analyzed criminal justice policy and documented the extent and nature of violence against women through small-scale studies and large-scale surveys. The feminist research agenda, which has focused on women as victims of male violence, has helped to create the momentum for various efforts and initiatives to reform sexual violence laws and criminal justice policies in the area of wife abuse, including mandatory arrest and sentencing laws and specialised family violence courts (Comack, 1999b).

WWW

Biographies of Canadian Women in Science, Government, Music, Literature, and Sport
www.collectionscanada.ca/women

At the same time, feminist initiatives to reform the criminal law have not been unambiguously endorsed (Currie, 1990; Snider, 1991, 1994; Busby, 1999), and feminists have debated whether reforming the criminal law, meant to address the real violence against women, has been an effective strategy for change. Comack suggests that the contemporary feminist project is now at a point where critical reflection is taking place, with one of the more recent feminist debates centring on whether any real advances have been achieved through criminal law reform, or whether "a strategic error has been made in engaging with the patriarchal state and legal system, especially the criminal justice system" (1993,

1). This debate explores the value of employing the criminal law to further feminist goals, including feminist initiatives to reform the criminal law in the area of wife abuse.

At issue is the question of whether criminal law reforms to address violence against women have been effective, as well as how "effectiveness" is to be measured, and finally, whether or not the feminist socialist project ought to engage at all with the state and the criminal justice system to further its goals of empowerment and transformation. Ursel (1991) argues that it is, in fact, possible for feminists to work with the "state" and the criminal justice system to improve the life conditions of women by lobbying for changes in the criminal law. Ursel advances this argument by examining the lobbying efforts of the Battered Women's Movement to strengthen spouse abuse laws in Manitoba, beginning with a 1983 directive from the Attorney General of Manitoba that instructed police to lay charges in all reported cases of spouse abuse. Prior to the 1983 directive, the onus was typically on the victim to request that charges be laid. Ursel argued that real changes with beneficial results for women have been produced as a result of the 1983 directive, including an increase in the number of men being charged with spousal assault, a decrease in the number of cases dismissed in court, and an increased percentage of offenders receiving court-imposed sanctions, including probation, mandatory counselling, and jail sentences. In addition, as Ursel also notes, the increased attention to the issue of wife abuse has also resulted in an increase in funding for wife abuse programs and an increase in community-based wife abuse services, as well as the creation of an office within the government to administer the funding.

Snider (1994), however, argues that feminist attempts to engage with the state in the area of criminal law reform have not only failed to improve the life conditions of women more generally, but have also served to direct attention away from strategies and tactics that have greater potential to empower and ameliorate women's lives. Snider points to some unintended consequences of mandatory arrest policies in the case of reports of spousal abuse, such as an increase in the number of women arrested, often for using violence to defend themselves, as well as women who find themselves facing contempt charges for refusing to testify against their abusers. In addition, when abusers are arrested, they tend to be young, economically marginal, minority males, who have themselves been subjected to the injuries of class, racism, and often childhood abuse. Snider argues that there is little evidence that mandatory response, arrest and charging policies have ameliorated the lives of women, or made them safer inside or outside the home (1998). Ultimately, Snider suggests that the criminal law is an inappropriate means of achieving social transformation (1991). She argues that feminist engagement with law reform should occur only under particular conditions to advance particular aims: to remove any remaining impediments that stand in the way of full legal equality for women, to prevent the passage of laws that will create new barriers, and to establish concrete rather than abstract rights such as concrete rights regarding universal medicare, daycare, or reproductive rights (Snider, 1994).

This debate helps to highlight the often contradictory nature of legal reforms and the difficulty of establishing which criteria are to be employed in assessing whether or not a legal reform is judged as successful. For example, is the criterion whether mandatory arrest serves to deter offenders (Faubert and Hinch, 1996)? How are we to measure deterrence, for example, and over what time period? Is the criterion that measures the success of a legal reform an increase in arrest rates (Ursel, 1991)? If so, what are the benefits that accrue from such an increase? Finally, is the feminist socialist project of ameliorating the lives of working class and marginalized women in keeping with involving more people, both men and women, with the coercive power of the criminal justice system (Snider, 1994)? That is, is the project itself flawed, and are reforms better sought through other avenues? These are obviously difficult questions to ask and to answer, and we see in the feminist criminology literature an attempt to come to terms with these questions, as well as with feminist socialist theory and practice more generally, as it is shaped, revised, and debated in the context of reforms to spousal abuse laws.

Left Realism

The final conflict perspective we will examine is that of left realism. Left realism was first developed in Britain in the late 1970s and early 1980s (Young, 1979, 1986; Young and Matthews, 1992; Lea and Young, 1984; Matthews and Young, 1992), and was subsequently taken up as an area of criminological inquiry by Canadian scholars (MacLean, 1991; Lowman and MacLean, 1992; DeKeseredy, 1991, 2003; Currie et al., 1990; Currie, 1991). In Britain, "left realism" was initially developed by Jock Young, John Lea, and Roger Matthews, who advanced a strong critique against what they described as "left idealism." Left idealism is a term coined by Young (1979) and is meant to include both instrumentalist and structuralist Marxist accounts of the state, law, and crime. Left realists are additionally critical of what they describe as conventional or orthodox criminology and argue that both Marxist and conventional interpretations are superficial accounts of crime. Specifically, left realists argue that for conventional criminology, crime is "simply antisocial behaviour involving people who lack values," while for Marxist criminology, crime is "proto-revolutionary activity, primitive and individualistic, but praiseworthy all the same" (Lea and Young, 1984, 96).

Left realists emphasize the need to examine the "square of crime," that is, the relationship between the offender, the victim, the police, and the public (Young and Matthews, 1992; Matthews and Young, 1992). Left realism emerged largely in response to the perceived failure of other types of criminology, including Marxist criminology, to pay attention to the serious harm generated by street crime, also described as "working-class crime." In Britain, left realists such as Young, Lea, and Matthews have argued, in essence, that Marxist critiques of capitalist society have not paid sufficient attention to the real suffering experienced by victims of street crime, particularly the poor and disadvantaged, who are typically the main victims of street crime. In this context, street crime means some form of injury committed directly by one or more specific individuals against the body or property of the victim, such as murder, rape, robbery, theft, vandalism, and burglary (Michalowski, 1991). In general, left realists argue that the victims of most crimes tend to be those from the most vulnerable segments of the community, and that crime is disproportionately distributed among the working class, women, and racial minorities. In addition, the majority of working class crime is intra-class, that is, both the offender and the victim tend to be from the same socio-economic strata (Lowman and MacLean, 1992; Young, 1986; Lea and Young, 1984).

Left realism takes its starting point in the observation that *crime really is a problem* for the working class and other marginalized groups in the community, and working class crime must therefore be "taken seriously" (Lea and Young, 1986). Taking crime seriously, for left realists, means developing a working class criminology that aims to both examine and offer practical solutions to the street crime that marginalized people experience. The strategy employed to examine the problem of crime for the working class is the victimization survey (see Chapter 4). One of the first victimization studies, the Islington Crime Survey (ICS), was conducted in inner-city London in 1985. Employing self-report data, these types of surveys attempt to measure public attitudes, perceptions, and beliefs about the extent and nature of street crime in the community and the effectiveness of police in dealing with it (Jones et al., 1986). With regard to offering practical solutions, left realists argue for a concrete crime control program, with the objective of offering non-repressive crime control policies (MacLean, 1991; Lea and Young, 1986). Crime control policies that have been endorsed by left realists include alternatives to prisons (such as community service, victim restitution, weekend prison sentences for working offenders); preemptive deterrence (encouraging citizens groups to cooperate with the police), transforming the police force into a police service accountable to the public; and "harnessing the energies of the marginalized" to create a "politics of crime control" (Lea and Young, 1986, 360–63; Young, 1992, 41–42).

Left realism has made some valuable contributions to the criminology literature, including sensitizing us to the amount and kinds of street crime and domestic violence experienced by the most marginalized and vulnerable members of society. In turn, left realism has been subject to a number of critiques. For example, Michalowski (1991) has argued that the left realist position is ahistorical; that is, left realism fails to take into consideration the political, economic, and cultural history of the society in which crime occurs. Can the square of crime (the relationship between victims, offenders, police, public) be fully understood by analyzing responses to local victimization surveys undertaken at a particular point in time and space? O'Reilly-Fleming (1996, 10) suggests that the left realism's advocacy for greater crime control may have the effect of "widening the net of social control" and may amount to little more than increasing state powers over the marginalized and disenfranchised groups under study. This has some interesting parallels with the feminist socialist debate described earlier that questioned whether engaging with the criminal justice system to strengthen criminal laws was in keeping with the feminist socialist project of ameliorating the lives of women. Finally, Mugford and O'Malley (1991: 23) argue that left realists make use of common sense notions (crime really is a problem), but neglect to transform these common sense notions into a defensible theoretical account.

Table 10.1 Conflict Theorists

Theory	*Theorists*	*Key Elements*
Cultural Conflict	Sellin	Crime occurs when individuals acting on the conduct norms of their own group are in violation of the conduct norms the dominant group has enacted into law.
Group Conflict	Vold, Quinney	Interest groups (Vold) or social groupings (Quinney) attempt to protect their own interests by influencing the creation and enforcement of the criminal law.
Instrumental Marxism	Quinney	The state and the legal system are instruments that can be directly manipulated by the capitalist class. The capitalist class can thus directly influence law and law formation.
Structural Marxism	Althusser, Poulantzas	The relative autonomy of the state functions to preserve the long-term interests of the capitalist system. This helps to explain why many laws are enacted that do not represent the immediate interests of the capitalist class.
Socialist Feminism	Eisenstein, Comack, Snider, Ursel	Draws upon both radical feminist and Marxist categories of analysis to explore the relationship between capitalism (class) and patriarchy (gender). Violence against women has been a major issue studied by Canadian socialist feminists.
Left Realism	Young, MacLean, DeKeseredy	Argues that crime really is a problem for the working class and must be taken seriously. Most working class crime is intra-class. Major methodological tool is the victimization survey. Argues for a concrete crime control program; endorses crime control policies which are not repressive.

Summary

- Conflict theory views societies as more divided by conflict than they are integrated by consensus.
- According to Sellin's cultural conflict theory, crime can be viewed as an expression of cultural conflict when individuals who act based on the conduct norms of their own group are in violation of the conduct norms that the dominant group has enacted into law.
- According to Vold's group conflict theory, crime occurs as a result of conflict between diverse interest groups. Vold makes use of group conflict theory to explain two general classes of group conflict that can result in criminal behaviour: first, crime that arises as a result of minority group behaviour, and second, crime that results from direct contact between groups struggling for the control of power in the political and cultural organization of society.
- Richard Quinney's group conflict theory explains criminality as arising from conflict between "segments" of society, which he defined as types of social groupings. The more powerful segments or social groups in society are able to secure and to protect their own interests by influencing the formulation, enforcement, and administration of criminal law. Quinney places

a greater emphasis than either Sellin or Vold on the unequal distribution of power in society.

- Instrumental Marxists view the state and the legal system as instruments that could be directly manipulated by the capitalist class. Instrumental Marxists thus maintain that laws are created and enforced in the interests of the ruling or capitalist class.
- Structural Marxists dispute the instrumentalist view that the state is the direct servant of the ruling or capitalist class and argue that the state and its institutions have a certain degree of independence from specific elites in the capitalist class. Structural Marxists point to the relative autonomy of the state to help explain why many laws are enacted that do not represent the immediate interests of the capitalist class.
- Socialist feminism offers a critique of both Marxism and radical feminism and offers a theory that attempts to integrate both class exploitation under capitalism and women's oppression under patriarchy. One of the major issues that Canadian feminist criminologists have studied has been violence against women. A recent debate in the feminist criminological literature focuses on feminist initiatives to reform the criminal law in the area of wife abuse.
- Left realists emphasize that crime really is a problem for the working class and other marginalized groups in the community, and that working class crime must be taken seriously. Left realists make use of victimization surveys to examine the problem of crime for the working class, with the objective of offering crime control policies that are not repressive.

QUESTIONS FOR CRITICAL THINKING

1. In what way is Quinney's understanding of conflict, in his early work, different from that of Sellin and Vold? In what way is it similar?
2. How does structural Marxism address the critiques of instrumental Marxism? Describe what is meant by "relative autonomy."
3. How does socialist feminism address the critiques of radical feminism and Marxism?
4. In discussing the notion of the "rule of law" and "equality of all before the law," Marxist theorists sometimes make use of the following quote by social critic Anatole France (1894): "The law in its majestic impartiality forbids both the rich and poor alike to sleep under bridges, to beg in the streets or to steal bread." What contradiction does France point out across the divide of a century? How might this quotation apply to the concept of law and ideology in Marxist thought?
5. The debate in the socialist feminist literature about the effectiveness of criminal law reform raises the issue of measurement criteria. Describe the different types of measurement criteria that might be employed to measure the effectiveness of reforms such as mandatory arrest for all reported cases of spousal abuse.

6. Left realists have argued for a concrete crime control program, with the objective of designing crime control policies that are not repressive. Is it possible to engage with the criminal justice system in the area of criminal law reform in a way that is not repressive for the groups that left realists study?

NET WORK

Go to the website of the Canadian Encyclopedia at www.thecanadianencyclopedia.com. Click on the link "Feature Articles." Under Subject Index, click on the "Economics & Labour" link. Here you will see links to 14 articles. Go to "Origins of Labour Day" and "Winnipeg General Strike." Explore the various links in these two articles, especially "working-class history" and "nine-hour movement."

1. As the link on "working class history" points out, "the consolidation of Canadian capitalism in the early 20th century accelerated the growth of the working class." What were some of the issues that the labour unions of the time were concerned about? What argument would structural Marxists make about the Industrial Disputes Investigation Act (1907)?
2. What was the nine-hour movement? Why was this movement considered to be unsuccessful? What would an instrumental Marxist argument say about the nine-hour movement?
3. When was the Winnipeg general strike and why is it considered a pivotal event in Canadian history? What was the Citizens' Committee of One Thousand, and how did it differ from the General Strike Committee? What would an instrumental Marxist argument point out about the ensuing events?

KEY TERMS

conduct norms; pg. 310
cultural conflict; pg. 311
group conflict; pg. 311
instrumental Marxism; pg. 317
patriarchy; pg. 326
radical feminism; pg. 326
relative autonomy; pg. 319
socialist feminism; pg. 327
structural Marxism; pg. 319

SUGGESTED READING

Comack, Elizabeth, and Stephen Brickey (eds.). (1991). *The Social Basis of Law: Critical Readings in the Sociology of Law.* Halifax: Garamond Press. An excellent collection of articles exploring socialist feminist and Marxist perspectives, including the Ursel (1991) and Snider (1991) articles referred to in this chapter. In addition, the volume contains a well-written and informative overview of the various approaches to the sociology of law.

Comack, Elizabeth (ed.). (1999). *Locating Law: Race, Class, Gender Connections.* Halifax: Fernwood Publishing. Another excellent collection of articles exploring various socialist feminist perspectives.

MacLean, Brian D., and Dragan Milovanovic (eds.). (1991). *New Directions in Critical Criminology.* Vancouver: Collective Press. A good assortment of articles on left realism with a Canadian emphasis.

McCormick, Christopher (ed.). (1992). *The Westray Chronicles: A Case Study in Corporate Crime.* Halifax: Fernwood Publishing. An edited collection exploring the Westray Mining disaster as a corporate crime.

McMullan, John. (1992). *Beyond the Limits of the Law: Corporate Crime and Law and Order.* Halifax: Fernwood Publishing. A Marxist approach to the analysis of corporate crime.

Pearce, Frank. (1976). *Crimes of the Powerful: Marxism, Crime and Deviance*, London: Pluto. An early and important study of criminal activities using a Marxist framework of analysis.

Pearce, Frank, and Steve Tombs (eds.). (1998). *Toxic Capitalism: Corporate Crime and the Chemical Industry.* Aldershot, England: Ashgate. A neo-Marxist informed analysis of corporate crime, including, especially, an examination of the tragic gas disaster at Bhopal in 1984.

Ratner, R. S., John McMullan, and Brian Burtch. (1987). "The Problem of Relative Autonomy and Criminal Justice in the Canadian State." In R. S. Ratner and John McMullan (eds.), *State Control: Criminal Justice Politics in Canada* (pp. 85–125). Vancouver: University of British Columbia Press. An informative article exploring Marxist issues, relative autonomy, and criminal justice in Canada.

Snider, Laureen. (1993). *Bad Business: Corporate Crime in Canada.* Toronto: Nelson Canada. A well-researched and informative Marxist study of corporate crime in Canada.

——. (1994). "Feminism, Punishment and the Potential of Empowerment." *Canadian Journal of Law and Society*, 9 (1):15–38. A critical analysis exploring the merits of engaging with the critical justice system for socialist feminist goals.

BIBLIOGRAPHY

Althusser, L. (1969). *For Marx.* New York: Vintage Press.

Armstrong, Pat, and Hugh Armstrong. (1985). "Beyond Sexless Class and Classless Sex: Towards Feminist Marxism." In Pat Armstrong, Hugh Armstrong, Patricia Connelly, and Angela Miles (eds.), *Feminist Marxism or Marxist Feminism: A Debate* (pp. 1–37). Toronto: Garamond Press.

Bartholomew, Amy, and Susan Boyd. (1989). "Towards a Political Economy of Law." In Wallace Clement and Glen Williams (eds.), *The New Canadian Political Economy* (pp. 212–39). Kingston: McGill University Press.

Bohm, Robert M. (1982). "Radical Criminology: An Explication." *Criminology* 19 (4):565–89.

Boyd, Susan B., and Elizabeth A. Sheehy. (1989). "Overview: Feminism and the Law in Canada." In Tullio Caputo, Mark Kennedy, Charles E. Reasons, Augustine Brannigan (eds.), *Law and Society: A Critical Perspective* (pp. 255–70). Toronto: Harcourt Brace Jovanovich.

Brickey, Stephen, and Elizabeth Comack. (1989). "The Role of Law in Social Transformation: Is a Jurisprudence of Insurgency Possible?" In T. Caputo, M. Kennedy, C. Reasons, and A. Brannigan (eds.), *Law and Society: A Critical Perspective* (pp. 316–30). Toronto: Harcourt, Brace, Jovanovich.

Busby, Karen. (1999). "Not a Victim until a Conviction Is Entered: Sexual Violence Prosecutions and Legal Truth." In Elizabeth Comack (ed.), *Locating Law: Race, Class, Gender Connections* (pp. 260–88). Halifax: Fernwood Publishing.

Cain, Maureen, and Alan Hunt. (1979). *Marx and Engels on Law.* London: Academic Press.

Chambliss, William, and Robert Siedman. (1982). *Law, Order and Power.* Reading: Addison-Wesley Publishing Company.

Comack, Elizabeth, and Stephen Brickey (eds.). (1991). *The Social Basis of Law: Critical Readings in the Sociology of Law.* Halifax: Garamond Press.

Comack, Elizabeth. (1993). *The Feminist Engagement with the Law: The Legal Recognition of the Battered Woman Syndrome.* Ottawa: Canadian Research Institute for the Advancement of Women.

———. (1999a). "Theoretical Excursions." In Elizabeth Comack (ed.), *Locating Law: Race, Class, Gender Connections* (pp. 10–68). Halifax: Fernwood Publishing.

———. (1999b). "New Possibilities for Feminism 'in' Criminology? From Dualism to Diversity." *Canadian Journal of Criminology* 41 (2):161–71.

Cook, Ramsey, and Wendy Mitchinson (eds.). (1976). *The Proper Sphere: Women's Place in Canadian Society.* Toronto: Oxford University Press.

Currie, Dawn. (1990). "Battered Woman and the State: From the Failure of a Theory to a Theory of Failure." *Journal of Human Justice* 1 (2):77–96.

———. (1991). "Realist Criminology, Women, and Social Transformation in Canada." In Brian D. MacLean and Dragan Milovanovic (eds.), *New Directions in Critical Criminology* (pp. 9–14). Vancouver: Collective Press.

Currie, Dawn, Walter S. DeKeseredy, and Brian D. MacLean. (1990). "Reconstructing Social Order and Social Control: Police Accountability in Canada." *The Journal of Human Justice* 2 (1):29–53.

Danner, Mona J. E. (1991). "Socialist Feminism: A Brief Introduction." In Brian MacLean and Dragan Milovanovic (eds.), *New Directions in Critical Criminology* (pp. 51–54). Vancouver: Collective Press.

DeKeseredy, Walter S. (1991). "Confronting Woman Abuse: A Brief Overview of the Left Realist Approach." In Brian D. MacLean and Dragan Milovanovic (eds.), *New Directions in Critical Criminology* (pp. 27–30). Vancouver: Collective Press.

———. (2003). "Left Realism on Inner City Violence." In Martin D. Schwartz and Suzanne E. Hatty (eds.), *Controversies in Critical Criminology* (pp. 29–41). Cincinnati, Ohio: Anderson.

Domhoff, G. William. (1970). *The Higher Circles: The Governing Class in America.* New York: Random House.

Einstadter, Werner, and Stuart Henry. (2006). *Criminological Theory: An Analysis of its Underlying Assumptions.* Lanham: Rowman & Littlefield Publishers Inc.

Eisenstein, Zillah. (1979). "Developing a Theory of Capitalist Patriarchy and Socialist Feminism." In Zillah Eisenstein (ed.), *Capitalist Patriarchy and the Case for Socialist Feminism* (pp. 5–40). New York: Monthly Review Press.

Faubert, Jacqueline, and Ronald Hinch. (1996). "The Dialectics of Mandatory Arrest Policies." In Thomas O'Reilly-Fleming (ed.), *Post-Critical Criminology* (pp. 230–51). Scarborough: Prentice Hall.

Gavigan, Shelley. (1999). "Poverty Law, Theory, and Practice: The Place of Class and Gender in Access to Justice." In Elizabeth Comack (ed.), *Locating Law: Race, Class, Gender Connections* (pp 207-30). Halifax: Fernwood Publishing.

Glasbeek, Harry. (1989). "Why Corporate Deviance Is not Treated as a Crime: The Need to Make Profits a Dirty Word." In T. Caputo, M. Kennedy, C. Reasons, and A. Brannigan (eds.), *Law and Society: A Critical Perspective* (pp. 126–45). Toronto: Harcourt, Brace, Jovanovich.

Goff, Colin and Charles Reasons. (1978). *Corporate Crime in Canada: A Critical Analysis of Anti-Combines Legislation.* Scarborough: Prentice Hall Canada.

Gold, David, Clarence Y. H. Lo, and Erik O. Wright. (1975). "Recent Developments in Marxist Theories of the Capitalist State." *Monthly Review* (October/November) 27:29–43/36–51.

Gordon, Robert, and Ian Coneybeer. (1999). "Corporate Crime." In N. Larsen and B. Burtch (eds.), *Law in Society: Canadian Readings* (pp. 101–27). Toronto: Nelson Thomson Learning.

Greenberg, David F. (1993). *Crime and Capitalism: Readings in Marxist Criminology* (2nd ed.). Philadelphia: Temple University Press.

Henry, Frank. (1986). "Crime—A Profitable Approach." In Brian Maclean (ed.), *The Political Economy of Crime* (pp. 182–203). Toronto: Prentice-Hall.

Hinch, Ron. (1983). "Marxist Criminology in the 1970s: Clarifying the Clutter." *Crime and Social Justice*19:65–74.

Hunt, Alan. (1993). *Explorations in Law and Society: Towards a Constitutive Theory of Law.* New York: Routledge.

Jones, Trevor, Brian MacLean, and Jock Young. (1986). *The Islington Crime Survey: Crime, Victimization and Policing in Inner-City London.* Aldershot, England: Gower Publishing Company.

Lea, John, and Jock Young. (1984). *What Is to be Done About Law and Order?* Harmondsworth: Penguin Books.

Lea, John and Jock Young (1986), "A Realistic Approach to Law and Order", In Brian D. MacLean (ed.), *The Political Economy of Crime: Readings for a Critical Criminology.* Ontario: Prentice-Hall Canada.

Lowman, John, and Brian D. MacLean. (1992). "Introduction: Left Realism, Crime Control, and Policing in the 1990s." In John Lowman and Brian D. MacLean (eds.), *Realist Criminology: Crime Control and Policing in the 1990s* (pp. 3–29). Toronto: University of Toronto Press.

MacLean, Brian. (1991). "The Origins of Left Realism." In Brian D. MacLean and Dragan Milovanovic (eds.), *New Directions in Critical Criminology* (pp. 9–14). Vancouver: Collective Press.

Mandel, Michael. (1987). "'Relative Autonomy' and the Criminal Justice Apparatus." In R. S. Ratner and John McMullan (eds.), *State Control: Criminal Justice Politics in Canada* (pp. 149–64). Vancouver: University of British Columbia Press.

Marx, Karl, and Friedrich Engels. (1992 [1848]). *The Communist Manifesto.* Oxford: Oxford University Press.

Matthews, Roger, and Jock Young. (1992). "Reflections on Realism." In Jock Young and Roger Matthews (eds.), *Rethinking Criminology: The Realist Debate* (pp. 1–23). London: Sage Publications.

McMullan, John. (1992). *Beyond the Limits of the Law: Corporate Crime and Law and Order.* Halifax: Fernwood Publishing.

Macphail, Andrew (1976). "On Certain Aspects of Feminism." In R. Cook and W. Mitchinson (eds.), *The Proper Sphere: Women's Place in Canadian Society* (pp. 301, 304). Toronto: Oxford University Press.

Messerschmidt, James. (1986). *Capitalism, Patriarchy, and Crime.* New Jersey: Rowman & Littlefield.

Michalowski, Raymond. (1985). *Order, Law and Crime: An Introduction to Criminology.* New York: Random House.

——. (1991). "'Niggers, Welfare Scum and Homeless Assholes': The Problems of Idealism, Consciousness and Context in Left Realism." In Brian D. MacLean and Dragan Milovanovic (eds.), *New Directions in Critical Criminology* (pp. 31–38). Vancouver: The Collective Press.

Miliband, Ralph. (1969). *The State in Capitalist Society.* London: Weidenfeld and Nicolson.

Mugford, Stephen, and Pat O'Malley. (1991). "Heroin Policy and Deficit Models." *Crime, Law and Social Change,* 15(1):19–36.

Okihiro, Norman. (1997). *Mounties, Moose and Moonshine: The Patterns and Context of Outport Crime.* Toronto: University of Toronto Press.

O'Reilly-Fleming, Thomas. (1996). "Left-Realism as Theoretical Retreatism or Paradigm Shift: Toward Post-Critical Criminology." In Thomas O'Reilly-Fleming (ed.), *Post-Critical Criminology* (pp. 1–25). Scarborough: Prentice Hall.

Pearce, Frank. (1976). *Crimes of the Powerful: Marxism, Crime and Deviance.* London: Pluto.

———. (1985). "Neo-Structuralist Marxism on Crime and Law in Britain." *The Insurgent Sociologist* 13:123–31.

———. (2001). "Crime and Capitalist Business Corporations." In Neal Shrover and John Paul Wright (eds.), *Crimes of Privilege: Readings in White Collar Crime* (pp. 35–48). New York: Oxford University Press.

Pearce, Frank, and Laureen Snider. (1995). "Regulating Capitalism." In Frank Pearce and Laureen Snider (eds.)., *Corporate Crime: Contemporary Debates* (pp. 19–47). Toronto: University of Toronto Press.

Pearce, Frank, and Steve Tombs. (1997). "Hazards, Law and Class: Contextualizing the Regulation of Corporate Crime." *Social and Legal Issues* 6 (1): 79-107.

Pearce, Frank, and Steve Tombs. (1998). *Toxic Capitalism: Corporate Crime and the Chemical Industry.* Aldershot: Ashgate.

Poulantzas, N. (1975). *Classes in Contemporary Capitalism.* London: New Left Books.

Prentice, Alison, Paula Bourne, Gail Cuthbert Brandt, Beth Light, Wendy Mitchinson, and Naomi Black. (1996). *Canadian Women: A History* (2nd ed.). Toronto, Harcourt Brace & Company.

Quinney, Richard. (1970). *The Social Reality of Crime.* Boston: Little, Brown and Company.

———. (1974). *Critique of the Legal Order.* Boston: Little, Brown and Company.

Sargent, Neil. (1991). "Law, Ideology and Social Change: An Analysis of the Role of Law in the Construction of Corporate Crime." In Elizabeth Comack and Stephen Brickey (eds.), *The Social Basis of Law: Critical Readings in the Sociology of Law* (pp. 289–309). Halifax: Garamond Press.

Sellin, Thorsten. (1938). *Culture Conflict and Crime.* New York: Social Science Research Council.

Smandych, Russell. (1985). "Marxism and the Creation of Law: Re-Examining the Origins of Canadian Anti-Combines Legislation 1890–1910." In Thomas Fleming (ed.), *The New Criminology in Canada: State, Crime and Control* (pp. 87–99). Toronto: Oxford University Press.

Snider, Laureen. (1979). "Revising the Combines Investigation Act: A Study in Corporate Power." In Paul Brantingham and Jack Kress (eds.), *Structure, Law, and Power: Essays in the Sociology of Law* (pp. 105–19). Beverly Hills: Sage Publications.

Snider, Laureen. (1987). "Towards a Political Economy of Reform, Regulation, and Corporate Crime", *Law and Policy,* 9 (1): 37-68.

Snider, Laureen. (1989). "Ideology and Relative Autonomy in Anglo-Canadian Criminology," *Journal of Human Justice,* 1 (1): 27-42.

———. (1991). "The Potential of the Criminal Justice System to Promote Feminist Concerns." In Elizabeth Comack and Stephen Brickey (eds.), *The Social Basis of Law: Critical Readings in the Sociology of Law* (pp. 238–60). Halifax: Garamond Press.

———. (1993). *Bad Business: Corporate Crime in Canada*. Toronto: Nelson.

———. (1994). "Feminism, Punishment and the Potential of Empowerment." *Canadian Journal of Law and Society* 9(1):15–38.

———. (1998). "Towards Safer Societies: Punishment, Masculinities, and Violence against Women." *British Journal of Criminology* 38 (1): 1-39.

———. (1999). "Relocating Law: Making Corporate Crime Disappear." In Elizabeth Comack (ed.), *Locating Law: Race, Class, Gender Connections* (pp. 183–207). Halifax: Fernwood Publishing.

Spitzer, Steven. (1975). "Towards a Marxian Theory of Analysis." *Social Problems* 22(5):638–51.

"Sweet Girl Graduates." (1976). In Ramsey Cook and Wendy Mitchinson (eds.), *The Proper Sphere: Women's Place in Canadian Society* (p. 123). Toronto: Oxford University Press.

Tierney, John. (1996). *Criminology: Theory and Context*. London: Prentice Hall.

Ursel, Jane. (1991). "Considering the Impact of the Battered Women's Movement on the State: The Example of Manitoba." In Elizabeth Comack and Stephen Brickey (eds.), *The Social Basis of Law: Critical Readings in the Sociology of Law*. Halifax: Garamond Press.

Vold, George. (1958). *Theoretical Criminology*. New York: Oxford University Press.

West, W. Gordon, and Laureen Snider. (1985). "A Critical Perspective on Law and the Canadian State: Delinquency and Corporate Crime." In Thomas Fleming (ed.), *The New Criminology in Canada: State, Crime and Control* (pp. 138–70). Toronto: Oxford University Press.

Young, Jock. (1979). "Left Idealism, Reformism, and Beyond." In Bob Fine, Richard Kinsey, John Lea, Sol Picciotto, and Jock Young (eds.), *Capitalism and the Rule of Law* (pp. 11–28). London: Hutchinson.

———. (1986). "The Failure of Criminology: The Need for a Radical Realism." In Roger Matthews and Jock Young (eds.), *Confronting Crime* (pp. 4–30). London: Sage Publications.

———. (1992). "Ten Points of Realism." In Roger Matthews and Jock Young (eds.), *Rethinking Criminology: The Realist Debate* (pp. 24–68). London: Sage Publications.

Young, Jock, and Roger Matthews. (1992). "Questioning Left Realism." In Roger Matthews and Jock Young (eds.), *Issues in Realist Criminology* (pp. 1–18). London: Sage Publications.

Contemporary Critical Criminology

11

Bryan Hogeveen and Andrew Woolford

UNIVERSITY OF ALBERTA AND UNIVERSITY OF MANITOBA

Alberta's economy has been booming for the past decade. With provincial coffers bursting at the seams, every Albertan received a $400 rebate cheque, and the government provided $45 million a year to support the horse racing industry. However, between 1999 and 2003, homelessness in Edmonton rose by 130 percent and the city has joined nine other major Canadian municipalities in declaring homelessness a national disaster (Edmonton, 2004). A growing number of destitute individuals are having to scrounge for the crumbs that remain after higher priority items such as horse racing get their cut. Alberta is not unique, and inequality and social suffering are not exclusively local problems. Around the globe, misery and hardship are prevalent. The current world situation is characterized by an enormous inequality of techno-scientific, military, and economic development, with the result being that "never have violence, inequality, exclusion, famine and . . . economic oppression affected as many human beings" (Derrida, 1994, 85).

What does this have to do with criminology? *Everything.* The downtrodden, the marginalized, and the impoverished make up the majority of individuals who are arrested by the police, represent the greatest number of inmates in our jails, and take up the bulk of spaces in the court docket. It seems that we inhabit an unjust world made up of enormous concentrations of wealth and power on one hand and masses of powerless people on the other. This situation raises many questions: Is this the best Canadians can hope for? If so, does this indicate a diminishment of political dreams and the loss of hope for social justice? If it is not, how do we move to a more just state? As you read this chapter, keep in mind the *face* of suffering—whether it be that of the homeless person Canadians hurry by on their way to enjoying a $4 Starbuck's coffee or that of a news story about the starving Ethiopian child so easily flipped past on a 60-inch plasma screen television—and ask what you are willing to give up to ameliorate social, economic, and political suffering.

These are the dilemmas critical criminology forces us to face. As citizens fully socialized into the social order, we rarely critically engage with our world but simply take it for granted. Inspired by promises of "freedom" and "justice," critical criminology attempts to draw attention to hidden and overlooked injustices scattered throughout *our* world. Critical criminology attempts to highlight inequalities, discrimination, and suffering and to relate these to the discipline of criminology. Social problems abound but are easily dismissed as someone else's responsibility. Critical criminology attends to the processes through which the social world restricts human freedom and choice. It attempts to assemble and create more "just" worlds with less misery or no misery: "the possibility daily withheld, overlooked or unbelieved" (Bauman, 2000).

Learning Objectives

After reading this chapter, you should be able to

- Explain what it means to be "critical" in critical criminology.
- Identify the origins of critical criminology in Canada in the New Criminology and the efforts of the Human Justice Collective.
- Understand Michel Foucault's approach to the concept of power and its importance to critical criminology.
- Describe how risk and actuarialism are prevalent in contemporary criminal justice practices and how this relates to the notion of the "risk society."
- Discuss cultural criminology and its contribution to critical criminology.
- Explain Pierre Bourdieu's "field theory" and its application to crime in the work of Loïc Wacquant.
- Define Giorgio Agamben's concept of the "state of exception" and explain its relationship to sovereignty.
- Describe Jacques Derrida's notion of "deconstruction" and how it is used in critical criminology.

What Is *Critical* about Critical Criminology?

Contemporary *critical* criminology promises to offer something critical. But what does this mean? To be certain, everyone is critical—at least to a certain extent. Indeed, as Kant stated over two centuries ago, our ethos (or distinguishing character) is one of criticism in which everything and everyone, it seems, is fair game (Kant, 1956; Martel et al., 2006). We cast judgment on movies ("*Pirates of the Caribbean* was the greatest movie of all time!"), clothing (both our own and, especially, that which belongs to others), and music ("Britney Spears does not sing particularly well"). Is this the pursuit in which critical scholars are engaged? Certainly not. However, defining exactly what meets and what fails to meet the "critical" bar is far more difficult than it might seem. If everyone is critical and capable of critique, what sets critical criminology apart?

Some schools of criminology have adopted an administrative approach to the question of crime and have produced policy-oriented knowledge directed toward regulating disruptions and disorders (Young, 1998). The products of this mainstream criminology/criminal justice (programs such as zero tolerance and broken-windows policing) appeal to politicians who promise an eager electorate that they will be "tough on crime and the causes of crime." Such scholarship is critical to the extent that it challenges existing criminal justice orthodoxy by suggesting that we focus on minimizing criminal opportunities rather than explaining criminal motivations. However, governments and criminal justice organizations can safely adopt this brand of "critical scholarship" within their existing infrastructure without fear that these suggestions and programs will significantly change existing mandates or practices. Government agencies are now promoting and, in some cases, soliciting this type of administrative scrutiny of policy and programming, because they view it as a path toward more efficient governance and control.

By contrast, the promise implied by "critical criminology" ensures a type of critique that prefers "to take the system to task rather than tinker with its parts" (Ratner, 1971, n.p.). Hogeveen and Woolford (2006) maintain that critique should not fall into the trap of conceiving of programs that work well within the existing criminal justice system, but critical criminologists should extend critique and thought beyond these limits. Indeed, criminal justice institutions that receive critical criminological scholarship favourably would invite their own destruction (Pavlich, 2005). Critical criminologists, then, practise a transformative brand of critique that confronts inequalities and social suffering with promises of more just outcomes.

So "critical" in critical criminology implies transformation through promises of justice. But what does it mean to be "critical"? That is, if critical criminology is transformative, does this imply that transformation and critique are identical? No. Critique is a means to a transformative (just) end. Thus, while we now know that the goal of critical criminology is justice, we are yet unaware of what "critical" means. When attempting to understand a *thing*, etymology (the origins of words) is often a productive starting point. George Pavlich (2000, 25), notes that "criticism," "crisis and critique relate to the Greek word *Krinein* which is associated with images of judgment (judge, judging), but also with deciding, separating out, discerning, selecting, differentiating, and so on." Interestingly, early medical officials closely associated notions of critique with *Krises*, which involved the art of diagnosing crisis stages in the development of an illness. Traces of this image have survived in common medical diagnoses of patients said to be in a *critical* condition (Pavlich, 2000).

Over many years, the broad meaning of the word *critical* has been reduced to such a degree that it is now almost exclusively associated with the act of judging. According to Williams, "What is significant in the development of *criticism*, and of the *critic* and *critical*, is the assumption of judgment as the predominant and even natural response" (1983, 85). Take the television program *American Idol* as an example of how the Western understanding of *critical* and *critique* have become whittled down to judgment. The program, for those who have never watched an episode, masquerades as a singing competition that features three "experts" who have been tasked with cutting down the hundreds of thousands of applicants to a select few and with providing feedback on individual performances. In many ways, Simon Cowell, the curmudgeon among the three judges, embodies the modern vision of critique as judgment. His comments have included these: "That's atrocious; that's simply not good enough," and "If your lifeguard duties were as good as your singing, a lot of people would be drowning." To the delight of the North American audience, Cowell expresses his displeasure about the seeming imperfections of the singers.

Judgmental critique derives its critical ammunition from the veracity of the *criterion* (or critical standard). Continuing with the *American Idol* example, Cowell holds the contestants up to a set of normative criteria for what counts as great singing. It is the criterion that allows him to render judgment ("That was atrocious"). Mainstream criminologists engage in a similar critical enterprise. For instance, many criminologists employ criterion such as recidivism rates as the standard against which to assess programmatic and legislative success or failure. Such judgmental criterion can then be employed to evaluate policing, correctional, and court practices. As you have learned already in Chapter 4, recidivism rates (the criteria) are not as robust and self-evident as once believed. Indeed, recidivism is hardly an irreproachable measure of re-offending rates after criminal justice intervention. Policing practices and a host of administrative conditions, including how long following their release offenders are tracked, are apt to artificially increase or reduce the criterion—the very foundation of much criminological judgment.

Critique typically implies that we are judging some *thing* against a normative standard held out as the epitome or the ultimate. Thus, when we claimed that Britney Spears does not sing particularly well, how did we render this assessment? We arrived at this judgment using Andrea Bocelli as our normative frame. Clearly, we must conclude—even if we prefer pop music to the operatic version—the latter can sing better than the former. This process and strategy fixes the critic as an expert judge who, because of a certain expertise (in music, in crime, etc.), is "deemed capable of authoritatively judging the true from the false, innocent from guilty, good from bad, progressive from regressive, and so on" (Pavlich, 2000, 74). Critique, as it is currently practised in criminology and elsewhere, is typically judgmental and reactionary.

Forms of critique that seek to challenge the criminal justice status quo are not always appreciated. However, Pavlich (2000) claims that there was a time when critical genres in criminology had considerable influence among politicians and policy-makers, especially following the publication and subsequent dissemination of Taylor, Walton, and Young's (1973) highly touted *The New Criminology*. Disenchanted with administrative brands of social science, administrators for a time looked to more radical brands of criminology for inspiration. In the spirit of 1960s radicalism, insight derived from critical questioning of the status quo was evident in governmental discourse and practice. Pleas to abolish prisons, insight into the crime-producing tendencies of the modern criminal justice process, and prisoners' rights discourses were prominent (van Swaaningen, 1997). But these days were quite brief; today administrative and liberal strains figure most prominently in criminological conferences and scholarly journals.

The reason "critical voices beyond the language of pragmatic technocracy are decidedly muted," especially when compared with critical debates less than three decades ago, is that critics have "failed to address that which distinguishes their radical precepts from proponents of administrative criminology: critique" (Pavlich, 1999, 70). In recent years, drawing on the insights of philosophers such as Michel Foucault, Pierre Bourdieu, Jacques Derrida, and Giorgio Agamben (among others), critical criminologists have called for a critical approach that goes beyond judgment. Instead of employing one or another yardstick from which to judge the success and failure of criminal justice policies, these scholars employ an art of critique that involves destabilizing seemingly well-anchored relations into new patterns of being that do not pander to established social logics or rely upon reactive judgments (Hogeveen and Woolford, 2006). A non-judgmental critical criminology would not render judgments about existing policy, programs, institutions, or societal structures. Rather it suggests "other" (just) ways of being in the world; "it would summon them, drag them from their sleep. Perhaps it would invert them sometimes—all the better" (Foucault, 1997).

Critical criminological critique attempts to move beyond complicity in government intrusion into the lives of the least powerful. It does not seek ways to better manage the poor and dangerous classes. Rather, it promises justice to those who are marginalized and discriminated against. Not justice, however, that seeks to punish; instead, it promises justice through emancipation. How willing are you to address suffering in your social world? What are you willing to do to ensure that children no longer suffer in silence on city streets and that drug-using women are no longer forced to sell their bodies to support their drug habits? There is much to do.

As we hope you will learn from the rest of this chapter, following the notion of criticism set out in this section, the critical criminologist is not "critical" because he or she is bad-tempered or unconstructive; rather, the negativity of criticism is intended to open your mind to new ways of thinking about and being in the world.

Critical Criminology in English Canada

Critical criminology in Canada was invigorated in 1973 with the arrival of *The New Criminology* by British criminologists Ian Taylor, Paul Walton, and Jock Young. In this wide-ranging critique of conventional criminology, Taylor, Walton, and Young identified starting points for a "new" criminology and criticized conventional criminology for supporting the political and economic status quo and for being individualistic in its orientation; that is, they decried conventional criminology for ignoring the structural causes of crime and focusing instead on biological and psychological factors. Taylor, Walton, and Young (1973, 270) recommended in contrast a "fully social" criminology that

a. *Understands crime within its wider socio-cultural context.* Crime is not merely an event that occurs between individuals but it takes place within broader social-structural and cultural conditions. Along these lines, a ghetto drug dealer is not just an individual seeking easy money—he may also be the product of a deindustrialized inner city that has been bled of all opportunities other than McJobs because capital investment has fled to the suburbs. He may also be immersed in patriarchal cultural conditions that associate masculinity with money, power, and violence, allowing him to obtain respect and credibility through drug dealing. These are just some of the structures that may influence his decision making.
b. *Examines the structural and political-economic dimensions that produce criminal behaviour.* Crime is not the result of "bad," abnormal, or poorly socialized people but stems from structural conditions that produce unequal opportunities, stigmatized populations, real and relative deprivation, and other concepts criminologists often credit as motivations for crime. For example, stigma and labelling occur not only at the micro-level when

authorities and significant others impose labels upon offenders and contribute to their secondary deviance (see Chapter 12) but also as the result of structural conditions that make certain individuals more likely to choose to commit crime, more likely to be caught, more likely to be punished, and therefore more likely to be labelled. This is all part of what Talor, Walton, and Young (1973, 274) refer to as a "political economy of social reaction."

c. *Probes the relationship between crime and the prevailing mode of production.* Crime occurs within societies defined by specific systems of economic production. What is defined as a crime, and the way that crime is punished, will often depend on this mode of production. For example, vagrancy was criminalized in Britain during the 17th century, in part because cheap labour was required for the factory system (Chambliss, 1969) to feed the profits of the ruling class and sustain the capitalist mode of production (see Box 2.3).
d. *Questions the role of power and conflict in shaping crime and criminal justice.* Crime is not simply the reflection of a societal consensus but instead is defined by the powerful and punished in a manner that suits their interests. Therefore, criminologists must not simply accept state-defined crime as a given. They must question its origins and the ways in which power is implicit in its formation and application.
e. *Engages in a materialist analysis of the development of law in capitalist societies.* Law is not simply a matter of societal consensus but is a function of the material conditions that define our society. Therefore, the law will contain contradictions because it is a reflection of dominant material interests. For example, gambling is illegal in a private club, but not in a government-run casino. Other forms of gambling, such as betting on "futures" in the stock market, may be encouraged by the government. Similarly, certain drug habits, such as alcohol and coffee, might be perfectly sociable and tolerated, if not encouraged. In contrast, others, such as marijuana, may be viewed as unproductive and criminalized.
f. *Takes a dialectical approach to analyzing how individuals both influence and are influenced by dominant social structures.* The New Criminology was not simply a shift to an objectivist standpoint holding that human action is fully determined by social structures. Instead, human agency and social structures each affect the other, meaning that although human actions are influenced by their cultural and political-economic conditions, humans can also act to change these conditions.

This approach inspired several Canadian criminologists to critically assess the liberal foundations of Canadian criminology. For example, in a provocatively titled article, "Inside the Liberal Boot," R. S. Ratner (1984) argued that Canadian criminologists had not risen to the challenge of the New Criminology and were guilty of ignoring social structures, failing to challenge state definitions of crime, and naively believing that the institutional apparatus of the criminal justice system could be easily adjusted to address systemic inadequacies and injustices.

Critical criminology soon spread to other venues. In 1985, Thomas O'Reilly-Fleming edited *The New Criminologies in Canada*, which was followed in 1986 by a special edition of the journal *Crime and Social Justice* dedicated to

Canadian critical criminology (edited by R. S. Ratner) and a conference in Vancouver on the "Administration of Justice" organized by Brian MacLean and Dawn Currie. By the late 1980s, Canadian critical criminologists had banded together to form the Human Justice Collective, a loose network of scholars assembled around their concerns with the narrow focus of mainstream criminology. Moreover, these scholars desired a criminology more sensitive to the criminogenic influences of capitalism, patriarchy, racism, and other social structures (Dekeseredy and MacLean, 1993). Out of the Human Justice Collective was born the *Journal of Human Justice*. In the first issue of this journal R. S. Ratner (1989, 6) defined critical criminology as follows:

> Although varied conceptions abound, we are all united around those premises that underscore the central role of power and conflict in shaping "criminal" outcomes, the range of vested interests that influence "crime", the need for a dialectical analysis of crime and social control that integrates materialist and idealist factors, the crucial importance of the state and equally important need to debunk state definitions of crime, and the necessity of devising a praxis that is not conditional on the imminent collapse of capitalist society.

This unity, however, was to be short-lived as funding challenges, personality conflicts, and scholarly differences made it difficult to sustain the Human Justice Collective and its journal. Initially, it had been intended that the *Journal of Human Justice* would fund itself through members of the collective adopting it as required reading in their courses. However, classroom use diminished and the journal was in a difficult financial position. In addition, personality conflicts had erupted within the collective, leading to schisms among members. In 1995, under these conditions, one of the editors, Brian MacLean, transported the journal to the Division of Critical Criminology at the American Society of Criminology. This move allowed for the journal's continued survival but also marked the end of its Canadian identity.

The growing eclecticism of critical criminology has produced a group of scholars who are difficult to unify under a single label. Initially, a key rift developed between two groups defined as "left realists" and "left idealists" (Young, 1979). Left idealists were said to begin their inquiry into crime from abstract premises (e.g., Marxist theory) rather than empirical work. For this reason, they were criticized by realists for minimizing the harm crime causes to the working class and for romanticizing criminals as a potentially revolutionary force. In contrast, left realists worked through local surveys of crime and victimization to try to move beyond partial criminological understandings that typically focused only on one aspect of crime: either the offender, state, public, or victim. Their objective was to take the fear of crime among the working classes seriously, and to answer and oppose the work of "right realists," who under the Thatcher, Reagan, and Mulroney governments had spread the popularity of punitive sanctions and administrative approaches. However, left realism did not achieve a sustained following among critical criminologists. For some, the reform-based agenda of left realism was viewed to compromise the critical thrust of critical criminology by participating in and legitimating the discourses of conventional criminal justice (Pavlich, 1999).

WWW

Division on Critical Criminology, American Society of Criminology
critcrim.org/node?page=1

The diversity of critical criminology in Canada would expand with the popularity of neo-Marxist and post-structuralist theories imported from continental Europe. The perspectives discussed in the rest of this chapter all derive from these origins and represent a shift in critical criminological theorizing away from distinctly political-economic perspectives. Although the premise that state-defined law must be challenged rather than replicated through criminological study remains, a great diversity of methodology and conceptualization now defines the Canadian critical criminological scene, which also includes the work of several of the feminist scholars discussed in Chapter 6. Recent efforts to unite these scholars at the 2000 and 2001 Canadian Sociology and Anthropology Association meetings, and a 2006 conference on the "criminological promise," have succeeded in once again establishing a network of critical criminological scholars. However, this network is better understood as an open and hospitable community of scholarship rather than a unified "collective" since it lacks the sense of common purpose that once animated the Human Justice Collective (Martel et al., 2006).

Governmentality and Power: Foucault and Criminology

Foucault did not regard himself as a significant contributor to the discipline of criminology. On the rare occasion when he did comment on criminology, he complained that its "garrulous discourse" and "endless repetitions" only served to relieve judges, police officers, and magistrates of their guilt for delivering pain and suffering on the guilty (Foucault, 1980, 47). Despite Foucault's disdain for the discipline, many scholars have applied his voluminous work toward the understanding of crime and its control. His penological treatise on the "birth of the prison"—*Discipline and Punish*—continues to inspire fresh criminological theorizing. More recently scholars have used his work on **governmentality.**

WWW

Foucault Resources
www.michel-foucault.com/

governmentality
The art of governing. It transcends and is considerably broader than the traditional understanding of government as a state-directed activity. Government, then, encompasses a wide array of techniques, within and outside of the state, intended to (re)shape and (re)direct human actions.

power
Power, for Foucault, extends beyond the state. It is not a quantity to hold or possess. It is, rather, relational, such that power is only ever evident in its exercise.

Foucault was born in Poitiers, France, in 1926. He died in 1984 from complications of HIV/AIDS. A philosopher and historian who wrote about the history of sexuality, prisons, governance, psychiatry, and knowledge systems, he is heralded for his unique work on **power**. Power, for Foucault, is evident only when it is *exercised.* He did not see it as something states or individuals could hold, accumulate, possess, or monopolize. In other words, can you show us what power looks like? Some may claim, and they often do, that money or wealth *is* power. Foucault would argue otherwise. For Foucault, money becomes power only when it is used or otherwise put into effect. Thus money in a bank account is of little purpose unless you can reach it or otherwise use it.

A further characteristic of the Foucauldian notion of power is that it is not solely negative or repressive. He instead preferred a more *positive* theory of power: not in terms of good or beneficial, but rather as creative. He argues that

> we must cease once and for all to describe the effects of power in negative terms: it "excludes," it "represses," it "censures," it "abstracts," it "masks," it "conceals." In fact power produces; it produces reality; it produces domains of object and rituals of truth. (Foucault 1979, 194)

Thus, rather than viewing power in a manner that exaggerates its negative elements, Foucault urged scholars to focus on what is created when power is exercised. What is the outcome when power is employed? What is created?

A third characteristic of the Foucauldian understanding of power is the emphasis he placed on **micro-powers** that are disseminated throughout the social world. Almost everywhere we turn, everywhere we go, power operates on our bodies and souls. It seems power is perpetually influencing our behaviour, often without our awareness. Consider your daily trip to university or college. Assuming that you are driving a vehicle of some sort, think about all the ways your behaviour is controlled while you drive. Traffic lights, signs, painted lines, photo radar, and the presence or absence of police all affect how we go about our drive.

micro-powers
Small and mundane relations of governance, which still have an appreciable effect on human behaviour. For example, the arrangement of a traditional classroom, with the professor or instructor at the front and all students facing her/him, is infused with power relations that rarely gain our attention.

Foucault is convinced that to intimately understand the operation of power we must shift our focus from the state to the dispersed spaces in which power operates. This is the essence of what Foucault called **discipline**. Discipline operates at the smallest level of detail and attends to the intricacies of human behaviour through **surveillance** and observation of individual functioning so as to increase the efficiency and usefulness of human actions. When thinking about discipline, it is the everyday and the mundane that are important. Fully understanding power involves examining it at its main point of application: the body. Remember back to when you were learning how to write using a pencil. Recall the teacher standing over you correcting your finger placement. S/he would watch you (surveillance) and correct your mistakes to make certain that you used the implement in the most efficient manner possible (positive power). To maximize the utility of our bodies and to allow hierarchal control and correction, this meticulous exercise of power is infinitely multiplied throughout the social world. As such, discipline requires that individuals be organized in space and time. Consider the timetable from public school. It provided a general framework for activity and organized our days. The timetable structured not only our *use* of time, but also the *space* we were to occupy at certain points in the day. The bell organized our behaviour. What happened when the bell sounded? Being conditioned to move according to the sounding of the bell, students would get up to leave, while the teacher attempted to quell the mass exodus. Thus time, space, and signals coexisted to discipline not only our minds but also our bodies (Hogeveen and Minaker, 2008).

discipline
A meticulous manner or method of training the body. It intends to ensure constant subjection and obedience. It involves hierarchal observation, normalizing judgment and examinations. Recall your grade school days when you were being taught to write: the teacher showed you how to hold the pencil, observed and corrected your faults, and examined your skill through quizzes and tests.

surveillance
The direct or indirect observation of conduct toward producing a desired outcome (i.e., conformity).

Foucault's analysis of discipline was criticized for (a) abandoning the state in its analysis and (b) its supposed tendency to characterize human subjects as "docile" (inactive) bodies as opposed to active agents (Garland, 1997). Foucault's later work on governmentality addressed many of these concerns (see Box 11.1). Governmentality, however, must not be reduced to its parliamentary forms (i.e., state government) but has wider application. For Foucault (1982, 221) governmentality

> must be allowed the very broad meaning which it had in the 16th century. Government did not refer only to political structures or the management of states; rather it designated the way in which the conduct of individuals or states might be directed; the government of children, of souls, of communities, of families, of the sick.

FOCUS

BOX 11.1 Restorative Justice as Governmentality

Restorative justice is a broad term used to describe a range of justice practices designed to involve victims, offenders, and community members in directly resolving the harms caused by crime. For some of its proponents, restorative justice is intended to empower communities and individuals to creatively solve their own problems, to remove justice control from the hands of the state and professionals, and to allow for a justice tailored specifically to the needs of victims, offenders, and community members. All of this is to occur within informal settings such as community centres, with victims, offenders, and their families and friends, as well as community members sitting in a circle to discuss what led to the crime and how its harm might be repaired.

In contrast to this representation of restorative justice as a community-led activity separate from the formal practices of the state, George Pavlich (2005) has described restorative justice as a form of governmentality. First, restorative justice can be viewed as governmentality because the participants in restorative justice meetings are encouraged to examine and reshape their conduct in relation to their experiences of crime and justice. Offenders are asked to take responsibility for their actions, victims are asked to express how the crime has affected them and to present reasonable demands for repair, and community members are asked to participate in the reintegration of the offender and the healing of the victim. Moreover, it is hoped that participation in restorative justice will transform the way these participants deal with conflict in the future. All of these aspects of restorative justice encourage individuals to accept and internalize restorative values and practices through which they might better govern themselves and their communities, thus freeing the state of this responsibility.

Second, restorative justice is a mode of governmentality because it fashions a way of understanding the world (and crime in particular) that makes the pursuit of "restorative" justice appear more rational and understandable to those involved. If restorative justice is to govern our behaviour, it must first shift how we think about crime and criminal justice. It does this by reframing or redefining core components of criminal justice. For Pavlich, this involves providing different answers to the questions:

a. What is governed? Unlike formal criminal justice, restorative justice claims to govern "harm" rather than "crime" since it is not the violations of the state's law but rather the harms suffered by individuals and communities that are of primary concern.
b. Who is governed? Those who are to be governed are all of those who have a stake in the crime and its effects—victim, offender, and community members—rather than just the offender.
c. Who governs? Whereas judges and lawyers are the individuals empowered through the practice of criminal justice, restorative justice seeks to give greater agency to victims, offenders and community members.
d. What is appropriate governing? Instead of focusing on the past, restorative governance should be directed toward the future. It is therefore less a question of punishing a wrongdoer and more an issue of creating a dialogue among stakeholders so that they can work out how to avoid repetition of the crime.

For Pavlich, the problem with this restorative justice governmentality is that it does not represent a true alternative to the criminal justice system. Instead, restorative justice is fundamentally dependent on the criminal justice system and criminal law. For example, although restorative justice shifts our attention to the harm suffered by victims and community members, it nonetheless relies on criminal law to define the acts that are to be considered harmful. Therefore, it restricts itself from addressing harms that are not codified within criminal codes (such as suffering caused by industrial pollution), as well as structural harms (such as the gender inequalities that result from patriarchal systems of domination).

Therefore, the study of governmentality should cast its gaze widely and address such broad questions as "how to govern oneself, how to be governed, how to govern others, by whom the people will accept to be governed, and how to become the best possible governor" (Foucault, 1991, 45). Summarizing governmentality all too briefly we could say that it is the "conduct of conduct" (Gordon, 1991, 2). Conduct denotes leading, directing, or guiding with some form of calculation about how this may be accomplished (as opposed to forcing and repressing). Government(ality) entails "any attempt to shape with some degree of deliberation aspects of our behaviour according to particular sets of norms and for a variety of ends" (Dean, 1999, 10).

Critical scholars have used Foucault's writings on governmentality to understand a wide range of state and non-state domains of governance. They have raised important insights about legal change and the centrality of law in the regulation of populations. They have also argued that critical criminology has been limited "by its emphasis on the state, and state-centred constructions of criminality, and by its failure to come to terms with how social injustices are reproduced through private institutions and modes of expertise that operate on the margins of the state and in the shadow of the law" (Lippert and Williams, 2006). For example, Randy Lippert and James Williams (2006) have looked to the margins of legal governance to explore how the rise of private security affects our social world. These authors maintain that critical scholarship should focus "less on how the machinery of the state is brought to bear on the production and control of individual subjects and offenders, and more on the myriad technologies of governance and their operation across diverse social fields" such as immigration and policing financial disorder (Lippert and Williams, 2006). Governmentality, then, draws scholarly attention to mechanisms *outside* the traditional state governmental machinery that structure and contour human behaviour. Recent years have witnessed the proliferation of private security firms that police a variety of venues, including the local mall, construction sites, and, as the upsurge in alarm companies continues, private dwellings. Moreover, as an extension of the American army, private security is now being called upon to assist in the Iraq war effort. A recent *Time* magazine article estimated that there are 100 000 contractors employed as bodyguards, snipers, translators, and interrogators (Bennett, 2007). They are also stationed at checkpoints and routinely transport supplies throughout Iraq (Bennett, 2007). By attending to the growth of private security "the governmentality literature presents a unique opportunity to expand the theoretical range and conceptual reach of critical criminology, and to enhance its capacity to reveal and interrogate forms of injustice and domination crafted on the margins of the state" (Williams and Lippert, 2006).

Actuarialism, Risk, and the Risk Society

Perhaps the greatest impact of Foucault's work on critical criminological studies has been on scholars' ability to understand how offenders' lives are increasingly organized around questions of **risk**. As we have seen already, Foucault

risk
The calculated probability of an eventuality.

actuarial
Refers to statistical calculations of risk across time and groups.

was fundamentally concerned with understanding how individuals were normalized through government and discipline—that is, how they were corrected and brought into line with the needs of the larger society (O'Malley, 1996). In the field of crime control, recent years have witnessed the emergence and proliferation of **actuarial** or "insurance" based strategies of governance and control. It seems Western criminal justice systems have become somewhat preoccupied with managing risks as police, probation, prisons, and halfway houses seek to minimize the likelihood of future offending (Bosworth, 2004). Toward this end, many institutions employ a variety of risk prediction tools, which are all part of what has been dubiously christened "actuarial justice" (Feeley and Simon, 1994).

Foucauldian-inspired theorists distinguish the everyday usage of the term *risk* from how it is construed as an actuarial (or insurance-based) technology. When we as citizens refer to risk it concerns the dangers and perils connected with an objective and often immediate threat—i.e., of being struck by lightning or having our house burglarized. However, this definition and understanding of risk has to be separated from its usage in actuarial terms where it indicates neither an "event nor a general kind of event occurring in reality, but a specific mode of treatment of certain events capable of occurring to a group of individuals" (Ewald, 1991). Risk, then, is the calculated probability of an eventuality. Think of the last time you purchased car insurance. The agent likely asked you a series of questions: What is your sex? How old are you? Where do you live? Where do you work? How far do you travel to work/school? These questions were then entered into a computer, which calculated your premium based on these factors. Agents ask these questions to derive a risk score. That is, by employing aggregated data (including accident reports and police statistics) collected over time and then comparing the aggregate to your indicators, insurance companies ascertain the probability of having to pay a claim on your behalf. If you are young, male and unemployed, your risk and insurance premium will be considerably higher than that of a married 40-year-old female who lives in the suburbs.

Events (car accidents) and populations (males, females, the elderly) are not inherent risks, but become constituted as "actuarial" risks through analyses and calculations of chance. Risk understood from a Foucauldian perspective, then, is constituted in relation to the aggregation of events over time and regulated through techniques such as higher insurance rates designed to contend with individual risk factors. Jonathan Simon (1988) maintains that risk-based technologies of governance have become dominant largely because of their efficiency and their ability to intensify the effectiveness of disciplinary technologies (O'Malley, 1996). Probabilistic calculation is particularly evident in the youth correctional field where the Youth Level of Service/Case Management Inventory (YLS/CMI) is employed. Andrews and Bonta (1998, 245) maintain that this tool is premised on the four principles of risk, need, responsivity, and professional discretion. First, the *risk* principle reflects the contention that criminal behaviour occurs in predictable patterns. Second, the *needs* principle implies that recidivism will be reduced through select targeting of criminogenic need through appropriate treatment programs. Third, given that many juvenile offenders suffer from attention deficit hyperactivity disorder, fetal alcohol spectrum disorder, or oppositional defiant disorder, responsivity is crucial to any "successful" treatment option and refers to the need for service providers to deliver treatment programs in a manner that is consistent with and appropriate to the offender's ability and learning style. Finally, *professional discretion* "strategically reasserts the importance of retaining professional judgment, provided that it is not used irresponsibly and is systematically monitored" (Hannah-Moffat and Maurutto, 2003, 3).

While at first blush actuarial strategies seem efficient and just, several factors raise questions about such assessments. Kelly Hannah-Moffat and Paula Maurutto (2003, 7) have found that correctional officials and practitioners fail to conceptualize "the problems intrinsic to this kind of needs assessment and how a failure to distinguish between risk and need can result in increased surveillance of youth." Although blending of risk and need is a problem, the problems of risk-based governance are particularly troubling when applied to female and non-white populations (Minaker and Hogeveen, 2008). Notably, "female offenders are more often deemed higher risk because of their risk to themselves, whereas high-risk male offenders are more likely to pose a risk to others" (Hannah-Moffat and Shaw, 2001). Risk assessment tools typically do not account for gender and cultural variation in offending and recidivism. For example, the tests do not adequately capture histories of physical, mental, or sexual abuse, prevalent among female youth. Moreover, risk assessment tools do not adequately address the broader socio-cultural and colonial context of Aboriginal youths (Hannah-Moffat and Shaw, 2001).

These Foucauldian notions of risk and actuarialism are occasionally combined with Ulrich Beck's concept of the "**risk society**." Beck admits that characterizing the present as the "risk society" may seem odd in light of the daily risks and dangers faced by people in pre-industrial societies—such as plagues, famine, and natural disasters. However, there is a qualitative difference between the looming hazards of our industrial present and those of earlier times. Beck suggests that today's hazards are not forces outside of us, but instead internal creations, and their danger originates from our own decision making (Beck, 1992, 98). Our technological development and scientific rationality have provided us with the tools to construct the means of our own destruction—nuclear power, environmental pollution, climate change, and an assortment of life-threatening chemicals, just to name a few dangers. Moreover, Beck does not suggest that we have necessarily witnessed a quantitative increase in risk; rather, we have come to organize our societies more around the fact of risk.

risk society
An emerging societal form characterized by the production and increased awareness of human-made "risks," such as nuclear destruction and environmental devastation. More importantly, the risk society is organized around the management of such risks.

This theoretical perspective comes to bear on critical criminology in at least two ways. First, social problems have increasingly come to be understood as "risks" to be *managed* rather than social "problems" to be *solved*. This shift in thinking is noticeable in criminological approaches that take crime to be inevitable and which, in response, prescribe various risk-reduction strategies to lessen crime's social costs. Along these lines, individuals are encouraged to become responsible for protecting themselves from opportunistic crimes through the techniques of "situational crime prevention" (O'Malley, 1992), whether by installing alarm systems in their homes or steering wheel locking mechanisms in their cars. As well, "three strikes" laws (see Box 12.1), which impose long-term prison sentences after a third criminal violation, are justified under a risk management logic as a means for warehousing repeat offenders who are perceived to pose too great a threat to the general public.

Second, risk thinking transforms criminal justice practices. Risk management strategies infiltrate judicial, correctional, and law enforcement institutions, tasking criminal justice professionals with the collection of aggregated risk data and with administering risk assessments to their charges. For example, Ericson and Haggerty (1997) note how policing practices have been affected by the demands of the risk society. They cite the case of a modern police officer investigating a traffic accident. The officer must now not only gather information pertinent to the courts and police records, but also to the insurance companies, the public health system, provincial vehicle registries, and the automobile industry. Under these new demands, Ericson and Haggerty report that a simple traffic accident "took one hour to investigate, and three hours to write about it, to account for it, and to bureaucratically process it" (Ericson and Haggerty, 1997, 24).

In alerting us to these broader social changes, the "risk society" thesis serves a critical criminological function by demonstrating the effects broad societal shifts toward increased insecurity have upon the ways we think about and react to matters of criminal justice. In this sense, crime and its response are not taken as givens, but as socially constituted phenomena that can be better understood by locating them in their wider social context. And by identifying this wider social context, we are thus able to critically assess proposed criminal justice "solutions" through an understanding of their historical contingency.

Cultural Criminology

WWW
Cultural Criminology
www.culturalcriminology.org/

The Social Reaction perspective (see Chapter 12) brought attention to crime as a process of social interaction involving victim, offender, bystanders, and criminal justice agencies in the construction of deviant meanings and identities. This insight has been absorbed and extended in the work of cultural criminologists who focus on crime as a cultural, rather than a legal, construct. These scholars turn their attention away from crime as a "real" phenomenon reflected in police data, victimization surveys, and other quantitative measures, and instead focus on "the debris of everyday life" (Morrison, 2007, 254) through an aesthetic and ethnographic engagement with their subject matter. In this manner, cultural criminologists do not accept crime simply as state-defined illegality; instead, they view it as a culturally negotiated phenomenon through which people create social meaning.

Hayward and Young (2004) identify five "motifs" of cultural criminology. First, cultural criminologists alert us to the importance of "adrenaline" in the commission of crime. In contrast, to rational choice theories that portray offenders as economic actors engaged in cost-benefit analyses of whether or not to break the law, cultural criminologists acknowledge that crime is *felt*. In other words, crime may be motivated by feelings of anger, insecurity, humiliation, or excitement. Moreover, the act of crime may produce a sensual and visceral rush that incites both panic and pleasure (Ferrell, 1998; Katz, 1988). Thus, although a potential car thief may make a *rational* choice not to steal your car because she or he is afraid that it might be a "bait car," the *attraction* of car theft may stem more from the desire to alleviate boredom through risk taking.

Second, cultural criminologists draw our attention to the "soft city" (Raban, 1974). This refers to the "underlife" of the city that hides beneath structured and rationally planned urban space. Whereas urban planning attempts to direct our everyday lives through policing strategies, the design of defensive urban space, and other modalities of social control, the "soft city" bubbles up as a realm of creativity and street-level possibility. While it may seem that we are free to go and do as we please in space, careful design contours our actions in very definite directions. Consider for example the layout of an Ikea store. The interior space has been mapped so that customers are forced to wander through all the showrooms before arriving at what they want to purchase. This is no accident. Ikea designers want us to see all their products on display, hoping this will make us want to purchase more than we intended. The "soft-city," by contrast, subverts planners' intentions. It is the space used, for example, by Critical Mass, to launch illegal bike rallies to confront our automobile culture and to illustrate how the daily commute is part of the depersonalized and routinized destruction of human sociability (Ferrell, 2004). As Ferrell (2004, 292) notes, "Critical Mass participants define their exuberantly collective bicycle rides not as traditional political protests, but as do-it-yourself celebrations enlivened by music, decoration and play." By resisting the boredom and repetition of the normal "protest march," Critical Mass seeks to reclaim the "soft city" of urban space through their theatrical rallies. Moreover, this challenge to the rigid ordering of city planning can provoke disproportionate responses from local authorities and expose the rigidity of public planning, as was the case at a 2006 Critical Mass rally in Winnipeg where police aggressively arrested several cyclists for disrupting traffic.

Third, cultural criminologists are interested in acts of "transgression" and rulebreaking that challenge the justness of laws. In this vein, a cultural criminologist might understand the spectacle of pro-cannabis protesters sparking joints on Parliament Hill not simply as individuals seizing the opportunity for public criminality, but rather as a collective act designed to challenge the criminalization of one leisure pursuit while others (e.g., alcohol, tobacco) go uncontested. Similarly, the Critical Mass rallies discussed above expose the over-regulated nature of modern urban life and the ways in which this over-regulation denies freedom of movement (as well as dedicated traffic lanes) to slower, less rushed, and less expensive vehicles.

Fourth, cultural criminologists propose a methodology founded upon an **attentive gaze**. This requires that researchers do more than sit back in their offices and peruse quantified crime data. They must engage in "an ethnography immersed in culture and interested in lifestyle(s), the symbolic, the aesthetic, and the visual" (Hayward and Young, 2004, 268). This requires that they enter into the world where crime occurs and where it is represented to better comprehend the experiential and interpretive dimensions of crime. For example, Maggie O'Neill (2004) employs a methodology she refers to as "ethno-mimesis," which draws on media such as photography, film, performance, theatre, and text to illustrate the complexity of the emotional lives of individuals. In one

attentive gaze
A methodological requirement that researchers immerse themselves in where crime occurs in the everyday world in order to better understand the ways in which crime is experienced and interpreted by individuals.

such study, O'Neill and Rosie Campbell encouraged sex workers to use art and writing to represent their "issues, concerns, experiences, and ideas for change" (O'Neill, 2004, 226). The final result was not only a written report, but also an art exhibit and information pamphlet, which collectively combined to allow community members to express, reflect upon, and relate to pressing local issues in a variety of creative ways.

dangerous knowledge
A form of knowledge that leaves no concept, notion, or idea untouched by criticism. To achieve this relentlessly critical stance, cultural criminologists will often turn to diverse sources of information (e.g., novels and street-level observation) as means to reveal alternative perspectives that might shake the foundations of our taken-for-granted assumptions about crime.

Finally, the knowledge produced by cultural criminology is argued to be **dangerous knowledge** because its purpose is to question all knowledge, including the status of criminology as an objective science. This might be achieved by drawing on unusual sources of knowledge. For instance, in his exploration of the crime of genocide, Wayne Morrison (2007) examines photographs snapped by Nazi police battalions, visits Belgian and Bangladeshi museums, and offers a reading of Joseph Conrad's famous novel *Heart of Darkness*. He uses these diverse sources to criticize criminology for its dependence on crimes defined and data generated by the state, and thereby its tendency to overlook crimes such as genocide that are perpetrated often by or beyond the state. In this sense, cultural criminology is a critical criminological project intended to relentlessly challenge the taken-for-granted assumptions of criminology and popular understandings of crime in order to expose how they are culturally constructed and delimited by a particular worldview.

A "Field Theory" of Criminology

field
A basic unit of social activity. The social world is divided into many fields (e.g., the "artistic" field, the "academic" field, or the "economic" field). Each field of activity is defined by its own market through which certain practices or dispositions are valued more than others. For example, in the artistic field one's possession of cultural knowledge about art history and technical mastery of artistic techniques is likely to be more valued than one's personal wealth.

habitus
A set of durable dispositions acquired through experience that allow one to achieve a "feel for the game" within a specific field of activity. These are internalized practices that serve as a "second nature" responsive to the immediate demands of everyday life.

The sociology of Pierre Bourdieu also provides insight into the cultural and economic conditions in which crime and our understanding of crime are produced, although on a much broader scale. The grounding concept of Bourdieu's theoretical corpus is that of the **field** (DiMaggio, 1979). Bourdieu's notion of the field can be likened to a battlefield or sports field. (Bourdieu, 1992). It is a space of conflict and competition wherein competitors, who each possess varying levels of social and economic power, vie for control. Nevertheless, the field is not even nor is it without pre-existing rules. Rather, participants encounter a field that is tilted to favour the already powerful (they will play downhill) and structured by predetermined rules that all must follow.

It is within a field of social activity, such as art, politics, or law, that a market defined by its own measures of value is established and it is in accordance with a field that actors seek the "profit of distinction" or, in other words, the awards associated with a display of competence (Bourdieu, 1991, 1990a, 1984). An actor's ability to display competence within a particular field depends, in part, upon his or her **habitus**. This is one's "feel for the game": that is, it refers to a set of "dispositions acquired through experience" (Bourdieu, 1990b, 9) that allow one to react to situations that arise within a particular field without the need to actively plot one's moves. Keeping with our sports analogy, imagine that in a game of hockey the skilled power forward Hogeveen finds a loose puck in a scrum in front of the net. In that instance, he automatically shifts the puck to his backhand and lifts it over the sprawling goalie, Woolford. Here, Hogeveen's dedication to his sport, and his practised experience of it, provide him the embodied knowledge necessary to succeed on the ice without needing to "overthink" his game (whereas Woolford's coach might advise him to work more on his hockey habitus).

The actor's "feel for the game" within the market relations of a specific field will vary, with those endowed with greater quantities of the forms of **capital** valuable within the field (e.g., economic, symbolic, cultural, or linguistic capital) more capable of transmitting an aura of competence (Brubaker, 1985). Thus, within a specific "game" or market situation actors come pre-equipped with differing amounts of capital, depending on their position(s) in the structural arrangements of society (e.g., level of education, occupation, age), and based on these factors are predisposed toward certain behaviours or practices. The valuational rules of the market ascribe these practices and behaviours with differing levels of profitability within the field, allowing some actors to feel more at home on their appointed terrain. To put this in simpler terms, if you are currently seeking a criminology degree this may be motivated by your desire to obtain employment in the legal or juridical field (e.g., as a police officer, lawyer, or probation worker). However, success in this field will depend on more than your possession of a criminology degree or your ability to extol Merton's strain theory. You will require possession of the forms of capital most valued within this field of activity. You will acquire some of this capital through your increased knowledge about the field of law, but you might also profit from the symbolic, linguistic, and cultural capital you have obtained through the practice of writing essays, making public presentations, and reading "classic" works of literature and philosophy. These latter forms of capital equip you with an aura of competence that communicates to your future employer that you are a "capable" person (see—essays, presentations, and readings *are* important!). However, it should be noted that due to our inequitable social structures some people enter university already in possession of a great deal of the capital needed to get a job within the juridical field and therefore are at an advantage. For example, an individual who was raised by a father/lawyer and mother/judge, who habitually thinks of the world in terms of law and adversarial justice, and who models his parents' ways of speaking and carrying themselves, is armed with a habitus that invests them with the capital needed to more easily navigate the legal profession.

capital
Each person enters a field of activity already possessed of certain powerful qualities or "capital." For example, a student who has a large vocabulary and is able to use this vocabulary competently will likely have an advantage in achieving a "feel for the game" within the academic field.

In criminological analysis, Bourdieu's field theory has been most influentially used by Loïc Wacquant. In his studies of American prisons and ghettos, Wacquant (1998, 2000, 2001) examines the meshing of these two institutions in the project of excluding African Americans from American society. It is within these "peculiar institutions" that we see the spatial segregation of those who lack, or possess negative forms of, capital. Indeed, the economic deprivation of ghetto residents is readily apparent. The decline of industrial employment within the urban core and the change toward a service-sector economy resulted in a loss of income opportunities for African American ghetto residents. But ghetto residents also possess what Wacquant refers to as **negative *symbolic* capital** and **negative *social* capital.**

negative *symbolic* capital
The way in which stigma cast upon a neighbourhood might be symbolically transferred to the neighbourhood's residents, placing them in a deficit with respect to their ability to improve their social standing.

negative *social* capital
The way in which one's network of formal social resources (e.g., organizations designed to provide social services) can be used to more effectively regulate and control rather than empower an individual.

Negative symbolic capital refers to the ways in which the ghetto is marked by a stigma that automatically devalues its residents by dint of their association with this neighbourhood. Moreover, their spatial concentration within the ghetto enables their territorial confinement, constraint, and institutional regulation. In other words, the ghetto becomes a means for controlling and administering to a population that is viewed to be subordinate and outside the labour force. Here, similarities between prison and ghetto become more evident, since prisons (in particular, U.S. prisons) increasingly serve to warehouse "recidivist" offenders who are assessed to be "incurable" and therefore unlikely to ever play a productive role in society.

"Social capital" refers to the resources one has at his or her disposal by virtue of being located within "a durable network of more or less institutionalized relationships of mutual acquaintance or recognition—or, in other words, to membership in a group" (Bourdieu, 1986, 248). Social capital can be "informal" (i.e., based on family, neighbourhood, or friendship networks) or "formal" (i.e., based on private or public formal organizations). Wacquant's (1998) concern is with how state-based formal social capital in the ghetto, in the form of civic goods and services such as welfare and public housing, has been turned toward the tasks of surveillance and exclusion rather than social integration and trust-building. For ghetto residents, this amounts to "negative social capital" since they are no longer empowered by participation in programs such as welfare services, as these programs have come to be directed toward the tasks of gathering further data about welfare recipients, placing further restrictions on their day-to-day lives, and generally increasing the social regulation of the poor.

This approach fits the label of "critical criminology" because it does not simply accept "criminalized" identities as constructed through the criminal law and its application. Instead, it seeks to identify the symbolic, cultural, and economic factors (e.g., habitus and capital) that empower dominant actors to create and apply criminal categories while simultaneously disempowering subordinate groups from resisting this criminalization because they lack the necessary forms of "capital" to achieve "profit" within various arenas of social action (or "fields").

Agamben—Sovereignty and the State of Exception

In political theory and public discourse the West is generally considered to be an asylum of human rights enmeshed within robust democracy (Ek, 2006). But this image has begun to erode in the wake of "exceptional" and seemingly extreme measures introduced after two planes piloted by terrorists slammed into the World Trade Center buildings in New York City on September 11, 2001. What are we to think about massive numbers of suspected terrorists being detained in Guantanamo Bay without ever being charged with an offence? To protect the public from similar future attacks, North American governments maintain that such practices are necessary. Moreover, in 2006, *USA Today* reported that the National Security Agency was "secretly collecting the phone call records of tens of millions of Americans," most of whom were not suspected of any crime. Typically wire taps and phone records are obtained by court order while gathering evidence against individuals suspected of crime.

Why do Americans not vehemently protest such efforts? It seems that citizens have become stoic; that is, whatever measures the government implements in the name of national security and, perhaps more important, the prevention of future terrorist attacks, are considered not only appropriate but welcome. The wave of repressions and concessions since 9/11 are typically made in the name of safety and protection of self and country. And the phone call database is no exception. A White House spokesperson reacted to such allegations in typical fashion: "The intelligence activities undertaken by the United States government are lawful, necessary and required to protect Americans from terrorist attacks" (Cauley, 2006).

Anything and everything (including torture?), it seems, is now permitted so long as the goal is the protection of the state and the public. Such a policy holds lethal implications. For example, after five suspected terrorist attacks left fifty-four dead and numerous wounded in the heart of London, an innocent man (Jean Charles de Menezes) was shot dead by police officers. Police Chief Sir Iain Blair, while disturbed by this tragedy, later admitted that more guiltless Londoners could lose their lives as police scoured the city for the suspected bombers. In effect, the police chief admitted that a mistake was made and stated that it could likely be made again in the future. How can we make sense of this? Giorgio Agamben, who has extended Foucault's work, has perhaps done more to assist scholars, activists, and the public in coming to terms with the post-9/11 world than any other academic.

Agamben's work is complex and not easily classifiable into a specific genre, although his writing has been heavily influenced by close readings of Foucault, Carl Schmitt, Walter Benjamin, and Saint Paul. Richard Ek (2006) concludes that since the Italian philosopher tends to extract the most "useful" conclusions from prominent and influential scholars and assembles them in a meaningful way, it might be best to read Agamben as an eclectic scholar. That is, one who does not rigidly hold to a single philosophical tradition, but instead integrates many ideas, concepts, and styles into his work.

Much of Agamben's work is grounded in a concern for and about the modern conditions of sovereignty. He takes his leave from Carl Schmitt, who defines political sovereignty in his now classic work *Political Theology*. For Schmitt and Agamben, the **sovereign** is the one who holds the power to declare a **state of exception** during which civil liberties (among other precautions) are suspended in the interests of defending and protecting the nation. That is, the sovereign is the one whom the juridical order grants the power to proclaim a state of exception. Declarations of this sort are typically issued after natural disasters, during wartime, and, especially, when the state is confronted by civil unrest. According to Schmitt (1985), the state of exception or emergency, as it is sometimes referred to, is declared when the sovereign deems suspension of the existing social order necessary in order that social order be restored. Typically, the state of exception is lifted once stability is returned.

sovereign
One who holds supreme power in a territory or space. Agamben, following Carl Schmitt, claims the sovereign is the one who is empowered to declare a state of exception.

state of exception
A period of time where the sovereign declares civil liberties suspended: typically in a time of national crisis.

Under Canada's National Emergencies Act (1988), which replaced the War Measures Act (1914), any national, provincial, or municipal government can declare a state of emergency. The Act defines an emergency as "an urgent and critical situation" that threatens Canadian citizens and the government's capacity to preserve Canadian "sovereignty, security and territorial integrity."

Declaring a state of emergency empowers the government to, among other things, prohibit travel and remove people from their homes. The most egregious invocation of such powers can be seen in the imprisonment and confiscation of the property of German and Ukrainian Canadians during World War I and Japanese Canadians during World War II. But, a world war is not a necessary condition for a state of emergency to be declared. Indeed, in the hunt for terrorists from the Front de libération du Québec (FLQ), soldiers in full battle attire raided homes of Quebecers, while tanks patrolled city streets in October 1970. Sparked by a seven-year-long series of bombings and kidnappings, Prime Minister Pierre Elliott Trudeau invoked the War Measures Act, which effectively suspended civil rights and afforded police wide-ranging powers of arrest and detention. After the dust settled, nearly 500 people had been arrested and detained but only 62 were ever formally charged.

How does this make sense? How can a government simply suspend your rights? The answer for Agamben lies in the fact that it is only by virtue of citizenship that modern states offer protections via human rights. At the same time, the nation's citizens are subordinated to the sovereign who could, at any time, decide to suspend these rights (Ek, 2006). That is, human rights are afforded by specific geo-political orders (e.g., Canada) and can be suspended only by the *de facto* sovereign. Thus, in the name of protection or defence of society and nation, the sovereign sets up the conditions under which he or she can abandon his or her subjects and return them to a state of **naked life**—unprotected by law and rights. When a state of emergency is declared, rights-bearing citizens are deemed enemies of the state and subject to exceptional and extreme measures. Thus, in the example cited above concerning the British police shooting of Menezes, sovereign decree granted "the police agents absolute sovereign power over him: the right, that is, to define within the instant, the confine between a life worth living and a life that does not deserve to live" (Minca, 2006).

naked life
For Agamben, naked life is akin to Homo Sacer—an individual who is excluded from possessing human rights, can be killed by anyone, yet cannot be sacrificed during a religious ceremony.

We should "ask ourselves if we are today witnessing a definitive paradigmatic break in conceptions of the relationship between countries and their citizens" (Minca 2006), if we are facing the creation of an enormous space of exception within which each and every one of us—through the temporary suspension of law and rights—can be potentially whisked away to a secret prison or camp. Do you think this cannot happen in Canada and that it is a horror tale confined to the United States, Britain, or some other nation? In Canada, Citizenship and Immigration can remove persons deemed threatening to the security and well-being of Canadians by issuing a Security Certificate under the Immigration and Refugee Act. Under this scheme both foreign nationals and permanent residents may be detained indefinitely without charge and without having full access to any evidence against them. Both detention and withholding evidence are justified, the Federal Court of Appeal ruled in 2004, in the interests of national security. Human rights are violated under this legislation, in a so-called haven of respect for humans—including the right to a speedy trial and innocence until a guilty finding.

Canadian Maher Arar's arrest as a suspected terrorist and his subsequent torture attests to the "paradigmatic break" described by Minca. Arar was born in Syria and immigrated to Canada in 1987. After earning a master's degree in computer engineering, he took a job as a telecommunications engineer in

Ottawa. Supported by RCMP "intelligence," U.S. officials detained Arar in 2002 on a stopover in New York after a vacation in Tunisia, charging that he possessed links to the terrorist organization al-Qaeda. After intense questioning, during which he was denied legal representation and phone calls, his wrists and ankles were shackled and he was taken to a nearby building where he was detained in a cell. The next morning he was roused only to face more intense interrogation before being put on a flight to Zurich, where he was once again scrutinized about his suspected terrorist ties. After three months of this sort of interrogation, Arar was deported to Syria, where he was detained and subsequently tortured (O'Connor, 2006). Arar was eventually released but only after spending a year in custody under very difficult conditions (see Box 11.2). For much of Arar's stay in Syria, the Canadian government made few efforts to help him.

FOCUS

BOX 11.2 Statements from Maher Arar's Interview with Amnesty International

I remember one of the immigration officers on the second day at the airport he asked me to voluntarily go to Syria—of course I refused—I explained to him why. And in one of the interviews at the embassy I explained at length that I would be tortured in Syria if I am sent back. They did not seem to care . . .

"I could not believe what I saw. I saw a cell almost the size of a grave. Three feet wide 6 feet deep and 7 feet high. And when I looked at him and said what is this he just did not say anything—he did this with his hands—so basically 'I have nothing to with that.' So I entered the cell and he locked the door. The cell had not light in it; it only had two thin mattresses (two thin blankets) on the ground. And I first thought they would keep me in that place, which I now call the grave, for a short period so that they could put pressure on me. But I was kept in that dark and filthy cell for about 10 months and 10 days. That was torture . . .

"The worst beating happened on the third day and they were trying to, you know, they were asking the same set of questions some times, some times more questions and they would beat me 3 or 4 times. They would stop, they would beat me again. They would ask questions; they would sometimes take me to another room where I could hear the other people being tortured. They would keep me there for a while. They would bring me back they would beat me again ask questions sometimes they would take me to the hallway and make me stand for a couple of hours blindfolded. That third day they wanted me, they kept telling me I had been to Afghanistan and I kept telling them no. And at the end of the day I could not take the pain any more and I falsely confessed of having been to Afghanistan. . . .

"In fighting this so-called war on terror what do we do with basic human rights? Do we throw them in the garbage and forget about our values that we pride ourselves with? Those are really the main points. And as I'm talking now, there are people, human beings being tortured . . .

"I think we have reached a point where we can confirm that these abuses, or this kind of torture is happening at different parts of the world at the behest of the CIA and the Bush Administration in general. So, there needs to be an action. Unless we do something about, it if we keep silent, if governments keep silent—in a way they are complicit."

Source: Amnesty International, "Real Lives—Maher Arar," http://web.amnesty.org/pages/stoptorture-reallives-maherarar-eng.

An egregious tragedy in all of this (and there is certainly more than one) is that Arar was not working with al-Qaeda or any other terrorist group (O'Connor, 2006). But under a state of exception such considerations—the juridical order and human rights—are of little import when compared to national security interests. It seems the evidence that linked him to terrorism and resulted in an innocent man being denied liberty and tortured was provided by his own country's national police force (the RCMP). In the wake of months of public and media scrutiny and fervour, former RCMP Commissioner Giuliano Zaccardelli appeared before the House of Commons Committee on Public Safety and National Security to confess that he knew his officers passed on false information about Arar to U.S. authorities in 2002—he previously gave misleading testimony that he was only made aware of this information in the fall of 2006! Zaccardelli subsequently resigned from the RCMP.

Maher Arar's handling by both Canadian and American officials prompted a commission of inquiry that was headed by Justice O'Connor (O'Connor, 2006). Confronted with nagging allegations of corruption and dereliction on the part of various government and police officials, in January 2007 Prime Minister Harper extended an official apology to Arar along with $10.5 million (plus legal fees) in compensation. More recently, Nipissing University bestowed an honorary degree on Arar, who now tours the country speaking about his suffering and the need for a greater concern for human rights.

Jacques Derrida: Deconstruction *Is* Justice

> Deconstruction, if such a thing exists, should open up. (Derrida, 1987, 261)

For Agamben and most others, sovereignty refers to a singular entity: to a head of state or some other similar type figure who can decide on the state of exception. Jacques Derrida (2005), in one of his last writings before his death in 2004, argued for a more open and wide-ranging definition. Keeping with the deconstructive ethic in which he worked throughout his life, Derrida attempted to open the concept of sovereignty up to other ways of thinking and relating. For him, sovereignty was intrinsic to each and all of us, insofar as the sovereign function is "anchored in a certain ability to do something" (Balke, 2005). Derrida was intent on undoing language and, in the process, peering behind discourse to reveal how it does not have a determinable meaning. He wanted to show that all language exceeds the boundaries of the taken-for-granted (e.g., sovereignty). **Deconstruction** attempts to reveal what is *really* going on in and through language. According to Derrida, we always say more than the surface of our language reveals.

deconstruction

An opening up of seemingly closed "things." It intends to encounter the hidden and excluded elements of language, meaning, and experience.

But what is deconstruction? Derrida frequently defined deconstruction in negative terms by referring to what it was not rather than what it *is*. For example, he argued, "deconstruction is not a method or some tool that you apply to something from the outside" (Derrida, 1997, 9). But what is it? We might say that deconstruction has to do with opening up given linguistic arrangements to the mostly silent, background suppositions that give words and phrases their meaning. Given Derrida's reticence, perhaps showing deconstruction at work would aid us here. As an example let us consider the word *promise*. What does this mean to you? When you promise your mother you will be home tonight for dinner, what are you doing? On the face of things you are giving her an assurance that you will sit down with her to eat this evening. Unless you are truly irresponsible, there is no reason to doubt the truth of your assurance. Humans typically relate to presence, to what is uttered. Nevertheless, what is unspoken in language (the perversion of the promise) is as important to determining meaning as what we hear from another. What would happen if you did not show up? Your mother would be upset that you broke your promise and others would certainly feel let down by your absence. Such perversions of the promise are as fundamental to its meaning as carrying through with the promised event. For a promise to be such, the statement must have the potential of falling through. If it does not, if what is assured is already guaranteed, there is no promise, only perfect conjugation of the assertion ("I will be home for supper") and the event. Again using the above example, if you promised your mum to come to dinner while sitting at the table with fork and knife in hand, you have not promised anything.

If we had only to consider the presence of speech, we could take everyone at their word and there would thus be no need for contracts, warranties, or oaths. Typically, however, when we hear language we do not attempt to read into it hidden meaning, but instead relate to what is laid out before us. However, and this is the important part, when speaking and writing we say much more than what is present on the page or in conversation. Deconstruction, then, attends closely to the unspoken elements that enable the central, or privileged, structure of a given meaning formation (Pavlich, 2007).

Underlying all language is a **trace**: the silent or absent element of language that provides words with an essential part of their meaning (i.e., perversion in the promise). The trace can be likened to a footprint or a comet. That is, when we observe a comet in the sky we are struck by the *presence* of the comet and/or tail. However, what is absent here is the comet's nucleus and essence, which is composed of rock and ice. When we observe a comet we are not privy to its essence—the nucleus remains hidden. The same can be said of language. No element, no idiom can function as a sign without at the same moment referring to another that is simply not present, but gives meaning to it (Derrida, 1981). While we are at liberty to separate out presence and trace for the purposes of reducing the promise to constituents, we (obviously) do not typically perform this operation.

trace
The mark of absence in words that is the necessary condition of thought and experience (Spivak, 1976).

Opening language up to its silent constituents (the trace) is at deconstruction's core. However, before passing such analysis off as a banal play of words and of little utility to *real* social problems let us consider the implications of "community" under the Youth Criminal Justice Act. Community-based sanctioning and interventions occupy pride of place in the act. The preamble, for example, states that

> WHEREAS members of society share a responsibility to address the developmental challenges and the needs of young persons and to guide them into adulthood; WHEREAS communities, families, parents and

> others concerned with the development of young persons should, through multi-disciplinary approaches, take reasonable steps to prevent youth crime by addressing its underlying causes, to respond to the needs of young persons, and to provide guidance and support to those at risk of committing crimes. (YCJA, preamble)

Without the insights of deconstruction we are apt to quickly read over the term *community* and be off to the next of the Act's many sections. Calls for community responsibility for youth crime may be laudable. However, given that the very essence of community is exclusionary, perhaps such enthusiasm should be tempered. That is, we cannot have a community—a school, a neighbourhood, a class, a town, or whatever other configuration—without exclusion. Those who belong define themselves in opposition to the excluded. If everyone were included under this or that community rubric, the term *community* would cease to hold meaning. "Community" designates divisions between and among people. Under the YCJA it is the young offenders—their deviance and criminality—who provide impetus for the creation of community in the first instance. For example, Youth Justice Committees, which are made up of community members who hear and adjudicate relatively minor crimes committed by youths, find their meaning and definition in the wrong doings of young people. A crime committed by a young offender brings this community together. Because of his or her contravention, the young person becomes not only the rationale for the formation of community, but, by virtue of the offence, its antithesis. George Pavlich (2005) maintains that this is the very essence of community, wherein "communities are identified—implicitly or explicitly—by exclusion." Before proclaiming this a meaningless play of words, we should be reminded of the repulsive consequences that may accrue when exuberance for and devotion to community has spilled over its limits: ethnic wars of annihilation have been waged, genocide has been carried out, and prisons have become overcrowded with the residues of such intolerance (Hogeveen, 2006).

broken windows policing
Just as houses with broken windows indicate that nobody cares about the neighbourhood, proponents of this policing style feel that tolerating minor misbehaviour will mean that residents will be afraid to use their streets. They feel that police should quickly deal with minor incivilities such as panhandling, vandalism, and other behaviours that contribute to fear of crime. Critics feel this policing style potentially discriminates against the poor.

justice
For Derrida, since it is perpetually deferred, justice cannot be defined adequately. It is not contained in or constrained by law. It is infinite. It is "to come."

Communities may derive their *raison d'être* in relation to a particularly deviant and troubling other. A string of car thefts or a proliferation of graffiti in a geographical space may inspire previously disorganized citizens to band together against this provocation. "Recent efforts to rid (affluent) neighbourhoods of prostitutes, the use of CCTV on busy city streets, **broken windows policing**, and gated neighbourhoods are poignant examples of community inspired attempts to exclude the 'other' while shoring up a privileged lifestyle. This regulation of the 'other' may contribute to and assist in shoring up the creation of community, but it also holds the insidious possibility of contributing to exclusionary practices which limit, rather than encourage, wider and more inclusive patterns of harmony" (Hogeveen, 2006, 295; Pavlich, 2005).

Through the examples of promises and community we can see that deconstructive critique involves "opening up" things up to examine what lies behind and beyond presence. However, there is one word that is not deconstructable: **justice**. In common parlance we use the term *justice* in a variety of ways: we have a justice system; there are Justices of the Peace; Canada boasts a federal Department of Justice; it is used in law and legislation to imply the impartiality of the system (e.g., the Youth Criminal *Justice* Act), and it is even a village

FOCUS

BOX 11.3 Crime Pays Off in Canada

Consider the assumptions made about "justice" in the following article: What are the sources of the reporter's dissatisfaction with the Canadian criminal justice system? What expectations does she have about justice and in what ways are they not being met? Also, note how she speaks as though her views represent taken-for-granted values that we all share and how she compares us (the "good" law-abiding and deserving) with youth offenders (the "bad," dangerous, and undeserving).

By Michele Mandel

Maybe this holiday weekend you're putting in another shift to help pay for your child's college tuition.

Maybe you are that student, worried about how you're going to put the cash together for school and your first apartment.

Or maybe you're a victim of crime, and you can't afford the counselling you so desperately need.

Too bad you're not a teen killer, because then you'd be showered—thanks to the Canadian government—with more than $100,000 a year.

It's called the Intensive Rehabilitative Custody and Supervision program or IRCS and for 24 of this country's worst youth offenders, the little-known federal justice program is akin to hitting the jackpot.

In return for accepting treatment for their mental issues, serious violent offenders can escape adult prison and do easy time instead in a youth facility, like Ontario's Sprucedale, while taxpayers spend $100,375 per inmate for academic courses, counselling, "life skills" and reintegration.

The theory is that these heavily damaged "kids" need intensive help if they are ever to find their way back into society.

What kind of help, you may ask?

Well, there was the $700 piece of wood we purchased for a killer who brutally beat and sexually assaulted 15-year-old Elisha Mercer under the Lorne Bridge in Brantford in 2001. According to a Sprucedale insider, the young murderer was given the lumber to fashion his very own homemade guitar.

"It makes us all want to vomit," says the employee, who doesn't want to be named. "The victims should be getting this money, not them."

When told by the Sun, Elisha's mom was outraged to learn what constitutes therapy for the killer of her only child. "It's ridiculous, absolutely ridiculous," Wilma Martin says. "These have been very hard years. My husband and I split up because of what happened, he took off and I was left to pay the mortgage and the bills. I came close to losing my home.

"I could have used $100,000."

Instead, Ottawa last year earmarked $3.4 million for the country's worst of the worst young murderers and rapists with psychological disorders.

In 2004, one of the first accepted into the new program was the 18-year-old Hamilton youth who had killed Jonathan Romero the year before. Romero, 18, had gone to Lime Ridge Mall to buy a Christmas present for his mom. Standing on the sidelines when his friend got involved in a fight, Romero was sucker punched by the youth and after falling to the ground, was savagely punched four more times in the head and neck. He died hours later in hospital.

A judge turned down the Crown's request for a 6½-year adult sentence for manslaughter and instead agreed to just 30 months in custody at Sprucedale. The young offender was deemed eligible for IRCS because—wait for it—he was diagnosed with attention deficit and hyperactivity disorder, post traumatic stress disorder and mood disorder.

If only every kid with ADD could get free one-on-one counselling and government-sponsored perks.

The Hamilton youth was assigned a "life coach" and various IRCS counselling programs. He was released four weeks ago to a six-month

(Continued)

FOCUS

BOX 11.3 Crime Pays Off in Canada (*Continued*)

reintegration period, but according to the Sprucedale worker, none of the expensive rehabilitation seemed to have any impact at all. "He felt no remorse whatsoever for his crime and anyone who worked with him over the last three years will tell you the same thing," he says. "He was a poster child for everything that was wrong with the system."

"Danger to society"

"Do I think he still poses a danger to society? You bet I do. At that summer camp, he didn't learn a thing."

The youth, stung by a previous article slamming easy time at Sprucedale, insists he's a changed man in a letter published in the Sun. "Every achievement that I completed here is to the memory of that boy."

According to his former worker, the letter is just another demonstration of how he's learned to talk the talk as well as how to use the IRCS program to his advantage.

Now 20, the Hamilton killer was boasting to everyone that the federal government will now be paying for his college tuition, laptop computer and his living expenses. On his $16,000 IRCS wish list, he also requested a plasma screen TV and new designer clothing. The insider says he doesn't know if those goodies were granted as well.

"All of this stuff," says the angry youth worker, "an average family can't afford and these kids are getting it for murdering other kids? It's unbelievable. The public needs to know."

Oh Canada, why are we such gullible souls?

Source: Michele Mandel, "Crime Pays off in Canada," *Toronto Sun*, July 1, 2007: http://torontosun.com/News/Columnists/Mandel_Michele/2007/07/01/4304140.html.

in Manitoba (located northwest of Brandon). Vengeance is by far the most commonplace understanding of justice (see Box 16.3). Here *justice* being done means an ethic of punishment that delivers obvious signs of unpleasantness to offenders. We live in an era where war, prison overcrowding, and vigilantism are justified in the name of justice. For example, the U.S. government has constructed Osama Bin Laden as a moral monster and a lunatic for crimes perpetrated upon the United States. All the while, the civilian and military death toll from the American campaign for "justice" mounts. The cost in dollars and human life are spiralling out of control, while domestic atrocities and oppressions are glossed over by a nation seeking justice. Now, as the philosopher Noam Chomsky (2003) suggests, the stance of the lunatic and monster are considered highly honourable, indeed obligatory, when "we" are seeking justice.

If these are all instances of "justice," how can Derrida say that it does not exist? It is because Derrida seeks a different kind of justice, one that goes beyond "right, a justice finally removed from the fatality of vengeance" (Derrida, 1994, 21). One of Derrida's most faithful followers, John Caputo (1997), puts the situation this way: "Justice is not a present entity or order, not an existing reality or regime; nor is it even an ideal *eidos* towards which we earthlings down below heave and sigh while contemplating its heavenly form. Justice is the absolutely unforeseeable prospect (a paralyzing paradox) in virtue in which the things that get deconstructed are deconstructed" (Caputo, 1997, 131). For Derrida, then, "justice appears as a promise, beyond law, and is itself incalculable, infinite and undeconstructable" (Pavlich, 2007, 989). It is not a thing or a person that we can hold up as exemplary or criterion for future generations. To maintain that Canada is a just nation or that we ourselves are just would be to conclude that our work is done. It would be the height of injustice to think that justice exists here in tolerant Canada in the midst of unimaginable suffering of First Nations people, the tragic abuse of female partners, and the expanding extremes of poverty and wealth—and we could go on (Caputo, 1997). But, you may conclude, the law is just . . . right? On the contrary, there are situations in which the application of law was legal but unjust (e.g., Arar, Menezes). This is not to say that law is unnecessary and that it is wrong in its conception. Only that law can be unjust in its application and in its fundamental opposition to justice.

In the work of Foucault, Cultural Criminology, Bourdieu, Agamben, and Derrida, as well as that of many other critical theorists not mentioned in this chapter, the common thread is one of questioning all taken-for-granted assumptions, shaking and disrupting our accepted notions, and exposing the injustices that lurk behind some of our most deeply held beliefs and time-tested practices.

Summary

- Critical criminology attempts to draw attention to hidden and overlooked injustices scattered throughout our world. Critical criminology seeks to highlight and genuinely grasp inequalities, discrimination, and suffering.
- Early critical criminology in Canada, inspired by Taylor, Walton, and Young's *The New Criminology*, maintained a focus on how economic power is implicated in the operations of criminal justice. Efforts to create a unified collective among Canadian critical criminologists were, however, cut short by several factors, including the growing diversity of critical criminology.
- Today's critical criminology does not maintain this dedication to a political economic approach to crime. Critique is less and less understood as a form of judgment gauged upon a fixed standard of evaluation and more as a means for disrupting and destabilizing taken-for-granted assumptions about and approaches to crime. The goal is not to prescribe a new social order but rather to create opportunities for unencumbered ideas and practices to arise and take form.
- Foucault has contributed to critical criminology through his work on power. For Foucault, power is not solely repressive—it is also productive. Through the tactics of discipline, surveillance, and governmentality, power shapes individuals so that they are transformed (or transform themselves) into more governable subjects.
- Actuarialism, risk, and the risk society are all terms used to understand the growing fixation on insurance-like evaluations of risk and harm in contemporary criminal justice practices. Through an understanding of the larger social context producing the "risk society," critical criminologists are able to challenge the logic of various risk-management approaches to criminal justice.

- Cultural criminology revives the ethnographic tradition in criminology and directs it toward discovering crime as a lived experience. Cultural criminologists investigate the cultural production of crime and our understandings of crime and thereby question popular notions about crime and criminal justice.
- Bourdieu's "field theory" alerts critical criminologists to the many forms of power that are amassed and the role they play in the domination over and definition of excluded and criminalized classes. Crime, therefore, is understood not only as a consequence of economic domination, but also of symbolic, cultural, and social domination.
- Giorgio Agamben points us to the power of the sovereign to define individuals as being outside of law. Thus built into law is the state of exception; that is, the sovereign's ability to suspend rights and protections. And through this concept criminal law is vividly revealed as a source of exclusion.
- Jacques Derrida's concept of deconstruction provides critical criminologists a tool for evaluating what is hidden or unspoken within social life and, in particular, criminal justice practices. It is a particularly powerful tool for unpacking the meanings hidden in fashionable criminal justice jargon, such as "community," "safety," and "security."

QUESTIONS FOR CRITICAL THINKING

1. In your view, what does it mean to be "critical"? Does your understanding of criticism align with the practices of critical criminology?
2. Is it enough to criticize, to expose the limits placed on our thinking about crime, or is it incumbent on the critical criminologist to devise a "solution" to the "problem" of crime?
3. Some have criticized critical criminologists for using a complex, academic discourse. In your view, is it the responsibility of scholars to place their thoughts in terms that everyone can understand? Are there ever situations where complex ideas demand complex language?
4. How might a critical criminologist put some of the concepts described in this chapter into practice? For example, imagine that you are the executive director of a not-for-profit agency that advocates for offender rights. How might the theories listed above help guide you in your efforts to secure better treatment for offenders both within prisons and upon release into the community?
5. How does the project of critical criminology differ from the other theories you have learned about in this text?

NET WORK

http://critcrim.org/ Homepage of the Critical Criminology Division of the American Criminological Society.

KEY TERMS

actuarial; pg. 350
attentive gaze; pg. 353
broken windows policing; pg. 362
capital; pg. 355
dangerous knowledge; pg. 354
deconstruction; pg. 360
discipline; pg. 347
field; pg. 354
governmentality; pg. 346
habitus; pg. 354
justice; pg. 362
micro-powers; pg. 347
naked life; pg. 358
negative *social* capital; pg. 355
negative *symbolic* capital; pg. 355
power; pg. 346
risk; pg. 349
risk society; pg. 351
sovereign; pg. 357
state of exception; pg. 357
surveillance; pg. 347
trace; pg. 361

SUGGESTED READING

Hogeveen, Bryan, Joane Martel, and Andrew Woolford (eds.). (2006). "Law, Crime and Critique," a special issue of the *Canadian Journal of Criminology and Criminal Justice* 48 (5). This collection brings together the work of critical criminologists who experienced the rise and demise of the Human Justice Collective with those trying to build a new network of Canadian critical criminologists. It offers examples from a variety of contemporary critical criminological perspectives.

O'Reilly-Fleming, Thomas (ed.). (1985). *The New Criminologies in Canada: State, Crime and Control*. Toronto: Oxford University Press. An early statement on the Canadian contribution to critical criminology, this volume illustrates the breadth and rigour of critical criminology in Canada during the 1980s.

Taylor, Ian, Paul Walton, and Jock Young. (1973). *The New Criminology: For a Social Theory of Deviance*. London: Routledge and Kegan Paul. This is the seminal text in critical criminology. The authors capture the critical ethos of the 1970s and the dissatisfaction that was emerging among like-minded criminologists worldwide.

BIBLIOGRAPHY

Andrews, D.A., and J. Bonta. (1998). *The Psychology of Criminal Conduct* (2nd ed.). Cincinnati, OH: Anderson Publishing Co.

Balke, Friedrich. (2005). "Derrida and Foucault on Sovereignty." *German Law Journal* 6(1):71–85.

Bauman, Zymunt. (2000). *Liquid Modernity*. Cambridge: Cambridge University Press.

Beck, Ulrich. (1992). "From Industrial to Risk Society: Questions of Survival, Social Structure and Ecological Enlightenment." *Theory, Culture, and Society* 9:97–123.

Bennett, Brian. (2007). "Outsourcing the War." *Time* 169(13): 36-40.

Bosworth, Mary. (2004). "Gender, Risk and Recidivism." *Criminology & Public Policy* 3(2):181–84.

Bourdieu, Pierre. (1984). *Distinction: A Social Critique of the Judgement of Taste*. Cambridge, MA: Harvard University Press.

——. (1986). "The Forms of Capital." In John Richardson (ed.), *Handbook of Theory and Research for the Sociology of Education*. New York: Greenwood Press, pp. 241–58.

——. (1990a). *The Logic of Practice*. Cambridge, MA: Polity Press.

——. (1990b). *In Other Words: Essays Toward a Reflexive Sociology*. Stanford, CA: Stanford University Press.

——. (1991). *Language and Symbolic Power*. Cambridge, MA: Harvard University Press.

——. (1992). *An Invitation to Reflexive Sociology*. Chicago: University of Chicago Press.

Brubaker, Rogers. (1985). "Rethinking Classical Theory: The Sociological Vision of Pierre Bourdieu." *Theory and Society* 14:745–75.

Caputo, John. (1997). *Deconstruction in a Nutshell: A Conversation with Jacques Derrida*. New York: Fordham.

Cauley, Leslie. (2006). "NSA Has Massive Database of Americans' Phone Calls." *USA Today* 11 May 2006.

Chambliss, William. (1969). "The Law of Vagrancy." In William Chambliss (ed.), *Crime and the Legal Process* (pp. 51–63). New York: McGraw-Hill.

Chomsky, Noam. (2003). *Hegemony or Survival: America's Quest for Global Dominance*. New York: Metropolitan Books.

Dean, Mitchell. (1999). *Governmentality: Power and Rule in Modern Society*. London: Sage.

Dekeseredy, Walter, and Brian D. MacLean. (1993). "Critical Criminological Pedagogy in Canada: Strengths, Limitations, and Recommendations for Improvements." *Journal of Criminal Justice Education* 4:361–76.

Derrida, Jacques. (1981). *Positions*. Chicago: University of Chicago Press.

——. (1987). "Some Questions and Responses" in N. Fabb (ed.), *The Linguistics of Writing: Arguments between Language and Literature*. Manchester: Manchester University Press.

——. (1994). *Specters of Marx: The State of the Debt, the Work of Mourning and the New International*. London: Routledge.

——. (2005). *Rogues: Two Essays on Reason*. Stanford: Stanford University Press.

DiMaggio, Paul. (1979). "Review Essay: On Pierre Bourdieu." *American Journal of Sociology* 84:1460–474.

Edmonton. (2004). Fact Sheet on Housing and Homelessness. http://intraspec.ca/Fact_Sheet-Housing-and-Homelessness.pdf. Accessed November 29, 2007.

Ek, Richard. (2006). "Giorgio Agamben and the Spatialities of the Camp." *Geografiska Annaler: Series B, Human Geography* 88(4):363–86.

Ericson, Richard, and Kevin Haggerty. (1997). *Policing the Risk Society*. Toronto: University of Toronto Press.

Ewald, Francois. (1991). "Insurance and Risk." In Graham Burchell, Colin Gordon, and Peter Miller (eds.), *The Foucault Effect: Studies in Governmentality*. Chicago: University of Chicago Press.

Feeley, Malcolm, and Jonathan Simon. (1994). "Actuarial Justice: The Emerging Criminal Law." In David Nelken (ed.), *The Futures of Criminology*. New York: Sage.

Ferrell, Jeff. (1998). "Criminological Verstehen." In Jeff Ferrell and Mark Hamm (eds.), *Ethnography at the Edge*. Boston: Northeastern University Press.

——. (2004). "Boredom, Crime and Criminology." *Theoretical Criminology* 8(3): 287–302.

Foucault, Michel. (1979). *The History of Sexuality*, Vol. 1. New York: Vintage.

———. (1980). *Power/Knowledge: Selected Interviews and Other Writings.* New York: Pantheon.

———. (1982). "The Subject and Power." In Hubert Dreyfus and Paul Rabinow (eds.), *Michel Foucault: Beyond Structuralism and Hermeneutics.* Chicago: University of Chicago Press.

———. (1991). "Governmentality." In Graham Burchell, Colin Gordon, and Peter Miller (eds.), *The Foucault Effect: Studies in Governmentality.* Chicago: University of Chicago Press.

———. (1997). *The Essential Works, 1954–1985, vol. 1, Ethics, Subjectivity and Truth.* New York: The New Press.

Garland, David. (1997). "Governmentality and the Problem of Crime: Foucault, Criminology, Sociology." *Theoretical Criminology* 1(2):173–214.

Gordon, Colin. (1991). "Introduction." In Graham Burchell, Colin Gordon, and Peter Miller (eds.), *The Foucault Effect: Studies in Governmentality.* Chicago: University of Chicago Press.

Hannah-Moffat, Kelly, and Paula Maurutto. (2003). *Youth Risk/Need Assessment: An Overview of Issues and Practices.* Ottawa: Department of Justice (http://www.justice.gc.ca/en/ps/rs/rep/2003/rr03yj-4/rr03yj-4.html).

Hannah-Moffat, Kelly, and Margaret Shaw. (2001). *Taking Risks: Incorporating Gender and Culture into the Classification and Assessment of Federally Sentenced Women in Canada.* Ottawa: Status of Women.

Hayward, Keith J., and Jock Young. (2004). "Cultural Criminology: Some Notes on the Script." *Theoretical Criminology* 8(3):259–73.

Hogeveen, Bryan. (2006). "Memoir of a/the Blind." *Punishment and Society* 8(4):469–76.

Hogeveen, Bryan, and Joanne Minaker. (2008). *Youth, Crime and Society: Critical Reflections.* Toronto: Pearson.

Hogeveen, Bryan, and Andrew Woolford. (2006). "Critical Criminology and Possibility in the Neoliberal Ethos." *Canadian Journal of Criminology and Criminal Justice* 48 (5):681–702.

Kant, Immanuel. (1956). *Critique of Pure Reason.* London: Everyman.

Katz, Jack. (1988). *Seductions of Crime: Moral and Sensual Attractions in Doing Crime.* New York: Basic Books.

Lippert, Randy, and James Williams. (2006). "Governing on the Margins: Exploring the Contributions of Governmentality Studies to Critical Criminology in Canada." *Canadian Journal of Criminology and Criminal Justice* 48(5):703–19.

Martel, Joane, Bryan Hogeveen, and Andrew Woolford. (2006). "The State of Critical Scholarship in Critical Criminology and Socio-Legal Studies in Canada: An Introductory Essay." *Canadian Journal of Criminology and Criminal Justice* 48 (5):633–46.

Minca, Claudio. (2006). "Giorgio Agamben and the New Biopolitical Nomos." *Geografiska Annaler: Series B, Human Geography* 88(4):387–403.

Morrison, Wayne. (2007). *Criminology and the New World Order.* London: Glasshouse.

O'Connor, D. (2006). *Report of the Events Relating to Maher Arar: Analysis and Recommendations of the Commission of Inquiry in the Actions of Canadian Officials in Relation to Maher Arar.* Ottawa: Queen's Printer.

O'Malley Pat. (1992). "Risk, Power and Crime Prevention." *Economy and Society* 21: 252–75

———. (1996). "Risk and Responsibility." In Andrew Barry, Thomas Osbourne, and Nikoas Rose (eds.), *Foucault and Political Reason: Liberalism, Neoliberalism and Rationalities of Government.* Chicago: University of Chicago Press.

O'Neill, Maggie. (2004). "Crime, Culture, and Visual Methodologies: Ethno-Mimesis as Performative Praxis." In Jeff Ferrell, Keith Hayward, Wayne Morrison, and Mike Presdee (eds.), *Cultural Criminology Unleashed*. London: Glasshouse.

O'Reilly-Fleming, Thomas (ed.). (1985). *The New Criminologies in Canada: State, Crime and Control*. Toronto: Oxford University Press.

Pavlich, George. (1999). "Criticism and Criminology: In Search of Legitimacy." *Theoretical Criminology* 3(1):29–51.

———. (2000). *Critique and Radical Discourses on Crime*. Aldershot: Ashgate.

———. (2005). *Governing Paradoxes of Restorative Justice*. London: Glasshouse Press.

———. (2007). "Deconstruction." *Blackwell Encyclopedia of Sociology*. London: Blackwell.

Raban, Jonathon. (1974). *The Soft City*. London: Hamilton.

Ratner, R. S. (1971). "Criminology in Canada: Conflicting Objectives." Unpublished Manuscript.

———. (1984). "Inside the Liberal Boot: The Criminological Enterprise in Canada." *Studies in Political Economy* 13: 145–64.

———. (1989). "Critical Criminology—A Splendid Oxymoron." *Journal of Human Justice* 1:3–8.

Schmitt, Carl. (1985). *Political Theology: Four Chapters on the Concept of Sovereignty*. Chicago: University of Chicago Press.

Simon, Jonathan. (1988). "The Ideological Effects of Actuarial Practices." *Law and Society Review* 22(4):772–800.

Taylor, Ian, Paul Walton, and Jock Young. (1973). *The New Criminology: For a Social Theory of Deviance*. London: Routledge and Kegan Paul.

van Swaaningen, Rene. (1997). *Critical Criminology: Visions from Europe*. London: Sage.

Wacquant, Loïc. (1998). "Negative Social Capital: State Breakdown and Social Destitution in America's Urban Core." *The Netherlands Journal of the Built Environment* 13-1:25–40.

———. (2000). "The New 'Peculiar Institution:' On the Prison as Surrogate Ghetto." *Theoretical Criminology* 4 (3):377–89.

———. (2001). "Deadly Symbiosis: When Ghetto and Prison Meet and Mesh." *Punishment & Society* 3(1):95–134.

Williams, Howard. (1983). *Kant's Political Philosophy*. Oxford: Blackwell.

Young, Jock. (1979) "Left Idealism, Reformism and Beyond: From New Criminology to Marxism" in B. Fine, R. Kinsey, J. Lea, S. Picciotto, and J. Young. *Capitalism and the Rule of Law*. London: Hutchinson, pp. 11–28.

———. (1998). "From Inclusive to Exclusive Society: Nightmares in the European Dream." In Vincent Riggiero, N. South, and Ian Taylor (eds.), *The New European Criminology: Crime and Social Order in Europe*. London: Routledge.

Interactionist Theories

12

Robert A. Stebbins

UNIVERSITY OF CALGARY

Strain and conflict theories deal with causes of crime at the level of social structure. Strain theorists related crime to variables such as cultural goals and the access to opportunities that was provided by society. For conflict theorists, the cleavages between different groups in society and the power relationships among these groups were critical in explaining criminality. Interactionist theories turn our attention to the smaller details of social life. They consider the ways in which crime is a consequence of our relationships with other people and of the social meaning of those relationships.

One of the most important concepts for interactionist theories of crime is the deviant career. This is the passage of an individual through the stages of one or more related deviant identities. This notion is at the heart of labelling theory, which explains how the social response to initial, tentative acts of deviance can move a person toward a deviant identity and a deviant career. The other important interactionist theory discussed in this chapter—differential association—outlines the ways in which people learn to be criminals through their interaction with other criminals and how they come to acquire a criminal identity.

Learning Objectives

After reading this chapter, you should be able to

- Describe primary and secondary deviation and explain how primary deviation can be transformed into secondary deviation.
- Understand the process of drift among juvenile delinquents.
- Explain the role of moral entrepreneurs in creating and enforcing the law.
- Discuss the various contingencies that criminals encounter in their deviant careers.
- Understand how people can be socialized into a life of crime.
- Outline the strengths and limitations of interactionist theories of deviance.

Interactionist theory in criminology centres on the interchanges people have with one another and on the meanings of these interchanges in the past, present, and future. Herbert Blumer (1986) notes that **symbolic interactionism**, the broader theory from which the interactionist theories of crime are derived, rests on three premises. First, people act toward the human and nonhuman objects in their lives according to the meanings that those objects have for them. Second, the meaning of those objects for each individual emerges from interactions between him or her and other people. Third, the meanings of objects learned in this manner are applied and occasionally modified as individuals

symbolic interactionism
A sociological perspective that focuses on the dynamics of how people interpret social situations and negotiate their meaning with others. It differs from more structurally focused perspectives in seeing individuals as actively creating the social world rather than just acting within the constraints of culture and social structure.

interpret how the objects and their meanings fit particular social situations with reference to them and their reasons for being there.

Much of this chapter is about criminal interactions, meanings, interpretations, and situations. Before turning to these processes, however, let us set the stage for discussion with a brief illustration of the three premises operating in the sphere of crime. The following interview with Allen, about 20 years old, shows how the meaning of a situation changed through social interaction with other people on the scene in an all-night drugstore:

> From what I understand from them, they didn't go in there with the intent to rob or beat anybody up or anything. I think they only really wanted to buy some gum and cigarettes, but by being drunk, they was talking pretty tough, and so the lady behind the counter automatically got scared. . . . The druggist . . . got a little pushy or ordered them out of the store, and by them being all fired up, naturally the next thing they did was jump on him.
>
> So now what do you have? You've got a drugstore. You've got a scared lady in the corner somewhere with her hands over her face. You've got a beat-up druggist laying on the floor. You've got three dudes that came in for chewing gum and cigarettes, but now they got two cash registers. So what do they do? They take the cash. Wasn't nothing to stop them, and it was there. Why would they leave it? They're thieves anyway and supposed to be hustlers. . . . There wasn't nothing to stop them, so they just took the money. (Katz, 1990)

The Deviant Career

labelling
According to labelling theory, deviance is not a quality of the act but of the label that others attach to the act. This raises the question of who applies the label and who is labelled. The application of a label and the response of others to the label may result in a person becoming committed to a deviant identity.

career
In common use, this refers to the sequence of stages through which people in a particular occupational sector move during the course of their employment. It has also been applied to analyzing the various stages of an individual's involvement with criminal activity.

Interactionism centres chiefly on what happens to criminals once their deviant activities commence. Interactionists have observed, for example, that some groups or individuals have enough power to force the label of deviant on other less powerful groups or individuals. The **labelling** process, however, is by no means accurate. It is not even always fair. Some people who have deviated escape public detection of their behaviour. Some who have not deviated are nonetheless labelled as having done so, despite their protests to the contrary. The application of the deviant label is sometimes subject to considerable negotiation between possibly deviant people and those in a position to apply the label of deviant to them.

Thus interactionist theory in criminology helps explain the establishment of moral rules, their application through labelling, and the long-term consequences of these two processes for deviants and for society. In interactionist theory, labelling and its consequences are viewed as unfolding within the deviant career.

A **career,** whether in deviance or a legitimate occupation, is the passage of an individual through recognized stages in one or more related identities. Careers are further composed of the adjustment to, and interpretations of, the contingencies and turning points encountered at each stage. For example, Short (1990) notes that careers in youth crime are likely to be prolonged after certain turning points are reached. One turning point is the early onset of delinquent activities; another is the development of an interest in drugs. The inability to find legitimate employment, a career contingency, also contributes to continued criminality. The type of offence, however, has been found to be unrelated to the length of careers in youth crime and even to the rate at which it is perpetrated. During the careers of young offenders and other deviants, there is a sense of continuity. This sense is fostered by the perception of increasing opportunities, sophistication, and perhaps recognition among one's associates for skill in, or at least commitment to, the special endeavour.

Primary Deviation

Edwin Lemert (1972) has contributed two important concepts to the study of deviant careers: **primary deviation** and **secondary deviation**. Primary deviation occurs with little change in the individual's everyday routine or lifestyle. In general, this will be the case when the individual engages in the deviance infrequently, has few compunctions about it, and encounters few practical problems when doing it. A person who occasionally smokes marijuana supplied by someone else exemplifies primary deviation.

primary deviation
Occurs when an individual commits deviant acts but does not adopt a primary self-identity as a deviant.

secondary deviation
Occurs when an individual accepts the label of deviant. This results in the adoption of a deviant self-identity that confirms and stabilizes the deviant lifestyle.

Primary deviation occurs in the early stages of the deviant career, between the first deviant act and some indefinite point at which deviance becomes a way of life and secondary deviation (discussed later) sets in. According to Matza (1969), one precondition of deviance is the willingness to engage in it. That is, the individual must have an affinity, innate or acquired, for the intended act (for example, theft, homicide, drug use). The affinity helps him or her choose among existing options. By way of illustration, imagine an individual who believes that the rich cheat others to get their money. This individual has an affinity for stealing from the rich. That affinity could lead the individual into crimes against the rich when faced with such unpleasant alternatives as poverty, unemployment, or tedious manual labour.

Behind the willingness to engage in deviance is a weak commitment to conventional norms and identities. At the same time, few young people have a strong value commitment to deviant norms and identities. Instead, they **drift** between the world of respectability and the world of deviance. They are "neither compelled to deeds nor freely choosing them; neither different in any simple or fundamental sense from the law abiding, nor the same; conforming to certain traditions in . . . life while partially unreceptive to other more conventional traditions" (Matza, 1990).

drift
A psychological state of weak normative attachment to either deviant or conventional ways.

Matza was writing about American males who were young offenders. He found these youths firmly attached to certain marginal, masculine, *subterranean traditions* or ways of life. They found satisfaction in drinking, smoking, renouncing work, being tough, and pursuing the hedonistic pleasures of "real" men. Matza's subjects looked upon themselves as grown and mature, but their behaviour was hardly a true picture of adult life in general in the United States.

Lemert explains how this peculiar orientation can set one adrift toward deviance:

> While some fortunate individuals by insightful endowment or by virtue of the stabilizing nature of their situation can foresee more distant social consequences of their actions and behave accordingly, not

> so for most people. Much human behaviour is situationally oriented and geared to meeting the many and shifting claims which others make upon them. The loose structuring and swiftly changing facade and content of modern social situations frequently make it difficult to decide which means will insure the ends sought. Often choice is a compromise between what is sought and what can be sought. . . . All this makes me believe that most people drift into deviance by specific actions rather than by informed choices of social roles and statuses. (Lemert, 1972)

Social control has failed for the groups of young offenders and young adults. This failure occurs because it is important for each deviant individual to be in good standing with his or her friends in the group. He or she attains good standing by honouring and practising the marginal, or subterranean, traditions that Matza describes. The quest for honour among peers helps explain how entire groups of youth can drift toward deviance (Hirschi, 1969).

It appears that much, if not all, of this is applicable to Canada. For instance, a comparative study conducted in California and Alberta indicates that ties to peers are important considerations among the sample of delinquent youth, while being in touch with home and school are valued much less (Linden and Fillmore, 1981).

The young offender subculture (see Chapter 10) is composed of many elements, some of the most important being the **moral rhetorics** (Schwendinger and Schwendinger, 1985) that are used to justify deviant behaviour. Each rhetoric consists of a set of guiding principles that is largely taken for granted, sometimes logically inconsistent, and always selectively applied according to the social situations in which youths find themselves. The rhetoric of *egoism* is most often used by those who still feel guilty about their deviant acts. These are typically early offenders, who have learned various ways to neutralize the **stigma** that comes with their behaviour, such as the claim that they steal in response to the greed and immorality of shopkeepers whose prices are unfair. Later young offenders are more likely to use the *instrumental* rhetoric to justify their acts. Here they stress the cunning and power that they can bring to bear against people who are otherwise more powerful and uncontrollable. Fraud, deceit, and violence are used in the pursuit of deviant aims whenever they appear to pay off, whenever they can take advantage of a weak moment in the lives of such people. The main point of this is that young offenders, like people in many other walks of life, can justify what they do. Though the law-abiding world sees it otherwise, the offenders have their own ways of defending their deviant acts as morally right.

moral rhetoric
In the study of crime, this is the set of claims and assertions that deviants make to justify their deviant behaviour. The moral rhetoric of a group is an important component of socialization into a deviant identity.

stigma
As used by Erving Goffman (1922–1982), a characteristic of an individual that is given a negative evaluation by others and thus distorts and discredits the public identity of the person. For example, a prison record may become a stigmatized attribute. The stigma may lead to the adoption of a self-identity that incorporates the negative social evaluation.

During the primary deviation stages of the deviant career, young offenders and young adults drift, in part, because they lack a value commitment to either conventional or deviant values. Value commitment is an attitude toward an identity, an attitude that develops when a person gains exceptional rewards from taking on that identity (Stebbins, 1970). Young men and women drifting between criminal and respectable pursuits have found few, if any, enduring benefits in either type of activity. Nonetheless, this pattern begins to change as they begin to have more contact with the agents of social control.

Agents of Social Control

The members of society who help check deviant behaviour are known as agents of social control. They include the police, judges, lawmakers, prison personnel, probation and parole officers, and ordinary citizens who take an active interest in maintaining law and order as they define it. Groups of ordinary citizens and lawmakers sometimes join hands in the capacity of **moral entrepreneurs**:

> Rules are the products of someone's initiative, and we can think of the people who exhibit such enterprise as *moral entrepreneurs*. Two related species—rule creators and rule enforcers—will occupy our attention. (Becker, 1963)

moral entrepreneur
Someone who is engaged in the process of defining new rules and laws or who advocates stricter enforcement of existing laws. Often such entrepreneurs will have some financial or organizational interest in particular definitions or applications of law.

The prototype of the rule creator, Becker observes, is the crusading reformer, whose dissatisfaction with existing rules is acute and who, therefore, campaigns for legal change (adding new laws or procedures and rescinding old ones) and, sometimes, for a change in attitude designed to produce what he or she considers proper behaviour. Canadian society is replete with crusades, both past and present. Different groups have sought to eliminate drug abuse, discourage the abuse of alcohol, reduce the availability of pornography, and stop the exploitation of women in the workplace. Organizations have been formed to stress the need for such things as protection against break and entry. Moral enterprise is currently at work in an attempt to curb electronic crime (for a further example, see Box 12.1).

To conduct an effective crusade, moral entrepreneurs must construct an argument that is capable of convincing the community that it has a deep and genuine threat in its midst. This process of collective definition (Spector and Kitsuse, 1987; Hewitt and Hall, 1973) centres largely on the "claims-making activities" of the entrepreneurs themselves. They

1. assert the existence of a particular condition, situation, or state of affairs in which human action is implicated as a cause;
2. define the asserted conditions as offensive, harmful, undesirable, or otherwise problematic to the society but nonetheless amenable to correction by human beings; and
3. stimulate the public scrutiny of the condition from the point of view advanced by the claims makers.

The claims are explained by quasi-theories that, unlike scientific theories, are selectively constructed to square with the point of view of the claims makers, are seldom responsive to **empirical evidence**, and contain simple explanations of complex and ill-defined problems.

empirical evidence
Evidence that can be observed through the senses. That is, it can be seen, touched, heard, smelled, tasted, and, to some extent, measured. This is the only form of evidence acceptable to science.

Moral entrepreneurs also enforce rules. The rules make it possible to apply norms to those who misbehave or step out of line. The entrepreneurs' legislated rules provide the enforcers (police, security personnel) with jobs and justifications for them. Since the enforcers want to keep these jobs, they are eager to demonstrate that enforcement is being carried out properly. Yet they also realize that there are more infractions than they can possibly prevent and guard against. Therefore, they must establish priorities. Thus,

> whether a person who commits a deviant act is in fact labelled a deviant depends on many things extraneous to his actual behaviour: whether the enforcement official feels that at this time he must make some show

FOCUS

BOX 12.1 Cracking Down on Crime: Could This Moral Entrepreneurship Happen in Canada?

Moral entrepreneurs often seek to increase the penalties for particular offences. For example, Mothers Against Drunk Driving (MADD) has lobbied very effectively to force the justice system to treat drinking and driving more seriously. While most people would probably support the efforts of MADD, other initiatives to make laws tougher have been more controversial. The most dramatic effort to increase penalties came in California with the passage of a very tough "three strikes you're out" law in 1994 and is far harsher than the legislation in any other state or Canada's dangerous offender legislation. The reason for the severity of the law was the power of the moral entrepreneurs responsible for its passage.

The law was passed during a period when fear of crime was high, even though crime rates had been declining for several years. The United States was becoming more politically conservative, and tougher laws were seen as the best way of dealing with the crime problem. The process that resulted in the California three strikes law began with the 1992 murder of Kimber Reynolds by a career criminal who was attempting to rob her (Vitiello, 1997). Her father, Mike Reynolds, worked with a judge to develop a draft of the three strikes legislation and lobbied to get the legislature to adopt it. While the Justice Committee initially defeated the bill, the kidnapping and murder of 12-year-old Polly Klaas by a repeat offender in 1993 galvanized public support for the bill. After thousands of Californians signed an initiative supporting his proposal, Mr. Reynolds returned to the legislature and was successful in getting the original bill passed with no modification. While the flaws of the legislation were well-known, in an election year few politicians were prepared to support any amendments to the bill for fear of being labelled "soft on crime" by their opponents. The legislation provides for a mandatory sentence of 25 years to life for a third felony conviction and a doubled sentence for those with a second felony conviction.

The consequences of the three strikes legislation can now be seen. By 2001, more than 50 000 offenders were serving time under this law. Nearly 7000 were convicted for "three strikes" and another 44 000 under a "second strike" provision that doubled the normal sentence. It costs billions of dollars to keep these people in prison, and these costs will escalate as the first three strikes offenders will not be released until 2019. By 2026, it is estimated that 30 000 three strikes offenders—a number that is close to the size of Canada's entire prison population—will be serving sentences of 25 years to life in California (King and Mauer, 2001). Most of these prisoners will be far past the age at which they represent any further threat to society but their incarceration will continue to take funds that might otherwise be used for education and health care.

As the following *Globe and Mail* editorial shows, many three strikes offenders have been sentenced for very minor offences:

> Some convicted felons have the book thrown at them. Leandro Andrade had an entire library thrown at him. He was sentenced to life in prison with no hope of parole for 50 years for the crime of trying to steal several videotapes worth a total of $153.54 (U.S.) from two different stores in California.
>
> This week, the U.S. Supreme Court upheld the sentence in a 5–4 decision. It reversed the ruling of the U.S. Court of Appeals for the Ninth Circuit, which had found the sentence unconstitutional because it amounted to "cruel and unusual punishment" under the Eighth Amendment of the U.S. Constitution.
>
> You might suspect there is more to the story than that, and you would be right. The majority on the Supreme Court, including Chief Justice William Rehnquist, Justice Sandra Day O'Connor and Justice Clarence

FOCUS

BOX 12.1 Cracking Down on Crime: Could This Moral Entrepreneurship Happen in Canada? *(Continued)*

Thomas, found ways, inch by tenuous inch, to justify a sentence that is on the face of it absurd, because the judges deferred to California's right to adopt and enforce its "Three Strikes and You're Out" law.

The law says that someone convicted of a felony, who has previously committed two serious felonies, must automatically receive a sentence of 25 years to life. . . . To an extent, the law is similar to the Canadian law that permits serial criminals to be declared dangerous offenders, and held indefinitely in prison, if they pose a foreseeably high risk to society. The idea of Canada's rule is to protect the public by locking up predictably dangerous recidivists, and if that were the sole effect of the California law, few would object to it.

In practice, the law can run amok. In 1995, Mr. Andrade was detained while leaving a Kmart store with five videotapes. A few days later, he tried to steal four tapes from another Kmart. He had previously been in and out of prison for theft and burglary. He said he took the videos to pay for his heroin habit. His state probation officer wrote: "He says when he gets out of jail or prison he always does something stupid."

So, not an ideal citizen. But not an obvious candidate for 50 years in prison without hope of parole.

Enter the three-strikes law. The prosecutor decided to treat the tape thefts as felonies rather than misdemeanours. The jury found that his conviction on three counts of first-degree burglary in 1982 qualified as "serious felonies" under the law. He received 25 years to life for each of the two tape thefts.

On Wednesday, the Supreme Court ordered him to serve the time. After all, it said, it's not as though he has no chance of parole; he will be eligible after 50 years. "The gross disproportionality principle reserves a constitutional violation for only the extraordinary case."

Forgive our slack-jawed incredulity. If this doesn't count as an "extraordinary case," what on Earth could? (The Supreme Court had one answer. It previously wrote that it might have trouble with a sentence of life imprisonment for "overtime parking.")

Justice David Souter, writing for his colleagues in the minority, had no problem with higher penalties for recidivists. However, he said, Mr. Andrade was a clear victim under the Eighth Amendment.

For a start, he received twice the sentence of a man who stole three golf clubs, though Mr. Andrade's offence was less serious and his criminal record less grave. "Andrade did not somehow become twice as dangerous to society when he stole the second handful of videotapes." And the judge wasn't impressed by the majority's note that Mr. Andrade will, after all, qualify for parole after 50 years—when he will be 87, if he lives that long.

"If Andrade's sentence is not grossly disproportionate," Judge Souter wrote, "the principle has no meaning."

The majority on the court may have prevailed with its states'-rights, tough-on-crime decision, but the absurdity of this case may help those in California—including a group called Families to Amend California's Three Strikes—to trim the ludicrous edges from the law.

Source: Editorial. "Where Shoplifting Means Life in Prison." *Globe and Mail* (Friday, March 7, 2003), p. A14. Other sources: Michael Vitiello. (1997). "Three Strikes: Can We Return to Rationality?" *Journal of Criminal Law and Criminology* 87 (Winter):395–482. Ryan S. King and Marc Mauer. (2001). *Aging Behind Bars: "Three Strikes" Seven Years Later*. Washington: The Sentencing Project.

> of doing his job in order to justify his position, whether the misbehaver shows proper deference to the enforcer, whether the "fix" has been put in, and where the kind of act he has committed stands on the enforcer's list of priorities. (Becker, 1963)

ethnic group
A group of individuals having a distinct subculture in common. An ethnic group differs from a race because it implies that values, norms, behaviour, and language, not necessarily physical appearance, are the important distinguishing characteristics.

It is no accident, then, that the least influential members of society (for example, the poor or certain **ethnic groups**) are often caught in the web of social control and labelled deviant out of proportion to their numbers. In other words, deviance is, in part, created by people in society. Moral entrepreneurs make certain laws, and the infraction of these laws constitutes deviance. Moral entrepreneurs also apply these laws to particular people, thereby labelling them as deviants of some sort. As Becker (1963) points out: "Deviance is not a quality of the act. . . . The deviant is one to whom that label has successfully been applied; deviant behaviour is behaviour that people so label."

But the rules are applied to some people and not to others; the application process is sometimes biased. Hence, some people remain at large as secret, or potentially identifiable, deviants. Others go through life falsely accused of antisocial acts. To discover why only certain groups of people are labelled deviant by dint of their actions, labelling theorists also study those who make the laws that deviants violate and the ways those laws are applied.

Those publicly labelled as deviant generally meet with some sort of community or societal reaction to their misdeeds (Lemert, 1951). Depending on the nature of the deviance, one or more of the following may be the deviant's fate: imprisonment, ostracism, fines, torture, surveillance, and ridicule. All labelled deviants soon discover that they must cope with a stigma.

A *stigma* is the black mark, or disgrace, associated with a deviant identity. It is part of the societal reaction inasmuch as it is a collective construction by the agents of social control and ordinary members of the community of the supposed nature of the unlawful act and the people who perpetrate it. As Goffman (1963) and Link and Phelan (2001) note, the collective image of stigma is constructed from social, physical, or psychological attributes that the deviant is believed to possess. In this connection, imputed possession of the attributes is far more important than actual possession.

Mark Watson (1984; and Wolf, 1991) found, after years of participation observation with outlaw motorcycle gangs, that their members had a mentality and background noticeably different from that imputed to them by the general public. They were not especially hostile to most social institutions, including government, education, and the family. Most members had finished high school and had held jobs from time to time. Some had gone to college, some were military veterans. Nearly every member had been married at least once. They were, to be sure, not particularly successful in these areas of life—which helped account for their tendency to live for the moment, to be impulsive. And although they were basically not violent men, it was important to them to be seen as "manly" in the most traditional sense of the term.

Secondary Deviation

The existence of moral rules and the societal reaction and stigma that occur when these rules are believed to have been violated set the stage for secondary

FIGURE 12.1 Relationship of Primary Deviance, Societal Reaction, and Secondary Deviance

deviation. Deviation becomes secondary when deviants see that their behaviour substantially modifies their ways of living. A strong desire to deviate, or a feeling of extreme guilt, can foster this redefinition of one's deviant activities. But being accused of deviance is typically the most influential factor behind the redefinition. Being labelled by the authorities as a murderer, rapist, prostitute, or cheque forger and being sanctioned for such behaviour forces the deviant to change his or her lifestyle drastically. As Lemert (1972) puts it, "This secondary deviant . . . is a person whose life and identity are organized around the facts of deviance."

What does a lifestyle of secondary deviation actually consist of? Stebbins (1997) defines lifestyle as

> a distinctive set of shared patterns of tangible behaviour that is organized around a set of coherent interests or social conditions or both, that is explained and justified by a set of related values, attitudes, and orientations and that, under certain conditions, becomes the basis for a separate, common social identity for its participants.

For example, drug addicts regularly buy or produce the drugs they use, habitually follow certain practices designed to prevent discovery by the authorities, and routinely consume the illicit substance thus acquired. Some addicts, prostitutes among them, justify this lifestyle as an escape from intolerable working conditions. The identity for an addict is pejorative, however, as the label "junky" clearly indicates. The relationship of primary deviance, societal reaction, and secondary deviance is portrayed in Figure 12.1.

Among the factors leading to secondary deviation is the tendency of society to treat someone's criminality as a **master status** (Becker, 1963). This status overrides all other statuses in perceived importance. Whatever laudable achievements the deviant might have, such as a good job or a successful marriage, he or she is primarily judged in the community by the fact of deviance. The statuses of work and family are treated as subordinate to the master status of deviance (see Box 12.2).

master status
A status that overrides all others in perceived importance. Whatever other personal or social qualities individuals possess, they are judged primarily by this one attribute. *Criminal* is an example of a master status that determines the community's identification of an individual.

Lack of success, or a perceived low probability of success, in attaining respectability among non-deviants may lead to interaction with other deviants. Here we shall consider a special aspect of this sort of interaction that takes place between the labelled deviant and the organized deviant group. There are several characteristics of this type of group life that stimulate or maintain such behaviour. These characteristics are effective partly because the wider community has rejected the deviant.

As Becker (1963) pointed out, the individual who gains entrance to a deviant group often learns from the group how to cope with the various problems

FOCUS

BOX 12.2 The Master Status of an Indian Mental Patient

Stigma In Everyday Life

During my first incarceration, they labelled me "schizophrenic" and "psychopathic." I was forced to wear "baby dolls"—the kind many prisoners wear. They also gave me insulin shock and electroshock. In Selkirk, I refused to conform to what the white majority staff wanted. The attendants responded by ridiculing me. They'd say things like, "Indians are all alike." I finally exploded and tried to fight back. I paid the price.

To get back at me, the staff gave me the cold wet pack treatment. They tied me up like a mummy, held my nose while they poured water down my throat so I couldn't swallow. They'd ask me if I'd had enough, and when I said no, they'd just keep me in the pack. I was in the pack for an hour or an hour-and-a-half for many days. Then they put me in a warm pack. Why did they use the pack on me? "Indians are violent."

I still refused to co-operate. Whenever they asked me to do something, I said, "No, I don't want to." On the ward, there was no such thing as "I don't want to." They continued to ridicule me. "We looked after you before the Indians did," they sometimes told me. At this point, I knew I wasn't welcome in white society. I stood alone.

Sometimes the guards beat me when I refused to cooperate. To cover up, they'd claim I had said things which I hadn't. If I told the head nurse the truth, the guards would threaten me with more bearings, so I lied to the nurse. That's what Selkirk and all the other psychiatric institutions taught me—to lie and manipulate.

Then they gave me twelve or more shock treatments. When I asked them why, they told me I had a "schizophrenic complex" or "schizophrenic tendencies." But I knew I wasn't "schizophrenic" and never was. They also gave me shock to forget: "We'll give him shock treatment so he'll forget he's an Indian." Amazingly, most of my memory came back—about 90 percent, but for a while I was afraid of being electrocuted. I was still not getting any treatment for my drinking.

Source: Lionel Vermette. "The 33 Years of the Lost Indian Walk." In Bonnie Burstow and Don Weitz (eds.), *Shrink Resistant: The Struggle against Psychiatry in Canada* (pp. 117–120). Vancouver: New Star Books.

associated with deviance. This makes being a deviant easier. Furthermore, the deviant acquires rationalizations for his or her values, attitudes, and behaviour, which come to full bloom in the organized group. While these rationalizations are highly varied, it is important to note that the very existence of rationalizations seems to point to the fact that some deviants feel a need to deal with certain conventional attitudes and values that they have also internalized.

Prus and Sharper (1991) quote one of their respondents, who was explaining how he developed the callous attitude prized by professional card hustlers:

> When I first got involved in hustling, my attitudes were less calloused [*sic*]. I might be at a stag of some sort and say some fellow is losing a little money. Through the course of the evening, talking back and forth, you find out that maybe he just got married, or that he has some kids and here he's writing cheques and I would slow down. If you pull something like this with a crew [of hustlers], the other guys will want to know what the hell you are doing! They're waiting for you to take him, and you're saying, "Well gee, the guy doesn't have much money." You would get the worst tongue lashing! The position they take is that

> "You can't have feelings on the road." And it's true, if you start saying to yourself, "Well, maybe I better not beat this guy or that guy," you would soon be out of business or at least you would really cut down on your profits.
>
> When a crew is on the road, they have no feelings for the other players. They say, "Well, if the sucker doesn't blow it to you, he's going to blow it to somebody else, so you might as well take him for his money. He's going to lose it one way or the other."

Because group forces operate to maintain and even promote deviance, it should not be assumed, as Goffman (1963) apparently does, that full-fledged deviants are always members of groups. There are some who reject the label of deviant during certain phases of their career, although they may be forced into that status. Some of these individuals spend part of their career trying to re-enter conventional life, often without success. Yet the fact that they refuse to identify themselves as deviant leads them to avoid others who are so labelled (for example, shoplifters and embezzlers). There are, moreover, some forms of deviant behaviour that, whatever the reason, are enacted alone. Rape is an example of this behaviour, as is some cheque forging. It is probably true, nevertheless, that deviance has collective support in most instances.

The amount and kinds of interaction that take place between the individual who is suspected of deviant behaviour and the agents of social control are extremely important for the future course of that person's deviant career. In fact, the interaction that takes place here makes up a major set of deviant career contingencies. A **career contingency** is an unintended event, process, or situation that occurs by chance; that is, it lies beyond the control of the individual pursuing the career. Career contingencies emanate from changes in the deviant's environment, his or her personal circumstances, or both. Movement through the career is affected by the contingencies the deviant meets along the way.

career contingency
An unintended event, process, or situation that occurs by chance.

Cohen (1965) has presented this process most clearly: alter (the agents of social control) responds to the action of ego (the deviant); ego in turn responds to alter's reaction; alter then responds to his perception of ego's reaction to him; and so forth. The final result is that ego's opportunity structure is in some way modified, permitting either more or fewer legitimate or illegitimate opportunities.

Where the opportunities for a deviant career are expanding, the steady growing apart of the deviant and the control agents leads to open conflict. Some proportion of these encounters lead in the opposite direction, however, resulting in some form of accommodation and a decrease in the opportunities for a deviant career (West, 1980).

This process of agent–deviant interaction is illustrated in the circumstances encountered by one of the respondents interviewed by Stebbins in a rare study of Canadian nonprofessional criminals:

> The respondent arrived in Toronto shortly after being released from prison in New Brunswick, only to be stopped while walking on a main street by two policemen in a prowl car. He was apparently immediately recognized and advised to return to his home province without further delay. But since he had just come from there, the respondent politely

> informed the police that he had important business in Toronto that would take a few days to accomplish, and after that he would consider leaving the city. This was not the sort of reaction the police were after, so they pressed their request again in a firmer manner. The respondent's reply was likewise more adamant, and the police left without success. That evening he was called from his rented room by his landlady only to be confronted by two different but "enormous" policemen who had just arrived in an ominous-looking police van. They again questioned him about his intentions to stay in Toronto, but the respondent, who could now see that he would probably remain in that city only in jail, replied that he had decided to return to New Brunswick after all. (Stebbins, 1976)

continuance commitment
Adherence to a criminal or other identity arising from the unattractiveness or unavailability of alternative lifestyles.

Another prominent contingency in secondary deviation is **continuance commitment**. Continuance commitment is "the awareness of the impossibility of choosing a different social identity . . . because of the imminence of penalties involved in making the switch" (Stebbins, 1976). Like the value commitment mentioned earlier in this chapter, continuance commitment helps explain a person's involvement in a deviant identity. Unlike value commitment, which explains this involvement by stressing the rewards of the identity, continuance commitment explains the involvement by describing the penalties that accrue from renouncing the deviant identity and trying to adopt a conventional identity.

As Ulmer (1994) notes, such penalties may be structural—they flow from the social structure of the community—or personal—they flow from the person's attitudes and sense of self. Stebbins's (1976) study of male, nonprofessional property offenders in Newfoundland reveals a number of commitment-related penalties of both types. As ex-offenders with prison records, the men in the study had difficulty finding jobs within their range of personally acceptable alternatives. The work they found was onerous, low in pay, and low in prestige. Many of the men had accrued sizable debts before they went to prison, which tended to discourage their return to a conventional livelihood upon release. Also penalizing were the questions from casual acquaintances about the nature of criminal life and the insulting remarks these people occasionally made about those who have been in jail. Even where their records were unknown, these nonprofessional offenders often heard people express unflattering opinions about men like them.

For these reasons and others, the man with a criminal record was often inclined to seek the company of those who understood him best—namely, other criminals—and to seek the way of life that afforded him at least some money and excitement—namely, crime. The police knew all this, and they would question local ex-offenders to determine whether they were possibly guilty of certain crimes. The ex-offenders, who were trying to "go straight," saw this as an additional penalty.

What is experienced as a string of penalties to the ex-offender is, from another perspective, a set of expressions of the societal reaction. In the everyday lives of ex-offenders, these expressions, when defined by the ex-offenders as penalizing, affect their deviant careers. The expressions force many of them into the company of other deviants. Here they find greater understanding for their circumstances. Here, also, is at least the possibility of a better living than they believe they can get in the conventional world.

What import does the process of continuance of commitment have for that of drift? Those teenagers and young adults who fail to drift out of crime into a more or less conventional way of life drift into a more or less solid commitment to crime. With a prison record and several years of secondary deviation, continuance commitment develops. Most deviants in this stage of their moral careers appear to be trapped in a self-degrading form of continuance commitment. The image they have of themselves is unflattering. It is one they wish they could abandon if only they could find a palatable way of leaving the world of crime (see also Schwendinger and Schwendinger, 1985).

But some criminals, including professional offenders, are quite attached to their deviant activities. Since the professionals find leaving crime for a conventional way of life no easier than it is for the nonprofessional offender, they are also committed to deviance. Nonetheless, theirs is a self-enhancing commitment. For the professionals, continuance commitment is of minor consequence, for they enjoy what they do and are disinclined to give it up.

Reactions to Commitment

Generally speaking, **self-enhancing commitment** presents no problem for deviants in spite of the fact that they are more or less forced to retain their social role. There is little motivation to leave this role for reasons of self-conception. Self-degrading commitment, however, presents a dramatically different situation. A number of alternatives are open to an individual committed to an identity in this manner.

self-enhancing commitment
Commitment leading to a better opinion of oneself.

First of all, a person motivated by **self-degrading commitment** has the objective alternative of redefining the values and penalties associated with the committed identity in such a way that he or she becomes attached to them. Basically, this alters the individual's perception of the balance of penalties. Such a psychological leap from self-degrading to self-enhancing commitment in the same deviant identity is exemplified by some in Shover's (1983) rare study of a sample of repeat offenders. These offenders wrestled with the frustrating gap between their legitimate aspirations and what they could actually achieve in life. Since conventional work offered them little, they turned to living from day to day, with crime being one of their more enjoyable activities.

self-degrading commitment
Commitment leading to a poorer opinion of oneself.

Without really switching to a form of self-enhancing commitment, it is occasionally possible for the deviant to adjust psychologically to self-degrading commitment. This depends, of course, on how strong a motivating force the current state of self-degrading commitment actually is for the deviant. Some types of mildly rejected deviants seem to manage this form of adaptation. Lemert (1972) refers to them as "adjusted pathological deviants." The subsequent development of character disorders is another possibility under these circumstances (Griffiths and Verdun-Jones, 1994). Successful adjustment apparently depends, in part, on the availability of a role for them to play in the community.

Lemert also considers "self-defeating and self-perpetuating deviance." He cites alcoholism, drug addiction, and systematic cheque forgery as examples of this sort of vicious circle of cause and effect, characterized by an almost complete absence of durable pleasure for those involved. Finally, if the desire to escape self-degrading commitment is exceptionally high, and none of the alternatives mentioned so far appeals to the committed individual, suicide becomes a prominent alternative. Perhaps this was the motive behind some or all of the 42 prison suicides reported by the Adult Correctional Services in Canada (Statistics Canada, 2003–04) for the period 2001 to 2004.

Undoubtedly, there are many other alternatives to self-degrading commitment besides the ones discussed here. Much, it seems, depends on the nature of the identity to which the deviant is committed. There are different ways in which commitment can manifest itself. Extensive research is still needed to isolate the kinds and circumstances of commitment and the various reactions to it.

For many deviants, however, commitment is not a lasting contingency in their careers once they become aware of their entrapment in that identity. In fact, this is one of the reasons for stating the case for commitment in subjective terms. The deviant feels this way, but this does not always correspond to the objective state of affairs. Criminological theory and research support this notion. For instance, Matza (1990) contends that delinquents generally end their deviant career at maturation, with very few continuing on to adult crime (for supporting evidence, see Shannon, 1988). West (1980) and Wolfgang et al. (1987) found that many adult criminals also mature out of their antisocial ways. This occurs when they take up a serious romantic relationship, find a legitimate job they like better than crime, or simply decide "to settle down" (see Chapter 13). Thus even deviants attached to their way of life often undergo disillusionment and shifts of interest (Sommers, 2001), which is what "maturation" means in everyday terms in the world of crime (Jankowski, 1991). There is always the possibility of therapy for alcoholics, gamblers, and drug addicts. And, of course, some deviance requires youthful vigour, a quality lost with increasing years (Inciardi, 1974).

Undoubtedly, the same can be said for many other committed identities. The worker committed to his or her job by a pension plan and seniority arrangements is often relieved of this condition if in no other way than by retirement. Divorce and remarriage are always possibilities for those in an unhappy union.

It is possible that self-enhancing commitment lasts longer than the self-degrading variety. Underlying this suggestion is the assumption that self-degrading commitment, while preferable to certain alternatives in the conventional world, is still undesirable in itself. A mortifying self-conception acts as a special penalty. It furnishes a significant part of the pressure to deal with an unpleasant state of affairs. Commitment to an identity or expectation that creates a negative self-image is viewed as a lesser-evil choice when initially compared with certain alternatives, and as a greater-evil choice when subsequently compared with certain others. The strength of the individual's desire to abandon an unpleasant status is an important consideration in determining whether the transition will be made.

Socialization into Crime

The theories of criminality discussed elsewhere in this book help explain why people start a life of crime. By contrast, interactionism has been interested chiefly in what happens to criminals once their deviant activities commence. Still, two areas of interactionist theory, though not causal, can be properly seen as contributions to the study of socialization into crime. They are the processes of differential association and acquisition of a **criminal identity**.

criminal identity
This social category is imposed by the community and correctly or incorrectly defines an individual as a particular type of criminal. The identity will pervasively shape his or her social interactions with others. It is similar in concept to master status.

Differential Association

Edwin H. Sutherland first set out his theory of differential association in the 1939 edition of *Principles of Criminology*. The statement he made in that edition differs little from the most recent version written by Sutherland and Cressey (1978). The theory consists of nine propositions that describe the complicated pattern of interaction Sutherland called **differential association**: (1) people learn how to engage in crime; (2) this learning comes about through interaction with others who have already learned criminal ways; (3) the learning occurs in small, face-to-face groups; (4) what is learned is criminal technique (for example, how to open a safe), motives, attitudes, and rationalizations; (5) among criminals, one important learned attitude is a disregard for the community's legal code; (6) one acquires this attitude by differentially associating with those who hold it and failing to associate with those who do not; (7) differential associations with criminals and non-criminals vary in frequency, duration, priority, and intensity; (8) learning criminal behaviour through differential association rests on the same principles as learning any other kind of behaviour; and (9) criminal behaviour is a response to the same cultural needs and values as non-criminal behaviour. For instance, one individual steals to acquire money for a new suit of clothes, while another works as a carpenter to reach the same goal. Consequently, tying societal needs and values to crime fails to explain it.

differential association
Developed by Edwin Sutherland in the 1930s, this theory argues that crime, like any social behaviour, is learned in association with others. If individuals regularly associate with criminals and are relatively isolated from law-abiding citizens, they are more likely to engage in crime themselves. They learn the specific skills needed to commit crime and the ideas that justify and normalize crime.

Based on what is known about the antecedents of crime, Sutherland's theory offers a valuable, albeit partial, explanation of theft, burglary, prostitution, and marijuana use. Also, differential association is often a major antecedent in the use of addictive drugs and dependence on alcohol. It may even play an explanatory role in some mental disorders.

However, many other factors, which dilute the importance of differential associations, must be considered when explaining these kinds of behaviour. For example, two processes discussed earlier in this chapter—drift and primary and secondary deviation—indicate that deviant motives and meanings are often gradually learned and tentatively applied and modified over time in interaction with both deviants and non-deviants. The motives and meanings are not mere causal antecedents of criminal acts and memberships in criminal groups (Davis, 1980). Another set of factors was recently reviewed by Birkbeck and LaFree (1993). Symbolic interactionism, they note, further contributes to our understanding of crime by directing attention to the motives and meanings operating in the situations in which crimes are committed. In this connection, Katz (1990) found that the expressive reasons behind many criminal acts such as thrill and enjoyment are as important as the instrumental reasons such as

FIGURE 12.2 Commitment

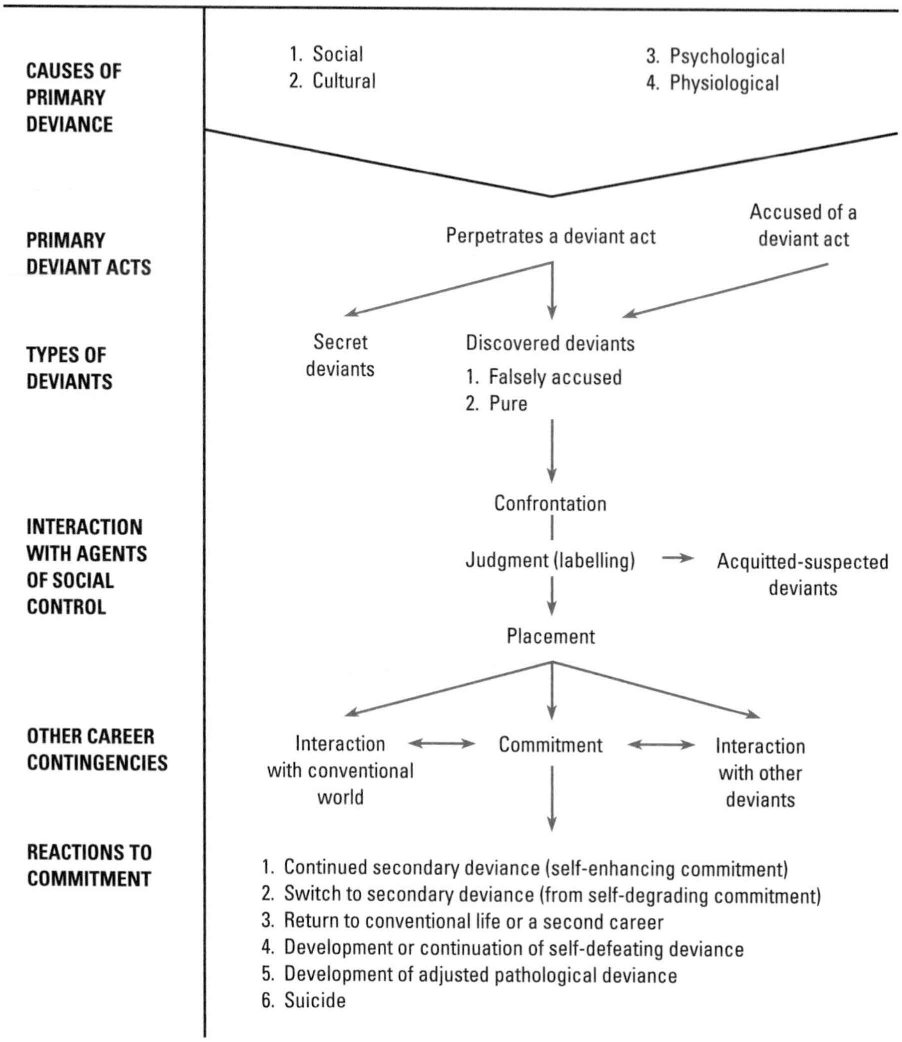

Source: Robert A. Stebbins. (1976). *Commitment to Deviance: The Nonprofessional Criminal in the Community*. Westport, Conn.: Greenwood Press, p. 66.

money and status. Additionally, precisely how a crime is committed and even which crimes are committed depend, in part, on decisions made on the spot by the criminal. These decisions may be made with reference to the possibility of being apprehended, serving a longer or shorter sentence, or enduring a hostile reaction from the community to the deviant act or acts.

Although various tests of the theory of differential association have been carried out, convincing support for it has always been blocked by the difficulty of operationalizing for empirical study some of Sutherland's key concepts (for example, frequency, intensity, and duration of criminal and non-criminal associations). Nonetheless, in Matsueda's (2001) words,

> differential association theory represents one of the most important theoretical traditions in criminology. Historically, the theory brought

> a sociological perspective to the forefront of criminology and, with his path-breaking work on white-collar crime, established Edwin Sutherland as perhaps the most important criminologist of his generation. . . . Over 50 years later, differential association theory continues to stimulate revisions, extensions, and original research into the causes of crime.

The major contribution of differential association is its emphasis on the role of ties to deviant peers in the persistence of a criminal career. Daniel Wolf, an anthropologist who rode with the Rebels, an Edmonton biker gang, described how the willingness of peers to stand up for one another can be critical in maintaining power in the face of violent opposition from competitors:

> For an outlaw biker, the greatest fear is not of the police; rather, it is of a slight variation of his own mirror image: the patch holder of another club. Under slightly different circumstances those men would call each other "brother." But when turf is at stake, inter-club rivalry and warfare completely override any considerations of the common bonds of being a biker—and brother kills brother. None of the outlaws that I rode with enjoyed the prospect of having to break the bones of another biker. Nor did they look forward to having to live with the hate–fear syndrome that dominates a conflict in which there are no rules. I came to realize that the willingness of an outlaw to lay down his life in these conflicts goes beyond a belligerent masculinity that brooks no challenge. When a patch holder defends his colours, he defends his personal identity, his community, his lifestyle. When a war is on, loyalty to the club and one another arises out of the midst of danger, out of apprehension of possible injury, mutilation, or worse. Whether one considers this process as desperate, heroic, or just outlandishly foolish and banal does not really matter. What matters is that, for patch holders, the brotherhood emerges as a necessary feature of their continued existence as individuals and as a group. (1991, 11)

There is a great deal of research evidence showing that having young offenders as friends is one of the strongest correlates of deviant behaviour. Several recent studies have also found that among at-risk youth, gang membership contributes to delinquency above and beyond the influence of associating with deviant peers. Sutherland's work helps us to understand why this is the case. Differential association theory also points to the need to learn the skills of committing certain crimes. These range from very simple techniques such as hitting a man over the head and stealing his watch to taking an unlocked bicycle to sophisticated computer crimes. According to Sutherland, people learn the necessary techniques and the motives, drives, rationalizations, and attitudes of deviant behaviour from others with whom they associate. Peter Letkemann (1973), for example, described how a former Canadian penitentiary resident learned the now-obsolete art of safecracking:

> Prior to doing his first "can" [safe] [he] bugged an older safecracker in prison "until he finally divulged how to do it." This instruction, he added was "not like a teacher–student, it was just a matter of discussion during work."

When he left the prison he went back to his regular partner and described to him what he had learned about safes. His partner said this was ridiculous but [he] persuaded him to come along: "I followed the instructions to the letter. It opened—we were both overcome with it all—the ease of it all!"

This first job had been a punch job [breaking into a safe without explosives]—technically the simplest. Following this [he] and his partner "opened many doors by trial and error." . . . This went on for four years; they had not yet used explosives, nor had they ever been caught punching safes. They became increasingly eager to try explosives since they found so many safes that couldn't be opened any other way.

During this time, [he] was associating with other safecrackers. . . . He eventually asked another safecracker whether he could borrow some grease [nitroglycerine]. "I wouldn't admit that I knew nothing about it." He obtained the grease and chose a small safe, but was unsuccessful. The next day, he discussed his problem with some more experienced safecrackers. He found he had used too long a fuse and was advised to use electric knockers [detonators]. This he did with success. (Letkemann, 1973, 136)

Criminal Identities

A *criminal identity* is a social category into which deviants are placed by others in the community and into which, eventually, they may place themselves. That is, the process of identification of an individual as deviant is a two-sided coin. Based on a variety of criteria (for example, appearance, actions, associates, and location), members of the community come to view someone as a particular kind of criminal. The woman wearing garish, suggestive clothing, who frequents a street corner in the red-light district, is identified as a prostitute. The man with long, unkempt hair, dirty jeans, and a black leather jacket who rides a Harley-Davidson motorcycle is identified, as we saw earlier, as a member of a gang bent on rape, violence, and drunkenness.

Moreover—and this is the other side of the coin—community identification of people tends to be very persuasive, even for the deviant. That is, with officials, neighbours, relatives, and others asserting that an individual is some sort of social outlaw, it becomes increasingly difficult for him or her to deny the charge. At the very least, the alleged prostitute must accommodate her everyday life to such opinion, whether or not she is selling sex. The biker has the same problem (Watson, 1984; Wolf, 1991).

Acquiring a community reputation, or identity, for unsavoury behaviour often helps to further individual criminality. This is especially likely to happen when the reputed criminal is forced into association with others of similar reputation and away from those who are "respectable." Once deviant ties are forged and non-deviant ties sufficiently weakened, the socializing potential of differential association begins to take effect. Interactionists see social interaction and definitions of situation as underlying the processes of identification and differential association.

Limitations

Like all theories of crime and deviance, interactionist theory has its limitations. That is to say, it is not in itself a complete explanation of crime. It falls well short of explaining all crime under all the conditions in which it is committed. Throughout this chapter, we have discussed the strengths of the theory (for a summary see Table 12.1). Drawing on Barry Glassner's (1982) review of the various critiques of this theory, we will now examine its limitations. These are discussed with reference to three categories: neo-Marxist, empiricist, and ethnomethodological. Each critique is also the nucleus of still another approach to the study of crime.

The Neo-Marxist Critique

The principal neo-Marxist objection to interactionist theory is that it fails to relate crime and other forms of deviance to the larger society. It fails to account for historical and contemporary political and economic interests. After all, deviant acts and careers do take place within such a context.

It is further charged that labelling theorists overlook the division between the powerful and the powerless in explaining deviance. Powerful members of society also violate laws and other norms even while establishing some of them in their role as moral entrepreneurs. Consider the case of Henri Marchessault, former head of the Montreal Police Drug Squad. In November 1983, he was convicted of stealing and selling hashish and cocaine, which were available to him from a police vault. He was a detective captain at the time (*Calgary Herald*, November 26, 1983).

The concept of moral entrepreneur and the categories of secret and falsely accused deviants suggest, however, that interactionists have some understanding of the power differences in society. Perhaps the fairest criticism is that they have failed to go as far as they might in linking power to such ideas as labelling, deviant career, and agent of social control. Still, the observation that labelling theory overlooks the larger social context of deviance is apt. This exposes the predominantly social-psychological character of the perspective.

TABLE 12.1 Interactionist Theories

Theory	*Theorists*	*Key Elements*
Labelling	Lemert Becker	Primary deviance is infrequent deviance that involves little change in routine or lifestyle. Secondary deviance occurs when deviance becomes a way of life and a part of the deviant's self-image.
Differential association	Sutherland	Crime and delinquency are primarily learned in interaction association with others in small, face-to-face groups. This involves learning the techniques of deviance and the justifications for deviant behaviour.

The Empiricist Critique

The empiricists find several research weaknesses in labelling theory and its empirical support. Glassner (1982) discusses three of these. First, interactionists are said by the empiricists to examine only, or chiefly, labelled deviants—those who have been *officially* identified as having deviated (charged and convicted, or examined and hospitalized). It is true that labelling theorists have frequently followed this narrow conception of the labelling process. Some deviants—for example, religious fanatics or occultists—are deviant and labelled by the community as such, even though they rarely if ever gain official recognition. This exposes interactionists to the criticism that community labelling makes no practical difference to the individual.

Second, the empiricists argue that labelling as a cause of deviance is inadequately conceptualized. This is a misunderstanding. As this chapter points out, labels are seen by interactionists as interpretations, not causes. The label of deviant is a career contingency, an event, a process, or a situation interpreted by the deviant as having a significant impact on his or her moral career.

Third, the empiricists claim that labelling theory lacks testable propositions. Consequently, data in this area can be explained in many different ways. Glassner notes that the empiricists hold that tests by quantitative, statistical means are the only definitive way of confirming propositions. Interactionists defend their approach by pointing out that qualitative methods, particularly participant observation, are more appropriate for the study of interaction, labelling, career, and self-conception. These phenomena rest on definitions of the situation, images of self and others, negotiations of reality, and similar processes that are difficult to measure and, therefore, largely unquantifiable. Nevertheless, qualitative research often proceeds from the intense examination of individual groups and cases. Such studies are difficult and time-consuming. As a result, there are relatively few of them. There is only suggestive, and still unconfirmed, evidence for many interactionist propositions.

The Ethnomethodological Critique

The ethnomethodologists and conversational analysts are the modern-day inheritors of the phenomenology of Alfred Schutz. (In fact, Glassner refers to them as "phenomenologists" in his review of interactionist theory.) The chief concern of the ethnomethodologists with labelling theory is its tendency to neglect this question: How do people make sense of their social world?

ethnomethodology
A sociological theory developed by Harold Garfinkel. Roughly translated, the term means the study of people's practices or methods. The perspective does not see the social world as an objective reality but as something that people must build and rebuild constantly in their thoughts and actions. Ethnomethodologists try to uncover the methods and practices that are used by people as they create the taken-for-granted world.

Kenneth Leiter (1980) defines **ethnomethodology** as the study of common-sense knowledge. Three phenomena are encompassed by this definition: ethnomethodologists study the stock of knowledge that people have of the social and physical world around them; with this stock of knowledge, people engage in common-sense reasoning about the events, processes, things, and characteristics experienced in everyday life; when people reason together on a common-sense basis, their thoughts often combine to form a suprahuman reality—a social reality. This social reality transcends the thoughts of those in the situation who are doing the reasoning.

Ethnomethodologists do not seek to confirm the validity of common sense. Rather, they note that whether common sense is scientifically right or wrong, it is the way in which "we experience the social world as a factual object" (Leiter, 1980). By studying these three phenomena, we find answers to the question of how people make sense of their social world.

However, the people of interest to the ethnomethodologist are not always deviant. Rather, ethnomethodologists are interested in how agents of social control and ordinary citizens make sense of deviants and deviant acts. Interactionists are accused of ignoring the ways in which the conventional world identifies and classifies morally offensive individuals and their behaviour. The important data for ethnomethodologists are the clues people use to identify kinds of deviants and deviant acts. People use this knowledge to reach such conclusions as "guilty" or "innocent." Studying these two processes demonstrates how we will construct special social realities—the realities of who did what to whom, at what time, and at what place.

To some extent, interactionists are guilty as charged. Although there are occasional hints of ethnomethodological thinking in the interactionist literature on deviance, there has been until recently a tendency to rely heavily on official definitions, or labels, of what and who is deviant. But even official definitions and their applications are informed by common sense. They, too, warrant ethnomethodological analysis.

Implications

The most profound implication of interactionist theory is practical only in a general sense. The theory offers a unique perspective on deviance, which enhances understanding of this phenomenon. For instance, observations on moral enterprise underscore the arbitrariness of criminal law and call attention to patterns of local and national power (though rarely to the extent neo-Marxists would like). Practically speaking, there is little that can be done to counteract most moral enterprise. But interactionist research, at least, exposes its existence.

On a more practical level, interactionist theory stresses the pernicious effects of the deviant label. These effects are of at least two types. One, the label (to the extent that the wider community is aware of it) makes re-entry into that community problematic after sanctioning. Non-deviants are inclined to avoid known deviants. They do so because their own reputations could be damaged from being seen with deviants and, possibly, because they are revolted by the deviant's lifestyle and moral behaviour. Deviants are more than rule violators. They are also outcasts.

Two, labels colour the judgments many people make of those who are labelled. Labels are names for stereotyped images. Both the images and the labels help non-deviants, including practitioners, define situations involving deviants. These two effects of the deviant label have led Empey et al. (1999), among others, to argue that the juvenile courts should be used as a last resort for only the most serious cases. Juvenile diversion and decriminalization programs are a practical response to this implication of interactionist theory. Canada's Youth Criminal Justice Act reflects this philosophy of minimal intervention, particularly for first offenders.

Interactionist theory calls attention to the deviant career as a set of factors that helps explain deviance beyond its initial causes. One practical implication stemming from this part of the theory is that, over time, people often become committed to certain lifestyles. To the extent that they have made substantial "side bets" (Becker, 1963) in one or more conventional identities, they are unlikely to deviate. Their possible deviance, if discovered and labelled, could ruin their reputations in the conventional world (for example, the politician exposed in the press for patronizing a prostitute). One antidote to initial or continued deviance, then, is to give people every possible opportunity to build a strong side bet in a "respectable" pursuit. By this reasoning, the juvenile should be encouraged to drift toward conventional interests. The adult ex-offender should also be encouraged to find non-criminal employment in new surroundings, away from his or her former deviant associates.

Summary

- Interactionist theory centres on the deviant interchanges people have with one another and the meanings of these interchanges in the present, past, and future.
- A deviant career is the passage of an individual through recognized stages in one or more related deviant identities.
- Primary deviation occurs in the early stages of the deviant career. Here, deviance is enacted with little change in the person's everyday routine or lifestyle.
- The deviant drifts between two moral worlds. In youth offender subcultures, deviance is facilitated by certain moral rhetorics and by other aspects of the subterranean tradition.
- Agents of social control help check deviant behaviour. Moral entrepreneurs create and enforce rules, the violation of which constitutes deviance. Thus some people are labelled deviant, whereas others are not.
- When the deviant sees his or her life as substantially modified by deviance, he or she has moved into secondary deviation. The rules are applied to some people and not to others. Those who are publicly labelled as deviant generally meet with some sort of community or societal reaction to their misdeeds. Labelled deviants may find they must cope with a stigma.
- Continuance commitment, or forcing a person to remain in an identity, is sometimes the outcome of these encounters. When self-degrading continuance sets in, it motivates those so affected to redefine commitment penalties or adjust in some other way to this unsettling frame of mind.
- Although the theory of criminal socialization has not been a central concern of the interactionist perspective, interactionists have contributed to the theory in two major ways. People learn crime through differential association with others who are already criminal. They are further socialized into it by acquiring a criminal identity by being placed in such a category by other people and by coming to accept (often grudgingly) this placement.

- Limitations to the interactionist theories have been noted by the neo-Marxists, empiricists, and ethnomethodologists. At the moment, however, none of these approaches has progressed beyond the concern with finding weaknesses in the interactionist perspective such that it could become a distinct orientation itself.
- Interactionist theory also has certain theoretical and practical implications. One of these is that, wherever possible, continuance commitment to deviance should be avoided for juveniles by avoiding the official label of criminal.

QUESTIONS FOR CRITICAL THINKING

1. Identify and describe a recent change in existing criminal law or a recent passing of a new criminal law that is founded in the efforts of a group of moral entrepreneurs.
2. Select a vulnerable category (e.g., lower-class male youths, Aboriginal peoples, Asian youths from immigrant families, motorcycle gangs) and develop an explanation of how they could be falsely accused of certain crimes. How does such an explanation relate to deviant identity?
3. What are some of the factors contributing to secondary deviation among heroin users?
4. Identify some of the legitimate "side bets" (Becker, 1963) people make that help them avoid committing criminal acts and that criminals might make to help them avoid further criminality.
5. Because of the influence of labelling theory, our society has become more sensitive to the costs of a deviant label. Can you think of measures that have been taken in our youth and adult courts to reduce the number of people who are officially labelled by those institutions?

NET WORK

Moral entrepreneurs are individuals or groups who try to have their personal values reflected in law and the legal process. Gun control is one issue that has seen groups of people with different viewpoints trying to influence lawmakers. Bill C-68, the Firearms Act, has been particularly controversial, and both sides have worked very hard to have their views accepted. On one side of the issue is the National Firearms Association, which strongly objects to the restrictions on the ownership and use of firearms that are part of Bill C-68. The website of this association is at **www.nfa.ca**.

On the other side of the debate is the Coalition for Gun Control. Some of the arguments in favour of gun control can be found at their website at **www.guncontrol.ca** and at the government's Canadian Firearms Centre website at **www.cfc-cafc.gc.ca**. On the government site, look particularly at the section "Information for the General Public."

1. What are the claims made by the two sets of moral entrepreneurs in this debate?

2. What do you think are some of the reasons for the conflicting views of the two sides in this debate?
3. What are some of the strategies that have been adopted by the National Firearms Association to fight the implementation of Bill C-68? Find some of the arguments used by the Coalition for Gun Control in their successful fight to convince the government to pass Bill C-68.

KEY TERMS

career; pg. 372
career contingency; pg. 381
continuance commitment; pg. 382
criminal identity; pg. 385
differential association; pg. 385
drift; pg. 373
empirical evidence; pg. 375
ethnic group; pg. 378
ethnomethodology; pg. 390
labelling; pg. 372
master status; pg. 379
moral entrepreneur; pg. 375
moral rhetoric; pg. 374
primary deviation; pg. 373
secondary deviation; pg. 373
self-degrading commitment; pg. 383
self-enhancing commitment; pg. 383
stigma; pg. 374
symbolic interactionism; pg. 371

SUGGESTED READING

Becker, Howard S. (1963). *Outsiders*. New York: Free Press. A collection of key articles written by Becker, several of which contain original statements on labelling, the deviant career, moral entrepreneurs, and types of deviants.

Foster, Janet. (1990). *Villains: Crime and Community in the Inner City*. London: Routledge. A field study of local and family traditions of petty crime among middle-aged and teenage males and females in southeast London.

Goffman, Erving. (1963). *Stigma*. Englewood Cliffs, N.J.: Prentice Hall. An essay on the nature and consequences of stigma for deviants, the handicapped, and those with physical blemishes.

Matza, David. (1990). *Delinquency and Drift*. New Brunswick, N.J.: Transaction. This book contains Matza's fullest development of the concepts of drift and subterranean tradition, as well as an introduction that links it with the 1964 edition.

Rubington, Earl, and Martin G. Weinberg (eds.). (2005). *Deviance: The Interactionist Perspective* (9th ed.). Boston: Allyn and Bacon. An anthology of theoretical and empirical articles written from the interactionist perspective.

BIBLIOGRAPHY

Becker, Howard S. (1963). *Outsiders: Studies in the Sociology of Deviance*. New York: Free Press.

Birkbeck, Christopher, and Gary LaFree. (1993). "The Situational Analysis of Crime and Deviance." In Judith Blake and John Hagan (eds.), *Annual Review of Sociology* 19. Palo Alto, Calif.: Annual Reviews, Inc.

Blumer, Herbert. (1986). *Symbolic Interactionism*. Berkeley: University of California Press.

Cohen, Albert K. (1965). "The Sociology of the Deviant Act." *American Sociological Review* 30:5–14.

Davis, Nanette J. (1980). *Sociological Constructions of Deviance* (2nd ed.). Dubuque, Iowa: Wm. C. Brown.

Empey, Lamar T., Mark C. Stafford, and Carter H. Hay. (1999). *American Delinquency: Its Meaning and Construction* (4th ed.). Belmont, Calif.: Wadsworth.

Glassner, Barry. (1982). "Labelling Theory." In M. Michael Rosenberg, Robert A. Stebbins, and Allan Turowetz (eds.), *The Sociology of Deviance*. New York: St. Martin's Press.

Goffman, Erving. (1963). *Stigma: Notes on the Management of Spoiled Identity*. Englewood Cliffs, N.J.: Prentice Hall.

Griffiths, Curt T., and Simon N. Verdun-Jones. (1994). *Canadian Criminal Justice* (2nd ed.). Toronto: Harcourt Brace Canada.

Hewitt, John P., and Peter M. Hall. (1973). "Social Problems, Problematic Situations, and Quasi-Theories." *American Sociological Review* 38:367–74.

Hirschi, Travis. (1969). *Causes of Delinquency*. Berkeley: University of California Press.

Inciardi, James A. (1974). "Vocational Crime." In Daniel Glaser (ed.), *Handbook of Criminology*. Chicago: Rand McNally.

Jankowski, Martin S. (1991). *Islands in the Street: Gangs and American Urban Society*. Berkeley, Calif.: University of California Press.

Katz, Jack. (1990). *Seductions of Crime: Moral and Sensual Attractions in Doing Evil*. New York: Basic Books.

Leiter, Kenneth. (1980). *A Primer on Ethnomethodology*. New York: Oxford University Press.

Lemert, Edwin. (1951). *Social Pathology*. New York: McGraw-Hill.

______. (1972). *Human Deviance, Social Problems, and Social Control* (2nd ed.). Englewood Cliffs, N.J.: Prentice Hall.

Letkemann, Peter. (1973). *Crime as Work*. Englewood Cliffs, N.J.: Prentice Hall.

Linden, Rick, and Cathy Fillmore. (1981). "A Comparative Study of Delinquency Involvement." *Canadian Review of Sociology and Anthropology* 18:343–61.

Link, Bruce G., and Jo C. Phelan. (2001). "Conceptualizing Stigma." In Karen S. Cook and John Hagan (eds.), *Annual Review of Sociology*, Vol. 27. Palo Alto, Calif.: Annual Reviews.

Matsueda, Ross L. (2001). "Differential Association Theory." In Patricia A. Adler, Peter Adler, and Jay Corzine (eds.), *Encyclopedia of Criminology and Deviant Behavior*, Vol. 1. Philadelphia: Brunner-Routledge.

Matza, David. (1969). *Becoming Deviant*. Englewood Cliffs, N.J.: Prentice Hall.

______. (1990). *Delinquency and Drift*. New Brunswick, N.J.: Transaction.

Prus, Robert C., and C. R. D. Sharper. (1991). *Road Hustler: Grifting, Magic, and the Thief Subculture* (expanded edition). New York: Kaufman and Greenberg.

Schwendinger, Herman, and Julia S. Schwendinger. (1985). *Adolescent Subcultures and Delinquency*. New York: Praeger.

Shannon, Lyle W. (1988). *Criminal Career Continuity*. New York: Human Sciences Press.

Short, James F. (1990). *Delinquency and Society*. Englewood Cliffs, N.J.: Prentice Hall.

Shover, Neal. (1983). "The Later Stages of Ordinary Property Offender Careers." *Social Problems* 31:208–18.

Sommers, Ira B. (2001). "Criminal Careers." In David Luckenbill and Dennis Peck (eds.), *Encyclopedia of Criminology and Deviant Behavior*, Vol. 2. Philadelphia: Brunner-Routledge.

Spector, Malcom, and John I. Kitsuse. (1987). *Constructing Social Problems*. Hawthorne, N.Y.: Aldine de Gruyter.

Statistics Canada. (2003–04). *Adult Correctional Services in Canada*, Cat. No. 85-211-XIE. Ottawa.

Stebbins, Robert A. (1970). "On Misunderstanding the Concept of Commitment: A Theoretical Clarification." *Social Forces* 48:526–29.

———. (1976). *Commitment to Deviance: The Nonprofessional Criminal in the Community*. Westport, Conn.: Greenwood.

———. (1997). "Lifestyle as a Generic Concept in Ethnographic Research." *Quality and Quantity* 31:347–60.

Sutherland, Edwin H., and David R. Cressey. (1978). *Principles of Criminology* (10th ed.). Philadelphia: Lippincott.

Ulmer, Jeffery T. (1994). "Revisiting Stebbins: Labeling and Commitment to Deviance." *The Sociological Quarterly* 35:135–57.

Watson, J. Mark. (1984). "Outlaw Motorcyclists: An Outgrowth of Lower Class Cultural Concerns." In Delos H. Kelly (ed.), *Deviant Behavior* (2nd ed.). New York: St. Martin's Press.

West, W. Gordon. (1980). "The Short Term Careers of Serious Thieves." In Robert A. Silverman and James J. Teevan, Jr. (eds.), *Crime in Canadian Society* (2nd ed.). Toronto: Butterworths.

Wolf, Daniel R. (1991). *The Rebels: A Brotherhood of Outlaw Bikers*. Toronto: University of Toronto Press.

Wolfgang, Marvin E., Terence P. Thornberry, and Robert M. Figlio. (1987). *From Boy to Man, from Delinquency to Crime*. Chicago: University of Chicago Press.

Social Control Theory

13

Rick Linden

UNIVERSITY OF MANITOBA

In this chapter, we begin by examining some of the early social disorganization theories exploring the relationship between social structure and deviance. These theories were very important, because along with Merton's work (Chapter 9) they challenged the earlier view that the sources of crime lay within the individual. Instead, they proposed that the structure and culture of the American city was responsible for deviant behaviour. Social disorganization theorists felt that disorganized communities did not provide meaningful employment to residents and did not have strong families, schools, and churches. This lack of effective social controls led to high rates of crime and other types of deviance. While the early theorists looked at the relationship between community characteristics and crime, later theorists focused more on the way the social bonds of individuals help to constrain crime and delinquency. Final sections of this chapter deal with some of issues surrounding control theory and with the policy implications of the theory.

Learning Objectives

After reading this chapter, you should be able to

- Understand the early social disorganization theories that sought to explain why crime rates were highest in neighbourhoods characterized by poverty, physical deterioration, and ethnic conflict.
- Know the importance of the social bonds of attachment, involvement, commitment, and belief in the causation of delinquency and crime.
- Explain the role of the family, the school, and the church in the causation of delinquency and crime.
- Describe the criticisms that have been made of social control theory and understand the validity of these criticisms.
- Understand the social policy implications of social control theory.

Social control theory assumes that human beings are neither good nor evil. Rather, we are born with the capacity to do wrong. Unlike most theories of criminality, control theory requires no special motivation to impel people to deviate. Since our natural propensity is to gratify ourselves with no concern for right and wrong, and since the "wrong" way may be the quickest and most efficient way of achieving our goals, it is conformity rather than deviance that must be explained. Other theorists ask, "Why do they do it?"; the control theorist is concerned with the question "Why don't we *all* do it?" The answer given by control theory is "We all would, if only we dared, but many of us dare not be-

social control theory
The theory that people do not become criminal because they do not want to jeopardize their bonds to conventional society.

cause we have loved ones we fear to hurt and physical possessions and social reputations we fear to lose" (Box, 1971, 140). All societies have developed ways of making people conform, and the control theorist is concerned with these processes that bind people to the social order.

Theories of Social Disorganization—Durkheim, Thrasher, and Shaw and McKay

Durkheim and Social Integration

The earliest social control theories explained how some types of social structure led to high rates of crime and deviance. Communities characterized by poverty, physical deterioration, and racial or ethnic conflict were too disorganized to exert effective control over the behaviour of residents. Social disorganization theorists included Durkheim, Thrasher, and Shaw and McKay.

social bond
The degree to which an individual has ties to his or her society. In Hirschi's theory, social bonds include attachment, commitment, involvement, and belief.

In his monograph *Suicide* (1951), Durkheim pointed out the importance of **social bonds** in the understanding of deviant behaviour. Egoistic suicide results from a situation in which a person's social ties are weakened to the extent that the person is freed from social constraints and acts only on the basis of private interests. Anomic suicide occurs when a lack of social integration, caused by factors such as rapid economic change, leaves a society without a clear system of moral beliefs and sentiments. In each case, social organization is weak, and the individual lacks moral guidance. If the rules are strong and if there is consensus about their validity, there will be little deviance. If the rules are weak and if there is minimal agreement about their applicability, society will be unable to regulate morality effectively, and deviance will be common. Without socially regulated goals, deviance is more likely, as people either pursue their aspirations without check or succumb to the mindlessness of pursuing unattainable goals.

We saw in Chapter 9 that in Merton's reformulation of anomie theory, he shifted from Durkheim's emphasis on a society's failure to define appropriate goals to an emphasis on the failure to define the appropriate means of reaching common culture goals, and on the unequal distribution of legitimate means of reaching these goals. More faithful to Durkheim's view of the effects of the social bond on deviance were the social disorganization theorists—among them Thrasher, and Shaw and McKay.

Thrasher and *The Gang*

WWW
National Youth Gang Center (U.S.A.)
www.iir.com/nygc/

Thrasher and Shaw and McKay (members of what became known as the "Chicago School") focused their attention on ecological studies of the city. Thrasher's classic study *The Gang* is still the most extensive study of juvenile gangs ever done. Thrasher located gangs both geographically and socially where there are breaks in the structure of social organization. They occur "in city slums characterized by physical deterioration, rapid succession of inhabitants, mobility, and disorganization; along economic and ecological boundaries; along political frontiers; . . . and during adolescence, an interstitial period between childhood and maturity" (Kornhauser, 1978, 51). Gangs arise spontaneously in areas where social controls are weak. Gangs are not necessarily delinquent, though delinquency will often be the natural result of the activities of groups of adolescents in communities where social institutions are not able to direct and control their behaviour (Thrasher, 1963). In the slum setting, delinquency was often the most exciting and interesting thing for these youths to do.

Shaw and McKay—Ecological Analysis

In one of the earliest sociological explanations of crime and delinquency, Shaw and McKay saw the origins of deviance not in the pathology of individuals, but in social disorganization. They concluded that the social structure of a community would affect its rates of crime and delinquency.

"Shaw and McKay: Social Disorganization Theory"
www.crimetheory.com/Soc1/Chic2.htm

In their ecological analyses of the city of Chicago, Shaw and McKay found that some areas had disproportionately high rates of officially recorded crime and delinquency. Rates were highest in slum areas near the city centre and generally declined as one moved outward. Areas with high crime and delinquency rates were characterized by "physical deterioration, decreasing population, high rates of dependency, [and a] high percentage of foreign-born and Negro population" (Thrasher, 1963, 361). In many of these neighbourhoods, crime rates remained high over a long period of time, even though the racial and ethnic characteristics of the residents changed as new waves of immigrants moved into the city. Shaw and McKay attributed these high rates of crime to the failure of neighbourhood institutions and organizations such as families, schools, and churches to provide adequate social controls. Like Thrasher, they also discussed the importance of exposure to the criminal subculture that developed in these areas and which attracted young people to deviant behaviour.

While control theory was not fully developed in the work of Thrasher and Shaw and McKay, from the 1930s to the 1960s subcultural and strain theories so dominated the field that there were very few additions to the social disorganization model (Kornhauser, 1978). Several reasons explain why control theory all but disappeared from the scene following this rather promising beginning. The most important of these was that the early research was methodologically flawed. The relationships among **independent variables** such as social class, mobility, and community diversity were consistent with social control theory, but they also were consistent with other perspectives such as strain theory, and Shaw and McKay never directly measured the degree of social control that existed in a particular community. They inferred, but did not demonstrate, that higher-income communities were better organized than were lower-class slums. The type of research done by Shaw and McKay was also subject to the problem of the **ecological fallacy**. For example, consider the finding that official crime rates are higher in lower-class than in middle-class areas. The conclusion usually drawn from this finding is that being a member of the lower class makes one more likely to become involved with crime. However, this inference is not necessarily true. Perhaps most crimes in lower-class areas are committed by middle-class residents of those census tracts. Perhaps the resident population is not responsible for crime at all. In his study of the impact of licensed hotels, bars, and shopping centres on Edmonton crime rates, Engstad (1975) showed

independent variable
A presumed cause of a dependent variable. If unemployment is thought to cause crime rates to increase, unemployment is the independent variable, and crime rates the dependent variable.

ecological fallacy
A research error made when data or information is gathered at a group level (the unemployment rate of various communities or neighbourhoods) and then conclusions are drawn about individuals (the unemployed person). Areas with high unemployment may have high crime rates, but this does not tell us that those crimes are necessarily committed by unemployed persons.

that certain facilities, which may be attractive to people from other parts of the city, provide opportunities for crime. Chambliss (1973) found that middle-class adolescents migrated to other parts of the city to commit their delinquencies. Finally, the vague and often value-laden term "social disorganization" fell into disrepute among sociologists.

Despite these problems, Thrasher and Shaw and McKay did lay the foundations for a control theory of crime and delinquency. They found that delinquents come from communities that are poorly organized and whose institutions are not well integrated. Families are unable to adequately socialize their children, and their schools are poor. These elements all reappear in the work of later theorists.

Early Social Control Theories—Reiss and Nye

Albert Reiss

While the social disorganization theorists had been concerned with controls at the community and family level, Reiss (1951) was the first to distinguish between *social* controls, which include ties to primary groups such as the family and to the community and its institutions, and *personal* controls, which have been internalized by an individual. If these controls are absent, if they break down, if they are in conflict, or if they cannot be enforced, delinquency will result. Using information collected in the court files of a group of male juvenile probationers, Reiss found that success or failure on probation was associated with the absence of both social and personal controls.

Ivan Nye

Theoretically, the work of Nye (1958) simply expanded on that of Reiss. However, methodologically, it represented a great advance. While Reiss had relied on court records of youths who were officially defined as delinquent, Nye developed a technique for measuring self-reported delinquency and gathered his data from a random sample of high school students in three small American cities. His book represented one of the first attempts at unravelling the causes of delinquency using this approach.

While Reiss did not elaborate on the theory underlying personal and social controls, Nye was quite explicit in stating his theoretical perspective. To Nye, "control theory assumes delinquency is not caused in a positive sense (motivated by the gains to be derived from it) but prevented (determined by the relative costs of alternative benefits). . . . Weak controls free the person to commit delinquent acts by lowering their cost relative to available alternatives" (Kornhauser, 1978, 140–41). Individuals are motivated to achieve certain goals as quickly as possible but are prevented from doing so by the laws and customs that societies establish to protect their members.

In expanding on Reiss's distinction between personal and social controls, Nye outlined four types of controls:

1. Direct control from outside, such as that imposed by the police and parents.
2. Internalized control, which is self-enforcing and is exercised through one's conscience. Violations of internalized values will cause a child to feel guilt.
3. Indirect control, which is a function of the degree to which a child has affective ties with parents and other conforming individuals. Fear of embarrassing or hurting the person to whom the child has ties encourages conformity.
4. Availability of alternative ways of reaching one's goals.

Nye considered the family to be the most significant group in the development of social controls. The extent to which the family enforced external controls and the degree to which family members got along with one another determined the extent to which a child would develop internal controls. The results of his research supported his hypotheses concerning the relationship between the family and delinquency. Children who came from families that were close and in which there was agreement on basic values were unlikely to be delinquent.

The work of Reiss and Nye provided a promising beginning for contemporary control theory and subsequent research received much more empirical support than did the theories of Merton, Cohen, Cloward and Ohlin, Miller, and Sutherland, which dominated the field. However, it took a number of years before control theory became widely accepted by criminologists as one of the major paradigms in explaining crime and delinquency.

Hirschi and the Social Bond

It was not until the publication of Travis Hirschi's *Causes of Delinquency* in 1969 that control theory began to receive renewed attention. Hirschi developed a clear and concise version of control theory and presented an empirical examination of his theory, demonstrating that it explained delinquency better than did competing theories. Like earlier control theorists, Hirschi postulates that individuals are more likely to turn to illegitimate means if their bond to society is weak or broken. For Hirschi, four interrelated aspects of the social bond constrain our behaviour: attachment, commitment, involvement, and belief.

Attachment

Attachment refers to the degree to which the individual has affective ties to other persons, particularly those who belong to their primary groups. If an individual is sensitive to the feelings of others and close to those others, this attachment will constrain his or her behaviour because that individual will not want to hurt or embarrass the people he or she likes. Those lacking such ties will not have to consider the feelings of others and will be free to deviate. Thus, youths who do not get along with their parents will be more free to commit acts of delinquency than those who are close to their families.

attachment
The degree to which an individual has affective ties to other persons. One of the social bonds in Hirschi's theory.

Commitment

commitment
The degree to which an individual pursues conventional goals. One of the social bonds in Hirschi's theory.

The essence of **commitment** lies in the pursuit of conventional goals. "The idea, then, is that the person invests time, energy, himself, in a certain line of activity—say, getting an education, building up a business, acquiring a reputation for virtue" (Hirschi, 1969, 20). If a person decides to engage in deviance, that person will be putting his or her investment at risk. Thus the student who has worked hard in school and who aspires to become a professional may avoid the temptations of delinquency for fear of jeopardizing this future career. However, the youth who is failing in school and who has no career aspirations may not feel as constrained. For the second youth, the immediate rewards of delinquency might outweigh the potential costs. Both commitments and attachments can change over time. For example, the phenomenon of maturational reform—as we get older, we behave better—can be explained by the fact that adults typically have a greater investment in conventional lines of activity than do adolescents so their deviance may have higher costs.

Involvement

involvement
The degree to which an individual is active in conventional activities. One of the social bonds in Hirschi's theory.

Hirschi felt that people's level of **involvement** has an impact on delinquency. According to control theory, if people are busy with conventional activities, they will not have time to engage in deviant behaviour. For example, if a student is busy at school and is involved in extracurricular activities, that student will not have as much opportunity to commit delinquencies as will peers who are not as involved.

Belief

belief
The degree to which an individual believes in conventional values, morality, and the legitimacy of law. One of the social bonds in Hirschi's theory.

Our **belief** in conventional values, morality, and the legitimacy of the law will constrain our behaviour. Unlike some conflict theorists, who believe that deviants are tied to value systems different from those of the rest of the population, Hirschi claims that society does have a common value system. However, individuals vary in the degree to which they believe they should obey the rules. While conflict theorists tell us that acts that are deviant from the perspective of those who have the power to make and enforce the rules are *required* by the beliefs of members of certain subcultures, the control theorist says that deviant acts are made possible by the *absence* of beliefs forbidding them.

For the most part, research has supported Hirschi's theory, particularly for the variables of attachment and commitment. Belief in the law has also been found to be related to delinquency (Gomme, 1985). The evidence concerning involvement is mixed in that involvement in school activities is related to lower involvement in delinquency, while participation in sports, hobbies, and part-time jobs is not (Hirschi, 1969).

Self-Control—The General Theory of Crime

Hirschi's early work focused on external sources of social control such as family, friends, and school. In 1990 Gottfredson and Hirschi published *A General Theory of Crime,* in which they proposed that individuals with low self-control have a greater propensity to commit crimes when they have the opportunity to do so. They will also be more likely to engage in other risky behaviour such as smoking, drinking, and dangerous driving. Gottfredson and Hirschi believe this theory applies to all types of crime.

Individuals who lack self-control are impulsive people who focus on the moment rather than planning for the future, who have unstable personal relationships, and who are less likely to feel shame or remorse when their actions hurt others. As Gottfredson and Hirschi have stated, when "desires conflict with long-term interests, those lacking self-control opt for the desires of the moment, whereas those with greater self-control are governed by the restraints imposed by the consequences of acts displeasing to family, friends, and the law" (1990, xvi).

Why do some people lack self-control? For Gottfredson and Hirschi, the answer lies in early childhood socialization. Children will have low self-control if they have poor relationships with their parents or if their parents do not have good parenting skills. Those who fail to develop self-control in childhood will be more likely to be involved in crime throughout their entire lives, so the impact of poor early socialization may persist for many years. Their behaviour will be constrained only by the lack of opportunities to commit crimes and other deviant acts.

Several Canadian researchers have studied the relationship between self-control and criminal behaviour. Using data collected during a nighttime roadside survey of Ontario drivers, Keane et al. (1993) found that men and women who were lower in self-control had higher levels of blood alcohol than other drivers. Sorenson and Brownfield (1995) also found a correlation between self-control and drug use. However, they found that ties to delinquent friends were correlated more strongly with drug use than any of their self-control variables. Marc LeBlanc (1997) has suggested that low self-control is just one of several psychological traits that should be a part of a comprehensive social control theory of offending. LeBlanc found that Quebec youths with "egocentric personalities"—a construct similar in some respects to Gottfredson and Hirschi's notion of low self-control—have weaker social bonds and higher levels of delinquency than their peers (LeBlanc et al., 1988). In their study of Edmonton youth, LaGrange and Silverman (1999) found that self-control explained part of the difference in delinquency involvement between males and females.

While some research does support this theory, other evidence suggests that it will not replace more traditional versions of control theory. In the general theory of crime, Gottfredson and Hirschi turned away from Hirschi's earlier view that ongoing social bonds will make involvement in crime and delinquency less likely. Instead, they proposed that early childhood experiences can produce low levels of self-control that will result in higher levels of deviance throughout the entire life course. However, Sampson and Laub (1993) have cast doubt on this hypothesis. They followed boys from ages 17 to 25 and found that those who developed adult social bonds, including stable jobs and cohesive marriages, were less likely to be involved in criminality than peers who did not develop these ties. Thus, rather than remaining stable over the life course, the propensity to deviate appears to be variable and to depend on changes in one's social bonds. Childhood patterns of deviance are not necessarily carried into adulthood. Several other studies, including the work by LaGrange and

WWW

"Risk or Threats to Children" National Crime Prevention Strategy
www.prevention.gc.ca/en/library/publications/children/risk/

Silverman (1999) and 21 studies reviewed by Pratt and Cullen (2000), suggest that self-control provides at best only a partial explanation of crime and delinquency and does not explain "all crime, at all times," as Gottfredson and Hirschi claim (117).

In the remainder of this chapter, we will look in detail at some of the research evidence bearing on control theory, discuss some issues with the theory, suggest ways in which the theory might be revised, and consider its social policy implications.

Family Relationships

Social control theory emphasizes family relationships since these provide children with the attachments that restrain their involvement in delinquency. Several aspects of family relationships are related to delinquency. Among these are strength of family ties, parental supervision and discipline, and the role model provided by parents.

WWW

"A Summary of Family Life, Delinquency, and Crime: A Policymaker's Guide" Office of Prevention, Texas Youth Commission
www.tyc.state.tx.us/prevention/family_life.html

Strength of Family Ties

Strong family ties are important in the development of the social bond. If parents are close to their children and provide a congenial atmosphere in the home, family relationships should act as a deterrent to delinquency. Children should be concerned about what their parents think of them and should be less likely to become involved in delinquency.

A number of studies confirm this view. Warm, affectionate family relationships are associated with low rates of delinquency, while mutual rejection and hostility are typical of the families of delinquents (Glueck and Glueck, 1950; Nye, 1958; Gove and Crutchfield, 1982). Some of this research has also found that conflict between the parents also characterizes the families of delinquents. A study of Edmonton youths discovered that boys who found their families attractive and who were concerned with pleasing their parents were less likely to be delinquent than boys who did not have such close ties to their parents (Kupfer, 1966).

Parental Supervision and Discipline

Children who are adequately supervised by their parents and whose parents discipline them in an appropriate fashion will have lower delinquency rates than will their peers who do not. Many studies have demonstrated the importance of parents' knowing what their children are doing and ensuring that they play with friends whom the parents consider suitable (Glueck and Glueck, 1950; Hirschi, 1969; West and Farrington, 1973; Wilson, 1980). Studies in Montreal and Edmonton have found that supervision was more strongly related to delinquency than any other family variable (Caplan, 1977; Biron and LeBlanc, n.d.; Kupfer, 1966).

Closely related to supervision is parental discipline. While critics of control theory have complained that the theory advocates the harsh treatment of children, control theorists do not view physical punishment as the major means of controlling behaviour. Rather, they see that "disapproval by people one cares about is the most powerful of sanctions. Effective punishment by the parent or major caretaker therefore usually entails nothing more than explicit disapproval of unwanted behaviour" (Gottfredson and Hirschi, 1990, 99–100). Studies have consistently found the disciplinary practices of delinquent families to be different from those of non-delinquent families. Families in which discipline was inconsistent or lax were much more likely to have delinquent children (Glueck and Glueck, 1950; West and Farrington, 1973). Children do not appear to learn from discipline unless it is administered in a clear, consistent manner.

There is also some evidence of an association between higher rates of delinquency and very strict discipline, particularly if it is associated with harsh physical punishment (Fischer, 1980) and if parental warmth and supportiveness is lacking (Simons et al., 2000). Very strict discipline is likely seen as unfair and may lead to feelings of frustration and resentment on the part of the child. Harsh punishment may be effective in gaining immediate compliance, but more moderate discipline is more effective in encouraging children to internalize a set of values that will ensure long-term compliance (Aronson, 1984).

In his study of youths in a poor inner-city community, Elijah Anderson describes how what he calls "street-oriented" parents—those who do not try to emulate the "decent-family model"—discipline their children:

> In these circumstances, a woman—or a man, although men are less consistently present in children's lives—can be quite aggressive with children, yelling at them and striking at them for the least little infraction of the rules she has set down. Often little, if any, serious explanation follows the verbal and physical punishment. This response teaches children a particular lesson. They learn that to solve any kind of interpersonal problem, one must quickly resort to hitting or other violent behaviour. (Anderson, 1994, 83)

The importance of parenting style is clearly shown in Canada's National Longitudinal Survey of Children and Youth (NLSCY), which is following the development of more than 23 000 children (Statistics Canada, 1998). The researchers asked the children's parents about their parenting styles, including punitiveness, hostility, consistency, and the amount of positive interaction. Parenting style had a strong correlation with relationship and behavioural problems in children. Children who were exposed to hostile or ineffective parenting in both the 1994 and the 1996 survey periods were *nine* times more likely to have behavioural problems than were children who were not exposed to these parenting styles. Parenting style, particularly hostile parenting, was more strongly related to behavioural problems than other factors, including income and family structure.

WWW

"National Longitudinal Survey of Children and Youth"
Statistics Canada
www.statcan.ca/Daily/English/981028/d981028.htm#ART1

Parental Role Model

In his formulation of control theory, Hirschi argued that ties to parents will act as a deterrent to delinquency involvement regardless of the criminality of the parents. However, there does appear to be a relationship between the criminality of the parent and that of the child. West and Farrington (1973) found that boys with at least one parent convicted of a criminal offence were more than twice as likely to become delinquent as those whose parents had no convictions. "Youthful crime often seems to be part of a family tradition" (West, 1982, 44). West does not feel that the parents deliberately transmit criminal values to their offspring because few of the children were involved in their parents' criminality, and the parents expressed disapproval of their children's involvement in delinquency. The relationship is at least partially explained by the fact that parents with criminal records were lax in applying rules and did not supervise their children effectively. In light of West's findings that criminal fathers were likely to be on social assistance and unemployment benefits and that this dependency was repeated among their sons, it would appear that families with criminal parents may have a variety of problems that are manifested in both parental criminality and poor family relationships. West and Farrington (1977) also suggest that part of the relationship may be due to labelling because an act of delinquency leading to arrest was more likely to result in a conviction if a boy came from a criminal family.

While direct modelling of parental behaviour does not appear to be a major cause of delinquency, it may be a factor in some types of offences. Rutter and Giller suggest that "criminal parents may provide a model of aggression and antisocial attitudes, if not of criminal activities as such" (1984, 183). The fact that a high proportion of abusive parents were themselves abused as children supports the view that family violence is learned in the home (Steinmetz and Straus, 1980). Abusive parents contribute to delinquency in another way. In a study of homeless youths in Toronto, Hagan and McCarthy (1997) found that some of their respondents were living on the streets in order to escape abuse at home. Once on the street, their need for food, shelter, and money led to delinquent behaviour.

Schooling

Like the family, the school plays a primary role in socialization and is an important determinant of delinquency. The school is a pervasive influence in a young person's life. For most of the year, children spend all day in classes and return to school after hours for other activities such as sports and dances. More important, the school is an arena in which an adolescent's performance is constantly being judged. Those who are successful enjoy the prestige conferred by teachers and parents as well as by many of their classmates. Those who fail may feel that they have been rejected by the adult world as well as by their peers (Polk and Richmond, 1972). For those who are successful in school and who enjoy their educational experience, the school provides a stake in conformity. However, those who fail do not have this stake and hence are more likely to become involved in delinquency. The correlation between school failure and delinquency is relatively strong and has been replicated in Canada (Gomme, 1985), Britain (Hargreaves, 1967), and the United States (Polk and Schafer, 1972).

The school affects delinquency in two distinct but interrelated ways. First, the school is "one of the fundamental determinants of an individual's economic and social position" (Polk and Schafer, 1972, 10). The school has taken over many of the occupational socialization functions that in earlier times were performed by the family. Formal educational qualifications have become the basis for entry into most occupations. Thus a child's experiences in school will have a profound impact on that child's future life chances. Second, the school is related to delinquency through its effects on child's daily life. For some, the experience is interesting, pleasant, and enriching. For others, it is irrelevant, degrading, and humiliating.

Both types of impact have an effect on a student's stake in conformity. Those whose school experiences will clearly not qualify them for meaningful occupations may not have the same degree of commitment as their peers whose expectations are higher. The daily consequences of failure and the resulting lack of attachment to the school also affect the child. In fact, research suggests that the daily problems of coping with school failure may be more strongly related to delinquency than is concern about the future. Linden (1974) found that measures reflecting present school status (whether the child liked school, finished homework, skipped school, valued good grades, and got along with teachers) were more highly correlated with delinquency than were measures of educational aspirations and expectations. Arum and Beattie (1999) showed that students who had a school environment with small class sizes and course work that was relevant to their lives had lower rates of adult incarceration than those with less positive school experiences, even when their education did not provide any labour market benefit. Using data from Canada's National Longitudinal Study of Children and Youth, Sprott (2004) found that the classroom environment had an impact on later delinquency. Children who attended an emotionally supportive classroom between the ages of 10 and 13 had lower rates of violence two years later. Further, those with an academically supportive classroom environment had lower levels of property crime over the same period.

Some criminologists see a broader relationship between schools and delinquency. From a structural perspective, the school "cuts adolescents off from participating in the social and economic life of the community: it reduces their commitments and attachments" (West, 1984, 169). Even within the school, the educational process involves the student in only a passive way. Polk and Schafer (1972) illustrate the irrelevance of the student role by asking what happens when a student dies. The student disappears without leaving a social ripple aside from family bereavement. The student's role is not one that has to be filled by someone else. This marginality may contribute to delinquency by leaving the adolescent relatively free of the commitments that constrain deviance.

Religion

Conventional wisdom has long held that people with strong religious commitment are not likely to become criminals. In the early penitentiaries that were the predecessors of our current prison system, Bible study was a major

Religion and Crime
Healthy Initiatives: Crime
www.healthyinitiatives.com/Research%20Summaries.htm

rehabilitative tool (Rothman, 1971). The first educational programs in prisons were intended to provide inmates with the basic literacy skills needed to read the Bible and other religious literature, which was expected to motivate the offender to mend his ways.

This view was supported by several early studies that showed a modest negative relationship between religious involvement and criminality. However, in 1969, Hirschi and Stark reported the results of a study that found that religious commitment was not related to delinquency. Neither church attendance, nor the belief in supernatural sanctions for rule breakers, nor the religiosity of parents was associated with delinquency. Because the work of Hirschi and Stark was methodologically superior to that of earlier researchers (and perhaps because of a secular bias among criminologists), the results of this study were commonly accepted as definitive. Most contemporary theories of the causes of crime do not consider religion to be an important factor.

However, subsequent studies found strong negative correlations between church attendance and delinquency (Higgins and Albrecht, 1977; Albrecht et al., 1977). How are we to reconcile these conflicting findings? One plausible answer has been given by Stark et al. (1982), who concluded that the key to resolving the contradiction was to look at differences in the communities studied. The studies that found there was no relationship between religiosity and delinquency were done in communities where religious participation was low, while the studies that found a relationship between religiosity and delinquency were done in communities that had high religious participation.

Stark et al. provided additional evidence to support this view. They compared samples of boys from Provo, Utah, where the church membership rate is very high, with boys from Seattle, where church membership rates are among the lowest in the United States. In Provo, the correlation (gamma) between church attendance and delinquency was –.45, while in Seattle, it was only –.13. This means that the relationship between attending church and not being involved in delinquency was much stronger in Provo than in Seattle. The relationship also holds for adult crime. In another paper (Stark et al., 1980), they found a negative relationship between church membership and crime rates for 193 U.S. cities. Stark et al. conclude that religiosity is related to reduced levels of involvement in crime and delinquency in communities where religion is important, but not in highly secularized communities.

individualistic
A theory that focuses on explaining the behaviour of individuals and using factors or features of the individual in explaining this behaviour.

Their explanation of this finding has broader implications for social control theory. Stark et al. believe that an **individualistic**, psychological view of the manner in which religion constrains behaviour has led researchers astray. Rather than looking at religion as affecting deviance through an individual's fear of religious sanctions, they suggest that "religion only serves to bind people to the moral order if religious influences permeate the culture and the social interactions of the individuals in question" (Stark et al., 1982). Religion will have its greatest impact where it binds its adherents into a moral community. In such a community, religious teachings will be salient and consistently reinforced. Under these circumstances, an individual is less likely to consider deviant behaviour. The costs to someone who decides to violate community norms may be high, and the likelihood of finding reference groups that support such a violation will be relatively low. Religion will have a greater impact if it is part of the community's institutional order than if it is a private matter.

It seems clear that religion constrains involvement in delinquent and criminal behaviour. However, this relationship is complex—it is greatest where there is a strong religious community; to some extent, it is mediated by one's relationships with family and friends (Elifson et al., 1983); and it has the most impact on behaviour (such as marijuana use) that may not be universally condemned by other segments of society (Linden and Currie, 1977).

Female Criminality

Since control theory views conformity rather than deviance as its central question, the fact that women have higher levels of conformity than men should have played an important part in the development of the theory. However, this has not been the case. While some control theorists have looked at female crime and delinquency, most have not looked explicitly at sex differences in the degree of adherence to social bonds. In fact, Hirschi excluded females from his analysis even though he had collected data from them.

Several studies comparing male and female delinquency have used a control framework. Typical of the results was Linden's (1974) finding, using Hirschi's California data, that social bond variables were correlated with the delinquency of both boys and girls, though the correlations were generally lower for girls. Part of the sex difference in delinquency was related to higher levels of parental supervision and a lower level of attachment to delinquent peers reported by girls, as compared with boys. However, there were still gender differences that could not be explained by control variables.

This type of research has been extended by Hagan et al. (1985). Since their work has been discussed at length in Chapters 5 and 6, it will be sufficient here to recall that the theory dealt with socially structured differences in sex roles and that parents were more likely to place controls on the activities of daughters than of sons.

Naffine (1987) has suggested an interesting new line of inquiry that may shed more light on the causes of female criminality. She is critical of the view of control theorists that "it is the stereotypically female qualities (passivity, compliance, dependence) which bond women to the conventional order" (131). She contends that law-abiding women are not simply passive creatures, clinging helplessly to conventional society. Instead, they are, to use Hirschi's description of conforming men, responsible, hardworking, engrossed in conventional activities and people, and perfectly rational in their calculation not to place all of this at risk by engaging in crime. Women are heavily involved in conventional activities, including both work and childrearing, and Naffine suggests their intense involvement in nurturing children provides them with more powerful attachments to the conventional order. While Naffine's thesis is only speculative, it should generate research that will have an impact on future versions of social control theory as well as on our understanding of female criminality.

Issues with Social Control Theory

The evidence we have reviewed in this chapter is generally supportive of control theory—in fact, many observers believe that empirical research provides more support for control theory than for its competitors. However, a number of issues have been raised about the theory that will be addressed in this section.

How Does Control Theory Explain Upper-World Crime?

Control theory has focused on street crime and juvenile delinquency, not on occupational crime committed by high-status adults. In fact, upper-world crime would appear to contradict control theory's emphasis on the role of commitment in preventing crime because high-status people have a great stake in conformity. However, control theory can be used to understand such crime.

In his analysis of the Watergate cover-up in the United States, Hagan (1985, 171–73) provided a control theory of upper-world crime. The Watergate affair took place over a two-year period from 1972 to 1974. It involved the attempt by highly placed U.S. government officials to conceal their involvement in an unsuccessful plot to break into the offices of the Democratic National Committee. Ultimately, these events led to the resignation of President Richard Nixon and to the imprisonment of a number of his senior advisors.

From a control perspective, such illegal events could have been prevented by the belief that such acts were wrong. However, our society has not clearly defined upper-world morality. Politicians and business leaders rarely receive more than token punishments for illegal activities and are more likely to see their behaviour as only technically wrong than to see it as criminal. Transcripts of tapes made by Nixon reveal no concern with morality or ethics. In the absence of moral constraints, "the occurrence of such behaviors will depend largely on the risk and rewards . . . associated with violating public and financial trust" (173). As you will see in Chapter 16, the rewards of upper-world crime are often very great. What, then, about the risks?

> The situational controls operative at the time of the initial Watergate offenses were inadequate. White House aides were able to manipulate funds and personnel for criminal political reasons with little expectation of detection. One reason why there was so little expectation of detection, of course, was that the criminals in this case were people who controlled the institutions of legal control (who could have been better positioned to deviate than those who controlled the FBI, the Justice Department, etc.?). Furthermore, once "caught," punishment became problematic in an atmosphere confused by promiscuous discussions of pardons. The uncertainties surrounding these events emphasize, then, the porous nature of the controls operative in one upperworld setting. (173)

In the next section of this chapter, you will learn that the theory has a message for those who wish to control deviance: monitor behaviour, recognize deviance, and punish deviant behaviour. While these principles are intended as advice for parents raising children, they are also applicable to upper-world crime.

As Hagan tells us: "If there is a message to the policy-minded in the Watergate experience . . . it is that checks and balances on power are crucial. Upperworld vocations, particularly politics and business, often carry with them a freedom to deviate unparalleled in the underworld. As control theory reminds us, unchecked freedom is a criminogenic condition" (173).

Does Everyone Have the Same Motivation to Deviate? The Role of Delinquent Peers

While control theory has been supported by research, critics have noted that a theory should also account for the motivation to deviate. To the control theorist, we would *all* be criminal or delinquent but for the restraints provided by social controls. However, this appears to be only a partial explanation. Several factors may increase the likelihood of deviance among those who lack ties to the conventional order (Box, 1981). We shall consider just one of these here—ties to deviant peers, which have been found to be strongly correlated to delinquency. For example, Sorenson and Brownfield (1995) found that ties to delinquent peers were a better predictor of drug use among Seattle youths than several measures of social control. Thornberry et al. (1993) studied a group of youths in Rochester, New York, and found that these youths were more likely to have committed delinquent acts while they were active members of juvenile gangs than they were either before or after their gang membership.

One way to deal with this is to integrate differential association (see Chapter 12) and control theories. These two theories present conflicting notions about the causation of crime and delinquency. For the differential association theorist, the crucial concept is ties to others; the pure control theorist claims that individuals with no ties to others—not even deviant others—are the most likely to become deviant.

Control theory conceives of an individual's social bond as having only a single dimension, weak to strong. When we incorporate differential association's emphasis on the importance of ties to deviant peers into the theory, however, we should see the social bond as multidimensional: conventional—weak to strong; unconventional—weak to strong. In bringing the two perspectives together, it is proposed that the first step is a weakness in the controls that bind an individual to the conventional system. An individual without these ties does not have to consider the consequences his or her actions will have on institutional and personal relationships. With the person "adrift" in this way (Matza, 1964), delinquency is a possible alternative. We are then faced with the problem of accounting for the motivation to commit acts of crime and delinquency (if we wish to go beyond the control theorists' reliance on natural motivation) and with explaining how one learns the techniques and rationalizations that facilitate deviance.

At least part of the answer to these questions can be found in differential association theory. We can postulate that the adolescent's lack of ties to the conventional order will increase the likelihood of association with deviant peers since the adolescent no longer has anything to lose by such affiliation. These ties will, in turn, increase the probability that the adolescent will be involved in deviance (see Figure 13.1).

FIGURE 13.1 Control-Differential Association Theory

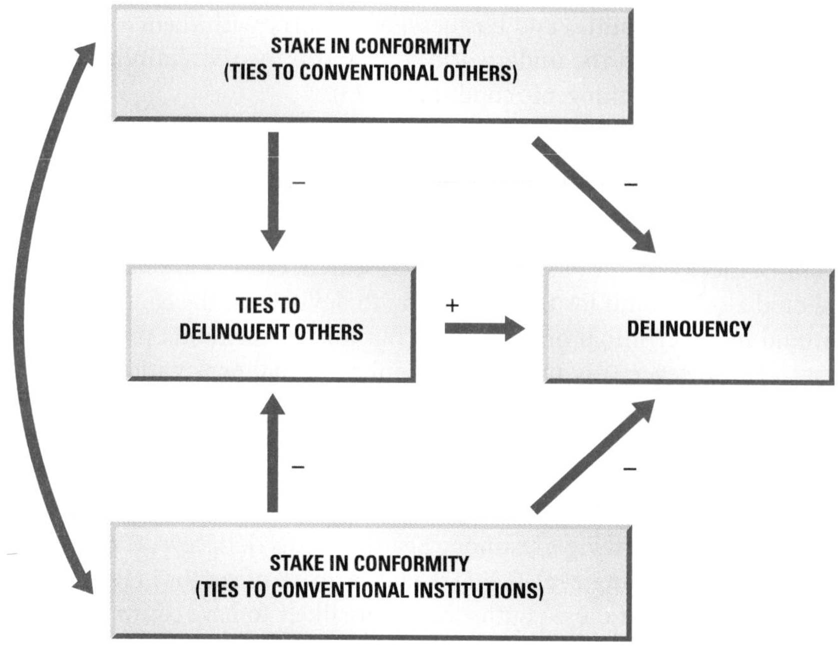

Source: Rick Linden and Cathy Fillmore. (1981). "A Comparative Study of Delinquency Involvement." *Canadian Review of Sociology and Anthropology* 18:343–61.

This extension of control theory explains more of the variation in delinquency than either of its parent theories alone (Linden and Hackler, 1973; Linden and Fillmore, 1981). However, both of these studies utilized cross-sectional data rather than the longitudinal data that are more appropriate to the sequential theory we have proposed. Recently Maume et al. (2005) have used longitudinal data to study the relationship between marriage, delinquent peer attachment, and marijuana use, and their research also supports the integrated theory. They found that desistance from marijuana was influenced by marriage and, to a lesser extent, by a reduction in ties to deviant peers following a person's marriage.

The sequential model proposed here is more consistent with control theory than with Sutherland's differential association. The control–differential association model does not necessarily entail the strong element of normative approval required by Sutherland's cultural deviance perspective. Even if this normative approval is not a factor, delinquency may be fun and profitable and is not disapproved of by the delinquent's peer group. The internal dynamics of the group are such that it would be difficult for a reluctant member not to go along. Several researchers (Short and Strodtbeck, 1965; Velarde, 1978), have found that delinquent boys may try to look "bad" or "tough" in front of the group, even though they may express different views privately, because each believes the others are committed to such values. "An individual delinquent may wonder if or even think that his/her friends are not committed to delinquencies, but he/she can never confront the others to be sure of the degree of commitment they have" (Velarde, 1978).

Other criminologists have also integrated control theory with competing perspectives. The most comprehensive extension of control theory has been carried out by Marc LeBlanc and several colleagues at the University of Montreal (LeBlanc, 1997; LeBlanc and Tremblay, 1985; Caplan and LeBlanc, 1985; Fréchette and LeBlanc, 1985). In addition to control and differential association variables, these researchers have also included the variables of external social control, personality traits, and the structural conditions of sex and social status. Most recently, Hardwick (2002) has shown that personality variables such as childhood temperament and self-control interact with social bonding variables and other social variables to produce delinquent and criminal behaviour. Because none of the theories you have studied in this text provides a complete explanation of crime and delinquency, it is likely that this integrative work will continue.

Is Control Theory a Conservative Theory of Crime?

There is no simple explanation of crime, but different perspectives can help to explain it. In the absence of any consensus, some criminologists have taken an ideological approach in which theories are accepted or rejected on the basis of whether they are sufficiently conservative or radical. Robert Bohm has observed that "political and value preferences, ideology, empiricism, and positivism . . . stand in the way of any unity between traditional and radical criminologists" (1987, 327). For example, some conflict criminologists have been very critical of theories of crime, such as control theory, which do not focus on the political and economic structures that produce crime.

To some degree, this critique is a fair one. Control theorists have emphasized people's immediate environment, and from the time of Shaw and McKay until recently, have not considered the political and economic structures of their communities. However, these critics mistakenly reject the theory rather than recognize the fact that control variables can be incorporated within a structural perspective. For example, Shaw and McKay pointed out the importance of community variables in the development of social bonds. The ways in which control theory explains individual differences in criminal involvement are compatible with any number of structural theories, including conflict theories, and provide the link between society and individual that structural theories lack.

While control theory focuses on an individual's relationships with social institutions, structural factors condition these relationships. Although crime involves the behaviour of individuals, it has its origins in the social structure in which these individuals live. Lynch and Groves point out that "persons are more likely to conform when they stand to gain by doing so. But to make conformity attractive, society must do something for the individual; it must provide minimal satisfaction for both human and culturally defined needs. Social structures that provide for these needs are more likely to encourage conformity" (1989, 78).

If social institutions work together to encourage and to support conforming behaviour, rates of deviance should be low. However, if these institutions do not work together and if individuals and groups are alienated from their society's institutions, rates of deviance will be high. Consider the problems faced by Canada's Aboriginal people. They have far less power and fewer resources than

WWW
"Manitoba Aboriginal Justice Inquiry 1991 Summary"
www.ajic.mb.ca/volume.html

FOCUS

BOX 13.1 The Mushuau Innu of Davis Inlet

On several occasions over the past 15 years, Canadians have been saddened by television images of young children sniffing gas in Davis Inlet in Labrador. The first incident was described by a team of researchers who studied the Mushuau Innu of Davis Inlet:

> One day in February 1992, six children in the Innu community of Davis Inlet in Labrador burned to death in a house fire. Almost a year later, six of their friends, depressed at the approaching anniversary of the tragedy and convinced that the ghost of a young Innu was telling them that they should end their own lives, barricaded themselves in an unheated shack in temperatures of −40 and tried to kill themselves by sniffing petrol. The local Innu policeman reached them in time and, with great presence of mind, videotaped their responses as they were removed to safety. Then, to show the world the horrors of life in Utshimassits (as the Innu call Davis Inlet), he passed the tape on to a television station.
>
> Over the next few days, his graphic pictures of wild-eyed children hurling themselves against the wall and screaming "Leave me alone! I want to die!" shocked Canada and made Utshimassits, after years of official neglect, the focus of national and international media attention. Journalists and television crews suddenly converged on Davis Inlet from all over North American and Europe to try to discover how a supposedly "modern" and enlightened country like Canada could produce such a vision of desolation and despair. They were scandalized by what they found.
>
> Utshimassits is a community living in almost unimaginable squalor and disarray. Rows of battered wooden shacks, looking more like a Third World refugee camp than a 'western' village, line unmade roads that for most of the year are no more than sheets of dirty ice. Virtually none of the houses — except for a handful belonging to non-Innu professionals like the priest, schoolteachers and nurses—have running water or mains drainage. Sewage is simply thrown onto the ground, where it is eaten by dogs or trampled by the gangs who roam the settlement. . . . These conditions are reflected in the appalling health and mortality statistics for Davis Inlet, where family breakdown, sexual abuse, drunkenness and alcohol-related disease, violence, accidents and self-harm have become endemic. (Samson et al., 1999, 6)

These problems did not exist prior to European colonization. Thus Samson and his colleagues conclude that the cultural and social disintegration of the Mushuau Innu has been caused by their past and current relationship with Canadian society. While many Aboriginal communities in Canada are healthy and thriving, particularly those that own valuable land and resources, many others share at least some of the problems of the Innu (see Shkilnyk, 1985).

How did colonialism cause the decline of a healthy people? The Mushuau Innu were successful nomadic hunters. However, colonial governments did not consider hunting to be an economically viable way of life and effectively forced the Innu to give up their centuries-old way of life and life in sedentary communities:

> After Newfoundland and Labrador joined Confederation in 1949, the federal government began to build new houses for the Innu. The houses were small (750 square feet), built close together and had few amenities. While equipped with tubs, toilets and sinks, the houses had no water or sewage services, few pieces of furniture and a single power outlet. Many families used hot plates or diesel fuel to start fires to warm their homes (Innu Nation, 1995). Gradually, the residents of Davis Inlet found themselves slipping out of touch with their traditional migratory way of life while having difficulty fully embracing a "modern" sedentary lifestyle. (Burns, 2006, 68)

After their initial settlement, the entire community was moved three times. The first move, in 1948, was a forced migration from Davis Inlet to

FOCUS

BOX 13.1 The Mushuau Innu of Davis Inlet *(Continued)*

Nutak, which was over 300 kilometres away (Denov and Campbell, 2002). The Innu were moved without their consent to a location far away from their traditional hunting grounds, ostensibly to improve their economic prospects. The band did not accept the move and walked back to their former location. In 1967, they were moved to an island on Davis Inlet, again for economic reasons. However, as with the earlier move, there were no economic opportunities on the island and they were isolated during the spring thaw and fall freeze-up when the island was accessible only by air. Their new houses lacked running water and sewer systems and quickly degenerated to Third World standards (Denov and Campbell, 2002). While the move was intended to help the Innu become more economically self-sufficient, there were few jobs in the area. Finally, in 2002–03, they were moved back to the mainland to a new community at Natuashish. The latest move was done with the consent of the Innu, and for the first time they were consulted about the structure of their new community.

In addition to the shift from a nomadic to a sedentary life, the horrible living conditions, and the disruption caused by the moves of the community, other factors have contributed to the problems of the Innu. Missionaries tried to replace traditional spiritual practices with Christianity. Massive hydroelectric projects, mining, and logging have destroyed part of the natural environment of the Innu without their approval and without compensation. All these changes have disrupted the cultural continuity of the people of Davis Inlet by altering their relationship with their traditional lands:

". . . land is of central importance to aboriginal culture, identity and well-being. Aboriginal people have a unique relationship with the land that guides their daily life and provides them with great meaning. . . . Isolating people from their traditional habitat, therefore, breaks the spiritual relationship with the land that exists within many aboriginal communities" (Denov and Campbell, 2002, 24). The Innu have been cut off from their ties to the land and their knowledge of how to survive on the land is not relevant to their sedentary lifestyle. "Displacement among the Innu can thus be seen as part of a painful process of dispossession and alienation of their society from the land and from the cultural and spiritual roots it nurtures, ultimately leading to a sense of powerlessness" (Denov and Campbell, 2002, 24).

This discontinuity (what Durkheim would call anomie) is particularly acute among young people. The school system is a major source of their problems. Schooling interfered with learning traditional skills and yet did not prepare them for mainstream jobs. Because the schools did not use the Innu language, many young people could not communicate with their Innu-speaking elders. Several generations of Innu have been cast adrift between two cultures and prepared for what Samson has called "a way of life that does not exist. . . . Many Innu have gradually become neither hunters nor 'modern' Canadians" (2003, 13) and as a result have strikingly high rates of suicide, gas sniffing, alcoholism, interpersonal violence, and vandalism. In the words of one young Innu: "We were taught in school to be doctors, nurses, store managers, teachers, that's what we were taught in school, to be one of those people. I was never taught to be a hunter or to learn about my culture, I was never taught like that, it was always the white culture that was focused in the school. . . . I see a lot of kids that have failed in school. . . They feel so ashamed about not learning to speak English and then they will start drinking, they will drink and drink, and a lot of those people are still drinking because they are ashamed, they don't know how to write, how to speak the language" (Samson et al., 1999, 22).

In looking at the tragic story of the Mushuau Innu, we can see the complementarity of the control and conflict approaches. At one level, members of groups with high rates of crime and other deviance typically lack the social bonds that might tie them to the social order. However, if we ask why the strength of social bonds is less among those who, like many Aboriginal people, are forced to live on the margins of society, we must turn to the work of conflict theorists and their analyses of the political and economic forces that have created the poverty, powerlessness, and inequality that shape their lives.

other Canadians. They must cope with systems of education and religion imposed from outside that are not compatible with Aboriginal customs and traditions. Forced attendance at residential schools and forced adoption outside the community have destroyed family ties, and crippling rates of unemployment mean no job ties. School curricula that are irrelevant to Aboriginal students weaken children's attachment to their schools. Many Aboriginal Canadians face daily encounters with racism. They must submit to government policies that have not allowed Aboriginal communities to achieve effective institutional integration. Under these conditions, strong social bonds are very difficult to develop, and the high rates of crime described in Chapter 5 can be expected. Manitoba's Aboriginal Justice Inquiry concluded: "From our review of the information available to us, including the nature of the crimes committed by aboriginal people, and after hearing the hundreds of submissions presented to us in the course of our hearings, we believe that the relatively high rates of crime among aboriginal people are a result of the despair, dependency, anger, frustration, and sense of injustice prevalent in aboriginal communities, stemming from the cultural and community breakdown that has occurred over the past century" (Hamilton and Sinclair, 1991, 91). The impact of structural conditions on social bonds and on rates of crime and other deviance is illustrated in the discussion of life in Davis Inlet, Labrador, in Box 13.1. By incorporating control elements within a structural perspective, the example demonstrates the complementarity of the control and conflict approaches.

Policy Implications of Control Theory

Early control theorists were strongly aware of the policy implications of their work. For example, Shaw established and worked for many years with the Chicago Area Project, trying to strengthen community ties in a slum area. To illustrate some of the possible uses to which the findings of research done from a social control perspective might be put, we can consider the role of the family and the school in delinquency prevention.

Policy Implications—The Family

Research has shown the importance of family relationships in the causation of delinquency. However, we are a long way from knowing what to do about this problem. How can we strengthen the family and make sure that parents love and care for their children? If anything, we are living in an era in which the family is becoming less stable as an institution.

While many of the problems in the family relationships of delinquents may require structural solutions, some small beginnings have been made in the task of trying to re-establish a bond between parent and child. One of the best examples of this is the work of Gerald Patterson and his colleagues at the Oregon Social Learning Center.

Oregon Social Learning Center
www.oslc.org/

Based on his experiences treating several hundred families of antisocial children and on detailed observation of interaction patterns within these families,

Patterson concluded that since "antisocial acts that are not punished tend to persist" (1980, 89), the key to changing the behaviour of these troublesome children was to punish their misdeeds. Hirschi observed that "this conclusion may come as no surprise to those millions of parents who have spent years talking firmly to their children, yelling and screaming at them, spanking them, grounding them, cutting off their allowances, and in general doing whatever they could think of to get the little bastards to behave; but it is exceedingly rare among social scientists, especially those who deal with crime and delinquency" (1983, 53).

While this approach might seem disturbingly authoritarian to some, Patterson is, in fact, merely advocating techniques used by families that are successful in avoiding delinquency. You will recall that parental supervision and disciplinary practices were strongly related to delinquent behaviour. Patterson has determined that the key aspects of this process involve several steps that have been summarized as "(1) monitor the child's behavior; (2) recognize deviant behavior when it occurs; and (3) punish such behavior" (in Hirschi, 1983, 55). In a properly functioning family, the parents understand this process, and the system is activated by the bonds of affection and caring between parent and child. The key is not just punishment—many parents of problem children were found to punish them more often and more harshly than did the parents of normal children. However, the parents of problem children did not know *how* to punish their children, and punishment actually made things worse. Discipline was used, but it was erratic and unpredictable and not directed specifically at the child's misbehaviour. "The failure of parents to use reasonable reinforcements contingent on steadily monitored behaviour places the child in a situation in which he comes to understand that he cannot control by his own actions what happens to him" (Wilson, 1983, 53). As a result, the children in effect train their parents (and others, such as teachers) to accept their misbehaviour.

Working with the families of pre-adolescent problem children, Patterson has taught parents how to shape their children's behaviour by using non-physical punishments (such as time-outs), by rewarding good conduct, and by interacting more positively as a family. This training process is often long and difficult. Many of the parents did not like their children, did not identify with the role of parent, and refused to recognize that their children were deviant (Patterson, 1980). Many were trying to cope with difficult economic and family situations as well as with the problems created by their antisocial children, and they resisted help.

Despite these problems, the results suggest that this program has potential. One evaluation showed that stealing was reduced from an average of 0.83 incidents per week to 0.07 incidents per week after the parent training program. The treatment effects persisted for six months, but within one year, stealing rates had gone back to pretreatment levels (Moore et al., 1979). This suggests that parental retraining may be necessary. Longer-term results were obtained with children diagnosed as aggressive, with whom program effects lasted longer than 12 months. The program also had a positive impact on siblings, indicating that the parenting skills of the parents had improved.

Richard Tremblay and his colleagues (1991) have evaluated a program similar to Patterson's in which preventive treatment was provided for disruptive

FOCUS

BOX 13.2 Parenting Delinquent Youths

"When I met him, he was six and a half years of age. There was nothing about his appearance that identified him as the boy who had set the record." The words are those of Gerald R. Patterson, a family therapist at the Oregon Social Learning Center in Eugene. The "record" to which he referred was the frequency—measured with painstaking care by the Learning Center's staff—with which Don, a small boy, displayed rotten behavior. Nearly four times a *minute* while in his home, Don would whine, yell, disobey, hit, or shove. When he was not at home, telephone calls from teachers and merchants would mark his progress through the neighborhood: "He left school two hours early, stole candy from a store, and appropriated a toy from a neighborhood child."

Don had "a sleazy look about him," Patterson wrote, "like a postcard carried too long in a hip pocket." His violent outbursts were frightening; any simple request or minor provocation would trigger obscene shouts, attacks on other children, or assaults on the furniture. His mother was tired, depressed, and nearly desperate as a result of coping unaided with this monster—no baby-sitter would take on the job of minding Don, whatever the pay. She nevertheless persevered, changing his wet sheets, bathing and dressing him, even feeding him, all the while talking to him in tones that vacillated between cajolery and scolding, murmurs and shouts. When her seemingly bottomless patience was at last at an end, she would threaten or hit him with a stick. That produced only temporary compliance. When the father was home, things were not much different. The shouting and fighting between Don and his younger brother continued, occasionally punctuated by the father slapping both children.

Children like Don are the youthful precursors not only of difficult teenagers, but sometimes of delinquents and adult criminals. The progression from violent, dishonest youngster to violent, dishonest teenager is not automatic, but it is common.

Source: James Q. Wilson. (1983). "Raising Kids." *The Atlantic* (October), p. 45.

kindergarten boys in a low-income community in Montreal. The treatment combined teaching social skills to the boys with training their parents to be consistent and constructive toward their children. Two years after the treatment, the treated boys reported less fighting and less theft than comparison groups of boys who did not receive the treatment. The classroom behaviour of the treated boys also showed improvement.

Programs like these may be too expensive to be implemented on a broad scale. However, given the high concentration of criminality in a relatively small proportion of families, they do have some potential for reducing crime rates. The demonstration that improved parenting can have an impact on misbehaviour should encourage those advocating structural changes (e.g., less unemployment) that are aimed at least in part at providing more family stability and programs (e.g., foster care) that provide substitute parents for children. The results also suggest that research should be done on other methods of increasing parenting skills, such as providing training in high schools and for the parents of newborn children.

The Schools and Social Policy

In their assessment of the role of the school in delinquency, Schafer and Polk suggest that the school fails in two ways: "The school not only fails to offset initial handicaps of lower-income and minority group children, but actively contributes to education failure and deterioration. If this is true, the school itself becomes an important active force in the generation of delinquency insofar as it is linked to failure" (1967, 236).

Research suggests that some schools and some teachers are better than others in helping children to function both academically and behaviourally. Rutter and Giller (1984) have suggested a number of factors differentiating good and bad schools. These include the standards and values set and maintained by the school; the degree to which students are allowed to participate in decision making; school and class size; staff turnover; and the degree of concentration of intellectually and socially disadvantaged pupils. Each of these factors has rather obvious policy implications.

A number of studies have looked at the impact of the teacher–student relationship on students' behaviour. British researchers (Hargreaves et al., 1975) have found that some teachers provoked deviance, while others were able to get students to cooperate. Failure to get along with teachers may weaken an adolescent's commitment to school. It may also affect grades by leading teachers to make negative judgments about a youth's abilities and character. Thus the classroom process may help to weaken an adolescent's attachment and commitment to the school.

Others have proposed changes in the type of curriculum and in the manner in which it is taught. Weis and Hawkins (1979) have recommended a greater use of programs such as performance-based education, which involves establishing learning goals for each student and developing individually paced programs with rewards for improvement. They also suggest the use of cross-age tutoring and other ways of involving students in the operation of the school to enhance their level of commitment.

Other research (Elliott, 1966; LeBlanc, 1983) suggests the importance of mechanisms for ensuring a transition from school to work, especially among those students who are not going on to university.

Schools must also ensure that their curriculum is relevant to the lives of their students. This was not achieved by the system of residential schools that has served Aboriginal youths in the Canadian North. A child who grows up in a small settlement on the Arctic coast will be flown south to Yellowknife or another southern point for high school. Besides being cut off from family and community, the student is educated into a way of life that is very different from that which exists in the home village. As a result, students may no longer fit into their home communities, but, at the same time, they are not completely acculturated into southern ways (Brody, 1975). Increasing rates of crime and other deviance among people who lack strong community ties can be consequences of this system.

It will not be easy to make changes in the schools to reduce the likelihood that students will get involved in delinquency and subsequent adult criminality.

TABLE 13.1 Social Control Theories

Theory	*Theorists*	*Key Elements*
Social disorganization theories	Durkheim Thrasher, Shaw and McKay	Deviance will be highest in disorganized communities that lack social controls.
Early social control theories	Reiss, Nye	Stresses the importance of personal controls, particularly those provided by the family.
Social bond theory	Hirschi	The four elements of the social bond: attachment, commitment, involvement, and belief.
General theory of crime	Gottfredson Hirschi	Individuals with low self-control have a greater propensity to commit crimes when they have the opportunity to do so.
Control-differential association theory	Linden	Lack of ties to the conventional order will increase the likelihood of association with deviant peers. These ties will, in turn, increase the probability of delinquency involvement.

It is hard to make significant changes in large institutions that must satisfy a number of different interest groups. Even if we could make changes quickly, we could not be certain that they would have the desired effect. For example, programs that separate misbehaving students may have unintended consequences. Schafer and Polk (1967) discuss a program in which students with academic and behaviour problems were placed in special classes and provided with individual instruction by specially selected teachers. The outcome of the program was negative—placement in a class with other poorly motivated students compounded their problems and further alienated them from the mainstream of school life. The students may also have suffered from being labelled as troublemakers.

Despite these potential problems, there is merit in trying to work within the school system. The research that has been done represents a promising beginning, but what is needed is a program in which the lessons learned are systematically applied to the schools on an experimental basis. The types of reforms that would be most likely to succeed would be beneficial to all students and possibly reduce delinquency as well.

Summary

- Rather than asking "Why do some people break the law?" social control theorists ask "Why don't we all do it?" The answer to this question lies in the processes that bind people to conventional society.
- Early theorists, including Thrasher and Shaw and McKay, looked at community-level controls. Disorganized communities that did not provide meaningful employment to residents and did not have strong families, schools, and churches could not provide adequate social controls and would have high rates of crime and other types of deviance.

- Later social control theories focused on the social bonds of individuals. Travis Hirschi described four interrelated aspects of the social bond that constrain our behaviour: attachment, commitment, involvement, and belief.
- Research on social control theory has pointed to the importance of the family and the school in restraining involvement in delinquency. While less research has been done with adults, it suggests that stable employment and a cohesive marriage are important factors.
- Among the criticisms of social control theory are these: it does not adequately explain white-collar crime; it does not account for the motivation to deviate; it is too individualistic; and it is too conservative.
- Recent theoretical work has returned to the social disorganization tradition and has once again linked societal and community factors to individual-level bonds.

QUESTIONS FOR CRITICAL THINKING

1. How could you apply the principles of social control theory to reduce the amount of white-collar and corporate crime in Canada?
2. Discuss three of the criticisms that have been made of social control theory. How would you defend the theory against these criticisms?
3. Several of the theorists discussed in this chapter have looked at the relationship between the community and crime. Starting with the example of the tragic situation in Davis Inlet, discuss some of the government policies that have led to high rates of crime and other types of deviance among Canada's Aboriginal people.
4. Based on your knowledge of social control theory, what changes would you make to the public school system to help reduce delinquency?

NET WORK

In 1998, the Canadian government established a $100-million fund to support the Aboriginal Head Start program. The program is intended to help reserve communities meet the educational, emotional, social, health, and nutritional needs of children under the age of six. Some early childhood education programs have proven very successful in reducing rates of crime and delinquency. You can find out more about Head Start at **www.acf.dhhs.gov/programs/hsb/**.

Using some of the evaluations you will find on this link, do the following exercises:

1. What has been the impact of Head Start programs on delinquency and crime? Are they a cost-effective way of reducing crime?
2. The most effective early childhood education program is the Perry Preschool program. Go to www.highscope.org/Content.asp?ContentId=219

What lessons can those running Head Start programs learn from the Perry Preschool program?

3. How important do you think it is to involve parents in Head Start programs? Does the research show that programs involving parents are more effective than those based only in the schools?

KEY TERMS

attachment; pg. 401
belief; pg. 402
commitment; pg. 402
ecological fallacy; pg. 399
independent variable; pg. 399
individualistic; pg. 408
involvement; pg. 402
social bond; pg. 398
social control theory; pg. 397

SUGGESTED READING

Gottfredson, Michael R., and Travis Hirschi. (1990). *A General Theory of Crime.* Stanford, Conn.: Stanford University Press. An extension of Hirschi's earlier work on social control theory, which includes an extensive discussion of the relationship between self-control and crime.

Hagan, John. (1994). *Crime and Disrepute.* Thousand Oaks, Calif.: Pine Forge Press. This book sets out Hagan's sociology of crime and disrepute showing the relationship between crime and the growing disparities of income and wealth. The book also describes the globalization of white-collar crime and provides a critique of the contemporary American justice system.

Hirschi, Travis. (1969). *Causes of Delinquency.* Berkeley: University of California Press. The classic statement of contemporary social control theory. Hirschi explains the theory and tests it against its major competitors.

Shkilnyk, Anastasia M. (1985). *A Poison Stronger Than Love: The Destruction of an Ojibwa Community.* New Haven, Conn.: Yale University Press. The book is a portrait of a community in trouble. It provides a graphic account of the social problems that affect a community after its social institutions have been destroyed.

Thrasher, Frederic M. (1963). *The Gang.* Chicago: University of Chicago Press. First published in 1927, this book remains the classic study of urban gang delinquency.

BIBLIOGRAPHY

Albrecht, Stan I., Bruce A. Chadwick, and David S. Alcorn. (1977). "Religiosity and Deviance: Application of an Attitude-Behavior Contingent Consistency Model." *Journal for the Scientific Study of Religion* 16:263–74.

Anderson, Elijah. (1994). "The Code of the Streets." *The Atlantic Monthly* (May):81–94.

Aronson, Elliot. (1984). *The Social Animal.* New York: W. H. Freeman.

Arum, Richard, and Irenee R. Beattie. (1999). "High School Experience and the Risk of Adult Incarceration." *Criminology* 37(3):515–36.

Biron, Louise, and Marc LeBlanc. "Family and Delinquency." Unpublished paper, Université de Montréal.

Bohm, Robert. (1987). "Comment on 'Traditional Contributions to Radical Criminology' by Groves and Sampson." *Journal of Research in Crime and Delinquency* 24 (November):324–31.

Box, Steven. (1971). *Deviance, Reality and Society*. London: Holt, Rinehart and Winston.

———. (1981). *Deviance, Reality and Society* (2nd ed.). London: Holt, Rinehart and Winston.

Brody, Hugh. (1975). *The People's Land*. Markham, Ont.: Penguin Books.

Burns, Ausra. (2006). "Moving and Moving Forward: Mushuau Innu Relocation from Davis Inlet to Natuashish." *Acadiensis* 2(Spring):64-84.

Caplan, Aaron. (1977). "Attachment to Parents and Delinquency." Paper presented at the annual meeting of the Canadian Sociology and Anthropology Association, Fredericton, N.B.

Caplan, Aaron, and Marc LeBlanc. (1985). "A Cross-Cultural Verification of a Social Control Theory." *International Journal of Comparative and Applied Criminal Justice* 9(2):123–38.

Chambliss, William. (1973). "The Saints and the Roughnecks." *Society* 11:24–31.

Denov, Myriam, and Kathryn Campbell. (2002). "Casualties of Aboriginal Displacement in Canada; Children at Risk among the Innu of Labrador." *Refuge* 20(2): 21–33.

Durkheim, Émile. (1951). *Suicide*. Translated by John A. Spaulding and George Simpson. New York: Free Press.

Elifson, Kirk W., David M. Petersen, and C. Kirk Hadaway. (1983). "Religiosity and Delinquency: A Contextual Analysis." *Criminology* 21:505–27.

Elliott, Delbert S. (1966). "Delinquency, School Attendance and Dropout." *Social Problems* 13 (Winter):307–14.

Engstad, Peter A. (1975). "Environmental Opportunities and the Ecology of Crime." In Robert A. Silverman and James J. Teevan (eds.), *Crime in Canadian Society* (pp. 193–211). Toronto: Butterworths.

Fischer, Donald G. (1980). *Family Relationship Variables and Programs Influencing Juvenile Delinquency*. Ottawa: Ministry of the Solicitor General.

Fréchette, M., and Marc LeBlanc. (1985). *Des délinquantes: émergence et développement*. Chicoutimi: Gaëtan Morin.

Glueck, Sheldon, and Eleanor Glueck. (1950). *Unraveling Juvenile Delinquency*. Cambridge, Mass.: Harvard University Press.

Gomme, Ian. (1985). "Predictors of Status and Criminal Offences Among Male and Female Delinquency in an Ontario Community." *Canadian Journal of Criminology* 26:313–23.

Gottfredson, Michael R., and Travis Hirschi. (1990). *A General Theory of Crime*. Stanford, Conn.: Stanford University Press.

Gove, Walter R., and Robert D. Crutchfield. (1982). "The Family and Juvenile Delinquency." *The Sociological Quarterly* 23:301–19.

Hagan, John. (1985). *Modern Criminology: Crime, Criminal Behavior and Its Control*. New York: McGraw-Hill.

Hagan, John, A. R. Gillis, and John Simpson. (1985). "The Class Structure of Gender and Delinquency: Toward a Power-Control Theory of Common Delinquent Behavior." *American Journal of Sociology* 90:1151–78.

Hagan, John, and Bill McCarthy. (1997). *Mean Streets: Youth Crime and Homelessness*. Cambridge: Cambridge University Press.

Hamilton, A. C., and C. M. Sinclair. (1991). *Report of the Aboriginal Justice Inquiry of Manitoba*. Vol. 1. Winnipeg: Queen's Printer.

Hardwick, Kelly. (2002). *Unravelling "Crime in the Making": Re-examining the Role of Informal Social Control in the Genesis and Stability of Delinquency and Crime*. Unpublished Ph.D. Thesis. University of Calgary.

Hargreaves, David H. (1967). *Social Relations in a Secondary School*. London: Routledge and Kegan Paul.

Hargreaves, David H., Stephen K. Hester, and Frank J. Mellor. (1975). *Deviance in Classrooms*. London: Routledge and Kegan Paul.

Higgins, Paul C., and Gary L. Albrecht. (1977). "Hellfire and Delinquency Revisited." *Social Forces* 55:952–58.

Hirschi, Travis. (1969). *Causes of Delinquency*. Berkeley: University of California Press.

———. (1983). "Crime and the Family." In James Q. Wilson (ed.), *Crime and Public Policy* (pp. 53–68). San Francisco: ICS Press.

Hirschi, Travis, and Rodney Stark. (1969). "Hellfire and Delinquency." *Social Problems* 17:202-13.

Keane, Carl, Paul S. Maxim, and James J. Teevan. (1993). "Drinking and Driving, Self-control and Gender: Testing a General Theory of Crime." *Journal of Research in Crime and Delinquency* 30:30–46.

Kornhauser, Ruth Rosner. (1978). *Social Sources of Delinquency*. Chicago: University of Chicago Press.

Kupfer, George. (1966). "Middle Class Delinquency in a Canadian City." Unpublished Ph.D. dissertation, Department of Sociology, University of Washington.

LaGrange, Theresa, and Robert Silverman. (1999). "Low Self-Control and Opportunity: Testing the General Theory of Crime as an Explanation for Gender Differences in Delinquency." *Criminology* 37(1):41–72.

LeBlanc, Marc. (1983). "Delinquency as an Epiphenomenon of Adolescence." In Raymond R. Corrado, Marc LeBlanc, and Jean Trepanier (eds.), *Current Issues in Juvenile Justice* (pp. 31–48). Toronto: Butterworths.

———. (1997). "A Generic Control Theory of the Criminal Phenomenon." In Terence P. Thornberry (ed.), *Developmental Theories of Crime and Delinquency* (pp. 215–85). New Brunswick, N.J.: Transaction Publishers.

LeBlanc, Marc, Marc Ouimet, and Richard Tremblay. (1988). "An Integrative Control Theory of Delinquent Behavior: A Validation 1976–1985." *Psychiatry* 51:164–76.

LeBlanc, Marc, and Richard Tremblay. (1985). "An Integrative Control Theory of Delinquent Behavior: A Validation 1976–1985." Paper presented at the annual meeting of the American Society of Criminology, San Diego.

Linden, Eric. (1974). "Interpersonal Ties and Delinquent Behavior." Unpublished Ph.D. dissertation, University of Washington.

Linden, Rick, and Raymond Currie. (1977). "Religiosity and Drug Use: A Test of Social Control Theory." *Canadian Journal of Criminology and Corrections* 19:346–55.

Linden, Rick, and Cathy Fillmore. (1981). "A Comparative Study of Delinquency Involvement." *Canadian Review of Sociology and Anthropology* 18:343–61.

Linden, Rick, and James C. Hackler. (1973). "Affective Ties and Delinquency." *Pacific Sociological Review* 16:27–46.

Lynch, Michael, and W. Byron Groves. (1989). *A Primer in Radical Criminology* (2nd ed.). Albany, N.Y.: Harrow and Heston.

Matza, David. (1964). *Delinquency and Drift*. New York: Wiley.

Maume, Michael, Graham Ousey, and Kevin Beaver. 2005. "Cutting the Grass: A Reexamination of the Link between Marital Attachment, Delinquent Peers and Desistance from Marijuana Use." *Journal of Quantitative Criminology* 21 (March): 27–53.

Moore, D. R., B. P. Chamberlain, and L. Mukai. (1979). "Children at Risk for Delinquency: A Follow-up Comparison of Aggressive Children and Children Who Steal." *Journal of Abnormal Child Psychology* 7:345–55.

Naffine, Ngaire. (1987). *Female Crime: The Construction of Women in Criminology*. Sydney: Allen and Unwin.

Nye, F. Ivan. (1958). *Family Relationships and Delinquent Behavior*. New York: Wiley.

Patterson, G. R. (1980). "Children Who Steal." In Travis Hirschi and Michael Gottfredson (eds.), *Understanding Crime: Current Theory and Research*. Beverly Hills, Calif.: Sage.

Polk, Kenneth, and F. Lynn Richmond. (1972). "Those Who Fail." In Kenneth Polk and Walter E. Schafer (eds.), *Schools and Delinquency* (pp. 55–69). Englewood Cliffs, N.J.: Prentice Hall.

Polk, Kenneth, and Walter E. Schafer. (1972). *Schools and Delinquency*. Englewood Cliffs, N.J.: Prentice Hall.

Pratt, Travis, and Francis T. Cullen. (2000). "The Empirical Status of Gottfredson and Hirschi's General Theory of Crime: A Meta-Analysis." *Criminology* 38(3):501–34.

Reiss, Albert J., Jr. (1951). "Delinquency as the Failure of Personal and Social Controls." *American Sociological Review* 16:196–207.

Rothman, David J. (1971). *The Discovery of the Asylum*. Boston: Little, Brown and Company.

Rutter, Michael, and Henri Giller. (1984). *Juvenile Delinquency: Trends and Perspectives*. New York: The Guilford Press.

Sampson, Robert J., and John H. Laub. (1993). *Crime in the Making: Pathways and Turning Points Through Life*. Cambridge, Mass.: Harvard University Press.

Samson, Colin. (2003). *A Way of Life That Does not Exist: Canada and the Extinguishment of the Innu*. London: Verso.

Samson, Colin, James Wilson, and Jonathan Mazower. (1999). *Canada's Tibet: The Killing of the Innu*. London: Survival.

Schafer, Walter E., and Kenneth Polk. (1967). "Delinquency and the Schools." In *The President's Commission on Law Enforcement and Administration of Justice, Task Force Report: Juvenile Delinquency and Crime* (pp. 222–77). Washington, D.C.: U.S. Government Printing Office.

Simons, Ronald, L.Chyi-In Wu, Kuei-Hsui Lin, Leslie Gordon, and Rand D. Conger. (2000). "A Cross-Cultural Examination of the Link Between Corporal Punishment and Adolescent Antisocial Behavior." *Criminology* 38:47–80.

Shkilnyk, Anastasia M. (1985). *A Poison Stronger Than Love: The Destruction of an Ojibwa Community*. New Haven, Conn.: Yale University Press.

Short, James, Jr., and Fred Strodtbeck. (1965). *Group Process and Gang Delinquency*. Chicago: University of Chicago Press.

Sorenson, Ann Marie, and David Brownfield. (1995). "Adolescent Drug Use and a General Theory of Crime: An Analysis of a Theoretical Integration." *Canadian Journal of Criminology* 37:19–37.

Sprott, Jane. (2004). "The Development of Early Delinquency: Can Classroom and School Climates Make a Difference?" *Canadian Journal of Criminology and Criminal Justice* 46:553–72.

Stark, Rodney, Daniel P. Doyle, and Lori Kent. (1980). "Rediscovering Moral Communities: Church Membership and Crime." In Travis Hirschi and Michael Gottfredson (eds.), *Understanding Crime: Current Theory and Research* (pp. 43–52). Beverly Hills, Calif.: Sage.

———. (1982). "Religion and Delinquency: The Ecology of a 'Lost' Relationship." *Journal of Research in Crime and Delinquency* 19:4–24.

Statistics Canada. (1998). "National Longitudinal Study of Children and Youth." *The Daily* (October 28).

Steinmetz, Suzanne K., and Murray A. Straus. (1980). "The Family as a Cradle of Violence." In Delos H. Kelly (ed.), *Criminal Behavior* (pp. 130–42). New York: St. Martin's Press.

Thornberry, Terence P., Marvin D. Krohn, Alan J. Lizotte, and Deborah Chard-Wierschem. (1993). "The Role of Juvenile Gangs in Facilitating Delinquent Behavior." *Journal of Research in Crime and Delinquency* 30:55–87.

Thrasher, Frederic M. (1963). *The Gang.* Chicago: University of Chicago Press.

Tremblay, Richard E., Joan McCord, Helene Boileau, Pierre Charlebois, Claude Gagnon, Marc LeBlanc, and Serge Larivee. (1991). "Can Disruptive Boys Be Helped to Become Competent?" *Psychiatry* 54:148–61.

Velarde, Albert J. (1978). "Do Delinquents Really Drift?" *British Journal of Criminology* 18.

Weis, Joseph G., and J. David Hawkins. (1979). *Preventing Delinquency: The Social Development Approach.* Seattle: Center for Law and Justice, University of Washington.

West, D. J. (1982). *Delinquency: Its Roots, Careers, and Prospects.* London: Heinemann.

West, D. J., and D. P. Farrington. (1973). *Who Becomes Delinquent?* London: Heinemann.

———. (1977). *The Delinquent Way of Life.* London: Heinemann.

West, W. Gordon. (1984). *Young Offenders and the State: A Canadian Perspective on Delinquency.* Toronto: Butterworths.

Wilson, Harriet. (1980). "Parental Supervision: A Neglected Aspect of Delinquency." *British Journal of Criminology* 20:30–39.

Wilson, James Q. (1983). "Raising Kids." *The Atlantic Monthly*:45–56.

PART III

Patterns of Criminal Behaviour

Many different types of behaviour are illegal but they vary widely in seriousness. Murder, for instance, is in a different category than not putting enough change in a parking meter. In Part 3, we look at some of the kinds of misconduct that frequently occur in Canada.

When the average citizen thinks of crime, the images that most commonly come to mind are the so-called street crimes—robbery, assault, break and enter, and so on. These are also the kinds of offences that occupy most of the time and attention of the criminal justice system. In Chapter 14, many of these crimes are discussed. The routine activities approach, an attempt to account for patterns of criminal victimization, is also discussed using data collected on these conventional crimes.

Chapter 15 looks at the "organized" criminals who are in the business of providing access to illegal goods and services. Chapter 16, the final chapter in the text, looks at crimes committed by "respectable" people: many of our leading citizens are white-collar criminals, and many of our largest businesses are corporate offenders. This chapter makes the important point that the power we give to those in positions of authority and ownership in modern corporations may encourage them to become involved in illegal activities that cause a great deal of social harm.

In Part 2, it was noted that the classification of theories into different categories is somewhat artificial. However, some classification system is useful in organizing the work of different theorists. In Part 3, different patterns of crime are described and they too are classified into types, though here as well there is overlap between the different categories.

Conventional or "Street" Crime

14

Daniel J. Koenig

FORMERLY OF UNIVERSITY OF VICTORIA

Rick Linden

UNIVERSITY OF MANITOBA

When most people think of crime, they have in mind offences such as murder, robbery, break and enter, assault, sexual assault, theft, and motor vehicle theft. These offences are sometimes called "street crimes" or **conventional crimes** to distinguish them from other categories of crime such as organized crime and white-collar and corporate crime.

conventional crime
Those traditional, illegal behaviours that most people think of as crime. Nonconventional crime may be organized crime, white-collar crime, political crime, etc.

Each of these conventional crimes involves an immediate and clearly identifiable victim and often results in a complaint to the police. In fact, much of the caseload of the police is made up of these offences. Most of the media reports about crime also focus on conventional crimes. In this chapter, police statistics and victimization survey data will be used to describe patterns of conventional crimes. Because these offences affect the lives of so many of us, it is important to learn as much about them as we can.

This chapter will also introduce you to a new perspective on crime that has its roots in the rational choice theory discussed in Chapter 7. In Part 2 of this text, you read about a variety of theories that try to explain why people break the law. These theories focused on the motivations of offenders. The theory introduced in this chapter, the routine activities approach to crime, looks instead at specific criminal events and so focuses more on the crimes than on the criminals. This approach to crime tells us that crime will not occur unless there is a motivated offender, a suitable target, and ineffective guardianship of that target. The theory does not compete with the others, as without motivated offenders no crimes would occur, but it looks at criminal events from a different perspective. As you will learn later in this chapter, the routine activities approach has been particularly useful in helping develop ways of preventing crime.

Learning Objectives

After reading this chapter, you should be able to

- Discuss the routine activities approach to crime and understand the role of the motivated offender, suitable target, and ineffective guardianship in any criminal event.
- Know who is most likely to be victimized by different types of conventional crime.

- Describe where the most important types of conventional crime are most likely to occur.
- Understand the legal definitions of each of the different types of conventional crime.
- Discuss how you can use your knowledge of causes and patterns of crime to develop prevention programs.

The Routine Activities Approach

After reading Part 2 of this book, you know that there are many competing explanations of why offenders commit crimes. In recent decades, many criminologists have also asked why one person is more likely than another to be *victimized* by crime. This has led to a search for patterns of crime, such as when and where it occurs, the immediate circumstances of crime, and the relationship between victims and offenders.

Hindelang et al. (1978) used this approach to develop what they called the **lifestyle/exposure theory** to account for personal victimization. This theory states that the lifestyle and routine activities of people place them in social settings with higher or lower risks of being victimized. For example, people who spend a lot of time in public places at night have a higher risk of being robbed than do people who spend most of their evenings at home. Similarly, people whose lifestyles put them in frequent contact with people who commit crimes are more likely to be victimized than those whose time is spent with law-abiding companions. For example, as you will see in Chapter 15, members of organized crime gangs likely have higher rates of homicide victimization than most other Canadians. They have chosen a lifestyle in which violence is used as a means of settling disputes and in which factors like the competition for the exclusive right to sell drugs in particular areas ensure that there will be many disputes to settle. While much of gang violence has been *between* competing gangs, it is also used as a means of settling accounts *within* gangs. Similarly, in several Canadian cities the police are currently investigating what appear to be the serial killings of prostitutes. The working conditions of street prostitutes, as well as their association with the drug culture, place them at very high risk of victimization.

lifestyle/exposure theory
A theory of victimization that acknowledges that not everyone has the same lifestyle and that some lifestyles expose people to more risks than others do. If you go to bed early, you are less at risk of robbery or assault than if you like to visit the bars several nights a week. Similar to *routine activities approach*.

Cohen and Felson (1979) made the assumptions of lifestyle exposure theory more explicit when they formulated the **routine activities approach** to crime. This approach begins with the observation that three factors must be present simultaneously for a crime to occur:

routine activities approach
A simple extension of the *lifestyle/exposure theory*, this approach assumes that crimes are the expected outcomes of routine activities and changing social patterns. For example, those with more property can expect to be the victims of property crime more often than those with less property. Young people who like to hang out in the evenings are more likely to be victims than are those who go to organized activities or remain at home to study.

- A *motivated offender*. Unless someone wants to commit a crime, it will not take place. Most of the theories of criminal behaviour that you studied in earlier chapters try to explain why some people are motivated to commit crimes.
- A *suitable target*. A theft will not take place unless there is property to steal and an assault cannot happen unless there is someone to attack.

- A *lack of guardianship* of that target. If a target is well-guarded, it will be much less likely to be victimized. **Effective guardianship** refers to actions such as removing ignition keys from a car and locking the door (by motorists), drawing a steel mesh curtain overnight across glass display windows of jewellery (by shopkeepers), and taking evening walks on busy, well-lit streets rather than walking alone in an isolated park or down a dark alley (by pedestrians).

effective guardianship
An aspect of the *routine activities approach* to understanding crime victimization that argues that three key factors are required for crime to happen: a motivated offender, a suitable target, and ineffective guardianship of that target. Effective guardianship would include having locks on bikes, security lights in the backyard, or putting goods in the trunk of the car. Measures like this can reduce the risk of being victimized.

Changes in any of these factors can lead to increases or decreases in crime. Thus even without additional motivated offenders, an increase in the number, the value, or the accessibility of suitable targets can result in increases in crime. For example, 30 years ago, electronic equipment was bulky, heavy, and difficult to carry. Today, potential criminals have the opportunity to steal laptop computers, portable CD and MP3 players, DVD players, automobile CD players, and other valuable electronics that weigh very little and that are easy to conceal. Cohen and Felson predicted that unless small, attractive items are carefully protected, theft rates will increase as these items become more common, and their data support this view. Less suitable targets are less frequently stolen. For example, Cohen and Felson observed that not many people steal refrigerators and washing machines because these are worth far less per pound than electronic equipment.

An example of the importance of suitable targets was the discovery by young people in Winnipeg and Regina that some models of Chrysler vehicles built in the 1990s were very easy to steal. As you will read later in this chapter, this discovery helped to fuel a boom in joyriding that saw rates of motor vehicle theft soar in both cities (Anderson and Linden, 2002). On the other hand, vehicles that are protected by electronic ignition immobilizers that make them virtually impossible to start without a key are very rarely stolen unless the owners leave their keys in the car. In another example, as the value of all types of metal rose dramatically in the middle of this decade, thieves started stealing things made of metal such as manhole covers, aluminum billboards and road signs, and stainless steel tanker trailers. In Prince George, B.C., thieves even tried to steal the head of a bronze statue of Terry Fox in order to recover the metal. People in New Brunswick and British Columbia have died because they cut into live power lines in an attempt to steal the copper wire.

To illustrate how changes in guardianship affect crime rates, Cohen and Felson showed that as daytime occupancy of homes decreased because of factors such as the increased employment of women outside the home and increases in the length of vacations, there was a substantial increase in daytime residential burglaries at the same time as the proportion of commercial burglaries declined. Thus besides explaining patterns of victimization, routine activities theory also offers a way of understanding changes in crime patterns over time. Crime trends are seen as the expected outcomes of routine activities and changing social patterns. Cohen and Felson take offender motivation as a given. Their objective was to demonstrate the relationship between crime trends and changes in **target suitability** and effective guardianship.

target suitability
Because of their vulnerability, some potential crime targets are more attractive than others. A home that is unlit, has shrubs blocking a view of the front door, and has no alarm system will be seen as a more suitable target than a well-protected home.

The research findings to be reported in this chapter are consistent with a routine activities approach. Before looking at specific types of crimes in detail, we will provide a brief overview of some of these findings.

Who

For most crimes of violence, including assault, robbery, and homicide, rates of both victimization and offending are highest among younger people, males, and those who spend a large number of evenings in activities away from the home. Statistics Canada's 2004 General Social Survey (GSS) revealed that the rate of violent victimization among those 15 to 24 was about twice that of those 35 to 44 and about 20 times that of those 65 and over (Gannon and Mihorean, 2005).

Income was also related to victimization. For example, theft of household property was much higher among respondents living in households with incomes in excess of $60 000 than in households with incomes under $15 000 per year. However, violent victimizations were 50 percent higher in the lowest household income category ($0 to $14 999) than in households with higher income. Marital status was another important variable. Rates of personal victimization for single or separated/divorced respondents were much higher than rates for those who were married or living common law. Aboriginal people had much higher rates of victimization than other Canadians, while the rates for visible minorities were slightly lower than average. Rates of violent victimization were about 2.5 times higher among people who identified themselves as gays and lesbians than among other Canadians (Gannon and Mihorean, 2005).

GSS results from 1993 also indicated that alcohol consumption and illicit drug use increase one's likelihood of being a victim of crime. Those who consumed 14 or more alcoholic drinks per week experienced twice as many incidents of personal victimization during the preceding 12 months as did non-drinkers (Wright, 1995). In addition, 26 percent of illicit drug users experienced a personal victimization, in contrast to only 10 percent of those who did not use any illicit substances during the preceding 12 months. For each type of violent victimization, a majority of victims thought that the crime was due to their own or someone else's alcohol or drug use. These findings are consistent with the fact that the western provinces, which have the highest rates of crime in Canada (see Chapter 5), also have the highest rates of alcohol and drug use problems (Veidhuizen et al., 2007).

If people with certain lifestyles are going to be more exposed to criminal victimization as they go about their routine activities, the probability of becoming a victim of crime will not be randomly distributed. People who have been victimized once, therefore, should have a higher probability of being victimized a second time than people who have not been victimized at all. These probabilities will change, of course, if the typical lifestyle and exposure of the already victimized person changes to reduce the risk of subsequent victimization.

Repeated victimization of the same victim (or victim's household), by both the same type of crime and different crimes, has been observed frequently in surveys both in the United States (U.S. Dept. of Justice, 1974a, 1974b; Hindelang et al., 1978; Sparks, 1981) and in Canada (Koenig, 1977; Sacco and Johnson, 1990). The 2004 GSS was no exception. Of those who stated that they had been victimized by a crime during the preceding 12 months, 40 percent reported that they had been victimized more than once. Such patterns provide support for the routine activities theory, as does the finding that the risk of violent victimization was significantly higher for those who participated in more evening activities outside the home.

Where

Thirty-eight percent of violent incidents reported in the 2004 GSS took place in bars, restaurants, malls, schools, hospitals, arenas, public transit, and so forth; 29 percent took place in or around a private residence (most often the victim's home); and about one-quarter took place in other public places such as on the street, in parks, or in parking garages (Gannon and Mihorean, 2005).

When

Personal victimizations were most likely to occur during the summer months (Wright, 1995). With longer days and warmer weather, people are more likely to place themselves at risk as suitable targets by being outdoors, or to have windows and doors open if they are at home. Another peak for some crimes occurs in December, when people are likely to increase their interpersonal contacts during the Christmas season by shopping, visiting, or going to parties.

The **incidence** per hour of most crimes is highest in the evening, particularly from 6 p.m. to midnight. These are the hours when effective guardianship is minimized: as darkness reduces visibility, and fewer people go about their routine activities in public places so there are fewer people to observe what is happening.

incidence
Incidence tells us the frequency of new occurrences of some event during a particular time period. For example, there were 605 criminal homicides in Canada in 2006.

Critique of Routine Activities Theory

Some criminologists have criticized routine activities theory on the grounds that it is not sufficiently theoretical. Because it takes the motivated offender as a given, it does not add to our understanding of the causes of criminality. Critics such as Jock Young maintain that ultimately crime can be controlled only if its origins are understood. If crime is due to injustice and inequality, these conditions must be corrected before crime can really be reduced (Young, n.d.).

To its critics, routine activities theory is too closely linked with an "administrative criminology" that has led to fragmented state actions to reduce crime that neglect the underlying social conditions that lead to crime. According to Young, raising the certainty of punishment, increasing the protection of targets, and imposing greater surveillance can make the world seem even more unfair to people who have been marginalized and already feel alienated. People do not necessarily behave as rationally as the routine activities theorists assume. A person does not "merely weigh up the sanctions positive and negative before him like the puppets believed by classical economists, he assesses these in terms of deprivation experienced in the past. As it is, inequalities in the economic sphere are reinforced and confirmed for a large number of the working class by the inequalities of justice in the streets and courts" (Young, n.d., 4).

However, Young does not totally reject the preventive measures proposed by routine activities theorists. He is aware that crime is an important quality of life issue for people in poor, high-crime neighbourhoods and recognizes that situational measures can help deal with this problem. He feels that "it is one thing to criticize the new administrative criminology for solely focusing on environmental control measures, it is another to discard these measures entirely. As I have agreed, if we are to understand the problem of crime we need to pay attention to both sides of the equation: causation and control" (Young, n.d., 59).

While Young does not reject situational crime prevention, he is correct in recognizing that it is not a complete solution to crime:

> the control of crime involves interventions on all levels: on the social causes of crime, on social control exercised by the community and the formal agencies, and on the situation of the victim. Furthermore, that social causation is given the highest priority, whereas formal agencies, such as the police, have a vital role, yet one which has in the conventional literature been greatly exaggerated. It is not the "Thin Blue Line", but the social bricks and mortar of civil society which are the major bulwark against crime. Good jobs with a discernable future, housing [projects] that tenants can be proud of, community facilities which enhance a sense of cohesion and belonging, a reduction in unfair income inequalities, all create a society which is more cohesive and less criminogenic. (Young, 1997, n.p.)

The use of criminological knowledge to prevent crime will be discussed more extensively later in this chapter. For now, in Box 14.1 you can read about the experiences of Stephen Schneider, a researcher who studied crime prevention in Vancouver's Downtown Eastside, one of Canada's most crime-ridden neighbourhoods. Schneider's experience in this community led him to a conclusion very similar to that of Young—that crime prevention programs eventually must be addressed through "a comprehensive strategy that ultimately is based upon a reinvigoration of civil society, the centrality of the local community in social problem solving, and the empowerment and participation of those who are in the most need. This means that a greater share of public resources and power be allocated to the local level and to the poorest communities in particular" (Schneider, 2007, 306). The work of Young and Schneider has led them to conclusions that are very different from politicians who falsely promise us that a bit of tinkering with the justice system will quickly end most of our street crime problems and their work helps to place the solutions suggested by routine activities theory in their proper perspective. These solutions will help, but they cannot overcome the serious social problems that are the root causes of crime.

Patterns of Specific Crimes

"Patterns of Crime" Malaspina University-College
web.mala.bc.ca/crim/stats/

To what extent is the routine activities approach to understanding crime consistent with known facts about patterns of specific types of crime? To answer that question, we will examine several types of conventional crimes that are commonplace or a source of public concern.

FOCUS

BOX 14.1 Vancouver's Downtown Eastside

The Downtown Eastside of Vancouver has one of Canada's highest urban crime rates. The area is extremely poor, many of the people are transient, and many of its residents have serious crime and addictions problems. Researcher Stephen Schneider describes his experiences with street crime during a period when he was doing fieldwork in the area for a study of community crime prevention.

"When first I moved to East Vancouver's Mount Pleasant neighbourhood to conduct participant observation research into crime and community safety for my doctoral dissertation, I had little idea how much 'participation' this research would actually entail. In the space of eight months, a bicycle was stolen from the balcony of my third-floor flat, the door of my apartment was jimmied open as part of an attempted break and enter, and there were two separate thefts from my car (both occurring in the 'secure' underground parking lot of the apartment complex). The final act was the torching of my building by a young arsonist who deliberately started a bonfire on the patio of his ground floor apartment that quickly spread throughout the wood-framed building, sending me scurrying into the night in my slippers with a draft of my dissertation protectively clutched to my chest. . . . Thinking my luck could not get any worse that night, I went in search of food, oblivious to my attire of sweatpants, a worn hockey jersey, and green corduroy slippers—the clothes I was wearing when I fled my burning building. My disheveled appearance did not go unnoticed by the legion of drug dealers who hounded me on every block, offering a smorgasbord of illicit pharmaceuticals" (2007, ix).

Murder and Other Criminal Homicides

Legal Meanings of Types of Homicide

Homicide is a legal term having somewhat different meanings in different countries and in different eras. In Canada, it is a general category that refers to an act in which the life of one person is lost at the hands of another. In Canada, criminal homicide refers to first- and second-degree murder, manslaughter, and infanticide.

Criminal homicide is classified as murder when the person who causes death means to cause death or means to cause bodily harm likely to result in death. Murder is first degree when the killing is planned and deliberate; when the victim is employed in certain occupations concerned with the preservation and maintenance of public order (for example, public police officer or correctional worker) and acting in that capacity; or when the killing occurs in connection with certain specific offences such as sexual assault, kidnapping, or hijacking. Other murders are second-degree murders. Manslaughter is a type of criminal homicide in which one person kills another in the heat of passion caused by a sudden provocation or when a person is too intoxicated to form intent. Infanticide is an archaic category of criminal homicide applying to deaths of newborn children caused by women who are in a disturbed state of mind as a consequence of giving birth.

Police statistics probably underestimate the true number of criminal homicides. Some missing persons, particularly young women and children, likely have been murdered. However, if neither a body nor other evidence of a murder is discovered, it is difficult to conclude that a specific missing person has been murdered. This has been tragically illustrated in the case of women who have gone missing from Vancouver's Downtown Eastside. This community has high rates of poverty along with serious problems of addiction, HIV/AIDS, and prostitution. Over a period of 25 years, a large number of women, most of whom were drug addicts working as prostitutes, disappeared and only recently has it been established that many of these women were murdered. For many years, the Vancouver police refused to treat the disappearances as possible homicide cases. The cases were difficult ones because many of the women were transients and some were not officially reported as being missing until years after they had last been seen on the street. However, in 2001 the police finally responded to pressure from relatives and friends of the missing women. They put together a list of 54 women and began to conduct an intensive investigation of their disappearances. This work finally resulted in the arrest of Robert Pickton, who has so far been charged with 26 murders. In 2007 he was convicted for six of these killings and may face trial for the rest later.

Incidence

What do police statistics tell us about homicide? There were 605 criminal homicides in Canada during 2006 (Silver, 2007). Criminal homicide should not be trivialized, but the risk should be kept in perspective. For example, there are six times more suicide deaths and five times more deaths from motor vehicle accidents than from homicides (Statistics Canada, 2003). During 2006, homicides accounted for much less than 1 percent of all violent crimes.

The Canadian criminal homicide rate for 2006 of 1.9 homicides per 100 000 population was down significantly from the peak of 3.0 recorded in 1975. Canada's homicide rate is somewhat higher than the rates in France and England (both 1.4) but far below that in the United States, where the homicide rate is about three times the Canadian rate.

In Canada, homicide rates are highest in the western provinces and in the territories and lowest in the Atlantic provinces. Among the provinces, Saskatchewan (4.1) had the highest rate followed by Manitoba (3.3) and Alberta (2.8). Prince Edward Island had only 1 murder in 2006, giving it a rate of 0.7 (Silver, 2007).

Pattern

Nationally, shootings (34 percent) and stabbings (30 percent) were the most frequent methods used to commit homicide in 2005 (Dauvergne and Li, 2006). The next most common methods were beatings (22 percent) and strangulation (7 percent). The proportion of homicides committed by firearms is lower in Canada than in the United States but higher than in the United Kingdom.

During 2005, 61 percent of Canadian homicides for which the location was known took place in a private residence, most commonly in the victim's residence (Dauvergne and Li, 2006). The location of Canadian homicides is consistent with the fact that homicide victims and their assailants usually know each other and that homicide is frequently the culmination of an argument that occurs as people go about their routine daily activities.

Contrary to impressions sometimes conveyed by news media and entertainment programs that focus on mass murder, 95 percent of homicide incidents reported to the police during 2005 involved a lone victim. Multiple-victim homicides were most commonly family related (Dauvergne and Li, 2006).

Gang-related homicides increased from 72 in 2004 to 107 in 2005, and have been steadily increasing since the early 1990s (Dauvergne and Li, 2006) when they averaged 22 a year—a figure that nearly tripled to 58 by 2000–01. Ontario has the most gang-related homicides (31) but there were also significant numbers in Alberta (26), Quebec (24), and British Columbia (16).

Victims

Most Canadian victims knew their assailants. In 2005, 33 percent of victims were killed by an immediate family member or relative, and 49 percent were killed by some other acquaintance. Only 18 percent were killed by a stranger.

Males are significantly more likely to be murdered than females (Dauvergne and Li, 2006). In 2005, 73 percent of homicide victims were male and 27 percent were female. Victims were relatively young. The peak age for male victims was 25 to 29 years and for female victims was 30 to 39 (see Figure 14.1). Seventeen percent of victims were Aboriginal people, who make up 3 percent of the Canadian population.

The differences in the age distribution between male and female homicide victims reflects differences in the nature of their victimization. Female victims are much more likely than male victims to be killed by an intimate partner. In 2005, 58 percent of female victims and 10 percent of male victims were killed by an intimate partner. By contrast, male victims were much more likely than women to be killed by strangers or by casual acquaintances. Thirty-three children under 12 were murdered in 2005; 59 percent were killed by a parent. Contrary to what you might assume from the extensive media coverage of child victims, only one child was killed by a stranger.

Over half the victims had consumed alcohol and/or drugs prior to the offence (Dauvergne and Li, 2006). Male victims were more likely than females to have used an intoxicant, a fact that is again consistent with the different patterns of victimization.

Suspects

Males made up 90 percent of those charged. Eighty-nine percent of those charged were adults, and only 11 percent were young offenders. The majority of accused were between the ages of 18 and 29, and the percentage of killers drops off sharply past 40 years of age. Twenty-three percent of suspects were Aboriginal. A study of homicide in Toronto showed that homicide rates for blacks were over four times higher than the overall homicide rate for that city (Gartner and Thompson, 2004). In recent years many of these Toronto homicides have occurred among poor young black youths as in the case discussed in Box 14.2.

FIGURE 14.1 Victim Homicide Rates by Age Group and Sex, Canada, 2005

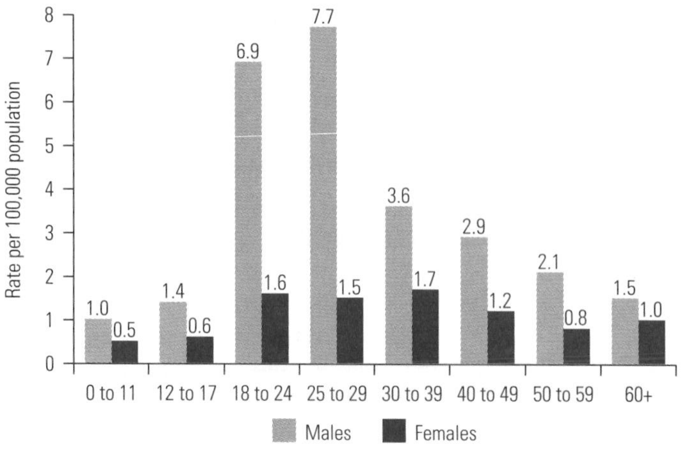

Source: Statistics Canada, Canadian Centre for Justice Statistics, Homicide Survey.

Alcohol and drugs play a significant role in homicide; nearly three-quarters of the accused were known to have consumed alcohol, drugs, or both at the time of the offence. The role played by alcohol is tragically illustrated by a recent case in which a 38-year-old Winnipeg man kicked a drinking companion to death because he got "bored" at a Valentine's Day drinking party (McIntyre, 2003). After his wife, daughter, and a family friend passed out, the man began kicking the friend in the head to try to wake her up. He continued to alternate between beating the woman and drinking throughout the rest of the evening until she finally died. The accused, who had a lengthy record of violence, pleaded guilty to manslaughter for the offence and received a sentence of five years in prison.

The overall pattern of Canadian homicide is consistent with a lifestyle/exposure, routine activities orientation. Homicide is often the final word in an argument arising between people who know each other and who are engaged in their normal activities. Even the location of homicide (most often the victim's own home) is where most people spend the greatest proportion of their time. Finally, both homicide suspects and victims are disproportionately young, male, and unmarried—characteristics that are associated with less structured lifestyles and higher levels of physical aggression.

The different patterns of male and female victimization are also consistent with this approach. Those who have the highest risk of victimization are young males who are users of alcohol and/or drugs and who are living lifestyles that include involvement with gangs or other criminal activities; all of these things expose them to a higher risk of homicide. Females are most likely to be killed by an intimate partner (or former partner); this is consistent with the more even age distribution of female victims (see Figure 14.1).

The Dynamics of Homicide

The routine activities perspective helps us understand the patterns of homicide and other crimes, but it does not tell us much about how and why these crimes actually occur. Why do some encounters between people result in homicide?

What are the dynamics of situations that result in the death of one or more of the persons involved? Following the interactionist approach (see Chapter 12), researchers have interviewed violent offenders and analyzed the accounts of homicides contained in police files to achieve a better understanding of the dynamics of the criminal event. David Luckenbill (1977) has examined the typical roles played by offenders, victims, and bystanders in situations that resulted in homicide. He looked at the social context in which homicides occurred and concluded that many of them were confrontations that escalated into "character contests"; that is, violence became a means of saving face for the individuals. These events tended to occur during leisure time while individuals were engaged in unstructured activities such as spending time at home with others, drinking in a tavern, or just hanging out on the street. In most cases, the individuals involved were with family, friends, or acquaintances. Often the victim and the offender had previous histories of disputes that led them to anticipate or even to seek out confrontation with the others involved. In some cases, one of the parties insulted the other either intentionally or inadvertently; in others, there was a refusal to carry out some requested action. This was interpreted as being offensive and rather than ignoring the insult or leaving the scene, the offended individual responded aggressively in order to save face. In some cases, other people at the scene either encouraged a violent response or did nothing to try to defuse the situation. These points are illustrated in one of Luckenbill's examples:

> The offender, victim, and three friends were driving in the country drinking beer and wine. At one point the victim started laughing at the offender's car which he, the victim, scratched a week earlier. The offender asked the victim why he was laughing. The victim responded that the offender's car looked like junk. The offender stopped the car and all got out. The offender asked the victim to repeat his statement. When the victim reiterated his characterization of the car, the offender struck the victim, knocking him to the ground. (1977, 181)

What is striking about this incident is just how trivial it was. A joking remark made among friends ultimately led to the death of one young man and a long prison sentence for another. This case is not like most of those you see on television or in movies or read about in the headlines, but it is more representative of the "typical" Canadian homicide than are the cases of Paul Bernardo or Clifford Olson that get so much of the media's attention. For a similar example of the circumstances surrounding a homicide, Box 14.2 describes the events leading to a recent murder in Toronto.

These cases illustrate the complexity of explaining criminal behaviour. At one level, the routine activities approach tells us that young males who engage in alcohol or drug use and other high-risk behaviours and who regularly associate with people with criminal records are more likely to be victimized by violent crime than other people. At another level, the interactionist perspective represented by Luckenbill allows us to understand the dynamics of the criminal event from the perspective of those involved. However, we still need to know more to adequately explain homicide and other serious crimes. We need to understand why some people respond violently, while others avoid such situations, walk away from them when they develop, or defuse the hostility with a friendly or

FOCUS

BOX 14.2 Doesn't Take a Lot to Get You Killed

TORONTO—When prosecutor Laura Bird began speaking yesterday, it sounded for all the world as though she had borrowed her story line from a violent video game or, in another age, a Bugs Bunny and Road Runner cartoon.

Hers was a tale of characters with childish nicknames who seethed with preening masculinity, nourished ridiculous grievances over months and whose ludicrous code of behaviour is redolent with more ritual gestures than a formal audience with royalty.

It would have been comic, but Ms. Bird was describing the real lives of real people and the terrible and senseless death of one of them.

Wayne Anthony Reid, a young black man, died in a hail of bullets on June 15 last year and, Ms. Bird said, he died because the friend he was with that night had, almost a full year earlier, either not nodded in respect, or not nodded vigorously enough, or not been seen to nod, in deference to a friend of the man now alleged to have killed him.

The prosecutor was delivering her opening address, designed to give jurors an overview of her case, in the second-degree murder trial of Leon Patrick Boswell. . . .

The victim, the alleged killer and their two friends either lived or grew up in the notorious housing complexes of the Jamestown area of northwest Toronto, a neighbourhood where territory is so clearly marked that, Ms. Bird said, "When you walked through the turf of someone else you were expected to acknowledge the other person in order to show your respect for them. Failure to nod, or otherwise hail them up, could be considered to be extremely disrespectful."

And, she said, "Disrespect was taken seriously and could be expected to result in violent retaliation" such that a code of silence envelops the whole community, "preventing citizens from coming forward to report crimes for fear that they may be next in line at the morgue."

Ms. Bird's story began in the late summer of the year 2000 when, she said, Mr. Reid's friend, one Shaun Sharp (known as Cookie), who was friends with various groups of young men in the area, was walking through Jamestown with a pal from another group.

This was the turf of Mr. Boswell's friend, Jermaine Grant (known as J-Bug), and Cookie apparently claims to have nodded at J-Bug, but J-Bug did not see him do it, and "confronted Cookie and accused him of disrespecting him." Cookie tried to explain that he had nodded, but J-Bug didn't believe him, and this marked the beginning of their bad relationship, and, allegedly, also of Mr. Reid's end.

The next time the two men saw one another, Ms. Bird said, "J-Bug demanded Cookie go around the corner with him, allegedly to talk," but Cookie "believed that J-Bug was carrying a gun, and that he would be killed" if he went. So he refused, which J-Bug purportedly took as a further disrespect.

By this time, Cookie was terrified of J-Bug, and the next time he spotted him, from inside a pool hall, he actually looked for a place to hide in case J-Bug "started shooting" through the windows.

"After this," Ms. Bird said, "the word on the street was that J-Bug was looking for Cookie. Cookie believed absolutely that J-Bug wanted him dead."

conciliatory remark. We also need to understand the social circumstances in which people learn to define violence as a way of resolving problems and why homicide is more prevalent among some segments of society than others. Can you think of some reasons why "respect" was so important to the young men involved in the homicide case discussed in this section? The theories you studied in Chapters 8 to 13 all shed some light on the complex issues involved in explaining homicide and other violent offences.

FOCUS

BOX 14.2 Doesn't Take a Lot to Get You Killed *(Continued)*

On June 15, Cookie was hanging around with Mr. Reid, who was now living in Mississauga but visiting his old neighbourhood of Jamestown that day.

The two men passed what was for them—neither were "model citizens," Ms. Bird said, and both were "low-level drug dealers"—a normal day. They had an impromptu party at Cookie's house, stood around talking in the sun, playing dominoes and drinking beer until it ran out, whereupon they headed out to buy more. En route, they spotted a girl, flirted with her and thought they had made arrangements to meet up with her later—and incurred the wrath of Mr. Reid's girlfriend, who spotted them with the girl and then chased them through the complex for a while.

Then they went back to Cookie's house, where Mr. Reid's girlfriend blasted him, partied some more until, later that evening, they headed out to try to meet up with the girl they had met. After a false start at finding her place, they decided to try Jamestown, what Ms. Bird called "the worst decision of their lives."

Cookie had barely parked the car when they were confronted by J-Bug and his friend, Mr. Boswell (known as Bluenose).

Now, at 26, Mr. Reid was older than the others, and had even known J-Bug as a child, and promptly stepped in, telling J-Bug and Mr. Roswell they were not going to bother Cookie so long as he was around. Cookie and Mr. Reid walked away, and as they did, Cookie told Mr. Reid that J-Bug wanted to kill him.

J-Bug and Mr. Boswell, now, were furious at being left, so they followed the two men, again confronting them. Again, Mr. Reid told them not to trouble Cookie, and again they walked away, highly disrespectful, Ms. Bird said, "particularly since all of this was happening on the turf of J-Bug" and Mr. Boswell.

Mr. Reid and Cookie continued on, through the narrow paths that wind through the complex of townhouses, and arrived at the home of the girl they had met hours earlier. They talked to her a while on the doorstep, she went in to answer the phone, and they were standing there when J-Bug and Mr. Boswell again showed up.

"They now proceeded to stare down" Cookie and Mr. Reid, Ms. Bird said. Mr. Reid was frustrated by now, and again told them to leave Cookie alone, but where J-Bug appeared to respect Mr. Reid, Mr. Boswell did not. Mr. Reid approached them, and again said he had been in Jamestown longer than either one of them.

At this point, J-Bug tried to lead Mr. Boswell away, Ms. Bird said, but Mr. Boswell "pulled out his revolver and fired five shots into the right side of Mr. Reid's body."

In the panic that followed, Cookie ran into the girl's house, Mr. Reid, bleeding, managing to follow him there. Cookie dragged him inside, shouted for someone to call 911 and then did so himself, but Mr. Reid died of his injuries in hospital some short time later. As Ms. Bird put it, "The bullets that ripped through his body had simply caused too much damage."

Source: Adapted from Christie Blatchford. (November 27, 2002). "Doesn't Take a Lot to Get You Killed," in *National Post*. Reprinted with permission of *National Post*.

Assaultive Behaviours

The patterns of assault are very similar to those of homicide, so we will not go through them in detail in this section but limit the discussion to considering how changes in citizen reporting practices can affect rates of reported assault. We will also consider two important issues related to family violence—child abuse and elder abuse.

The Increased Incidence of Assault in the 1980s and 1990s

Assaults increased rather dramatically through the 1980s and early 1990s, but have remained relatively stable since 2000. It is likely that some of this increase in police-reported assault is attributable to increased reporting of assaults to the police rather than to an increase in assaultive behaviour. Many behaviours that are now reported to the police and treated as crimes were in the past considered to be private or non-criminal matters. Domestic assaults, child abuse, schoolyard fights, sibling violence, and elder abuse are examples (as are date rape, child molesting, and unwanted touching, in the case of sexual assaults). Zero-tolerance policies, which require the police to lay charges in domestic violence cases, are responsible for much of the increase in recorded assaults (Linden, 1994). These policies mean that incidents that would not previously have been recorded by the police are recorded now and become part of UCR assault statistics.

Family Violence—Child Abuse and Elder Abuse

The most widely discussed type of family violence is domestic assault, which has been discussed in Chapter 6. However, there are several other types of family violence, including violence against children and elder abuse.

Child Abuse

Violence against children has typically been studied more from a child welfare than a criminological perspective. Consequently, past studies have tended to lump together both criminal and non-criminal types of behaviour under the rubric of "child abuse and neglect." In recent years, the issue of parental discipline has been raised by those who feel that physical punishment should not be allowed. While the courts have thus far supported the rights of parents to discipline their children, they have been setting limits on the nature of physical punishment. Box 14.3 discusses the judge's ruling in a case in which parents and their minister insisted that physical punishment of children was required by their religion. In this ruling the judge upheld the rights of the Children's Aid Society to remove the children from their home. In a later ruling, the judge prohibited the parents from using physical punishment. While there is societal consensus that severe forms of child abuse are wrong, there is still much disagreement about whether parents should be able to physically discipline their children.

Elder Abuse

The abuse of elderly people can take place in both domestic and institutional living situations. Moreover, like child abuse, there are many types of abuse that are not necessarily violations of any criminal law. Some types of neglect such as psychological abuse are examples of antisocial behaviours that may not be criminal matters. Others such as physical violence and financial manipulation violate the criminal code.

The 1999 General Social Survey interviewed more than 4000 seniors who were living in private households and asked if they had experienced emotional abuse, financial abuse, and physical and sexual abuse in the previous five years

FOCUS

BOX 14.3 Judge Rules for CAS in Aylmer Spanking Case

A judge says that while the seizure of seven children from their home two years ago for fear they were being spanked was "very traumatic," a child welfare worker did not violate anyone's constitutional rights.

The worker had "reasonable and probable grounds to believe the children were in need of protection," Ontario Court Justice Eleanor Schnall said in written reasons supporting her ruling last October to admit certain evidence in the so-called "spanking case" in Aylmer, Ont.

Michael Menear and Valerie Wise, lawyers for the parents, had argued that evidence gathered by child welfare worker Shelley West was inadmissible because it was gathered in violation of the constitutional rights of their clients.

West "is not to be faulted for taking the action she did," Schnall wrote in reasons dated last Thursday.

"The rights of the parents cannot be elevated to be paramount to the rights of the children," Schnall said.

The parents had also argued that West should not have interviewed the children without their consent.

But Schnall called that "sheer nonsense."

"No community, or society, could reasonably agree with the concept that a parent who sexually abuses or physically mistreats a child should be entitled to give his/her consent to the interviewing, or examination of the child by a member of a Children's Aid Society."...

Family and Children's Services of St. Thomas and Elgin County officials said Schnall's ruling "affirms that the right of children to be protected from abuse and neglect takes precedence over any other procedural rights for parents."

"We are pleased that Ontario's child protection legislation, regulations and accepted practice has not been compromised by the procedural arguments put forward by the parents' lawyers," Steve Bailey, executive director of the agency, said Monday in a release.

The children, devotees of a religious group called the Church of God, were taken kicking and screaming from their home in early July 2001 when child welfare workers, with the assistance of police, seized the children after the mother refused to promise she would stop using objects to discipline them.

The parents insisted they were acting in accordance with Biblical principle when they hit the children with objects, including a broken metal fly swatter described as the "spanking stick."

The children were returned home about three weeks later after their parents agreed, on an interim basis, to refrain from physical discipline and to seek medical care when necessary.

Section 43 of the Criminal Code has allowed spanking in Canada since 1892, but only for the purpose of "correction" and only within the bounds of what it calls "reasonable force."

The courts over the years have interpreted the law—which withstood a constitutional challenge earlier this year—as forbidding the use of inanimate objects such as paddles, sticks or wooden spoons.

Ultimately, Schnall will decide if the children need protection, and if so, what form it should take.

Source: Adapted from Peter Cameron. (March 3, 2002). "Judge Rules for CAS in Aylmer Spanking Case." Reprinted with permission of The Canadian Press.

(Dauvergne, 2003). Seven percent of seniors reported having experienced one of these forms of abuse from an adult child, caregiver, or spouse. Emotional abuse was the most common form reported, followed by financial abuse and physical and sexual abuse. Additional data were obtained from police records for 2000 (Dauvergne, 2003). According to these data, about 25 percent of reported offences were committed by family members. Common assault was the most frequently reported offence committed against elderly victims by family members, followed by uttering threats and more serious levels of assault. Robbery was the most commonly reported crime committed by a non-family member. While rates of victimization for seniors are lower than for the rest of the population, the consequences can be much more severe. For example, seniors may be dependent on their caregivers and unable to readily escape a dangerous or threatening situation. Also, the consequences of victimization may be more serious. A young person who is knocked down by a stranger may get up unharmed, while an older person may be seriously hurt in a similar incident. Similarly, an elderly person who loses money to theft or fraud will not be able to replace the money as easily as a younger person who is still in the labour market.

While lifestyle factors are associated with most types of assault, major exceptions to this generalization are spousal assaults, child abuse, and assaults on the elderly. The home does not appear to be a place of effective guardianship for these victims. This is because so many of these assaults are of a domestic nature, perpetrated by a current or former spouse or parent, or a current or former dependent child who may have easy access both to the home and to the victim. Such assaults can also be quite severe, possibly because of the non-rational, emotional affect that motivates them. However, it is likely that for most Canadians, the home remains a place of relative safety if one considers the rate of assault in various locations *per hour of risk (or exposure).*

Robbery

Like assault, robbery is considered a violent crime. It occurs when there is threatened or actual use of force or of a weapon in conjunction with taking, or attempting to take, something from another person. But robbery is a much rarer crime than assault. Police statistics for 2006 showed 10 percent of all violent crimes were robberies.

Incidence

The police-reported rate of robberies in 2006 was 94 per 100 000 Canadians (Silver, 2007). About half of robberies involve no weapon; weapons other than firearms are more likely to be used in the remainder. The incidence of robbery has been declining and dropped by about 12 percent between 1996 and 2006.

Victims

In the 2004 GSS, males were more likely than females to report being victimized by robbery. Victimization rates among urban residents and those 15 to 24 were also much higher than the average. The experience of being robbed can be a very difficult one. While most robberies do not result in injury, some victims are very seriously injured and most victims suffer some emotional damage. Injuries are more likely if the victim resists the robbery. Over 60 percent of the victims interviewed by Gabor et al. (1987) reported physical symptoms because of the robbery, including chronic nervousness, insomnia, nightmares, headaches, and eating problems as well as psychological symptoms such as fear, distrust, and aggressiveness. In most cases these symptoms lasted seven months or more.

Offenders

Robbery is the only violent crime typically committed by strangers. Janhevich (1998) reported that during 1996, five out of six victims were robbed by strangers. Almost nine out of ten persons charged with robbery in 1997 were males, and three out of eight were young offenders. The median age of female offenders (16) was considerably below that of male offenders (21) (Kong, 1998b).

The robberies depicted in movies such as *Ocean's Thirteen* show highly skilled crews of specialists stealing millions of dollars after months of intensive planning and practice. However, real robberies typically involve young, unsophisticated substance abusers who rarely spend more than a few minutes planning their offences and whose take is at best a few hundred dollars (Desroches, 1995). The typical targets are not banks or casinos, but vulnerable small businesses such as gas bars and convenience stores. Frequently, the victim is just a person who happens to be walking down the street when the robber decides he needs more money. Robberies can be dangerous for both victim and offender, and the chances of being caught and punished are considerably higher than for most other crimes of financial gain. In their study of robberies in Montreal and Quebec City, Gabor et al. (1987) found that in about three-quarters of the cases, the robbers did not try to disguise themselves. Although there were a few large robberies, two-thirds involved $500 or less. The vast majority of cases involved one (41 percent) or two (46 percent) offenders; the average age of offenders was 22 years.

Gabor and his colleagues asked a number of armed robbers about their motivations for committing the offence. Not surprisingly, the principal motives were financial:

> It's the fastest and most direct way to get money. There's no thrill in getting it. It's for the cash, the money that I do it. (Gabor et al., 1987, 63)

However, some robbers also enjoyed the thrill of committing a robbery and the power that the robber had over the victim:

> When I have a gun in my hands, nothing can stop me. It makes me feel important and strong. With a revolver you're somebody.
>
> It's funny to see the expression of people when they have a .38 in their face. Sometimes when I went home at night I thought of it and laughed. I know that it's bad to say that. Maybe I was just fascinated. (Gabor et al., 1987, 63)

No special training or skills are required to commit a robbery, and most robbers appear to underestimate the risks of being caught. Thus, robbers may see the crime as an easy way to accomplish their goals.

Gabor and his colleagues also examined why some of the robbers they interviewed decided to stop committing robberies. Occasional offenders felt that the modest rewards were not worth the long sentences involved or the risk to themselves and to others. Chronic offenders were older and decided to quit because they did not want to spend increasingly longer sentences in jail and because the criminal lifestyle was no longer as attractive as it had been when they were younger. Some of those who gave up robbery completely ended their involvement in crime; others switched to different offences such as fraud and drug trafficking, which they felt were more lucrative and less risky.

Robbery is one of the few crimes in which researchers have been able to study the differences in motivation between male and female offenders. Many different studies have explored the idea that male criminality is a result of men "doing masculinity." That is, they use crime to validate their manhood. Much less is known about the link between gender and criminality for women. Brookman and her colleagues interviewed men and women who had been incarcerated for robbery in England. They concluded that males and females shared several common motivations for committing the offence. A primary motivation was to obtain money for drugs and also to support other aspects of a life focused on partying. Men and women also reported that respect was an important factor. One woman told the researchers that "[violence on the streets] it's not to do with drugs . . . [it's to do with] respect. . . . It's like the clothes you wear, a lot of them [gang members] have been in and out of jail, I think that's why I've got respect, because I've been in and out of jail, survived. If you're a survivor [you do] stupid things like fighting. I got respect when I did that street robbery" (Brookman et al., 2007, 7). However, the women were not as likely as men to use intimidation and the threat of force to carry out their robberies, while the women were more likely to have a weapon particularly when they were robbing male victims: "Due to the social definition of gender and gender abilities in the minds of *both* offender and victim, female physical threats must be backed up with a weapon to be taken seriously" (Brookman et al., 2007, 21). The women were also more likely to target middle-class victims who would be more likely to submit to their threats than would more streetwise victims.

Pattern

Most robberies occur between 6 p.m. and 6 a.m., usually before midnight. Forty-three percent took place on the street (Gannon and Mihorean, 2005). Over half of robbery victims felt that their robbery was related to alcohol or drug use by the accused. Thus it is not surprising that over half of the victims reported that they engaged in 30 or more evening activities outside the home in a typical month. While we must avoid blaming victims, it is apparent that these people's routine activities place them at greater risk of robbery than those who rarely went out in the evening. Box 14.4 discusses how changes in guardianship are affecting bank robberies.

Break and Enter

People sometimes confuse robbery with break and enter (or burglary, as it is also called). The difference between the two is simple. Robbery involves face-to-face contact with the threat of force. Break and enter involves stealth. The typical burglar seeks to avoid all contact with anybody in the residence or building that is being illegally entered.

FOCUS

BOX 14.4 The End of Bank Robberies?

Routine activities theory would predict that if targets become less attractive or if guardianship becomes more effective there should be less crime. This is exactly what has happened to bank robberies, which used to be a major problem in Canada. In fact, two decades ago, Montreal was the bank robbery capital of North America. Well-organized and well-armed gangs were responsible for as many as 900 bank robberies a year in that city and often took their skills on the road to rob banks and jewellery stores in Toronto and other cities. Often gangs of four men would carry out precisely coordinated bank robberies. One of the men would remain in the getaway car, another would stand guard at the door with a sawed-off shotgun and count out the time remaining to the other two men who were gathering up the money. The gang assumed that the alarm had been sent to the police as soon as they entered the door, so it was critical to finish the job and leave as quickly as possible. However, the number of bank robberies in Montreal has declined to about 100 per year and has also been declining in the rest of the country (Ha, 2002). The Montreal police department has abolished its specialized holdup squad, which had attracted some of the city's best police officers.

What has caused this dramatic decline in bank robberies? According to Tu Thanh Ha (2002), a number of factors were involved. First, banks have less cash on hand because of changes in banking patterns. Most people now have their paycheques deposited directly into their bank accounts so banks no longer have long lineups of people cashing their cheques at the end of the week. Also, many Canadians do their banking by using automatic teller machines, debit cards, or the Internet and do not depend on getting cash at the tellers' counter. Second, banks have developed more effective security methods, including time-release locks and closed-circuit camera systems. Finally, the police make arrests in 80 to 90 percent of bank robberies (McLean, 2000), and the courts have become tougher on firearms offences, so many of the robbers have decided crimes such as drug selling are easier ways of making money.

Incidence and Patterns

The rate of break and enters has declined dramatically in Canada. From its peak of 1550 break and enters for every 100 000 Canadians in 1991, the rate has declined dramatically to 768 per 100 000 in 2006 (Silver, 2007; Kowalski, 2000). In 2002, almost six of ten break and enters targeted private residences; most of the remainder targeted commercial businesses (Wallace, 2003b). In 2006 the highest rates were in the northern territories, followed by Saskatchewan, British Columbia, and Manitoba (Silver, 2007).

The 1999 GSS reported that 21 percent of property stolen from residences consisted of audiovisual equipment. This was followed by household tools, appliances, or furniture (18 percent), and bicycles (14 percent) (Mihorean et al., 2001).

It is unusual for stolen property to be returned as only 12 percent of stolen items were even partially recovered (Gannon and Mihorean, 2005). Experienced burglars generally steal for income rather than for excitement. Consequently, they steal expensive, portable, and compact items that can easily be disposed of or sold. If such items are not available in a burgled location, often nothing will be taken. Indeed, in 1999 nothing was reported stolen in almost 20 percent of break-ins (Kowalski, 2000). The Insurance Information Centre of Canada (2007) reported that the average claim by home owners for losses (including damages) from break and enters amounted to $3568 in 2004, and for commercial businesses, $6497. Overall, the Insurance Bureau of Canada reported that residential and commercial claims from break and enters cost the industry $290 million in 2000 (Savoie, 2002), down from a loss of $434 million in 1992 (Kong, 1998a).

Most break and enters are not cleared by arrest. In 1999, only 16 percent of break and enters resulted in an arrest. Ninety-two percent of those charged with break and enter in 1999 were male, and about 40 percent were youths 12 to 17 (Kowalski, 2000).

Victims of break and enter found the experience very upsetting. Forty-one percent were angry, and substantial numbers were upset, shocked, or confused (22 percent) after their home had been burglarized (Gannon and Mihorean, 2005).

A Crime of Opportunity

Research findings suggest that break and enter is largely a crime of opportunity. It is motivated less by the prospect of a large gain than by the perception of a low risk of being caught. This is consistent with the finding that 30 percent of residential break and enters occurred in the summer months of June, July, and August, when school is out and people are most likely to be taking holidays (Wright, 1995). The perceived risk of being caught is heavily influenced by the lifestyle factors of the household occupants, by whether entrance accesses are secured, and by whether a dwelling is occupied or seems to be occupied.

The high frequency of attempted rather than completed break and enters would also suggest that potential targets are selected haphazardly rather than through careful planning. Clearly, many attempted break-ins are unsuccessful, presumably because of inopportune circumstances. Mayhew (1984) has suggested that such unsuccessful burglaries tell us about the value of security and target hardening. While target hardening such as enhanced hardware and security systems may not deter burglary attempts, these measures may prevent such attempts from being successful.

Bennett and Wright (1984a; 1984b) asked older, experienced burglars which factors influenced their choices of targets. They found that the prospect of a large gain was less often a consideration than the certainty that there was something present worth taking. Ease of entry was not reported to be a major consideration (though it will be recalled that many attempts at break-in apparently are foiled once begun). The majority of these older, experienced burglars also stated that they would be deterred, either conditionally or unconditionally, by the presence of dogs. The authors concluded that the major consideration in target selection was factors affecting risk: burglars would be deterred if they believed that someone was home and by the apparent "surveillability" or visibility of entrance accesses from nearby overlooking buildings or by passers-by and neighbours. For example, when Wright and Decker asked their respondents to describe unsuitable targets, most said they would avoid targets in areas where it looked like neighbours would look out for each other. Older people were considered to be especially likely to report suspicious behaviour to the police:

> The thing is if you got a lot of elderly people on one block, that'll get you killed mostly. . . . I wanted to do [a burglary] over here by the bakery shop, but that's a retired area. Almost everybody that live on that block is retired and they constantly lookin' out windows and watchin' [out] for each other. Ain't nothin' you can do about that. (Wright and Decker, 1992, 87)

In other words, a major factor in the risk of break and enter is the degree to which one's lifestyle decreases the exposure of the household through effective guardianship.

Motor Vehicle Theft

Motor vehicle theft is one of the few crimes that increased during the late 1990s and early 2000s. While other property crimes declined by 38 percent between 1991 and 2001, vehicle theft increased by 10 percent. There were nearly 160 000 vehicles stolen in 2006, a decrease of 2 percent from the previous year. As with most other offences, rates of vehicle theft are highest in the territories and the western provinces and lowest in Atlantic Canada. Only about 13 percent of motor vehicle thefts result in an arrest. Those arrested are most frequently young males. Forty percent are between 12 and 17 and almost 90 percent are male (Wallace, 2003a).

We usually think of vehicle theft as a property crime, and it does cost Canadians about $1 billion per year (Wallace, 2003a). However, this offence also causes a significant number of injuries and deaths as a high proportion of stolen cars become involved in accidents. Many of those killed and injured were young people. Research conducted by the National Committee to Reduce Auto Theft (Miceli, 2002) found that between 1999 and 2001, 81 people were killed and 127 people suffered serious injuries because of collisions involving stolen vehicles. In April 2003, a particularly bad crash occurred that differed from the typical stolen vehicle accident only in the number of victims. The car was driven by a 13-year-old.

> Scars at the base of a cherry tree in full white blossom along Chilliwack River Road and a small wooden cross are the only signs left of a nightmare car crash in which six young people were trapped, screaming, inside a burning car. . . . Six youths died after the car they were riding in flew off the road and crashed head-on into the tree. It happened at about 10 p.m. Sunday near Cultus Lake when an unregistered, unlicenced car carrying six youths missed a sharp turn and lost control, said Chilliwack RCMP Constable David Aucoin. As soon as the car hit the tree, a fire ignited in the engine and quickly spread into the passenger area, where the six youths—aged 12 to 16—were trapped, Aucoin said. . . . Chilliwack RCMP would not release the age of the driver, but said the crash initially killed three boys, ages 12, 13, and 15, and two girls, aged 14 and 16. As well, a 12-year-old boy who had been on life support at B.C. Children's Hospital in Vancouver died Monday evening. (Read and O'Brian, 2003, A1)

Challinger (1987) has suggested there are three different types of motivations for motor vehicle theft: profit, transportation, and recreation. Those who steal for *profit* are often professional criminals who sell the vehicles, many of which are exported to foreign countries, or "chop" the vehicles to sell the parts. *Transportation* refers to offenders who steal cars in order get from one place to another or who use the stolen vehicle to commit another crime. *Recreational* theft is often called joyriding. This form of theft involves stealing cars for the fun of it and driving them around. This is often done in the company of friends.

The national increase in vehicle theft has largely been due to increases in thefts for joyriding and transportation. We know this because a high percentage of the cars are recovered and because many are older vehicles that have little commercial value. The increase in vehicle theft has been concentrated in a few communities and has actually declined in many other areas. Between 1991 and 2001, rates of theft quadrupled in Winnipeg, tripled in Regina, and doubled in Hamilton and London (Wallace, 2003b). In fact in 2006, Winnipeg had the highest rate of auto theft in North America. What explains this dramatic rise? A research study conducted in Winnipeg tells us a great deal about the dynamics of auto theft in some parts of Canada.

The most common vehicles stolen in Winnipeg since 2000 were Dodge Caravans and Plymouth Voyagers built prior to 1995, and 1995 and 1997 Dodge Neons. About 95 percent of all cars stolen in the city are recovered, most within 24 hours. The pattern of these thefts indicates that most are stolen by young people and are used for joyriding or for transportation from one part of the city to another. Anderson and Linden (2002) studied a group of young offenders who were incarcerated for vehicle theft and found that many did it just for the thrill. One of the respondents said he stole cars "for a joyride . . . for the rush!" and another reported that "[stealing cars] is addicting. When you find something you're good at, you want to keep doing it." Peer influences played an important role in vehicle theft. Often cars were stolen by groups of friends, and over half the respondents reported that they had taken part in contests to see who could steal the most cars over a given period of time. Many of the young people said they sometimes took cars for basic transportation. The young offenders were also asked why they selected particular targets. As suggested by the pattern of thefts, the majority of offenders felt that Chrysler products were the easiest to steal. Although recent models are much more difficult to take, older model Chrysler vehicles can be entered and started in a few seconds using only an ordinary screwdriver.

The reason thefts increased so rapidly in Winnipeg was that vehicle theft had become part of the culture among many of the city's young people. After a few young people learned how easy it was to steal some models of cars and realized that the probability of arrest was very low, they told their friends and schoolmates and the number of people willing to steal cars grew quickly. Children in some neighbourhoods learned to steal cars at a very early age (a number of children under 12 have stolen dozens of vehicles), and a peer culture developed that focused on car theft. This culture was reinforced by the mass media as well as by peer groups. Most of the interviewed youth played video games such as "Grand Theft Auto" that glamorized stealing cars and using them to create mayhem on the streets. Several also said that movies such as *Gone in 60 Seconds* had helped teach them some of the techniques of stealing cars.

The dramatic increase in vehicle thefts in Winnipeg can be partially explained by the routine activities approach. The focus on vehicle theft among some segments of the city's youth culture led to an increase in the number of young people who were motivated to steal cars and trucks. The lack of anti-theft protection on older vehicles means that a huge number of easy targets are available, and in many parts of the city it is very difficult to guard these targets effectively, as most vehicles are stolen from parking lots and from the street, where there is little scrutiny. With the development of an urban subculture that highly valued the skill and excitement involved in stealing cars, the stage was set for a dramatic increase in vehicle theft.

The fact that almost all cars in Winnipeg, Regina, and several other cities are quickly recovered suggests that they fit this model of auto theft. However, patterns vary across the country. For example, in Montreal only 42 percent of cars were recovered in 2001. This suggests that theft in Montreal is more likely to involve professional thieves who are selling the cars or taking them apart in order to sell the parts. Tremblay et al. (1994) have explained that the greater incidence of professional vehicle theft in Quebec is likely due to circumstances that have led to an orderly market for stolen cars and car parts in that province. From the routine activities perspective, the existence of such a market would increase the attractiveness of auto theft for those interested in making money, hence increasing the number of motivated offenders.

Preventing Crime

You will recall that Cohen and Felson stated that three components—target suitability, ineffective guardianship, and a motivated offender—must converge in space and time for a crime to occur. Routine activities theorists have focused on the first two of these in developing crime prevention initiatives and have developed a type of crime prevention called situational crime prevention, while others have focused on reducing the number of motivated offenders.

Situational Crime Prevention

There is a large body of research evidence showing the success of *situational crime prevention*. Changes in technology and new policies and programs have created methods of greatly reducing certain crimes. Many Canadian women were bothered by obscene phone callers until caller ID systems made it very easy to determine who was calling. Most models of new cars have very low rates of theft because they have immobilizers that make them virtually impossible to steal without having the keys or using a towtruck. About three decades ago, robberies of city bus drivers declined dramatically when transit systems installed very sturdy fare boxes and implemented exact change systems so the drivers did not have to carry cash. Researchers in the United Kingdom found that people who were victims of break-ins were often victimized again within a few weeks of the initial crime. In response, they worked with victims to improve home security measures by installing better locks and they established "cocoon" Neighbourhood Watch programs that enlisted the help of the victims' immediate neighbours. Subsequent break and enter rates declined dramatically compared with similar areas that did not have this follow-up.

situational crime prevention
Premised on the belief that most crime is opportunistic rather than being the outcome of those driven to commit a crime no matter what the circumstances. This form of prevention attempts to reduce the opportunities for crime rather than just relying on the police after the crime has occurred. An example is the exact fare system used on buses, which removes the opportunity to rob the driver.

Situational crime prevention is premised on the belief that much crime is opportunistic and contextual rather than on the belief that offenders are driven to commit a crime no matter what. Clarke (1995) has summarized steps people can take to reduce the opportunities for crime by requiring more effort on the part of potential offenders, increasing their risks of apprehension, or reducing the likely payoff of committing an offence (see Table 14.1). While most of Clarke's examples involve increasing guardianship, some also entail making the target less attractive. For example, the first category in the table includes ways of hardening the target, which means making it more difficult to steal. Steering locks are the devices that lock automobile steering wheels in one position until the key is placed in the lock, and slug rejector devices are mechanisms in parking meters and vending machines that reject artificial coins (which are called slugs). Both of these innovations have been shown to reduce crime. Several of the items in Table 14.1, including ID badges, baggage screening, security guards, closed-circuit TV systems, and changes in rules and regulations are among the measures that have been implemented or augmented to increase guardianship at airports and other vulnerable locations since the September 11, 2001, attack on the World Trade Center. Can you think of other changes that have been made to reduce the likelihood of this type of crime in the future?

WWW

Institute for the Prevention of Crime
www.socialsciences.uottawa.ca/ipc/eng/

Although defensive measures can be expected to produce an overall reduction in crime because some crime is opportunistic, some crime will simply be displaced from one victim or location to another. While some offenders are opportunistic—that is, they do not seek out potential targets but will take advantage of a target that presents itself—others are highly motivated. Offender motivation or motivated offenders must also be a focus of crime-prevention activities.

Reducing Motivated Offenders

Crime Prevention Through Social Development

crime prevention through social development
An approach to crime prevention that focuses on reducing the number of motivated offenders by changing the social environment. Examples include preschool education programs and effective parenting training; also called crime prevention through social development.

Many criminologists argue that resources need to be targeted at social interventions that will deflect individuals at risk from becoming motivated offenders. This approach is labelled **crime prevention through social development.** Social development programs are intended to reduce the pool of motivated offenders by altering the conditions that breed crime. These programs try to focus on factors that make people, and particularly children, at risk of criminal activity. Many of these have been mentioned in Part 2 of this book and include personality factors, family problems, peer issues, and school and community factors (Wasserman et al., 2003).

The social development approach to crime tries to deal with the root causes of crime through programs and activities that are "intended to increase

TABLE 14.1 Twelve Techniques of Situational Prevention

Increasing the Effort	*Increasing the Risks*	*Reducing the Reward*
1. **Target hardening**	5. **Entry/exit screening**	9. **Target removal**
Steering locks	Baggage screening	Removable car radio
Slug rejector device	Automatic ticket gates	Exact change fares
2. **Access control**	Merchandise tags	Phonecard
Fenced yards	6. **Formal surveillance**	10. **Identifying property**
Entry phones	Security guards	Property marking
ID badges	Burglar alarms	Vehicle licensing
3. **Deflecting offenders**	Speed cameras	Personal identification numbers for car radios
	7. **Surveillance by employees**	
Tavern location	Park attendants	11. **Removing inducements**
Street closures	Pay phone location	Graffiti cleaning
Graffiti board	Closed-circuit TV systems	Rapid repair
4. **Controlling facilitators**	8. **Natural surveillance**	"Bum-proof" bench
	Street lighting	12. **Rule setting**
Gun controls	Defensible space	Customs declaration
Credit card photo	Neighbourhood watch	Income tax returns
Caller ID		Hotel registration

Source: Adapted from Ron Clarke. (1995). "Situational Crime Prevention." In Michael Tonry and David Farrington (eds.), *Building a Safer Society: Strategic Approaches to Crime Prevention*. Chicago: University of Chicago Press, pp. 91–150.

positive . . . motivations, attitudes or behaviour in individuals by influencing their experiences in areas such as family life, education, employment, housing or recreation" (Waller and Weiler, 1984, 4). Social development strategies are often targeted at young people, who appear to be the most amenable to intervention and who make up the next generation of offenders.

There are a wide variety of different social development programs. Some have tried to improve the parenting skills of high-risk parents, while others have provided job training and employment for young people who are cut off from the labour market because they live in poor communities. One of the most promising areas is the provision of preschool programs for children from deprived backgrounds. One of the few social development programs that has undergone a long-term evaluation is a Michigan program called the Perry Preschool Project. The students were 123 black children from poor families. Children aged three and four attended a preschool with an active learning curriculum five mornings a week, and teachers visited the children's homes once a week. The program lasted 30 weeks each year. A control group did not receive these services. Like the earlier Head Start program, this project sought to remedy the impact of the children's impoverished backgrounds on their later school success.

WWW

Perry Preschool Program
www.highscope.org/Content.asp?ContentId=219

The most recent follow-up of the Perry Preschool project looked at the participants at age 40 (Schweinhart et al., 2005). Far fewer of the program participants than controls had been arrested five or more times (36 percent versus 55 percent) and had less than half the arrest rate for drug offences (14 percent vs. 34 percent). The program group had higher incomes, were more likely to own their own homes, and were less likely to have been on welfare. They had greater educational achievement and lower rates of illiteracy. Program group members were more likely to have had stable marriages and females had lower rates of out-of-wedlock births. The costs of the program were more than recovered because of gains in reduced welfare costs and increased earnings of the graduates. Schweinhart et al. estimate that the saving was over $17 for every dollar invested in the program. Those responsible for this program strongly suggest that the intervention must be made while the children are young and must be thorough enough to overcome the range of disadvantages faced by the participants. The Canadian government has responded to this research by establishing early childhood education programs in a number of communities and by establishing a national Aboriginal Head Start program.

Selective Incapacitation

Another group of criminologists, and many politicians, take a very different approach to crime reduction. They feel that the best way to reduce crime is to make the justice system harsher so that crime is deterred, or to lock up dangerous offenders for lengthy periods of time. The latter approach is known as **selective incapacitation.**

selective incapacitation

A philosophy of incarceration that argues that some offenders might have to be incarcerated not for what they have done, but to prevent future harm to the community. This depends on the community's ability to identify those who might re-offend. Some also argue that it is unfair to punish people for what they might do rather than for what they have done. Selective incapacitation is provided for under dangerous offender legislation.

incapacitation

The policy of locking offenders in jail to prevent them from repeating their crimes.

violent predator

An offender who has a very high rate of offending for serious and violent crimes.

Proponents of this strategy feel that crime will be reduced if society locks up the most chronic motivated offenders in order to prevent them from committing further offences. These ideas are based on research conducted during the 1980s by the Rand Corporation which claimed that the U.S. crime rate could be significantly reduced if the most active criminals were **incapacitated** through incarceration. Chaiken and Chaiken (1984) studied 2000 male prison and jail inmates in the United States. They found a high volume of crime committed by 15 percent of their sample, who reported committing a combination of robberies, assaults, and drug deals. These prisoners, whom they labelled **violent predators,** had an average age at first incarceration of less than 23, and they had been committing serious crimes, especially violent crimes, for at least six years. They had considerably more total arrests than other offenders, including those much older than themselves. Moreover, they had spent considerable time in juvenile facilities and were more likely than other offenders to have been granted parole and to have had it revoked. Finally, they were also more socially unstable than other offenders and were unlikely to be regularly employed, to be married, or to have other family obligations. Drug use, particularly multiple drug use involving heroin or barbiturates, is often characteristic of violent predators. The 20 percent of highest-risk offenders in the Chaikens' sample had, on the average, robbery rates 65 times as high as those predicted to be in the lowest 20 percent of offenders; burglary rates 66 times as high; auto theft rates 346 times as high; and drug dealing rates 5 times as high. From these data, many policy makers drew the inference that locking high-rate offenders in jail for long periods would have a significant impact on a community's overall crime rates.

Most countries have laws that enable the state to incarcerate serious habitual offenders for lengthy periods. Canada's dangerous offender legislation provides for indefinite sentences for dangerous offenders. This sentence is reviewed after seven years and every two years thereafter. In order to be considered a dangerous offender, a person must have committed a serious personal injury offence such as sexual assault, aggravated assault, or manslaughter and must be judged to constitute a risk to others based on the brutality of the crime, the offender's previous pattern of aggressive violent behaviour, or a failure to control sexual impulses.

In most jurisdictions, very few offenders are sentenced under these provisions. (For example, in 2000 there were 276 dangerous offenders in Canadian prisons.) An exception is California's "three strikes and you're out" law, which mandates a life sentence for a third felony conviction. This has resulted in bizarre sentences, including two cases where men will spend the rest of their lives in prison, one for stealing a slice of pizza and the other for shoplifting a small package of meat. The incapacitation strategy is also very expensive. California's taxpayers will eventually be spending $6 billion each year to keep a large number of aging offenders in prison (Skolnick, 1994). This punishment may seem to be far too harsh, at least for minor felonies, but in 2003 the U.S. Supreme Court ruled that it did not violate the Constitutional protection against cruel and unusual punishment in two cases involving one defendant who received a sentence of 25 years without parole for stealing three golf clubs and a second defendant who was given two consecutive 25-year sentences (50 years in all) for stealing nine videotapes in two separate incidents (see Box 12.1).

Ethical Concerns

Some criminologists strenuously object to such proposals for selective incapacitation. They argue that it is unjust to sentence a person to a long term in prison not for something that person has done, but for what that person might do if he or she were not imprisoned. This is particularly true considering the fact that there tends to be a high rate of **false positives** (50 to 60 percent of the total) in most predictive studies, including the original Rand Corporation study on which the Chaikens' study was modelled. As von Hirsch (1984, 177) expressed it: "The 'false positive'—that is, the person erroneously designated to be a future recidivist—loses his liberty on account of an injury that he will not in fact commit."

false positive
When trying to identify dangerous offenders (or other phenomena), researchers often make mistakes. One category of mistakes is known as a false positive. A false positive is identifying offenders as dangerous (and possibly keeping them incarcerated or denying them parole) when they are actually not dangerous.

Others respond that the "false positive" has lost his or her freedom for what he or she has done. The issue is for how long the offender's freedom will be lost. They contend that it is appropriate for society to protect itself by assigning longer terms to offenders whose profiles suggest a disproportionate likelihood of re-offending. Unfortunately for proponents of selective incapacitation, recent research by Auerhahn (1999) has shown that the measures used to predict which offenders should be incarcerated for long periods do not work. She concludes that sentencing is a very poor method of trying to reduce crime rates. Despite this research, incapacitation policies in the United States have resulted in that country having rates of incarceration that are among the highest in the world. Locking up so many people has likely led to some crime reduction (although there are few differences between states such as California with very tough measures and those such as New York that do not), but the financial and human costs have been enormous. There is ample evidence that investing the same amount of money in social development programs would have been a far more cost-effective way of reducing crime (Waller, 2006).

FOCUS

BOX 14.5 A Public Health Model or Harm Reduction Approach to Substances

Some argue that the easiest and most effective crime-prevention action would be to adopt a public health rather than a criminal approach for controlling substance use and abuse (Moore, 1995). For example, many people have concluded that the war on drugs has been an expensive failure and have recommended that treatment would be a better way to deal with the drug problem (British Columbia, 1995).

The B.C. Attorney General's Co-ordinated Law Enforcement Unit (CLEU) (1992a) estimated that the cost of illicit drug use within British Columbia for 1989 was at least $349 million (or roughly $100 per every resident in the province). Most of these costs were justice-related, including drug law-enforcement services ($67.9 million) and the policing of non-drug crimes, such as break and enter or crimes of violence, that were related to illicit drug use ($151 million). Indeed, CLEU (1992b) estimated that 60 percent of non-drug crime in British Columbia is drug-related. As a concrete example, CLEU (1992b, 55) cited one police officer who recounted "the case of a woman in Vancouver who supports her $1,400 per day habit with prostitution, stealing from tricks, shoplifting, forging cheques, theft and drug dealing." In contrast to these huge enforcement costs, CLEU (1992a) reckoned that in 1989, British Columbia taxpayers spent only $13.8 million on provincial programs directed at the prevention of substance abuse, of which a minuscule $1.8 million was directly targeted at the prevention of illicit drug use.

Moreover, the criminalization of drugs has fostered an environment in which contaminated needles are exchanged among users and reused. One result of this is what British Columbia's Provincial Health Officer described as "the epidemic of deaths and infections related to injection drug use" (Millar, 1998, 2). By 1996, drug overdoses had become the leading cause of death among adults between the ages of 30 and 49 within British Columbia.

The criminalization of part of the drug trade has opened an extremely lucrative market for groups of criminals to organize crime (see Chapter 15), as did Prohibition on both sides of the border early in the twentieth century. This, in

Summary

- Conventional or street crime includes the offences of homicide, assault, sexual assault, robbery, break and enter, motor vehicle theft, personal theft, and household theft.
- Patterns of conventional crime can be understood with the help of lifestyle/exposure and routine activities theories. Lifestyle/exposure theory points out that the lifestyle and activities of some people place them at higher risk for crime victimization. Routine activities theory is based on the observation that crime results from the simultaneous presence of a motivated offender, a suitable target, and ineffective guardianship of that target.
- Property crimes tend to be committed disproportionately against those whose lifestyles leave their possessions least effectively guarded.
- Violent crimes are committed disproportionately against people who are exposed to individuals who have a high level of physical aggression.

FOCUS

BOX 14.5 A Public Health Model or Harm Reduction Approach to Substances *(Continued)*

turn, breeds numerous related crimes, ranging from thefts to murders, as well as corruption of public officials, sometimes including police.

A harm reduction approach to this problem would be to minimize criminal victimization and criminal justice system costs, as well as to reduce drug-related fatalities, disease, and health-care costs by providing heroin to addicts under controlled conditions. In 1997, the Swiss established a permanent harm reduction policy following a three-year experiment with this practice that saw falling death rates and criminal involvement, as well as improved health, housing, and employment on the part of 1100 addicts. The Dutch have followed suit, although they had already been tolerating hard drug centres under controlled conditions in some cities.

The election of Larry Campbell (now Senator Larry Campbell) as mayor of Vancouver in 2003 helped to ensure that a harm reduction strategy was adopted in that city. Campbell is a former RCMP chief superintendent who became the Chief Coroner of British Columbia and who was the model for the television series *Da Vinci's Inquest*. In the mid-1990s, Campbell was one of the first public figures to advocate a harm reduction approach to addiction. The Four Pillars approach to drug problems (enforcement, treatment, prevention, and harm reduction) was a key part of his election platform. Canada's first safe injection site (called Insite) opened in Vancouver in 2003. The federal licence for the Insite was due to expire at the end of 2007 and was extended by the government for an additional six months. The final decision was not known when this chapter was written, but there was speculation that the government was planning to deny a licence renewal despite the fact that there was a substantial body of research showing the benefits of the program. Among these benefits were a reduction in deaths (500 drug users overdosed at Insite over a two-year period, but none died because the site has medical supervision) and increased enrolments in treatment programs that resulted from Insite referrals (Globe and Mail, 2007).

- Alcohol and drug use increase the likelihood of victimization. There are two fairly distinct patterns of risk. One high-risk group are people whose family members cannot control their anger. The second group are people whose lifestyle places them in social settings with young males who use alcohol and/or drugs.
- The routine activities approach leads to a number of crime reduction strategies. These include situational measures, crime prevention through social development, and incapacitation of high-rate offenders.

QUESTIONS FOR CRITICAL THINKING

1. Understanding patterns of crime means that you can reduce your chances of becoming a victim of crime if you change certain aspects of your lifestyle. Some people argue that they should not have to change the way they dress, work, or play to avoid being victimized. What do you think?

2. As a student at a university or college, how do you assess your risk of victimization? What changes could you or others make that might reduce your chances of being a crime victim?
3. Canada has been restricting the distribution of some drugs for almost a century, but illegal drugs are readily available across the country. Do you think that a public health model or a criminal model would be more effective for reducing harm from drug use? What are some of the weaknesses of the public health approach?
4. Is the media's portrayal of violence causally related to crime on the part of some offenders? Why or why not?
5. How do you think that social, economic, cultural, or technological changes in society will affect crime in five years' time? Why?

NET WORK

In this chapter, you have learned about the routine activities approach to crime. This approach has had an impact on the nature of crime prevention programs in North America and Europe by drawing attention to the role of the attractiveness of the target and the importance of effective guardianship. To see how these insights are used in crime prevention, go to the website of a major U.S. report on the effectiveness of crime prevention programs at **www.ncjrs.gov/works/**.

Go to Chapter 7 "Preventing Crime at Places." Find three projects that are intended to reduce the attractiveness of the target and three projects that increase effective guardianship. Have these projects been successful in reducing crime?

KEY TERMS

conventional crime; pg. 429
crime prevention through social development; pg. 452
effective guardianship; pg. 431
false positive; pg. 455
incapacitation; pg. 454
incidence; pg. 433
lifestyle/exposure theory; pg. 430
routine activities approach; pg. 430
selective incapacitation; pg. 454
situational crime prevention; pg. 452
target suitability; pg. 431
violent predator; pg. 454

SUGGESTED READING

American Psychological Association Commission on Violence and Youth. (1993). *Violence & Youth: Psychology's Response. Volume 1: Summary Report of the American Psychological Association Commission on Violence and Youth*. Washington, D.C.: American Psychological Association Public Interest Directorate. This is a wide-ranging investigation of the ways in which violence affects youth and includes recommendations for pro-social transformations of media content.

Erickson, Patricia G., Diane M. Riley, Yuet W. Cheung, and Patricia A. O'Hare (eds.). (1997). *Harm Reduction: A New Direction for Drug Policies and Programs*. Toronto: University of Toronto Press. A variety of contributions concerned with the emerging approach of "harm reduction." As implied by its name, the focus is on whatever is most effective at reducing harm, whether it be legal, public health, or other approaches.

Statistics Canada. *Juristat*. A serial that reports the latest available information about various facets of the Canadian criminal justice system.

Tonry, Michael, and David Farrington (eds.). (1995). *Crime and Justice: A Review of Research, Volume 19. Building a Safer Society: Strategic Approaches to Crime Prevention*. Chicago: University of Chicago Press. State-of-the-art reviews about various approaches to crime prevention, including community-based approaches, situational crime prevention, developmental crime prevention, and public health approaches.

Waller, Irvin. 2006. *Less Law, More Order: The Truth About Reducing Crime*. Westport: Praeger. A good up-to-date discussion of crime prevention by one of Canada's foremost experts in this field.

BIBLIOGRAPHY

Anderson, Jeff, and Rick Linden. (2002). "Pilot Study of Juvenile Auto Theft Offenders in Winnipeg." Unpublished manuscript, University of Manitoba.

Auerhahn, Kathleen. (1999). "Selective Incapacitation and the Problem of Prediction." *Criminology* 37(4):703–34.

Bennett, Trevor, and Richard Wright. (1984a). *Burglars on Burglary*. Brookfield, Vt.: Gower Publishing.

———. (1984b). "Constraints to Burglary: The Offender's Perspective." In Ronald Clarke and Tim Hope (eds.), *Coping with Burglary* (pp. 181–200). Boston: Kluwer-Nijhoff Publishing.

British Columbia, Province of, Ministry of Attorney General, Co-ordinated Law Enforcement Unit (CLEU). (1992a). *The Costs Associated with Illicit Drug Use in British Columbia in 1989*. Victoria: The Queen's Printer.

———. (1992b). *Updates on Drug-Related Projects* (April, 1992). Victoria: The Queen's Printer.

———. (1995). *Report of the Task Force into Illicit Narcotic Overdose Drug Deaths in British Columbia*. Victoria: The Queen's Printer.

Brookman, Fiona, Christopher Mullins, Trevor Bennett, and Richard Wright. 2007. "Gender, Motivation and the Accomplishment of Street Robbery in the United Kingdom." *British Journal of Criminology*. Advance Access published, 7 July, 2007, doi:10.1093/bjc/azm029.

Chaiken, Marcia R., and Jan M. Chaiken. (1984). "Offender Types and Public Policy." *Crime and Delinquency* 30(2):195–226.

Challinger, D. (1987). "Car Security Hardware—How Good Is It?" *Car Theft: Putting on the Brakes, Proceedings of Seminar on Car Theft*. Sydney: National Roads and Motorists' Association and the Australian Institute of Criminology.

Clarke, Ron. (1995). "Situational Crime Prevention." In Michael Tonry and David Farrington (eds.), *Building a Safer Society: Strategic Approaches to Crime Prevention* (pp. 91–150). Chicago: University of Chicago Press.

CLEU. See British Columbia, Province of, Ministry of Attorney General, Co-ordinated Law Enforcement Unit.

Cohen, Lawrence E., and Marcus Felson. (1979). "Social Change and Crime Rate Trends." *American Sociological Review* 44:588–607.

Dauvergne, Mia. (2003). "Family Violence Against Seniors." *Canadian Social Trends* (Spring):10–14. Ottawa: Statistics Canada.

Dauvergne, Mia, and Geoffrey Li. (2006). "Homicide in Canada, 2005." *Juristat* 26(6). Ottawa: Statistics Canada.

Desroches, Frederic J. (1995). *Force and Fear: Robbery in Canada*. Toronto: Nelson.

FBI. See U.S. Department of Justice, FBI.

Gabor, Thomas, Micheline Baril, Maurice Cusson, Daniel Elie, Marc LeBlanc, and Andre Normandeau. (1987). *Armed Robbery: Cops, Robbers, and Victims*. Springfield: Charles C. Thomas.

Gannon, Maire, and Karen Mihorean. (2005). "Criminal Victimization in Canada, 2004." *Juristat* 25(7). Ottawa: Canadian Centre for Justice Statistics.

Gartner, Rosemary, and Sara Thompson. (2004). "Trends in Homicide in Toronto." In Bruce Kidd and Jim Phillips (ed.), *From Enforcement and Prevention to Civic Engagement: Research on Community Safety* (pp. 28–39). Toronto: University of Toronto Centre of Criminology.

Globe and Mail. (2007). "Safe Injection Sites: Renew Insite's Licence." 27 August: A12.

Ha, Tu Thanh. (2002). "The Demise of the Bank Heist." *The Globe and Mail*, 11 November: A1, A7.

Hindelang, Michael J., Michael R. Gottfredson, and James Garofalo. (1978). *Victims of Personal Crime: An Empirical Foundation for a Theory of Personal Victimization*. Cambridge, Mass.: Ballinger Publishing.

Insurance Bureau of Canada. (2007). Personal correspondence concerning claims data.

Janhevich, Derek E. (1998). "Violence Committed by Strangers." *Juristat* 18(9). Ottawa: Canadian Centre for Justice Statistics.

Koenig, Daniel J. (1977). "Correlates of Self-Reported Victimization and Perceptions of Neighbourhood Safety." In Lynn Hewitt and David Brusegard (eds.), *Selected Papers from the Social Indicators Conference, 1975* (pp. 77–90). Edmonton: Alberta Bureau of Statistics.

Kong, Rebecca. (1998a). "Breaking and Entering in Canada, 1996." *Juristat* 18(5). Ottawa: Canadian Centre for Justice Statistics.

———. (1998b). "Canadian Crime Statistics, 1997." *Juristat* 18(11). Ottawa: Canadian Centre for Justice Statistics.

Kowalski, Melanie. (2000). "Break and Enter, 1999." *Juristat* 20(13). Ottawa: Statistics Canada.

Linden, Rick. (1994). "Deviance and Crime." In Lorne Tepperman, James E. Curtis, and R. J. Richardson (eds.), *The Social World* (3rd ed.). Whitby: McGraw-Hill Ryerson.

Luckenbill, David. (1977). "Criminal Homicide as a Situated Transaction." *Social Problems* 25(2):176–86.

Mayhew, Pat. (1984). "Target-Hardening: How Much of an Answer?" In Ronald Clark and Tim Hope (eds.), *Coping with Burglary* (pp. 29–44). Boston: Kluwer-Nijhoff Publishing.

McIntyre, Mike. (2003). "Girl, 12, Saw Father Deliver Fatal Beating." *Winnipeg Free Press* 12 March:A3.

McLean, Gene. (2000). "The New Age of Bank Security." *Canadian Banker* 107(4).

Micelli, Matthew J. (2002). *A Report on Fatalities and Injuries as a Result of Stolen Motor Vehicles (1999–2001).* Project 6116: National Committee to Reduce Auto Theft.

Mihorean, Karen, Sandra Besserer, Dianne Hendrick, Jodi-Anne Brzozowski, Catherine Trainor, and Stacie Ogg. (2001). *A Profile of Criminal Victimization: Results of the 1999 General Social Survey.* Ottawa: Minister of Industry.

Millar, John S. (1998). *HIV, Hepatitis, and Injection Drug Use in British Columbia: Pay Now or Pay Later.* Victoria: Office of the Provincial Health Officer.

Moore, Mark H. (1995). "Public Health and Criminal Justice Approaches to Prevention." In Michael Tonry and David Farrington (eds.), *Building a Safer Society: Strategic Approaches to Crime Prevention* (pp. 237–62). Chicago: University of Chicago Press.

Read, Nicholas, and Amy O'Brian. (2003). "Six Youths Killed in Horrific Car Crash." *The Vancouver Sun*, 29 April:A1.

Sacco, Vincent F., and Holly Johnson. (1990). *Patterns of Criminal Victimization in Canada.* Ottawa: Statistics Canada (Housing, Family and Social Statistics Division), Minister of Supply and Services Canada.

Savoie, Josee. (2002). "Crime Statistics in Canada, 2001." *Juristat* 22(6). Ottawa: Statistics Canada.

Schneider, Stephen. (2007). *Refocusing Crime Prevention: Collective Action and the Quest for Community.* Toronto: University of Toronto Press.

Schweinhart, L. J., J. Montie, Z. Xiang, W. S. Barnett, C. R. Belfield, and M. Nores. (2005). *Lifetime Effects: The High/Scope Perry Preschool Study Through Age 40.* Ypsilanti: The High/Scope Press.

Silver, Warren. (2007). "Crime Statistics in Canada, 2006." *Juristat* 27(5). Ottawa: Statistics Canada.

Skolnick, Jerome N. (1994). "Wild Pitch: 'Three Strikes You're Out' and Other Bad Calls on Crime." *The American Prospect* 17 (Spring):30–37.

Sparks, Richard F. (1981). "Multiple Victimization: Evidence, Theory and Future Research." In National Institute of Justice, *Victims of Crime: A Review of Research Issues and Methods.* Washington, D.C.: U.S. Dept. of Justice.

Statistics Canada. (2003). "Canadian Statistics—Age Standardized Mortality Rates." Ottawa: Statistics Canada, Health Statistics Division. www.statcan.ca/english/Pgdb/health30c.htm. Accessed 25 April, 2003.

Tremblay, Pierre, Yvan Clermont, and Maurice Cusson. (1994). "Jockeys and Joyriders: Changing Patterns in Car Theft Opportunity Structures." *British Journal of Criminology* 34(3):307–21.

U.S. Department of Justice. (1974a). *Crime in Eight American Cities.* Advance Report. Washington, D.C.: U.S. Dept. of Justice.

———. (1974b). *Crimes and Victims: A Report on the Dayton-San Jose Pilot Study of Victimization.* Washington, D.C.: U.S. Dept. of Justice.

Veidhuizen, Scott, Karen Urbanoski, and John Chairney. (2007). "Geographical Variation in the Prevalence of Problematic Substance Use in Canada." *Canadian Journal of Psychiatry* 52 (7) 426–33.

von Hirsch, Andrew. (1984). "The Ethics of Selective Incapacitation: Observations on the Contemporary Debate." *Crime and Delinquency* 30(2):175–94.

Wallace, Marnie. (2003a). "Motor Vehicle Theft in Canada—2001." *Juristat* 23(1). Ottawa: Statistics Canada.

Wallace, Marnie. (2003b). "Crime Statistics in Canada, 2002." *Juristat* 23(5). Ottawa: Statistics Canada.

Waller, Irvin. 2006. *Less Law, More Order.* Westport: Praeger.

Waller, Irvin, and Dick Weiler. (1984). *Crime Prevention Through Social Development: An Overview with Sources.* Ottawa: Canadian Council on Social Development.

Wasserman, Gail, Kate Keenan, Richard Tremblay, John Coie, Todd Herrenkohl, Rolf Loeber, and David Petechuk. (2003). *Risk and Protective Factors of Child Delinquency.* Washington: Office of Juvenile Justice and Delinquency Prevention.

Wright, Christine. (1995). "Risk of Personal and Household Victimization: Canada, 1993." *Juristat* 15(2). Ottawa: Canadian Centre for Justice Statistics.

Wright, Richard T., and Scott H. Decker. (1992). *Burglars on the Job: Streetlife and Residential Break-Ins.* Evanston: Northeastern Books.

Young, Jock. (n.d.). "The Left and Crime Control." http://www.malcolmread.co.uk/JockYoung/. Accessed 4 September, 2007.

Young, Jock. (1997). "Left Realism: Radical in its Analysis: Realist in Its Policy." In M. Maguire, R. Morgan, and R. Reiner, *The Oxford Handbook of Criminology* (2nd ed.). Oxford: Clarendon Press. http://www.malcolmread.co.uk/JockYoung/leftreal.htm, Accessed 4 September, 2007.

Organized Crime

15

Rodney T. Stamler

ASSISTANT COMMISSIONER RCMP (RTD)

Over the past century, governments in North America and their enforcement agencies have become increasingly concerned about organized crime. In recent years organized crime groups have become more powerful because of the massive profits they have acquired from supplying illicit goods and services to a willing public. The illegal monopolistic business enterprises run by organized criminals are able to survive and grow as public demand for the illicit goods and services continues to increase. Legitimate competitors are excluded because these markets are illegal, while illegitimate competitors are controlled by force.

In this chapter, you will learn about the nature and extent of organized crime in Canada. Organized criminals are involved in a wide range of activities, including selling illegal drugs, extortion, immigration fraud, pornography, international stock and bank fraud, money laundering, and environmental crimes such as transporting and dumping hazardous waste. For a variety of reasons, the most successful organized crime groups are ethnically based. The major exceptions to this are outlaw motorcycle gangs, whose participation in organized crime has increased significantly over the past 20 years. The chapter concludes with a discussion of some of the strategies that might help to reduce the growth of organized crime.

Learning Objectives

After reading this chapter, you should be able to

- Describe the characteristics of organized crime and the difficulties of arriving at a precise definition of organized crime.
- Understand the roots of organized crime and the reasons that organized crime is such a profitable activity.
- Understand why many successful criminal organizations are ethnically based and why outlaw motorcycle gangs are a major exception to this trend.
- Describe the history and structure of the major organized crime groups operating in Canada.
- Explain why money laundering is such an important part of organized crime.
- Discuss the most effective ways of reducing organized crime in Canada.

What Is Organized Crime?

It is difficult to provide a precise definition of organized crime. In the past several years legislative authorities both in Canada and around the world have enacted various definitions of organized crime in order to comply with the United Nations Convention on Transnational Organized Crime. For the most part legal definitions have tended to be very narrow and limited in an attempt to define those involved in major organized crime activity.

Authors, criminologists, and legislative drafters have tried to develop all-encompassing definitions of organized crime that would include every type of crime group. Such definitions are of necessity very broad and general. Some definitions have tried to distinguish organized crime groups from petty thieves, armed robbers, and others who are involved in criminal activity. Other definitions have used the partnership or business-entity approach, which stresses organizational effort, planning, leadership, division of work, and co-operation. Still other definitions have focused on the social elements involved in organized crime and have emphasized the family-type organization in which members pledge their lifelong loyalty, trust, and obedience (Pennsylvania Crime Commission, 1980).

Some definitions of organized crime clearly delineate one organized crime network, while others confine themselves to one particular element of organized crime. Several authors, after studying or examining street gang activity, have described these groups as if they operate autonomously from any other group or level of authority. These authors tend to reach the mistaken conclusion that organized crime is not organized at all, but is a collection of uncontrolled bandits, outlaws, and crooks who work together at times in order to co-exist in the unfriendly street environment. This conclusion can be reached only if one fails to examine carefully all crime groups that operate in a given territory, from the top of the hierarchy to the street-level gang. Street groups tend to be the most visible part of an organized crime network, but, like an iceberg, the highly organized elements remain hidden from public view. Only a careful examination of the cash flow from street crimes will identify the entire criminal organization.

Jean-Pierre Charbonneau states that the underworld is not an organization but an environment. This environment consists of crooks, bandits, dealers, and outlaws of every description. Within this milieu, a multitude of gangs, clans, or organizations exist or co-exist. Some are powerful, well organized, and stable; others are loose and haphazard and may include temporary coalitions of odd-job criminals and journeyman crooks.

Margaret Beare concludes that "organized crime is a process or method of committing crimes, not a distinct type of crime in itself" (1996, 14). She goes on to say, "Organized crime is *ongoing* activity, involving a *continuing criminal conspiracy*, with a *structure greater than any single member*, with the potential for *corruption and/or violence* to facilitate the criminal process" (15).

On April 21, 1997, the Parliament of Canada passed Bill C-95 and amended the Criminal Code to create the offence of participation in a criminal organization through the commission or furtherance of certain indictable offences for the benefit of the organization. While it is still not an offence to belong to a criminal organization, Parliament did define a *criminal organization* as well as a *criminal organization offence*. In amending the Criminal Code of Canada, Parliament defined criminal organization as

> any group, association or other body consisting of five or more persons, whether formally or informally organized, having as one of its primary activities the commission of an indictable offence . . . and any or all of the members of which engage in or have within the preceding five years engaged in the commission of a series of such offences.

In 1998 the Solicitor General of Canada used the following definition of organized crime:

> Economically motivated illicit activity undertaken by any group, association or other body consisting of two or more individuals, whether formally or informally organized where the negative impact of said activity could be considered significant from an economic, social, violence generation, health and safety and/or environmental perspective. (Porteous, 1998, 2)

The INTERPOL (International Police Organization) definition adopted by the General Assembly of the member countries in 1998 defined organized crime as follows:

Interpol—Organized Crime
www.interpol.int

> Any enterprise or group of persons engaged in a continuing illegal activity which has as its primary purpose the generation of profits irrespective of national boundaries.

In 1999, The United Nations adopted a new convention entitled International Transnational Organized Crime; at the present time over 120 countries have ratified this convention. The convention requires countries to enact national law that will coordinate the international control of organized crime. With more international coordination on the subject of organized crime, it has become increasingly important to distinguish organized crime from other similar criminal activities such as terrorism and other hate-related group activities. The United Nations convention defined *organized crime* as follows:

UN Convention on International Transnational Organized Crime
www.unodc.org/palermo/convmain.html

> Organized Crime consists of groups which are bound together by language, culture and includes groups that come together for political objectives and become involved in criminal activity that produces revenue.

It becomes clear that an all-encompassing definition of organized crime must be very general if it is to include all crime groups from the street-level operators to the top-level financiers. These definitions do not adequately describe or express the complexities of major regional, national, or international crime organizations such as the Mafia, the Triads, and the North American outlaw motorcycle gangs. These organizations, with their binding ethnic ties or their binding common interests, have developed rituals and codes of conduct and secrecy that provide them with the protection and security to continue as distinctive criminal societies.

Whether for legal or academic purposes, one could do no better than to use the description developed by the U.S. Bureau of Alcohol, Tobacco and Firearms (Pennsylvania Crime Commission, 1980):

> "Organized Crime" refers to those self-perpetuating, structured, and disciplined associations of individuals, or groups, combined together for the purpose of obtaining monetary or commercial gains or profits, wholly or in part of illegal means, while protecting their activities through a pattern of graft and corruption.

Organized crime groups possess certain characteristics which include but are not limited to the following:

1. Their illegal activities are conspiratorial;
2. In at least part of their activities, they commit or threaten to commit acts of violence or other acts that are likely to intimidate;
3. They conduct their activities in a methodical, systematic, or highly disciplined and secret fashion;
4. They insulate their leadership from direct involvement in illegal activities by their intricate organizational structure;
5. They attempt to gain influence in government, politics, and commerce through corruption, graft, and illegitimate means;
6. They have economic gain as their primary goal, not only from patently illegal enterprises such as drugs, gambling, and loan sharking, but also from such activities as laundering illegal money through and investment in legitimate business.

When we analyze the various definitions of organized crime that have been developed for academic or legal purposes we can clearly state that organized crime is an on going illegal business activity. This activity may involve what appears to be, or is in fact, a partnership, a corporation, or a sole proprietorship that is supplied by wholesalers or distributors. These may be wholesalers who purchase goods or services from other entities, who may be importers or manufacturers. If the entire business line or a portion of it is illegal, that business is an organized criminal activity and the individuals who are involved in it constitute an organized crime group. It does not matter whether the business entity sells contraband alcohol, smuggled cigarettes, or illicit drugs. The law will not enforce their contracts and their profits must be laundered to be used legitimately. In some cases, the enforcement of contracts or laundering of money actually becomes a related organized crime activity. A number of related criminal enterprises can flow from the unlawful business—for example, bribery, extortion, murder, or money laundering. While these activities are related, they can be illegal business enterprises in themselves. Thus the activities of a "Murder Incorporated" may be a stand-alone organized crime activity or it may be a way that one criminal group enforces its own directives. A money-laundering service could be a stand-alone business entity operating like a bank to service a number of criminal groups or could be directly connected to one criminal group to launder the illegal profits of that group only.

A group of thugs who break legs or cause bodily harm for various reasons but with no intention of obtaining financial gain or benefit is not organized crime. The infamous Ku Klux Klan would likely not be classified as part of organized crime, but could be classified as a terrorist group. A terrorist group that is involved only in a political struggle is not organized crime, unless it is also involved in illegal activities to raise funds to support its terrorist activities. An otherwise legitimate manufacturing corporation, on the other hand, which knowingly becomes involved in supplying organized crime with goods or services will certainly become part of organized crime activity, even though its main business may be supplying legal goods or services to a legitimate market. For example, the German government has prosecuted a German domestic tobacco manufacturing company for selling cigarettes to organized criminals for their contraband markets (Mansell and Boyes, 2003).

What Distinguishes an Organized Crime Group from a Terrorist Group?

Since September 11, 2001, many countries of the world, including Canada, have enacted new legislation to deal with acts of terrorism. In 2002 the Parliament of Canada enacted The Anti-Terrorism Act, which strengthened a number of criminal laws with respect to terrorism. This enactment created the Terrorist Financing Act and a new government agency called Fintrac. The Act also amended the Criminal Code, the Official Secrets Act, the Canada Evidence Act, the Proceeds of Crime (Money Laundering) Act and a number of other Acts, and enacted the Charities Registration (Security Information) Act. These laws have provided new definitions for terrorism and terrorist groups. In the process of restricting the financing of terrorist groups, the legislation has provided new methods for identifying and curbing money laundering, which will also apply to organized crime groups. Most of these criminal laws now conform to the various United Nations conventions. Because a terrorist in one country may be deemed a freedom fighter in the next country, it becomes increasingly important to distinguish terrorist groups from organized crime groups, particularly when enforcing organized criminal activity at the international level. There are, of course, many instances when a crime group involved in organized criminal activity, such as the manufacture and distribution of illicit drugs, also becomes involved in political struggles that include acts of terror. The profits from this organized crime activity will be directly used to finance the political acts of terror. In other instances, terrorist groups will join forces with organized crime groups to further their respective objectives.

When a terrorist group has all the elements that protect it from identification, it may easily become connected with organized crime activity. On the other hand, if funding for a terrorist group comes directly from a government or if it obtains voluntary financial support from the public, it will not be classified as organized crime. If a terrorist group becomes involved in the commission of crimes that produce revenue or profits, that group will be included in the definition of organized crime.

WWW

Department of Justice—Anti-Terrorism Act
www.justice.gc.ca/en/anti_terr/

WWW

UN Convention on Terrorism,
untreaty.un.org/English/Terrorism.asp

WWW

"Al Capone" Marilyn Bardsley, The Crime Library
www.crimelibrary.com/capone/caponemain.htm

How Organized Is Organized Crime?

Organized crime can encompass a wide range of crime groups. However, there has been a long debate about the extent to which criminal organizations fit these criteria. On one side of the debate are those who view organized crime in North America as a monolithic alliance of crime families whose members are of Italian descent. The activities of each of these families are firmly controlled by its bosses and by a commission made up of the men who control its most powerful families (Cressey, 1969). On the other side are researchers who feel that there is no centralized direction or leadership. Organized crime consists of local crime gangs, whose activities sometimes lead them to work with other groups. For example, Reuter (1983) studied bookmaking, numbers gambling, and loan sharking in New York City. He found that the Mafia did not dominate these enterprises. None of the three illegal markets was centrally controlled, and bookmaking was particularly competitive and decentralized.

The most sensible approach to the question is to recognize that the level of organization can vary widely depending on the time, place, and type of offence. Organized crime is a very broad term and can apply to a wide range of groups, from those that are structured and organized to those with fluid memberships that sporadically work together to carry out specific criminal activities. Haller (1990) has found that many illegal enterprises are run as partnerships rather than as complex bureaucracies. He suggests that even the famous Capone gang was actually a complex set of partnerships directed by Al Capone, his brother Ralph, and two colleagues. These senior partners worked with many other different men to establish a variety of bootlegging, gambling, and vice activities in the Chicago area during the 1920s.

Haller concludes that the degree of organization involved in selling illegal goods and services is influenced by two factors. The first is the internal economics of the type of crime. For crimes such as the manufacture, importation, and distribution of illegal drugs, cooperation and coordination are required to get the product to the consumer. Other crimes such as gambling require cooperation to share the risk as street-level gamblers might not have sufficient capital to absorb a short period of heavy losses, even though the odds are strongly in their favour in the long run. The second is the involvement of law enforcement officials and politicians in supporting criminal activities. Where officials and criminals work together, competition is controlled, and there is a stable climate for illegal activity. This makes it more likely that crime groups will be well organized.

The Roots of Organized Crime

Many of the activities of organized crime result from the demand by the "law-abiding" citizenry for illegal goods and services such as illicit drugs, contraband cigarettes and alcohol, and prostitution. The opportunity of serving these illicit markets has determined the structure and scope of organized criminal activities. Consider drug trafficking, which is now the most lucrative of organized criminal activities. The basis of this activity is a public demand for a product,

FOCUS

BOX 15.1 The "Virtual Corporation"

In comments at a conference on global organized crime, James Woolsey, the former director of the U.S. Central Intelligence Agency, described how drug cartels may be the model for 21st-century organizations.

One could look at how drug traffickers are developing and sustaining the European market for cocaine as a model of a successful multinational business. Latin American groups know that Italian and other European groups control the drug distribution networks in Europe, networks built up over 40 years to accommodate the flow of heroin. Italian groups know that cocaine is increasing in popularity in Europe. And both groups know that cocaine sells in Europe for two to three times the U.S. price, meaning there are enormous profits to be made.

As a result, Latin American groups provide the drugs, using groups in Venezuela, Brazil, and Argentina to transship cocaine to newer markets in Europe, while distribution remains in the hands of European—primarily Italian—organized crime.

Thus the "virtual corporation" touted by management theorists as the leading contender to the dominant entrepreneurial structure of the next century takes shape: drug traffickers develop a loose network of independent companies; they share information, skills, costs, and market access and position themselves to maximize profits by working cooperatively (Woolsey, 1994, 138–39).

Source: Adapted from Rick Linden. (1994). "Crime and Deviance." In L. Tepperman, J. Curtis, and J. Richardson (eds.), *The Social World* (3rd ed.). Toronto: McGraw-Hill Ryerson, pp. 188–229.

in this case a drug such as cocaine, marijuana, or heroin. Governments of most countries have made the production, sale, and possession of these drugs illegal. Those using the drug (many of whom are addicts) have a very strong desire for it, which cannot be met by any other product, so there is a high demand for the drug. Those who are prepared to run the risk of breaking the law can charge a premium for it because competition has been restricted by laws forbidding the legal distribution of the drug.

The nature of the illicit marketplace also determines the structure of organized crime. If one intends to break into homes and to steal and sell computers and video recorders, the largest criminal network required is the thief and a "fence" who will pay for and distribute the stolen articles. However, much more is required to move a drug from the fields of Peru or Afghanistan to the streets of Vancouver and Toronto. Elaborate organizations must be established for this type of activity, including financiers, buyers, sellers, and people to transport the drug across international borders.

Many types of criminal activity flow out of the illicit market structure. In order to maintain or increase their share of the market, organized criminals may use violence to discourage competition. Recent gang-related shootings in any number of American cities are the result of competition for markets by rival groups. In 1991, 18 persons were shot in the Chinatown area of Toronto in battles between Chinese and Vietnamese gangs. Nine of the victims died of their wounds. Most of those shot were of Vietnamese origin (Canada, 1992).

FOCUS

BOX 15.2 The Origins of an Illicit Market Structure

Over the past few years, taxes on cigarettes and alcohol have driven the prices of these products so high that Canadians have shifted their demand to lower-priced product that is smuggled from other countries. This demand for smuggled cigarettes and alcohol has produced revenue opportunities for Canadian organized crime groups.

When governments impose high taxes on a consumer product, they create a demand for a cheaper product. Organized criminals step forward to meet that demand and black markets are created. This pattern was at the heart of the contraband tobacco crisis that gripped Canada in the early 1990s. In 1985, there was virtually no contraband tobacco for sale in Canada. However, tobacco taxes rose steeply and by 1993 a legally sold carton of cigarettes cost about $50 compared with the $22 for an untaxed carton sold on the black market. Thus the Canadian government helped to create a booming market for smuggled cigarettes. The government did not criminalize tobacco, but attempted to reduce its consumption by imposing high taxes on it. Smuggled cigarettes saved consumers money and were lucrative for the smugglers. The federal and provincial governments were the big losers. By 1993, 30 percent of the cigarettes sold in Canada were illegally supplied. The tax revenue lost to the federal government was more than $1 billion. Smuggling was particularly out of control in Quebec, where law enforcement officials estimated that up to one-third of the cigarettes smoked were purchased illegally.

The role of government in this matter went beyond simply imposing taxes. When it did so, the federal government was aware that smuggling would increase. Most of the cigarettes smuggled into Canada are manufactured here and exported to the United States, where smugglers purchase them and bring them back illegally. The government sought to control the export of Canadian cigarettes by imposing a tax on all cigarettes exported from Canada.

Cigarette smuggling has now become a worldwide phenomenon. Organized crime has established international markets for smuggled cigarettes where products of every brand and blend can be purchased. If brands are not available from legitimate manufacturers they are counterfeited and introduced to the marketplace through extensive illegal wholesale operations situated in various duty-free ports around the world. Mediterranean and Caribbean locations have become extremely popular for this type of shipping operation. Cigarettes are shipped to these locations and then redirected to the prime market areas of the world. The entire operations are managed and controlled by various organized crime groups. The areas these shipments come from now include Canada, the United States, Europe, and Asia. Contraband cigarettes have become the source of revenue for crime groups in Afghanistan, Pakistan, the Balkans, and other countries of Eastern Europe where profits from this market area are fuelling terrorist activities.

The World Health Organization attempted in 2003 to develop an international convention to control the manufacture and international distribution of cigarettes in an attempt to control the worldwide cigarette contraband problem. The convention is currently on hold and is not expected to be adopted in the near future. The convention was expected to be similar to the 1961 Single Convention on Narcotic Drugs. The plan was that the export and import of tobacco products would be controlled by permits issued by government agencies to ensure that all tobacco products, including cigarettes, are under government control when shipped from a manufacturer in one country to a wholesaler in another country.

Because many law enforcement officials believed that this type of control would not be successful in stopping cigarette smuggling and would actually assist organized crime in developing their own manufacturing and distribution systems similar to those that were developed to produce and distribute illicit drugs in spite of the United Nations narcotic control conventions, the idea of an international convention to control tobacco products has been shelved for the time being.

In Quebec, territorial wars among biker gangs resulted in more than 60 deaths between 1995 and 1999. Gangland shootings and bombings were regular occurrences. Violence is also used to ensure that debts are paid and other obligations are met. Normal legal systems for enforcing contracts cannot be used by organized criminals because the object of the contract is usually illegal and therefore would not be enforced in a court of law. Therefore, force and intimidation is used. In addition, there is a need to conceal the illegal activities. The enormous profits that can be earned from the illicit market lead to activities such as laundering money to conceal the source, loan sharking, and investment in legitimate businesses, which then come under the control of criminal syndicates. Finally, in order to prevent the legal system from interfering with these illegal activities, officials may be bribed to ignore them.

World Health Organization—Tobacco Draft Convention
www.who.int/gb/fctc/PDF/inb6/einb65.pd

While such corruption is widespread in many countries, it is not common in Canada. Even though our politicians have not always been completely honest, there have been relatively few instances of systematic corruption involving organized criminals, police, court officials, and politicians, as has occurred in the United States. Sacco (1986) has given a number of reasons for this: political power in the United States is highly decentralized, which makes it easier to corrupt people holding certain key offices; in the United States, there are a large number of elected political, law enforcement, and court officials, many of whom are associated with political "machines" financed by organized crime; Canadians have been less inclined to try to control moral behaviour through laws than Americans have been, so there are fewer opportunities to establish illicit markets. To these we might also add the fact that our law enforcement agencies and court officials have worked very hard to maintain their reputations for honesty and have seldom been involved in organized corruption.

Who Is Involved in Organized Crime?

With the exception of outlaw motorcycle gangs, most organized crime groups are ethnically based. In North America, just about every major ethnic group has participated in organized crime over the years—Irish, English, Italians, Jews, French Canadians, Blacks, Chinese, Gypsies, Chicanos, and many others (Dubro, 1985).

The Italian-based Mafia groups are perhaps the most widely known and publicized crime organizations in the Western world. The term *Mafia*, which was originally used to identify a specific Sicilian crime group, is now commonly used to identify any ethnic or regionally based crime organization. The Colombian Mafia, the Turkish Mafia, and the Asian Mafia are all major international crime groups, but they have no direct connection as members of the Italian-based Mafia.

There are several reasons for the ethnic connection in organized crime. You will recall from the discussion of strain theory (Chapter 9) that when people are denied legitimate access to common culture goals such as financial success, they may turn to criminal ways of achieving these goals. Frequently, minority groups have been denied access to legitimate success because of the barriers of discrimination and poverty. While visible ethnic minorities actually have lower crime rates than other Canadians (Thomas, 1992), some members of these groups choose organized crime as a way of achieving financial success.

Once this choice has been made, several structural factors increase the likelihood of ethnically based groups succeeding in the highly competitive world of organized crime. First, today's major internationally connected crime organizations started at the family or local level. It was the strong family or cultural connection that permitted these organizations to enforce their code of conduct and secrecy to counter any intrusive action from law enforcement. As the crime groups grew in size, their members moved to other regions. This migration served to broaden the base of the crime groups by adding new territories, which, in turn, resulted in the expansion of their illegal operations. Ethnic-based crime groups, which are now situated in different regions of the world, use their ties in these expanded territories to develop their international connections and penetrate the illicit markets of the world. In this way, crime groups have the advantage of developing efficient international illegal distribution systems for illicit goods and services. At the same time, they are able to set up international money laundering schemes that are used to hide and distribute their illegal profits.

Besides facilitating international networks, ethnic ties may benefit organized crime groups in other ways. For example, members of some ethnic groups have interpersonal ties, which make it difficult for strangers to infiltrate their organizations. Racial and language differences also make law enforcement much more difficult.

Biker gangs do not base their affiliation on ethnic ties, but have other bonds that exclude others and ensure the cooperation of members. Daniel Wolf, an anthropologist who succeeded in joining an Edmonton biker gang, has observed that "after repeated attempts, the police have long since discovered that infiltrating an outlaw club is a long, arduous, and risky process when it is being done for 'professional' reasons." Infiltration of the gangs is difficult. "They have an internal discipline that makes it dangerous," said a police officer. "It's an area we have trouble infiltrating. The conditions of initiation make it almost impossible . . ." (Wolf, 1991, 14).

Despite the apparent dominance of particular groups in activities such as gambling or illicit drug distribution, we should not think that doing away with any group will reduce organized crime in a community any more than closing Chrysler would seriously reduce car sales. Organized crime exists because of market demand. Groups like the Italian Mafia or the Chinese Triads may meet some of this demand at a particular time and place because their organization gives them a competitive advantage. However, if they were put out of business, other groups would quickly replace them (Sacco and Kennedy, 1994).

Major Organized Crime Groups in Canada

Major international organized crime groups have found it profitable, over the years, to establish a base of operations in Canada. In addition, crime groups that originated in Canada have grown and established ties with related groups in other parts of the world. At present, there are at least seven major types of crime groups operating in Canada. The history and development of these groups can be largely attributed to the fact that Canada has a long and open border with the United States. This allows easy access for criminals and illicit goods to move from one country to the other. Also, Canada, like the United States, enjoys a multicultural society, which extends ethnic ties to all regions of the world.

The most prominent internationally connected crime organizations with established crime bases in Canada include the Italian Mafia; Triads and other Asian organized crime groups; the South American, Colombian, and Mexican cartels; outlaw motorcycle gangs; and the Russian Mafia and other eastern European crime groups.

RCMP Organized Crime
www.rcmp-rc.gc.ca/qc/infos_gen/publications/bilan_2004/crime_e.htm

The Italian-Based Mafia

The **Mafia** organizations of Italy are major criminal societies that are permanent, secret, and powerful. The first Mafia-style organization in Italy was the Camorra. This group was established in Sicily in the 19th century and was a direct offshoot of the 15th-century hill bandits who formed a guerrilla force known as the Garduna. The Camorra based itself on a hierarchical system of control, with the godfather at the top of the hierarchy and soldiers at the bottom. Income was derived from protection rackets, robbery, murder for hire, blackmail, kidnapping, and loan sharking. Its members were recruited from prisons. New members to the Camorra were required to serve probationary periods before entering the ranks of the society. Eventually, the Camorra gave way to the Sicilian Mafia, which had a family-based recruitment system. This organization became a powerful crime syndicate (Maclean, 1974).

Mafia
Originally used to identify a specific Sicilian crime group. It is now commonly used to identify any ethnic or regionally based crime organization.

In the late 19th century, members of the Sicilian Mafia found their way to the United States, Canada, and Australia. As they became established in their new homelands, they began to carry out their traditional patterns of criminal activity. Mafia members sent letters threatening serious injury or death to the recipients. The letters were signed with the outline of a black hand. This was the earliest report of organized crime activity in North America, and the "black hand" became synonymous with the Mafia (Glaser, 1978).

The first city in the United States in which a Mafia group became established as a criminal society was New Orleans. New York City became the second area, and from there, Mafia groups were quickly formed in other parts of the eastern United States (Glaser, 1978). The Mafia groups controlled gambling, narcotics, and other rackets. They became deeply involved in political patronage in Harlem and Brooklyn. By 1917, they dominated the illegal activities that took place throughout New York.

Mafia groups surfaced in Ontario as early as 1906. In this era, Toronto, Hamilton, and the Niagara Peninsula became the centres of Canadian Mafia activity. In 1909, the arrest of five so-called Black-Handers in Hamilton was a major event (Dubro, 1985). By 1920, the Mafia gangs in southwestern Ontario had increased in number and size. By 1921, murders, bombings, and extortion were common occurrences.

Prohibition in the United States caught the Mafia by surprise. They could not quickly adjust their illegal operations to supply illicit alcohol to the public.

This resulted in other organized crime groups forming in the United States. In Chicago, New York, and other major cities, the groups involved in the manufacture, importation, and sale of illicit alcohol began to reap huge profits. These new organized crime groups quickly took over power and control at the expense of the Mafia.

Street wars between gangs trying to acquire or maintain control of valuable territorial rights continued for a decade. Organized crime groups with a variety of ethnic backgrounds emerged. There were Irish gangs in bootlegging, Jewish groups in money laundering, and the original Mafia families trying to regain control. In the 1930s, Lucky Luciano brought together a federation of North American Mafia families, which covered every major city in the United States and Canada. He made alliances with other major ethnic groups, which resulted in a unified crime syndicate. In the United States, this syndicate has been termed La Cosa Nostra (LCN). It invested its illegal profits in legitimate businesses, which included legal gambling casinos in Nevada and Cuba. Meyer Lansky became the chief money launderer and banker for the syndicates. He perfected money laundering systems through secret-numbered bank accounts in tax havens (Maclean, 1974).

By the 1930s, LCN was firmly based in Montreal, Toronto, and Vancouver. The Italian Mafia, as one of its main ethnic components, operates very much like a corporate entity. The godfather, capo, or family boss takes the position of the chief executive officer. The underbosses, or lieutenants, act as vice-presidents and head the various branches of the organization. These branches may be engaged in different types of criminal activity. Soldiers are given licences to operate in specific territories and are authorized to carry out specified types of criminal activity. They are required, in return, to pay a percentage of their profits to the management level of the organization. The upper levels of this criminal organization invest their laundered proceeds into legitimate business entities. They prefer to appear as legitimate business executives within their communities.

According to Carrigan (1991), pressure resulting from a U.S. Congressional committee in 1951 caused the Mafia to move its gambling headquarters to Montreal. Those involved were well connected with both the American and Italian Mafias, as well as with Quebec politicians and police. The international affiliations later facilitated drug smuggling from Montreal to the United States. The Quebec Crime Probe report of 1977 concluded that the Italian Mafia still existed in Montreal and that this organization was a significant factor in organized crime. The report went on to state:

> This secret society was reserved for criminals of Sicilian and Italian ancestry . . . and is a direct descendant of similar secret societies which did and do exist in southern Italy. This statement is supported by many meetings between Mafiosi leaders from all over America and elsewhere, particularly Italy.

The report describes the background and scope of the Cotroni-Violi Mafia family of Montreal, and describes how members of this group were recruited and selected. The report pointed out that a number of employees or independent partners of this crime family provided the infrastructure for an association of criminals from different ethnic backgrounds. Some of these associates were

French Canadians, Jews, Anglo-Saxons, Slavics, and Blacks, and were under the authority and control of this one Mafia family (Quebec, 1977).

In recent years, the territory controlled by Paolo Violi, who was shot to death in 1978, has been split between Montreal's Rizzuto family and Toronto's Cuntrera-Caruana family. The latter group controlled one of the world's largest drug-trafficking networks.

Although the Italian Mafia remains a powerful organization, its influence has been reduced over the past decade. In the United States, many of the old bosses have died or been imprisoned, and young new leaders must deal with aggressive competition from other criminal groups. For example, the majority of heroin sold in North America is imported through Asian drug trafficking networks rather than through the Mafia-controlled French Connection route from Turkey to France and then to Montreal and New York (Dubro, 1992). In Italy, magistrates and police have conducted a concerted campaign against the Mafia, which has resulted in the conviction of hundreds of criminals and has implicated scores of politicians, government officials, and businesspeople. Public outrage over the ambush murders of prosecutors Giovanni Falcone and Paolo Borsellino in 1992 has forced the government to continue the investigations despite the natural reluctance to implicate government officials and their friends (Stille, 1995).

The Criminal Intelligence Service Canada (CISC) states that there are three main Italian-based organized crime groups that participate in significant criminal activities: the Sicilian Mafia, the 'Ndrangheta, and the U.S. branch of the Cosa Nostra. Their presence in Canada is particularly prominent in Ontario and Quebec with varying levels of activity in other provinces. These Italian-based crime groups maintain close ties with Asian and Eastern European-based organized crime and with Colombian and other South American groups as well as with various domestic criminal organizations. In particular, outlaw motorcycle gangs in Quebec, Ontario, and British Columbia have had a historical relationship with the Italian-Canadian crime families. These crime families are involved in a number of different organized crime activities including drug trafficking, smuggling, contraband distribution, money laundering, illegal gaming (including Internet gaming), extortion, loan sharking, prostitution, counterfeiting money and high-end products, and stock market manipulation. Unlike outlaw motorcycle gangs, the Italian-based Mafia maintains a very low profile in Canada. Its members mostly engage in legitimate commercial business activity to conceal their criminal activities. They participate in regular social and cultural activities in their community with the express purpose of maintaining the appearance of being respectable and legitimate to their neighbours and their community (Criminal Intelligence Service Canada, 2002; 2003; 2004; 2005; 2006; 2007).

WWW

Criminal Intelligence Service Canada
www.cisc.gc.ca/index_e.htm

Outlaw Motorcycle Gangs

Motorcycle gangs began to form in North America during the late 1940s. These motorcycle enthusiasts were, for the most part, ordinary individuals who enjoyed cycling for part-time recreation. They formed the American Motorcycle Association (AMA), which, in turn, sponsored tours, races, and rallies.

On July 4, 1947, the AMA sponsored one such event. It was a tour through California called the Gypsy Tour. On the same day, the town of Hollister, California, situated 60 miles south of Oakland, held its annual motorcycle "dirt hill climb races." In previous years, small groups of motorcycle enthusiasts from the surrounding area attended these annual races. On this occasion, however, more than 3000 AMA riders invaded the small town. The AMA participants included a number of different motorcycle clubs, including a group known as Booze Fighters and another called Hells Angels. Some violent clashes broke out, causing the police to arrest many of the bikers involved. A number of police officers and bikers were seriously injured. Broken beer bottles and damaged property left the main street of the small town in a shambles.

In the days following this event, the AMA publicly drew a distinction between the legitimate members of the AMA and the now newly classified renegades. The association characterized 99 percent of its members as clean-living folks enjoying a pure sport. It condemned the other 1 percent as antisocial barbarians. The renegade groups exploited this event by publishing this condemnation with bold defiance. They developed a motorcycle patch called the "one-percenter." This patch is still worn in addition to regular "colours" and identifies the member as an "outlaw biker." This single incident clearly served to unify and develop a unique type of major organized crime society in North America. Hollywood, with the film version of the Hollister riots entitled *The Wild One* and such movies as *Easy Rider* and *Hells Angels on Wheels*, gave the motorcycle gang a distinctive image by romanticizing the outlaw biker. New chapters of outlaw groups subsequently formed in almost every part of the United States and Canada (Canada, 1980).

All groups function in the same general manner. They are tightly organized, and their hierarchical system maintains a highly exclusive control over a particular territory alone or through alliances with other clubs. Smaller gangs often find it more expedient to support a larger, better-organized gang.

A gang member can never fully retire from the group. New members are recruited with care to ensure that agents or informants of law enforcement or rival gangs do not penetrate the group easily. A "striker," in biker parlance, is a would-be member aspiring to join the group. Strikers are recruited from "hangers-on" who generally ride with the gang on their tours or runs but at the back of the pack. Strikers may occasionally enter the club headquarters, but only to carry out minimal tasks. This period of "apprenticeship" may last as long as six months. Several criminal acts will likely have to be committed by the striker to the satisfaction of the peers. In addition, he may be required to attack or embarrass a rival gang member.

Crimes of violence are committed by gang members to establish territory, expand their membership through mergers, intimidate the public, or for "entertainment purposes." Most groups are involved in major traditional organized-enterprise crime activities such as extortion, prostitution, and drug trafficking. These activities can be very lucrative. Carrigan (1991) discusses one member of the Grim Reapers in Calgary who had 23 prostitutes working for him. He owned property worth over $600 000 and was once arrested with more than $200 000 in cash in his possession. Bikers are mainly responsible for the manufacture and sale of illicit chemical drugs such as ecstasy, methamphetamine (speed), and PCP (angel dust). They traffic in all types of illicit drugs, including marijuana, hashish, cocaine, and chemically manufactured drugs. In Canada the street value from the sale of these illicit drugs amounts to billions of dollars (Canada, 1985).

For many years, biker gangs in Quebec have been among the most violent in North America. The most notorious incident occurred in March 1985 when six members of the Laval chapter of the Hells Angels were murdered by some of their colleagues who suspected them of dealing drugs outside the gang. Another biker, Yves (Apache) Trudeau, became a Crown informer and witness when he learned he was also a target. Trudeau later pleaded guilty to 43 counts of manslaughter and may have been involved in as many as 40 other deaths.

The Canadian groups connect with their American and European counterparts to facilitate their drug trafficking operations. Unlike members of other crime organizations, outlaw bikers are usually visibly identifiable as belonging to a particular group. Yet evidence of their illegal activities is difficult for law enforcement to obtain. The very structure of outlaw motorcycle groups, their internal discipline, their intimidating behaviour, and other violent actions are the tools they use to protect themselves from prosecution. Potential witnesses and informants become the special targets of the gangs. Their intimidating approach and their barbaric behaviour make the public cautious in confronting the groups, even when they are committing crimes.

The Criminal Intelligence Service Canada (CISC) reported that outlaw motorcycle gangs across Canada, particularly the Hells Angels, are engaged in money laundering, intimidation, assaults, murder, fraud, theft, counterfeiting, extortion, prostitution, escort agencies and strip clubs, after-hours clubs (selling alcohol illegally), telemarketing and the possessing and trafficking of illegal weapons, stolen goods, and contraband. Hells Angels remain the largest and most criminally active organized motorcycle gang in the country with 35 full chapters. Members of this biker gang continue to be extensively involved in the importation and trafficking of cocaine; the cultivation and exportation of high-grade marihuana, and, to a lesser extent, the production and trafficking of methamphetamine; and the trafficking of ecstasy and other illicit synthetic drugs. Organized motorcycle gangs in Canada continue to be involved in violence, ranging from intimidation and assault to attempted murder and murder. Incidents of violence between the Hells Angels and another motorcycle gang, the Bandidos, continue (see Box 15.3). Several high-profile cases of intimidation against victims of crime, witnesses, and law enforcement across the country demonstrate the extent to which the gang will attempt to protect its members from law enforcement. In western Canada, the Hells Angels have dominated over the other outlaw motorcycle gangs and are in control of most gang-related organized crime activity. They continue to be extensively involved in the importation and trafficking of cocaine and the cultivation and trafficking of cannabis (marijuana). They have a strong connection with the Italian-based Mafia in eastern Canada and have similar connections with Asian organized crime groups. The Hells Angels are increasingly joining alliances with various ordinary street gangs. These street gangs often perform lower-level criminal activities and security duties for the outlaw motorcycle gangs (Criminal Intelligence Service Canada, 2002; 2003; 2004; 2005; 2006; 2007).

FOCUS

BOX 15.3 Bikers Fighting for Place Behind Bars

Police in Montreal have, to say the least, a unique problem. Members of rival motorcycle gangs, the Rock Machine [now the Bandidos] and Hells Angels, when they are not blowing one another to smithereens, are tripping over themselves to get into jail.

In this, the Year of the Pig, the bikers' turf war has reached new heights of ferocity. For almost two months, gang members have been killed in car bombings at a rate of one a week, supplemented by the occasional machine-gun slaying and stabbing.

It's one of those paradoxes of a wintry city such as Montreal: it's too cold and snowy even for bikers, so they tend to drive trucks and minivans.

Earlier this month, when Claude (Le Pic) Rivard of the Hells Angels stopped his 4X4 at a red light, a family van pulled alongside and he died in a hail of machine-gun fire. (Those sliding doors and tinted windows are popular not only with parents but also with contract killers.) A couple of weeks earlier, the Plymouth Voyageur of Bruno (Boom Boom) Bandiera of the Rock Machine went up in a fireball. Between the two incidents, fellow Rock Machinist Daniel Senésac was blown to bits as he planted a bomb in a rival's van.

Aside from the regular bombing and shooting work, members of the leather-clad set are committing petty crimes in a bid to be sent to Bordeaux prison in east-end Montreal, the newest battleground in the nasty spat between the rival gangs.

The way the guards' union tells it, the Rock Machine, the more sophisticated and ruthless of the two, controls Bordeaux, and the Hells Angels, a more old-fashioned bikers' group, controls Parthenais prison, also in the east end. Despite their differences in philosophy—something like the difference between the Liberals and Conservatives—neither group takes losing lightly, so the leaders have sent reinforcements to settle a few scores behind bars.

Now, why would a group such as Rock Machine, which already controls a goodly part of the drug trade in the city, including business in Montreal's glitziest bars, care about a filthy, rundown prison such as Bordeaux?

Well, consider that the jail, built in 1913 with a capacity of 800, is now home to 1014 prisoners, one of the most captive drug-consuming clienteles in the world. Prisoners will smoke, swallow and inject just about any illegal substance they can get their hands on, and they will pay dearly for the distraction.

Demand is so high, prison officials report, that pushers have taken to lobbing drug-filled tennis balls over the fence at Bordeaux, not to mention the prisoners and visitors who smuggle the booty in more traditional manners. Again, the guards' union estimates that the drug trade at Bordeaux exceeds $7-million, annually.

As it turns out, members of Rock Machine and Hells Angels, despite being purveyors of libertarian notions such as drug decriminalization, are not fond of free-market competition. Those who have the misfortune to be selling drugs in a prison that is not controlled by their gang suffer swift and harsh retribution. So, in recent weeks, the infirmary at Bordeaux has been a high-traffic area.

In an attempt to defuse the tension, members of Rock Machine and Hells Angels have been segregated in separate wings of the prison, and their leaders have been shipped to jails elsewhere in the province. Prison officials also conducted a full-scale sweep of the establishment.

They found a "pen gun" (a small pipe rigged to fire a .22-calibre bullet), a number of knives, a steel bar and numerous bits of lethally sharpened wood and glass. How someone manages to smuggle a pickaxe through a strip search boggles the mind, but there was one of those in a cell too.

Serge Ménard, the Public Security Minister, called his visit to Bordeaux on Friday "one of the most traumatizing experiences I've ever lived through." And he stayed for less than an hour.

Source: André Picard. "Bikers Fighting for Place behind Bars." *The Globe and Mail* (February 21, 1995), A8. Reprinted with permission from *The Globe and Mail*.

A number of outlaw motorcycle gangs who have become involved in highly successful crime enterprises have found it even more profitable to take on the public appearance of successful businessmen rather than the image of outlaw bikers. From their disguised position, they find it useful and more effective to use corruption than brute force to expand their enterprises' crime interests. Perhaps what is evolving is a second-level crime group in the fashion of the Triad society or the Italian-based Mafia.

Triads and Other Asian Organized Crime Groups

Just as the Mafia was founded as a guerrilla movement in Sicily, so the earliest Triad societies came into existence in Fukien Province in China in the latter part of the 17th century. They began as resistance fighters against the Manchu invaders. Although the societies' original purpose was self-protection and opposition to various Chinese dynasties, they eventually developed into crime groups (Bresler, 1980).

As the membership of the Triad societies grew, they dispersed throughout Southeast Asia. Their members were bound together by an intricate system of rituals, oaths, passwords, and a ceremonial intermingling of their blood. During the politically turbulent years of China's history, with the rise and fall of various governments, the **Triads** entrenched themselves in criminal activity for profit. This move provided them with the power to ensure their continued existence as a society. Like the Mafia, the Triads engaged in criminal activities such as gambling, narcotics trafficking, prostitution, loan sharking, and extortion.

Triads
These Chinese groups came into existence in the 17th century as resistance fighters against the Manchu invaders. They eventually developed into crime groups.

With Chinese migration to North America, it was not long before the Triads began to develop within North American communities. In Canada and the United States, the gangs followed the basic Triad principles they had followed in China. They formed cellular groups, which were controlled by certain members operating within each group. They retained a secretive system by not disclosing details of criminal activity to other cells.

The various cells often join together for specific purposes such as opposing other groups in their attempts to acquire or maintain control over territory. Behind each cell, which is directly involved in crime activity, is a second group or cell, which provides support but is not directly involved in the criminal activity. The members of these types of cells are, however, former members of the crime cells. They are the advisors to the crime group and their approval must be solicited before any major criminal enterprise is carried out by the crime cells. The Triad groups remain almost exclusively within the Chinese communities, and very little of their criminal activity, except their illicit drug distribution activities, directly affects members of the wider public.

The Southeast Asian region involving the tri-border area of Burma, Laos, and Thailand, commonly known as the Golden Triangle, has been a major supplier of heroin to the Western world (though in recent years much of the world's heroin has been produced in Afghanistan (United Nations Office on Drugs and Crime, 2007). The Triad organizations acquired control of this illegal operation and developed major illicit drug distribution systems throughout the world. They made direct connections with Triad groups in Canada, the United States, and Europe.

Hong Kong has been the centre for Triad groups throughout the world. Drug-trafficking activities have made them wealthy and powerful, and many have invested their funds in legitimate enterprises. The colony of Hong Kong came under the control of the Chinese mainland government in 1997, and this has likely led to further migration by many who were not anxious to reside under the rule of the People's Republic of China. Organized crime groups, or those who have profited from this activity, are likely continuing to relocate to other parts of the world. This will, in all likelihood, further broaden the base of these organized crime syndicates.

Organized crime groups originating in Vietnam and Japan pattern themselves along the lines of Chinese Triads. The Japanese Yakuza (gangsters) are professional racketeers in Japan specializing in blackmail, extortion, and the sale of illicit drugs and guns. The Vietnamese crime groups originated during the Vietnam War, where they specialized in the sale of black-market goods and illicit drugs. When the war ended, many gang members immigrated to North America. Both crime groups, attracted by the lucrative profits derived from extortion and from drug trafficking and other **consensual crime**, have emerged in Canada and the United States. Several Asian gangs, notably the Big Circle boys, have developed a business smuggling illegal immigrants into Canada and the United States. Dubro (1992) claims that this business is almost as lucrative as heroin smuggling, and the potential penalties are much less severe.

consensual crime
Any crime in which the "victim" is a willing participant (drug use, prostitution, etc.).

Criminal Intelligence Service Canada states that members of Asian organized crime travel frequently nationally and internationally. This travel demonstrates the wide scope of their criminal activities and is also an attempt to avoid law enforcement scrutiny. Like the outlaw motorcycle gangs, the Asian crime groups recruit street and youth gangs, which they use as a labour pool for their criminal activities, for security, and as a source of recruits. There are a number of active Asian-based street gangs in British Columbia, Ontario, and Quebec. Some members of street gangs graduate to performing criminal activities for organized crime groups, typically through street-level crimes, violence, and drug trafficking. They are involved in the international illicit trade in drugs, firearms, and illegal human migrants. The Asian groups across the country remain extensively involved in the large-scale importation and trafficking of drugs.

Vietnamese-based groups continue to be extensively involved in the large-scale cultivation and exportation of marijuana through residential growing operations across Canada, particularly in British Columbia. Vietnamese-based marijuana operations have rapidly expanded eastward across the country to Ontario. Through marijuana brokers, the Hells Angels and Vietnamese-based crime groups control approximately 85 percent of the marijuana production and distribution in British Columbia. It is conservatively estimated that there are 15 000 to 20 000 grow operations in the Lower Mainland of British Columbia. Profits from the marijuana industry are frequently funnelled into other criminal activities. According to intelligence gathered from one operation, high-level gang members of Chinese descent bought marijuana from Vietnamese-based drug-trafficking gangs to transport to the United States. The Asian groups are heavily involved in manufacturing designer drugs such as ecstasy. They continue to be involved in extortions, home invasions, kidnappings, illegal migrant smuggling operations, theft, shoplifting, prostitution, assaults,

FOCUS

BOX 15.4 Canadian Alleged to Be Running Empire from Jail

By Adrian Humphreys

Bankers, businessmen, investment brokers and a man linked to the royal family of Italy were among those arrested in Europe yesterday as police announced an attack on an underworld financial empire allegedly controlled from jail by Canada's top Mafia boss.

A series of raids across Italy and France saw police freeze 500-million euros ($689-million) worth of assets, seize 22 companies and charge 17 men, presenting a decidedly white-collar face of the Mafia.

The controlling mind behind it all was Vito Rizzuto of Montreal, Italian authorities allege.

Police in Italy issued an arrest warrant for Rizzuto, who is currently in prison in the United States for three gangland slayings. Also wanted are four men in Canada—including Rizzuto's father, Nicolo, who is similarly in jail in Montreal awaiting trial.

"We believe that even from jail they are able to control the organization," said Silvia Franze, an investigator with the Direzione Investigativa Antimafia in Rome. "We blocked a lot of bank accounts and money," Ms. Franze told the *National Post.* "We have seized many companies and hundreds of millions of Euros all around the world because we believe that behind these companies is Vito Rizzuto."

Also arrested was Mariano Turrisi, 53, the president and founder of Made in Italy Inc., an export marketing group. He is heard on wiretaps speaking with Rizzuto, police allege. . . .

Italian legal documents in the case dramatically portray Vito Rizzuto as being a global superboss.

From their origins in Italy the Rizzutos moved to Canada, where they "gave birth to a transnational society" that worked to unite the Italian Mafias and create "overseas cells," a document from the Rome anti-Mafia prosecutor's office alleges.

The organization sought to "manage and control the economic activities connected to the acquisition of contracts in public works" and to "commit a series of crimes—killings, international drug trafficking, extortion, frauds, smuggling, stock-market manipulation, insider trading and criminal transfer of securities," it alleges.

The group used several companies listed on European and North American stock markets, including one registered in Vancouver, to develop business projects linked to gold mines in Canada and Chile, authorities allege. . . .

The masses of money come from rampant international drug trafficking, authorities say, including a company that used leather clothing to mask the smell of narcotics from drug-sniffing dogs. . . .

Despite the allegations of high-finance and political connections, the charges stem from a small-time mob-linked swindle north of Toronto in 2001. That allowed police in Ontario to install wiretaps in Montreal. . . .

It was shortly after those wiretaps were turned on that police tracked regular contact between gangsters in Montreal and men in Italy. That information was forwarded to Italian authorities, who, in turn, placed several suspects under surveillance.

The Italian probe brought two startling sets of allegations.

The first were announced in 2005 and accused Rizzuto and former Montreal construction engineer Giuseppe Zappia (known for building the Olympic Village for the 1976 games) of conspiring to use illicit money to build a bridge connecting the island of Sicily to mainland Italy.

The bridge was one of the largest public works projects in Italy and the consortium was allegedly prepared to invest $6-billion to complete it.

The second series of charges are those announced yesterday in Rome.

"We found there were cells here in Italy controlled by Vito Rizzuto . . . ,"Ms. Franze said.

The Rizzuto organization has formed a "Sixth Family," a Mafia clan based in Montreal that has overshadowed the Mafia's notorious Five Families of New York. Recent allegations of their presence abroad place them as one of the world's most robust criminal cartels.

National Post, with files from Paul Cherry, CanWest News Service, ahumphreys@nationalpost.com.

illegal gambling, loan-sharking, and the production of counterfeit currency, software, manufactured goods, and credit cards. The groups are also involved in the laundering of criminal proceeds and the investment of laundered money into legitimate businesses (Criminal Intelligence Service Canada, 2002; 2003; 2004; 2005; 2006; 2007).

The Russian Mafia and Eastern European Crime Groups

There are fears that organized crime is threatening the future of Russia. Organized criminals have been among the main beneficiaries of the transition from a communist to a capitalist economy. After the end of the Communist regime in 1991, conditions were ideal for criminals. Russia is in the midst of wrenching social change and has suffered from a troubled economy and political uncertainty. The social institutions developed under the Communist Party have disappeared or have been drastically weakened. In a country where every move was once controlled by the state police, law enforcement officials are now struggling to maintain control over the rapidly rising organized crime rate.

In his analysis of the rise of the Russian mafia, Handelman concluded that Russian officials "tried to develop a free market before constructing a civil society in which such a market could safely operate. . . . Many activities that are considered unlawful according to Western norms, such as organized crime, are not specifically prohibited" (1994, 89). Criminal gangs were quick to fill the vacuum left by the fall of the old order. They eagerly embraced the new agenda and began to sell goods and services that were unavailable through other sources.

Statistics about organized crime cannot be very precise. Criminals try to hide their actions, and the agencies that keep such statistics may have reasons to exaggerate or to minimize criminal activities. Recognizing these inaccuracies, a study by the U.S. Department of Energy's Office of Threat Assessment provides an indication of the scope of the problem in Russia (Hersh, 1994). The study found 4000 different organized crime groups or gangs inside Russia. Organized crime groups owned half of Russia's commercial banks and similarly high proportions of other businesses. One-quarter of these groups had ties to other groups inside or outside the country, and many worked closely with corrupt police and government officials.

The close relationship between criminals and government officials is particularly troubling. The criminal establishment had existed in Russia during the Communist regime, and government officials had benefited from its operations. However, the nature of the relationship has changed. The extent of the influence of the Mafia following the 1991 coup is suggested by the comment that "pre-coup, the government kind of ran the criminals. After-coup, the criminals are kind of running the government" (Raine and Cilluffo, 1994, 121).

In addition to its economic impact, organized crime has had a profound effect on public safety. Contract killings have added to Russia's skyrocketing murder rate, and there are fears that organized criminals may be involved in trying to export nuclear weapons material and technology to other countries. The inability of government to control the problem has reduced the confidence of people in the democratic system of government. The globalization of crime means that Russian organized crime has had a direct impact on Canada.

The Criminal Intelligence reports outline that in Canada, organized crime includes groups originating in the former Soviet Union, Poland, Hungary, Romania, Bulgaria, and the former Yugoslavia. Among these groups, power tends to be concentrated among those whose origins can be traced to the territory of the former Soviet Union. These include groups originating not only in Russia proper but also in Belarus, Ukraine, Transcaucasia (such as Georgia and Chechnya), and the former Soviet Central Asia. The centre of this activity in Canada is southern Ontario. These groups are also reported to be active in the larger urban centres of Quebec and British Columbia and are known for their entrepreneurial and opportunistic tendencies. They will engage in any type of criminal activity or attempt to penetrate any market sector they view as being vulnerable for exploitation. These crime groups are involved in a wide spectrum of criminal activity, ranging from various street-level crimes to more sophisticated economic crimes requiring specific technological expertise. To give the appearance of legitimacy, they have utilized bona fide businesses as fronts for their illegal activities. The groups have maintained a close relationship with the Italian-based Mafia, the Asian-based crime groups, and the outlaw motorcycle gangs. This association allows them to reach criminal markets that would otherwise be inaccessible to them. Unlike other organized crime groups that have been observed to participate in either vehicle or commodities smuggling, these groups are extensively involved in both activities. These crime groups play a significant role in organized theft and export of automobiles in Canada. In addition, they are extensively involved in the smuggling of stolen consumer goods, from Canada and the United States to the former Soviet Union and other European countries, via both legitimate business and criminal operations (Criminal Intelligence Service Canada, 2002; 2003; 2004; 2005; 2006; 2007).

South American, Colombian, and Mexican Cartels

The Colombian organized crime syndicates are situated in most cities in Colombia but are centred in Bogota, Medellin, and Cali. Although all Colombian crime families are involved in traditional organized crime activity in Colombia, their Canadian operations are centred on illicit drug trafficking. Their cocaine and marijuana crime families are organized along the same pattern as the Italian Mafia—a corporate organizational style. Each of these syndicates has related groups that act as investors, bankers, and lawyers. In addition, most have logistics experts, exporters, chemists, and specialists in wholesaling, retailing, and market development. They have separate groups that provide support services in the areas of manufacturing, transportation, distribution, finance, and security. Few of the group members are aware of the others who are involved. The loss of one member or even a whole group does not threaten the stability or security of the remaining parts. The managers or top end of each crime organization are completely removed from physical trafficking activities. They have related groups operating in the Caribbean and in major cities in the United States as well as in Canada. In addition, they have established a strong presence in Spain to facilitate cocaine distribution throughout Europe. Recent linkages with organized crime groups in Russia have increased this European foothold.

Mexican crime groups have emerged as major distributors of illicit drugs to the United States and Canada. These groups connect directly with Colombian crime families, who at one time supplied at least 75 percent of the cocaine that is consumed in Canada and the United States and who now channel much of that illicit market through Mexico. This market amounts to a multibillion-dollar business.

Members of both the Mexican and Colombian crime families are assigned to foreign illicit distribution networks on a rotational basis. Members will move into a Canadian city for a period of six months and then return to Mexico or South America and be replaced by other members. This system of constantly changing membership makes it more difficult for law enforcement to identify the size and specific drug-trafficking activities of the group.

WWW

CATO Institute—Foreign Policy Briefing

www.cato.org/pubs/fpbriefs/fpb87.pdf

These crime families effectively control illicit cocaine distribution in South America, the Caribbean, Europe, the United States, and Canada. They are continually expanding to develop distribution networks in other parts of the world. Their propensity to be highly organized and to commit violent crimes such as serious assaults and homicide in an effort to acquire new territory has made them potentially the most dangerous crime groups in the world. Over the past few years, the Colombian and Mexican governments, with assistance from the United States, have moved more aggressively against the cartel groups. Some leaders, including the notorious Pablo Escobar, have been killed and others imprisoned. However, Colombia remains a major cocaine supplier. With new alliances with Mexican cartels, the South American crime groups will continue to dominate crime activity in the Americas and Europe for some time to come.

Other Canadian Ethnic-Based Crime Groups

In Canada, as in the United States, many citizens or residents, because of their individual cultural backgrounds, have strong family or ethnic ties to other regions of the world. When certain organized crime enterprises emerge in those other regions, it becomes profitable for those crime groups to establish bases in Canada, and Canadian citizens or residents become members of the illegal enterprise.

Major illicit drug distribution systems controlled by strong organized crime groups currently exist in the Southwest Asian area of Pakistan, Iran, and Afghanistan; in Lebanon; and in India. These networks have now established connections with groups in Canada, the United States, South America, and Europe. Illicit drugs are supplied to Canadian-based groups, which then sell the illicit product to any other organized crime groups, which in turn distribute the drugs in their own established territories.

Some drug-trafficking groups in drug-source countries are involved in national political violence. In such cases, there is the merging of organized crime and terrorism through the common interest of trafficking illicit drugs. The drug–terrorism link not only increases revenues for political purposes but also intensifies the political effect of the terrorist group through connections (usually ethnic) with another group that has traditionally been involved only in enterprise crime activity.

Most organized crime groups in Canada are becoming increasingly involved in criminal activity that manipulate technology and utilize the Internet to facilitate financial frauds. Credit card "skimming," e-commerce site hacking, and fraudulent credit card purchases are examples of how they exploit technology, including the Internet (Criminal Intelligence Service Canada, 2002; 2003; 2004; 2005; 2006; 2007).

The Nature of Consensual Crime Activity

When governments use the law to curtail the distribution and supply of goods or services that are reasonably high in public demand, a so-called black market results. In this market, the traders or businesspeople become the criminals, and their business entities become the crime organizations. They will operate without regard to territorial boundaries, taxation systems, or regulations that control legitimate trade and commerce. The cost of corruption for bribes and payoffs, and contracts for intimidation and extortion, will be the only price crime organizations will pay directly to maintain their base of control. In this environment, the consumer will pay the highest price for the lowest-quality product that the market will bear, and the crime organization will achieve its prime objective—to accumulate profit and power.

Although organized crime groups derive profits from a wide range of criminal activity including kidnapping, robbery, theft, and fraud, in North America their most sought-after criminal ventures involve consensual-type crimes. Crimes related to drug trafficking, gambling, prostitution, and pornography produce massive profits yet leave no victim behind to complain to law enforcement authorities that a financial loss has been incurred. When the criminal act has been committed, the crime group members are relatively free to use the proceeds for their own benefit. Without a victim to bring a complaint to the attention of the police and without a legitimate legal owner to bring an action of recovery for loss of property, the consensual crime will occur without creating an incident or a visible social problem in the community. Consensual crime produces more income for crime organizations than any other type of criminal activity. Drug trafficking alone accounts for most of the proceeds obtained from consensual-type crime such as prostitution, gambling, pornography, smuggling, and loan sharking.

The profitability of drug trafficking can be demonstrated by examining the increase in value of illicit drugs as they progress from the producer or manufacturer to the consumer. While the farmer who produces illicit opium may make several thousands of dollars from the annual harvest, the organized criminals who sell heroin in the illegal markets of the world will make billions of tax-free dollars annually. Judge Jean L. Dutil stated that the trade in narcotics pours tens of millions of dollars into the coffers of traffickers in Canada, financing their operations in other fields and permitting them to spread their criminal activity over a much larger area (Charbonneau, 1976; Dubro, 1985).

Like the illicit drug trade, contraband smuggling has become a major source of revenue for organized crime. Most of the criminal groups in Canada are involved, both separately and cooperatively, in smuggling operations. While tobacco and alcohol remain the most popular commodities, the range of products is constantly increasing. The only consideration is the potential of the commodity to command a maximum profit. Among the most recent goods being smuggled are jewellery and precious stones, stolen vehicles, weapons, cigars, and illegal immigrants. A substantial market for each of these products or services exists, either within or outside of Canada. One organization, whose alleged leader was arrested in the United States and is the subject of a Canada-wide arrest warrant, was responsible for smuggling tobacco and alcohol from the United States to Canada. It is estimated that this group made as much as $100 million in profits in five years (Criminal Intelligence Service Canada, 1997).

Money-Laundering Schemes

One of the few ways that a street gang's illegal activities can be connected to a national or international organized crime group is by tracing the money flow from the street-level crimes. In most organized crime groups, the transfer of the profits or proceeds is the only tangible link between the unlawful acts and the top-level organizers and planners of the group. Thus movements of funds are carefully concealed through the use of specially devised transfer systems. These systems are usually called " money laundering schemes."

Although there are a wide variety of money laundering schemes, the most difficult to penetrate and, therefore, the most popular are those that utilize secret banking and corporate facilities in tax-haven countries.

It is now recognized by international law enforcement organizations that the only successful way to identify and prosecute organized crime figures is to trace the proceeds of crime from the source to the ultimate beneficiaries. James Dubro found that

> when the Commissos [a notorious Toronto Mafia family] got involved in land deals they concentrated on hidden titles, a money laundering operation to hide the sources of profits made from drugs and contract murders. In one documented case, Remo and Commisso were in secret partnership with Alberto Bentivogli in owning a Toronto restaurant, as well as 23 acres in Richmond Hill and land in Burlington. (Dubro, 1985)

In another case, law enforcement officers from the United States, Canada, Hong Kong, Singapore, and Thailand attempted to identify and seize money being transferred from North America to Thailand via the Netherlands, Hong Kong, and Singapore. They followed the transfer of $2 million, derived from heroin sales in western United States and Canada, and transported in cash lots, first to the Netherlands and then to Hong Kong, where it was deposited in a bank. From this bank, it was transferred to a Chinese Hong Kong import–export company that operated primarily as an underground money laundering service for the Southeast Asian Chinese community.

When the funds were received by the import–export company in Hong Kong, a corresponding credit appeared with another related import–export company in Singapore. Instructions from the company in Singapore caused a further paper transfer to occur in Thailand, where the last transaction in the chain occurred. Cash was then paid to an unidentified individual, and it was believed that the funds were moved to northern Thailand to the benefit of a major drug trafficking organized crime group. No assets were seized as a result of this investigation, but it was established that over $52 million had been moved through this one laundering system. Similar laundering systems also exist for other ethnically based organized crime groups (Stamler, 1984).

Although Europeans have been using protected banking facilities in Switzerland since the early 19th century, in North America, tax havens have grown in popularity in recent times as one of the few means of placing funds beyond the reach of government authorities or tax collectors. This guarantee of financial privacy became attractive to a wide variety of persons, including those whose primary interest was not necessarily to avoid taxes. It was not long before crime organizations found the sanctuary of tax havens too inviting to ignore. With the development of multinational banking systems and international business and commerce, it became easy to develop sophisticated laundering schemes designed to move money obtained directly from criminal activity into the foreign banks protected from intrusion by law enforcement officials. For the organized criminal, this financial privacy is an indispensable aid in concealing the proceeds of crime. Many countries and territories, at times unwittingly, provide this type of protection.

These countries and territories allow easy access to banking institutions with secret-numbered accounts; they also have extended corporate and secrecy laws to allow the establishment of an unlimited number of beneficially owned corporations. These so-called offshore corporations or international business corporations are operated by local agents or lawyers but manipulated by the beneficial owners. When these corporate entities are combined with several numbered bank accounts, a maze of financial transactions can be structured in a way that makes the tracing of assets a very complex task. If questionable funds are then moved from one tax-haven jurisdiction to another, using the combination of beneficially owned corporations with secret-numbered bank accounts, the complexities are significantly increased.

Current favourite money laundering spots include Panama, the British Virgin Islands, the Channel Islands, the Turks and Caicos Islands, and the Cayman Islands. These countries and territories have extremely permissive financial regulations that enable them to attract money laundering businesses. For example, the tiny Cayman Islands has more than 500 banks that handle massive amounts of money. Total assets held by Cayman banks in 1994 were about $430 billion (United Nations, 1998).

An investigator working with a BBC TV crew visited one of the Cayman banks:

> I sat with the chairman of the bank and he described for me how to set up offshore in a way which the U.S. government could not follow what

FOCUS

BOX 15.5 Unloading Dirty Money—A Complex Process

Money laundering is a complex process. This is illustrated by a case described by Margaret Beare in her book *Criminal Conspiracies: Organized Crime in Canada*. The case involved a large North American cannabis distribution network headed by Timothy Neeb and Robert Brook. Neeb and Brook were assisted in their laundering efforts by several professionals, including Toronto lawyer Donovan Blakeman. After several years of investigation, Brook was arrested and persuaded to testify against others involved in his network. For his protection, he is now in a witness relocation program. This case demonstrates the difficulty faced by police departments in their investigations of money laundering.

Brook estimated that between 1982 and 1987, the Neeb/Brook criminal organization exchanged $100 million through Friedberg Exchange in Toronto. (In the latter period, they were exchanging $1 million per week.) This exchange house played a critical role. The profits from drug sales were converted into U.S. dollars and bearer cheques from Friedberg Currency Exchange. Bearer cheques were used in offshore bank deposits to avoid the suspicions that large cash deposits would arise. (Although less conspicuous than large amounts of cash, these bearer cheques should have alerted authorities and bank officials; bearer cheques are very uncommon in legitimate transactions because they can be stolen and cashed by anyone who has them in their possession.) Some of the U.S. dollars and bearer bonds were then flown by Blakeman to Brown Shipley Inc. in Jersey Island and England, to First Trust Corporations in St. Kitts, and to Switzerland for deposit into corporate accounts. From these corporate accounts, they were transferred to corporations in the United States, Canada, Switzerland, the Caribbean, and England.

Flight records revealed that on occasion Neeb, Blakeman, and their accountant acted as couriers for these funds, flying them personally to the second stage of what was usually a long route back home. If the Caribbean was to be the destination, the three men would rent a Learjet from Toronto's Pearson International Airport. The remaining U.S. dollars went to the United States, Mexico, and South America for the purchase of more cannabis shipments. Blakeman recognized the benefits of using international tax havens and numerous overseas corporations as vehicles for routing cash back into the criminal's hands that they could not otherwise use (RCMP case files).

> I did. He went on to explain how I could move money out of the United States by writing checks to corporations he and his bank had set up . . . in the United States to receive money from people who wanted to hide it. He described how I could then, through a Caymanian corporation whose ownership was completely concealed, open up brokerage accounts and trade on stock markets anywhere I wanted to. Then finally, he described to me how I could bring money back into the United States without its being traced. (Blum, 1994)

Laundering schemes used to move illegally obtained funds vary as widely and are as complex as legitimate business and commercial transactions. Through a variety of transactions, cash can be secretly transferred anywhere in the world. This includes the use of corporations, business entities, or phony business transactions, all done under the guise of a legitimate commercial enterprise (United States Government, 1983).

FOCUS

BOX 15.5 Unloading Dirty Money—A Complex Process *(Continued)*

The Role of Lawyers

In both the Outrage and IOU projects, lawyers and ex-lawyers played a critical role. Donovan Jackson Blakeman was the main money launderer for the Neeb/Brook organization. Blakeman became involved in the organization in 1979 and retired his law practice in 1981. His role was to "manage" the illicit profits by incorporating domestic and international corporations: maintaining numerous foreign and domestic bank accounts; and concealing, laundering, and investing (in real estate in Ontario, Florida, and elsewhere) millions of dollars of criminal proceeds.

The corporations alone were registered in Liberia, the Cayman Islands, the Isle of Man, the British Virgin Islands, Ontario, Florida, and North Carolina. A chart, titled by the criminals "What We Got!—Spaghetti Jungle," was seized from Blakeman's residence. The police identified 62 Canadian corporations directly or indirectly related to accused persons in this organized criminal group. Blakeman explained to Neeb his procedure of taking the illicit funds overseas and making deposits in various banks to the credit of numerous corporations. These funds would then be repatriated to North America through offshore accounts and investments in other offshore corporations. As only an indication of their property holdings, Neeb and Brook through Blakeman owned 148 lots in West Palm Beach, Florida. Bank accounts were located in Jersey, the Channel Islands, Switzerland, St. Kitts, Bahamas, the Cayman Islands, Ontario, and the United States.

Major funds were put into the Brown Shipley Inc. accounts in various company names. The companies were set up with little capital and got advances through use of the "spaghetti jungle" maze of corporate entities for financing. The investigation indicated that 62 Canadian corporations, 30 U.S. corporations, and 18 foreign corporations were used (directly or indirectly) to facilitate the movement of drug money. In total, $13,408,845.00 was deposited to Brown Shipley.

Source: Margaret Beare. (1996). *Criminal Conspiracies: Crime in Canada*. Toronto: ITP Nelson, pp. 208–10.

Controlling Organized Crime

Legalization of Illicit Goods and Services

Legalizing the products and services supplied to meet a public demand is one of the most effective means of curbing the profits and income of crime groups. This factor has, in turn, a direct effect on the development, growth, and continuation of organized crime within a society.

Volstead Act
Passed by the United States Congress on October 28, 1919, the legislation prohibited the manufacture and sale of alcohol in the United States. Since a ready market existed for this prohibited good, organized crime in America gained a ready foothold.

There is no doubt that when the United States Congress passed the countrywide **Volstead Act** on October 28, 1919, prohibiting the manufacture and sale of alcohol, organized crime moved into the business and became the major supplier of what had then become an illegal product. From 1920 to 1933, organized crime groups in the United States grew and flourished from the profits derived from the sale of illicit alcohol, only because it was a product prohibited by the government.

The United States stayed dry (at least legally) until 1933. In the 13 years that the sale of alcohol was prohibited in the United States, profits from the sale of illicit alcohol topped all other income from unlawful activity. When Prohibition ended, crime groups turned to gambling, illicit drugs, and prostitution as the high-income enterprises.

In more recent times, gambling laws in North America have been liberalized. In most Canadian provinces, gambling provides a significant portion of government revenues. In fact, some say that governments are now as addicted to gambling as are compulsive gamblers. An interesting example of how government has moved into this formerly criminal enterprise is the Pick 3 lottery. To win, you must pick a three-digit number matching the one drawn by the government lottery agency. Several years ago, this game was called the numbers racket and was the most common form of gambling in many low-income neighbourhoods. The main differences between the two are that criminals paid out a higher share of the take than the government does and that the profits now go back to the population and not into the pockets of organized criminals. With the decline in gambling revenues, organized crime is now focusing on other activities such as illicit drugs, pornography, extortion, immigration fraud, money laundering, smuggling, and international stock and bank frauds.

United Nations—Convention on Transnational Organized Crime
www.unodc.org/unodc/en/crime_cicp_convention.html

Although the liberalization of liquor and gambling laws in both Canada and the United States reduced the income for organized crime from those illegal activities, the dramatic increase in the demand for illicit drugs since the 1960s has more than filled the gap. Beginning in the early 1980s, drug trafficking clearly became one of the most profitable enterprises for organized crime (Canada, 1983; 1984; 1985).

Legalizing illicit drugs may, however, prove more difficult than legalizing alcohol or gambling. Canada, along with 130 countries of the world, has ratified several United Nations conventions agreeing to prohibit the manufacture, distribution, and sale of narcotic drugs except for medical, scientific, or research purposes. At this time, the trend at the United Nations is toward maintaining control over the manufacture and distribution of illicit drugs. In this international environment, it would be extremely difficult for one country to legalize the use of any illicit drugs other than for the purposes authorized by the UN conventions. The Netherlands has set up zones in which illicit drugs may be distributed for personal use without police intervention, but they have not legalized the distribution and sale of these drugs throughout the country. In Canada, the federal government gave temporary approval for a safe injection site in Vancouver. Such special zones, however, are not entrenched in law but only in police tolerance and discretion. They do not curb the activities of organized crime since the illicit drugs that are sold in these areas are produced and delivered by organized crime.

Enforcement

An effective police investigation must be proactive, especially when it is directed against an organized crime group involved in consensual crime. It must include a number of lawful covert law enforcement techniques. These covert techniques include the use of paid informants, trained undercover police officers, electronic surveillance equipment to surreptitiously record the private conversations of organized crime members, and covert physical surveillance techniques. The police and enforcement authorities must have an adequate witness protection program available so that potential witnesses will be protected from any acts of intimidation or violence by the organized crime groups. The use of financial investigations to trace, freeze, seize, and forfeit the proceeds of crime will serve to remove the profits of the criminal enterprise. This type of investigation will also assist in gathering evidence to implicate top levels of organized crime with the criminal activity carried out by the group.

Unfortunately, organized crime investigations are very expensive. Because infiltration of groups is usually impossible, the police must rely on wire taps and constant surveillance. An investigation that resulted in the arrests in Toronto, Montreal, Italy, and Mexico of the leaders of one of most powerful Sicilian crime families, the Cuntrera-Caruana group, was nearly terminated for financial reasons. The difficulties of such investigations were outlined as follows by Staff Sergeant Larry Tronstad, the RCMP officer who headed the day-to-day investigation: "These guys change phones every week; it was a huge problem. At one point we had over 100 pay phones wired hoping to get these guys. They are extremely surveillance conscious" (Appleby and Cheney, 1998, A1, A2).

Another problem was tracing the money used to purchase millions of dollars' worth of cocaine: "The money was originating in Italy, then moving to Switzerland, then to Miami, then to Caracas, then to Mexico and then on to here [Toronto]. And in each of these countries they had a network set up, opening and shutting bank accounts before we're even there" (Appleby and Cheney, 1998, A1, A2).

Limitations on police resources mean that many of the activities of organized crime groups are never investigated.

National Criminal Laws and Procedures

The enactment of new criminal laws over the past several years has provided new tools for law enforcement to combat both organized crime and terrorism in Canada. The Proceeds of Crime (Money Laundering) and Terrorist Financing Act, together with new regulations, established the Financial Transaction and Report Analysis Center of Canada (FINTRAC). This agency, under the Ministry of Finance, now receives and collects reports on suspicious financial transactions, as well as other information relevant to money laundering. Under the provisions of this Act, financial institutions and other identified private business entities are required to report all suspicious financial transactions and all money movements that are specifically outlined in the regulations. The information that is then collected and analyzed is supplied to Canadian law enforcement and intelligence agencies.

In 1997, the legislature of Quebec introduced legislation to prevent real estate from being used as a fortified or barricaded residence, which is often associated with outlaw motorcycle gangs. A similar law has since been passed by the Ontario legislature. Manitoba, on the other hand, uses The Civil Remedies

Manitoba Civil Remedies Against Organized Crime
web2.gov.mb.ca/laws/statutes/ccsm/c107e.php

B.C. Ministry of Public Safety and Solicitor General News Release: New Law Targets Organized Crime
www2.news.gov.bc.ca/nrm_news_releases/2005PSSG0011-000260.htm

Against Organized Crime Act to prevent biker gangs and other organized crime groups from setting up legitimate businesses. Under the legislation police apply for court orders to cancel or withhold liquor licences and dissolve businesses that are intended to be used to advance the objectives of crime organizations. In addition to Quebec and Manitoba, Ontario, British Columbia, and Alberta have civil forfeiture laws.

National criminal laws and procedures along with provincial legislation are being improved to help ensure that organized crime is not able to profit from the proceeds generated by criminal activity, no matter where a crime has occurred. Canada has enacted criminal laws that make it an offence to possess the proceeds of crime. This means that it is an offence to possess anything that was obtained or derived directly or indirectly from the commission of an indictable offence or from any act committed anywhere, which, if committed in Canada, would be classified as an indictable offence. This law, combined with the laws of conspiracy, makes it possible to prosecute in Canada anyone who conspires to possess proceeds of crime within Canada, even if all the conspirators are outside Canada.

Besides empowering an attorney general to obtain an order to seize or restrain the proceeds of crime and request forfeiture, the Criminal Code makes it an offence for anyone to launder the proceeds of crime. This includes employees of banks and financial institutions. The current laws and regulations provide law enforcement with considerable authority to investigate organized crime and seize and forfeit the proceeds of crime.

International Cooperation

In 2000, the United Nations developed a convention against transnational organized crime. This convention has now been adopted by more than 120 countries.

New national laws will be required in each country to conform to the convention. These new laws and programs will make it easier for law enforcement in each country to identify and prosecute organized criminals who are operating at the international level from a base in one or two countries.

The convention also requires that national laws include in their definition of organized crime groups all persons and entities that supply and assist organized crime. This means that otherwise legitimate organizations that supply goods or services to organized crime that are subsequently distributed unlawfully will be caught up in the definition of organized crime activity. For example, the tobacco manufacturing company that sold cigarettes that it knew were being distributed in an unlawful manner in another country will likely be prosecuted for money laundering, because the proceeds of the smuggling operation obtained by the organized crime groups were used to purchase the next supply of cigarettes. If a conviction for money laundering is achieved, the entire amount of funds that the manufacturer received will be subject to seizure and forfeiture. In addition the manufacturer will likely be prosecuted for receiving the proceeds of crime. This situation will likely apply to any other goods or services that follow a similar pattern.

Unfortunately, as law enforcement develops more capabilities, so do the wealthy and powerful organized crime groups of the world. In the meantime, governments will likely continue to outlaw goods and services that the public demands. Organized crime will continue to build sophisticated international supply chains to bring those goods and services to a waiting public willing to part with their funds.

Summary

- The demand for illegal goods and services influences the presence, size, and structure of organized crime.
- The phenomenon of organized crime is best described as the operation of illegal business entities, members of which are bound together because of their group interest and because of their desire to profit from illegal activity.
- There are a number of major organized crime groups in Canada. These groups have connections with groups in many other countries and use these connections to distribute their illicit goods and services.
- Crime organizations establish territorial distribution areas and utilize extortion and corruption to develop regions under their control and enforce their rules.
- Organized crime groups launder their illegal profits through countries whose laws are designed to protect bank and investment records. Often laundered profits are invested in legitimate businesses.
- Government control over organized crime is exercised through police enforcement and prosecution through the courts. However, because of its global nature, organized crime cannot be fought without international action and co-operation.
- The only certain way to reduce the influence of organized crime is to reduce the demand for the illicit goods and services that organized crime groups supply.

QUESTIONS FOR CRITICAL THINKING

1. Discuss the role played by governments in the creation of organized crime. Using cigarette smuggling as an example, describe several actions the government could take to reduce the profits of organized crime.
2. Why do most successful organized crime groups tend to be ethnically based?
3. Think about the theories of crime causation you studied in earlier chapters of this book. Which of these theories provides the best explanation of organized crime?
4. Find some reference material in the library or on the Internet on Russian organized crime groups. Why did these groups become so powerful in such a short time after the end of the Communist regime? How does their existence threaten the future of democracy in Russia?

5. If you were an advisor to the government of Canada, what actions would you recommend to reduce the impact of organized crime?
6. What distinguishes organized crime from terrorism?

NET WORK

There is a good deal of material about organized crime on the Internet. A good place to start is the website of York University's Nathanson Centre on Transnational Human Rights, Crime and Security at **www.yorku.ca/nathanson/Links/links.htm.** This site has an extensive bibliography that can be searched by keyword. It also has many links to other sites.

Using the links on this site, answer the following questions:

1. Organized crime groups based in Russia are becoming more powerful. Discuss the latest information about the spread of these groups into Canada and other countries. What are the major illegal activities of Russian/Eastern European organized crime groups?
2. What new opportunities does globalization offer to organized crime? Why are organized crime groups in a good position to take advantage of these opportunities?
3. What is narcoterrorism? How does it differ from traditional organized crime?

KEY TERMS

consensual crime; pg. 480
Mafia; pg. 473
Triads; pg. 479
Volstead Act; pg. 489

SUGGESTED READING

Beare, Margaret E. (1996). *Criminal Conspiracies: Organized Crime in Canada*. Toronto: ITP Nelson. The first systematic and comprehensive examination of organized crime in Canada written by the former director of York University's Nathanson Centre on Transnational Human Rights, Crime and Security. The book describes the characteristics of those who get involved in organized crime and the changing nature of international organized crime, and addresses the issues of how law enforcement agencies can best deal with the problem.

Block, A. A. (1990). *Perspectives on Organized Crime*. Dordrecht, The Netherlands: Kluwer Academic Publishers. This book presents some interesting essays on some of the more recent activities of organized crime. These include toxic waste disposal and financial crimes such as tax evasion.

Carrigan, O. D. (1991). *Crime and Punishment in Canada: A History*. Toronto: McClelland and Stewart. Chapter 4 of this book is a very entertaining and informative chapter on the history of organized crime in Canada.

Cressey, D. R. (1969). *Theft of the Nation*. New York: Harper and Row. This book is drawn from Cressey's research for the influential President's Commission on Law

Enforcement and the Administration of Justice. He presents his view that there was a national cartel that controlled organized crime in the United States.

Criminal Intelligence Service Canada. (2002). *Annual Report on Organized Crime in Canada.* Ottawa: Department of Supply and Services. An annual review of organized crime in Canada. Updates are available on the Internet at www.cisc.gc.ca.

Criminal Intelligence Service Canada. (2004). *Annual Report on Organized Crime in Canada.* Ottawa: Department of Supply and Services. An annual review of organized crime in Canada. Updates are available on the Internet at www.cisc.gc.ca.

Criminal Intelligence Service Canada (2006). *Annual Report on Organized Crime in Canada.* Ottawa: Updates are available on the Internet at www.cisc.gc.ca.

Criminal Intelligence Service Canada (2007). *Annual Report on Organized Crime in Canada.* Ottawa: Department of Supply and Services. An annual review of organized crime in Canada. Updates are available on the Internet at www.cisc.gc.ca.

Dubro, J. (1992). *Dragons of Crime.* Markham: Butterworths. A very readable and objective discussion of the history and activities of Asian gangs in Canada. Dubro is one of Canada's more experienced observers of organized crime.

Lavigne, Yves. (1987). *Hells Angels: Taking Care of Business.* Toronto: Deneau and Wayne. A fascinating book about the history of the Hells Angels and their Canadian operations.

Reuter, P. (1983). *Disorganized Crime.* Cambridge: MIT Press. One of the relatively few detailed research studies on organized crime. Reuter, an economist, examines the illegal markets of bookmaking, numbers gambling, and loan sharking. His results question the widely held view that the Italian Mafia has maintained firm control over these activities.

Wolf, D. R. (1991). *The Rebels: A Brotherhood of Outlaw Bikers.* Toronto: University of Toronto Press. A rare ethnographic study of a biker gang written by a Canadian anthropologist. Wolf claims that the Rebels, a group based in Alberta and Saskatchewan, commit minor criminal offences but were not involved in organized crime.

BIBLIOGRAPHY

Appleby, Timothy, and Peter Cheney. (1998). "Police Hit Crime Family." *Globe and Mail,* 16 July:A1, A2.

Beare, Margaret E. (1996). *Criminal Conspiracies: Organized Crime in Canada.*Toronto: ITP Nelson.

Blum, J. (1994). "Global Financial Systems Under Assault: Countering the $500 Billion Conspiracy." In L. P. Raine and F. J. Cilluffo (eds.), *Global Organized Crime: The New Empire of Evil* (pp. 22–25). Washington: The Center for Strategic and International Studies.

Bresler, Fenton. (1980). *The Trial of the TRIADS: An Investigation into International Crime.* London: Weidenfeld and Nicolson.

Canada. (1980). "No Biker Problems in Canada?" *Royal Canadian Mounted Police—Gazette.* Ottawa: RCMP:42:10.

———. (1983). *RCMP National Drug Intelligence Estimate 1982.* Ottawa: Queen's Printer.

———. (1984). *RCMP National Drug Intelligence Estimate 1983.* Ottawa: Queen's Printer.

———. (1985). *RCMP National Drug Intelligence Estimate 1984/5.* Ottawa: Queen's Printer.

———. (1992). *Organized Crime Committee Report. Ottawa*: Criminal Intelligence Service Canada.

Carrigan, O. D. (1991). *Crime and Punishment in Canada: A History.* Toronto: McClelland and Stewart.

Charbonneau, Jean-Pierre. (1976). *The Canadian Connection.* Ottawa: Optimum Publishing Company.

Cressey, D. R. (1969). *Theft of the Nation.* New York: Harper and Row.

Criminal Intelligence Service Canada. (1997). *Annual Report on Organized Crime in Canada.* Ottawa: Department of Supply and Services Canada.

———. (2001). *Annual Report on Organized Crime in Canada.* Ottawa: Department of Supply and Services Canada.

———. (2002). *Annual Report on Organized Crime in Canada.* Ottawa: Department of Supply and Services Canada.

———. (2003). *Annual Report on Organized Crime in Canada.* Ottawa: Department of Supply and Services Canada.

———. (2004). *Annual Report on Organized Crime in Canada.* Ottawa: Department of Supply and Services Canada.

———. (2005). *Annual Report on Organized Crime in Canada.* Ottawa: Department of Supply and Services Canada.

———. (2006). *Annual Report on Organized Crime in Canada.* Ottawa: Department of Supply and Services Canada.

———. (2007). *Annual Report on Organized Crime in Canada.* Ottawa: Department of Supply and Services Canada.

Dubro, James. (1985). *Mob Rule: Inside the Canadian Mafia.* Toronto: Macmillan.

———. (1992). *Dragons of Crime.* Markham: Butterworths

Dutil, Jean L. (1977). Quebec Police Commission, Report of the Commission of Inquiry on Organized Crime in Quebec, "The Fight Against Organized Crime in Quebec."

Glaser, Daniel. (1978). *Crime in Our Changing Society.* New York: Holt, Rinehart and Winston.

Haller, M. H. (1990). "Illegal Enterprise: A Theoretical and Historical Interpretation." *Criminology* 28:207–35.

Handelman, S. (1994). "The Russian 'Mafiya.'" *Foreign Affairs* 73:83–96.

Hersh, S. M. (1994). "The Wild East." *The Atlantic Monthly* (June):61–86.

Maclean, Don. (1974). *Pictorial History of the Mafia.* New York: Pyramid Books.

Mansell, Ingrid, and Roger Boyes. (2003). "Hamburg Police Raid Reemtsma Offices." *The Times of London* 15 January.

Pennsylvania Crime Commission. (1980). *A Decade of Organized Crime.* Pennsylvania State Printer.

Porteous, Samuel. (1998). *Organized Crime Impact Study: Highlights*, prepared for the Ministry of the Solicitor General, Canada.

Quebec. (1977). *The Fight Against Organized Crime in Quebec.* Quebec: Éditeur Officiel.

Raine, L. P., and F. J. Cilluffo (eds.). (1994). *Global Organized Crime: The New Empire of Evil.* Washington: The Center for Strategic and International Studies.

Reuter, P. (1983). *Disorganized Crime.* Cambridge: MIT Press.

Sacco, Vincent F. (1986). "An Approach to the Study of Organized Crime." In Robert A. Silverman and James J. Teevan (eds.), *Crime in Canadian Society* (3rd ed.) (pp. 214–26). Toronto: Butterworths.

Sacco, V. F., and L. W. Kennedy. (1994). *The Criminal Event.* Scarborough: Nelson Canada.

Stamler, Rodney T. (1984). *Background Document—Proceeds of Drug Trafficking.* Vienna: United Nations Division of Narcotic Drugs Report. DND/Wp 1984/9.

Stille, A. (1995). *Excellent Cadavers: The Mafia and the Death of the First Italian Republic.* New York: Pantheon.

Thomas, D. (1992). *Criminality Among the Foreign Born: Analysis of Federal Prison Population.* Ottawa: Immigration and Employment Canada.

United Nations. (1998). "UN Laundering Report: A Global View." *The Report on Crime and Profiteering* 2(3):20–22.

United Nations Office on Drugs and Crime. (2007). *2007 World Drug Report.* New York: United Nations Office on Drugs and Crime.

United States Government. (1983) (February). Permanent Subcommittee on Investigations. *Crime and Secrecy: The Use of Offshore Banks and Companies.* Washington, D.C.: U.S. Government Printing Office.

Wolf, D. R. (1991). *The Rebels: A Brotherhood of Outlaw Bikers.* Toronto: University of Toronto Press.

Woolsey, R. J. (1994). "Global Organized Crime: Threats to U.S. and International Security." In Linnea P. Raine and Frank J. Cilluffo (eds.), *Global Organized Crime: The New Empire of Evil* (pp. 134–44). Washington: The Center for Strategic and International Studies.

16 Corporate and White-Collar Crime

John Hagan

NORTHWESTERN UNIVERSITY

Rick Linden

UNIVERSITY OF MANITOBA

Most of us know far more about street crime and organized crime than we do about corporate and white-collar crime. While cases such as the multibillion-dollar Enron bankruptcy and the Conrad Black trial (see Chapter 1) have raised the profile of these crimes, few Canadians are aware of the harm that is done by corporate and white-collar criminals. In fact, these crimes are much more costly in dollar terms than street crime is. The $6 billion lost to investors in the Bre-X fraud discussed later in this chapter is far more than the money lost in all the robberies in Canadian history. Few bank robbers get away with more than a few thousand dollars, but Julius Melnitzer, an Ontario lawyer, defrauded banks and friends of $90 million to support his lavish lifestyle. Corporate and white-collar crimes also cause a large number of deaths and injuries. Laureen Snider (1988) reported that occupational deaths were the third leading cause of death in Canada and attributed at least half these deaths to unsafe and illegal working conditions.

The topic of white-collar crime raises some important issues in the field of criminology. The term itself, introduced by Edwin Sutherland (1940) more than a half-century ago, may be one of the most popularly used criminological concepts in everyday life. However, despite its popularity, there is uncertainty about the precise meaning of the term. This is less important than the fact that the concept of white-collar crime has forced a reconsideration of some very basic criminological assumptions.

No longer is it possible to take for granted the way in which crime itself is defined. No longer can the official data collected on crime by agencies of crime control be accepted uncritically. No longer can it be assumed that the poor are necessarily more criminal than the rich. The criminological enterprise has taken on new form and substance now that the topic of white-collar crime has become a central part of our thinking. This chapter will consider issues of class, crime, and the corporations; the social organization of work; and legal sanctions. Each is part of the topic of white-collar crime.

Learning Objectives

After reading this chapter, you should be able to

- Describe the concept of white-collar crime and explain the impact the notion of white-collar crime had on the discipline of criminology.
- Understand the occupational and organizational components of white-collar crime.
- Explain the physical and social harm caused by white-collar crime in Canada.
- Analyze how the structure of the modern corporation facilitates criminal activity.
- Understand the nature and extent of occupational crime.
- Understand the causes and consequences of our weak laws concerning corporate and white-collar crime.

The Extent and Nature of Corporate and White-Collar Crime

The Extent of Corporate and White-Collar Crime

The business section in your daily paper normally deals with stories involving new business developments, company profits, mergers, and other related matters. However, in recent years criminal matters have become a routine part of business reporting. To give you some idea of the extent of corporate and white-collar crime, consider the following stories from the May 9, 2003, edition of the business section of the *Globe and Mail*:

- Two Ontario men were charged with theft and fraud because of activities in the mid-1990s that resulted in over $40 million in losses. Mark Eizenga and James Sylvester were accused of selling shares to support investments in Cuba and the Caribbean. Investors were allegedly misled by the pair, and most of the money has disappeared.
- Stock traders working for a unit of the Royal Bank were accused of placing stock orders late in the day in order to artificially inflate the closing price of a stock at the end of a reporting period. This would help to make the performance of a stock portfolio look more positive than it actually was.
- The Ontario Securities Commission has accused a Peterborough man of collecting at least $25 million by falsely guaranteeing individuals a high rate of return on investments.
- There is a flaw in Microsoft's Internet Passport service that could make it possible for computer hackers to gain access to the accounts of customers visiting Internet shopping sites. The system also controls access to Microsoft's Hotmail system. The security flaw placed Microsoft in possible violation of a U.S. Federal Trade Commission order to ensure that personal

consumer information was protected by the Passport system. The order resulted from previous problems with the system.

- Rupert Murdoch, owner of a global media empire that includes Fox TV, appeared before a U.S. Congressional committee seeking approval of a takeover of DirecTV, which is the largest provider of satellite television in the United States. Critics fear that the deal would violate competition laws by allowing Murdoch's company to use its huge size to force smaller competitors out of business.
- The U.S. government is pursuing fraud charges against HealthSouth Corporation, the largest owner of physical therapy clinics and rehabilitation clinics in the United States. Many of the company's executives have pleaded guilty to making fraudulent reports that made the company appear to be more profitable than it actually was. This inflated the stock price. Many investors who bought the stock because of its apparent profitability lost most of their money when the fraud was revealed.
- A New York stockbroker was accused of using his clients' money to pay off former employees who had threatened to reveal his illegal stock trading. He had been previously charged with "churning" investors' accounts. "Churning" is the practice of making unnecessary trades to generate higher commissions.
- The Dutch company Ahold NV, one of the world's largest supermarket companies, lowered its earnings estimates by $880 million after these earnings had been artificially inflated by some of its American executives in order to make the company's performance look better than it really was.
- The U.S. Securities and Exchange Commission is looking into potential accounting fraud charges against Qwest Communications, a large phone company. The company overstated its revenues by $2.2 billion over a three-year period ending in 2001.
- Halliburton Company, once run by U.S. Vice-President Dick Cheney, admitted paying $2.4 million in bribes to an official of the Nigerian government in order to get tax breaks for its operations in that country.

In addition to these stories involving violations and possible violations of criminal laws and securities regulations, there were also several articles dealing with ethical and regulatory issues. Among these were stories dealing with the need for better regulation of the stock market; the debate over the need to better regulate complex financial instruments known as derivatives; ethical questions about whether it was proper for Gerry Schwartz, the chief executive of the large Canadian company Onex, to appoint his wife to the board of directors of his company; the problems that were created for the Calgary-based oil company Talisman when it was accused of producing revenues that helped the Sudanese government to repress its own people in a civil war; a discussion of the reluctance of major pharmaceutical manufacturers to provide low-cost AIDS drugs for developing countries that cannot afford to pay for these treatments; and the ethics of Molson's sex-laden campaign for Bavaria beer.

More recently, the *Globe and Mail* has published another significant list of occupational crimes, but this time it is in the sports section rather than in the business news. On July 25, 2007, several sports scandals made the headlines:

- National Basketball Association referee Tim Donaghy resigned from the league after being accused of betting on basketball games, including some that he had refereed. He was also accused of providing inside information to gamblers. Donaghy subsequently pleaded guilty to two charges.
- Barry Bonds was nearing Hank Aaron's Major League Baseball home run record. While Bonds broke the record later that season, his accomplishment was tarnished by accusations that he used muscle-building steroids to help him develop his hitting power. Bonds was later charged with lying to a grand jury about his alleged steroid use. Many other Major League Baseball players have also been accused of using drugs to help their performance.
- Top cyclist Alexandre Vinokourov was sent home after testing positive for performance-enhancing drugs while riding in the Tour de France, the world's most prestigious cycling event. Later that week race leader Michael Rasmussen was also sent home because of suspicion that he had used doping to improve his performance. The race has been dogged by doping allegations for years, and in 2006, race winner Floyd Landis was disqualified after a positive drug test.
- Officials of Formula One motor racing team McLaren-Mercedes were accused of illegally obtaining confidential technical documents from the rival Ferrari team. McLaren-Mercedes and its star drivers Fernando Alonso and Lewis Hamilton had been the leading racing team in 2007. Ultimately, McLaren-Mercedes were fined $100 million for their offence.

Corporate espionage in the sports world did not end with the McLaren-Mercedes incident. Later in 2007, New England Patriot coach Bill Belichick, one of the National Football League's most successful coaches, was fined $500 000 for using a video camera to spy on an opposing coach during a game and Chinese officials were caught filming a Danish women's soccer team meeting through a two-way mirror prior to the Denmark–China match in the Women's World Cup, which took place in China. Obviously the pressure to win is sufficient to overcome any sense of ethics and fair play that some sports executives and athletes might possess.

The sheer volume of these stories clearly shows that corporate and white-collar crime is a major problem. Although most of these stories will remain on the business pages, many others that you will read about in this chapter have become front-page news. The public is finally starting to become aware of the harm being done by corporate and white-collar criminals.

The Nature of Corporate and White-Collar Crime

Corporate and white-collar offenders have found many ways to make money. Figure 16.1 shows the range of offences committed by corporations and by individuals in the course of practising legitimate occupations. We will not discuss all these different crimes, but in the rest of this chapter you will first learn about corporate crimes and then about crimes committed by individual practitioners.

Class, Crime, and the Corporations

Occupation, Organization, and Crime

white-collar crime
An important concept in criminology but one with changing definitions. As used by Edwin Sutherland in 1940, the concept referred to corporate behaviour that caused social harm and for which there was a legal sanction. This sanction need not be criminal; it could be regulatory. Since that time, criminologists have also included the illegal actions of executives or employees who commit crimes against their employer or use organizational resources to gain personal benefit.

WWW
Scams and Frauds RCMP Site
www.rcmp-grc.gc.ca/scams/index_e.htm

occupational crime
Refers to individuals who violate the law in the course of practising a legitimate occupation.

organizational or corporate crime
White-collar crime committed with the support and encouragement of a formal organization and intended at least in part to advance the goals of that organization.

WWW
"Get Tough on Corporate Crime" Aaron Freeman and Craig Forcese, Democracy Watch On-line
www.web.net/dwatch/camp/corpcr94.html

White-collar crimes are often committed through, and on behalf of, corporations. The involvement of corporations in crime has been recognized at least since the early part of this century, when E. A. Ross (1907) wrote of a new type of criminal "who picks pockets with a 'rake-off' instead of a jimmy, cheats with a company prospectus instead of a deck of cards, or scuttles his town instead of his ship." Particular actions of corporations have been criminal offences in Canada since 1889 (Casey, 1985). However, it was not until after the Great Depression that Edwin Sutherland (1940) finally attached a lasting label to these offenders in his influential paper "White-Collar Crime." Sutherland proposed in this paper that white-collar crime be defined "as a crime committed by a person of respectability and high social status in the course of his occupation."

Since Sutherland came up with this term, there has been confusion about the role of *occupation* and *organization* in the study of white-collar crime. For example, Wheeler and Rothman (1982) note that two influential works—Clinard's (1952) and Hartung's (1950) studies of black-market activities during World War II—defined white-collar crime in two rather different ways. Clinard defined white-collar crime occupationally, as "illegal activities among business and professional men," while Hartung included an organizational component, defining such crimes as "a violation of law regulating business, which is committed for a firm by the firm or its agents in the conduct of its business." A distinction is still often drawn today (see, for example, Coleman, 1985, 8) between "**occupational crime**—that is, white collar crime committed by an individual or group of individuals exclusively for personal gain," and "**organizational crime**—white collar crimes committed with the support and encouragement of a formal organization and intended at least in part to advance the goals of that organization." Organizational crime is also known as **corporate crime.**

The problem is that the occupational and organizational components of many white-collar crimes cannot be easily separated. Clinard and Yeager (1980) make this point with the example of a Firestone tire official who aided his corporation in securing and administering illegal political contributions benefiting the corporation, but then embezzled much of the funds for himself. The illegal activities of lawyers (Reasons and Chappell, 1985) are another common form of white-collar crime in which it is often difficult to separate the individual component from what is done for and through the law firm. Nonetheless, it is important to note that locating white-collar offenders in their ownership and authority positions in occupational and organizational structures is a key part of the class analysis of white-collar crime (Geis, 1984; Hagan and Parker, 1985; Weisburd et al., 1990). Sutherland's emphasis on "respect" and "status" in defining white-collar crime opens up the issue of class position and the role it plays in any understanding of white-collar crime. A key element of social class is the power to commit major white-collar crimes that only ownership

FIGURE 16.1 Types of Corporate and White-Collar Crime

Crimes Against the Public

Corporate and Business Crime

- Price-fixing (conspiring on contract bids or on prices for selling to the public)
- Manipulation of stocks and securities
- Commercial and political bribery and rebates
- Patent and trademark infringements
- Misrepresentation and false advertising
- Fraudulent grading, packaging, and labelling
- Tax fraud
- Adulteration of food and drugs
- Illegal pollution of the environment

Crimes by Individual and Professional Practitioners

- Obtaining fees, payments, or charges through fraud and deception
- Deceiving or defrauding patients, clients, customers
- Immoral practices in relations with clients
- Unprofessional conduct and malpractice
- Falsification of statements on vital documents

Crimes within the Organization

Offences Against the Organization

- Theft of funds by employees
- Theft of inventory by employees

Offences Against Employees

- Violation of workplace health and safety laws
- Violation of labour laws
- Discriminatory employment practices
- Harassment

Source: Adapted from Ronald Akers. (1973). *Deviant Behavior: A Social Learning Approach.* Belmont: Wadsworth: 180–81. Reprinted with permission of the author.

and authority positions in occupational and organizational structures can make possible.

Sutherland (1945) insisted that insofar as there exists a "legal description of acts as socially injurious and legal provision of a penalty for the act," such acts are, for the purposes of our research and understanding, crime (cf., Tappan, 1947). This is the case even though many such acts go undetected and unprosecuted. For example, many stock and securities frauds can be prosecuted under provincial securities legislation or under the Criminal Code of Canada. The former are considered "quasi-criminal" statutes. Yet the behaviours prosecuted under either body of law may be identical. It is an act of prosecutorial discretion that determines whether these behaviours are defined clearly and officially as crimes. Sutherland insisted that such acts of official discretion were not relevant to the categorization of these behaviours for the purposes of research. In either case, the behaviours were to be regarded as criminal. Such a position can make a major difference in the relationship observed between class and crime.

Consider the issue of deaths and accidents that result from events in the workplace. Occupational deaths outnumber deaths resulting from murder (Sharpe and Hardt, 2006). While it cannot be assumed that most of these deaths result from the illegal actions of employers, there nonetheless is good reason to believe that many are not simply the result of employee carelessness.

One estimate (Reasons et al., 1981) holds that more than one-third of all on-the-job injuries are due to illegal working conditions, and that about another quarter are due to legal but unsafe conditions. At most, one-third of all such accidents are attributed to unsafe acts on the part of employees. There are numerous well-documented examples of employers intentionally, knowingly, or negligently creating hazards. These include failing to follow administrative orders to alter dangerous situations and covering up the creation and existence of such hazards. The penalties for these offences are very light. For example, Reasons et al. discuss the case of Quasar Petroleum of Calgary, which was fined $15 000 for violating safety regulations when three men died while cleaning out a tank containing toxic fumes. The men were not provided with protective equipment nor were they trained to recognize the need for such equipment.

The case of asbestos poisoning involving administrative decisions within the Johns-Manville Corporation is but one of the best-known examples. Swartz (1978) notes that asbestos has been recognized as a serious health hazard since the turn of the century. Nonetheless, people working with it were not informed, and the government bureaucracy and the medical community ignored the hazard. At the Johns-Manville plant in Toronto, company doctors regularly diagnosed lung diseases among the asbestos workers, but they never told the workers that their lung problems were related to asbestos. Many of the workers subsequently died of asbestos-related illnesses. In 2005, asbestos-related deaths accounted for nearly one-third of workplace fatalities in Canada (Sharpe and Hardt, 2006).

The construction industry also has high rates of death and injury because of failure to implement workplace health and safety regulations. For example, in two Manitoba cases one company was fined $75 000 because of the death of a bridge painter who was working on a platform with no guard rails, and another was fined $27 500 for its role in the death of a young worker who was electrocuted when he was allowed to work on a high-voltage light fixture while the wires were live (McIntyre, 2001). Swartz (1978) concludes that these deaths should be recognized as a form of murder, or what is sometimes called "corporate homicide." However, as with the Westray mine disaster (Box 16.1), corporate executives are almost never held personally responsible for their negligence. At most, their companies are ordered to pay small fines.

This chapter does not attempt to debate the fine points in the definition of corporate homicide or to establish with any precision how many such homicides occur. It is enough to note that such deaths occur in considerable numbers. Of immediate interest here is the meaning of corporate homicide, and crimes like it, for the relationship between class and crime.

Social Class and Crime

To pursue this interest, a fundamental point must first be made about more conventional forms of crime and delinquency. There is increasing evidence that a relatively small number of offenders account for a rather large proportion of serious street crimes (Greenwood, 1982; Wolfgang, 1972). The difficulty of including such persons in conventional research designs has probably obscured the relationship that exists between class position and this type of criminality.

A parallel point may be true of many kinds of white-collar crime. For example, crimes such as corporate homicide may occur much more frequently among particular employers in particular kinds of industries. The mining, asbestos, and construction industries are examples that have already been noted. It may be difficult to pinpoint such employers in conventional research designs, and this may obscure the relationship between class position and this type of criminality.

Implicit in the preceding references to street crimes and corporate homicide is the high likelihood that crime is not a unidimensional concept. That is, these are different kinds of crime that likely have different connections to the concept of class. Among adults, class probably is negatively related to making the direct physical attacks involved in street crimes of violence, and class probably is positively related to causing harms less directly through criminal acts involving the use of corporate resources. Similarly, among juveniles, it may be that some common acts of delinquency (for example, forms of theft that include the illegal copying of computer software and music and the unauthorized use of credit and bank cards) are related positively to class (Cullen et al., 1985; Hagan et al., 1985; Hagan and Kay, 1990), while less frequent and more serious forms of delinquency are negatively related to class (see Chapter 5). The study of white-collar crime and delinquency provides increasing reason to believe that measures of class are connected to crime and delinquency in interesting, albeit complicated, ways.

Why do higher-status people get involved in criminal behaviour? Shover and Hochstetler (2006) suggest three cultural components of middle- and upper-class life that may shape their criminality: a competitive spirit; arrogance; and a sense of entitlement. The unethical acts of many of the sports figures described at the beginning of this chapter were carried out in order to help them win. Athletes are told that "winning is the only thing" and some respond to this pressure by cheating. According to Shover and Hochstetler, employees at Enron (a corporation discussed later in this chapter) were continuously evaluated and 15 percent were always rated unacceptable. They feel that this competitive pressure and the resulting insecurity of employees helped to foster a culture that encouraged misconduct. The fact that success in business is often measured by the size of one's salary can help to explain why executives who are already making huge salaries will break the rules so they can make even more money.

Shover and Hochstetler propose that people who are used to power and authority can develop an arrogance that convinces them that the rules that apply to the rest of us do not apply to them. Conrad Black was very explicit in contrasting his abilities and position with those of people who were not among the rich and powerful. You will recall from Chapter 1 that Black was expelled from Upper Canada College for several offences, including selling copies of final

FOCUS

BOX 16.1 Westray—A Disaster of Criminal Proportions

In the early morning of 9 May 1992 a violent explosion rocked the tiny community of Plymouth, just east of Stellarton, in Pictou County, Nova Scotia. The explosion occurred in the depths of the Westray coal mine, instantly killing the 26 miners working there at the time" (Richard, 1997, vii). These words begin the report of a judicial inquiry into the Westray mine explosion that tells a shocking story of corporate and government misconduct that resulted in one of the largest occupational disasters in Canadian history.

Glasbeek and Tucker (1994) point out that the Westray explosion was not an accident, but like other occupational health and safety damage was the result of conscious decisions by those responsible for the safety of the miners. This conclusion was reinforced by the title of Justice Richard's inquiry: *The Westray Story: A Predictable Path to Disaster.*

While the explosion was not an accident, nobody intended to kill the miners. Rather, their deaths were the result of "a complex mosaic of actions, omissions, mistakes, incompetence, apathy, cynicism, stupidity, and neglect" (Richard, 1997, viii). The inquiry concluded that Westray managers "displayed a certain disdain for safety and appeared to regard safety-conscious workers as the wimps in the organization" (Richard, 1997, ix).

The mine was built in an area that was known to be treacherous because of geological faults and high levels of methane gas. However, only minimal safety precautions were taken. The mine owners and governments were more concerned about the economics of mining than about protecting the workers. While there were safety standards that should have been maintained, the government relied on the company to meet these standards and provided very limited compliance inspections. The company, Curragh Corporation, was having financial difficulties and put pressure on Westray to increase production levels in order to increase company revenues. Safety violations were common and some miners quit; others stayed because of the lack of alternative employment in the province. The state of safety of the mine was eloquently summed up by Justice Richard:

examinations. In his memoirs he justified his actions by describing his reaction to the school staff:

> All those who, by their docility or obsequiousness, legitimized the excesses of the school's penal system, the several sadists and few aggressively fondling homosexuals on the faculty, and the numerous swaggering boobies who had obviously failed in the real world and retreated to Lilliput where they could maintain their exalted status by contract threat of battery: all that gradually produced in me a profound revulsion. (Olive, 2007, 1)

He was not humbled by the criminal charges against him that led to his conviction in 2007:

> Canadians suspect, if only intuitively, the corruption of the American prosecutorial system and I have made the transition from being perceived as a plutocrat to an underdog. . . . I am undaunted. . . . When the case is exposed as the unmitigated farrago of lies and defamations that it is, the exhilaration at having defeated the most powerful organization in the world—not just the so-called Justice Department, but the SEC,

FOCUS

BOX 16.1 Westray—A Disaster of Criminal Proportions *(Continued)*

> I find that the source of ignition was sparks struck by the cutting bits of the continuous miner working in the Southwest 2 section of the mine. But it became apparent as the Inquiry proceeded that conditions at Westray were of greater significance to what happened than was the source of the ignition. Had there been adequate ventilation, had there been adequate treatment of coal dust, and had there been adequate training and an appreciation by management for a safety ethic, those sparks would have faded harmlessly. (1997, 3)

Despite clear evidence of these violations, the government did not exercise its responsibility under the Mineral Resources Act and shut down the mine until it was safe.

Five employees of the Nova Scotia Natural Resources Department and the Department of Labour were fired for their role in the explosion, but nobody from the mining company will ever be held legally responsible for the Westray tragedy. Clifford Frame, president of Curragh Corporation, refused to testify at the inquiry and was never charged with any offence. Mine managers Gerald Philips and Roger Parry were charged with manslaughter and criminal negligence, but these charges were stayed by the Nova Scotia government on the grounds that a conviction was unlikely. This is but one of many cases that illustrate the inability of our laws to control corporate crime. The weakness of the current law was addressed by Justice Richard in recommendation 73 of his report:

> The government of Canada . . . should institute a study of the accountability of corporate executives and directors for the wrongful or negligent acts of the corporation and should introduce in the Parliament of Canada such amendments to legislation as are necessary to ensure that corporate executives and directors are held properly accountable for workplace safety. (1997, 57)

To date, the government has shown no willingness to redress this long-standing weakness in our criminal law.

> IRS, and their Canadian quislings as well—will be very great and I will resume my career fortified. (Olive, 2007, 1)

A sense of entitlement also plays a role in motivating corporate and white-collar criminals. Shover and Hochstetler cite research that showed that doctors who had been convicted of defrauding the U.S. Medicare system felt that they were entitled to the money they took illegally because of their status as doctors. Many corporate executives who have been accused of criminality have long histories of using their position for their own benefit in a manner that would not be allowed for any of their subordinates. Once again a quote from Conrad Black illustrates this sense of entitlement. In the 1980s Black was trying to take for himself funds that were in his employees' pension plan; he accused them of stealing from him and used this accusation to support his claim on the money (a battle Black later lost in court):

> It's sometimes difficult to work myself into an absolute lachrymose fit about a work force that steals on that scale. . . . We are not running

a welfare agency for corrupt union leaders and a slovenly work force. (Olive, 2007, 1).

2002 Fraud and Misconduct Survey KPMG
www.kpmg.ca/en/services/advisory/forensic/fmdSurvey2002.html

White-Collar Crime and the Social Organization of Work

Not all white-collar crimes are committed by white-collar persons. For example, much embezzlement is committed by relatively low-status bank tellers (Daly, 1989). However, if it is true that white-collar crime is positively related to class position, it is also reasonable to ask why it should be so. The answer may lie in the power derived from ownership and authority positions in the occupational and organizational structures of modern corporations. These positions of power carry with them a freedom from control that may be criminogenic. That is, to have power is to be free from the kinds of constraints that may normally inhibit crime. As will be seen, the modern corporation facilitates this kind of freedom with the presumed goal of enhancing free enterprise but with the unintended consequence of encouraging and facilitating crime.

Crime and the Corporation

The organizational form of the corporation is crucial to understanding most corporate crime (Ermann and Lundman, 1982; Hagan, 1982; Reiss, 1980). As Wheeler and Rothman (1982) succinctly note, the corporation "is for white-collar criminals what the gun or knife is for the common criminal—a tool to obtain money from victims." Of course, the importance of the corporation is not restricted to the world of crime. From the Industrial Revolution on, it has become increasingly apparent that "among the variety of interests that men have, those interests that have been successfully collected to create corporate actors are the interests that dominate the society" (Coleman, 1974). This reference to men in particular is not accidental, for corporate entities are disproportionately male in employment, ownership, and control. Our interest is in developing an understanding of the link between the power of the corporate form and the criminogenic freedom that this powerful structure generates.

The corporation itself is a "legal fiction," with, as H. L. Mencken aptly observed, "no pants to kick or soul to damn." That is, the law chooses to treat corporations as **juristic persons**, making them formally liable to the same laws as "natural persons." Some of the most obvious faults in this legal analogy become clear when the impossibility of imprisoning or executing corporations is considered. However, there are more subtle differences between corporate and individual actors with equally significant consequences.

juristic person
The legal concept that corporations are liable to the same laws as natural persons. Treating corporations as individuals raises practical difficulties for legal enforcement and punishment.

For example, the old legal saw tells us that the corporation has no conscience or soul. Stone (1975) describes the problem well:

> When individuals are placed in an organizational structure, some of the ordinary internalized restraints seem to lose their hold. And if we

> decide to look beyond the individual employees and find an organizational "mind" to work with, a "corporate conscience" distinct from the consciences of particular individuals, it is not readily apparent where we would begin—much less what we would be talking about.

Stone goes on to suggest some interesting ways in which the corporate conscience and corporate responsibility could be increased (see also Nagorski, 1989). However, the point is that these mechanisms, or others, have not been put in place. Corporate power in this sense remains unchecked, and it is in this sense criminogenic.

The problem is in part the absence of cultural beliefs to discourage corporate criminality (Geis, 1962). C. Wright Mills (1956) captured part of the problem in his observation that "it is better, so the image runs, to take one dime from each of ten million people at the point of a corporation than $100 000 from each of ten banks at the point of a gun." Nonetheless, there is some evidence that cultural climates vary across time and regimes. For example, Sally Simpson (1986), who studied antitrust violations in the United States between 1927 and 1981, found that such violations were more common during Republican than Democratic administrations. However, even when condemnatory beliefs about corporate crime have been strong, there have been too few controlling mechanisms in place to impose their controlling influence effectively.

Many modern global corporations are huge, with hundreds of thousands of employees and many layers of bureaucracy. It is very difficult for the members of the boards of directors who are responsible for corporate governance to know many details concerning the daily operations of the corporation. Stone (1975) points out that top officers and directors, theoretically, are liable to suit by the corporation itself (via a shareholders' action) if they allow a law violation to occur through negligence. However, the courts have not imposed a duty on directors to uncover corporate wrongdoing. This provides an incentive for senior managers and directors to remain uninformed about illegal activities.

Canadian law in this area has been tested in the case of YBM Magnex, a company that ostensibly sold a variety of products, including industrial magnets and bicycles, primarily to eastern European markets. Starting its Canadian life as a shell corporation on the Alberta Stock Exchange, YBM Magnex stock rose in value from 85 cents to $20 in less than three years. It was included as one of the stocks used in the prestigious Toronto Stock Exchange 300 index and had a total share value of about $1 billion. Several eminent Canadians served on its board of directors, including former Ontario premier David Peterson. However, despite this face of respectability, the company had a very shady background. The company was controlled by Semion Mogilevich, one of Russia's most powerful organized criminals (Howlett, 2002). YBM Magnex had been investigated in Britain for a variety of offences, including money laundering. In Canada, the RCMP had been investigating the company since it was established in 1995 (Rubin, 1999). Stockholders' investments disappeared in May 1998 when the Ontario Securities Commission stopped all trading in the company's shares. Auditors had refused to accept the company's financial statements, and

U.S. law enforcement officials had raided the company's Pennsylvania headquarters investigating charges of fraud and money laundering. Directors and auditors of the company were sued for $635 million and were charged by the Ontario Securities Commission with withholding information from the public concerning the fact that the company was under investigation for its ties to organized crime. In 2003 the Ontario Securities Commission banned five of the former directors of YBM Magnex from becoming directors or officers of any companies for periods ranging from five years to life. Other directors, including former premier Peterson, were not punished. Shareholders also recovered some of their money through lawsuits against company executives. While the penalties were not nearly as harsh as those in U.S. cases, there is some evidence that boards of directors are now taking their roles more seriously and programs have been set up to train directors how to perform their supervisory roles more effectively.

How widespread is the use of "executive influence from afar" and "executive distancing and disengagement" in corporate criminality? Two intriguing studies (Baumhart, 1961; Brenner and Molander, 1977) suggest that the problem is large. The latter of these studies reports that the percentage of executives who indicate an inability to be honest in providing information to top management has nearly doubled since the earlier research, done in the 1950s. About half of those surveyed thought that their superiors frequently did not wish to know how results were obtained as long as the desired outcome was accomplished. Furthermore, the executives surveyed "frequently complained of superiors' pressure to support incorrect viewpoints, sign false documents, overlook superiors' wrongdoing, and do business with superiors' friends" (Brenner and Molander, 1977).

executive disengagement
The custom by which lower-level employees assume that executives are best left uninformed of certain decisions and actions of employees, or the assumption that executives cannot be legally expected to have complete control over their individual staff.

The bankruptcy of Britain's Barings Bank provides another example of **executive disengagement**. Barings Bank, which had been controlled by the same family since 1762, was brought down by the actions of a 28-year-old trader in the bank's Singapore office. Nicholas Leeson lost almost $1 billion of the company's money on financial derivatives, which were essentially bets on the future performance of the Tokyo stock market. When the Tokyo market fell, Barings collapsed when it could not cover the losses. The size of this gamble was in violation of British banking laws. While bank officials were quick to blame Leeson for the entire affair, it is very likely that senior bank officials at least tacitly approved of Leeson's trading activities. Several financial experts have suggested that the profits Leeson had previously made for Barings led bank officials to allow him to risk their shareholders' money by making illegal trades (Drohan, 1995). Some Canadian banks have recently faced similar problems with unauthorized trading, but not nearly on the scale of the Barings losses.

The Criminogenic Market Structure

Corporate crime research suggests not only a growing freedom at the top of organizations from the need to know and accept responsibility for criminal activity below, but also a growing pressure from managers that is also criminogenic. Farberman (1975) has referred to such pressures in the automotive industry and in other highly concentrated corporate sectors as constituting a **criminogenic market structure**. The crime-generating feature of these markets is their domination by a relatively small number of manufacturers who insist that their dealers sell in high volume at a small per-unit profit. Dealerships that fail to perform risk the loss of their franchises in an industry in which the alternatives are few. A result is high pressure to maximize sales and minimize service. More specifically, Farberman suggests that dealers in the car industry may be induced by the small profit margins on new cars to compensate through fraudulent warranty work and repair rackets. The connection between these findings is that the executives of the automotive industry can distance themselves from the criminal consequences of the "forcing model" (high volume/low per-unit profit) they impose. The result is an absence of control over repair and warranty frauds at the dealership level.

criminogenic market structure
An economic market that is structured in such a way that it tends to produce criminal behaviour.

The scale of the crimes that access to corporate resources makes possible will now be considered. In an intriguing study, Wheeler and Rothman (1982) categorized white-collar offenders into three groups: those who committed offences alone or with affiliated others using neither an occupational nor an organizational role (individual offenders); those who committed offences alone or with affiliated others using an occupational role (occupational offenders); and those who committed offences in which both organization and occupation were ingredients (organizational offenders). The results of this study indicate in a variety of ways the enormous advantages accruing to those who use formal organizations in their crimes. For example, across a subset of four offences, the median "take" for individual offenders was $5279, for occupational offenders $17 106, and for organizational offenders $117 392. In a parallel Canadian study, Hagan and Parker (1985) reported that securities violators who make use of organizational resources commit crimes that involve larger numbers of victims and are broader in their geopolitical spread. Why the organizational edge? Wheeler and Rothman (1982) answer with an example:

> Represented by its president, a corporation entered into a factoring agreement with a leading . . . commercial bank, presenting it with $1.2 million in false billings over the course of seven months; the company's statements were either inflated to reflect much more business than actually was being done, or were simply made up. Would the bank have done this for an individual? Whether we conclude that organizations are trusted more than individuals, or that they simply operate on a much larger scale, it is clear that the havoc caused when organizations are used outside the law far exceeds anything produced by unaffiliated actors.

Just as the organizational form has facilitated economic and technological development on a scale far beyond that achieved by individuals, so too has this form allowed criminal gains of a magnitude that men and women acting alone would find hard to attain.

The structure of the modern corporation allows a power imbalance to prevail in which those individuals at the top experience a relative freedom, while those at the bottom often experience pressure applied from the top that encourages various kinds of white-collar crime. The point has also been made that the corporate form itself can be used effectively to perpetrate "bigger and better

FOCUS

BOX 16.2 Criminal Misconduct: Alan Eagleson's Abuse of Power

In recent years, sentences of imprisonment have become more likely for high-status offenders. For example, Alan Eagleson, former head of the National Hockey League Players' Association, received an 18-month jail sentence after pleading guilty to multiple fraud offences. Eagleson was released on day parole after serving four months of his sentence and was on full parole after six months. Eagleson was also removed from the Order of Canada, thrown out of the Hockey Hall of Fame, and disbarred by the Law Society of Upper Canada. Some of Eagleson's offences are described by Jim Silver in a review of a book by Russ Conway, a U.S. journalist whose investigative work convinced the police to take on the case:

Russ Conway is a practitioner of the art, too little seen in Canada and especially among sportswriters, of muck-raking investigative journalism. And there's so much Eagleson muck to be raked. Eagleson wore at least four different hats while President of the National Hockey League Players Association [NHLPA]: union president, player agent, international hockey impresario, and close friend of NHL owners and management. As one former player said: "He wears so many hats I think even he gets screwed up sometimes."

Players complained about him for years, but Eagleson bullied and embarrassed any player with the temerity to ask questions about his conduct of union affairs, and put his own hand-picked, non-elected, yes-men on the union executive.

Disability Scams

[Eagleson's conduct] was criminal. For example, Eagleson ripped off players who suffered career-ending injuries.

The Jim Harrison case is revealing. Harrison's back was shot. He could scarcely walk, much less play. The Blackhawks jerked him around. He filed a grievance through Eagleson, head of the NHLPA and Harrison's agent. But Eagleson was also the agent for Chicago coach and general manager and long-time pal Bob Pulford, and Pulford was employed by Eagleson's yachting companion and Florida neighbour, Blackhawk owner Bill Wirtz. The grievance, as per the collective agreement negotiated by Eagleson, was heard by another pal, NHL President John Zeigler, "whose salary was paid by Wirtz and the other owners." The deck was stacked. Eagleson "cut a private deal with Pulford to the benefit of the Blackhawks and the detriment of his client." So much for Jim Harrison.

In another instance Eagleson convinced injured Boston Bruin player Mike Gillis to pay him, Eagleson, 15 percent of whatever was received from Gillis' disability insurance. Securing the claim, Eagleson intoned, would be tough. Yet Conway reveals that the meeting at which this deal was struck occurred *after* Eagleson had already been notified by the insurer that Gillis' claim had been approved. Eagleson was paid $41,250 for that scam.

crimes" than can be achieved by individuals acting alone. Access to these corporate resources is a unique advantage of class positions involving ownership and authority in business organizations. It is in this sense that it can be said that in the world of the modern corporation, the social organization of work itself is criminogenic.

Corporate Accounting Scandals

While corporate crime has always been a major problem in North America, the new millennium saw scandals that shocked even the most avid supporters

FOCUS

BOX 16.2 Criminal Misconduct: Alan Eagleson's Abuse of Power *(Continued)*

Bobby Orr

The Bobby Orr story is also revealing. It was as agent of the great Boston defenceman that Eagleson first came to prominence, and he used his relationship with Orr to build a huge stable of players for whom he acted as agent. In 1976 Eagleson negotiated Orr's sale to Chicago, to Eagleson's close pal Bill Wirtz, even though Orr did not want to leave the Boston Bruins and Boston tried desperately to hold him. Boston even offered Orr an 18.5 percent ownership stake in the franchise—worth $16 million US by 1994. Eagleson never informed Orr of this offer, but instead lied to Orr that Boston did not want him. What kind of financial gain Eagleson made from this deal Conway does not know, though it likely was substantial. Orr clearly was the loser. When in 1980 he finally severed his ties with Eagleson, his agent and financial manager, Orr was effectively bankrupt—his taxes and legal and accounting bills exceeded his assets.

Pension Scams

NHL veterans have been financially hurt by the pension scams and Conway brings the story up to the present. NHL pensions have been the worst in major professional sport. Eagleson touted himself as the savior of the players' pension plan. Money earned from international hockey tournaments organized by Eagleson was, the players and the public were repeatedly told, to go to the NHL players' pension fund, when in fact it appears those earnings were used merely to reduce the NHL's contribution. The owners benefited, not the players. Similarly, surpluses in the fund were being used to reduce the owners' contribution, with Eagleson's approval.

Lining His Pockets

As Conway reveals, this wasn't the half of it. Not only were profits from international hockey benefiting owners, rather than players, but also Eagleson himself was lining his pockets. He and his family and his associates and his companies apparently made millions in contracts associated with the tournaments, while "the Eagle" ran a sophisticated scheme involving the sale of rinkboard advertising, hundreds of thousands of dollars in proceeds which he apparently salted away in Swiss bank accounts. All the while Eagleson was insisting to players and the public that he never earned a cent from international hockey.

Source: Jim Silver. (1996). "Review of Game Misconduct: Alan Eagleson and the Corruption of Hockey." *Canadian Dimension* 30 (4) (July–August).

of free enterprise. Several of America's largest corporations, including energy company Enron and the telecommunications company WorldCom, went bankrupt, stock markets crashed, and one of the world's largest accounting companies was forced out of business. What caused what one observer has called a "scandalous rot" (DeCloet, 2002)?

While each of the bankrupt companies had different problems, an overall explanation must start with the way in which corporate executives are paid. Many companies provide their senior executives with stock options that allow the executive to purchase shares in his or her company at a later date for a price that is guaranteed at the time the options are issued. This means that if the stock goes up in the future, the executive can buy it at the guaranteed price and keep the difference between the issue price and the value of the stock at the time it is purchased. If the stock goes down, the executive will not have to use the option, so will not lose money. The intent of stock options is to provide executives with an incentive to work hard and raise the company's value. This will ensure that the company's shareholders benefit from the company's growth. Many companies also pay their senior employees very large bonuses if the company meets specified profit targets.

While some executives took a long-term perspective and worked to build up the value of their companies, other executives took a short-term approach that proved disastrous for their shareholders. They used a variety of short-term measures to raise both company profits and the stock price so they could make enormous profits on their stock options and bonuses very quickly. For example, "Chainsaw Al" Dunlap (named for his willingness to reduce costs by firing employees) was the chief executive officer (CEO) of the household appliance company Sunbeam. Dunlap's aggressive methods included artificially inflating sales figures so the company's profits appeared higher than they actually were. Sunbeam eventually went bankrupt and Dunlap was fired and fined $15 million, which was only a share of the illegal gains he made from Sunbeam stock.

Dunlap was the not the last CEO of a major company to run into trouble because of his pursuit of millions of dollars. During the late 1990s, the stock market rose dramatically and CEOs became corporate superstars. Many paid themselves enormous sums of money, and pay levels for CEOs of large companies reached $50 to $100 million per year. This star system convinced executives that they deserved these high levels of pay even when their companies were losing money. The greed of senior executives led directly to two of the largest bankruptcies in American history: Enron and WorldCom.

The Collapse of Enron

How did those responsible for Enron cost their investors $63 billion? Enron was once a pipeline company that delivered natural gas. This business was very profitable, but to CEO Kenneth Lay and his senior executives it was a boring business that did not have the potential for quick growth in profits. They developed a business model that involved trading futures contracts that are essentially bets on the future prices of commodities such as natural gas, electricity, and pulp and paper. Initially, this new focus proved very profitable, and the value of the stock climbed quickly until Enron was the seventh-largest company in the United States. Senior executives promised investors that the good times would continue. However, the company moved into riskier areas and at some stage the new business model broke down. To keep the company growing, Enron executives began to use illegal financial measures to make it appear as though profits were continuing to increase. Some of these complex measures involved the company selling its own assets to itself and showing the "profits" from this sale in its revenues. The company also tried to hide its debts by transferring them to outside "partnerships" that had actually been established by Enron.

Enron developed what can only be described as a culture of greed. Many senior Enron employees acted like children in a candy store and took massive personal profits from the financial schemes organized by the company. For example, several finance department employees invested $125 000 of their own funds in one of Enron's illegal financial transactions and made $30 million in only a few months (Butler, 2002). Executives were not content with the millions of dollars they had taken from the company. As the illegal schemes began to unravel and the company began to slide into bankruptcy, Enron paid $681 million to 140 top executives, including $67 million to CEO Kenneth Lay, who continued to encourage employees and members of the public to buy Enron stock even as he and his executives stripped the company of much of its remaining capital (Kranhold and Pacelle, 2002). Ultimately, creditors, stockholders, and other Enron employees suffered the loss of this money when the financial arrangements fell apart.

Enron executives must take most of the blame for the company's demise and many have received very lengthy jail terms. However, they also had help from the managers of other large corporations. The Arthur Andersen accounting firm, one of the world's largest, allowed Enron's many lapses of legal and ethical standards to slip by its auditors in order to help it obtain lucrative consulting contracts with Enron. Many of Wall Street's largest banks and brokerage firms collaborated with Enron in order to profit from stock commissions, consulting contracts, and interest from loans. One of Canada's largest banks, CIBC, was accused of helping Enron with its fraudulent financial dealings. While not admitting any wrongdoing, in 2005 CIBC paid $2.4 billion to settle a lawsuit in which CIBC was accused of helping Enron to hide its financial dealings.

WorldCom

The Enron debacle was quickly followed by an even larger bankruptcy. The failure of WorldCom, the largest long-distance telephone service provider in the United States, cost investors a massive $175 billion, as its share value dropped from $64.50 a share to only 83 cents (Kadlec, 2002). WorldCom, led by CEO Bernard Ebbers, a former Edmonton milkman, admitted it overstated earnings by $3.8 billion over a period of 15 months. That is, the company reported earning $3.8 billion more than it actually made. While the Enron fraud was very complex, WorldCom used a simple method of inflating its non-existent profits. It simply treated its everyday expenses (mainly payments to local phone companies for using their services to complete calls) as capital investments that could be written off over a period of several years. This made its profits look higher than they really were because it did not have to deduct these expenses from the money it took in from its customers. This would be like you pretending that you are paying your tuition over a period of four years instead of in the current academic year. This pretence could make your accounts look better than they really are, but eventually you are going to have to account for the missing money. In the case of WorldCom, that revelation led to a collapse in the company's stock. Ebbers, the company's CEO, is now serving a 25-year prison sentence and has lost most of the fortune he made from his company.

A final footnote in this ongoing story is that Arthur Andersen, the global company that was responsible for auditing Enron, WorldCom, and several other companies accused of misleading accounting, was found guilty of a felony count of obstructing the Securities and Exchange Commission's investigation into Enron. Several Andersen employees had shredded documents and tried to persuade others to cover up the scandal. Following the verdict, the company announced that it was going out of business. It was victim of a corporate culture in which generating revenue for the company became a greater concern than protecting the public by doing its job competently.

Canada's Nortel

In 2000 Nortel, a Canadian-based telecommunications company was the most valuable company in Canada. Its shares were valued at $124 each, but unfortunately for investors its financial statements greatly overstated the company's revenues. At a time when the market for technology stocks was collapsing, revelations that Nortel was not as profitable as it had claimed to be, along with a realization that the company had been mismanaged and had greatly overpaid for smaller companies that it had purchased, drove its shares below $1. While some shareholders lost 99 percent of their investments, John Roth, Nortel's CEO, retired after cashing in most of his shares at the top of the market. Executives who followed Roth were given bonuses if they could return Nortel to profitability. Nortel did report a profit in 2003 and the executives were given nearly $300 millions in bonus payments. However, in 2004 the company revealed that most of the profits were due to faulty accounting and company shareholders again suffered a devastating loss. In 2007, civil charges were laid against seven former Nortel executives by the U.S. Securities and Exchange Commission over these accounting irregularities, but Canadian legal officials and regulators have thus far failed to act. This pattern of inaction by Canadian authorities is common, as Canadian authorities and legislators have not taken corporate crime nearly as seriously as their U.S. counterparts.

Consumer Safety Issues

Beginning in the 1960s the consumer movement began to make sure that manufacturers were held accountable for the safety of their products. Ralph Nader's book *Unsafe at Any Speed*, which described the deaths and injuries caused by the faulty design of the General Motors Corvair automobile, helped to focus the public's attention on consumer safety. Widely publicized cases like the calculation by Ford executives that it would be cheaper to pay for lawsuits brought by the families of Ford Pinto drivers who had been burned to death in accidents than to fix the fuel tank design flaw that caused the fires, and the production of Firestone tires that came apart at high speed, led to tougher safety regulations and convinced companies that it was good business to manufacture safe products. Over the next 40 years, governments became more active in regulating consumer goods and products became much safer.

In 2007, people who took product safety for granted were surprised to learn of several incidents in which unsafe products manufactured in China were being sold in the North American market. The first was the melamine-contaminated pet food that you read about in Chapters 1 and 10 of this text. The second was the sale of counterfeit Colgate toothpaste in discount stores throughout Canada. The toothpaste contained chemicals that were potentially harmful to users. The third scandal involved children's toys, including Elmo, Big Bird, and Dora, that were recalled by manufacturers because of safety concerns. Within a few months Mattel, the maker of Fisher-Price toys, was forced to issue three recalls involving millions of toys. Some of the toys had lead paint, which can be poisonous, while others had design flaws, including loose magnets that children could swallow.

The toy recall provides an example of a criminogenic market structure that has come about because of globalization. Mattel manufactures most of its toys in China not because the Chinese manufacturers were higher quality or more innovative than North American factories. Manufacturing is done offshore because it is cheaper to build toys in low-wage countries than in Canada or the United States, so companies like Mattel can make higher profits because their production costs are lower. Low wage levels and an absence of environmental and workplace health and safety regulations mean that it is much cheaper to manufacture toys in China. However, in China the toy companies contract out their production to local companies where quality control is difficult to maintain. The president of Mattel blamed Chinese manufacturers for the safety problems, but in fact the responsibility must be shared more broadly.

Some of the blame does fall on China, which has a booming industrial sector in which regulation is lax and where corruption and bribery are common. In order to encourage economic expansion, the government tacitly approves of a wide range of illegal practices. However, despite Mattel's attempt to blame the Chinese, the toy company is also at fault. It is hardly a secret that quality control is not nearly as effective in China as it is in North American factories. Thus the toy companies are ultimately responsible for doing sufficient testing of their Chinese-made products to ensure that they are safe, but they have obviously not done enough. And what about the role of the Canadian and American governments? There are toy safety regulations, but we know that unless regulations are actively enforced some businesses will ignore them. Neither country does routine testing of toys, leaving that task to the toy companies. Unfortunately, even if safety violations are found, neither country is likely to impose any sanctions against the violators. Ultimately, it is the consumer who will enforce safety regulations. If Mattel and other companies have to keep issuing safety-related recalls, customers will eventually stop putting their children at risk by buying these companies' products and will turn to more reliable suppliers.

White-Collar Crime and Legal Sanctions

Given the distribution of freedom and pressure that has been identified within the structure of the modern corporation and the power this gives to those who run it, the question that recurs is this: What does the law do to remedy the potential for abuse? This question raises issues of legal liability and the enforcement of law.

"We have arranged things," writes Christopher Stone (1975), "so that the people who call the shots do not have to bear the full risks." This, in a nutshell, is the consequence of the limited liabilities borne by modern corporate actors:

> Take, for example, a small corporation involved in shipping dynamite. The shareholders of such a company, who are typically also the

> managers, do not *want* their dynamite-laden truck to blow up. But if it does, they know that those injured cannot, except in rare cases, sue them as individuals to recover their full damages if the amount left in the corporations' bank account is inadequate to make full compensation. . . . What this means is that in deciding how much money to spend on safety devices, and whether or not to allow trucks to drive through major cities, the calculations are skewed toward higher risks than suggested by the "rational economic corporation/free market" model that is dreamily put forth in textbooks. If no accident results, the shareholders will reap the profits of skimping on safety measures. If a truck blows up, the underlying human interests will be shielded from fully bearing the harm that they have caused. And then, there is nothing to prevent the same men from setting up a new dynamite shipping corporation the next day; all it takes is the imagination to think up a new name, and some $50 in filing fees. (462–63)

It may be conceded that large corporations are not quite as free as the small corporation in the example to dissolve and reconstitute their operations. However, the separation of shareholder and management interests gives rise to a related problem of liability. Damage judgments against corporations are taken from the companies' revenues and rarely affect the salaries of the managers who made the decisions leading to the penalties. Thus the shareholders suffer for the misdeeds of corporate managers while the managers are shielded by the corporate structure.

These discussions raise the broader issue of how and why the law is used to control white-collar crime. It has already been seen that civil remedies are not very effective. We turn now to criminal sanctions. How does the state decide what kinds of upper-world indiscretions will be called criminal? The most interesting work that has been done on this issue in Canada involves the development of anticombines legislation. Given the powerful economic interests involved in forming the **monopolistic enterprises** this legislation presumably seeks to prevent, one might wonder how an **anticombines law** was ever passed in the first place. Goff and Reasons (1978) indicate that the initiative for the original legislation in 1899 "came not from the general populace but from small businessmen, who felt their firms were at the mercy of big business interests." However, more recently Smandych (1985) has noted that a "Royal Commission on Labour and Capital" created for the purpose of investigating industrial conditions in Canada interviewed and recorded testimony from numerous trade-union representatives and workers. This testimony, cited in the report of the commission in 1899, specifically sought legislation against monopolistic practices, and Smandych argues that "the possibility that worker demands for the elimination of combines went unnoticed by the government of the day is extremely doubtful."

monopolistic enterprise
Any corporation that controls all, or the majority, of the market for a particular product or service.

anticombines law
In order to protect the principle of competition, valued by all liberal, capitalistic societies, laws have been created to prevent and punish corporations that work together to reduce competition.

Smandych goes on to conclude that "the first flourishing of Canadian anticombines legislation was the product of an essential confrontation between labour and capital, and of the state's effort to find an acceptable solution." None of this is to say, as later noted, that this legislation was strong or effective. Quite the contrary, as Snider (1979) observes. Efforts over the years to strengthen the legislation with "proconsumer and procompetition" amendments regularly "were weakened or eliminated in the face of business opposition." Smandych, Snider, Goff, and Reasons are all agreed that this legislation has done less than it promised to reduce monopolistic practices and to punish those who promote them. In fact, many have argued that the laws are almost totally ineffective. Prosecutions are rarely successful, and when they are, the fines are so low that they do not act as an effective deterrent to anticompetitive behaviour. Not surprisingly, business has lobbied very strongly against changes to combines legislation.

Steven Box (1981) has noted another way in which the law favours corporate offenders:

> Some people benefit more than others from these laws. . . . By the criminal law's constructing *particular* definitions of murder, rape, robbery and assault other acts, which are in many ways very similar, are excluded, and these are just the acts more likely to be committed by more powerful individuals. Thus the criminal law defines only some types of killing as murder: it excludes, for example, deaths which result from acts of negligence such as employers' failure to maintain safe working conditions in factories and mines. . . . The criminal law includes only some types of property deprivation as robbery: it excludes, for example, the separation of consumers from part of their money that follows manufacturers' malpractices or advertisers' misrepresentations. . . . The criminal law defines only some types of violence as criminal assault: it excludes those forms of assault . . . resulting from working in a polluted factory environment where the health risk was known to the employer but concealed from the employee. (48–49)

But what of the white-collar offenders who are held criminally liable and processed through the criminal justice system? Are they liable to as severe sanctioning as individual actors? Notions of "equality before the law" are perhaps nowhere more subjective in meaning than in their application to the sentencing of white-collar offenders (Hagan and Albonetti, 1982). This is reflected in at least two kinds of comments made by judges about the sentences they impose for white-collar crimes. It is reflected first in the suggestion that white-collar offenders experience sanctions in a different way from other kinds of offenders, and second in the assertion that different kinds of sanctions are appropriate in white-collar cases.

The view, common among judges, that white-collar offenders experience sanctions differently is well summarized in Mann et al.'s (1980) conclusions after interviewing a sample of judges who have tried such cases: "Most judges have a widespread belief that the suffering experienced by a white-collar person as a result of apprehension, public indictment and conviction, and the collateral disabilities incident to conviction—loss of job, professional licenses, and status in the community—completely satisfies the need to punish the individual." This belief persists in the face of findings from a recent study by Benson (1989, 474) that "although they commit the most serious offences, employers and managers are least likely to lose their jobs after conviction for a white-collar crime." The argument for white-collar leniency endures in the minds of judges and others: the defendant, having suffered enough from the acts of prosecution and conviction, does not require a severe sentence. However, the sentence must still provide a deterrent. Mann et al. (1980) conclude that most judges seek a compromise in resolving this dilemma. "The weekend sentence, the very short jail term, and the relatively frequent use of amended sentences (where a judge imposes a prison term and later reduces it) are evidence of this search for a compromise."

It is important to acknowledge the disputed role of fines in sentencing white-collar offenders. Posner (1980) asserts that "the white-collar criminal . . . should be punished only by monetary penalties." His argument is that if fines are suitably large, they are an equally effective deterrent and cheaper to administer, and therefore socially preferable to imprisonment and other afflictive punishments. It has already been noted that corporate entities are liable to little else than fines. However, Mann et al. (1980) find judges to be skeptical of the effectiveness of fines. The sense that emerges from this research is that judges are acutely aware of the issues of deterrence, disparity, and discrimination in the sentencing of white-collar offenders, and that they attempt to respond to these issues by fashioning sentences that combine sanctions in a compromise fashion. Consistent with this view, Hagan and Nagel (1982) found, in a sentencing study covering the period from 1963 to 1976 in the Southern District of New York, that judges attempted to compensate for the shorter prison terms given to white-collar offenders by adding probation or fines to their sentences. Similarly, fines were most frequently used in conjunction with prison and probation sentences. In any case, all these findings suggest that white-collar offenders are advantaged by the specific types and combination of legal sanctions that are imposed on them.

However, both in Canada and the United States, there is some evidence that the mid-1970s brought a new and somewhat harsher attitude toward white-collar crime. Katz (1980) speaks of a "social movement against white-collar crime" that began in the United States in the late 1960s, and the evolution of public opinion documents an increasing concern with the occurrence of such crimes (Cullen et al., 1982; Schrager and Short, 1978). This new concern seems at least in part to have been a response to incidents such as the American experience with Watergate and the Canadian experience with a major scandal involving dredging contracts. It was illustrated by the "proactive" prosecutorial policies of several U.S. attorneys (Hagan and Nagel, 1982) and in the increased prosecution of large-scale securities violations in Ontario (Hagan and Parker, 1985). In 1987 the Canadian government replaced the Environmental Contaminants Act with new legislation that provides for fines of up to $1 million per day and jail terms of up to five years for guilty executives. Further, the government of Ontario has increased the fine for insider trading of securities from $25 000 to $1 million, and it has increased the possible jail term from one to two years.

So there *appears* to be a move toward tougher legal sanctions for white-collar offences. Of course, charges must be laid before sanctions can be imposed, and the power of corporations and of persons in high social-class positions makes the decision to prosecute problematic (see Benson et al., 1988). Wheeler et al. (1982) have sought to demonstrate that policies like those described above have led to the more severe sentencing of high-status white-collar offenders.

Hagan and Palloni (1983) concur in reporting an increased use of imprisonment with white-collar offenders after Watergate, but they also indicate that the length of these prison sentences was unusually short. The Canadian study of the enforcement of securities laws in Ontario (Hagan and Parker, 1985) reveals a similar pattern of trade-offs in the severity with which white-collar offenders are treated. Overall, treatment of white-collar offenders seems to have been lenient in the past, and despite some examples of harsher sentences, there is no unambiguous evidence that this situation has changed markedly. Even where white-collar offenders have received prison sentences, they typically obtain parole very early in their terms.

In recent years the massive losses due to the failures of companies such as Enron and WorldCom have led to harsher treatment of corporate criminals in the United States. These crimes led to a serious loss of confidence in the stock market—why would someone want to invest money in companies whose earnings reports could not be trusted? This had a major impact on the economy as investors moved their money out of the stock market. The scandals were so pervasive that it became obvious that major changes were needed in regulation and corporate governance, and governments in the United States have become more involved in regulating corporations and making their laws tougher. They have also put more resources into investigating and prosecuting corporate crime. Many senior executives have been publicly arrested and taken into custody in front of the media in so-called "perp walks," designed to show the public that politicians have acted. The jail sentences received by high-profile offenders in cases such as Enron and WorldCom have been very harsh, so there is at least anecdotal evidence that the new guidelines are having an impact. However, there is no evidence that Canadian courts have become more punitive toward corporate criminals and the police and securities regulators have not made much effort to clean up the business world. Even Jim Flaherty, the federal Minister of Finance, has said that Canada's securities regulations are ineffective. The fact that Conrad Black (see Chapter 1) was prosecuted in the United States rather than in Canada is indicative of the fact that the U.S. justice system is now much tougher on corporate malfeasance cases than is the Canadian system.

Occupational Crime

In the rest of this chapter you will learn about crimes that are committed by individuals who violate the law in the course of practising a legitimate occupation. As with corporate crime, at the heart of much occupational crime is a violation of positions of trust (Shapiro, 1990).

Unprofessional Conduct and Malpractice

Historically we have known little about unprofessional conduct and malpractice among groups such as lawyers and doctors because most of it has been dealt with privately by the governing bodies of professional associations. However, in recent years society has become less tolerant of professional deviance. Complainants have become more vocal and more violations have come to the attention of the public. Governments have also been more willing to prosecute in cases that involve violations of the criminal law.

Every occupation includes people who are willing to violate legal or ethical codes for their own benefit. However, the problem is made worse when those responsible for regulating the conduct of individual practitioners fail to do their job. The examples of sexual abuse by members of the clergy and malpractice by doctors illustrate how the failure by church and medical authorities to respond to complaints against members of their professions has led to much greater harm being done.

Perhaps the most widely publicized cases of unprofessional conduct over the past decade have involved sexual abuse by members of the clergy. In Canada, the Anglican Church has been named as a co-defendant in over 1200 complaints from former students of Indian residential schools, and several Catholic priests have been convicted of sexual assault charges in which the victims were former residential school students. Aboriginal children who attended residential schools have not been the only victims of abuse. The first major case to come to the attention of the Canadian public involved the Mount Cashel Orphanage in St. John's, Newfoundland, which was run by members of the Christian Brothers order. Abuse at the orphanage was hidden for many years. In 1975 a police investigation heard testimony such as this statement from a former resident:

> I am 11 years old. . . . I have been at Mount Cashel Orphanage for about five years. I am happy at the orphanage except for Brother Burke, Brother Ralph and Brother English. I don't like Brother Burke because he beats me across my bare backside with a stick about three days ago Brother Burke took me into a closet and made me pull down my pants he hit me five or six times across my backside with a stick. He beat me because I threw a after shave tin into the garbage and it made a noise and Brother Burke was watching T.V. Both Brother Ralph and Brother English on seven or eight times have caught a hold of me and have felt my legs and felt my bird. Sometimes this has happened when I have been in bed. Brother Ralph would sit down on the bed and feel my bird inside my pyjama pants. Most times Brother English would feel my bird when I was in the dining Hall he would do it sometimes when I was in bed. (Law Commission of Canada, 2000, 28)

Survivors Network of Those Abused by Priests
www.survivorsnetwork.org

When the police who conducted this investigation recommended laying charges against members of the Christian Brothers, the chief of the Royal Newfoundland Constabulary ordered them to change the report and refused to allow charges. As a result, no further action was taken until a Royal Commission was established in 1989 following a series of public complaints from former residents of the orphanage. The commission found that senior Catholic Church officials who knew about the abuse covered up accusations of sexual and physical abuse. The commission also concluded that the police chief and a provincial deputy minister also covered up the abuse. Following the Royal Commission, 15 members of the Christian Brothers were charged and both the Newfoundland government and the Christian Brothers order have been forced to make multimillion-dollar payments to abuse victims.

The failure of church officials in Newfoundland to deal with abusive clergy is by no means unique. Former Boston cardinal Bernard Law resigned his post in 2002 after facing criticism that he had failed to act in many cases of sexual misconduct by priests. Not only did he fail to take action, but he covered up many instances of misconduct and reassigned several priests who had been accused of abusing children to positions where they would continue to work with children. A number of these priests reoffended, including Father John Geoghan, who has been accused of fondling or raping 150 children. Geoghan received a sentence of nine to ten years for one case, and by 2002 the Catholic Church had paid out over $10 million in settlements with 86 victims. Geoghan had been moved to a number of parishes in the Boston area in response to complaints, but the Church otherwise took no action until after the case had received wide publicity.

Medical doctors have been accused of sexual misconduct with patients as well as other violations, ranging from false billing to ethical lapses in the treatment of patients. Perhaps the most serious violations by doctors involve malpractice. Most doctors are competent professionals, but accusations of malpractice are not uncommon. For example, in 2001, patients began 917 legal actions against physicians, although typically only about one-third of these actions are successful (Canadian Medical Protective Association, 2007). Examples of cases that have resulted in action against doctors include one Manitoba doctor who was sanctioned for sewing beads into the stitches of an Aboriginal woman, and an American doctor who was convicted of assault for carving his initials into a patient (Henderson, 2000). In one rather bizarre case, a South Carolina doctor was fined and reprimanded for using an amputated foot as bait in his crab trap (*Vancouver Sun*, 2000).

One tragic case of malpractice involved a Winnipeg surgeon who specialized in pediatric cardiac surgery. In 1994, 12 young children died while undergoing surgery at the Health Sciences Centre. A judicial inquiry into the case found that at least five of the deaths were likely preventable (Sinclair, 2000). The inquiry determined that the surgeon was at fault, but the inquiry also blamed the hospital, which failed to ensure that the surgeon was qualified, and his supervisors, who failed to take action even when there were complaints about his performance. Part of the problem in this case was a culture of secrecy surrounding the work of the doctor. Parents had great difficulty getting any information about the pediatric cardiac surgery program, and nurses who complained about the program were ignored. While no charges were laid as a result of this inquiry, the doctor is no longer doing cardiac surgery and Manitoba now sends pediatric cardiac cases to Alberta, where the surgical failure rate is extremely low.

The failure by professional licensing and regulatory bodies to hold their members accountable has seriously harmed clients and patients. For example, gynaecologist and obstetrician Dr. Richard Neale lost his surgical privileges in British Columbia after a series of complaints. However, rather than being removed from the profession, he was allowed to retrain for six months and then to return to his surgical duties. In 1981, an Ontario patient died as a result of Dr. Neale's incompetence, but he continued to operate and to injure patients until he was finally banned from practice in 1985 as a result of the 1981 case.

Leaving Canada, he continued to practise in England, where he had a complication rate five times higher than that of his colleagues (Wente, 2000). Even though British authorities had been warned about Neale, they did not remove him from practice until 2000. Following his removal from practice, he was the subject of more than 100 complaints from women in England and another 60 in Canada.

Betrayal of trust can occur in many professions. In 2003, the *New York Times* reported that Jayson Blair, one of its reporters, had plagiarized and fabricated much of the information in dozens of stories he had written. His "eyewitness" reports from distant states were actually written in his New York apartment. The government was considering laying fraud charges against Blair. More serious were the crimes of Robert Courtney, a Kansas City pharmacist who received 30 years in prison for diluting medicine used for cancer chemotherapy. This meant that hundreds of patients did not receive the required doses of their medication. One test showed that a prescription contained only 1 percent of the proper dose of medication. Courtney profited by selling the diluted medicine for the normal price and selling the rest to other customers. Many of the patients died, though it will never be clear whether their cancer would have killed them even if they had received the proper medication.

Investment and Securities Fraud

Many Canadians rely on financial advisors to help them prepare for their retirement. In most cases, this is a good idea, but unfortunately not all advisors can be trusted. For example, Patrick Kinlin received a five-year prison sentence after pleading guilty to 54 counts of fraud for defrauding a number of Ontario residents, many of them senior citizens, of $12.5 million. He was very close to these victims, one of whom was his own aunt; he attended family weddings with them and frequently bought them gifts. However, instead of investing his clients' money, he was spending it on his own lavish lifestyle. It is unlikely that any of the victims will receive compensation, as Kinlin has declared bankruptcy (Gadd, 2000). Kinlin died of heart disease shortly after beginning his sentence, but at the time of his death he was under investigation for a pension fraud scheme using prison computers (Canadian Broadcasting Corporation, 2001b). In another case, a Montreal land developer committed suicide prior to his trial on charges of stealing $100 million from two Quebec religious orders of nuns. Jean-Alain Bisaillon used the money, which the nuns had invested to pay for their retirements, to pay for fancy hotels, private jets, jewellery, and a hunting lodge. A lawyer who worked with Bisaillon was sentenced to five years in prison for his role in the case.

Another type of securities fraud is insider trading. Insider trading occurs when someone, usually an owner or employee of the company, receives information about the company that is not available to the general public. It is unlawful to buy or sell stock using this information because this would give the insider an advantage over other investors. In 2000, Glen Harvey, former president of Alberta-based Golden Rule Resources, was sentenced to one year in jail and fined $3.95 million for trading $4 million worth of company stock while withholding assay results showing that the company had almost no gold on one of its properties. When the news was finally released, the company shares dropped by over half. Harper was only the second person to be sentenced to jail in Canada for insider trading (Canadian Press, 2000) and successful prosecutions for this offence are rare.

A third type of investment fraud is the "pump and dump." In this scam, stock promoters take a worthless company, invent a story about the company, then tell that story in order to get people to buy the stock. If they are successful, the stock price will rise and the promoters will sell their shares for a profit and other investors will be left only with worthless shares. The story of Bre-X, the most expensive stock fraud in Canadian history, is described in Box 16.3.

Internet Fraud

White-collar criminals have never been slow to adopt new technologies. As the Internet becomes more prevalent and as more people use it to conduct economic transactions, Internet crime will become more common. Some individuals have found it profitable to advertise on Internet auction sites such as eBay, to collect cheques from purchasers, and then to fail to deliver the promised article. Others have used spam e-mail to get people to order products such as Norton Anti-Virus. Some of these spam advertisers deliver a pirated copy of the software that cannot be registered or updated; others simply use the customer's credit card number to order other goods. Other entrepreneurial criminals swindle funds through phony investment schemes or sell phony products. An innovative former community college student found another way to use the Internet to commit fraud. Mark Jakob put out a false press release over the Internet about alleged problems at Emulex Corporation. The stock immediately dropped by about 60 percent. Jakob had sold the stock short (a way of "betting" that the stock would go down) and made a profit of over $350 000 when it dropped after his press release. Although the stock eventually regained its value, investors who sold as it was declining lost a total of $110 million. Jakob received a jail sentence of 44 months and was forced to return the money he had made on the transaction (U.S. Securities and Exchange Commission, 2001).

Another Internet fraud victimized Cryptologic, a Canadian firm that develops software for Internet gambling. In 2001, a computer hacker broke into the company's servers and altered Cryptologic's programs for online slot machines and craps games at two Web casinos to ensure that players would always win. As a result, several online gamblers made a total of $1.9 million.

Tax Fraud

The Auditor General of Canada estimated that the amount of money lost to tax cheats in 1997 was $12 billion (Auditor General of Canada, 1999), a sum greater than the budget of the Department of National Defence. The income tax system in Canada is one that requires all taxpayers to report their incomes honestly. However, they clearly do not do so, and there is evidence that in some occupations, the rate of non-compliance is as high as 90 percent (Gabor, 1994).

How do so many people avoid taxes? People who are working at jobs where all their income is paid by an employer have little opportunity to avoid tax because the employer deducts the tax and reports salary information to the

FOCUS

BOX 16.3 Bre-X: The Anatomy of a Stock Fraud

The speculative segment of the Canadian stock market has had a very bad reputation. *Forbes* magazine once called Vancouver the "scam capital of the world" because of the fraudulent stocks that were sold on the Vancouver Stock Exchange. Governments have not been willing to regulate the activities of some of the more aggressive stock promoters. Perhaps, then, it is fitting that Canada was the home of one of the world's largest stock swindles.

According to the autopsy report that marked the end of one of history's largest frauds: "Testimonies of witnesses and existing evidence indicate that victim Michael Antonius [*sic*] de Guzman did not fall by accident but that he deliberately ended his life by dropping himself from the helicopter" (Wells, 1998, 29). Michael de Guzman was the chief geologist of Bre-X, a Canadian gold mining company that claimed to have discovered one of the world's largest gold mines in Indonesia. Shortly after de Guzman's death, assay reports revealed that there was no gold and that the Bre-X property was worthless. Investors collectively lost $6 billion when the market for Bre-X stock collapsed.

Mines have been "salted" for hundreds of years. Owners of a worthless property could attract investors by scattering gold at the mine site or by adding it to rock samples after they had been collected. Despite this long history of fraud and deception, investors around the world fell for the story of Bre-X. Many of these investors lost their life savings, and at least one killed himself after Bre-X stock collapsed.

Bre-X was built on a flimsy structure of lies. However, the greed of those who hoped to make a fortune on the company's stock led many to ignore the risks and warning signs and to believe the story spun by the Bre-X principals and by their supporters in the financial world. Jennifer Wells describes the press release by company president David Walsh, a man whose career as a stock promoter had been, up until Bre-X, a disaster:

> The Walsh press release described the prospect as a "deposit," which it was not, the presumed gold resource as "reserves," which they were not, and said that drilling on the property by the previous tenant had yielded numerous intersections of more than two grams of gold per tonne, which was a lie. It also projected the potential of the property at 20 million tonnes at more than 2 grams per tonne of gold, which was absurd. (1998, 122)

government. However, a large segment of the working population has jobs that enable them to hide income. Many of you have likely worked as servers in the restaurant industry or have friends who work in this field. Since much of the income of servers comes from tips, the employer usually does not keep a record of this income, so many servers do not pay tax on this portion of their earnings. Another major source of under-payment is the construction industry. Unscrupulous contractors will offer customers a reduced price if the customer will pay them in cash so they will not have records of income that could be uncovered through an audit. These workers are part of what is called the "underground economy," whose size in 2006 was estimated at $52 billion based on the Auditor General's conclusion that the underground economy represents about 4.5 percent of Canada's Gross Domestic Product. Another important part of the underground economy is buying smuggled goods, particularly cigarettes and alcohol, in order to avoid Canadian taxes.

FOCUS

BOX 16.3 Bre-X: The Anatomy of a Stock Fraud (*Continued*)

In his attempt to raise exploration money, Walsh was essentially announcing that he had a producing gold mine, even though the company had not yet begun to explore the property.

After initial samples from the property showed no signs of gold, somebody, most likely de Guzman, began salting the samples. Not surprisingly, these samples were more successful, and Bre-X officials used the results to increase regularly their estimates of the amount of gold on the property. As the mythical gold reserves increased, the stock began to soar. Shares that once sold for six cents per share were soon worth hundreds of dollars.

In addition to the problems with the mine, Bre-X also had to contend with the corrupt Indonesian government, which eventually took nearly half of the project. Investors did not panic, however, because company officials simply doubled their estimates of the amount of gold. Investors were comfortable that they had not really lost anything even though over half their investment had been assigned to the Indonesians and to a large mining company selected by the Indonesian government (Wells, 1998).

The involvement of this company, Freeport McMoRan, spelled the beginning of the end for Bre-X and its investors. When Freeport carried out its own testing program, assay results showed there was no gold on the Bre-X property. The last nail was hammered into the Bre-X coffin by Graham Farquharson, an independent analyst whose report concluded:

> The magnitude of the tampering with core samples that we believe has occurred and resulting falsification of assay values at Busang, is of a scale and over a period of time and with a precision that, to our knowledge, is without precedent in the history of mining anywhere in the world. (Wells, 1998, 368)

Nobody will ever be punished for the Bre-X fiasco. De Guzman committed suicide and David Walsh died of natural causes in 1998. John Felderhof, the company's chief geologist, was acquitted of fraud charges in 2007. Lawsuits from unhappy investors will continue, but the company is bankrupt and nobody associated with Bre-X has the resources to replace the billions of dollars lost by investors.

Surveys suggest that many people would be willing to cheat on their taxes and do not strongly disapprove of others who commit this offence (Gabor, 1994). People often feel that tax fraud is justifiable because of their view that taxes are too high and governments are just taking money that rightfully belongs to the taxpayer. Many Canadians were particularly upset when the GST was implemented, and there is some evidence that people in businesses such as contracting turned to the underground economy as a way of avoiding the GST.

Other types of tax fraud have involved exaggerating income tax deductions. Over one hundred thousand Canadians have had their claims for charitable deductions rejected by the Canada Revenue Agency because they were grossly inflated. People who donated funds to phony charities would receive tax receipts for many times the value of their donation. About $1.4 billion in tax revenue was lost because of this scam (Donovan, 2007) and it was highly unlikely that any of the donated money actually reached people in need.

Political Corruption

While Canadian politicians have been more honest than their counterparts in many other countries, we have still had our share of political scandals. In 1873, just six years after Confederation, the government of John A. Macdonald was forced to resign over allegations of bribery in the selection of a contractor to build and operate the Canadian Pacific Railway. Perhaps the most corrupt political regime in Canada was that of Maurice Duplessis, who was the premier of Quebec for most of the period between 1936 and 1959. He created a powerful political machine that routinely violated election rules and violated many of Quebecers' basic rights, such as the right to freedom of political expression. In addition, his supporters used inside information to make money on the stock market and accepted financial kickbacks from people who wanted to do business with the Quebec government (Corrado, 1996).

Raymond Corrado (1996) has documented many of the corrupt activities engaged in by members of Brian Mulroney's Conservative government between 1984 and 1993. Mulroney's use of patronage was widespread, as political supporters were given government jobs and contracts, often without any competitions. Although this practice is not illegal, it set the tone for other misconduct. Several of his cabinet ministers and MPs were forced to resign after being charged with bribery and influence peddling and many other Conservative Party officials were prosecuted for similar offences in connection with party fundraising activities. There were also many allegations that the government interfered with the judicial process in an attempt to cover up some of these illegal activities. Dissatisfaction with the ethical standards of Prime Minister Mulroney and his colleagues was one reason that the federal Conservative Party was almost wiped out in the 1993 election.

The most recent major scandal involved the Liberal government of Prime Minister Jean Chrétien. In 2002, a newspaper ran a story about a Montreal advertising company that had received over half a million dollars for a report that was never completed. The federal Auditor General investigated the matter and concluded that there had been massive misspending in a government program that provided federal funding for the sponsorship of events, most of which were in the province of Quebec. In many cases, money was given to companies that did not actually do any work for the government. The Auditor-General concluded: "I think this is such a blatant abuse of public funds that it is shocking. I am actually appalled by what we've found" (Canadian Broadcasting Corporation, 2004, n.p.).

Following this report, an inquiry commission headed by Justice John Gomery was established to further investigate what had become known as the Sponsorship Scandal. After many months of public testimony, Justice Gomery's report was released in 2005. The report concluded that over $150 million of taxpayers' money was given by the Liberal government to five advertising and communications companies in Quebec with ties to the federal Liberal Party, and in many cases nothing was done by these companies to earn the money. Several of the executives who received this money subsequently made large donations to the Liberal Party and paid the salaries of Liberal party workers. Justice Gomery concluded that "whether legal or illicit, there was at least an implicit link between the contributions [to the Liberal party] and the expectation that the government contracts would be awarded" (2005, 79). Thus government money appears to have been returned to the party to use for its own purposes.

The report laid some of the blame for the scandal on Prime Minister Chrétien, his chief of staff Jean Pelletier, and Public Works Minister Alfonso Gagliano, all of whom failed to ensure that government funds were spent properly. While no elected officials were charged, one government official and several of the marketing executives have been convicted and sentenced to jail for their roles in this affair. Justice Gomery stated that his report "chronicles a depressing story of multiple failures to plan a government program appropriately and to control waste—a story of greed, venality and misconduct both in government and advertising and communications agencies, all of which contributed to the loss and misuse of huge amounts of money at the expense of Canadian taxpayers. They are outraged and have valid reasons for their anger" (Gomery, 2005, xix).

Corruption is only one type of government malfeasance. Many countries are governed by politicians who abuse their citizens by repressing dissent and denying people their basic human rights. These problems are obviously most prevalent in dictatorial regimes such as Zimbabwe and China, but even democratic societies are not immune. During U.S. president George Bush's "War on Terror" following the attacks on New York's World Trade Center on September 11, 2001, the government imposed a series of restrictions on civil liberties. Legislation such as the Patriot Act and the Protect America Act has allowed the government to open people's mail and to carry out wiretaps and other types of electronic surveillance without the judicial supervision required by the Constitution. Suspected terrorists were held in a U.S. military base in Guantanamo Bay, Cuba, rather than in the United States so that American laws would not apply, and prisoners were tortured and humiliated by U.S. soldiers at the Abu Ghraib prison in Iraq. As you read in Chapter 11 (see Box 11.2), Maher Arar was stopped at a New York airport by U.S. officials on his way home to Canada and deported to Syria, where he was tortured because he was suspected of terrorist activities. These charges were groundless and were based on false information passed on to the United States by Canadian authorities.

Blue-Collar Crime

The concept of white-collar crime also fits many people who wear blue collars. Because of this, some have suggested that the term *occupational crime* may be a better one to use. Many tradespeople defraud the government by doing work "off the books" to avoid provincial sales tax and the GST. Some blue-collar businesses have very bad records of consumer fraud. For example, Robert Sikorsky (1990) documented an appalling degree of misconduct in the automobile repair business. Travelling across Canada, he visited 152 repair shops. Before each visit, he disconnected the idle air control in his car, triggering a warning light on the instrument panel. The repair was obvious and very simple—reinsert the connector. Over half the shops Sikorsky visited performed unnecessary work, overcharged him for work that was done, or lied about the work that had been done. In one case he was presented with an estimate of $570. A similar study was conducted by David Menzies (2000). In this case a mechanic disabled one of the sparkplugs on a car that was otherwise in good working order. In each case Menzies requested and paid for an engine diagnosis that ranged in price from $69 to $103, so there was ample information available to do the repair that should have cost about $20. Menzies visited only four Toronto repair shops, but his study reinforced Sikorsky's findings. Only one shop, a Honda dealership, repaired the problem without recommending any further work. Of the other three, Goodyear estimated the repair would cost $234, Speedy Auto Service estimated $300, and Canadian Tire estimated $648 would be required to return the car to working order.

Employee Fraud

Corporations are also often the victims of crime. A 2001 survey sponsored by the accounting company Ernst & Young found that about 25 percent of the Canadian workforce reported either having committed fraud against their employer or witnessing someone committing fraud during the previous year. Given these numbers, it is not surprising that an earlier survey of employers found that 80 percent reported having been victimized by employee fraud (Canadian Broadcasting Corporation, 2001a). Examples of frauds reported to Ernst & Young include taking kickbacks from suppliers in exchange for contracts, creating phony invoices and collecting the money, stealing company property, and stealing cash from the company. Canadian retailers estimate that in 2001 they lost $1 billion to employee theft, almost as much as their losses from shoplifting and other types of customer theft. To put this figure in perspective, the Retail Council of Canada reported that in 2002, losses due to robberies were $5.6 million and losses from credit card fraud were $204 million (2002). Corporations of all sizes are victimized, but often the toll has been greatest on small companies. For example, there have been reports of many small restaurants going out of business because of theft of money and food by staff. Lisa Leduc interviewed Ottawa restaurant employees about ways of "scamming" their employers. One of the interviewees described some of these methods:

> A manager would bring in his friends, a table of, let's say, eight, and [they would have] wings and beer, and he would go into the cooler where the beer was and grab it when the bartender wouldn't even notice, and [there would be] free dinner and beer for this person's friends. . . . Also, people weren't punching in drinks and [were] pocketing the money. Cooks [were] taking food home, all staff [were] taking dishes and cutlery. (Quoted in Gabor, 1994, 78–79)

In recent years technology and changes in financial practices have made larger corporations more vulnerable to the actions of individual employees. Earlier in this chapter you read about the illegal trades by Nicholas Leeson that drove Barings Bank into bankruptcy. Since the Leeson case, there have been several others where an individual trader has done significant harm to his company. Toronto's Stephen Duthie lost $182 million through unauthorized trading that was essentially gambling with his company's money. Duthie would have received a huge bonus if his gamble had succeeded in making large profits for his company. However, the trades lost money, and Duthie's employer, Phoenix Trading and

Research, was forced to close. These cases have become so common that the term *rogue trader* has been invented to describe the actions of people like Leeson and Duthie.

Leeson and Duthie were able to carry out their illegal trades because their companies did not properly supervise them. Many other organizations, including governments, have also been victimized because they did not exercise proper control over their employees. Between 1999 and 2003, Paul Champagne, a mid-level bureaucrat in Canada's Department of National Defence, was able to swindle $146 million from contracts he administered before he was caught.

Summary

- The study of white-collar crime has altered our view of some of the major issues in criminology. Most importantly, it has demonstrated that the relationship between class and crime is more complicated than early criminologists had believed. Our theories of crime must account for the crimes of the privileged as well as for the crimes of the poor.
- Even when they come to the attention of the authorities, white-collar crimes are often not reported in official crime statistics because they are dealt with under quasi-criminal statutes.
- Corporations are instruments that enable people to commit crimes that are vast in scope. The financial and physical costs of corporate crimes are very high.
- The structure of the modern corporation provides managers with a great deal of freedom from control. This has the unintended consequence of encouraging crime. In some industries, high-level managers demand such unreasonably high levels of profit that their subordinates feel pressured to break the law.
- While corporations are subject to legal regulation, the laws that govern them are weak. Even when punishment is administered, it is often so light that it does not act as a deterrent but is an accepted cost of doing business.
- There is some evidence that penalties for white-collar offenders are increasing in the United States, but this does not appear to be the case in Canada.
- One of the major contributions to many types of occupational crime is the failure of professional organizations to adequately control the behaviour of their members. Another is the fact that many people do not strongly condemn crimes such as tax fraud.

QUESTIONS FOR CRITICAL THINKING

1. The argument is made in this chapter that the structure of the corporation facilitates crime. What changes could be made in the organization and operation of corporations that would increase corporate responsibility?

2. Why do you think the government has refused to implement laws that would hold corporate officials responsible for their actions in cases like the Westray mine explosion?
3. In previous chapters of this text, you have studied a number of theories of criminal behaviour. Select one of these theories and assess how well it explains white-collar and corporate crime.
4. Some judges give light sentences to white-collar offenders because they feel that these offenders have already suffered from the publicity surrounding their conviction and because their employment prospects have suffered. Do you feel that these are appropriate sentencing criteria?
5. Can you think of three different actions that might be taken by governments and/or corporations to reduce the amount of white-collar and corporate crime in Canada?

NET WORK

There are several websites dealing with fraud. Two of the best are **www.scambusters.com** and **www.fraud.org**.

1. Go to these websites and briefly describe three different types of fraud. How can each of these frauds best be prevented?
2. How have the white-collar criminals who carry out these frauds adapted to new communications technology?

KEY TERMS

anticombines law; pg. 518
criminogenic market structure; pg. 511
executive disengagement; pg. 510
juristic person; pg. 508
monopolistic enterprise; pg. 518
occupational crime; pg. 502
organizational or corporate crime; pg. 502
white-collar crime; pg. 502

SUGGESTED READING

Coleman, J. W. (2006). *The Criminal Elite: Understanding White Collar Crime* (6th ed.). New York: St. Martin's Press. Coleman focuses on the "culture of competition" as well as inequities of class and power to explain and suggest remedies for white-collar crime.

Ermann, M. David, and Richard Lundman. (2002). *Corporate and Governmental Deviance: Problems of Organizational Behavior in Contemporary Society* (6th ed.). New York: Oxford University Press. A collection of readings that combines classic papers by James Coleman, Albert Reiss, Edwin Sutherland, Gilbert Geis, and Marshall Clinard with more recent research and analysis.

Glasbeek, Harry. (2002). *Wealth by Stealth*. Toronto: Between the Lines. Glasbeek provides a lawyer's perspective on corporate crime. The book shows how corporations are criminogenic organizations that protect owners from legal sanctions. It also provides some suggestions for reforming the law to make corporations more accountable.

Reasons, C., L. Ross, and C. Paterson. (1981). *Assault on the Worker: Occupational Health and Safety in Canada*. Toronto: Butterworths. This book provides a critical analysis of the complicated issues surrounding death and injury in the workplace, with a particular emphasis on the Canadian experience.

Reiman, Jeffrey. (2007). *The Rich Get Richer and the Poor Get Prison: Ideology, Class and Criminal Justice* (8th ed.). Boston: Allyn and Bacon. An inquiry into the failure of the American criminal justice system—its causes, mechanisms, and moral implications. The causes as well as the consequences of white-collar crime are a part of this story.

Shover, Neal, and John Paul Wright. (2001). *Crimes of Privilege: Readings in White-Collar Crime*. New York: Oxford University Press. A reader incorporating some of the classic articles on white-collar crime as well as a number of recent articles that describe some of the famous scandals of the 1990s. The book applies the rational-choice perspective to white-collar crime.

Snider, Laureen. (1993). *Bad Business: Corporate Crime in Canada*. Scarborough: Nelson. A very thorough review of corporate crime theory and research in Canada. The book has a strong focus on issues concerning the social and legal control of corporate crime.

BIBLIOGRAPHY

Akers, Ronald. (1973). *Deviant Behavior: A Social Learning Approach*. Belmont: Wadsworth.

Auditor General of Canada. (1999). "The Underground Economy Initiative." *Report of the Auditor General of Canada*. Ottawa: Office of the Auditor General of Canada.

Baumhart, Raymond. (1961). "How Ethical Are Businessmen?" *Harvard Business Review* 39:5–176.

Benson, M. L. (1989). "The Influence of Class Position on the Formal and Informal Sanctioning of White-Collar Offenders." *Sociological Quarterly* 30:465–79.

Benson, M. L., W. J. Maakestad, F. T. Cullen, and G. Geis. (1988). "District Attorneys and Corporate Crime: Surveying the Prosecutorial Gatekeepers." *Criminology* 26:505–18.

Box, Steven. (1981). *Deviance, Reality and Society* (2nd ed.). Toronto: Holt, Rinehart and Winston.

Brenner, S. S., and E. A. Molander. (1977). "Is the Ethics of Business Changing?" *Harvard Business Review* 55:57–71.

Butler, Steve. (2002). "Colossal Enron Collapse a Good Thing for the Rest of Us." *Winnipeg Free Press* 22 February:A15.

Canadian Broadcasting Corporation. (2001a). "Study Shows Employee Fraud Prevalent in Workplace." http://cbc.ca/cgi-bin/templates/print.cgi?/news/2001/01/08/workplace_fraud010108. Accessed 9 January, 2001.

Canadian Broadcasting Corporation. (2001b). "Swindler Patrick Kinlin Dies in Prison." http://www.cbc.ca/news/story/2001/03/06/tor_kinlindeath030601.html. Accessed 15 September, 2007.

Canadian Broadcasting Corporation. 2004. "Auditor-General's Report 2004." http://www.cbc.ca/news/background/auditorgeneral/report2004.html. Accessed 10 September, 2007.

Canadian Medical Protective Association. (2007). *2006 Annual Report*. Ottawa: Canadian Medical Protective Association.

Canadian Press. (2000). "CEO Jailed for Insider Trading." *Winnipeg Free Press* 19 September:B8.

Casey, John. (1985). "Corporate Crime and the State: Canada in the 1980s." In Thomas Fleming (ed.), *The New Criminologies in Canada* (pp. 100–101). Toronto: Oxford University Press.

Clinard, Marshall. (1952). *The Black Market: A Study of White Collar Crime*. New York: Holt, Rinehart and Winston.

Clinard, Marshall, and Peter Yeager. (1980). *Corporate Crime*. New York: Free Press.

Coleman, James. (1974). *Power and the Structure of Society*. New York: W.W. Norton.

——. (1985). *The Criminal Elite*. New York: St. Martin's Press.

Corrado, Raymond. (1996). "Political Crime in Canada." In Rick Linden (ed.), *Criminology: A Canadian Perspective* (3rd ed.) (pp. 459–93). Toronto: Harcourt Brace.

Cullen, Francis, Martha Larson, and Richard Mathers. (1985). "Having Money and Delinquency Involvement: The Neglect of Power in Delinquency Theory." *Criminal Justice and Behavior* 12(2):171–92.

Cullen, Francis, Bruce Link, and Craig Polanzi. (1982). "The Seriousness of Crime Revisited: Have Attitudes Toward White Collar Crime Changed?" *Criminology* 20:83–102.

Daly, Kathleen. (1989). "Gender and Varieties of White-Collar Crime." *Criminology* 27:769–93.

DeCloet, Derek. (2002). "Deceit Began This Scandalous Rot." *National Post* 11 July.

Donovan, Kevin. (2007). "$1.4B Tax Scams Nail Donors." *TheStar.com*, (29 September).

Drohan, Madelaine. (1995). "Barings Was Warned of Risk." *The Globe and Mail* 6 March:A1.

Ermann, M. David, and Richard Lundman. (1982). *Corporate Deviance*. New York: Holt, Rinehart and Winston.

Farberman, Harvey. (1975). "A Criminogenic Market Structure: The Automobile Industry." *Sociological Quarterly* 16:438–57.

Gabor, Thomas. (1994). *Everybody Does It*. Toronto: University of Toronto Press.

Gadd, Jane. (2000). "Fraud Artist Jailed for Bilking Seniors." *The Globe and Mail* 11 January:A1, A8.

Geis, Gilbert. (1962). "Toward a Delineation of White-Collar Offenses." *Sociological Inquiry* 32:160–71.

——. (1984). "White Collar Crime and Corporate Crime." In Robert F. Meier (ed.), *Major Forms of Crime*. Beverly Hills: Sage.

Glasbeek, Harry, and Eric Tucker. (1994). "Corporate Crime and the Westray Tragedy." *Canadian Dimension* (January–February):11–14.

Goff, Colin, and Charles Reasons. (1978). *Corporate Crime in Canada*. Scarborough: Prentice Hall.

Gomery, Mr. Justice John. (2005). *Who Is Responsible? Fact Finding Report*. Montreal: Commission of Inquiry into the Sponsorship Program and Advertising Activities.

Greenwood, Peter. (1982). *Selective Incapacitation*. Santa Monica, Calif.: Rand.

Hagan, John. (1982). "The Corporate Advantage: The Involvement of Individual and Organizational Victims in the Criminal Justice Process." *Social Forces* 60 (4):993–1022.

Hagan, John, and Celesta Albonetti. (1982). "Race, Class and the Perception of Criminal Injustice in America." *American Journal of Sociology* 88:329–55.

Hagan, John, A. R. Gillis, and John Simpson. (1985). "The Class Structure of Gender and Delinquency: Toward a Power-Control Theory of Common Delinquent Behavior." *American Journal of Sociology* 90:1151–78.

Hagan, John, and Fiona Kay. (1990). "Gender and Delinquency in White-Collar Families: A Power-Control Perspective." *Crime and Delinquency* 36(3):391–407.

Hagan, John, and Ilene Nagel. (1982). "White Collar Crime, White Collar Time: The Sentencing of White Collar Criminals in the Southern District of New York." *American Criminal Law Review* 20(2):259–301.

Hagan, John, and Alberto Palloni. (1983). "The Sentencing of White Collar Offenders Before and After Watergate." Paper presented at the American Sociological Association Meetings, Detroit.

Hagan, John, and Patricia Parker. (1985). "White Collar Crime and Punishment: The Class Structure and Legal Sanctioning of Securities Violations." *American Sociological Review* 50(3):302–16.

Hartung, Frank E. (1950). "White Collar Offenses in the Wholesale Meat Industry in Detroit." *American Journal of Sociology* 56:25–34.

Henderson, Tanya. (2000). "Delivered and Signed." http://abcnews.go.com/onair/2020/2020_000428_zorro_feature.html. Accessed 12 May, 2003.

Howlett, Karen. (2002). "The Two Faces of YBM Magnex." *The Globe and Mail* 29 December:B13.

Kadlec, Daniel. (2002). "WorldCon." *Time* (8 July):15–20.

Katz, Jack. (1980). "The Movement against White-Collar Crime." In Egon Bittner and Sheldon Messinger (eds.), *Criminology Review Yearbook*, Vol. 2. Beverly Hills: Sage.

Kranhold, Kathryn, and Mitchell Pacelle. (2002). "Enron Paid Top Managers $681 Million, Even as Stock Slid." *The Wall Street Journal* 17 June: B1, B4.

Law Commission of Canada. (2000). *Restoring Dignity: Responding to Child Abuse in Canadian Institutions*. Ottawa: Law Commission of Canada.

Mann, Kenneth, Stanton Wheeler, and Austin Sarat. (1980). "Sentencing the White Collar Offender." *American Criminal Law Review* 17(4):479.

McIntyre, Mike. (2001). "Deaths Cost Firms Dearly." *Winnipeg Free Press* 3 March:A1, A4.

Menzies, David. (2000). "Looking for Mr. Goodwrench." *National Post* 23 September.

Mills, C. Wright. (1956). *The Power Elite*. New York: Oxford University Press.

Nagorski, Zygmunt. (1989). "Yes, Socrates, Ethics Can Be Taught." *New York Times* 12 February:F2.

Olive, David. "An Anthology of Black Quotes." *Toronto Star* 11 March. http://www.thestar.com/News/article/190677. Accessed 16 September, 2007.

Posner, Richard A. (1980). "Optimal Sentences for White Collar Criminals." *American Criminal Law Review*: 409–18.

Reasons, Charles, and Duncan Chappell. (1985). "Crooked Lawyers: Towards a Political Economy of Deviance in the Profession." In Thomas Fleming (ed.), *The New Criminologies in Canada*. (pp. 206–22). Toronto: Oxford University Press.

Reasons, C., L. Ross, and C. Paterson. (1981). *Assault on the Worker: Occupational Health and Safety in Canada*. Toronto: Butterworths.

Reiss, Albert. (1980). *Data Sources on White Collar Law Breaking*. Washington: National Institute of Justice.

Retail Council of Canada. (2002). *2001 Canadian Retail Security Report*. Toronto: Retail Council of Canada.

Richard, Justice K. Peter. (1997). *The Westray Story: A Predictable Path to Disaster*, Executive Summary. Halifax: Government of Nova Scotia.

Ross, E. A. (1907). *Sin and Society*. Boston: Houghton Mifflin.

Rubin, Sandra. (1999). "RCMP Investigated YBM in Early 1995." *The Financial Post* 9 January.

Schrager, Laura, and James F. Short. (1978). "Toward a Sociology of Organizational Crime." *Social Problems* 25(4):407–19.

Shapiro, Susan P. (1990). "Collaring the Crime, Not the Criminal: Reconsidering the Concept of White-Collar Crime." *American Sociological Review* 55:346–65.

Sharpe, Andrew, and Jill Hardt. (2006). "Five Deaths a Day: Workplace Fatalities in Canada, 1993-2005." CSLS Research Paper 2006-04. Ottawa: Centre for the Study of Living Standards.

Shover, Neal, and Andy Hochstetler. (2006). *Choosing White-Collar Crime.* New York: Cambridge University Press.

Sikorsky, Robert. (1990). "Highway Robbery: Canada's Auto Repair Scandal." *Reader's Digest* (February):55–63.

Silver, Jim. (1996). "Review of *Game Misconduct: Alan Eagleson and the Corruption of Hockey.*" *Canadian Dimension* 30(4) (July–August).

Simpson, Sally. (1986). "The Depression of Antitrust: Testing a Multilevel, Longitudinal Model of Profit-Squeeze." *American Sociological Review* 51:859–75.

Sinclair, Judge Murray. (2000). *The Report of the Manitoba Pediatric Surgery Inquest.* Winnipeg: Provincial Court of Manitoba. www.pediatriccardiacinquest.mb.ca. Accessed 12 May, 2003.

Smandych, Russell. (1985). "Marxism and the Creation of Law: Re-Examining the Origins of Canadian Anti-Combines Legislation, 1890–1910." In Thomas Fleming (ed.), *The New Criminologies* (pp. 87–99). Toronto: Oxford University Press.

Snider, Laureen. (1979). "Revising the Combines Investigation Act: A Study in Corporate Power." In Paul J. Brantingham and Jack M. Kress (eds.), *Structure, Law and Power: Essays in the Sociology of Law* (pp. 105–19). Beverly Hills: Sage.

———. (1988). "Commercial Crime." In Vincent F. Sacco (ed.), *Conformity and Control in Canadian Society* (pp. 231–83). Scarborough: Prentice Hall.

Stone, Christopher. (1975). *Where the Law Ends: The Social Control of Corporate Behavior.* New York: Harper and Row.

Sutherland, Edwin. (1940). "White Collar Criminality." *American Sociological Review* 5:1–12.

———. (1945). "Is 'White Collar Crime' Crime?" *American Sociological Review* 10:132–39.

Swartz, Joel. (1978). "Silent Killers at Work." In M. David Ermann and Richard Lundman (eds.), *Corporate and Governmental Deviance* (pp. 114–28). New York: Oxford University Press.

Tappan, Paul. (1947). "Who Is the Criminal?" *American Sociological Review* 12:96–102.

U.S. Securities and Exchange Commission. (2001). *Securities and Exchange Commission v. Mark S. Jakob.* www.sec.gov/litigation/litreleases/lr17094.htm. Accessed 12 May, 2003.

Vancouver Sun. (2000). "Doctor Baited Crab Trap with Human Foot." 9 August: A3.

Weisburd, David, Elin Waring, and Stanton Wheeler. (1990). "Class, Status and the Punishment of White-Collar Criminals." *Law and Social Inquiry* 15(2):223–46.

Wells, Jennifer. (1998). *Fever: The Dark Mystery of the Bre-X Gold Rush.* Toronto: Viking.

Wente, Margaret. (2000). "Dr. Bloody and Mr. Whizzo." *The Globe and Mail* 25 July: A17.

Wheeler, Stanton, and Michael Rothman. (1982). "The Organization as Weapon in White Collar Crime." *Michigan Law Review* 80(7):1403–26.

Wheeler, Stanton, David Weisburd, and Nancy Bode. (1982). "Sentencing the White Collar Offender: Rhetoric and Reality." *American Sociological Review* 47:641–59.

Wolfgang, Marvin. (1972). *Delinquency in a Birth Cohort.* Chicago: University of Chicago Press.

Glossary

acephalous society
Literally "headless," meaning that the society is without any formalized or institutionalized system of power and authority. Collective decisions are made in a variety of ways, including informal community gatherings, which will change according to circumstances.

actuarial
Refers to statistical calculations of risk across time and groups.

actus reus
All of the elements contained in the definition of a criminal offence—other than the mental elements (**mens rea**).

administrative record
Collection of information about individual cases, such as statistics concerning what is common among individual cases. An administrative record contains information that can be the basis of statistics, provided that clear procedures are developed for handling the data and generating statistical descriptions.

anomie
A concept developed by Émile Durkheim (1858–1917) to describe an absence of clear societal norms and values. Individuals lack a sense of social regulation: people feel unguided in the choices they have to make. American sociologist Robert Merton (1910–2003) used the term more narrowly to refer to a situation in which people's goals—what they wanted to achieve—were beyond their means. Their commitment to the goal was so strong that they would adopt deviant means to achieve it.

anticombines law
In order to protect the principle of competition, valued by all liberal, capitalistic societies, laws have been created to prevent and punish corporations that work together to reduce competition.

Antisocial Personality Disorder
A personality disorder that involves disregard for the rights of others, as well as impulsive, irresponsible, and aggressive behaviour.

assumption of discriminating traits
The view that offenders are distinguished from non-offenders by, for example, their high levels of impulsiveness and aggression.

assumption of offender deficit
The view that offenders who break the law have some psychological deficit that distinguishes them from normal law-abiding citizens.

atavism
Cesare Lombroso (1836–1909) believed that some criminals were born criminals; they were atavistic. This suggested that they were throwbacks to an earlier stage of human evolution and that this limited evolutionary development meant that they were morally inferior. This inferiority could be identified through a series of physical **stigmata**.

attachment
The degree to which an individual has affective ties to other persons. One of the social bonds in Hirschi's theory.

attentive gaze
A methodological requirement that researchers immerse themselves in where crime occurs in the everyday world in order to better understand the ways in which crime is experienced and interpreted by individuals.

autonomic reactivity
A measurement of the extent to which an individual's physical organism reacts to external stimuli.

belief
The degree to which an individual believes in conventional values, morality, and the legitimacy of law. One of the social bonds in Hirschi's theory.

bourgeois class
The term *bourgeois class*, or bourgeoisie, was used by Marx to refer to the capitalist or ruling class in modern societies.

broken windows policing
Just as houses with broken windows indicate that nobody cares about the neighbourhood, proponents of this policing style feel that tolerating minor misbehaviour will mean that residents will be afraid to use their streets. They feel that police should quickly deal with minor incivilities such as panhandling, vandalism, and other behaviours that contribute to fear of crime. Critics feel this policing style potentially discriminates against the poor.

Canadian Centre for Justice Statistics
A division of Statistics Canada, formed in 1981, with a mandate to collect national data on crime and justice.

capital
Each person enters a field of activity already possessed of certain powerful qualities or "capital." For example, a student who has a large vocabulary and is able to use this vocabulary competently will likely have an advantage in achieving a "feel for the game" within the academic field.

career
In common use, this refers to the sequence of stages through which people in a particular occupational sector move during the course of their employment. It has also been applied to analyzing the various stages of an individual's involvement with criminal activity.

career contingency
An unintended event, process, or situation that occurs by chance.

Charter—Charter of Rights and Freedoms
Part of the Constitution Act of 1982, the Charter came into effect in April 1982. The Charter provides protection for a wide range of individual rights typical of liberal democracies that until this time were protected by common law rather than constitutional guarantee. As a part of the Constitution of Canada, the Charter cannot be changed without the consent of both Parliament and provincial legislatures. The Charter includes provisions to protect freedoms of speech, conscience, and religion; protection against unreasonable search and seizure; rights to due legal process; and mobility and minority language rights.

class conflict theory
Laws are passed by members of the ruling class in order to maintain their privileged position by keeping the common people under control.

classical conditioning
A basic form of learning whereby a neutral stimulus is paired with another stimulus that naturally elicits a certain response; the neutral stimulus comes to elicit the same response as the stimulus that automatically elicits the response.

Classical School
Considered to be the first formal school of criminology, Classical criminology is associated with 18th and early 19th century reforms to the administration of justice and the prison system. Associated with authors such as Cesare Beccaria (1738–1794), Jeremy Bentham (1748–1832), Samuel Romilly (1757–1818), and others, this school brought the emerging philosophy of liberalism and utilitarianism to the justice system, advocating principles of rights, fairness, and due process in place of retribution, arbitrariness, and brutality.

collective solidarity
Similar in meaning to Émile Durkheim's term *mechanical solidarity*, this refers to a state of social bonding or interdependency that rests on similarity of beliefs and values, shared activities, and ties of kinship and cooperation among members of a community.

commitment
The degree to which an individual pursues conventional goals. One of the social bonds in Hirschi's theory.

common law
The common law tradition found in English Canada derives from feudal England, where it had become the practice for the king to resolve disputes in accordance with local custom. Customs that were recognized throughout the country were called common custom, and decisions made by the king and by subsequent courts set up to settle disputes became known as common law. Common law is considered a source of law. Also, the body of judge-made laws that has evolved in areas not covered by legislation.

community psychology
A perspective that analyzes social problems, including crime, as largely a product of organizational and institutional characteristics of society. It is closely related to sociology.

conduct norms
Specification of rules or norms of appropriate behaviour generally agreed upon by members of the social group to whom the behavioural norms apply.

conflict perspective
Sociological perspectives that focus on the inherent divisions of societies based on social inequality and the way these social divisions give rise to different and competing interests. The central assumption is that social structures and cultural ideas tend to reflect the interests of only some members of society rather than society as a whole. This contrasts with consensus or functionalist perspectives that assume a foundation of common interest among all members of society. Marxism and feminism are examples of conflict perspectives.

consensual crime
Any crime in which the "victim" is a willing participant (drug use, prostitution, etc.).

consensus perspective
Also known as *functionalism*, the foundation of this perspective is the assumption that societies have an inherent tendency to maintain themselves in a state of relative equilibrium through the mutually adaptive and supportive interaction of their principal institutions. The approach also assumes that effective maintenance of a particular form of society is in the common interest of all its members.

consensus theory
Laws represent the agreement of most of the people in society that certain acts should be prohibited by the criminal law.

conservative approach
An approach that understands "difference" between men and women as biologically based sex differences. Women are viewed as "naturally" inferior or unequal to men.

conspiracy
An agreement by two or more persons to commit a criminal offence.

continuance commitment
Adherence to a criminal or other identity arising from the unattractiveness or unavailability of alternative lifestyles.

conventional crime
Those traditional, illegal behaviours that most people think of as crime. Non-conventional crime may be organized crime, white-collar crime, political crime, etc.

correlate
Any variable that is related to another variable. Age and sex are the two strongest correlates of crime.

correlation
A relationship that exists when two or more variables are associated.

counselling
Procuring, soliciting, or inciting another person to commit a crime.

counting procedure
In any statistical system, there must be consensus on how to count units and data elements. This is not as easy an issue as it appears. For example, if an offender goes on a break-and-enter spree and steals from a half dozen houses, is this to be counted as one incident or six?

crime
Conduct that is prohibited by law and that is subject to a penal sanction (such as imprisonment or a fine).

crime prevention through social development
An approach to crime prevention that focuses on reducing the number of motivated offenders by changing the social environment. Examples include preschool education programs and effective parenting training.

crime rate
When studying crime, if a researcher wishes to compare the amount of crime over time or between communities of different sizes, it is not enough to just do a gross count of the amount of crime. To get around the problems involved with this, criminologists calculate crime rates (or rates of incarceration, conviction, or recidivism). This is done by dividing the amount of crime by the population size and multiplying by 100 000. This produces the standard rate per 100 000, but occasionally it is useful to calculate a rate per million or some other figure when looking at less frequently occurring offences.

criminal attempt
A criminal attempt occurs when an individual does—or omits to do—anything for the purpose of carrying out a previously formed intention to commit a crime. The conduct in question must constitute a substantial step toward the completion of the crime that is intended.

criminal identity
This social category is imposed by the community and correctly or incorrectly defines an individual as a particular type of criminal. The identity will pervasively shape his or her social interactions with others. It is similar in concept to **master status**.

criminal law
A body of jurisprudence that includes the definition of various crimes, the specification of various penalties, a set of general principles concerning criminal responsibility, and a series of defences to a criminal charge.

criminal procedure
A body of legislation that specifies the procedures to be followed in the prosecution of a criminal case and defines the nature and scope of the powers of criminal justice officials.

criminogenic market structure
An economic market that is structured in such a way that it tends to produce criminal behaviour.

criminology
The body of knowledge regarding crime as a social phenomenon. It includes the processes of making laws, of breaking laws, and of reacting to the breaking of laws. Its objective is the development of a body of general and verified principles and of other types of knowledge regarding this process of law, crime, and treatment.

cultural conflict
A theory that attempts to explain certain types of criminal behaviour as resulting from a conflict between the conduct norms of divergent cultural groups.

cultural construction
A perspective on a subject that is shaped by cultural assumptions rather than having a natural or objective basis. For example, concepts of masculine and feminine suggest how men and women should behave, but very few of these gender differences are determined by biological sex.

cultural explanation
An explanation for crime that is phrased in terms of the culture of the subgroup or the culture of that nation.

culturally prescribed aspiration
A rejection of the notion that aspirations are entirely self-created; rather, they are defined by culture and transmitted by other members of the society.

dangerous knowledge
A form of knowledge that leaves no concept, notion, or idea untouched by criticism. To achieve this relentlessly critical stance, cultural criminologists will often turn to diverse sources of information (e.g., novels and street-level observation) as means to reveal alternative perspectives that might shake the foundations of our taken-for-granted assumptions about crime.

dark figure of crime
The amount of crime that is unreported or unknown. The total amount of crime in a community consists of crimes that are known or recorded and the dark figure of crime. Criminologists have used differing methods (such as victimization surveys) to try to decrease the amount of unknown or unrecorded crime.

data element
What, specifically, is to be collected. Operational issues may require more detail than the statistical system does. Also, statistical needs may require that operational agencies collect data that they do not need (or do not think that they need) for operational purposes. In any statistical system, there must be detailed agreements on exactly what is to be collected.

deconstruction
An opening up of seemingly closed "things." It intends to encounter the hidden and excluded elements of language, meaning, and experience.

deterrence
As used in criminal justice, it refers to crime prevention achieved through the fear of punishment.

differential association
Developed by Edwin Sutherland in the 1930s, this theory argues that crime, like any social behaviour, is learned in association with others. If individuals regularly associate with criminals and are relatively isolated from law-abiding citizens, they are more likely to engage in crime themselves. They learn the specific skills needed to commit crime and the ideas that justify and normalize crime.

diffuseness of roles
A characteristic of relatively simple societies in which people encounter one another in a variety of overlapping roles—there is little occupational specialization and no clear separation of private and public spheres of life. People are continuously reminded of their extensive bonds with others.

discipline
A meticulous manner or method of training the body. It intends to ensure constant subjection and obedience. It involves hierarchal observation, normalizing judgment and examinations. Recall your grade school days when you were being taught to write: the teacher showed you how to hold the

pencil, observed and corrected your faults, and examined your skill through quizzes and tests.

drift

A psychological state of weak normative attachment to either deviant or conventional ways.

duress

Duress may be a defence to a criminal charge when the accused was forced to commit a crime as a consequence of threats of death or serious bodily harm made by another person.

ecological fallacy

A research error made when data or information is gathered at a group level (the unemployment rate of various communities or neighbourhoods) and then conclusions are drawn about individuals (the unemployed person). Areas with high unemployment may have high crime rates, but this does not tell us that those crimes are necessarily committed by unemployed persons.

economic determinism

The theory that all the main features of a society, including its cultural ideas and social organization, are chiefly shaped by its form of economic organization.

effective guardianship

An aspect of the **routine activities approach** to understanding crime victimization that argues that three key factors are required for crime to happen: a motivated offender, a suitable target, and ineffective guardianship of that target. Effective guardianship would include having locks on bikes, security lights in the backyard, or putting goods in the trunk of the car. Measures like this should reduce the risk of being victimized.

ego

A psychoanalytical term that denotes the rational part of the personality. It mediates between the **id** and the **superego** and is responsible for dealing with reality and making decisions.

electrodermal response

Electrical activity of the sweat glands in the skin. Tests of electrodermal activity have indicated correlation between skin conductivity and tendency to delinquency, aggressiveness, and recidivism.

empirical evidence

Evidence that can be observed through the senses. That is, it can be seen, touched, heard, smelled, tasted, and, to some extent, measured. This is the only form of evidence acceptable to science.

ethnic group

A group of individuals having a distinct subculture in common. An ethnic group differs from a race because it implies that values, norms, behaviour, and language, not necessarily physical appearance, are the important distinguishing characteristics.

ethnomethodology

A sociological theory developed by Harold Garfinkel. Roughly translated, the term means the study of people's practices or methods. The perspective does not see the social world as an objective reality but as something that people must build and rebuild constantly in their thoughts and actions. Ethnomethodologists try to uncover the methods and practices that are used by people as they create the taken-for-granted world.

etiological factor

A factor that encourages or causes a particular outcome. For example, addiction to hard drugs is a factor that can lead people into prostitution or criminal behaviour; being raised in a violent home is a factor that can lead to violent behaviour or being victimized by violence.

executive disengagement

The custom by which lower-level employees assume that executives are best left uninformed of certain decisions and actions of employees, or the assumption that executives cannot be legally expected to have complete control over their individual staff.

extraversion

A personality characteristic associated with sociability, impulsiveness, and aggression.

false positive

When trying to identify dangerous offenders (or other things as well), researchers often make mistakes. One category of mistakes is known as a false positive. A false positive is identifying offenders as dangerous (and possibly keeping them incarcerated or denying them parole) when they are actually not dangerous.

feminist approach

Understands "difference" between men and women as structurally produced by inequalities of class, race, and gender that condition and constrain women's lives.

feudalism

A system of economic and social organization found historically in several areas of the world. In western Europe, feudalism was at its height between about 1000 and 1500. The usual economic foundation of the system was the feudal manor, an agricultural organization that included a central farm owned by the landlord and small land holdings for a class of bonded farm labourers (serfs). The serfs were required to work the central manorial farm and to provide the lord with produce and money payments in return for their right to use the land. The system gradually declined as cities and towns grew and power became centralized in nation-states under monarchies.

field

A basic unit of social activity. The social world is divided into many fields (e.g., the "artistic" field, the "academic" field, or the "economic" field). Each field of activity is defined by its own market through which certain practices or dispositions are valued more than others. For example, in the artistic field one's possession of cultural knowledge about art history and technical mastery of artistic techniques is likely to be more valued than one's personal wealth.

free trade zone

A specially designated geographical area within a nation that is exempt from the regulations and taxation normally imposed on business. These zones are intended to facilitate cross-border production and trade. Examples of these zones are found along the United States–Mexico border, where they are referred to as *maquilladora.*

Gemeinschaft

A German word, translated as "community," used by sociologist Ferdinand Tönnies (1855–1936) to define an **ideal type** or model of a society in which social bonds are personal and direct and there are strong shared values and beliefs. Characteristic of small-scale, localized societies, it is in contrast to **Gesellschaft**, which refers to complex, impersonal societies.

gender-ratio problem

Poses the question of why are there sex differences in rates of arrest and types of criminal activity between men and women.

generalizability problem

Raises the issue of whether mainstream theories of crime—which have largely been developed with men in mind—can be made to "fit" women.

Gesellschaft

A German word, translated as "society-association," used by Ferdinand Tönnies (1855–1936) to refer to an **ideal type** or model of a society in which social bonds are primarily impersonal, instrumental, and narrow. Characteristic of large-scale, complex societies, with a strict division between private and public spheres of life, it contrasts to the community-oriented life of the **Gemeinschaft**.

governmentality

The art of governing. It transcends and is considerably broader than the traditional understanding of government as a state-directed activity. Government, then, encompasses a wide array of techniques, within and outside of the state, intended to (re) shape and (re)direct human actions.

gross counts of crime

A count of the total amount of crime in a given community, making no distinction between crime categories.

group conflict

A theory that attempts to explain certain types of criminal behaviour as resulting from a conflict between the interests of divergent groups.

habitus

A set of durable dispositions acquired through experience that allow one to achieve a "feel for the game" within a specific field of activity. These are internalized practices that serve as a "second nature" responsive to the immediate demands of everyday life.

human capital

The talents and capabilities that individuals contribute to the process of production. Companies, governments, and individuals can invest in this capital, just as they can invest in technology and buildings or in finances.

human rights

The minimum conditions required for a person to live a dignified life. Among the rights set out by the Universal Declaration of Human Rights are the right to life, liberty, and security of the person; the right to be free of torture and other forms of cruel and degrading punishment; the right to equality before the law; and the right to the basic necessities of life.

hunting and gathering society

Probably the earliest form of human society that still persists in remote regions of the world, to some extent. These societies have an economic base that rests on the use of the naturally occurring animal and plant resources of the environment. They do not practise agriculture or raise animals.

id

A psychoanalytical term that denotes the most inaccessible and primitive part of the mind. It is a reservoir of biological urges that strive continually for gratification. The **ego** mediates between the id and the **superego**.

ideal type

An abstract model of a classic, pure form of social phenomenon. It is a model concept and does not necessarily exist in exact form in reality. An example is Ferdinand Tönnies's (1855–1936) dichotomy **Gemeinschaft** and **Gesellschaft**.

ideology

A linked set of ideas and beliefs that act to uphold and justify an existing or desired situation in society. Ideologies offer explanations and justifications of features of society such as the distribution of wealth, status, and power.

incapacitation

The policy of locking offenders in jail to prevent them from repeating their crimes.

inchoate crime

A criminal offence that is committed when the accused person seeks to bring about the commission of a particular crime but is not successful in doing so. The three inchoate offences in the Criminal Code are attempt, conspiracy, and counselling.

incidence

Incidence tells us the frequency of new occurrences of some event during a particular time period. For example, there were 605 criminal homicides in Canada in 2006.

independent variable

A presumed cause of a dependent variable. If unemployment is thought to cause crime rates to increase, unemployment is the independent variable, and crime rates the dependent variable.

individual pathology

A term used to refer to biological or psychological explanations of criminal or deviant behaviour by individuals. The assumption is that the deviant behaviour of individuals can be at least partly explained by some physical or psychological trait that makes them different from normal law-abiding citizens.

individualistic

A theory that focuses on explaining the behaviour of individuals and using factors or features of the individual in explaining this behaviour.

instrumental Marxism

In this perspective, the state is viewed as the direct instrument of the ruling or capitalist class. Instrumentalism is based on the notion that the processes of the superstructure are determined by the economic base.

intoxication

Intoxication caused by alcohol and/or other drugs may be a defence if it prevents the accused from forming the intent required for a specific intent offence, such as murder or robbery.

involvement

The degree to which an individual is active in conventional activities. One of the social bonds in Hirschi's theory.

juristic person
The legal concept that corporations are liable to the same laws as natural persons. Treating corporations as individuals raises practical difficulties for legal enforcement and punishment.

justice
For Derrida, since it is perpetually deferred, justice cannot be defined adequately. It is not contained in or constrained by law. It is infinite. It is "to come."

labelling
According to labelling theory, deviance is not a quality of the act but of the label that others attach to the act. This raises the question of who applies the label and who is labelled. The application of a label and the response of others to the label may result in a person becoming committed to a deviant identity.

legal definition of crime
Crime is an act that violates the criminal law and is punishable with jail terms, fines, and other sanctions.

levels of aggregation
This refers to how data are to be combined. Do we want city-level, provincial, or national data? Among other things, data aggregation requires common rules, allowing confidence in the **reliability** and **validity** of the measures used.

liberal approach
Distinguishes sex (biological) from gender (cultural) and sees differences between men and women as resulting from gender roles and socialization patterns.

lifestyle/exposure theory
A theory of victimization that acknowledges that not everyone has the same lifestyle and that some lifestyles expose people to more risks than others do. If you go to bed early, you are less at risk of robbery or assault than if you like to visit the bars several nights a week. Similar to **routine activities approach**.

longitudinal study
This measures relationships between variables over a period of time. For example, one might follow a group of males from birth to age 30 to measure their involvement with the criminal justice system over time.

Mafia
A term originally used to identify a specific Sicilian crime group. It is now commonly used to identify any ethnic or regionally based crime organization.

master status
A status that overrides all others in perceived importance. Whatever other personal or social qualities individuals possess, they are judged primarily by this one attribute. Criminal is an example of a master status that determines the community's identification of an individual.

maturational reform
The observation that involvement in crime tends to decrease as people age.

mens rea
Criminal intent. The mental elements (other than voluntariness) contained in the definition of a criminal offence.

methodology
The study or critique of methods. There are many philosophical issues about the use of a particular method or about positivism or measurement itself.

micro powers
Small and mundane relations of governance, which still have an appreciable effect on human behaviour. For example, the arrangement of a traditional classroom, with the professor or instructor at the front and all students facing her/him, is infused with power relations that rarely gain our attention.

middle-class measuring rod
A phrase suggesting that children and young people from the lower class often find themselves in situations in which they are measured against middle-class standards.

mistake of fact
Mistake of fact may be a defence where the accused person acts under the influence of an honest mistake in relation to any of the elements of the **actus reus** of the offence charged.

mode of production
The dominant form of social and technical organization of economic production in a society. Historically, a variety of modes of production can be distinguished based on both technology and the structure of social relationships.

modelling
A form of learning that occurs as a result of watching and imitating others.

monopolistic enterprise
Any corporation that controls all, or the majority, of the market for a particular product or service.

moral development theory
Refers generally to theories of individual psychology that investigate how moral reasoning emerges in the individual and develops as the individual matures.

moral entrepreneur
Someone who is engaged in the process of defining new rules and laws or who advocates stricter enforcement of existing laws. Often such entrepreneurs will have some financial or organizational interest in particular definitions or applications of law.

moral rhetoric
In the study of crime, this is the set of claims and assertions that deviants make to justify their deviant behaviour. The moral rhetoric of a group is an important component of socialization into a deviant identity.

mutual conversion
A phrase suggesting that conversion to deviance (and perhaps to other lifestyles) is not a solitary activity but is achieved through a process of interaction with others.

naked life
For Agamben, naked life is akin to *Homo sacer*—an individual who is excluded from possessing human rights, can be killed by anyone, yet cannot be sacrificed during a religious ceremony.

NCRMD
The special verdict of "not criminally responsible on account of mental disorder." In order to be found NCRMD, it must be proved on the balance of probabilities that, because of mental disorder, the accused lacked the capacity to appreciate the nature and quality of the act or omission in question or of knowing that it would be

considered morally wrong by the average Canadian.

necessity
Necessity may be a defence to a criminal charge when the accused person commits the lesser evil of a crime in order to avoid the occurrence of a greater evil.

negative social capital
The way in which one's network of formal social resources (e.g., organizations designed to provide social services) can be used to more effectively regulate and control rather than empower an individual.

negative symbolic capital
The way in which stigma cast upon a neighbourhood might be symbolically transferred to the neighbourhood's residents, placing them in a deficit with respect to their ability to improve their social standing.

norms
Established rules of behaviour or standards of conduct.

objective *mens rea*
The **mens rea** elements of a criminal offence are considered to be objective if they are based on a determination of whether a reasonable person, in the same circumstances and with the same knowledge as the accused, would have appreciated the risk involved in the accused's conduct and would have taken steps to avoid the commission of the **actus reus** elements of the crime in question.

occupational crime
Refers to individuals who violate the law in the course of practising a legitimate occupation.

operant conditioning
The basic process by which an individual's behaviour is shaped by reinforcement or by punishment.

opportunity structure
Opportunity is shaped by the way the society or an institution is organized or structured.

organizational or corporate crime
White-collar crime committed with the support and encouragement of a formal organization and intended at least in part to advance the goals of that organization.

over-representation
A group that has a number of its members in some condition in greater numbers than their population would suggest. If a group makes up 20 percent of the population, then a researcher might predict, other things being equal, that they would represent 20 percent of offenders.

paramount chieftainship
A political system similar to a kingdom that brings together a number of partly autonomous villages or communities under the hierarchical rule of a grand chief.

party to a crime
The Criminal Code specifies that one is a party to—and liable to conviction of—a criminal offence if one actually commits it; aids and/or abets it; becomes a party to it by virtue of having formed a common intention with others to commit a crime; or counsels the commission of an offence that is actually committed by another person.

patriarchy
A system of male domination that includes both a structure and an ideology that privileges men over women. Stresses the systemic nature of the oppression of women. For example, men exercise control over women both overtly by objectifying women's bodies in pornography and covertly in the form of a "monogamous heterosexuality" that legitimates male control over women and children and reinforces the ideology that women are dependent on men for both their economic and sexual needs.

population
All members of a given class or set. For example, adult Canadians, teenagers, Canadian inmates, or criminal offenders can each be thought of as populations. Populations are difficult to study because we cannot find all the members (heroin addicts) or because there are too many in the population to address all of them. Social scientists avoid this problem by gathering a **sample** from the population and then generalizing from the sample to the population.

Positive School
The first scientific school consisting of the Italian criminologists Cesare Lombroso (1836–1909), Raffaelo Garofalo (1852–1934), and Enrico Ferri (1856–1929). They supported the assumptions of positivism and argued that criminality is determined—the effect in a cause–effect sequence—and that the mandate of criminology should be to search for these causes. It was believed that with the exception of those deemed to be born criminals, the discovery of the causes of crime would allow for effective treatment.

power
Power, for Foucault, extends beyond the state. It is not a quantity to hold or possess. It is, rather, relational, such that power is only ever evident in its exercise.

primary deviation
Where the individual commits deviant acts but does not adopt a primary self-identity as a deviant.

provocation
Provocation may be a partial defence to a charge of murder (if successful, it reduces the offence from murder to manslaughter). The required elements of provocation are (i) that the accused responded to a wrongful act or insult that was of such a nature that an ordinary person would have been likely to lose the power of self-control and (ii) that the accused acted "on the sudden and before there was time for his (or her) passion to cool."

radical feminism
A perspective that views the problem of gender inequality and of women's subordination in society as rooted in the institution of patriarchy.

reaction formation
In Freudian terms, it is an adaptation in which the **ego** unconsciously develops attitudes and interests the direct opposite of those in the **id** striving for expression. In Albert Cohen's theory, lower-class children who cannot succeed when measured by middle-class criteria collectively reverse these values and obtain status by doing the opposite.

regulatory offences
Regulatory offences arise under legislation (either federal, provincial, or territorial) that regulates inherently legitimate activities connected with trade, commerce, and industry or with everyday living (driving, fishing, etc.). These offences are not considered to be serious in nature and usually carry only a relatively minor penalty upon conviction.

relative autonomy
A term used in the structural Marxist perspective to indicate that the state has a certain amount of independence from the capitalist class and is therefore able to enact laws that are not in the immediate interests of the capitalist class.

relative deprivation
Relative deprivation and absolute deprivation are often contrasted. Absolute deprivation refers to the inability to sustain oneself physically and materially. However, in relative terms, deprivation is not judged against some absolute standard of sustainability but against deprivation in relation to others around you. You may have sufficient money to meet your needs and even meet them adequately, but you may feel relatively deprived because others around you have more.

reliability
Identifies one of the standards (another being **validity**) against which the tools used to measure concepts are judged. Reliability refers to consistency of results over time. If a bathroom scale is used to measure the concept of weight, one must ask: Is this tool (the bathroom scale) reliable? Does it provide consistent results? Notice that the bathroom scale or any other measure may be reliable and yet be inaccurate.

risk
The calculated probability of an eventuality.

risk society
An emerging societal form characterized by the production and increased awareness of human-made "risks," such as nuclear destruction and environmental devastation. More importantly, the risk society is organized around the management of such risks.

role convergence
One explanation for the rising crime rate among women has been that their roles have become similar to (converged with) those of men.

routine activities approach
Similar to the **lifestyle/exposure theory**, this approach assumes that crimes are the expected outcomes of routine activities and changing social patterns. For example, those with more property can expect to be the victims of property crime more often than those with less property. Young people who like to hang out in the evenings are more likely to be victims than are those who go to organized activities or remain at home to study.

sample
A group of elements (people, offenders, inmates) selected in a systematic manner from the population of interest.

secondary deviation
Occurs when an individual accepts the label of deviant. This results in the adoption of a deviant self-identity that confirms and stabilizes the deviant lifestyle.

selective incapacitation
A philosophy of incarceration that argues that some offenders might have to be incarcerated not for what they have done, but to prevent future harm to the community. This depends on the community's ability to identify those who might re-offend. Some also argue that it is unfair to punish people for what they might do rather than for what they have done. Selective incapacitation is provided for under dangerous offender legislation.

self-defence
The Criminal Code permits the use of force in self-defence in certain circumstances where the individual concerned becomes the object of an unlawful assault. Where the individual acted in self-defence without intending to inflict death or grievous bodily harm on the assailant, it must be shown that no more force was used than was necessary in the circumstances. Where the individual concerned inflicted death or grievous bodily harm, then it must be shown that he or she acted under a reasonable apprehension of death or grievous bodily harm and under a reasonable belief that he or she had no alternative but to employ lethal force.

self-degrading commitment
Commitment leading to a poorer opinion of oneself.

self-enhancing commitment
Commitment leading to a better opinion of oneself.

self-report study
A method for measuring crime involving the distribution of a detailed questionnaire to a sample of people, asking them whether they have committed a crime in a particular period of time. This has been a good method for criminologists to determine the social characteristics of offenders.

seriousness rule
If there are several crimes committed in one incident, only the most serious crime is counted. UCR1.0 uses the seriousness rule.

sexism
Attributing to women socially undesirable characteristics that are assumed to be intrinsic characteristics of that sex.

situational crime prevention
Premised on the belief that most crime is opportunistic rather than being the outcome of those driven to commit a crime no matter what the circumstances. This form of prevention attempts to reduce the opportunities for crime rather than just relying on the police after the crime has occurred. An example is the exact fare system used on buses, which removes the opportunity to rob the driver.

social bond
The degree to which an individual has ties to his or her society. In Hirschi's theory, social bonds include **attachment**, **commitment**, **involvement**, and **belief**.

social control theory
The theory that people do not become criminal because they do not want to jeopardize their bonds to conventional society.

social structure
The patterned and relatively stable arrangement of roles and statuses found within societies and social institutions. The idea of

social structure points out the way in which societies, and institutions within them, exhibit predictable patterns of organization, activity, and social interaction.

socialist feminism
A perspective that views women's exploitation under capitalism and oppression under patriarchy as interconnected. Neither the class structure of capitalism nor patriarchal gender relations are given priority in socialist feminism, rather gender and class relations are viewed as mutually dependent.

socialization
The interactive process whereby individuals come to learn and internalize the culture of their society or group.

sovereign
One who holds supreme power in a territory or space. Agamben, following Carl Schmitt, claims the sovereign is the one who is empowered to declare a state of exception.

sovereignty
The authority possessed by the governing individual or institution of a society. Sovereign authority is distinct in that it is unrestricted by legal regulation since the sovereign authority is itself the source of all law.

state
As defined by Max Weber (1864–1920), the state is an institution that claims the exclusive right to the legitimate exercise of force in a given territory through the use of police to enforce laws or the army to maintain civil stability. While there have been stateless societies, most complex societies have state systems of formal government and administrative bureaucracies.

state of exception
A period of time where the sovereign declares civil liberties suspended: typically in a time of national crisis.

Statistical School
Associated with early social scientists such as Adolphe Quetelet (1795–1874) and André-Michel Guerry (1802–1866), who began to explore the structure of emerging European societies with the assistance of statistical methods. While their early use of statistics is important, they also developed a **structural explanation** of crime and other social problems.

stigma
As used by Erving Goffman (1922–1982), a characteristic of an individual that is given a negative evaluation by others and thus distorts and discredits the public identity of the person. For example, a prison record may become a stigmatized attribute. The stigma may lead to the adoption of a self-identity that incorporates the negative social evaluation.

stigmata
Physical signs of some special moral position. Cesare Lombroso (1836–1909) used the term to refer to physical signs of the state of **atavism** (a morally and evolutionary inferior person).

strain theory
The proposition that people feel strain when they are exposed to cultural goals that they are unable to obtain because they do not have access to culturally approved means of achieving those goals.

stratification
A social division of individuals into various hierarchies of wealth, status, and power. There is disagreement about how to describe stratification systems; some sociologists favour the concept of class and others discuss status differentiations.

structural explanation
An explanation for crime that focuses on **social structure** (usually this refers to inequality, poverty, or power differentials). For example, the patriarchal structure of the family might help explain the abuse of women and children within the family.

structural Marxism
In this perspective, the state is viewed as acting in the long-term interests of capitalism as a whole, rather than in the short-term interests of the capitalist class. Structuralism rejects the belief that law is an instrument of the capitalist class.

subculture
A group of people who share a distinctive set of cultural beliefs and behaviours that differs in some significant way from that of the larger society.

subjective *mens rea*
The **mens rea** elements of a criminal offence are considered to be subjective if they are based on a determination of "what actually went on in the accused person's mind." The forms of subjective *mens rea* are intention and knowledge; recklessness; and wilful blindness.

superego
A psychoanalytical term that denotes the ethical and moral dimensions of personality; an individual's conscience. The **ego** mediates between the superego and the **id**.

surveillance
The direct or indirect observation of conduct toward producing a desired outcome (i.e., conformity).

surplus
The excess of production over the human and material resources used up in the process of production. In simple societies, there was often little if any surplus since the production from hunting and gathering was entirely used up in subsistence. With the development of animal herding and settled agriculture, production exceeds immediate subsistence needs, and social inequality and class division become possible when particular individuals or groups are able to take control of this surplus.

symbolic interactionism
A sociological perspective that focuses on the dynamics of how people interpret social situations and negotiate their meaning with others. It differs from more structurally focused perspectives in seeing individuals as actively creating the social world rather than just acting within the constraints of culture and **social structure**.

target suitability
Because of their vulnerability, some potential crime targets are more attractive than others. A home that is unlit, has shrubs blocking a view of the front door, and has no alarm system will be seen as a more suitable target than a well-protected home.

theory
All sciences use theory as a tool to explain. It is useful to think of theory as a conceptual model of some aspect of life. We may have a theory of mate selection, of the

emergence of capitalist societies, of criminal behaviour, or of the content of dreams. In each case, the theory consists of a set of concepts and their nominal definition or assertions about the relationships between these concepts, assumptions, and knowledge claims.

token economy

A behaviour therapy procedure based on operant learning principles. Individuals are rewarded (reinforced) for positive or appropriate behaviour and are disciplined (punished) for negative or inappropriate behaviour.

trace

The mark of absence in words that is the necessary condition of thought and experience (Spivak, 1976).

transnational corporation

A corporation that has sales and production in many different nations. As a result of their multinational reach, these corporations are often thought to be beyond the political control of any individual nation-states.

Triads

These Chinese groups came into existence in the 17th century as resistance fighters against the Manchu invaders. They eventually developed into crime groups.

tribalism

Where social bonds are based primarily on people's real or assumed common descent from an ancestor or group of ancestors, and this shared identification distinguishes the group from outsiders. In such societies, all social relationships tend to be direct and quasi-familial.

true crime

A "true crime" occurs when an individual engages in conduct that is not only prohibited but also constitutes a serious breach of community values: as such, it is perceived by Canadians as being inherently wrong and deserving of punishment. Only the Parliament of Canada, using its criminal law power under the Constitution Act, 1867, may enact a "true crime."

Tudor

Refers to the period of English history from 1485 to 1603, when the nation's monarchs were descended from Owen Tudor and Catherine (1401–1437), widow of Henry V.

Uniform Crime Reports (UCR)

Since 1962, Canada has had a Uniform Crime Reporting system developed by Statistics Canada and the Canadian Association of Chiefs of Police. This system is designed to provide a measure of reliability for crime statistics through providing police agencies with a standardized set of procedures for collecting and reporting crime information.

validity

The extent to which a tool or instrument (questionnaire, experiment) actually measures the concept the researcher claims to be interested in and not something else. For example, measuring people's feet to learn about the concept of intelligence, on the surface at least, does not seem valid.

value

A collective idea about what is right or wrong, good or bad, and desirable or undesirable in a particular culture.

victimization survey

A survey of a random **sample** of the population in which people are asked to recall and describe their own experience of being a victim of crime.

violent predator

An offender who has a very high rate of offending for serious and violent crimes.

Volstead Act

Passed by the United States Congress on October 28, 1919, this legislation prohibited the manufacture and sale of alcohol in the United States. Since a ready market existed for this prohibited good, organized crime in America gained a ready foothold.

white-collar crime

Crime that is committed by middle- and upper-class people in the course of their legitimate business activities. This concept has had changing definitions. As used by Edwin Sutherland in 1940, the concept referred to corporate behaviour that caused social harm and for which there was a legal sanction. This sanction need not be criminal; it could be regulatory. Since that time, criminologists have also included the illegal actions of executives or employees who commit crimes against their employer or use organizational resources to gain personal benefit.

Credits

Chapter 1

Page 17: John Hagan, *The Disreputable Pleasures: Crime and Deviance in Canada*, 3rd ed. (1991), Toronto. Reproduced with permission of McGraw-Hill Ryerson Ltd.

Chapter 2

Page 33: Rupert Ross. "Leaving Our White Eyes Behind: The Sentencing of Native Accused." [1989] 3 *Canadian Native Law Reporter* 1 at 4.
Page 38: Rupert Ross. "Leaving Our White Eyes Behind: The Sentencing of Native Accused." [1989] 3 *Canadian Native Law Reporter* 1 at 5–6.
Page 49: William Chambliss. (1988). *Exploring Criminology*. New York: MacMillan, pp. 109–11. Reprinted with permission of the author.
Page 58–59: "Prologue to Law in Canada: Dynamics and Roots" by DeLloyd J. Guth, in DeLloyd J. Guth and W. Wesley Pue (eds), *Canada's Legal Inheritances*, Canadian Legal History Project, Faculty of Law, University of Manitoba, Winnipeg, 2001, pp. xxx–xxxv. Reprinted with permission of the author.

Chapter 4

Page 113: Adapted from Statistics Canada "Canadian Crime Statistics," Catalogue 85-205-X, Chapter 6. Released October 13, 2004, URL: http://www.statcan.ca/bsolc/english/bsolc?catno=85-205-X&CHROPG=1.
Page 116: Adapted from Statistics Canada, "Crime Statistics in Canada, 2005" by Maire Gannon. Catalogue no. 85-002-XIE, Vol. 26, no. 4, page 16. Released July 20, 2006, URL: http://www.statcan.ca/bsolc/english/bsolc?catno=85-002-X&CHROPG=1.
Page 117: Adapted from Statistics Canada, *The Daily*, Catalogue 11-001, Homicides, 2005, November 8, 2006, URL: http://www.statcan.ca/Daily/English/061108/d061108b.htm
Page 118–119: Adapted from Statistics Canada *Juristat*, Catalogue 85-002-X, Crime Statistics in Canada, 2005, Vol. 26, no. 4, page 16, Released July 20, 2006, URL: http://www.statcan.ca/bsolc/english/bsolc?catno=85-002-X&CHROPG=1.
Page 121–122: Adapted from Statistics Canada, *Juristat*, Catalogue 85-002-X, Criminal Victimization in Canada, 2004, Vol. 25, no. 7, page 1, Released November 24, 2005, URL: http://www.statcan.ca/bsolc/english/bsolc?catno=85-002-X&CHROPG=1.
Page 123: Adapted from Statistics Canada, *Juristat*, Catalogue 85-002-X, Criminal Victimization in Canada, 2004, Vol. 25, no. 7, Figure 11, page 17, Released November 24, 2005, URL: http://www.statcan.ca/bsolc/english/bsolc?catno=85-002-X&CHROPG=1.
Page 123–124: Adapted from Statistics Canada, *Juristat*, Catalogue 85-002-X, Criminal Victimization in Canada, 2004, Vol. 25, no. 7, Figure 12, page 19, Released November 24, 2005, URL: http://www.statcan.ca/bsolc/english/bsolc?catno=85-002-X&CHROPG=1.
Page 125: Adapted from Statistics Canada, *Canadian Centre for Justice Statistics Profile Series*, Catalogue 85F0033M, Canadians Use of Crime Prevention Measures, 2004, no. 12, Table 1, page 10, Released November 23, 2006, URL: http://www.statcan.ca/bsolc/english/bsolc?catno=85F0033M&CHROPG=1.

Chapter 5

Page 140: Adapted from Statistics Canada, *Juristat*, Catalogue 85-002-X, Crime Statistics in Canada, 2003, Vol. 24, No. 6, Figure 1, page 3, Released July 28, 2004, URL: http://www.statcan.ca/bsolc/english/bsolc?catno=85-002-X&CHROPG=1.
Page 141: Adapted from Statistics Canada, *Juristat*, Catalogue 85-002-X, Crime Statistics in Canada, 2003, Vol. 24, No. 6, Figure 2, page 3 , Released July 28, 2004, URL: http://www.statcan.ca/bsolc/english/bsolc?catno=85-002-X&CHROPG=1.
Page 145: Adapted from Statistics Canada, *Juristat*, Catalogue 85-002-X, Crime Statistics in Canada, 2003, Vol. 24, No. 6, Table 9, page 25, Released July 28, 2004, URL: http://www.statcan.ca/bsolc/english/bsolc?catno=85-002-X&CHROPG=1.
Page 146: Adapted from the Statistics Canada, "Canadian Crime Statistics," Catalogue 85-205-X, Released December 10, 2001, URL: http://www.statcan.ca/bsolc/english/bsolc?catno=85-205-X&CHROPG=1.
Page 150: © Correctional Services Canada. 2004. Reproduced with the permission of the Minister of Public Works and Government Services Canada, 2007.
Page 153: Adapted from Statistics Canada, *Juristat*, Catalogue 85-002-X, Victimization and offending among the Aboriginal population in Canada, Vol. 26, No. 3, Table 5, page 28, Released June 6, 2006, URL: http://www.statcan.ca/bsolc/english/bsolc?catno=85-002-X&CHROPG=1.
Page 169: Adapted from Statistics Canada, *Juristat*, Catalogue 85-002-X, Homicide in Canada, 2005, Vol. 26, No. 6, Table 5, Released November 8, 2006, URL: http://www.statcan.ca/bsolc/english/bsolc?catno=85-002-X&CHROPG=1.

Page 171: Adapted from Statistics Canada, *The Daily*, Catalogue 11-001, Crime statistics, 2006, July 18, 2007, URL: http://www.statcan.ca/Daily/English/070718/d070718b.htm

Chapter 6

Page 193–194: Reprinted with permission of the author.
Page 200: Reprinted with permission of the author.

Chapter 8

Page 251: From Sociology In Our Times (with InfoTrac) 2nd Edition by KENDALL. 1999. Reprinted with permission of Wadsworth, a division of Thomson Learning: www.thomsonrights.com. Fax 800 730-2215.
Page 253: Reprinted from *The Psychology of Criminal Conduct* with permission. Copyright 1994 Matthew Bender & Company, Inc., a member of the LexisNexis Group. All rights reserved.
Page 261–262: From *Psychology and the Legal System* 2nd Edition by Wrightsman. 1991. Reprinted with permission of Wadsworth, a division of Thomson Learning: www.thomsonrights.com. Fax 800 730-2215.
Page 264–265: Copyright by The Canadian Press.
Page 268: Reprinted with permission of the author.

Chapter 11

Page 359: © Amnesty International Publications, 1 Easton Street, London WC1X 0DW, UK http://www.amnesty.org.
Page 363–364: © Sun Media Corp.

Chapter 12

Page 376–377: Reprinted with permission from *The Globe and Mail.*
Page 386: Robert A. Stebbins. (1976). *Commitment to Deviance. The Nonprofessional Criminal in the Community.* Westport, Conn.: Greenwood Press, p. 66.

Chapter 13

Page 412: Rick Linden and Cathy Fillmore. (1981). "A Comparative Study of Delinquency Involvement," *Canadian Review of Sociology and Anthropology* 18:343–61.
Page 418: James Q. Wilson. (1983). "Raising Kids," *The Atlantic* (October), p. 45.

Chapter 14

Page 438: "Victim homicide rates by age group and sex, Canada, 2005," adapted from Statistics Canada publication *Juristat*, Homicide in Canada– 2005. Catalogue 85-002-XIE, Vol. 26, no. 6, Figure 8, page 9.
Page 440–441: Adapted from Christie Blatchford. (November 27, 2002). "Doesn't Take A Lot to Get You Killed," in the *National Post*. Reprinted by permission of the *National Post.*
Page 443: Copyright by The Canadian Press.

Chapter 15

Page 469: Adapted from Rick Linden. (1994). "Crime and Deviance." In L. Tepperman, J. Curtis, and J. Richardson (eds.), *The Social World* (3rd ed.). Toronto: McGraw-Hill Ryerson, pp. 188–229.
Page 478: Reprinted with permission from *The Globe and Mail.*
Page 481: Material reprinted with the express permission of: *National Post* Company, a CanWest Partnership.
Page 488–489: From *Criminal Conspiracies: Organized Crime in Canada*, 1st Edition by Beare. 1995. Reprinted with permission of Nelson, a division of Thomson Learning: www.thomsonrights.com. Fax 800 730-2215.

Chapter 16

Page 503: Adapted from Ronald Akers. (1973). *Deviant Behaviour: A Social Learning Approach.* Belmont, Wadsworth, pp. 180–181. Reprinted with permission of the author.
Page 512–513: Jim Silver. (1996). "Review of Games Misconduct: Alan Eagleson and the Corruption of Hockey" in *Canadian Dimension*, 30(4), July–August.

Index

Page numbers in italics refer to figures and tables.

Aaron, Hank, 501
Aboriginal Head Start program, 454
Aboriginal over-representation, explanations of, 155–59
Aboriginal people
  alcohol abuse effects on, 162
  over-representation in criminal justice system, 152–55, *153*
Aboriginal women, in Canadian prisons, 194
Abram, K.M., 270
Abu Ghraib prison, 529
Abuse
  alcohol, 162
  child, 442
  elder, 442–44
  of power, 287, 288, 512
Accounting scandals, corporate, 512–14
ACCS. *See* Adult Criminal Court Survey (ACCS)
Acephalous societies, 31
Achievement Place, 260
Actual incidents, 113
Actuarialism, risk and, 349–52
Actus reus, 1, 76–78
  of bigamy, 90
  of conspiracy, 88
  of criminal attempt, 87, 88
Adler, Freda, 191
Administrative record, 107
Adult Correctional Services, in Canada, 384
Adult Criminal Court Survey (ACCS), 109, 128–29, 139
Advisor systems, in small-scale societies, 36–37
Agamben, Giorgio, 342, 356–60, 365
Age
  as correlate of crime, 139–44, *140, 141*
  crime types by, *140, 140–42, 141*
  homicide by, *438*
  maturational reform, 142–44
Ageton, Suzanne S., 140, 165
Aggregation, levels of, 107
Agnew, Robert, 289, 299–301
Ahold NV, 500
Akers, Ronald L., 258, 259, *503*
Alberta Stock Exchange, 509
Alcohol abuse, impact on Aboriginal people, 162
Allodi, F., 269
Alonso, Fernando, 501
al-Qaeda, 359, 360
Althusser, L., 319
AMA. *See* American Motorcycle Association (AMA)
American Bar Association, 196
American Idol, 341–42
American Motorcycle Association (AMA), 475–76
American Psychiatric Association, 269
  DSM-IV-TR of, 262–64
American Revolution, 294
American Society of Criminology, 345
American Sociological Association, 15
American Sociological Review, 293
Amir, Menachem, 199
Amnesty International, Maher Arar's interview with, 359
Anderson, Elijah, 296–300, *297,* 405
Andrews, Donald A., 144, *253,* 304, 350
An Essay on Crimes and Punishments, 224
Angell, Robert, 221
Anglican Church, 522
Animal cruelty laws, 23
Anomie, 283, 284
  functions of, 283–84
  normlessness and, 283–84
Anslinger, Harry, 48
Anticombines law, 518
Antisocial personality disorder, 260–67
Anti-terrorism Act, 74, 467
Arar, Maher, 358–60
  interview with Amnesty International, 359
Arthur Andersen accounting firm, 288, 515–16
Arum, Richard, 407
Asian organized crime groups, 479–82
Aspiration(s)
  culturally prescribed, 284
  means and, 284–90
Assault, in 1980s and 1990s, 442
Assaultive behaviours, 441–44
Association, differential, 385–88, *386*
Assumption of discriminating traits, 248
Assumption of offender deficit, 248
Atavism, 233
  concepts of, 184
Attachment, 401
Attempt, criminal, 86–88
Attentive gaze, 353
Auerhahn, Kathleen, 455
Auger, Brian, 4–5
Autonomic reactivity, 257
Autonomy, relative, 319, 544
Avoidable harms, victims of, 51–52

Backman, J.G., 140
Bandidos, 477, 478
Bandura, A., 257
Bank robberies, end of, 447
Bankruptcy, Enron, 498
Baring's Bank, 510, 530
Baron, S.W., 167
Bartol, C.R., 256
Battered Women's Movement, 328
Beare, Margaret, 464, 488–89
Beattie, Irenee R., 407
Beaver, Kevin, 412
Beccaria, Cesare, 224–28, 230
Becker, Howard S., 48, 189, 378–80
Beck, Ulrich, 351
Begin, Menachem, 18
Behaviour(s)
  assaultive, 441–44
  criminal. *See* Criminal behaviour
  regulation of, 14–15
Belichick, Bill, 501
Belief, 402
  community of, 33–34
Bell, Laurie, 4
Bell, Richard A., 232
Bell-Rowbotharn, B., 166
Benjamin, Walter, 357
Bennett, Bill, 287
Bennett, Trevor, 448
Benson, M.L., 519
Bentham, Jeremy, 224
Bentivogli, Alberto, 486
Bernardo, Paul, 11, 262, 264–65, 439
Bernard, Thomas, 286, 289
Bertrand, Marie-Andrée, 184
Bigamy
  actus reus of, 90
  mens rea of, 90
Big Circle boys, 480
Bin Laden, Osama, 364

Biological theories, in early 20th century, 236–43, *242*
Bird, Laura, 440
Birkbeck, Christopher, 385
Bisaillon, Jean-Alain, 524
Black Act of 1723, 44
Black, Conrad, 6–9, 498, 505, 507–8, 521
Black-Handers, 473
Blackhawks, 512
Blackstone, Sir William, 198
Blackwell, Tom, 265
Blair, Jayson, 524
Blair, Sir Iain, 357
Blakeman, Donovan Jackson, 488, 489
Blatchford, Christie, 441
Blue-collar crime, 529–30
Blumer, Herbert, 300, 371
Bocelli, Andrea, 342
Boeree, C. George, 255, 257
Bohm, Robert, 413
Boileau, Helene, 417
Boldt, E.D., 158
Bond(s), social, 398, 401–4
Bonds, Barry, 501
Bonta, James, *253*, 271, 304, 350
Borsellino, Paolo, 475
Borum, R., 270, 272
Bourdieu, Pierre, 342, 354, 365
Bourgeois ascendance, consolidation of, 46–47
Bourgeois class, 44
Bowlby, J., 250
Box, Steven, 149, 519
Boydell, B., 166
Braithwaite, John, 59, 140, 302–3
Break and enter, 446–49
  as crime of opportunity, 448–49
  incidence of, 447–48
  patterns of, 447–48
Bre-X, 525–27
Bre-X fraud, 498
Brief Jail Mental Health Screen, 269
Brison, Scott, 19
British North America Act, 59
Brodeur, Paul, 52
Brodsky, S.L., 266, 269
Broken window policing, 362
Bronson, Diane, 200
Brookman, Fiona, 446
Brook, Robert, 488
Brownfield, David, 403, 411
Brown, Lester, 56
Brown, Stephen, 52
Buck v. Bell, 238
Bundy, Ted, 247, 260–62
Burgess, R.L., 259
Bush Administration, 359
Bush, George W., 287–88
Buttell, F.P., 254

CACSW. *See* Canadian Advisory Council on the Status of Women (CACSW)
Cain, Maureen, 192
Calgary Herald, 10
Cameron, Peter, 443
Campbell, Larry, 457
Campbell, Rosie, 354
Canada Evidence Act, 467
Canada Revenue Agency, 527
Canada's Legal Inheritances, 58–59
Canadian Aboriginal people, over-representation in criminal justice system, 152–55, *153*
Canadian Advisory Council on the Status of Women (CACSW), 199
Canadian Centre for Justice Statistics (CCJS), 104, 107, 120, 128, 131
Canadian Centre on Substance Abuse (CCSA), 161
Canadian Charter of Rights and Freedoms, 69
  impact on criminal law, 73–75
  terrorism and, 74–75
Canadian Constitution, 70
Canadian Criminal Justice Statistics, 109–10, *110, 111*
Canadian Environmental Protection Act, 70–71
Canadian ethnic-based crime groups, 484–85
Canadian Imperial Bank of Commerce (CIBC), 288
Canadian Pacific Railway, 528
Canadian prisons, Aboriginal women in, 194
Canadian Sportfishing Industry Association, 23
Canadian Veterinary Medical Association, 23
Canadian women, struggle for vote by, 321–22
Capital, 355
  "criminal," 295
  human, 295
  negative social, 355
  negative symbolic, 355
  social, 356
Capone, Al, 468
Caputo, John, 364
Caputo, Tullio, 219
Career(s), 372
  deviant, 372–84
Career contingency, 381
Carlen, Pat, 192, 195
Carrier's Case of 1473, 45
Carrigan, O.D., 474, 476
Carrington, P.J., 142
Cartel(s)
  Colombian, 483–84
  Mexican, 483–84
  South American, 483–84
Castro, Fidel, 18
Catholic Church, 221, 523
Catlin, G., 120
Causes of Delinquency, 401
CCJS. *See* Canadian Centre for Justice Statistics (CCJS)
CCSA. *See* Canadian Centre on Substance Abuse (CCSA)
Census Metropolitan Areas, 170
Centralized state, emergence of, 43–44
Chaiken, Jan M., 454–55
Chaiken, Marcia R., 454–55
Challinger, D., 450
Chambliss, John, 48
Chambliss, William, 320, 400
Champagne, Paul, 531
Charbonneau, Jean-Pierre, 464
Chard-Wierschem, Deborah, 411
Charge(s), criminal, 88–97. *See also* Defence(s)
Charities Registration (Security Information) Act, 467
Charkaoui v. Canada, 75, 76
Charlebois, Pierre, 417
Charter of Rights and Freedoms, 229
Chaulk case, 90
Check, J.V.P., 257–58
Cheney, Dick, 287, 500
Cherry, Paul, 481
Chesney-Lind, Meda, 190
Chicago Sun-Times, 7
Chieftainships, paramount, 41–42
Child abuse, 442
Child and Family Canada, 257
Children's Aid Society, 442, 443
Children's Wish Foundation, 287
Chopyk, Vanessa, 203, 206–7
Chrétien, Jean, 528, 529
Christian Brothers, 522
Church of God, 443
"Churning" investors' accounts, 500
CIA, 359, 469
CIBC. *See* Canadian Imperial Bank of Commerce (CIBC)
Circle of Justice, 61
Circular reaction, 300
CISC. *See* Criminal Intelligence Service Canada (CISC)
Citizenship and Immigration, 358
Civil law, 30
Civil Remedies Against Organized Crime Act, 491–92
Civil War, 49
Clarke, Ron, 452
Class(es)
  bourgeois, 44
  crime effects of, 302
  social, 504–8
Class conflict theorists, 20
Class conflict theory, 20
Classical conditioning, 255
Classical School, 224–29
  assessing contributions of, 227–29
  current status of, 230–31
  legal reform and, 227
  limitations of, 227–29

Classical theorists, 226, 230–31
Classical theory of crime, 225–27, *242*
Clastner, D.S., 258
Cleckley, H., 263
CLEU. *See* Co-ordinated Law Enforcement Unit (CLEU)
Clinard, Marshall, 502
Clingempeel, W.G., 248
Cloward, Richard, 292–96, *293*, 303
Coalition, of merchants and monarchs, 44–45
Code of the Street: Decency, Violence, and the Moral Life of the Inner City, 296–98, *297*
Coercion, strain and, 289–90
Cohen, Albert K., 251, 296–300, *297*, 381
Cohen, Lawrence E., 430, 431, 451
Collective solidarity, 31–32
Colson, Elizabeth, 32
Colombian cartels, 483–84
Colvin, Mark, 289, 295, 299–300
Comack, Elizabeth, 48, 203, 206–7, 327
Combines Investigation Act of 1889, 54, 319
Commerce, 45–46
Commitment, *386*, 402
  continuance, 382
  reactions to, 383–85
  self-degrading, 383
  self-enhancing, 383
Commitment to Deviance: The Nonprofessional Criminal in the Community, *386*
Common law, 43, 73
Community(ies), 362
  defined, 362
  Inuit, 38
  Ojibway, 33, 38
  opportunities in, 291–92, *291*
  Type I, 291
  Type II, 291–92
  Type III, 292
  Type IV, 292
Community of belief, in small-scale societies, 33–34
Community psychology, 249
Competition Act, 72
Complicity, of criminology, 198–99
Comte, Auguste, 232
Conditioning
  classical, 255
  operant, 259–60
Conduct, unprofessional, 521–24
Conduct norms, 310–11
Conflict(s)
  cultural, 311, *331*
  group, 311, *331*
  of values, 69
  vs. consensus theories of law, 19–21
Conflict approach, *17*, 20–21
Conflict perspective, 282
Conflict Tactics Scale (CTS), 205–7
Conflict theories, 310–38
  cultural, 310–11
  group, 311–15
Conflict theorists, *331*
Conger, R.D., 273
Congress, U.S., 489
Conrad, Joseph, 354
Consensual crime, 480
Consensual crime activity, nature of, 485–86
Consensus, law and, 48
Consensus approach, *17*, 20
Consensus perspective, 282
Consensus theorists, 20, 282
Consensus theory, 20
Conservative approach, to women's crime, 184–87
Conservative theory, of crime, 413–16
Consortium, described, 197
Conspiracy, 88
  actus reus of, 88
  mens rea of, 88–89
Constitution Act of 1867, 70
Consumer safety issues, 516–17
Contagion(s), group, 300
Contemporary critical criminology, 339–70. *See also* Critical criminology
Contingency, career, 381
Continuance commitment, 382
Contract(s), 45–46
  legal, 45
Contribution to the Critique of Political Economy, 316
Control
  shift to opportunity structures, 290–96, *291*, *294*
  social, 375–78
Control-differential association theory, *412*, *420*
Controlled Drugs and Substances Act, 13, 71n, 72
Conventional ("street") crime, 429–62
  assaultive behaviours, 441–44
  break and enter, 446–49
  defined, 429
  homicides, 435–41, *438*
  motor vehicle theft, 449–51
  murder, 435–41, *438*
  patterns of, 434
  prevention of, 451–56, *453*
  robbery, 444–46
  routine activities approach to, 430–33
  "when" in, 433
  "where" in, 433
  "who" in, 432–33
Convergence, role, 148–49
Conversion(s), mutual, 297, 300
Conway, Russ, 512
Cooke, Josh, 11
Cook, T.D., 257
Cooperation, international, 492–93
Co-ordinated Law Enforcement Unit (CLEU), 456
Copernicus, Nicolaus, 232
Corporate accounting scandals, 512–14
Corporate crime, 325, 498–536
  extent of, 499–501
  legal sanctions and, 517–21
  nature of, 501, *503*
  social organization of work and, 508–17
  types of, *503*
Corporation(s)
  transitional, 54
  transnational, 51
Corrado, Raymond, 528
Correctional Services of Canada, 144, 269
Correlate(s), defined, 137–39
Correlates of crime, 137–82. *See also* Correlates of criminal behaviour
Correlates of criminal behaviour, 137–82
  age, 139–44, *140*, *141*
  drug misuse, 159–62
  maturational reform, 142–44
  race, 149–59, *150*, *153*
  region, 169–72, *169*, *171*
  sex, 144–49, *145*, *146*
  social class, 163–68
Correlation, defined, 137–38
Corruption, political, 528–29
Costner, Herbert, 293
Côté, G., 269
Cotroni-Violi Mafia, 474–75
Council(s), elders', 40–41
Counselling, 85
  crime over Internet, 86–87
  offence not committed, 85–86
Counting crime, 103–36
  controversies over, 104–7, *105*
Counting procedures, 107, 128–29
Court(s), 128
  vs. police UCR survey data, 129
Courtney, Robert, 524
Court of Star Chamber, 224
Courts-based data, defining of, 128
Cowell, Simon, 341–42
Cows, Pigs, Wars, and Witches, 225
Craddick, R., 266
Craig, Wendy M., 304
Craven, W., 270
Creighton case, 79–82
Cressey, David R., 385
Cressey, Donald, 9, 139
Crime(s)
  age-related, *140*, *140–42*, *141*
  amount of, 110–11
  basic elements of, 76–83
  blue-collar, 529–30
  causation of, 12
  Classical theory of, 225–27
  class mix and reduction of, 302
  consensual, 480
  conservative theory of, 413–16
  continuum of, 16–18, *17*
  conventional, 429–62. *See also* Conventional ("street") crime
  corporate, 325, 498–536. *See also* Corporate crime

correlates of, 137–82. *See also* Correlates of criminal behaviour
counselling of, 85–87
counting, 103–36, *105*
cracking down on, 376–77
dark figure of, 111
defined, 12, 15, 68–69
described, 224
early theories of, *242*
explanations of, 217–426
Eysenck's theory of, 255–56
food-related, 24–25
functions of, 283–84
future of, 131–32
gender-ratio problems in, 190–91
generalizability problem in, 190
gross counts of, 114
human rights violations as, 16
inchoate, 85
intelligence and, 239–43, *242*
legal definition of, 15
mainstream theories of, 188–90
media and, 10–11
mental illness and, 267–73, *272*
occupational, 502–4, *503,* 521–31, 543
opportunistic, 288–89
organizational, 502
organized, 463–97. *See also* Organized crime
party to, 84
patterns of, 434–35
paying off in Canada, 363–64
physical characteristics and, 236–39
of powerful, 324–26
of powerless, 323–24
prevention of, 451–56, *453*
psychological theories of, 248–60, *251, 253*
race and, 149–52, *150, 153*
reasons for studying, 9–11
relativity of, 19
situational, 451–52, *453*
social class and, 504–8
social definition of, 18–19
social distribution of, 12
socialization into, 385–88, *386*
social structure of, 229–32
societal reactions to, 12–13
society and, 1–216
"street," 429–62. *See also* Conventional ("street") crime
theories of women's, *208*
"true," 72
upper-class, 302–3
upper-world, 410–11
violent, 3–6
white-collar, 6–9, 15–16, 498–536
women's, 184–90, *208*
Crime: Its Causes and Remedies, 234
Crime and Social Justice, 344–45
Crime groups
Eastern European, 482–83
ethnic-based, 484–85
Crime of opportunity, break and enter as, 448–49
Crime prevention through social development, 452–54
Crime rate, 104
neighbourhood variation in, 172
Crime Times, 268
Criminal(s), defined, 12
Criminal attempt, 86–88
actus reus of, 87, 88
mens rea of, 86–88
Criminal behaviour
correlates of, 137–82. *See also* Correlates of criminal behaviour
drug misuse and, 159–62
extraverts and, 255–56
patterns of, 12, 430–33
"Criminal capital," 295
Criminal charge, defences to, 88–97. *See also* Defence(s)
Criminal Code, 19, 52, 68–69, 71–77, 80, 81, 84–86, 90, 91, 93–95, 97, 108, 113–14, 129, 144, 145, 149, 183, 201, 219, 227, 443, 464–65, 467, 492, 503
Criminal Conspiracies: Organized Crime in Canada, 488–89
Criminal court, international, 96–97
Criminal homicides, 435–41, *438. See also* Homicide(s)
classification of, 435–38, *438*
Criminal identity, 385, 388
"Criminal imbeciles," 240
Criminal Intelligence reports, 483
Criminal Intelligence Service Canada (CISC), 475, 477, 480
Criminality
female, 409
psychological perspectives on, 247–81. *See also* Psychological theories
Criminalized women, 192–95
Criminal Justice Statistics, future of, 131–32
Criminal Justice System
over-representation of Canadian Aboriginal people in, 152–55, *153*
statistics on, 107–10, *110, 111*
Criminal law, 30, 68–102
Canadian Charter of Rights and Freedoms impact on, 73–75
defined, 70
federal legislation, 70–72
judge-made, 72–73
quasi-, 72
sources of, 70–73
substantive, 71
use of, 85–88
Criminal laws and procedures, national, 491–92
Criminal misconduct, 512–13
Criminal norms, 311
Criminal offence, becoming party to, 83–85
Criminal organization(s). *See also specific organization*
defined, 465
Criminal organization offence, defined, 465
Criminal procedure, 71
Criminogenic market structure, 510–12
Criminologist(s), defined, 9
Criminology
Classical School of, 224–29
complicity of, 198–99
contemporary critical, 339–70. *See also* Critical criminology
cultural, 352–54
defined, 1, 3, 9, 68
described, 9–14
discipline of, 12–13
early theories of, 219–46
eugenics and, 238
as evolving discipline, 21-25
feminism and, 183–215
feminist, 327
"field theory" of, 354–56
green. *See* Green criminology
Marxist conflict perspectives in, 315–26
in Nazi Germany, 241
New, 344
objectives of, 9
Critical criminology
contemporary, 339–70
described, 340–43
in English Canada, 343–46
Critical Mass, 353
Critique of the Legal Order, 318
Croall, Hazel, 24
Crutchfield, Robert, 285
CSI, 10
CTS. *See* Conflict Tactics Scale (CTS)
Cullen, Francis T., 232, 292, 294–95, 404
Cultural conflict, 311
theorists of, *331*
Cultural conflict theory, 310–11
Cultural construction, of rape, 195–97
Cultural criminology, 352–54
Cultural explanation, 155
Culturally prescribed aspiration, 284
Culture(s), classification of, 30
Culture, Conflict, and Crime, 310
Cuntrera-Caruna family, 475
Curragh Corporation, 506–7
Currie, Dawn, 345

Daly, Kathleen, 190
Dangerous knowledge, 354
Danner, Mona J.E., 327
Dark figure of crime, 111
Darwin, Charles, 232
Darwinism, Social, 184, 241, 242
Darwin's Theory, 232
Data element, 107
Daviault case, 92
Da Vinci's Inquest, 457

Davis Inlet, Mushuau Innu of, 414–15
Decision rules, 129
Decker, Scott T., 448–49
Deconstruction, 360
  is justice, 360–65
Defence(s)
  to criminal charge, 88–97
  duress, 92–93
  general, 90–91
  intoxication, 91–92
  mental disorder, 89–90
  mistake of fact, 90–91
  necessity, 92–93
  provocation, 94
  self-defence, 94–95
de Guzman, Michael, 526–27
Dei Delitti E Delle Pene, 230
Delinquency and Opportunity, 293
Delinquent Boys: The Culture of the Gang, 296
Delinquent peers, social control theory and, 411–13, *413*
Delinquent youths, parenting of, 418
Demers, D.J., 159
Democratic National Committee, 410
Department of Justice, 362
Department of Labour, 507
Department of National Defence, 525, 531
Dependence, mutual, in small-scale societies, 32–33
Deprivation, relative, 290–91
Derrida, Jacques, 342, 360–65
Desroches, Fred, 295
Deterrence, 228
  general, 231
  specific, 230–31
Development
  moral, 252–54, *253*
  social, 452–54
Deviance(s)
  continuum of, 16–18, *17*
  general model of, 285
  types of, 16–18, *17*
Deviant Behavior: A Social Learning Approach, 503
Deviant career, 372–84
  symbolic, 371
Deviation
  primary, 373–74
  secondary, 373, 378–83, *379*
Devil, 221
Diagnostic and Statistical Manual of Mental Disorders (DSM-IV-TR), of American Psychiatric Association, 262–64
Dickson, Donald, 48
Dietz, Park, 262
Differential association, 385–88, *386*
Diffuseness of roles, 32
DirecTV, 500
Direzione Investigativa Antimafia, 481
Dirty money, unloading of, 488–89
Disability scams, 512
Discipline, 347
  parental supervision and, 404–5
Discipline and Punish, 346
Discretion(s), professional, 351
Discriminating traits, assumption of, 248
Disengagement, executive, 510
Disorganization, social, 398–400
Dispute settlement
  return to original forms of, 57–61
  in small-scale societies, 34–37
  traditional Inuit and Ojibway, 38
  transformation in forms of, 40–42
Division of Labor in Society, 283
Dobson, James, 261
Doman Industries, 287
Donaghy, Tim, 501
Dove, Adrian, 240
Dowie, Mark, 51
Doyle, Daniel P., 408
Drabinsky, Garth, 287
Drabman, R.S., 257
Dracula, 235
Drift, 373
Drug misuse, criminal behaviour and, 159–62
Drumheller Penitentiary, 4
DSV-IV-TR. *See Diagnostic and Statistical Manual of Mental Disorders* (DSM-IV-TR)
Dubro, James, 480, 486
Dumont, J., 155
Dunham, L. Joe, 283
Dunlap, "Chainsaw Al," 514
Duplessis, Maurice, 528
Duress, defence for, 92–93
Durkheim, Émile, 200, 283–84, 293
  general model of deviance of, 285
  social integration and, 398
Duthie, Stephen, 530
Dutil, Jean L., 485

E. coli poisoning, 24
Eagleson, Alan, 512–13
Early social control theories, 400–1, *420*
Eastern European crime groups, 482–83
Easy Rider, 476
Ebbers, Bernard, 287, 515
École Polytechnique, 200
Ecological analysis, of Shaw and McKay, 399–400
Ecological fallacy, 399
Economy, token, 260
Effective guardianship, 431
Egalitarian family, 188
Ego, 250, *251*
Eisenstein, Zillah, 326
Eizenga, Mark, 499
Ek, Richard, 357
Elder abuse, 442–44
Elders' councils, 40–41
Element(s), data, 107
Elliott, Delbert S., 26, 140, 165
Emotional restraint, in Ojibway community, 33
Empirical evidence, 375
Empiricist critique, of interactionist theories, 390
Employee fraud, 530–31
Emulex Corporation, 525
Energy Services Group, 53
Engel, Friedrich, 317
English Canada, critical criminology in, 343–46
English Civil War of 1642–48, 46
Engstad, Peter A., 399–400
Enlightenment, 223
Enron, 288, 513, 521
  bankruptcy of, 498
  collapse of, 514–15
Enron trial, 287
Enterprise(s), monopolistic, 518
Entrepreneur, moral, 375
Entrepreneurship, moral, 376
Environmental Contaminants Act, 520
Equitas, 53
Ericson, Richard, 352
Ernst & Young, 530
Ethical concerns, 455
Ethnic-based crime groups, 378, 484–85
Ethnic group, 378
Ethnomethodological critique, of interactionist theories, 390–91
Ethnomethodology, 390
Eugenics
  criminology and, 238
  defined, 238
Euthanasia, 69
Evans, John, 103, 120
Evidence, empirical, 375
Evil spirits
  sin and, 220
  wrongdoing and, 220
Ewen, R.B., 250–51
Exception, state of, 356–60
Executive disengagement, 510
Explanation(s)
  cultural, 155
  structural, 156
Extraversion, 255
Extravert(s), criminal behavior and, 255–56
Eysenck, H.J., 248, 255, 267
Eysenck Personality Inventory, 267
Eysenck's model, 266
Eysenck's theory of crime and personality, 255–56

Fact(s), mistake of, 90–91
Facts on File, 52
Fagan, J., 161
Faith, Karlene, 192
Falcone, Giovanni, 475
Fallacy(ies), ecological, 399
False positive, 455

Family(ies)
egalitarian, 188
patriarchal, 188
social control theory and, 416–18
Family and Children's Services, 443
Family relationships, 404–6
Family ties, strength of, 404
Family violence, 442–44
Family Violence Court, 203
Farberman, Harvey, 510–11
Farnworth, M., 165
Farquharson, Graham, 527
Farrington, D.P., 256, 406
FDA (Food and Drug Administration), 325
Federal Court of Appeal, 358
Federal legislation, 72
criminal law and, 70–72
Felson, Marcus, 430, 431, 451
Female criminality, 409
Feminism, 183–215
radical, 326
social, 326–29, *331*
Feminist approach, 192
Feminist criminology, 327
Feminization of poverty, 193
Ferrell, Jeff, 353
Ferrero, William, 184
Ferri, Enrico, 232
Feudalism, 42
tribalism to, 42
Field, defined, 354
"Field theory," of criminology, 354–56
Figlio, Robert M., 384
Fillmore, Cathy, *412*
Financial Transaction and Report Analysis Center of Canada (FINTRAC), 467, 491
FINTRAC. *See* Financial Transaction and Report Analysis Center of Canada (FINTRAC)
First Nation's people, 365
Fischer, C.S., 161
Fisheries Act, 72
Fisher, J., 147
Fitzgerald, Robin, 145
Five Hundred Delinquent Women, 184
Flaherty, Jim, 521
Florida State University, 261
Food(s), crimes related to, 24–25
Food and Drug Administration (FDA), 48, 325
Food and Drugs Act, 72
Forbes, 526
Forces of production, 316
Formation(s), reaction, 300
Fortune, W.H., 262
Foucault, Michel, 342, 346–49, 365
Fox, J., 148
Fox TV, 500
Frame, Clifford, 11, 507
Franze, Silvia, 481
Fraud
Bre-X, 498
employee, 530–31
Internet, 525
investment, 524–25
securities, 524–25
stock, 526–27
tax, 525–27
Fréchette, M., 131, 141
Freeport McMoRan, 527
French Revolution, 229
Frenschkowski, JoAnne, 193–94
Freud, Sigmund, 232, 249–50, *251*
Friedberg Currency Exchange, 488
Friedman, Lawrence, 50

Gabor, Thomas, 130, 444, 445
Gagliano, Alfonso, 529
Gagnon, Claude, 417
Gang(s)
outlaw motorcycle, 475–79
types of, 293
Gannon, Maire, *105*
Garfinkel, Harold, 390
Garofalo, Raffaelo, 232
Gayme case, 201
Gaze, attentive, 353
Geen, R.G., 257
Gelles, Richard, 205–6
Gelsthorpe, Lorraine, 190
Gemeinschaft, 31, 34
"Gender," vs. sex, 187
Gendered violence, 205–8, *208*
Gender-ratio problem, in mainstream theories of crime, 190–91
General deterrence, 231
Generalizability problem, in mainstream theories of crime, 190
General Motors, 516
General Social Survey (GSS), 120, 207
highlights of, 121–22
of Statistics Canada, 432
General theory, of crime, *420*
General Theory of a Crime, 402
Geoghan, John, 523
Gesellschaft, 31, 45
Giffen, P.J., 295
Giller, Henri, 419
Gilligan, Carol, 253
Gillis, A.R., 409
Gillis, Mike, 512
Glasbeek, Harry, 506
Glassner, Barry, 389, 390
Glatman, Harvey Murray, 265
Globe and Mail, 499, 500
Glueck, Eleanor, 184, 185
Glueck, Sheldon, 184, 185
Goddard, Henry, 239–40
Goff, Colin, 50, 319, 320, 518–19
Goffman, Erving, 374, 378, 381
Golden Rule Resources, 524
Golding, S.L., 271
Gomery, John, 528, 529
Gone in 60 Seconds, 451
Gordon, R.A., 163
Goring, Charles, 236–37
Gorofalo, James, 430
Gottfredson, Michael R., 143, 144, 402–3, 430
Gould, Stephen Jay, 233, 235
Governmentality
defined, 346
power and, 346–49
restorative justice as, 348
Graham, James, 48
Grant, Jermaine, 440
Gray, Barbara, 60
Great Depression, 502
Great Law of Peace, 61
Greenberg, D., 143
Greenberg, David F., 315, 323–24
Green criminology, 1, 21–25
described, 22–24
issues in, 24–25
Griffiths, G.B., 236
Grim Reapers, 476
Gross counts of crime, 114
Group(s)
Eastern European crime, 482–83
ethnic-based, 378
ethnic-based crime, 484–85
homicide by, *438*
interest, 47
organized crime, 467, 472–85
terrorist, 467
Group conflict, 311
theorists of, *331*
Group conflict theory, 311–15
Group contagion, 300
Groves, W. Bryon, 413
GSS. *See* General Social Survey (GSS)
Guardianship, effective, 431
Gudjonsson, G.H., 248
Guerry, André-Michel, 163, 229
Gunn, J., 270
Guze, S., 269
Gypsy Tour, 476

Habitus, 354
Hagan, John, 15, 16–18, *17,* 48, 144, 158, 167, 188, 289–90, 295, 406, 409, 410, 498, 511, 520, 521
Haggerty, Kevin, 352
Hails, J., 270
Hakeem, M., 267
Hale, C., 149
Haller, M.H., 468
Halliburton, 53–54, 288, 500
Hall, Jerome, 45
Hamilton, Lewis, 501
Hannah-Moffat, Kelly, 351
Hanson, K., 271
Hardwick, Kelly, 413
Hare, Robert D., 256, 263–68, *263*

Harken Energy, 288
Harm(s), avoidable, 51–52
Harm reduction approach to substances, 456–57
Harper's Weekly, 196
Harris, Marvin, 225
Harris, Mike, 22, 288
Harrison, Jim, 512
Harris, S.L., 260
Hartnagel, T.F., 148, 159, 171, 257
Hartung, Frank E., 502
Harvey, Glen, 524
Havemann, P., 162
Hawkins, J. David, 419
Hayward, Keith J., 352
Hazardous Products Act, 72
Health Sciences Centre, 523
HealthSouth Corporation, 500
Heart of Darkness, 354
Heidensohn, Frances, 184, 185, 188
Heilbrun, A.B., Jr., 266
Hells Angels, 476–78, 480
Hells Angels on Wheels, 476
Henry VIII, 44
Hibbert case, 93
Himelfarb, Alexander, 103
Hindelang, Michael J., 130–31, 144–45, 163, 250, 430
Hirschi, Travis, 126, 129–31, 143, 144, 189, 404–5, 409
  social bond and, 401–4
Hobbes, Thomas, 225
Hochstetler, Andy, 505, 507
Hockey Hall of Fame, 512
Hodgins, S., 269
Hoebel, E., 34
Hoffman-Bustamante, Dale, 187
Hofstadter, 232
Hogan, Margaret Monahan, 238
Hogeveen, Bryan, 339, 341, 354–55
Hollinger International, 6–9
Holmes, Oliver Wendell, 238
Homicide(s)
  dynamics of, 438–41
  incidence of, 436
  legal meanings of, 435–38, *438*
  pattern of, 436–37, 446
  rates by age, group, and sex, *438*
  suspects of, 437–38, *438*, 440
  types of, 435–38, *438*
  victims of, 437
Homicide Survey, 162
Homolka, Karla, 262, 264–65
Hooker, Richard, 223
Hooton, Ernest A., 237
Horton, R.W., 257
House of Commons, 54, 199
House of Lords, 7
Hudson's Bay Company, 58
Huitt, Bill, 259
Human capital, 295
Human Justice Collection, 345
Human rights, 16
Human rights violations, 16
Human social organization, patterns of, 30–37
Humphreys, Adrian, 481
Hungle, Terry, 287
Hunt, Alan, 321
Hunting and gathering society, 31
Husband, immunity from rape, 197–98
Hydro-Québec case, 70
Hylton, J.H., 156

ICS. *See* Islington Crime Survey (ICS)
Id, 250, *251*
Idealist(s), left, 345
Ideal type, 31
Identity(ies), criminal, 385, 388
Ideology, 106
Illegitimate opportunity structures, 292–96, *293*
Illicit goods, legislation of, 489–90
Illicit market structure, origins of, 470
Illicit services, legislation of, 489–90
"Imbecile(s)," criminal, 240
Immigration and Refugee Protection Act (IRPA) 74, 358
Incapacitation, 454
  selective, 454–56
Inchoate crime, 85
Inchoate offences, 85–88
Incident(s)
  actual, 113
  property, 113
  total Criminal Code, 113
  violent, 113
Independent variable, 399
Indian Act, 20
Indian Conditions, 162
Indians and the Law, 152
Industrial Revolution, 508
Inequality, evolution of, 39
Instrumental Marxism, 317–18
  theorists of, *331*
Insurance Bureau of Canada, 448
Integration, social, 398
Intelligence, crime and, 239–43, *242*
Intensive Rehabilitative Custody and Supervision (IRCS) program, 363
Interactionism, symbolic, 371
Interactionist theories, 371–96
  empiricist critique of, 390
  ethnomethodological critique of, 390–91
  implications of, 391–92
  limitations of, 389–91, *389*
  neo-Marxist critique of, 389
  types of, *389*
Interest groups, laws and, 47–51
International cooperation, 492–93
International criminal court, 96–97
International Police Organization (INTERPOL), 169, 465
Internet, counselling crime over, 86–87
Internet fraud, 525
INTERPOL (International Police Organization), 169, 465
Intoxication, defence for, 91–92
Inuit community, dispute settlement in, 38
Investment fraud, 524–25
Invisibility of women, 184–95
Involvement, 402
IQ tests, controversy over, 240
IRCS program. *See* Intensive Rehabilitative Custody and Supervision (IRCS) program
IRPA. *See* Immigration and Refugee Protection Act (IRPA)
Islington Crime Survey (ICS), 330
Italian-based Mafia, 473–75

Jacobsen, D., 270
Jail Screening Assessment Tool, 269
Jakob, Mark, 525
James, J.T.L., 155
Janhevich, Derek E., 445
Japanese Yakuza, 480
Jarvis, G.K., 172
Jeffery, Clarence Ray, 43, 259
Jennings, W.S., 254
Jensen, G.F., 258
Jerusalem Post, 7
Jiang, Wenran, 325
Johns-Manville Corporation, 52, 504
Johnson, Holly, 149, 192, 195
Johnston, L.D., 140
Journal of Human Justice, 345
Judge-made criminal law, 72–73
Juke Report, 238
Juristat, 139
Juristic person, 508
Justice, 362
  deconstruction is, 360–65
  restorative, 57–61, 348
Justice Committee, 376
Justice system(s), Canada vs. U.S., 10

Kallikak, Martin, 239
Kant, Immanuel, 340
Katz, Jack, 385, 520
Keane, Carl, 403
Kedward, H., 269
Kendall, Diana, *251*
Kendzierski, D.A., 257
Kennedy, L.W., 170
Kent, Lori, 408
"Kernel of crime," 234
Kilkenny, R., 254
Kin-based redress, 35–36
King, Joan, 235
King John, 43
Kinlin, Patrick, 524
Kirsch, Philippe, 96
Klaas, Polly, 376
Klein, Dorie, 184

Kmart, 377
Knights of Labour, 50, 320
Knowledge, dangerous, 354
Kobrin, Sol, 291–92, 295
  typology of community structures implicit in, 291–92, *291*
Koenig, Daniel J., 429
Kohlberg, L., 252–54, *253*
Konty, Mark, 285
Krahn, H., 143
Kramer, R., 253
Krohn, Marvin D., 131, 411
Ku Klux Klan, 467
Kushner, S., 270

Labelling, 372
Laberge, Danielle, 192
Labour
  productive, 327
  wage, 327
Labour of serfs, 44
La Cosa Nostra (LCN), 474
Ladinsky, Jack, 50
LaFree, Gary, 385
LaGrange, Theresa, 403–4
Lamb, H.R., 271
Landis, Floyd, 501
Landon, P.B., 267
Lansky, Meyer, 474
LaPrairie, C.P., 154, 156–57
Larivee, Serge, 417
Latimer, Tracy, 69
Latiner, Robert, 69
Lauderdale, Pat, 60
Lavallee case, 95
Law(s)
  animal cruelty, 23
  anticombines, 518
  civil, 30
  commerce-regulating, 45–46
  common, 43, 73
  conflict vs., 19–21
  consensus and, 48
  contracts and, 45
  criminal, 30, 68–102. *See also* Criminal law
  formulation of, 30
  interest groups and, 47–51
  origins and role in society, 12, 29–67
  rape-related, 49–50
  regulation by, 47–51
  vagrancy, 49
  violence against women–related, 201–3
Law, Bernard, 523
Law, M., 271
"Law of the hammer," 105
Law Society of Upper Canada, 512
Lay, Kenneth, 514–15
LCN. *See* La Cosa Nostra (LCN)
Lea, John, 329
Leacock, Stephen, 321
Learning, social, 259
LeBlanc, Marc, 131, 140–41, 144, 166, 403, 413, 417
Leduc, Lisa, 530
Lee, G.W., 171
Leeson, Nicholas, 510, 530
"Left idealists," 345
Left realism, 329–30, *331*
  theorists of, *331*
"Left realists," 345
Legal contracts, 45
Legal definition of crime, 15
Legal reform, Classical School of, 227
Legal sanctions, corporate crime and, 517–21
Leger, G., 120
Legislation
  federal, 72
  of illicit goods and services, 489–90
  provincial, 72
  rape-related, 49–50
  regulatory, 72
  territorial regulatory, 72
Legitimacy, state, 55–57
Leiter, Kenneth, 390
Lemert, Edwin, 373, 379, 383–84
Lenski, Gerhard, 30
Leonard, Eileen, 188, 190
Leon, Jeffrey, 48
Letkemann, Peter, 387–88
Levels of aggregation, 107
"Levels of analysis" perspective, 249
Levy, Madeleine, 46
Lewis, Dorothy, 262
Liberal approach, to women's crime, 187–88
Liberal Party of Canada, 285–86
Life
  naked, 358
  street, 295
Lifestyle/exposure theory, 430
Lilly, J. Robert, 232
Lime Ridge Mall, 363–64
Linden, Eric, 407
Linden, Rick, 219, *251*, 397, 409, *412*, 469, 498
Lindros, Eric, 287
Link, Bruce G., 378
Lippert, Randy, 349
Lippincott, E.C., 257
Livent, Inc., 287
Lizotte, Alan J., 411
Locke, John 225
Lombroso, Cesare, 184, 231, 233–38
  Positive School and, 232–36
Lord Black of Crossharbour, 7
Losel, F., 267
Luckenbill, David, 439
Lynch, Michael, 413

Macdonald, John A., 528
MacLean, Brian, 345
MacLeod, Linda, 199
Macphail, Andrew, 321–22
MADD. *See* Mothers Against Drunk Driving (MADD)
Mafia
  Cotroni-Violi, 474–75
  defined, 471
  described, 473
  Italian-based, 473–75
  Russian, 482–83
  Sicilian, 475
Malamuth, N.M., 257–58
Male violence against women, law's role in condoning, 197–98
Malott case, 95
Malpractice, unprofessional conduct and, 521–24
Malvo, Lee Boyd, 11
Mandel, Michele, 363–64
Mann, Kenneth, 519–20
Manson, Charles, 247, 260–62
Marchak, Patricia, 54
Marchessault, Henri, 389
Marginal opportunity structures, 294–96
Market structure
  criminogenic, 510–12
  illicit, 470
Martineau case, 80, 84–85
Marxism, 327
  instrumental, 317–18, *331*
  structural, 319–23, *331*
Marxist conflict perspectives, in criminology, 315–26
Marx, Karl, 316–17
Master status, 379
Matsueda, Ross L., 386–87
Mattel, 517
Matthews, Roger, 329
Maturational reform, 142–44
Matza, David, 373, 384
Maume, Michael, 412
Maurutto, Paula, 351
Mayhew, Henry, 229
McCarthy, Bill, 167, 290, 295, 406
McConnell case, 96–97
McCord, John, 417
McDonald, Angus, 265
McKay, 398–400, 413
  ecological analysis of, 399–400
McKay, H.D., 172
McLaren, Mercedes, 501
McMullan, John, 324
Means, aspirations and, 284–90
Mechanical solidarity, 31–32
Media
  crime and, 10–11
  public perceptions of crime and, 130
Medieval society, 221
Ménard, Serge, 478
Mencken, H.L., 508
Mens rea, 1, 76, 78–83
  of bigamy, 90
  of conspiracy, 88–89
  of criminal attempt, 86–88

for murder, 94
objective, 79–82
regulatory offences and, 82–83
subjective, 79–82
Menstruation, 186
Mental disorder, as defence to criminal charge, 89–90
Mental illness, crime and, 267–73, *272*
Menu Foods, 24
Menu Foods Income Fund, 324, 325
Menzies, David, 530
Mercer, Elisha, 363–64
Merchant(s), coalition of monarchs and, 44–45
Merton, Robert K., 189, 283–90, 293, 299, 304, 397, 398
strain theory of, 355
Messinger, H.B., 172
Messner, Steven F., 286, 287, 301
Methodology, 104
Mexican cartels, 483–84
Michalowski, Raymond, 31, 325, 330
Microanomie, 285
Micro-powers, 347
Middle-class measuring rod, 296
Milhorean, Karen, *105*
Miliband, Ralph, 47, 318
Mills, C. Wright, 509
Mineral Resources Act, 507
Ministry of the Solicitor General of Canada, 120
Minnesota Multiphasic Personality Inventory (MMPI), 267
Misconduct, criminal, 512–13
Missionary Church of Christ, 6
Mistake of fact, defence for, 90–91
MMPI. *See* Minnesota Multiphasic Personality Inventory (MMPI)
Mobilization for Youth Project, 303
Modelling, 256–57
Mode of production, 30, 316
Modern state, dilemma and challenge for, 56–57
Modern state systems, 42–55
Mogilevich, Semion, 509
Monahan, J., 269
Monarch(s), coalition of merchants and, 44–45
Money, dirty, 488–89
Money-laundering schemes, 486–89
Monopolistic enterprise, 518
Montesquieu, 225
Montreal Massacre, 200–1
Montreal Police Drug Squad, 389
Montreal Social Welfare Court, 141
Monture Angus, Patricia, 194
Moral development
Kohlberg's theory of, 252, *253*
theories of, 252–54, *253*
Moral development theory, *272*
Moral entrepreneur, 375
Moral entrepreneurship, 376
Moral rhetoric, 374
Morash, M., 254
Morris, Allison, 188, 190
Morrison, Wayne, 354
Most serious offence (MSO), 113, 128–29
Mothers Against Drunk Driving (MADD), 376
Motivated offenders, reducing of, 452–54
Motor vehicle theft, 449–51
Mount Cashel Orphanage, 522
Mounties, Moose, and Moonshine: The Patterns and Context of Outport Crime, 312
MSO. *See* Most serious offence (MSO)
Mugford, Stephen, 59, 330
Muirhead, G.K., 155, 157
Muir, Leilani, 240
Mulroney, Brian, 345, 528
Murder, 435–41, *438*
mens rea for, 94
Murdoch, Rupert, 500
Murray, Jane Lothian, *251*
Murray, S., 120
Mushuau Innu of Davis Inlet, 414–15
Mutual conversion, 297, 300
Mutual dependence, in small-scale societies, 32–33

Nader, Ralph, 516
Naffine, Ngaire, 188–90, 409
Nagel, Ilene, 520
Naked life, 358
Narcotic Control Act, 71
Natalizia, Elena, 191
Nathan, P.E., 260
National Basketball Association, 501
National Commission on Correctional Health Care, 269
National Committee to Reduce Auto Theft, 449
National criminal laws and procedures, 491–92
National Emergencies Act, 357
National Football League, 501
National Hockey League Players Association (NHLPA), 512
National Longitudinal Survey of Children and Youth (NLSCY), 145, 405, 407
National Post, 7, 481
National Security Agency, 356
Native Counselling Services of Alberta, 155
Nazi Germany, criminology in, 241
Nazi Party Congress, 241
NCRMD. *See* Not criminally responsible on account of mental disorder (NCRMD)
'Ndrangheta, 475
Neale, Richard, 523–24
Necessity, defence for, 92–93
Neeb/Brook criminal organization, 488–89
Neeb, Timothy, 488
Negative social capital, 355
Negative symbolic capital, 355
Neighbourhood(s), crime rate variation by, 172
Neighbourhood Watch programs, 452
Neoclassical theory, *242*
Neo-Marxist critique, of interactionist theories, 389
Nettler, Gwynne, 139, 142, 163, 299
Neuroticism, 255
New Criminology, 344
Newman, J.P., 266, 267
Newman, Katherine, 35
Newton, Isaac, 232
New York Times, 325, 524
NHLPA. *See* National Hockey League Players Association (NHLPA)
Nicholls, T.H., 269
Nietzel, M.T., 262
1999 General Social Survey, 442–44
Nixon, Richard, 410
NLSCY. *See* National Longitudinal Survey of Children and Youth (NLSCY)
Norm(s), 14
conduct, 310–11
criminal, 311
Norman Invasion (1066), 43
Normlessness, anomie and, 283–84
Nortel, 286, 516
Northern Telecom, 286
Northwestern University, 498
Norton Anti-Virus, 525
Not criminally responsible on account of mental disorder (NCRMD), 89–90
Nova Scotia Bar Society, 10, 130
Nova Scotia Resources Department, 507
"Novel theory," 235
Nye, F.I., 164
Nye, Ivan, 400–1

Objective *mens rea,* 79–82
O'Brien, R.M., 147
Occupational crime, 502–4, *503,* 521–31
Ocean's Thirteen, 445
O'Connor case, 202–3
O'Connor, Sandra Day, 360, 376
Offence(s)
criminal, 83–85
inchoate, 85–88
not committed, 85–86
regulatory, 72, 82–83
Offender(s)
motivated, 452–54
women as, 204–5
Offender deficit, assumption of, 248
Office of Threat Assessment, of U.S. Department of Energy, 482–83
Official Secrets Act, 467
OFY. *See* Opportunities for Youth (OFY)
Ogloff, R.P., 269
Ohlin, Lloyd, 293, *294,* 303

Ojibway community
  dispute settlement in, 38
  emotional restraint in, 33
Okihiro, Norman, 312
Olley, M.C., 269
Olson, Clifford, 11, 247, 260, 262, 267, 268, 439
O'Malley, Pat M., 140, 330
O'Neill, Maggie, 353–54
Onex, 500
Ontario Securities Commission, 499, 509–10
Ontario Superior Court, 194
Ontario Works Act, 193–94
Operant conditioning, 259–60
Operant conditioning theory, *272*
Opportunistic crimes, of powerful persons, 288–89
Opportunities for Youth (OFY), 303–4
Opportunity(ies), crimes of, 448–49
Opportunity structures, 290
  illegitimate, 292–96, *294*
  marginal, 294–96
  shift from control to, 290–96, *291, 294*
Order of Canada, 512
O'Reilly-Fleming, Thomas, 330, 344
Organization, crime and, 502–4, *503*
Organizational crime, 502
Organized crime, 463–97
  controlling of, 489–93
  described, 464–67
  enforcement for, 490–91
  organization of, 468–71
  persons involved in, 471–72
  roots of, 468–71
Organized crime groups, 472–85
  Asian, 479–82
  vs. terrorist group, 467
Orr, Bobby, 513
Osgood, D.W., 140
Ouimet, M., 172
Ousey, Graham, 412
Outlaw motorcycle gangs, 475–79
Over-representation, 152
  Aboriginal, 155–59

Palloni, Alberto, 521
Paramount chieftainships, 41–42
Parental role model, 404–5
Parental supervision, discipline and, 404–5
Parenting, of delinquent youths, 418
Parker, Patricia, 511
Parliament of Canada, 70, 72, 199, 202–3, 464, 467
  federal, jurisdiction of, 13
Parole Board, 159
Parry, Roger, 11, 507
Parthenais prison, 478
Party to a crime, 84
Paterson, C., 504
Patriarchal family, 188
Patriarchy, 195, 326
Patriot Act, 529
Patriote rebellion of Quebec, 59
Patterson, Gerald R., 416–18
Paul, Saint, 357
Pavlich, George, 341, 342, 348, 362
PCL-R. *See* Revised Psychopathy Checklist (PCL-R)
Pearce, Frank, 324, 325
Pearson Airport, 93
Pearson, Patricia, 205, 206, 208
Peer(s), delinquent, 411–13, *413*
Penal Code of 1791, 228
Penal sanction, 68
Penetanfuishene Mental Health Centre, 264
Pension scams, 513
Perka case, 92–93
Personality
  antisocial, 260–67
  Eysenck's theory of, 255–56
  Freud's theory of, 250, *251*
Personality theory, *272*
Perspective(s)
  conflict, 282
  consensus, 282
Pétel case, 95–97
Peterson, David, 509
Pfohl, Stephen J., 222
Phelan, Jo C., 378
Phillips, Gerald, 11, 507
Phoenix Trading and Research, 530–31
Physical characteristics, crime and, 236–39
Piaget, Jean, 252
Picard, André, 478
Platt, Anthony, 48
PMS. *See* Premenstrual syndrome (PMS)
Poaching, big game, 312
Poisoning, *E. coli,* 24
Police incident-based data, defining of, 128
Police UCR survey data, vs. courts, 129
Policing, broken windows, 362
Political corruption, 528–29
Political Theology, 357
Polk, Kenneth, 407, 419, 420
Pollak, Otto, 184–86, 205
Polsky, Ned, 106–7
Population, 105
Positive School, *242*
  contribution of, 235–36
  described, 232
  Lombroso and, 232–36
Posner, Richard A., 520
Poulantzas, N., 319
Poverty, feminization of, 193
Power
  abuse of, 287, 288, 512
  defined, 346
  governmentality and, 346–49
  social, 37, 39
Powerful persons
  crimes of, 324–26
  responding to opportunistic crimes of, 288–89
Powerless persons, crimes of, 323–24
Pratt, Travis, 404
Predator(s), violent, 454
Premenstrual syndrome (PMS), 187
Primary deviation, 373–74
Principles of Criminology, 385
Prison(s)
  Aboriginal women in, 194
  Abu Ghraib, 529
  Parthenais, 478
Proceeds of Crime (Money Laundering) Act, 467
Proceeds of Crime (Money Laundering) and Terrorist Financing Act, 491
Production
  forces of, 316
  modes of, 30, 316
  social relations of, 316
Productive labour, 327
Professional discretion, 351
Property incidents, 113
Prostitution, 194–95
Protect America Act, 529
Protestant Reformation, 221
Prototypical psychopath, 268
Provincial legislation, 72
Provocation, defence for, 94
Prus, Robert C., 380
Psychoanalytic theory, *272*
Psychological perspectives, on criminality, 247–81. *See also* Psychological theories
Psychological theories
  of crime, 247–81, *251, 253, 272*
  Eysenck's theory of crime and personality, 255–56
  moral development, 252–54, *253, 272*
  operant conditioning, 259–60, *272*
  personality, *272*
  psychoanalytic, 249–52, *251, 272*
  psychopathy, *272*
  social learning, 256–58, *272*
Psychology, community, 249
Psychopath(s), prototypical, 268
Psychopathy, *272*
Psychoticism, 255
Public perceptions of crime, media and, 130
Pulford, Bob, 512

Quasar Petroleum, 504
Quebec, patriote rebellion of, 59
Quebec Crime Probe report of 1977, 474
Queen's College Journal, 321, 322
Queen's University, 265
Quetelet, Adolph, 163, 229–31
Quimet, M., 142
Quinney, Richard, 168, 303, 314–15, 318
Quinsey, Vern, 265
Qwest Communications, 500

R. v. Hamilton, 86–87
R. v. Latimer, 69
R. v. Malmo-Levine; R. v. Caine, 71
R. v. Morgentaler, Smolig and Scott, 73

R. v. Olan, Hudson and Hartnett, 73
R. v. Sharpe, 74–75
Race, as correlate of crime, 149–59, *150, 153*
Radical feminism, 326
Radler, David, 7–9
Radzinowicz, Sir Leon, 235
Rafter, Nicole, 191
Rand Cooperation, 454–55
Random sample, 120
Rape
  cultural construction of, 195–97
  husband's immunity from, 197–98
Rape legislation, analysis of history of, 49–50
Rappaport, J., 249
Rasmussen, Michael, 501
Rate(s), crime, 104
Ratner, R.S., 345
RCMP. *See* Royal Canadian Mounted Police (RCMP)
Reaction(s), circular, 300
Reaction formation, 297, 298, 300
Reactivity, autonomic, 257
Reader's Digest, 301
Reagan, Ronald, 345
Realism, left, 329–30, *331*
Realist(s), left, 345
Reasons, Charles, 50–52, 319, 320, 504, 518–19
Rebels, 387
Record(s)
  administrative, 107
  to statistics, 107–8
Redress
  self-based, 35–36
  in small-scale societies, 35–36
Reed, Hayter, 20
Reeves, Keanu, 11
Reform, maturational, 142–44
Region, as correlate of crime, 169–72, *169, 171*
Regulation
  failure in, 51–55
  by law, 47–51
Regulatory legislation, territorial, 72
Regulatory offences, 72
  mens rea and, 82–83
Rehnquist, William, 376
Reid, C.L., 248
Reid, Wayne Anthony, 440–41
Reinforcement, defined, 259
Reiss, Albert, 400–1
Relationship(s), family, 404–6
Relative autonomy, 319
Relative deprivation, 290–91
Reliability, 104
Religion, 407–9
Reppucci, N.D., 248
Respondeat superior, 50
Restorative justice, 57–61
  as governmentality, 348
  prospects and future directions for, 60–61
Restraint(s), emotional, 33
Retail Council of Canada, 530
Reuter, P., 468
Revised Psychopathy Checklist (PCL-R), 263, *263*
Reynolds, Kimber, 376
Reynolds, Mike, 376
Rhetoric, moral, 374
Rice, Marnie, 264
Riel Rebellion, 20
Risk(s)
  actuarialism and, 349–52
  defined, 349
Risk society, 351
  actuarialism and, 349–52
Rivard, Claude (Le Pic), 478
Rizzuto, Vito, 481
Robbery, 113, 444–46
  bank, 447
  incidence of, 444
  offenders of, 445–46
  victims of, 44–45
Robertson, M., 269
Rock Machine, 478
Rock, Paul, 217n
Rodgers, Karen, 192, 195
Roesch, R., 269–71
Rogers, Kimberly, 193–94
Role(s), diffuseness of, 32
Role convergence, sex and, 148–49
Rome Diplomatic Conference, 96
Romero, Jonathan, 363–64
Rome Statute, 96
Romilly, Samuel, 224
Rosenfeld, Richard, 286, 287, 301
Rosenhaft, Eve, 241
Rose, Stephen, 303
Ross, E.A., 502
Rossi, Peter, 43
Ross, L., 504
Ross, Rupert, 32, 33, 37, 38, 58
Roth, John, 516
Rothman, Michael, 502, 508, 511
Routine activities approach, to street crime, 430–33
Routine activities theory, critique of, 433–34
Royal Bank, 499
Royal Canadian Mounted Police (RCMP), 13, 360, 491, 509
Royal Commission, 522
Royal Newfoundland Constabulary, 522
Royal Proclamation of 1763, 59
Rule(s), 14–19, *17. See also* Law(s)
  making of, 19–21
  seriousness, 112
"Rule of law," legitimacy of, 55
Russian Mafia, 482–83
Rutter, Michael, 419
Ruzic case, 93–94

Sacco, Vincent F., 471
Sample, 120
  random, 120
Sampson, R.J., 172
Sand brothers, 3–6
Saskatchewan Liberal Party, 84
Sault Ste. Marie case, 83
Scam(s)
  disability, 512
  pension, 513
"Scam capital of the world," 526
Scandal(s), corporate accounting, 512–14
Schafer, Walter E., 407, 419, 420
Schmitt, Carl, 357
Schnall, Eleanor, 443
Schneider, Stephen, 434–35
Schoenfeld, C.G., 250
School(s), social control theory and, 419–20, *420*
Schooling, 406–7
Schutz, Alfred, 390
Schwartz, Gerry, 500
Schwendinger, Herman, 15, 16
Schwendinger, Julia, 15, 16
Scoring rule, MSO and, 128–29
Seaboyer case, 201
Seattle Crisis Clinic, 261
Secondary deviation, 373, 378–83, *379*
Securities and Exchange Commission, 288, 515–16
Securities fraud, 524–25
Security Certificate, under Immigration and Refugee Act, 358
Selective incapacitation, 454–56
Self-based redress, 35–36
Self-control, 402–4
Self-defence, defence for, 94–95
Self-degrading commitment, 383
Self-enhancing commitment, 383
Self-report studies, 126–31, *127*
Self-restraint, in small-scale societies, 32, 33
Sellin, Thorsten, 43, 310–11, 314–15
Senésac, Daniel, 478
September 11, 2001, World Trade Center–New York City on, 74, 287, 288, 301, 452, 529
Serf(s), labour of, 44
Seriousness rule, 112
Sex
  as correlate of crime, 144–49, *145, 146*
  crime trends between, 144–48, *145, 146*
  differences between, 144–48, *145, 146*
  "gender" vs., 187
  homicide by, *438*
  role convergence, 148–49
Sexism, 184
Sex trade work, 194–95
Sharper, C.R.D., 380
Sharp, Shaun, 440
Shaw, 398–400, 413
  ecological analysis of, 399–400
Shaw, C.R., 172
Sheldon, William, 238
Sherbrooke Record, 7

Shippensburg University of Pennsylvania, 255, 257
Short, James F., 372
Short, J.F., Jr., 164
Shover, Neal, 383, 505, 507
Sicilian Mafia, 473, 475
Siedman, Robert, 320
Sikorsky, Robert, 529
Silber, D.E., 269
Silver, Jim, 513
Silverman, Robert, 403–4
Simon, Jonathan, 350
Simon, Rita J., 148, 191
Simourd, Linda, 144
Simpson, John, 409
Simpson, Sally, 509
Sin, evil spirits and, 220
Situational crime prevention, 451–52
  twelve techniques of, *453*
Skinner, B.F., 259
Skogan, W., 120
Slum(s)
  "stable," 291
  "transitory," 291–92
Smadych, Russell, 320
Small-scale societies, 31–34
  absence of surplus, stratification, and state in, 34
  advisor systems in, 36–37
  community of belief in, 33–34
  dispute settlement in, 34–37
  mutual dependence in, 32–33
  redress in, 35–36
  self-restraint in, 32, 33
  transformation to state societies, 37–42. *See also* State societies
Small, Shirley, 48
Smandych, Russell, 50, 518–19
Smart, Carol, 184, 186, 188, 192, 197
Smith, D.A., 147
Snider, Laureen, 48, 50, 51, 54, 320, 324, 328–29, 498, 518
Social bond, 398
  aspects of, 401–4
  Hirschi and, 401–4
Social bond theory, *420*
"Social capital," 356
Social capital, negative, 355
Social class
  as correlate of crime, 163–68
  crime and, 504–8
Social control, agents of, 375–78
Social control theory, 397–426. *See also* Deviance
  as conservative theory of crime, 413–16
  described, 397–98
  early, 400–1, *420*
  family and, 416–18
  family relationships, 404–6
  female criminality, 409
  issues with, 410–16, *412*
  policy implications of, 416–18
  religion, 407–9
  schooling, 406–7
  schools and, 419–20, *420*
  types of, *420*
  upper-world crime and, 410–11
Social Darwinism, 184, 241, 242
Social development, crime prevention through, 452–54
Social disorganization theories, 171, 398–400, *420*
Social distribution, of crime, 12
Social feminism, 326–29
  theorists of, *331*
Social integration, Durkheim and, 398
Socialization, 250
  into crime, 385–88, *386*
Social learning, defined, 259
Social learning theory, 256–58, *272*
Social organization, patterns of, 30–37
Social organization of work, corporate crime and, 508–17
Social power, emergence in state societies, 37, 39
Social Reaction perspective, 352
Social relations of production, 316
Social structure, 284
  crime and, 229–32
Societal reactions, to crime, 12–13
Society(ies)
  acephalous, 31
  crime and, 1–216
  hunting and gathering, 31
  medieval, 221
  origins and role of law in, 12, 29–67
  risk, 349–52
  small-scale, 31–34. *See also* Small-scale societies
  strain as feature of, 286–88
  Triad, 479–82
Sociopath, defined, 262
"Soft city," 353
Solicitor General Canada, 120
Solidarity
  collective, 31–32
  mechanical, 31–32
"Somatotype" theory, 238
Sorenson, Ann Marie, 403, 411
Souter, David, 377
South American cartels, 483–84
South Park: Bigger, Longer & Uncut, 10
Sovereign, 357
Sovereignty, 43
  state of exception and, 356–60
Specific deterrence, 230–31
"Specific intent," 91
Spencer, Herbert, 232
Spirit(s), evil, 220
Spitzer, Stephen, 323
Sprott, Jane, 407
Sprucedale, 363–64
"Stable slum," 291
Stamler, Rodney T., 463
Standard Metropolitan Statistical Areas, 164
Stanford, Leland, 287
Stanford University, 257, 258
Staples, David, 4
Stark, Rodney, 408
State, 30
  absence in small-scale societies, 34
State(s)
  eclipse of, 51–55
  laws of, 47
  modern, 56–57
State legitimacy, crisis in, 55–57
State of exception, sovereignty and, 356–60
State societies
  evaluation of inequality in, 39
  transformation from small-scale society to, 37–42
  emergence of social power in, 37, 39
State systems, modern, 42–55. *See also specific types*
Statistic(s)
  on Criminal Justice System, 107–10, *110, 111*
  from records to, 107–8
Statistical School, 229–32
  described, 229
Statistics Canada, 104, *105, 110,* 113, 120, 150, 152, *153, 169,* 201
  GSS of, 432
  Violence Against Women Survey of, 166
Statute of Wills, 44
Steadman, H.J., 269
Stebbins, Robert A., 371, 379, 382, *386*
Steffensmeier, D., 147, 149
Stigma, 374
Stigmata, 234
Stock fraud, anatomy of, 526–27
Stoker, Bau, 235
Stone case, 78, 94
Stone, Christopher, 51, 508–9, 517
Strain(s)
  coercion and, 289–90
  as feature of individuals, 289
  as feature of society, 286–88
Strain theories, 282–309, *297*
  assessing of, 299–301
  convergence with other perspectives, 300–1
  defined, 282
  of Merton, 355
  policy implications of, 303–4
  static state of, 299–300
  uses of, 301–3
Stratification, 31
  absence in small-scale societies, 34
Straus, Murray, 205–6
"Street" crime, 429–62. *See also* Conventional ("street") crime
Street life, 295
Strongquill, Dennis, 4–6
Structural explanations, 156

Structural Marxism, 319–23
  theorists of, *331*
Study(ies), self-report, 126–31, *127*
Subculture(s), 293
  of power abuse, 287, 288
Subjective *mens rea*, 79–82
Substance(s), harm reduction approach to, 456–57
Substantive criminal law, 71
"Suburbia," 292
Suedfeld, P., 267
Suicide, 284, 398
Suitability, target, 431
Superego, 250, *251*
Supervision, parental, 404–5
Supreme Court of Canada, 13, 69–71, 73–75, 78, 80, 81, 83, 84, 86–87, 89, 90, 92, 93, 95–97, 201, 202, 238, 377
Surplus, absence in small-scale societies, 34
Surveillance, 347
  defined, 545
Survey(s), victimization, 120–26, *123–25*, 128
Sutherland, Edwin, 9, 15, 139, 189, 293, 498, 502, 503
Swartz, Joel, 504
Sylvester, James, 499
Symbolic capital, negative, 355
Symbolic interactionism, 371

Tanner, Julian, 143, 151
Tarde, Gabriel, 228
Target suitability, 431
Task Force on Aboriginal Peoples in Federal Corrections, 154, 156
Task Force on Federally Sentenced Women, 204
Tate murders, 261
Tax fraud, 525–27
Taylor, Ian, 189, 342–44
Teevan, J.J., 257
Telegram, 7
Teplin, L.A., 269–71
Territorial regulatory legislation, 72
Terrorism, Canadian Charter of Rights and Freedoms and, 74–75
Terrorist Financing Act, 467
Terrorist group, vs. organized crime group, 467
Thatcher case, 84
Thatcher, Colin, 84
Thatcher, Margaret, 345
The Betrayal of the Poor, 303
The Communist Manifesto, 317
The Criminality of Women, 184, 186
The Female Offender, 184
The Gang, 398–99
The Mask of Sanity, 263
The Matrix, 11
The Mismeasure of Man, 235
The New Criminologies in Canada, 344
The New Criminology, 189, 342, 343
Theoretical Criminology, 311
Theorist(s)
  class conflict, 20
  conflict, *331*
  consensus, 20, 282
Theory(ies)
  biological, 236–43, *242*
  class conflict, 20
  Classical, 225–27, *242*
  conflict, 310–38. *See also* Conflict theories
  consensus, 20
  conservative, 413–16
  control-differential association, *420*
  of crime, *242*
  of criminology, 219–46
  Darwin's, 232
  defined, 106
  early, *242*
  Eysenck's, 255–56
  general, *420*
  interactionist, 371–96. *See also* Interactionist theories
  lifestyle/exposure, 430
  moral development, 252–54, *253, 272*
  neoclassical, *242*
  novel, 235
  old, 230–31
  operant conditioning, *272*
  personality, *272*
  psychoanalytic, 249–52, *251, 272*
  psychological, 248–60, *251, 253*
  routine activities, 433–34
  social bond, *420*
  social control, 397–426. *See also* Social control theory
  social disorganization, 171, 398–400, *420*
  social learning, 256–58, *272*
  "somatotype," 238
  strain, 282–309, *297*. *See also* Strain theories
  of women's crime, 184–90, *208*
Théroux case, 76
The Social Reality of Crime, 314
The State in Capitalist Society, 47
"The struggle for survival," 232
"The survival of the fittest," 232
The Unadjusted Girl, 184
The Westray Story: A Predictable Path to Disaster, 506
The Wild One, 476
Thibert case, 94
Thomas, Clarence, 376–77
Thomas, D., 151
Thomas, Jennifer, 139
Thomas, M.H., 257
Thomas, S.V., 257
Thomas, W.I., 184–85
Thornberry, Terence P., 131, 384, 411
Thrasher, Frederic M., 398
Tierney, John, 317
Tigar, Michael, 46
Time, 349
Tittle, C.R.,
Token econo
Tönnies, Ferd
Toronto Police
Toronto Star, 151
Toronto Stock Exc
Toronto Youth Cri
  Survey, 151
Torture, witchcraft an
Total Criminal Code in
Trace, 361
Trade-Marks Act, 72
Transitional corporation, p
"Transitory slum," 291–92
Transnational corporation, 51
Tremblay, Richard E., 304, 417–
Triad(s), 479
Triad societies, 479–82
Tribalism, 37, 39
  to feudalism, 42
Tribble, S., 166
Tronstad, Larry, 491
Trudeau, Pierre Elliott, 19, 358
Trudeau, Yves (Apache), 477
"True crimes," 72
Tucker, Eric, 506
Tudor, 57
Turrisi, Mariano, 481
20th century, biological theories in, 236–43, *242*
2004 Canadian Addiction Survey, 159
2004 General Social Survey in Canada, 144

UCR2 Incident-based Survey, 112
UCR Aggregate (UCR1.0) Survey, 112, 113
UCRs. *See* Uniform Crime Reports (UCRs)
UCR system. *See* Uniform Crime Report (UCR) system
Ulmer, Jeffery T., 382
"Underlife" of the city, 353
Uniform Crime Reporting Incident-Based Survey, 128
Uniform Crime Reports (UCRs), 111
  categories of, 113
  described, 111
  most serious offence rule, 113
Uniform Crime Report (UCR) system, 103
United Nations, 465, 467, 470, 492
United Nations Convention on Transnational Organized Crime, 464
United States, justice system of, 10
Université de Montréal, 304
University Magazine, 322
University of Alberta, 325, 339
University of British Columbia, 264
University of California, 288
University of Manitoba, 339, 397, 498
University of Minnesota, 267
University of Montreal, 413
University of Washington, 261, 293
Unprofessional conduct and malpractice, 521–24

...mmission,

...w, origin and evolution of, 49
...State University, 259
...tine Golf Invitational, 287
...alentine, Mark, 287
Validity, 104
Value(s), 20
  conflict of, 69
Vancouver Stock Exchange, 526
Vancouver Sun, 268
Variable(s), independent, 399
VAWS. *See* Violence Against Women Survey (VAWS)
Verdun-Jones, N., 155, 157
Vermette, Lionel, 380
Victim(s), women as, 204–5
Victimization surveys, 120–26, *123–25*, 128
Villemez, W.J., 163
Vinokourov, Alexandre, 501
Violation(s), human rights, 16
Violence
  among diverse populations, 127, *127*
  family, 442–44
  gendered, 205–8, *208*
  by Winnipeg Police Servcie, 203
Violence against women, 195–203
  breaking silence, 199–200
  complicity of, 198–99
  cultural construction of rape, 195–97
  law's role in condoning male, 197–98
  recent developments in law's response to, 201–3
Violence Against Women Survey (VAWS), of Statistics Canada, 166, 201
Violent incidents, 113
Violent predator, 454

..., Paolo, 475
...C.A., 147
...rge, 311–15
..., 489
...ew, 455
...omen, 321–22
...a Argument Against,
..., Loïc, 355, 356
..., Andrew, 300
...age labour, 327
Waite, Emily, 43
Walsh, David, 526–27
Walters, Vivienne, 50–51
Walton, Paul, 189, 342–44
War Against Women report, 204
War Measures Act, 357, 358
"War on Iraq," 287–88
War on Poverty, 303
"War on Terror," 529
Warren, M.Q., 250
Warr, M., 144
Watergate, 521
Watson, Mark, 378
Weber, Max, 30
Weis, Joseph G., 130–31, 419
West, D.J., 406
Westray Mine disaster, in Stellarton, Nova Scotia, 11, 506–7
West, W. Gordon, 48, 166, 384
Wetzell, Richard, 241
Wheeler, Stanton, 502, 508, 511, 520
"When," in patterns of criminal behaviour, 433
When She Was Bad: Violent Women and the Myth of Innocence, 205
"Where," in patterns of criminal behaviour, 433
White-collar crime, 6–9, 15–16, 498–536
  as crime, 15–16
  defined, 502
  nature of, 501, *503*
  types of, *503*
White, Helene Raskin, 301
"Who," in patterns of criminal behaviour, 432–33
Wholesale Travel Group Inc. case, 83
Widom, Cathy Spatz, 266, 267
Wife Battering in Canada: The Vicious Circle, 199
Wildlife Act, 312
Williams, Howard, 341
Williams, James, 349
William the Conqueror, 43, 44
Wilson, James Q., 228, 418
Winnipeg Police Service, 207
  violence by, 203

Wirtz, Bill, 512
Witchcraft, torture and, 225
Without Conscience, 267
Wolf, Daniel, 387, 472
Wolfgang, Marvin E., 43, 384
Wolf, Leonard, 235
Women. *See also* Female criminality; Violence against women
  Aboriginal, 194
  criminalized, 192–95
  invisibility of, 184–95
  struggle for vote by, 321–22
  as victims and offenders, 204–5
Women in Trouble, 204
"Women problem," 186
Women's crime
  conservative approach to, 184–87
  liberal approach to, 187–88
  theories of, 184–90, *208*
Women's liberation thesis, 191–92
Women's Rights, 322
Women's World Cup, 501
Wood, Linda, 203, 206–7
Wooldredge, J., 172
Woolford, Andrew, 339, 341
Woolsey, James, 469
"Workfare" programs, 193
WorldCom, 288, 513, 515–16, 521
WorldCom trial, 287
World Health Organization, 470
World War I, 240, 358
World War II, 298, 358, 502
Wortley, Scot, 151
Wright, Richard T., 448–49
Wrightsman, L.S., 262
Wrongdoing, evil spirits and, 220
Wynne, D.F., 159

Yakuza, 480
YBM Magnex, 509–10
Yeager, Peter, 502
YLS/CMI. *See* Youth Level of Service/Case Management Inventory (YLS/CMI)
Young, Jock, 189, 329, 342–44, 352, 433–34
Young Offenders Act, 59
Youth(s), delinquent, 418
Youth Court Survey, 128–29
Youth Criminal Justice Act, 59, 361, 391
Youth Justice Committees, 362
Youth Level of Service/Case Management Inventory (YLS/CMI), 350
Youths in Achievement Place programs, 260

Zaccardelli, Giuliano, 360
Zappia, Giuseppe, 481
Zedong, Mao, 18
Zeigler, John, 512
Zepeda-Cordera, Diego, 6
Zilborg, Gregory, 220